Praise for Frances FitzGerald's
FIRE IN THE LAKE
The Vietnamese and the Americans in Vietnam

Winner of the National Book Award
Winner of the Pulitzer Prize
Winner of the Bancroft Prize

"An extraordinary book . . . partly a history of South Vietnam, partly a study of American policy there, and partly an account of what this policy has done to a people we have destroyed in order to save from Communism. *Fire in the Lake* is all these and much more: a compassionate and penetrating account of the collision of two societies that remain untranslatable to one another, an analysis of all those features of South Vietnamese culture that doomed the American effort from the start, and an incisive explanation of the reasons why that effort could only disrupt and break down South Vietnam's society — and pave the way for the revolution that the author sees as the only salvation. . . . Miss FitzGerald's analysis should help us understand why even apparent battlefield successes of 'our side' provide, in the long run, no way of saving the unsavable. It should also, by its very depth and by its admirable style — cool empathy, restrained indignation, quiet irony, devastating vignettes — help us realize the monumental scope of what went wrong and what we did wrong. . . . A fine book." — Stanley Hoffmann, *New York Times Book Review*

"Frances FitzGerald writes with the controlled fire of one whose Inner Light is hot, yet tempered by the cool ice of Reason and Fact. . . . There has been to this point no book on recent Vietnam with the power and conviction of *Fire in the Lake*. Compared to Miss FitzGerald's prodigious effort, all previous studies, of whatever persuasion, pale into insignificance." — David Brudnoy, *National Review*

"FitzGerald is a wonderful reporter and writer, with an eye for the telling detail." — Jim Miller, *Newsweek*

"A superbly dramatic and informative account of current events on the other side of the globe. It is also a depth analysis, supported by a compelling thesis, of why events have proceeded as they have and why the drama is proving not only a tragedy for the people of Vietnam but also for the American people as well. . . . FitzGerald has unusual gifts as a narrator of large historical events. . . . The impact of her history is overwhelming."

— Christopher Lehmann-Haupt, *New York Times*

"Rarely have we been able to regard the Vietnamese and their divided country from the standpoint of an essential unity of culture, tradition, and ethnic identity. That is what makes *Fire in the Lake* such an important departure. . . . Miss FitzGerald's basic complaint is that the American failure in Vietnam has been our inability to perceive that all along 'the enemy' has been the people. And so the *Fire in the Lake*, the revolution being waged by the North and the Front, may be the only one capable of restoring order and unity to the wartorn society of Vietnam."

— Laurence Stern, *Washington Post Book World*

"The best part of *Fire in the Lake* describes how the Americans, as they defoliated the countryside, proceeded to corrupt the cities: to turn a land of farmers into a ghetto of refugees, shoeshine boys, and prostitutes. . . . By the end of the book, FitzGerald has presented two Vietnamese societies with nothing in common: that of the villages and that of the *bidonvilles*. The 'infra-structures' the American army rooted out were the traditional values of the ancestral culture. With so many families scattered and gone, these values are unlikely to become the basis of a new political order — Marxist or Confucian or otherwise."

— Tom Geoghegan, *New Republic*

"This is the richest kind of contemporary history; it places political and military events in cultural perspective. . . . FitzGerald is superb at clarifying the differences between Vietnamese and American cultures. . . . This is the best book on Vietnam."

— *New York Times* "Books of the Century

Books by Frances FitzGerald

Fire in the Lake:
The Vietnamese and the Americans in Vietnam

America Revised:
History Schoolbooks in the Twentieth Century

Cities on a Hill:
A Journey Through Contemporary American Cultures

Way Out There in the Blue:
Reagan, Star Wars and the End of the Cold War

Vietnam: Spirits of the Earth
with photographs by Mary Cross

FIRE IN THE LAKE

The Vietnamese and the Americans in Vietnam

Frances FitzGerald

Little, Brown and Company
Boston   New York   London

Originally published in hardcover by Little, Brown and
Company, August 1972
First Back Bay paperback edition, July 2002

Portions of this book appeared originally in *The New Yorker,*
in slightly different form.
Excerpts from testimony to the Joint Economic Committee
of Congress, January 1971, reprinted with permission of the
Boston Globe.
Quotations from *The Economics of Insurgency in the Mekong
Delta of Vietnam* by Robert L. Sansom © 1970 by MIT.
Reprinted with permission of the MIT Press, Cambridge,
Massachusetts.
The *I Ching,* or *Book of Changes,* translated by Richard
Wilhelm, rendered into English by Cary F. Baynes, Bollingen
Series XX (© 1950 and 1967 by Bollingen Foundation),
reprinted by permission of Princeton University Press:
pp. xlix–li and various small quotations.

ISBN 0–316–28423–8 (hc)/0–316–15919–0 (pb)
LIBRARY OF CONGRESS CONTROL NUMBER 72–186966

Q-MART

PRINTED IN THE UNITED STATES OF AMERICA

To the memory of
my father
and
Paul Mus

Note on the Title

Fire in the Lake comes from the *I Ching*, the Chinese Book of Changes, and it is the image of revolution. This image, like all of the others in the Book of Changes, is almost as old as China itself; for Vietnamese it forms the mental picture of change within the society.

The following note on the hexagrams and the Book of Changes comes from the introduction by Richard Wilhelm in the *I Ching* (Princeton University Press, 1967), pp. xlix-li.

At the outset the Book of Changes was a collection of linear signs to be used as oracles. In antiquity, oracles were everywhere in use; the oldest among them confined themselves to the answers yes and no. This type of oracular pronouncement is likewise the basis of the Book of Changes. "Yes" was indicated by a simple, unbroken line and "No" by a broken line. However, the need for a greater differentiation seems to have been felt at an early date, and the single lines were combined in pairs. To each of these combinations a third line was then added. In this way the eight trigrams came into being. These eight trigrams were conceived as images of all that happens in heaven and on earth. At the same time, they were held to be in a state of continual transition, one changing into another, just as transition from one phenomenon to another is continually taking place in the physical world. Here we have the fundamental concept of the Book of Changes. The eight trigrams are symbols standing for changing transitional states; they are images that are constantly undergoing change. Attention centers not on things in their state of being — as is chiefly the case in the Occident — but upon their movements in change. The eight trigrams therefore are not representations of things as such but their tendencies in movement. . . .

In order to achieve a still greater multiplicity, these eight images were combined with one another at a very early date, whereby a total of sixty-four signs was obtained. Each of these sixty-four signs consists of six lines, either positive or negative.

Preface

I went to South Vietnam in February 1966, and remained there until November of that year to write articles for the *Atlantic Monthly*, the *New York Times* Sunday Magazine, the *Village Voice*, *Vogue*, and other periodicals. My arrival in Saigon coincided with the Honolulu Conference and with the beginning of the Buddhist struggle movement of 1966. The succeeding political crisis within the Saigon government dramatically exposed the rift between the Vietnamese political reality and the American ambitions for the anti-Communist cause in the south. In the following months my attempt was to follow this rift and to try and understand the politics of Vietnam and the effect of the American presence and the war on Vietnamese society.

At the time there was little American scholarship on Vietnam and few Americans were engaged in a serious effort to understand the political, economic, and social issues at stake for the Vietnamese. Happily, not long after my arrival, I came across a copy of Paul Mus's important work on Vietnamese culture and the French war, *Sociologie d'une guerre*. The book not only answered a great number of questions the American experience raised, but it indicated an entirely new way of asking them. Upon my return to the United States I was fortunate enough to meet Professor Mus and to have the opportunity to study Vietnam under his guidance. I owe most of what I have learned to his wisdom and generosity.

My thanks also go to Mr. Joseph Buttinger for the use of his library and to the editors of the *Atlantic* for their kind encouragement.

— Saigon, 1972

Abbreviations

AID   (United States) Agency for International Development

ARVN   Army of the Republic of (South) Vietnam

DRVN   Democratic Republic of (North) Vietnam

GVN   Government of (South) Vietnam

MAAG   (United States) Military Assistance Advisory Group

MACV   (United States) Military Assistance Command, Vietnam

NLF   National Liberation Front

PRP   People's Revolutionary Party

USOM   United States Operations Mission

Contents

Contents

III. CONCLUSION

I

The Vietnamese

1

States of Mind

For ten years we have been engaged in negotiations, and yet
the enemy's intentions remain inscrutable.
— Hoang Dieu (1829–1882).
A letter from the commander
of the citadel of Hanoi to the
emperor just before the citadel's seizure by the French and
the suicide of its commander.

*The emperor of China sits on a raised dais in a vast hall thronged
with the mandarins in their embroidered robes. The hall itself lies
within the maze of a palace as large as any city on the earth; a
thousand elephants and countless foot soldiers guard its towering
stone walls, for the great halls of the palace contain such a wealth of
precious metals that the emperor himself cannot count it, and its
libraries enclose all the wisdom of the earth. Past the guards and in
through the glittering streets there rides today a man on a shaggy
horse wearing the outlandish dress of a barbarian. The man is a
chieftain in his own country, but he is as poor as any beggar in the
palace. He has ridden across the length of the known world to
Peking, still it seems to him that the road from the palace gates to
the interior is longer and more dangerous than any he has traveled.
He does not even know how to name the great beasts and the
shining metals that surround him, nor could he, the navigator of the
earth, find his way back to the gates unaided. And yet the emperor
and all his mandarins are waiting for him in the great hall, for there
has been some trouble in the chieftain's country that, despite the
efforts of all the Chinese armies of the border, threatens to spread to
the surrounding provinces.*

Somewhere, buried in the files of the television networks, lies a series of pictures, ranging over a decade, that chronicles the diplomatic history of the United States and the Republic of Vietnam. Somewhere there is a picture of President Eisenhower with Ngo Dinh Diem, a picture of Secretary McNamara with General Nguyen Khanh, one of President Johnson with Nguyen Cao Ky and another of President Nixon with President Thieu. The pictures are unexceptional. The obligatory photographs taken on such ceremonial occasions, they show men in gray business suits (one is in military fatigues) shaking hands or standing side-by-side on a podium. These pictures, along with the news commentaries, "President Nixon today reaffirmed his support for the Thieu regime," or "Hanoi refused to consider the American proposal," made up much of what Americans knew about the relationship between the two countries. But the pictures and news reports were to a great extent deceptions, for they did not show the disproportion between the two powers. One of the gray-suited figures, after all, represented the greatest power in the history of the world, a nation that could, if its rulers so desired, blow up the world, feed the earth's population, or explore the galaxy. The second figure in the pictures represented a small number of people in a country of peasants largely sustained by a technology centuries old. The meeting between the two was the meeting of two different dimensions, two different epochs of history. An imagined picture of a tributary chieftain coming to the Chinese court represents the relationship of the United States to the Republic of Vietnam better than the photographs from life. It represents what the physical and mental architecture of the twentieth century so often obscures.

At the beginning of their terms in office President Kennedy and President Johnson, perhaps, took full cognizance of the disproportion between the two countries, for they claimed, at least in the beginning, that the Vietnam War would require only patience from the United States. According to U.S. military intelligence, the enemy in the south consisted of little more than bands of guerrillas with hardly a truck in which to carry their borrowed weapons. The North Vietnamese possessed anti-aircraft guns and a steady supply of small munitions, but the United States could, so the officials promised, end their resistance with a few months of intensive bombing. In 1963 and 1965 few Americans imagined that a commitment to war in Vietnam would finally cost the United States billions of dollars, the production of its finest research and development laboratories, and fifty-five thousand American lives. They did not imagine that the Vietnam War would prove more politically divisive than any foreign war in the nation's history.

In one sense Presidents Kennedy and Johnson had seen the disproportion between the United States and Vietnam, but in another they did not see it at all. By intervening in the Vietnamese struggle the United States was attempting to fit its global strategies into a world of hillocks and hamlets, to reduce its majestic concerns for the containment of Communism and the security of the Free World to a dimension where governments rose and fell as a result of arguments between two colonels' wives. In going to Vietnam the United States was entering a country where the victory of one of the great world ideologies occasionally depended on the price of tea in a certain village or the outcome of a football game. For the Americans in Vietnam it would be difficult to make this leap of perspective, difficult to understand that while they saw themselves as building world order, many Vietnamese saw them merely as the producers of garbage from which they could build houses. The effort of translation was too great.

The televised pictures of the two chiefs of state were deceptive in quite another way: only one of the two nations saw them. Because of communications, the war was absurd for the civilians of both countries — but absurd in different ways. To one people the war would appear each day, compressed between advertisements and confined to a small space in the living room; the explosion of bombs and the cries of the wounded would become the background accompaniment to dinner. For the other people the war would come one day out of a clear blue sky. In a few minutes it would be over: the bombs, released by an invisible pilot with incomprehensible intentions, would leave only the debris and the dead behind. Which people was the best equipped to fight the war?

The disparity between the two countries only began with the matter of scale. They seemed, of course, to have come from the same country, those two figures in their identical business suits with their identical pronouncements. "The South Vietnamese people will never surrender to Communist tyranny," "We are fighting for the great cause of freedom," "We dedicate ourselves to the abolition of poverty, ignorance, and disease and to the work of the social revolution." In this case the deception served the purposes of state. The

Chinese emperor could never have claimed that in backing one nomad chieftain against another he was defending the representative of Chinese civilization. But the American officials in supporting the Saigon government insisted that they were defending "freedom and democracy" in Asia. They left the GIs to discover that the Vietnamese did not fit into their experience of either "Communists" or "democrats."

Under different circumstances this invincible ignorance might not have affected the outcome of the war. The fiction that the United States was defending "freedom and democracy" might have continued to exist in a sphere undisturbed by reality, a sphere frequented only by those who needed moral justification for the pursuit of what the U.S. government saw as its strategic interests. Certain "tough-minded" analysts and officials in any case ignored the moral argument. As far as they were concerned, the United States was not interested in the form of the Vietnamese government — indeed, it was not interested in the Vietnamese at all. Its concerns were for "containing the expansion of the Communist bloc" and preventing future "wars of national liberation" around the world. But by denying the moral argument in favor of power politics and "rational" calculations of United States interests, these analysts were, as it happened, overlooking the very heart of the matter, the issue on which success depended.

The United States came to Vietnam at a critical juncture of Vietnamese history — a period of metamorphosis more profound than any the Vietnamese had ever experienced. In 1954 the Vietnamese were gaining their independence after seventy years of French colonial rule. They were engaged in a struggle to create a nation and to adapt a largely traditional society to the modern world. By backing one contender — by actually creating that contender — the United States was not just fighting a border war or intervening, as Imperial China so often did, in a power struggle between two similar contenders, two dynasties. It was entering into a moral and ideological struggle over the form of the state and the goals of the society. Its success with its chosen contender would depend not merely on U.S. military power but on the resources of both the United States and the Saigon government to solve Vietnamese domestic problems in a manner acceptable to the Vietnamese. But what indeed were Vietnamese problems, and did they even exist in the terms in which Americans conceived them? The unknowns made the whole enterprise, from the most rational and tough-minded point of view, risky in the extreme.

In going into Vietnam the United States was not only transposing itself into a different epoch of history; it was entering a world qualitatively different from its own. Culturally as geographically Vietnam lies half a world away from the United States. Many Americans in Vietnam learned to speak Vietnamese, but the language gave no more than a hint of the basic intellectual grammar that lay beneath. In a sense there was no more correspondence between the two worlds than that between the atmosphere of the earth and that of the sea. There was no direct translation between them in the simple equations of x is y and a means b. To find the common ground that existed between them, both Americans and Vietnamese would have to re-create the whole world of the other, the whole intellectual landscape. The effort of comprehension would be only the first step, for it would reveal the deeper issues of the encounter. It would force both nations to consider again the question of morality, to consider which of their values belong only to themselves or only to a certain stage of development. It would, perhaps, allow them to see that the process of change in the life of a society is a delicate and mysterious affair, and that the introduction of the foreign and the new can have vast and unpredictable consequences. It might in the end force both peoples to look back upon their own society, for it is contrast that is the essence of vision.

The American intellectual landscape is, of course, largely an inheritance from Europe, that of the Vietnamese a legacy from China, but in their own independent development the two nations have in many respects moved even further apart from each other. As late as the end of the nineteenth century Americans had before them a seemingly unlimited physical space — a view of mountains, deserts, and prairies into which a man might move (or imagine moving) to escape the old society and create a new world for himself. The impulse to escape, the drive to conquest and expansion, was never contradicted in America as it was in Europe by physical boundaries or by the persistence of strong traditions. The nation itself seemed to be less of a vessel than a movement. The closing of the frontier did not mean the end to expansion, but rather the beginning of it in a new form. The development of industry permitted the creation of new resources, new markets, new power over the world that had brought it into being. Americans ignore history, for to them everything has always seemed new under the sun. The national myth is that of creativity and progress, of a steady climbing upward into power and prosperity, both for the individual and for the country as a whole. Americans see history as a straight line and themselves standing at the cutting edge of it as representatives for all mankind. They believe in the future as if it were a religion; they believe that there is nothing they cannot accomplish, that solutions wait somewhere for all problems, like brides. Different though they were, both John Kennedy and Lyndon Johnson accepted and participated in this national myth. In part perhaps by virtue of their own success, they were optimists who looked upon their country as willing and able to right its own wrongs and to succor the rest of the world. They believed in the power of science, the power of the will, and the virtues of competition. Many Americans now question their confidence; still, the optimism of the nation is so great that even the question appears as a novelty and a challenge.

In their sense of time and space, the Vietnamese and the Americans stand in the relationship of a reversed mirror image, for the very notion of competition, invention, and change is an extremely new one for most Vietnamese. Until the French conquest of Vietnam in the nineteenth century, the Vietnamese practiced the same general technology for a thousand years. Their method of rice culture was far superior to any other in Southeast Asia; still it confined them to the river-fed lowlands between the Annamite cordillera and the sea. Hemmed in by China to the north and the Hindu kingdom of Champa to the south, the Vietnamese lived for the bulk of their history within the closed circle of the Red River Delta. They conquered Champa and moved south down the narrow littoral, but they might by American or Chinese standards have been standing still, for it took them five centuries to conquer a strip of land the length of Florida. The Vietnamese pride themselves less on their conquests than on their ability to resist and to survive. Living under the great wing of China, they bought their independence and maintained it only at a high price of blood. Throughout their history they have had to acknowledge the preponderance of the great Middle Kingdom both as the power and as the hub of culture. The Vietnamese knew their place in the world and guarded it jealously.

For traditional Vietnamese the sense of limitation and enclosure was as much a part of individual life as of the life of the nation. In

what is today northern and central Vietnam the single form of
Vietnamese settlement duplicated the closed circle of the nation.
Hidden from sight behind their high hedges of bamboos, the villages stood like nuclei within their surrounding circle of rice fields.
Within the villages as within the nation the amount of arable land
was absolutely inelastic. The population of the village remained
stable, and so to accumulate wealth meant to deprive the rest of the
community of land, to fatten while one's neighbor starved. Vietnam
is no longer a closed economic system, but the idea remains with the
Vietnamese that great wealth is antisocial, not a sign of success but
a sign of selfishness.

With a stable technology and a limited amount of land the traditional Vietnamese lived by constant repetition, by the sowing and
reaping of rice and by the perpetuation of customary law. The
Vietnamese worshiped their ancestors as the source of their lives,
their fortunes, and their civilization. In the rites of ancestor worship
the child imitated the gestures of his grandfather so that when he
became the grandfather, he could repeat them exactly to his grandchildren. In this passage of time that had no history the death of a
man marked no final end. Buried in the rice fields that sustained his
family, the father would live on in the bodies of his children and
grandchildren. As time wrapped around itself, the generations to
come would regard him as the source of their present lives and the
arbiter of their fate. In this continuum of the family "private property" did not really exist, for the father was less of an owner than a
trustee of the land to be passed on to his children. To the Vietnamese the land itself was the sacred, constant element: the people
flowed over the land like water, maintaining and fructifying it for
the generations to come.

Late in the war — about 1968 — a Vietnamese soldier came with
his unit to evacuate the people of a starving village in Quang Nam
province so that the area might be turned into a "free fire zone."
While the villagers were boarding the great American helicopters,
one old man ran away from the soldiers shouting that he would
never leave his home. The soldiers followed the old man and found
him hiding in a tunnel beside a small garden planted with a few
pitiful stunted shrubs. When they tried to persuade him to go with
the others, he refused, saying, "I have to stay behind to look after
this piece of garden. Of all the property handed down to me by my
ancestors, only this garden now remains. I have to guard it for my

grandson." Seeing the soldiers look askance, the old man admitted that his grandson had been conscripted and that he had not heard from him in two years. He paused, searching for an explanation, and then said, "If I leave, the graves of my ancestors, too, will become forest. How can I have the heart to leave?"

The soldiers turned away from the old man and departed, for they understood that for him to leave the land would be to acknowledge the final death of the family — a death without immortality. By deciding to stay he was deciding to sacrifice his life in postponement of that end. When the soldiers returned to the village fourteen months later, they found that an artillery shell had closed the entrance to the tunnel, making it a grave for the old man.[1]

Many American officials understood that the land and the graves of the ancestors were important to the Vietnamese. Had they understood exactly why, they might not have looked upon the wholesale creation of refugees as a "rational" method of defeating Communism. For the traditional villager, who spent his life immobile, bound to the rice land of his ancestors, the world was a very small place. It was in fact the village or *xa*, a word that in its original Chinese roots signified "the place where people come together to worship the spirits." In this definition of society the character "earth" took precedence, for, as the source of life, the earth was the basis for the social contract between the members of the family and the members of the village. Americans live in a society of replaceable parts — in theory anyone can become President or sanitary inspector — but the Vietnamese lived in a society of particular people, all of whom knew each other by their place in the landscape. "Citizenship" in a Vietnamese village was personal and untransferable. In the past, few Vietnamese ever left their village in times of peace, for to do so was to leave society itself — all human attachments, all absolute rights and duties. When the soldiers of the nineteenth-century Vietnamese emperors came to the court of Hue, they prayed to the spirits of the Perfume River, "We are lost here [*depaysée*] and everything is unknown to us. We prostrate ourselves before you [in the hope that] you will lead us to the good and drive the evil away from us."[2] The soldiers were "lost" in more than a geographical sense, for without their land and their place in the village, they were without a social identity. To drive the twentieth-century villager off his land was in the same way to drive him off the edges of his old life and to expose him directly to the political movement that could best provide him with a new identity.

During the war the village *dinh* or shrine still stood in many of the villages of the south as testimony to the endurance of the traditional political design of the nation. In prehistoric times, before the advent of national government, the *dinhs* referred to the god of the particular earth beneath the village. In assuming temporal power, the emperors of Vietnam took on the responsibility to perform the rites of the agriculture for all the Vietnamese villages and replaced the local spirits with the spirits of national heroes and genii. Under their reign the *dinh* contained the imperial charter that incorporated the village into the empire, making an ellision between the ideas of "land," "Emperor," and "Vietnamese." The French brushed away the sacred web of state, but they did not destroy this confluence of ideas. The Vietnamese call their nation *dat nuoc*, "earth and water" — the phrase referring both to the trickle of water through one rice field and the "mountains and rivers" of the nation.

Like the Celestial Empire of China, the Vietnamese empire was in one aspect a ritual state whose function was to preside over the sacred order of nature and society. At its apex the emperor stood as its supreme magician-god endowed with the responsibility to maintain the harmonious balance of the *yin* and the *yang*, the two related forces of the universe. His success in this enterprise (like that of the villagers in the rites of ancestor worship) depended upon the precision with which he followed the elaborate set of rituals governing his relations with the celestial authorities and the people of the empire. To act in conformity with the traditional etiquette was to insure harmony and prosperity for the entire nation. In A.D. 1129 the Emperor Ly Than Tong proclaimed to the court: "We have little virtue; we have transgressed the order of Heaven, and upset the natural course of events; last year the spring was blighted by a long rain; this year there is a long drought. . . . Let the mandarins examine my past acts in order to discover any errors or faults, so that they may be remedied."[3] In analyzing these disasters the emperor blamed them on his deviation from Tao, the traditional way, which was at once the most moral and the most scientific course.

As Americans are, so to speak, canted towards the future, the traditional Vietnamese were directed towards the past, both by the small tradition of the family and the great tradition of the state. Confucianism — the very foundation of the state — was not merely a "traditional religion," as Judaism and Christianity are the traditional religions of the West. Originating in a society of ancestor worshipers, it was, like ancestor worship itself, a sacralization of the past. Unlike the great Semitic prophets, Confucius did not base his teachings on a single, contemporary revelation. "I for my part am not one of those who have innate knowledge," he said. "I am simply one who loves the past and is diligent in investigating it."[4] According to tradition, Confucius came to his wisdom through research into the great periods of Chinese civilization — the Chou empire and its predecessors in the distant past. Tradition presents the Master not as a revolutionary but as a true reactionary. Arriving at certain rules and precepts for the proper conduct of life, he did not pretend to have comprehended all wisdom, but merely to have set up guideposts pointing towards the Tao or true way of life. For him the Tao was the enlightened process of induction that led endlessly backwards into the past of civilization. The Tao may have been for him a secular concern, a matter of enlightened self-interest. ("The Master never spoke of the spirits," reported his disciples, leaving the question moot.) But for later Confucians it had a sacred weight reinforced by magic and the supernatural.

For traditional Vietnamese, formal education consisted of the study of the Confucian texts — the works of the Master and the later commentaries. To pass beyond the small tradition of the family and the village was therefore not to escape the dominion of the past, but to enter into it more fully. The mandarins, the literate elite, directed all their scholarship not towards invention and progress, but towards a more perfect repetition of the past, a more perfect maintenance of the status quo. When a French steamship was sighted off the shores of Vietnam in the early nineteenth century (or so the story goes) the local mandarin-governor, instead of going to see it, researched the phenomenon in his texts, concluded it was a dragon, and dismissed the matter.[5]

As long as Vietnamese society remained a closed system, its intellectual foundations remained flawless and immobile. Quite clearly, however, they could not survive contact with the West, for they were based on the premise that there was nothing new under the sun. But the coming of the French posed a terrible problem for the Vietnamese. Under the dominion of the old empire the Vietnamese were not members of a religious community (like the Christians of Byzantium or the Muslims of the Abbasid caliphate) but participants in a whole, indivisible culture. Like the Chinese, they considered those who lived outside of its seamless web to be by definition barbarians. When the Vietnamese conquered peoples of other cultures — such as the Chams — they included these people within the structure of empire only on condition of their total assimilation. The peoples they could not assimilate, they simply surrounded, amoeba-like, and left them to follow their own laws. The various montagnard tribes that lived beyond the zone of wet-rice cultivation retained their own languages, customs, and governments for thousands of years inside Vietnam. But with the arrival of the French forces in the nineteenth century the Vietnamese confronted a civilization more powerful than their own; for the first time since the Chinese conquest in the second century B.C. they faced the possibility of having to assimilate themselves. Confucianism was, after all, not merely a religion or an arbitrary morality, but a science that operated inside history. Confucius said, "If it is really possible to govern countries by ritual and yielding, there is no more to be said. But if it is not really possible, of what use is ritual?"[6] The rituals and the way of life they confirmed did not help the Vietnamese defend themselves against the French, and thus certain mandarins concluded they had to be abandoned. As the French armies swept across the Mekong Delta, Phan Thanh Giang, the governor of the western provinces, reconciled this logic with his loyalty to the nation by committing suicide and ordering his sons not to serve the French but to bring up their children in the French way.[7]

Similarly, those mandarins who decided to resist the French saw the foreign armies as a threat not only to their national sovereignty and to their beliefs, but to their entire way of life. The southern patriots warned their people:

Our country has always been known as a land of deities; shall we now permit a horde of dogs and goats to stain it?
The moral obligations binding a king to his subjects, parents to their children, and husbands to their wives were highly respected. Everyone enjoyed the most peaceful relationships.
Our customs and habits were so perfect that in our country, in our ancestors' tombs, and in our homes, all things were in a proper state.
But from the moment they arrived with their ill luck,
Happiness and peace seem to have departed from everywhere.[8]

And the mandarins were correct: the French occupation changed the Vietnamese way of life permanently. Since the Second World War the Vietnamese have been waging a struggle not merely over the form of their state but over the nature of Vietnamese society, the very identity of the Vietnamese. It is the grandeur of the stakes involved that has made the struggle at once so intense and so opaque to Westerners.

Just before the fall of the Diem regime in 1963 the American journalists in Vietnam wrote long and somewhat puzzling analyses of the Buddhist demonstrations, in which they attempted to explain how much the rebellion against Diem owed to "purely religious" motives, how much to "purely political" ones. Like most Westerners, these journalists were so entrenched in their Western notion of the division of church and state that they could not imagine the Vietnamese might not make the distinction. But until the arrival of the European missionaries there was never such a thing as a church in Vietnam. Shaped by a millennium of Chinese rule and another of independence within the framework of Southeast Asia, the "Vietnamese religion" was a blend of Confucianism, Taoism, and Buddhism sunken into a background of animism. More than a "religion" in any Western sense, it was the authority for, and the confirmation of, an entire way of life — an agriculture, a social structure, a political system. Its supernatural resembled one of those strange metaphysical puzzles of Jorge Luis Borges: an entire community imagines another one which, though magical and otherworldly, looks, detail for detail, like itself. In the courts of Hue and Thanglong, organization-minded genii presided over every government department and took responsibility for the success or failure of each mandarin's enterprise. (During a long period of drought in the seventeenth century the Emperor Le Thai Ton ordered his mandarins: "Warn the genii on my behalf that if it doesn't rain in three days, I will have their tablets boiled and thrown in the river so as to prevent my people from uselessly throwing away their money on them.")[9] In the villages the peasants recognized hosts of local spirits and ghosts as well as the official genii delegated by the mandarins. In Paul Mus's words, religion was the "spiritualization of the community itself" and "the administration of Heaven." The "religion," in some sense, was the state and vice versa — except that the emperor was not the representative of God on earth, but rather a collective moral personality, a representation of the sacred community to itself.

For the Vietnamese today as in centuries past, each regime — each state or political movement — has its own "virtue," its own character, which, like that of a human being, combines moral, social, and political qualities in a single form. Whether secular parties or religious sects, all modern Vietnamese political movements embrace a total design for the moral life of the individual and the social order of the nation. With Ngo Dinh Diem, for instance, this spherical Confucian universe showed up continually through the flat surfaces of Western language. He spoke of himself as the chosen of Heaven, the leader elected to defend Vietnamese morality and culture. The Buddhist leaders had much the same pretensions, and even for the Vietnamese Communists, the heirs to nineteenth-century Western distinctions between church and state, between one class and another, the society retains its moral impulse, its balanced Confucian design.

Never having known a serious ideological struggle in their history, many Americans persisted in thinking of the Vietnamese conflict as a civil war, as a battle between two fixed groups of people with different but conceivably negotiable interests. But the regional conflict existed only within the context of a larger struggle that resembled a series of massive campaigns of conversion involving all the people in the country and the whole structure of society. Owing to the nature of the old society, the struggle was even more all-encompassing than the European revolutionary wars. Americans, and indeed most Westerners, have lived for centuries with a great variety of institutions — with churches, with governments, with a patriarchal family, with industrial concerns, trade unions and fraternities, each of which offered a different kind of organization, different kinds of loyalties — but the Vietnamese have lived with only three: the family, the village, and the state.[10] As the family provided the model for village and state, there was only one type of organization. Taken together, the three formed a crystalline world, geometrically congruent at every level. The mandarins, for instance, were known as the "fathers of the people," and they stood in the same relationship to the emperor (himself the "son of Heaven") as the Vietnamese son stood to his father. Recruited by competitive examination, they moved closer to the emperor, that is, higher in the great imperial family, as they passed through the grades of the examination system. The village was a more informal organization — a Vietnamese deviation from the orthodox Chinese model — but it reflected a similar hierarchical design. The "government" of the family, the village, and the empire derived from one single set of instructions. Thus a change in one implied a change in all the others.[11]

To American officials throughout the war it seemed absolutely unreasonable that the non-Communist sects and political factions could not come to some agreement, could not cooperate even in their opposition to the Communists. But then the Americans had been brought up in a pluralistic world, where even the affairs of the family are managed by compromise between its members. In the traditional Vietnamese family — a family whose customs survived even into the twentieth century — the father held absolute authority over his wife (or wives) and children. The Vietnamese woman by custom wielded a great deal more power than her Chinese sister, but the traditional Chinese-based law specified that the patriarch governed his wife and children as he governed his rice fields. In theory, though not by customary practice, he could dispose of them as he wished, and they had no recourse against him.[12] The emperor held a similar power over the great family of the empire. By law the trustee of all the rice lands,[13] he held them for the villages on condition of their productivity and good behavior. Without a priesthood or independent feudal aristocracy to obstruct the unified field of his power, he exercised authority through a bureaucracy of mandarins totally dependent on him. Though Vietnam was often divided between warlord families, the disputes were never resolved by a sharing of power — by treaties such as the dukes of Burgundy made with the kings of France — but always by the restoration of an absolute monarch. Even after Vietnam had been divided for two centuries between the Trinh dynasty in the north and the Nguyen in the south, the Vietnamese would not acknowledge the legitimacy of both sovereigns. To do so would have been to assert that the entire moral and social fabric of the community had dissolved. As a family can have only one father, so the nation could have only one emperor to preside over its one Tao or way of life.

Good conduct, then contentment; thus calm prevails. Hence there follows the hexagram of PEACE. Peace means union and interrelation.

In the *I Ching*, the ancient Chinese Book of Changes, lie all the clues to the basic design of the Sino-Vietnamese world. As the commentary to the verse explains, the Chinese character translated as "peace" implies not only the absence of conflict, but a positive union conducive to prosperity and contentment. To the Vietnamese of the twentieth century "peace" meant not a compromise between various interest groups and organizations, but the restoration of a single, uniform way of life. The Vietnamese were not interested in pluralism, they were interested in unanimity.

Since the Second World War one of the main reasons for the hostility of American intellectuals to Communism has been the suppression of intellectual freedom by Communist leaders in the Soviet Union and the Eastern European countries. In an attempt to rally Americans to the Vietnam War U.S. officials and their sympathizers took pains to argue that the Vietnamese Communists came from the same totalitarian mold. The difficulty with their argument was, however, that the non-Communist Vietnamese leaders believed in intellectual freedom no more than the Communists — a fact that would seem to indicate that their attitudes were founded not in ideology but in culture.

Intellectual freedom, of course, implies intellectual diversity. Westerners tend to take that diversity for granted, for the Western child, even of the narrowest background, grows up with a wide variety of authorities — parents, teachers, clergy, professional men, artists, scientists, and a host of other experts. The traditional Vietnamese child, however, grew up into a monolithic world composed of the family and its extensions in the state. For him there was no alternative to the authority of the father and no question of specialized knowledge. The education of a mandarin was greater, but hardly more diverse, than that of the rice farmer, for the Confucian tradition provided a personal philosophy, a religion, a technology, and a method of managing the state. For the mandarin there was no such thing as "pure science" or "knowledge for its own sake." There was (somewhere) a single correct answer to every question; the mandarin therefore studied in order to learn how to act.

The Vietnamese have lived with diversity for over a century, but the majority — including many of those brought up with French education — still perceive the intellectual world as uniform and absolute. While teaching at the Saigon university in 1957 one young American professor discovered at the second session of his course on comparative government that several students had memorized large sections of their first reading assignment. Pleased but somewhat bewildered, he asked them to finish their work on Machiavelli and turn to Montesquieu. The next day after class the students came to him in open rebellion. "What do you mean?" they asked angrily. "What do you mean by teaching us one thing one day and one thing the next?" The students could not conceive that government could be a matter of opinion. Either a government had worked or it had not, and if it had not worked, then it was not a proper subject for study. Ho Chi Minh said in answer to the question "What is the aim of study?": "One must study in order to remould one's thinking . . . to foster one's revolutionary virtues. . . . Study is aimed at action: the two must go hand in hand. The former without the latter is useless. The latter without the former is hard to carry through."[14]

In trying to teach comparative government, the American professor had, of course, assumed that his Vietnamese students possessed certain analytical tools: a conceptual framework, for instance, that allowed them to abstract the idea "government" from all the various instances of government that have existed in the world. In his course he would often be working from the general to the particular by a process of deductive logic. (A republic has certain characteristics, this state has the same characteristics, therefore it must be a republic.) What he did not realize was that his logic was hardly more universal than the forms of government he was discussing, and that most Vietnamese have an entirely different organization of mind.

The Chinese system of orthography, used by the Vietnamese until the mid-nineteenth century,[15] was not, like the Roman alphabet, composed of regular, repeatable symbols. It was built of particulars. The ideograms for such abstract notions as "fear" or "pleasure" were composed of pictures of concrete events (the pictures of a man, a house, and so on) and to the highly literate these events were always visible within the larger word. The writing was therefore without abstraction, for each word has its own atmosphere, impossible to translate into Western languages and irreducible to categories. Each word was a thing-in-itself.[16] Traditional Vietnamese education accorded with its medium. The child did not learn "principles" from his parents, he learned how to imitate his father in his every action. Confucius said, "When your father is alive, discover his project and when he is dead, remember his actions. If in three years you have not left the road followed by your father, you are really a son full of filial piety."[17] In his formal education the child encountered not a series of "disciplines" but a vast, unsystematized collection of stories and precepts. In the Confucian texts instructions on how to dress and write poetry were juxtaposed with injunctions to such virtues as patience and humility. Each precept, independently arrived at by a process of induction (the Confucian researches into the past), had its own absolute importance for the proper conduct of life. Phrased, perhaps, as a moral absolute, the precept still depended for authority on the success it was thought to have conferred in the past. Confucian logic was, in a sense, pure pragmatism applied over a vast distance in time. In reading the Confucian precepts the child arrived not at a theory of behavior but at a series of clues to the one true way of life.

At the end of his scholarly book, *Viet Cong*, Douglas Pike, an American official and the leading government analyst of the National Liberation Front, breaks out of his neutral tone to conclude: "The NLF and the people it influenced lived in a muzzy, myth-filled world of blacks and whites, good and evil, a simplistic world quite out of character with the one to which the Vietnamese was accustomed. . . . Here, one felt, was tomorrow's society, the beginning of 1984, where peace is war, slavery is freedom, the nonorganization is the organization."[18] American officials might, perhaps, legitimately criticize the National Liberation Front, but they have had, as in this instance, a curious tendency to criticize what is most typically and essentially Vietnamese. A world where there is no clear air of abstraction, no "principles" and no "theories," cannot but seem "muzzy" and "myth-filled" to Westerners. The Vietnamese Communist leaders differ from the non-Communists only in that they have successfully assimilated the Western conceptual framework and translated it into a form of intellectual organization that their less educated compatriots can understand. Like Mao's *Thoughts,* the NLF's "Three Silences" and "Six Duties of a Party Member" correspond exactly to the Confucian precepts. Taken together, they do not form an "ideology" in the Western sense, but the elements of a Tao, or, as the Vietnamese now call it, a "style of work," a "style of life." As for the NLF being "tomorrow's society, the beginning of 1984, where peace is war, slavery is freedom," it is not perhaps so different from the United States government — at least on the subject of Vietnam. In 1970, for instance, President

Nixon called the American invasion of Cambodia a "step towards peace" and his firm stand behind President Thieu a firm stand "for the right of all the South Vietnamese people to determine for themselves the kind of government they want."[19] The difference between the two is simply that Americans have traditionally distinguished between objective truth and political persuasion, description and project, whereas the Vietnamese have not — at least not in the same manner.

Westerners naturally look upon it as sinister that the children of North Vietnam and the NLF zones of the South learn to read and do arithmetic from political material. But "politics," or "government" in the widest sense of the word, was also the basis for the traditional education. Confucianism was, first and foremost, a philosophy of social organization. The Confucian texts, for instance, provided the foundation for the imperial law. (Is not the law . . . true virtue? asked one of the nineteenth-century intellectuals. "In the law we can . . . find complete expositions of the three duties [of a prince, a father, and a husband] and of the five constant virtues [benevolence, righteousness, propriety, knowledge, and sincerity] as well as the tasks of the six ministries [of the central government]."[20]) As one historian has pointed out, the texts established a social contract between the government and the governed, for in order to claim legitimacy the emperor would have to echo Confucius's "I invent nothing, I transmit," thus acknowledging the limitations on his personal power. To learn how to read was therefore already to learn the management of the state. Because the Confucian texts formed the whole of civil education, the bias of the intellectuals was towards these "human sciences," towards practical instruction in the governing of society. To the traditional Confucian scholars all knowledge led back into the political and moral world of man. Mathematics and the physical sciences were no exceptions for, as scientists, the Confucians understood the universe as a unified "field" in which the movements of heaven and earth directly affect human society. The aim of the physical sciences was to plot these movements, these changes, so that man might put himself in tune with the world and with his fellow men. The mandarins, for instance, studied astrology in order to learn the political outlook for the nation: the appearance of comets or the fall of meteorites presaged the smaller disturbances of man. While man could do nothing by himself, he could with intelligence discern the heavenly movements and put his own smaller sphere in accord with the larger one. In China, after a dynastic struggle, the new emperor coming to power would break the instruments of the court musicians in the conviction that they, like the old dynasty, were out of tune with the universe — that they had in some sense caused the rebellion. Similarly, the new emperor would initiate the "rectification of names" so that the words he used for the affairs of state should (unlike those of his predecessor) perfectly accord with the magical etiquette governing the relations of man and nature.

At the time of the Buddhist struggle in 1966 the Buddhist leaders claimed, "Ninety percent of the Vietnamese are Buddhists . . . the people are never Communists," while the NLF leaders claimed by contrast, "The struggle of the religious believers in Vietnam is not separate from the struggle for national liberation." The two statements were mutually contradictory, and an American might have concluded that one or both of their proponents was telling an untruth. But neither the Buddhists nor the NLF leaders were actually "lying," as an American might have been under similar circumstances. Both groups were "rectifying the names" of the Vietnamese to accord with what was no longer the "will of Heaven" but "the laws of history" or "the spirit of the times." They were announcing a project and making themselves comprehensible to their countrymen, for whom all knowledge, even the most neutral observation, is to be put to use.[21]

With this intellectual framework in mind it is perhaps easier to see why the pilots of the People's Republic of China should read Mao's *Thoughts* in order to learn how to fly an airplane. The Vietnamese Communists look upon technology as an independent discipline in certain respects, but they insist that political education should be the basis for using it. During the period of conflict and change in their society, this emphasis on politics is not, perhaps, as unreasonable as it seems to most Americans. Without political education it proved useless or destructive for the cadets of the Saigon air force to learn how to fly airplanes.

For Americans the close relationship the Vietnamese draw between morality, politics, and science is perhaps more difficult to understand now than at any other time in history. Today, living in a social milieu completely divided over matters of value and belief, Westerners have come to look upon science and logic alone as containing universal truths. Over the past century Western philosophers have worked to purge their disciplines of ethical and metaphysical concerns; Americans in particular have tended to deify the natural sciences and set them apart from their social goals. Under pressure from this demand for "objective truth," the scholars of human affairs have scrambled to give their own disciplines the authority and neutrality of science. But because the social scientists can rarely attain the same criteria for "truth" as physicists or chemists, they have sometimes misused the discipline and taken merely the trappings of science as a camouflage for their own beliefs and values. It is thus that many American "political scientists" sympathetic to American intervention in Vietnam have concluded that the NLF's subordination of science and "objective truth" to politics has its origins in Communist totalitarianism.

For Westerners who believe in the eternal verity of certain principles the notion of "brainwashing" is shocking and the experience is associated with torture. But in such societies as those in Indonesia, China, and Vietnam, it is in one form or another an activity of every political movement. Under the traditional Vietnamese empire there was only one truth, only one true way. And all modern Vietnamese parties have had to face the task of changing the nature of the "truth." Among people with an extremely pragmatic cast of mind, for whom values depend for their authority upon success, the task has implied a demonstration that the old ways are no longer useful, no longer adapted to the necessities of history. During the course of the war both the Saigon government and the NLF held "re-education" courses for defectors and prisoners, with varying degrees of success. Those Americans who objected to the process (and most Americans singled out the NLF) saw it in European terms as the forcible destruction of personality, a mental torture such as Arthur Koestler described in *Darkness at Noon*. But to the Vietnamese, Communist and non-Communist, it did not imply torture at all, for the reason that they have a very different kind of commitment to society than do Westerners.

And it is this commitment that lies at the basis of intellectual organization. Unlike the Westerner, the Vietnamese child is brought up not to follow certain principles, but to accept the authority of certain people. The "Three Net Ropes" of the traditional society consisted in the loyalty of the son to his father, of the wife to her husband, and the mandarin to his emperor. The injunctions to filial piety and conjugal obedience were unconditional. Traditional Vietnamese law rested not upon the notion of individual rights, but the notion of duties — the duty of the sovereign to his people, the father to his son, and vice versa. Similarly, the Confucian texts defined no general principles but the proper relationship of man to man. Equal justice was secondary to social harmony. This particular form of social contract gave the individual a very different sense of himself, of his own personality. In the Vietnamese language there is no word that exactly corresponds to the Western personal pronoun I, *je, ich.* When a man speaks of himself, he calls himself "your brother," "your nephew," "your teacher," depending upon his relationship to the person he addresses. The word he uses for the first person (*toi*) in the new impersonal world of the cities originally denoted "subject of the king."[22] The traditional Vietnamese did not see himself as a totally independent being, for he did not distinguish himself as acutely as does a Westerner from his society (and by extension, the heavens). He did not see himself as a "character" formed of immutable traits, eternally loyal to certain principles, but rather as a system of relationships, a function of the society around him. In a sense, the design of the Confucian world resembled that of a Japanese garden where every rock, opaque and indifferent in itself, takes on significance from its relationship to the surrounding objects.

In central Vietnam, where the villages are designed like Japanese gardens, a young Vietnamese district chief once told this writer that he had moved a group of villagers from a Liberation village to his headquarters in order to "change their opinions." He had not lectured the villagers on the evils of Marxism and he did not plan to do so; he would simply wait for them to fall into relationship with his political authority. Had the villagers, of course, received an adequate political education, his waiting would be in vain. A "hardcore" NLF cadre would understand his community to include not only the village or the district but all of Vietnam. His horizons would be large enough in time and space to encompass a government-controlled city or years of a harsh, inconclusive war. But with regard to his refugees, the district chief was probably right: the old people and the children had left their NLF sympathies behind them in the burning ruins of a village only two miles distant.

In the old society, of course, a man who moved out of his village would find in his new village or in the court of Hue the same kind of social and political system that he had left behind him. During the conflicts of the twentieth century, however, his movement from one place to another might require a change of "ideology," or of way of life. In 1966 one American official discovered an ARVN soldier who had changed sides five times in the war, serving alternately with three NLF units and three GVN battalions. Clearly this particular soldier had no political education to speak of and no wider sense of community. But even for those that did, the possibility of accommodation and change remained open. When asked by an American interviewer what he thought of the GVN, one Front defector found it necessary to specify that "with the mind of the other regime" (i.e., that of the NLF) he felt it was bad for the people. At that point he was preparing himself to accept a new interpretation.

Such changes of mind must look opportunistic or worse to Westerners, but to the Vietnamese with their particular commitment to society it was at once the most moral and the most practical course. Indeed, it was the only course available, for in such situations the Vietnamese villager did not consider an alternative. In the old language, a man depended upon the "will of Heaven"; it was therefore his duty to accommodate himself to it as well as possible. In a letter to his subordinates of the southern provinces Phan Thanh Giang described this ethic of accommodation in the most sophisticated Confucian terms:

It is written that he who lives according to Heaven's will is in the right way; he who departs from Heaven's will is wrong. To act according to Heaven's will is to act according to one's reason. Man is an intelligent animal created by Heaven. Each animal lives according to its proper nature, like water which seeks its own level or fire which spreads in dry places. . . . Man to whom Heaven has given reason should endeavor to live according to that reason.[23]

In conclusion Phan Thanh Giang requested that his officials surrender without resistance to the invading French forces. "The French," he wrote, "have huge battleships, full of soldiers and armed with powerful cannons. . . . It would be as senseless for you to assail [them] as for the fawn to attack the tiger. You would only draw suffering upon the people whom Heaven has entrusted to your care."[24] Loyal to the Vietnamese emperor, Phan Thanh Giang could not so easily accommodate himself to necessity. Branding himself as a traitor, he chose the same course that, throughout history, his predecessors had taken at the fall of dynasties. Suicide was the only resolution to the unbearable conflict between loyalty to the emperor and obligation to what he saw as the will of Heaven, to the will of the community as a whole.

But such protests against the will of Heaven were only for the mandarins, the moral leaders of the community. They were not for the simple villager, for as Confucius said, "The essence of the gentleman is that of wind; the essence of small people is that of grass. And when a wind passes over the grass, it cannot choose but bend."[25] In times of political stability the villager accommodated himself to the prevailing wind that clearly signaled the will of Heaven. Only in times of disorder and uncertainty when the sky clouded over and the forces of the world struggled to uncertain outcome, only then did the peasant take on responsibility for the great affairs of state, and only then did the leaders watch him carefully, for, so went the Confucian formula, "The will of Heaven is reflected in the eyes and ears of the people."

This ancient political formula clarified the basis on which twentieth-century Vietnamese, including those who no longer used the old language, would make their political decisions. Asked which side he supported, one peasant from a village close to Saigon told a Front cadre in 1963: "I do not know, for I follow the will of Heaven. If I do what you say, then the Diem side will arrest me; if I say things against you, then you will arrest me, so I would rather carry both burdens on my shoulders and stand in the middle." Caught between two competing regimes, the peasant did not assert his right to decide between them, rather he asked himself where his duty lay. Which regime had the power to claim his loyalty? Which would be the most likely to restore peace and harmony to his world? His decision might be based on personal preference (a government that considered the wishes of the people would be more likely to restore peace on a permanent basis). But he had, nonetheless, to make an objective analysis of the situation and take his gamble, for his first loyalty lay neither with the Diem regime nor the NLF but with the will of Heaven that controlled them both. At certain periods *attentisme* was the most moral and the most practical course.

As a warning to Westerners on the difficulties of understanding the twentieth-century conflict in Vietnam, Paul Mus told an ancient Chinese legend that is well known to the Vietnamese. There was trouble in the state of Lu, and the reigning monarch called in

Confucius to ask for his help. When he arrived at the court, the Master went to a public place and took a seat in the correct way, facing south, and all the trouble disappeared.[26]

The works of Vo Nguyen Giap are but addenda to this legend, for the legend is the paradigm of revolution in Vietnam. To the Vietnamese it is clear from the story that Confucius was not taking an existential or exemplary position, he was actually changing the situation. Possessed of neither godlike nor prophetic authority, he moved an entire kingdom by virtue of his sensitivity to the will of Heaven as reflected in the "eyes and ears of the people." As executor for the people, he clarified their wishes and signaled the coming — or the return — of the Way that would bring harmony to the kingdom. For the Hoa Hao and the Cao Dai, the traditionalist sects of the south that in the twentieth century still believed in this magical "sympathy" of heaven and earth, political change did not depend entirely on human effort. Even the leaders of the sects believed that if they, like Confucius, had taken "the correct position," the position that accorded with the will of Heaven, all Vietnamese would eventually adopt the same Way, the same political system that they had come to.

Here, within the old spiritualist language, lies a clue as to why the Vietnamese Communists held their military commanders in strict subordination to the political cadres. Within the domestic conflict military victories were not only less important than political victories, but they were strictly meaningless except as reflections of the political realities. For the Communists, as for all the other political groups, the vehicle of political change was not the war, the pitch of force against force, but the struggle, the attempt to make manifest that their Way was the only true or "natural" one for all Vietnamese.* Its aim was to demonstrate that, in the old language, the Mandate of Heaven had changed and the new order had already replaced the old in all but title. When Ho Chi Minh entered Hanoi in August 1945, he made much the same kind of gesture as Confucius had made in facing south when he said (and the wording is significant, for he was using a language of both East and West), "We, members of the Provisional Government of the Democratic Republic of Viet-Nam solemnly declare to the world that Viet-Nam

---

* "The English word 'struggle,' a pale translation of the Vietnamese term *dau tranh,* fails to convey the drama, the awesomeness, the totality of the original." (Douglas Pike, *Viet Cong,* p. 85.)

has the right to be a free and independent country — and in fact it is so already. The entire Vietnamese people are determined to mobilize all their physical and mental strength, to sacrifice their lives and property in order to safeguard their independence and liberty."[27] His claims were far from "true" at the time, but they constituted the truth in potential — if he, like Confucius, had taken the "correct position." For the Confucians, of course, the "correct position" was that which accorded with the will of Heaven and the practice of the sacred ancestors. For Ho Chi Minh the "correct position" was that which accorded with the laws of history and the present and future judgment of the Vietnamese people.

> *Fire in the lake: the image of REVOLUTION.*
> *Thus the superior man*
> *Sets the calendar in order*
> *And makes the seasons clear.*
>
> — *I Ching*[28]

In August 1945 the whole city of Hanoi turned about on itself within the space of a few days. The highest officials of the Emperor Bao Dai's government fled, and their subordinates joined the Viet Minh. In a city that the French had thought passive, acquiescent to foreign rule, there were suddenly Viet Minh flags in every window and vast crowds cheering for the independence of Vietnam.[29] In Hue in 1966 at the beginning of the Buddhist struggle, much the same phenomenon occurred. Overnight the Buddhists, led by the brilliant rhetorician Thich Tri Quang, took over the administration of the city. Arriving at their desks the next day, the American officials suddenly found that the city government was at war with Saigon — though its personnel had hardly changed and there had been no violence. By the beginning of the next week the troops of the ARVN First Division stationed near the city had either fled, complied with the Buddhists, or given their active support to the struggle against their own command in Saigon.

Time after time Westerners have been surprised by the suddenness of political change in Vietnam, by its seeming lack of motivation. But the motivation is always there. It is just that, given the commitment the Vietnamese have to their society, it remains hidden, and for the majority of the people, hidden even below the surface of consciousness, until in the old language the will of

Heaven manifests itself and the success of the rebellion appears assured. At that moment the wind shifts, and if all goes for the best, the whole society changes from unanimity to unanimity. In such a change, the element of personal leadership is of the highest importance, for the Vietnamese do not look upon government as the product of a doctrine, a political system that hangs somewhere over their heads, but as an entire way of life, a Tao, exemplified by the person of the ruler.

Over the years those American officials concerned with the Saigon government occupied themselves almost exclusively with the development of policies and programs, with organization and reorganization. That the Vietnamese showed much less interest in the programs than in the people who ran them proved a continual source of discomfort to the Americans. This discomfort they manifested in their complaints about the "underdevelopment" of Vietnamese politics. In part, of course, this American preoccupation with programs and instrumentalities arose out of the ground rules of their involvement in Vietnam. (Officially, the U.S. government was "not interfering in Vietnamese domestic politics.") In part, however, it came from the basic American — or Western — view of government as a complex machine. Americans tend to speak of "governmental machinery" and to look upon the problem of government as one of programming the machinery correctly to attain the goals desired. For Americans it is ideas, principles, and organization that count: men are replaceable and their "personalities" almost incidental to their functions. (In Vietnam it was simply embarrassing that gossip about the Vietnamese generals described the workings of the government better than all of their organizational charts.) But the Vietnamese look at government in a very different light. To them it is not merely one organization among others, but a complete enterprise that comprehends much of what Westerners would consign to personal life and private morality. In looking for a leader they look not merely for a man with ideas and administrative skills; nor do they, as many Americans assumed, look only for a charismatic figure, a magical authority. They look for a man who expresses in his life how the government and the society ought to behave. In coming to the court of Lu, Confucius made no speeches and gave no orders. He gave the people a picture of the "correct" way of life; he showed them what had to be done.

The Vietnamese Communists understood policies and programs

as well as anyone else in Vietnam, but they, and in particular Ho Chi Minh, made an effort to present a picture of "correct behavior" to the people. Dressed usually in shorts and rubber sandals, the North Vietnamese leader lived as simply as a peasant in order to show that his revolution would inaugurate a truly popular regime. The same dress on Lenin would have been sheer affectation. But for Ho Chi Minh and his representatives to the people it was a necessity, for the Vietnamese do not differentiate between a man's style and his "principles," between his private and public "roles": they look to the whole man.

It was this very coherency of man and society that was to Westerners the most bewildering and unsympathetic aspect of the Vietnamese — Communists, Buddhists, and Catholics alike. In his biography of Ho Chi Minh, Jean Lacouture observed:

However ruthlessly the people of North Vietnam may be governed, it would be wrong not to indicate how fully Ho has managed to identify with his fellow countrymen, and what an unusual relationship he has established with them. He is forever addressing ordinary citizens in an easygoing or fatherly tone, forever distributing oranges or other tidbits to the children. This is partly play-acting — why deny it? The character he projects is too well rounded to be entirely spontaneous, and his large red handkerchief has too often dabbed at dry eyes.[30]

While generally admiring of the North Vietnamese leader, Lacouture could not get over the suspicion that he was "playing a part," that he was, to put it more harshly, insincere. Lacouture was right in a sense. But the very terms he chose to describe Ho Chi Minh showed exactly how Westerners and Vietnamese differ in their view of the function of the individual. To Westerners, of course, "sincerity" means the accord between a man's words or actions and his inner feelings. But to Vietnamese, for whom man is not an independent "character" but a series of relationships, "sincerity" is the accord between a man's behavior and what is expected of him: it is faithfulness not to the inner man, but to the social role. The social role, in other words, is the man. To many Vietnamese, therefore, Ho Chi Minh was perfectly sincere, since he *always* acted in the "correct" manner, no matter what effort it cost him. And it was the very consistency of his performance that gave them confidence that he would carry the revolution out in the manner he indicated. Ironically enough, because of this very intimate relation of man to society, it was precisely those Vietnamese military men, such as Nguyen Cao Ky, who had no notion of a political system and who did not therefore "hide their feelings" or practice the Confucian "self-control," who seemed to Westerners the most likable, if not the men most fit for the job of government.

The Confucian world was rationalist rather than mystical, characterized by the ethical bureaucrat-scholar rather than by the heroic tribal chieftain. In times of crisis the Vietnamese looked for a particular kind of leader. A Hitler or a Joseph McCarthy or an Abraham Lincoln would have had no success in Vietnam, for they did not conform to the model laid down in the depths of Vietnamese history.

At the beginning of the first Indochina war Paul Mus asked an old friend of his, a Vietnamese intellectual, whether he supported the Emperor Bao Dai or Ho Chi Minh. "Ho Chi Minh," said the intellectual. "Ho Chi Minh because he is pointed, whereas Bao Dai is circular like a drop of water. Like water, he will rot everything he touches. What we want is pointed fire and flames like Ho Chi Minh." As Mus explained, the traditional Vietnamese, like so many peasant people, saw history not as a straight-line progression[31] but as an organic cycle of growth, fruition, and decay; for them these seasonal changes were associated with textures and pictures — the images as old as China itself. In times of prosperity and stability the empire appeared circular — the image of water and fecundity, or a time when, in the words of the great Vietnamese poet, Nguyen Du, "The emperor's virtues spread like rain over all the land, penetrating deeply into the hearts of men." Inevitably times would change: rich and secure, the dynasty would isolate itself from the people and grow corrupt — the image of degeneration, the stagnant pool. Then revolution would come — the cleansing fire to burn away the rot of the old order. At such times the Vietnamese would look for a leader who, in his absolute rectitude, his puritanical discipline, would lead the community back to the strength and vigor of its youth. And it was this picture that the Viet Minh and the Viet Cong presented to the Vietnamese of the twentieth century.

This view of history does much to explain the fact — so long puzzling to American officials — that a peasant people who otherwise seemed to resist change and innovation could turn to the most radical of revolutions. For Westerners, even Marxists, who see history as a progression, revolution is an alarming prospect. The very word implies a mechanical operation — and one that more or less escapes human control. Revolution for Westerners is an abrupt reversal in the order of society, a violent break in history. But the Vietnamese traditionally did not see it that way at all. For them revolution was a natural and necessary event within the historical cycle; the problem of revolution was merely one of timing and appropriateness.

Times change and with them their demands. Thus the seasons change in the course of a year. In the world cycle also there are spring and autumn in the life of peoples and nations, and these call for social transformations.
— *I Ching*[32]

Vietnamese history was far from uneventful, but it was without movement of the sort that took place in Europe over the same millennium from the accession of Charlemagne to the industrial revolution. Distant from the seat of empire, the traditional villager did not fear the coming of a new regime, for like leaves in the Celestial Book the dynasties were bound to a common base in the traditional agriculture and the traditional Way. What the villager did fear was a difficult transition, an interregnum of social disorder and violence in which the conflict broke through the bamboo hedges of the village and disturbed the cycle of the rice. As long as the revolution passed over quickly, he had no reason to be conservative. Secure within his own landscape, he could accommodate himself to the dynasties that came and went like the seasons passing through the heavens. To him revolution meant no alarming break from the past, but simply a renewal. The Chinese character for revolution meant in its original sense an animal's pelt, which is changed in the course of a year by molting.[33]

In the twentieth century the Westerners are probably correct: revolution in Vietnam now implies a change of structure and a modulation in history. But the question remains whether it, too, is not in its own way appropriate. The French and the Americans tried to stop the revolution, and in doing so they created an interregnum of violence unparalleled in Vietnamese history. In the end the Vietnamese may reject them and their intervention as an organism rejects a foreign body. As one Vietnamese scholar told a Frenchman, "If you want so much to be in Vietnam, just wait a bit and perhaps in your next reincarnation you will be born Vietnamese."

2

Nations and Empires

Tzu-lu said: "The ruler of Wei has been waiting for you in order with you to administer the government. What will you consider the first thing to be done?"

The Master replied: "What is necessary is to rectify names. If names be not correct, language is not in accord with the truth of things. If language not be in accord with the truth of things, affairs cannot be carried on to success."

Saigon in 1966 was, as always, a city of rumors. It breathed rumors, consumed only rumors, for the people of Saigon had long since ceased to believe anything stated officially as fact. Rumor was the only medium. Among the stories of comets falling and bombing halts there was that year one rumor that stood out from all the rest. A work of art, a Fabergé among rumors, it was so embellished with circumstantial evidence of murders and secret meetings, so exquisitely crafted of inference, coincidence, and psychological truth, that its purveyors established its value without question. The central theme of the rumor was that Premier Nguyen Cao Ky and a number of other highly placed politicians in Saigon belonged to a secret society formed in northern Vietnam before the Indochina war. The aim of this society was now to subvert the Saigon government and enlist the Americans in helping the North Vietnamese to conquer the south.[1] The rumor had a certain undeniable attraction in that year when the Saigon government lost control of central Vietnam and two southern politicians were shot by unknown assailants in the streets. Few Americans, however, fully appreciated it, for as they saw it, the story had a certain internal logic for the southerners — a logic that went as follows: Premise: All northerners are alike.

Premise: Nguyen Cao Ky is a northerner. Conclusion: Nguyen Cao Ky is an agent of the Politburo in Hanoi.

Having thus reduced the rumor, most Americans would then proceed to attack it on the grounds that it was not true — a conclusion which, while undoubtedly correct, left something to be desired. The story of Oedipus was not true either, but it did describe a certain fundamental dilemma in the most graphic manner possible. In this case the dilemma was that although the United States claimed to be supporting the right of self-determination for the South Vietnamese people, it was in fact supporting a government of northerners who, to judge by their performance, were aiding and abetting their Communist compatriots. Clearly the rumor was an attempt by the Vietnamese to reconcile the claims of the U.S. State Department with the evidence before their own eyes.

Over the years American government officials have assembled a number of theories that present similar contradictions with practice — not only in the matter of Vietnamese politics, but in that of the whole political geography of Southeast Asia. In trying to persuade the American public to support the war in Vietnam, they invested twenty-five years of political rhetoric in the establishment of certain propositions about the nature of the area. On the strategic plane they held South Vietnam to be the second in a series of domino-countries that in their black-and-white uniformity stood in a row beginning at the Chinese border and ending at the foot of Southeast Asia. If South Vietnam were to "fall to the Communists," then it was more than likely that Cambodia, Laos, Thailand, and Malaya (and then, successively, the Philippines, Indonesia, and Australia) would "fall to the Communists" in their proper order. Just what nationality these Communists might be was not exactly clear, as U.S. officials often warned in the same breath of Chinese aggression, of North Vietnamese aggression, and of Khrushchev's "wars of national liberation" around the world. The indefinite nature of this threat notwithstanding, the peoples of Asia (so the officials insisted) had called upon the United States to help them in their common struggle for freedom and against Communism.

On the more detailed scheme of official reasoning, Vietnam was thought to be composed of two countries: a) North Vietnam, which was Communist and therefore intent upon invading the south; and b) South Vietnam, which was "a member of the Free World family striving to preserve its independence from Communism." The

United States became involved in Vietnam because the South Vietnamese government, under the terms of the SEATO pact, asked for American help against armed aggression by a foreign power — North Vietnam. The South Vietnamese government was having certain internal difficulties, but the United States would not be interfering in its domestic political affairs. Its sole purpose was to defend South Vietnam from outside attack. Its intervention would be limited, for with some American help, the Saigon government would in time build a democratic nation as strong as the Democratic Republic of Vietnam in the north. The United States was bombing South Vietnam in order to help its people build a strong, democratic government.

Whether or not the American officials actually believed their own propositions, they repeated them year after year with a dogged persistence and a perfect disregard for all contradictory evidence. In the course of a decade these propositions were transmuted into fact: fact, that is, for large sections of the American public; fact for the AID economists promoting such schemes as the cooperation of South Vietnam, Laos, Cambodia, and Thailand on a Mekong River development project; fact in those realms of the Pentagon where systems analysts planned to end the insurgency with an electronic barrier circling South Vietnam. Ten years of American political rhetoric about North Vietnamese aggression and anti-Communist solidarity in Southeast Asia left even Washington insiders like Clark Clifford ill-prepared for such events as the Joint Chiefs' request for a total of seven hundred thousand American troops in Vietnam and the refusal of the "Free World" countries to help the South Vietnamese government unless the United States paid them to do so. For most Americans, Southeast Asia came to look like the most complicated place in the world. And naturally enough, for the American official effort to fit the new evidence into the old official assumptions was something like the effort of the seventeenth-century astronomers to fit their observations of the planets into the Ptolemaic theory of the universe.

On the official propositions about Southeast Asia rest all the strategic wisdom of, and the moral justification for, the American war in Vietnam. This being the case, it is interesting to take a look at those propositions in the light of the political history on which they are based. What was Vietnam's relationship to China and to the other countries around her? What was the relationship between

northern and southern Vietnam, and what, precisely, was Vietnamese nationalism? To answer these questions it is necessary to go
back beyond 1954 to see how Vietnam initially developed as a
nation, how Vietnamese society changed as a result of the French
colonial occupation, and how Ho Chi Minh and his compatriots
fought and won the struggle for independence. While history does
not give precise answers, it does give certain clues, certain indications as to the shape of the future. Vietnam is, after all, much older
than the "threat of Communism," and below the ideological conflict
lie older oppositions, older lines of force that articulate that conflict profoundly.

Unlike the other countries of Southeast Asia, Vietnam has always
lived in the orbit of China. First as a Chinese colony and then as a
small tributary state, Vietnam was until the fifteenth century no
more than a planet in the great solar system of the Celestial Empire.
Vietnam came out of China and survived as a nation in a strange —
and strangely stable — balance of attraction and repulsion.

In 207 B.C. a Chinese warlord marched into the Red River Delta
and opened an avenue to the south by which a century later the
imperial armies would take his kingdom of Nam Viet for a Chinese
colony. Vietnamese national mythology places several "Vietnamese"
kingdoms in the Delta before the coming of the Chinese, but
scholars now maintain that the region previously contained only a
flux of tribes and feudalistic principalities, whose populations came
from a variety of ethnic sources, tangentially related to the Vietnamese. Like the French or the English, the Vietnamese are not a
"pure race" but a nation created within a particular landscape by a
political process. According to ethnologists, the Vietnamese derive
not from a single Chinese tribe, but from a mixture between tribes
of Mongolian and Austro-Indonesian origin; their language has
grown from both Chinese and Southeast Asian roots. In the third
and fourth centuries B.C. the Red River Delta sustained two kingdoms, Au Lac and Van Lang, whose people the Chinese called
simply southern, or *Yuéh* (*Viêt* in Vietnamese). During the ten centuries of Chinese suzerainty the Viêt peoples settled slowly into a
new ethnic and cultural pattern. Vietnamese history began in Chinese writing, and the Vietnamese nation took shape along the
political and cultural lines of force emanating from China.

Given the Chinese capacity for empire-building, it is somewhat
remarkable that the Vietnamese had a history at all. Hardly more

broad-minded than the emissaries of other imperial powers, the first Chinese governors made no distinction between the Viêt tribes of the Delta and those that inhabited what is today Yunnan and Canton. They regarded them all as savages whose religion and customs showed only a pitiful lack of cultural development. Enlightened rulers, these governors took up the Chinese burden of educating the Viêt peoples to behave as much like the Chinese as possible. The Celestial Empire was universal, so they considered their *mission civilisatrice* to be a comprehensive project that would end with the complete assimilation of all the southern peoples into the body of the empire. Ten centuries later a Chinese historian might well have judged that they had succeeded. The Viêts had adopted Chinese technology and the Chinese religions; their aristocracy sent its sons to compete for the mandarinate in the regional examinations. With his long imperial perspective the historian would probably have persisted in his opinion even when in the tenth century this same aristocracy raised troops to expel the armies of the declining T'ang dynasty from the Red River Delta. Such warlord revolts had occurred many times before in the Delta, just as they had occurred throughout China in times of imperial weakness. But the historian would have been wrong: the Vietnamese were then in the process of taking their independence from China. When, forty years later, the armies of the Sung dynasty descended to reconquer the Red River Delta, they confronted not the scattered forces of the warlords but the united armies of a man who called himself the emperor of Vietnam, the Land to the South.

Just why the Vietnamese alone among the *Viêt* tribes should have resisted grafting onto the great trunk of China remains a matter of scholarly debate. The most southerly of the Viêt peoples, they alone possessed a distinct territory: the circle of mountains all but isolated the Red River Delta. But the Chinese empire had broken through so many natural frontiers. Of course, even after ten centuries the inhabitants of the Delta had not become precisely Chinese — but then neither had the peoples of what is today Yunnan and Canton. Secreted within the demotic language of every southern tribe, the old gods and the old customs lingered like the memories of early childhood. How much more the Vietnamese differed from their northern conquerors was a matter of subtle distinction, a difference of degree that approached a change in quality. From the tenth century onwards they defended themselves from China with a ferocity that perhaps could only come from a consciousness of the fragile borders of their identity. In the great patriarchate of the empire Vietnam was the unfilial son.

•

The Emperor of the South rules over the rivers and mountains of the southern country.
This destiny has been indelibly registered in the Celestial Book.
How dare you, rebellious slaves, come violate it?
You shall undoubtedly witness your own and complete defeat.[2]

The declaration of Vietnamese independence was in itself ironic. Writing in Chinese, the great Vietnamese military leader, Ly Thuong Kiet, rebuked the Chinese for claiming sovereignty over a state whose very identity depended on her relationship to the Empire of the Center. But then the claim to independence was no more paradoxical than the method of achieving nationhood.

Like their rivals, the Ly princes were warlords. They took control of the Red River Delta shortly after the first war for independence, in A.D. 1010. They united the nation and established a dynasty — but only at the price of rebuilding the entire apparatus of government by which the Chinese had ruled them. Though fervent Buddhists, they called upon the sacred powers of the Confucian tradition to establish a claim to legitimacy. Through the institution of the mandarinate with all its rank and ritual, they persuaded the other warlord families to give up their armies and compete for power as dutiful sons within the one great household of the empire. In effect the Ly took on the role of the Chinese governors, adopting the Chinese universal empire in order to reject the universalism of the Chinese. After a new war with China in the fifteenth century the court poet to the hero-emperor Le Loi wrote in defense of Vietnamese autonomy:

Our state of Dai Viet [Greater Vietnam] is indeed a country wherein culture and institutions have flourished. Our mountains and rivers have their characteristic features, but our habits and customs are not the same from north to south. Since the formation of our nation by the Trieu, Dinh, Ly and Tran, our rulers have governed their empire in exactly the same manner in which the Han, T'ang, Sung and Yuan did theirs.[3]

In other words, according to the poet, the justification for Vietnamese national independence rested on the double foundation that while Vietnamese "habits and customs" differed from those of the Chinese, their governments conformed most faithfully to the Chinese models. Five centuries later Ho Chi Minh invoked the same reasoning to explain Vietnam's relation to China within yet another universalist system:

The Chinese Communist Party, under Mao Tse-tung's leadership, succeeded in combining the universal truth of Marxism-Leninism with the revolutionary practice of China, thereby taking steps proper to the Chinese society. . . . At present, in building socialism, although we [the Vietnamese] have the rich experiences of brother countries, we cannot apply them mechanically because our country has its own peculiarities.[4]

Given the geographical and cultural proximity of Vietnam to China, it is perhaps understandable that the two major historical changes within Vietnamese society — the building of a Confucian state in the tenth to eleventh centuries and the Communist revolution in the twentieth — should follow the same pattern. In both cases the Vietnamese leaders assumed Chinese political culture while rejecting, or at least attempting to reject, Chinese political domination. The relationship of Vietnam to China runs not only through lines of force but through the deep channels of a civilization.

Today Vietnam's continued success in maintaining her independence from China rests on a very different set of conditions than it did in the past. In medieval times the mountains and the limited technology of war served as insulation for Vietnam. Now the Vietnamese can defend themselves only by opening themselves out to other countries. Ho Chi Minh, who spent many years in France, China, and the Soviet Union in preparation for the struggle for independence against the French, understood that Vietnam's survival depended upon her putting an end to her isolation. During his lifetime he counseled his countrymen to become internationalists, to learn from other nations and to take from them what would be useful in the development of their small and backward country. In the 1950's and 1960's he looked to the Soviet Union and to Eastern Europe to compete with China for influence in Vietnam. But the French and then the American war restricted his choices and threatened from time to time to close off even those apertures he had made onto the rest of the world.[5]

Historically the Vietnamese have been accustomed to isolation

and to encirclement by larger rival powers. Until the fifteenth
century Vietnam remained confined to the Red River Delta, to the
small basin of arable land pressed against the China Sea. To the
south the great kingdom of Champa, the last on the arc of Hindu
states that ran eastward from India, occupied the coastal plain of
what is today central Vietnam. Always hostile to the Vietnamese,
the Chams had warred with them throughout the period of their
colonization by the Chinese, threatening occasionally in the slow
lurch of the military balance to crush them and take over their
territories. Only when Vietnam had gained her independence and
closed her border with China did she grow strong enough to check,
and finally turn, the waves of invasion from the south. In the fifteenth century, after defeating an invasion by the Ming dynasty, the
Emperor Le Loi began the "March to the South," the succession of
military campaigns by which, a century later, the Vietnamese
armies would reduce the kingdom of Champa and push the frontiers
of Vietnamese settlement down to the bottom of the Annamese
littoral.

As the Vietnamese empire breached the Gates of Annam, near the
17th parallel, its whole history changed course. From a small kingdom that had looked only north towards China, Vietnam became a
major power in Southeast Asia. During the seventeenth century the
Vietnamese entered the nearly virgin plains of the Mekong Delta,
and under pressure from a continual growth of population pushed
south to the Gulf of Siam and west across the Bassac river deep into
the kingdom of the Khmers.

Once the Vietnamese had reached the plain of Southeast Asia,
they entered into the battle for territory that the kingdoms of the
south had intermittently waged across the lowlands for the centuries of their history. These wars seemed to have no end and no
beginning. Like the wars in Europe before the Reformation, they
went on through the rise and decline of a dozen kingdoms. At the
time the Vietnamese entered the conflict, the fortunes of Siam were
in the ascendant over those of the princedoms of Laos and the other
two Buddhist states, Burma and Cambodia, the kingdom of the
Khmers. Though beset by Burmese armies from the west, Siam was
in the process of building an empire out of the territories of Laos
and Cambodia. From the point of view of Laos and Cambodia, the
Vietnamese arrived at exactly the right moment — except that they
too had territorial ambitions. After a series of battles with the Thais

that lasted over a century, the Vietnamese concluded a treaty with Siam whereby the Khmer kingdom recognized the suzerainty of both empires and gave each of them rights over the provinces adjoining their territories. Laos was similarly embattled and overcome. At last one Lao prince offered himself as a vassal to the Vietnamese emperors in Hue and ceded some of his territory to the capital beyond the mountains in return for protection from the Thais, against whom he had no geographical defenses.

These eighteenth- and nineteenth-century wars seemed like ancient history to most Americans in Vietnam, but they were very much present in the minds of the Southeast Asian leaders during the American war. In the intervening period of eighty years the five countries had held a merely artificial peace — a peace imposed by the British and the French colonial administrations. With the coming of independence the old territorial disputes broke out again, fired by the same old fears and ambitions. Even the balance of power remained much the same. Prince Sihanouk of Cambodia remarked in 1961:

Westerners are always astonished that we Cambodians are not disturbed by our future in which China will play such a powerful role. But one should try to put himself in our place: in this jungle, which is the real world, should we, simple deer, interest ourselves in a dinosaur like China when we are more directly menaced, and have been for centuries, by the wolf and the tiger, who are Vietnam and Thailand?[6]

In the 1950's and 1960's the Cambodians and the Lao had only one hope for maintaining their independence, and that was for one or more of the great powers to insure their territorial integrity against their two more powerful neighbors. In 1954 France, Britain, the Soviet Union, and China made an agreement at Geneva to this end. In 1962 the United States appeared to take over the protective role of France and Britain by agreeing, tacitly in the case of Cambodia, overtly in the case of Laos, to support neutralist regimes in both countries acceptable to the Communist powers. Later, however, in the pursuit of the Vietnam War it was to wreck these agreements and destroy the fragile basis on which the independence of Laos and Cambodia rested. Prince Sihanouk of Cambodia and Souvanna Phouma of Laos did their best to maintain neutrality and resist participation in the war. But like Belgium or Poland, their countries were finally helpless before the larger powers. Their

future depended on an overall political settlement. Thailand, however, being larger and more distant from the conflict, had somewhat
more leverage. The military-supported regime in Bangkok granted
all the American requests for bases and staging areas in return for
princely sums of American aid. Their bargain did not, however,
entail an ideological commitment to the Americans or even full
support for the American war in Vietnam. The Bangkok politicians
had no interest whatsoever in helping the Vietnamese, Communist
or non-Communist. Their obligation to the United States for feeding
and strengthening them domestically was strictly limited by their
desire not to interfere while the Vietnamese destroyed each other
and by their calculations as to the final outcome of the conflict. There
is an old Thai proverb to the effect that it is worthwhile to try and
help an elephant that is trying to stand up, but perfectly useless to
help one that happens to be falling down.

It was one of the inconsistencies of American public relations that
while the American officials painted over these acute national differences with the rubric of "Asian dominoes" or "Free World Allies,"
they simultaneously brought into sharp relief the differences between northern and southern Vietnamese. The American public
thus had the impression that while all Southeast Asians were alike
— that nationality stood for little among them — the South Vietnamese were a nation distinct from the northerners. Certainly there
were differences between the two groups of Vietnamese, but these
were small by comparison with the separate culture and the thousand years of history that distinguished the Vietnamese from the
Thais and the Cambodians. For until the eighteenth century there
was no such thing as southern Vietnam. The demilitarized zone at
the 17th parallel, drawn by the members of the Geneva Conference
in 1954, corresponded roughly to the line that for a millennium and a
half had marked the border of Vietnam and the kingdom of
Champa. Only in the fifteenth century did the Vietnamese break
through that border and begin their colonization of the south.
Gradually, as the nation expanded, it lost its political cohesion, and
for a period of time the 18th parallel marked the division between
two warring Vietnamese states. It was during this period and afterwards under the colonial regime that the southerners grew slowly
away from the northerners. In the twentieth century the southerners
had different accents and to some extent different customs from the
northerners. But would this difference sustain a new political divi-

sion of the country? From the American point of view the question was not simply whether the difference was great enough, but whether it implied southern strength and independence. The question is political in the most profound sense. To answer it it is necessary first to have some notion of the foundations of the precolonial Vietnamese state and the changes that occurred within that part of Vietnamese society that colonized the south.

In his defense of Vietnamese sovereignty Le Loi's court poet himself pointed out the sources of the weakness of the Vietnamese state from its beginnings. On the one hand, he said, the early Vietnamese monarchs governed their country in exactly the same manner as the classical Chinese dynasties. On the other hand, the Vietnamese "habits and customs" differed from those of the Chinese. The contradiction was an important one, for the reason that the Confucian government was essentially a family affair. The Chinese empires achieved their breadth and duration largely by virtue of the extraordinary length of their patrilineal loyalties. Even today Chinese who have lived in Thailand, Indonesia, or Vietnam for generations maintain their attachments to relatives in China and, by extension, to China herself. Up until the twentieth century a Chinese aristocrat might have understood his family loyalties to include everyone in his district or canton — or other noblemen a thousand miles away. But the Vietnamese of the empire drew their boundaries closer to home. Even in the Red River Delta, the region of Chinese occupation, the peasants worshiped their ancestors only to the ninth generation. After ramifying through several nuclear families, their clans would split apart into separate hierarchies unbound by any tie of community.

As a result of this difference in "habits and customs," the Vietnamese government had never operated in exactly the same manner as the Han, the T'ang, and the Sung, even during its first four hundred years of stability. The emperors followed the rituals of state (each gesture a *déjà vu*) so that time would not flow through the empire, but the "natural order" of the universe did not hold throughout the society. "The laws of the emperor are less than the customs of the village," runs the best-known of Vietnamese adages. In Vietnam it was the village rather than the clan that stood as the primary community. The village was an informal association of families. An institution peculiar to Vietnam, it had probably developed during the period of Chinese occupation as a response to the decline of the feudalistic principalities. At that point it had served to weld the small and otherwise autarchic families into communities large enough to meet the demands of the traditional rice culture. The village was always the efficient unit of local government, but in the fifteenth century, when the court abandoned the village mandarinate and retired the lowest order of its officials from the villages, it became a quasi-autonomous unit.

In the 1960's the shells of the central Vietnamese settlements — even voided and half-destroyed by the war — showed what strength the villages must have had in that traditional landscape. The villages of northern and central Vietnam stood like small fortresses in the center of their rice fields, closed off from the world by bamboo hedges. When the mandarin rode out from the stone ramparts of his citadel, he traveled quite alone, a fish out of the water of the population. The mandarin was more an ambassador from the court than a governor in his own domain. He had only the authority to negotiate with the village council for the amount of taxes and the number of army recruits to be submitted to the empire. If the negotiations broke down, he had no resort except the final one of calling in the imperial troops and burning down the hedges of the village.[7]

Almost self-sufficient, the villages required from the government only the planning of large-scale public works (the dikes) and external defense. Their councils of notables, selected by co-optation from among the senior, the well-educated, and the wealthy men of the village, conducted their external affairs, organized their religious and social life, and managed their administrations. The councils reserved a certain proportion of the land for common use, organized cooperative enterprises, and apportioned the common burden of the tax and the draft. The councils were organized hierarchically on the pattern of the Confucian family, yet they retained enough flexibility to adjust the economic as well as the purely Confucian relationships between various families. Rather than referring misdemeanors and petty disputes to the mandarins, they dealt with them themselves on the basis of informal, customary law. For below the brittle network of family relationships lay the reality of the land and its production of rice. In times of war or revolution the villages shut like oysters, protecting their essential substance from the disorder of the outside world.

In their very self-sufficiency the villages gave Vietnam hidden powers of resistance. In times of war they provided not only a source of recruitment for the regular army but a base for guerrillas. Their high bamboo hedges shut out strangers better than any jungle redoubt. When the guerrilla slipped into the village, he became invisible among other men.[8] Because he belonged to the village, he had a ready-made system of logistics and supply, a community that trusted and cooperated with him against all enemies from the outside. In the path of the Chinese armies, as in the path of the French Expeditionary Corps several centuries later, the guerrillas carried out a scorched earth policy with the consent of the villagers. When the empire was divided during the Mongol invasion, the villages themselves opposed the Chinese until national leadership was restored. This deep, underground resistance constituted an important element of the Vietnamese national identity. It was one of the "habits and customs" that distinguished the Vietnamese. As an eighteenth-century Chinese emperor said: "The Vietnamese are indeed not a reliable people. An occupation does not last very long before they raise their arms against us and expel us from their country. The history of past dynasties has proved this fact."[9]

The independence of the villages gave strength to the nation, but it proved nonetheless an obstacle to the maintenance of a national government. For Le Loi's poet to compare the early Vietnamese dynasties to the T'ang and Sung of China was, after all, to elevate his own country into a different dimension: the "empire" of the Ly and the Tran was no larger than a single Chinese province. The Vietnamese state remained stable for as long as it remained within the circle of the Red River Delta, but once it breached the Gates of Annam it began to suffer the consequences of its original political frailty. In the year 1400 the general Le Qui Ly, who had saved his country from the last of the Chinese invasions, turned his army north from the frontier and overthrew the Tran emperor, and laid claim to the Mandate of Heaven. But the great mandarins refused to support him, and the empire shattered along the same faults that had opened during the war for independence. Irreconcilable, the powerful families of Vietnam rose like thunderheads in an electrical storm — their division giving the Chinese a new opportunity to launch an invasion and occupy the country. Only after two decades of guerrilla warfare did the new military hero, Le Loi, succeed in uniting them under his command and driving the Chinese out of Vietnam.

The rebellion of Le Qui Ly did not destroy the Confucian empire, but it did signal the difficulty that future emperors would have in maintaining central control. The Vietnamese empire rested upon smaller units than did the Chinese, and so the danger of its breaking apart was always greater. When the armies of the successful new Le dynasty undertook the conquest of Champa, it was the villages rather than the state that conducted the colonization of the land to the south. From the now crowded plains of the Red River Delta, colonies of the young and the landless set out to pioneer the new territories. These colonies would be supported by the parent-villages until they became self-sufficient; then they would flesh out and close in upon themselves.[10] In this process of amoebic repro-duction the mandarinate could only certify an accomplished fact by granting the new villages charters of their incorporation into the empire. The difficulty of controlling these colonies naturally in-creased as they migrated away from the circle of the northern delta and down the thin strip of coastal plain to the Mekong.

Broken laterally by the foothills of the Annamites, the ribbon of cultivable land in what is today central Vietnam is only three hun-dred miles wide at its greatest extent and forty-five miles wide at its narrowest. As the imperial armies fought their way down through the kingdom of Champa, they left behind them a new line of settle-ment six hundred miles long. In their seasonal campaigns they could only temporarily secure the stretch of lowland. Isolated within the short valleys, the villages offered easy targets to bandits who made their bases in the jungled slopes of the foothills. Under local military pressure the thin web of loyalty that bound them to the empire would snap off. With time the blood lines that bound the villagers to their ancestors in the north would similarly break and be forgotten. As the frontiers of settlement drew further and further from the capital, the Le emperors began to lose control of their territory in a more and more permanent manner. The bandits secured agricultural bases and turned their guerrilla bands into full-fledged armies. The most successful among them established their own bureaucracies of mandarins and, securing the villages against their smaller rivals, entered into a competition with the Le monarchy. By the beginning of the seventeenth century two warlord families, the Trinh and the Nguyen, had succeeded in eliminating all other contenders and in partitioning the country between them. The Trinh took control of the Red River Delta; the Nguyen withdrew to the Annamese coast to rule that part of the country that continued to expand southward. Though both remained determined to reunify the empire — still under the nominal suzerainty of the Le dynasty — their all-out civil war settled slowly into a boundary dispute. At the end of the seventeenth century they broke off hostilities at a wall built by the Nguyen across the narrow Gates of Annam at the 18th parallel. Once the most powerful and strictly Confucian of all the dynasties, the Le lived out their days as sacred prisoners in the imperial citadel, their empire divided between the northern and the southern warlord-kings.

Like the "temporary" demilitarized zone created by the Geneva powers in 1954, the "temporary" wall built by the Nguyen had more than a military significance. The March to the South had altered the substance as well as the dimensions of the Vietnamese empire. As a result of the original distance between village and court, the nation had expanded at the price of its Confucian organization.

Generally speaking, Confucian society consisted of two separate groups, the small, literate elite and the mass of the peasantry. The link between the two was the village "notables," who sent their sons to study the Confucian texts and to compete in the national examinations for a place in the bureaucracy. These "notables," in turn, instructed the villagers in Confucian patterns of behavior. After centuries of Confucian government — Chinese as well as Vietnamese — the villages of the Red River Delta possessed strong traditions of family solidarity, Confucian literacy, and loyalty to the empire. But even in the north the villages acted as reservoirs for an older folk culture. Secreted within the oral tradition were all the legends of an ancient world where nature ran countercurrent to the tidy designs of the Confucian heaven. Within the bamboo hedges of the villages, tree spirits and stone spirits and anarchic female spirits competed with the genii of the empire for influence over the villagers. (Père Léopold Cadière, the distinguished French anthropologist, came upon the following situation in a village in central Vietnam in the nineteenth century. The guardian of a village *dinh* had been persuaded by the villagers that *con tinh*, a dangerous female spirit who walked without feet, had come to inhabit a large tree by the edge of the river. Since she, the restless soul of a virgin, was known to seduce men and pluck their souls out of their mouths, he became very much concerned for the peace of mind of his mandarin-genii. In order that she should not disturb the genii he began to make offerings of flowers and glutinous rice to her tree. His successor, however, suppressed the cult with the explanation that he had "seen the *con tinh* following around a lot of local demons of no account." In other words, a clear victory for Confucianism and the cosmopolitan tendency in the village.[11]) The village scholars studied the Confucian texts until they believed they believed in self-control, filial piety, and the virtues of the mandarin administration, but they lived nonetheless within a local underground of belief and custom that all but contradicted the official discipline. From a political point of view this meant that they were continually divided between parochialism and nationalism, the virtues of self-reliance and those of obedience to the emperor.

As the villages moved out from the Red River Delta, away from the base circle of the empire, the influence of Confucian culture diminished progressively within them. The mandarins of the Le and the Nguyen followed them south, but the warlords and bandits disrupted their royal administration and left the intellectual elites to sink back into the village traditions, into the small anarchy of the old culture. The withdrawal of the Confucian notables from the universalist tradition exposed the villages more and more to the particular influences of the places where they settled. The change became most apparent as they moved from the narrow coastal plain of central Vietnam into the Mekong Delta.

Unlike northern and central Vietnam, the Mekong Delta lies full in the framework of Southeast Asia. With their conical mountains, their sudden outcropping of rock formed by glacier and volcano, the northern regions of Vietnam seem to belong to China. But the low alluvial plains of the south flow directly into the deltas of Cambodia and Thailand without a break in soil or climate. At the time of the Vietnamese conquest the Mekong Delta was a vast, flooded territory, uninhabited but for a scattering of Khmer villages. As the Vietnamese moved into it, they dispersed to settle in clusters on the high ground of the marshes or along the banks of the tributary rivers. Suddenly freed of the old land pressures, their pioneer villages lost their fortress aspect and along with it the disciplined social organization that gave the northern villages their political strength. In the village below Saigon studied by the American anthropologist, Gerald Hickey, the village notables could trace their patrilineage back only to the fifth generation, the rest of the vil-

lagers only to the third.[12] In Hickey's term, the villages had gone
through a "cultural washout" as they moved from north to south. By
the time of the French arrival they had only the unity of a series.

During the American war the villages no longer played the important role they once had, but by that time the difference in their
organization had left its mark even on the character of their inhabitants. The Vietnamese need no anthropologist to tell them that there
are differences between northerners and southerners. The differences are clichés, endless source of jokes and, occasionally, of
hostility. One southern member of the Viet Minh who had regrouped to the north in 1954 under the terms of the Geneva
Agreements gave examples of these clichés in describing the relations between the northerners and the southerners in his unit. The
southerners, he said, "are used to being free and extravagant in their
expenses. After working hours they get together to go eat or play
guitars and sing." The northerners, on the other hand, "are very
economical in their expenses and not very generous in their relations
with friends." While the southerners like to fight among themselves
and to argue about matters of policy, the northerners "obey their
leaders, and in the meetings they are ready to respond to any motto
or any way. . . . [They] try to keep their present positions and
thirst for fame." This difference in life-style, said the soldier, provoked continual arguments within the unit. "Those northern stinkers
are miserly," the southerners complained. "They consider money as
a big wheel. They are cowards like land crabs. . . . [They are]
servile flatterers, always nodding to show their submission and
never conceiving any idea of fighting for their rights." The northerners in anger blamed the southerners for never being satisfied
with anything and for fighting among themselves all the time.
"Those southern guys," they said, "only know how to have fun. They
do not have Revolutionary Ethics. Their fighting standpoint is
weak."[13]

The soldier's account is reminiscent of Aesop's fable of the ant
and the grasshopper: the grasshopper sings all summer long and
mocks the drudgery of the ant, but when winter comes the grasshopper must beg the ant for food. As a southerner, the soldier
weights his account in favor of the southerners; still, the picture he
presents is telling. In general it is true that the northerners have
more discipline than the southerners. Brought up in a country where

the land is scarce for everyone, they tend to be hard workers, careful of waste and expense. Theirs is a tightly knit, patriarchal society, and they, more than the southerners, are aware of their obligations to others and responsive to authority. On the whole they are less spontaneous than the southerners, more given to formality; they see themselves always with respect to their place within society. In Freudian terms, they tend to be more repressed than the southerners; politically, they are more inclined to community action and to the whole notion of government as the fulfillment of a society.

These characteristics — as described by the Vietnamese themselves — ought perhaps to have given pause to the Americans who wished to oppose south against north. While the contrast between the people of each region is too broad to show up at the level of the individual, it has continually manifested itself in the political history of the country. By backing a regime in the south, the United States was taking on what had historically been the weakest part of the country. The south represented anarchy in contrast to the order of the north.

The disintegration of Confucian society in the south had immediate consequences for the government of the south in the nineteenth century, for the Confucian culture was the single foundation of the state. Inflexible Confucians, the Nguyen princes continued to rule in precisely the same manner as their predecessors, making no adjustment for the change in the society beneath them. At the end of the eighteenth century a massive peasant rebellion led by three brothers from the village of Tay Son (in what is now Binh Dinh province) swept across the central and southern provinces. After a short resistance the Nguyen family fled — their last surviving heir taking refuge with the enemy in Siam. Brilliant military commanders, the Tay Son brothers,[14] in a series of lightning campaigns, marched up the length of the coastal plain, broke through the Gates of Annam, and conquered the Trinh dynasty in the north. In the view of many historians, their revolt initially had the aspect of a true social revolution that pitted the peasants and merchants against the mandarins and large landowners. But the brothers failed to consolidate their victories by making social reforms or creating a replacement for the Confucian system of government. Their supporters quickly became disillusioned and apathetic. When a few years later the surviving heir to the Nguyen began a new offensive in the south, the peasants, who had formerly sustained the Tay Son, withdrew from the struggle and allowed the new dynasty to fall before the old one.[15]

All Vietnamese look to historical precedents for the events of their own day. Thus the southern gentry of the 1950's and 1960's looked with hope upon the restoration of the Nguyen monarchy as a precedent for their own struggle. In the late eighteenth century the southern Nguyen emperor Gia Long reaped the Tay Son's military harvest and reconquered the country from south to north. The surviving Le monarch deposed, Gia Long in 1802 succeeded in unifying Vietnam from the Chinese border to the Gulf of Siam for the first time in history. Despite this achievement, the Nguyen restoration boded poorly rather than well for the twentieth-century southerners. In the first place Gia Long's military victories rested less on brilliant generalship or popular enthusiasm than on artillery and advisers loaned to him by foreigners. In the second place, rather than correct the political mistakes of his predecessors, he and his successors exaggerated them by creating an administration that was not simply North Vietnamese in style, but Chinese. Abolishing the Le code that had accommodated the "habits and customs" of the Vietnamese, the Nguyen promulgated a new set of laws modeled on those of the Ming and the Ch'ing dynasties of China. On the stele before the Temple of Literature near their new capital of Hue, they had inscribed: "It belongs to the sovereign to decide matters of ritual" and "The religion of the Sage is immutable as Heaven."[16] The religion might be immutable, but the country itself had changed. In the south the villagers so recently settled into the broad rich plains of Southeast Asia possessed no firm commitment to the empire or to its rituals. In time, perhaps, the mandarins descending from the imperial court might have "pacified" the southerners and included them within the circle of empire. But the French did not allow them the necessary period of generations. Only forty years after the accession of Gia Long a small French naval force landed near Saigon. The French column marched straight through the oldest of the southern provinces and severed them from the empire.[17]

For those southerners interested in historical analogies, the French conquest of Vietnam provided a whole series of parallels to the American intervention a century later. To begin with, the French involvement in Vietnam was a gradual process. The French made a series of decisions, none of which could be singled out as the

sole cause of armed intervention. French missionaries and merchants came to Vietnam to pursue their respective vocations as early
as the seventeenth century. The merchants failed to establish themselves — in part because of the poverty of Vietnamese trade beside
that of the other Far Eastern countries, in part because of Vietnamese resistance. But the Catholic fathers persisted and founded a
strong mission in Vietnam. For a long time the French government
in Paris considered Vietnam not worth the effort of subduing — it
offered few commercial advantages. But by the mid-nineteenth
century the British, Spanish, and Portuguese had made extensive
conquests in Southeast Asia and the Pacific, and the French naval
commanders in the Far East began to see Vietnam as vital to their
imperial mission in Asia.[18] Like the American commanders of the
twentieth century, they were concerned not so much with Vietnam
itself as with China, where France was already engaged in commercial competition with the other European powers. Their occupation
of Saigon and the surrounding provinces, finally authorized by the
French government, gave them a base on the Pacific and the opportunity to search for a southern river route to China. When they discovered to their great disappointment that the Mekong was
unsuitable for navigation (and in any case did not originate in
China), they turned their sights towards the Red River Delta. In
1873 a young adventurer called Francis Garnier, under the aegis of
local officials, sailed up the river, declared it open to international
trade, and bombarded Hanoi as well as all the Vietnamese towns and
garrisons along the shores. The adventure was frowned upon by the
authorities in Paris. It was not until ten years later that Paris authorized the conquest of the Red River Delta and the bombardment of
Hue. The justification the French officials chose for this armed intervention was the missionary account — greatly exaggerated — of persecution of the Catholic missionaries by the Vietnamese emperor.
Because the missionaries had for more than a century directed a
steady stream of propaganda to Paris about their valiant, but sometimes thwarted, efforts to civilize the natives, this religious pretext
was more or less accepted by those who performed the conquest.
Like many Americans in the twentieth century, the French conquerors truly believed they were helping the Vietnamese by occupying
their country.

Had the French naval forces met a concerted national resistance
from the Vietnamese — even such a campaign as Gia Long waged

against the Tay Son — they might have finally failed to convince Paris of the desirability of a military conquest. But the country fragmented beneath them. At the same time that the French were moving across the Mekong Delta a rebellion, sponsored by French missionaries, broke out in the north, and the emperor chose to accede to the French demands for the cession of the southern provinces rather than divert the imperial armies from the revolt. As a result, the resistance to the French in the south came not from the court but from the local governors, who raised the villages to wage guerrilla warfare against the ensconced French troops. The southern mandarins were finally defeated. Fleeing north, they found the center of the empire in a state of chaos, riven by pirate bands, invading Chinese troops, and a new rebellion, this time led by the anti-Catholic mandarins against the supine court. When twenty years later the French decided to make their move against the north, the imperial armies gave little resistance to the French Expeditionary Corps. A year after the death of the Emperor Tu Duc the French installed their own protégé, Dong Khanh, in the court of Hue; the young sovereign, Ham Nghi, appointed by the Vietnamese regents, fled into the mountains with a few loyal mandarins to carry on a long but finally hopeless resistance in the jungles. By the time of Ham Nghi's submission, the Mekong Delta under its new name of Cochin China had been a French colony for over twenty years.

At the beginning of the American war in Indochina certain American scholars of Vietnam argued against U.S. support for a regime in Saigon on the grounds that the Communists had already "captured" the forces of nationalism. Their intentions were to defend Ho Chi Minh, but their argument merely hardened the semantic paradox created by the administration officials who defined "Communism" and "nationalism" as mutually exclusive terms. "Nationalism" in Vietnam did not wait like a brass ring to be "captured" by the most energetic pursuer: it had to be created. After seventy years of French rule in the north, and ninety years in the south, even the idea that it ought to be created was not shared by all Vietnamese. "Vietnam" had, after all, disappeared. Since the French conquest there had been only "Indochina"[19] — a loose federation that included the kingdoms of Laos and Cambodia along with the three *pays* of what had been Vietnam: Cochin China, Annam, and Tonkin. Many of those brought up on French maps would be deceived by this new administrative nomenclature. The Francophile

Vietnamese were misled by it, but so also was the Comintern, which in the 1930's made a false start with the "Indochinese Communist Party." On the other hand, many Vietnamese — the Catholics being the prime example — saw the Vietnamese people, but only some of them, as forming the basis for a political movement. Many Vietnamese were "nationalists" in the sense that they looked forward to the disappearance of French rule, but few conceived of the creation of a nation-state and only one group succeeded in organizing on a national basis. Regionalism, class interests, or a traditional outlook defeated the rest of them. Because the French decided to contest Vietnamese independence, these defects showed up very plainly at the moment of engagement. Among all the anticolonial political movements, only the Viet Minh actually created a "nation" strong enough to defeat the French armies. Apart from the specific political organization the Viet Minh made from the society as it emerged from French occupation, "Vietnam" was no more than a theory.

By the end of the Second World War no one, not even the handful of Vietnamese royalists, hoped to reconstruct the old empire. In the years of their occupation the French had altered Vietnam to the point where, like Humpty Dumpty, it could not be put back together again. Their aim had been to preserve rather than to change Vietnamese society, but the changes occurred in any case, and largely as a result of economic measures.

Once they had conquered Vietnam, the French looked to their new colony to become a source of raw materials for their burgeoning industrial plant and a buyer for their manufactured goods. But in the mid-nineteenth century Vietnam was only a potential source. To achieve the common aim of all colonialist countries, France first had to transform what was essentially a subsistence economy serving the Vietnamese peasants and landlords into an economy that produced surpluses for the international market. Given the particular geography of the country, the French enterprise consisted of the creation of large plantations and the development of mines to extract the rich deposits of coal, zinc, and tin. The restriction of Vietnamese trade to French markets came as a corollary. To encourage and support the establishment of French colonists and entrepreneurs, the French administration built roads, canals, railroads, and market cities linking the Vietnamese interior with the shipping routes. These public works benefited the French almost exclusively at the time, but the French officials financed them largely by an increase of taxes on the Vietnamese peasantry. Following metropolitan practice, they levied taxes in money instead of kind, and upon trade in commodities more than upon property values and capital. They also established a government monopoly on salt, alcohol, and opium, and raised the prices on these goods to six times what they had been before the occupation.[20] The result was a sudden growth in the number of landless and impoverished people — people ready to accept employment in the French plantations and mines under the most exploitative of terms. The French, however, took this new work force for granted, understanding it to be the normal complement of poor people that existed in this "backward" country.

The economic enterprise of the French naturally entailed certain changes in the administration of the country. In the north and the center the French governed indirectly through the mandarinate. But the French could not reconcile their desire for an active state with the traditional Vietnamese state that governed largely by ritual. The mandarins had no part of the new activity of development with the result that their powers declined until they were serving merely as a front for a French administration that grew every day in size and importance. The second innovation, perhaps more important to the mass of the people, was that the colonial regime usurped the right of the village council to conduct the census and make up the tax rolls. With one stroke of the pen it broke through the traditional anonymity of the villages and shattered their collective responsibility. Left without any binding obligations to the community, many of the village "notables" seized the communal land for their own private property and used their judicial powers to terrorize the other villagers. Seeing this corruption (and imagining it eternally thus) the French then deprived the village councils of their power and substituted election for co-optation as a method of selecting the village chiefs. This second "reform" merely served to exaggerate the effects of the first since it replaced the natural leaders of the villages with men who, election or no election, depended for their power on the colonial administration rather than the people of the villages.[21] These political disturbances were not, however, obvious to those who did not live in the villages — and particularly not to the paternalistic French colonials who believed in the maintenance of native traditions. Though undermined, the surfaces of the old political order remained intact as a deception to the French of the next generation and to much of the new Vietnamese elite as well.

Not only did the French destroy the very foundation of traditional politics, but they did so in such a way as to render Vietnam less homogeneous than ever. Under the principle of divide and rule they left Vietnam as they had conquered it, administering each of the *pays* under its original status: Cochin China as a colony, Tonkin (the Red River Delta) as a direct protectorate, and Annam (central Vietnam) as an indirect protectorate, under the rule of the emperor. These administrative distinctions hardly touched the life of the peasantry, but they had a strong influence on the development of a new Vietnamese elite and on the future of Vietnamese nationalism.

By 1946 the French colonial officials could with some justice claim a special status for Cochin China. At the time of the French conquest the Vietnamese villages had just begun to thicken through the lower Mekong Delta: the land lay open for a classical enterprise in plantation colonialism. Building an arterial system of roads and canals, the French administration sold the new territories off in lots of any dimension to the French and the Vietnamese planters who had the capital to pay for them. With the introduction of new crops, principally rubber and sugar, and the development of a capitalized rice production, Cochin China became a larger exporter of agricultural produce. On a strip of marshland near the old Chinese trading port of Cholon the French built a new city as the central market for all Indochina. Saigon, "the Paris of the Orient," belonged more to the metropolis than it did to the interior. The same was true of the administration. Because the mandarins had fled north at the time of the conquest, the French had no choice but to recruit and train a new cadre of civil servants with no experience of the traditional government. They brushed away the thin web that bound the villages to Hue and to the empire, centralized the administration, and shaped it along Western bureaucratic lines. After ninety years of French rule, Vietnamese society in the south took on an entirely different construction from that in the north and center: the majority of the population was landless, dependent for wages or tenant's rights on the French and their Vietnamese protégés. The old elite had vanished, giving place to a small but very wealthy class of Vietnamese landlords and civil servants.

By the end of the Second World War few of the educated Cochin Chinese had either the disposition or the resources to take up arms against the French. They had no attachments to the precolonial government. Their fathers and grandfathers were raised out of the villages by the French and had vowed loyalty to France even before the old empire succumbed. With no tradition of mandarin culture, they had modeled themselves on their conquerors, many of them turning Catholic and building up large estates in the Delta. After several generations they had severed all but their economic ties with the country people — and for the maintenance of those ties they depended upon the French regime. *Assimilés,* they looked to Paris rather than Hue or Hanoi as the center of civilization; they looked to Paris for political reform. Saigon in the 1920's and 30's was a ferment of "Constitutionalists," socialists, Trotskyites, and cells of the French Communist Party. Though quite as radical in rhetoric as their counterparts in France, most of these new political groups — often more cliques than parties — focused their sights on reform that would make them the equal of the French colonists rather than on Vietnamese national independence. Accordingly, the French found these groups easy to appease with better work laws for the small urban working class and consultative councils for the wealthy. Those that seemed dangerous the Sûreté disposed of easily, for, having relied on the French, the southern radicals had built no power base in their own countryside, whose rural society they considered backward and reactionary.

In Cochin China the true anticolonial sentiment came not from the educated elite, but from the lower echelons of society — from the small farmers, merchants, and civil servants who had been touched only by the backwash of French culture. Semi-educated, culturally unfocused, their leaders lived in the disputed zone between the foreign city and the villages of the interior. In 1925 a group of second-rank civil servants discovered in their consultations with a spiritualist medium a spirit that revealed itself as the Cao Dai, or supreme god of the universe. Within a year the group had developed into a sect celebrating the "third amnesty of God" — the first amnesty being that of Christ and Moses, the second that of Buddha and Lao Tzu, and the third that appearance revealed through their spiritualist mediums. Using as their symbol the Masonic eye of God, the Cao Dai worshiped all the world's religious leaders and placed such figures as Jeanne d'Arc and Victor Hugo along with the Taoist gods in their panoply of minor saints. The small merchant who became the first grand master of the sect built up a religious organization modeled on that of the Catholic Church and a secular administration with nine ministries that owned land, dispensed welfare, and conducted education and public works. By the end of 1926 the Cao Dai had twenty thousand adherents scattered throughout Cochin China and comprising a number of Vietnamese civil servants.[22]

Little short of miraculous, the growth of the Cao Dai church showed to what extent the French presence had disturbed the traditional society of the countryside. The peasantry, once almost self-sufficient, had come to depend on the landowners, the Chinese merchants, the French administrators, and the fluctuations of the international rice market. Some of the peasants had left the land to become civil servants or small merchants. The village governments were unable to deal with the distant and incomprehensible forces at work in the society. They had lost much of their hold over the people — as had the whole system of beliefs that supported their authority. (Why worship the ancestors or the mandarin-genii when they demonstrably had no power over the future?) The Cao Dai and its cousin sect, the Hoa Hao, offered alternatives. They offered first a means of re-establishing the spiritual communion between man, heaven, and earth that the French with their abstract finances and their secular bureaucracy had swept away. A synthetic religion, Cao Daiism enhanced its largely traditional format with certain ideas and symbols associated with the European power over man and nature. It promised to renew the old patriarchate and the old sense of communal identity by welding together a new and larger community from the ruins of the clans and the villages.[23]

With its elaborate rites, its pyramidical hierarchy, and its multiplicity of spirits, the Cao Dai filled much the same space that the Confucian state had occupied. The Hoa Hao, on the other hand, rose out of a landscape still new to Vietnam. Its prophet, Huynh Phu So, whom the French called the "mad bonze," came from the northwest corner of the Delta, from the region west of the Bassac river, where the Vietnamese had settled among Cambodians and colonized the vast, uninhabited wasteland of mountain, scrub, and marsh. Since the days of the Nguyen empire the region had been a refuge and a breeding ground for prophets, magicians, and faith healers, and for the secret societies that flourished in the underground of the Confucian orthodox world. In the 1830's a philosopher called Phat Thay Tay-An had predicted that "men from the West" would destroy the Vietnamese empire. His teachings, widely propagated, became the basis for two local revolts against the French in 1875 and 1913, and the basic education of Huynh Phu So.[24] In 1939, the year of signs in the heavens, So, a sickly young man who had trained with the most famous of the sorcerers, became possessed of the spirit and was miraculously cured. From that moment on he preached of his revelation about the Enlightened Sage who, after the departure of the French, would come to rule the Vietnamese in the brotherhood of the Three Religions. By his teachings and his book of oracles and prayers, he showed the way to a species of reformed Buddhism based on the common people and expressed through internal faith rather than elaborate ritual. The Hoa Hao religion (the name is that of So's home village) required no pagodas, no expensive ceremonies for birth and death such as the Confucian ancestral cult demanded. One of the four prayers of the day was devoted to "the mass of small people," whom So hoped would have "the will to improve themselves, to be charitable, and to liberate themselves from the shackles of ignorance."[25] The Hoa Hao doctrine was both progressive and democratic by contrast with the traditional beliefs of many of the Delta villagers. Indeed, within a milieu of poor farmers and sharecroppers oppressed by high rents and taxes, it seemed to point to a revolutionary social movement. In 1940 the French arrested So, and after a futile attempt to silence him by removing him to another village, they committed him to an insane asylum, where after a few months he converted the Vietnamese psychiatrist in charge of his case. The prophet was released the next year, but escaped a new French attempt to exile him through the intervention of the Japanese. During the Second World War he continued to make converts and to build up a small army with arms supplied by the Japanese. (He escaped the opprobrium of being called a "Japanese puppet" by prophesying the defeat of Japan well before the end of the war.) After a short-lived period of "coexistence" with the Viet Minh, the Hoa Hao troops foolishly attacked a Viet Minh stronghold and there was mutual bloodletting for a period of years. In 1947 the Viet Minh command assassinated their prophet and earned the hostility of what was then an important political force in the Delta.[26]

The prewar French hostility to the sects — the Cao Dai as well as the Hoa Hao — arose out of the suspicion that they were subversive organizations intent upon raising a peasant rebellion against colonial rule. This suspicion was largely unfounded. The main achievement of the sects was to fill in the traditional social and religious gaps the French had left open in substituting their colonial administration and economic system for that of the old empire. The sects built up secular administration and military forces during the Second World War, but they did not intend to take on the French directly by military force. They were merely waiting for the will of Heaven to change, at which point (so they were convinced) the French would disappear and all the Vietnamese would become Cao Dai or Hoa Hao. Their true rival was not so much the French state as the Catholic Church in Vietnam that under the very eyes of the French clergy had developed much the same kind of political control over its adherents as the native sects possessed. But even with the Catholic Church, rivalry did not imply conflict: heaven was either with them or it was not. Traditionalist, mystical, the sects were the real voices of the Mekong Delta, of the Vietnamese who had left behind them in Tonkin and Annam the philosophic strain of Mahayana Buddhism and rationalist Chinese social thought. The Delta would not on its own give rise to a revolution.

Having neither agricultural nor industrial potential, the second *pays*, Annam, did not interest the French. Hue, the seat of the emperor, remained alone with its past, walled in by its court rituals, its illusions of empire. In a country of poor farmers and poor aristocrat-scholars, it became a haven for the old Confucian values, for a fierce traditionalism, and a concomitant xenophobia. While the emperor and the mandarins of the court gave their submission to the French, many of the central Vietnamese scholars withdrew from the capital and continued their resistance in the provinces. In the 1880's and 1890's Phan Dinh Phung and others led armed revolts against the French in the provinces of Nghe An and Ha Tinh. A participant in one of these early revolts, a scholar called Phan Boi Chau, left Vietnam in the early years of the twentieth century to look for foreign support for an anticolonial movement. Chau was a monarchist who saw the necessity for modern education and reform. Looking for foreign assistance and education for Vietnamese students, he went to Japan, the only country in Asia to become a modern nation on its own terms. Along with the Prince Cuong De, his chosen contender for the throne, Chau remained in exile for most of his life. He was unable to obtain substantial help from either the Chinese or the Japanese, and he was restricted from playing an active role in Vietnam by his own Confucian elitist notions of politics. His followers founded the Dai Viet or "Greater Vietnam" Party, a small secret society that was eventually to attract a number of the highly placed Vietnamese civil servants. But the early central Vietnamese resistance movements bore other kinds of fruit. They created a tradition of anti-French activity, particularly in the provinces of Nghe An and Ha Tinh. Ho Chi Minh was born in Nghe An in 1890, the son of a provincial mandarin. During the 1920's a group of civil servants in the Nghe-Tinh region created the Tan Viet, the New Vietnam Revolutionary Party. But as time went on and the French established themselves throughout the rest of the country, Annam gave place to Tonkin as the center of the anti-colonial struggle, the new territories to the Red River Delta, which had been the old base of empire.

The north, too, had suffered from the colonial regime. Because the northern delta possessed no new land available for development, the French had simply expropriated the village land to build their own farms. With the addition of a heavy tax burden the economic squeeze on the peasantry became acute. Few Vietnamese in Tonkin profited from French enterprises, as they did in Cochin China. The new wealth of Tonkin lay in her minerals and her cheap labor, and the mines belonged exclusively to the French. In the 1930's Tonkin possessed the only industrial base in Vietnam — a collection of mines and several factories for the production of textiles and cement. It also possessed the beginnings of an industrial proletariat. The wages paid to the mine and factory workers ought in some measure to have compensated for the agricultural dislocations, but they did not, for while the wages were calculated on the basis of the barter economy of the village, the taxes and the prices of goods were calculated on the moneyed city economy. The French pocketed the difference.[27] For the sake of survival many of the industrial workers divided their time between the factories, where they could earn money for taxes, and the villages, where they could raise food. This continual coming and going created a link between the modern city and the traditional countryside that did not exist in the south.

In Annam the French had left the mandarins to themselves, but in Tonkin they created the beginnings of a new class — not a group of wealthy landowners, as in the south, but a middle class composed of administrators and professional men.[28] Under the pressure of the First World War they had found it necessary to break into the traditional educational system and train Vietnamese to fill the secondary levels of the colonial and commercial administrations. After that war they abolished the Confucian schools throughout Vietnam and replaced them with a small primary education system, two lycées, and the faculties of law and medicine at the University of Hanoi. In Tonkin, where the loyalties of the mandarins to the old regime remained as strong as they did in the center, the new students grew up on a dangerous blend of modern Western education and Vietnamese tradition. As one historian has contended, the French in this respect made a most impolitic calculation: the Western-educated students were few in number, but by the 1930's there were still too many of them to fill the available jobs.[29] In particular there were too many schoolteachers, for, believing in the unconditional value of French education, the French trained schoolteachers without regard for their own economic priorities. They trained such men as Vo Nguyen Giap to educate his own compatriots to become Frenchmen. The chief difficulty was that while the schoolbooks spoke of liberty, equality, and fraternity, the French in Vietnam did not apply those principles to the Vietnamese. Because the French left no opportunities open for the educated class, the effect of modernization in Tonkin was to split the society on different lines than in Cochin China — not city/country, or modern/traditional, but French/Vietnamese.

In the 1920's a group of political organizations very different from their predecessors began to emerge in Vietnam, and mainly out of the north. Their memberships remained small, but they were composed largely of French-educated civil servants, schoolteachers, and professional men who saw the need for a social program and for the participation of the mass of the people. Their aim was not merely to rid the country of the French but to bring about revolutionary change in the life of the society. Among these parties numbered the Tan Viet and the Viet Nam Quoc Dan Dang, the Vietnam Nationalist Party, or VNQDD, and the Communist Party of Indochina. Of the three the VNQDD was by far the most prominent in the 1920's. Modeled on the Chinese Kuomintang, it attracted some thousand adherents in the area of Hanoi to undertake a program of anti-French agitation and terrorism. But like the Tan Viet, it suffered from parochialism and from the lack of a well-thought-out political and social strategy.[30] The French police arrested most of its leading members in 1930–1932, and the rest went into exile in China to survive through the Second World War only by the grace of the Chinese Kuomintang. In 1925 Ho Chi Minh founded the Revolutionary Youth League which was to be the nucleus of the Indochinese Communist Party. Initially the League undertook a much less adventurous policy of building up committees in the three *pays* and converting many of the other radicals. In 1930, just as the worldwide depression hit Vietnam, forcing down the price of rice and plunging the small farmers throughout Vietnam into bankruptcy, the Party undertook its first large-scale action with the organization of workers and peasants in the Nghe-Tinh region. The results were spectacular. For a year the people of the region demonstrated against the colonial regime, assassinated local officials, created a government of village soviets, and carried out a land reform. The revolt did not spread to other areas of the country, and from a historical perspective it might be said to have been premature, for the French still possessed the force to put it down in a most brutal manner.[31] But the Communist Party survived, gained experience, and waited for a new opportunity to emerge.

The opportunity came as a result of the Second World War. The war marked a caesura in Vietnamese history as it did in that of most countries. After the fall of France in 1940 Japan took over French Indochina by diplomatic fiat. The Vichyite governor sent by Paris to Saigon agreed to continue to administer the territory while the Japanese used its ports for military bases and its raw materials for trade within the Greater East Asian Co-Prosperity Sphere. In the spring of 1941 Ho Chi Minh and his comrades founded the Vietnam Independence League or the Viet Nam Doc Lap Dong Minh Hoi, known as the Viet Minh, and with the cooperation of the Tho, one of the montagnard tribes of the north, built up bases in the mountains and assembled a small guerrilla force to combat the Japanese. While Ho's policy was in line with that of the Chinese Communists, his support came from one of the warlords under the nominal suzerainty of Chiang Kai-shek, who dominated the provinces just across the Vietnamese border.

The Viet Minh's opportunity arrived with a sudden change in the status of the country in 1945. A few months before the Allied landings in the south, the Japanese overthrew the French administration in a sudden *coup de force*, and set up an "independent"

Vietnamese government over Tonkin and Annam, composed of the local Vietnamese functionaries and under the aegis of the current Nguyen emperor, Bao Dai. In mid-August, 1945, Ho Chi Minh moved into Hanoi with a thousand men and, given no resistance, proclaimed the establishment of the Democratic Republic of Vietnam. The French moved quickly into Cochin China with their British allies. But it was the Chinese Nationalists that under the Potsdam Agreements occupied northern Vietnam for seven months following the allied landings. When the period was up and the French made ready to move back into the north, Ho Chi Minh had already been ensconced in Hanoi and Hue for nine months claiming to represent the sovereign nation of Vietnam.

Since the autumn of 1940 our country has ceased to be a colony and had become a Japanese outpost . . . we have wrested our independence from the Japanese and not from the French. The French have fled, the Japanese have capitulated, Emperor Bao Dai has abdicated, our people have broken the fetters which for over a century have tied us down; our people have at the same time overthrown the monarchic constitution that had reigned supreme for so many centuries and instead have established the present Republican government.[32]

Ho Chi Minh's claim for Vietnamese independence was not just the legalistic rationale it seemed to many Frenchmen at the time. Despite its haphazard character, the Japanese coup had made a profound impression on the Vietnamese. In escaping out of Hanoi at that moment in history, Paul Mus, a Free French agent and scholar of Asian religions, had seen its effect on the villages: the day before the coup the French were the respected masters of the country, the day after it they were uninvited guests with the worst of reputations. Later, Mus realized that he had witnessed one of those strange shifts in Vietnamese life where the resentment, so long repressed, turns suddenly to revolt. To the Vietnamese the sight of French surrendering to Asians meant that the French had, as it were, lost their winning streak; in the old language, the will of Heaven had changed and the French were no longer the rulers of the country.[33] This shift was felt by the ministers of the Bao Dai government, the former faithful servants of the French, as much as by the most traditional of the villagers.[34] For the Vietnamese it was now merely a question of time before the French disappeared altogether. Incomprehensible as it was to the French, this conviction was to remain with most Vietnamese throughout the war for independence. The issue was merely who now possessed the Mandate of Heaven.

Ho Chi Minh's revolution in Hanoi succeeded mainly because there was nothing to oppose it. Apart from the Viet Minh, the country had no national leaders ready to assert independence and take control of the government. The Japanese-sponsored government in Hanoi was no more than a group of functionaries with no political experience and no ideas for the future. Presented with a *fait accompli* by the Viet Minh, many of the officials joined the new movement; the Emperor Bao Dai himself proposed to serve it for a time, and three northern Catholic bishops added their approval. The test of Ho Chi Minh's government lay not in domestic political confrontation but in a military trial with the French armies — in the war that Ho Chi Minh hoped to avoid. Not long after the French reoccupation of the south the North Vietnamese leader began negotiations with the French authorities in Saigon and Paris.[35] For a time there seemed a possibility that the French would grant the Vietnamese their independence: the Free French commanders in the south had little sympathy with the local Vichyites, and the coalition government in Paris included the supposedly anti-imperialist left-wing parties. But gradually the negotiations broke down. The French Communists and socialists defected to the imperialist cause, now a matter of national pride for the newly liberated France, and the French colonial authorities deliberately sabotaged the diplomatic bargaining process. In February 1947 the French army took control of Hanoi, and the Viet Minh, now numbering some one hundred thousand throughout the country,[36] retreated to their bases in the countryside and prepared for a war of resistance.

Seven years later in 1954, no one, and particularly not the French, deny the existence of an independent nation-state in Vietnam. Ho Chi Minh's Democratic Republic had all the attributes of a nation-state, including the essential one of an army capable of making it too expensive and too dangerous for the French to continue their occupation of the country. What was not so well appreciated by the Americans as by the French who had fought the war was that the new Vietnamese government had a stronger claim to legitimacy than did most governments in Southeast Asia. To win the war, Ho Chi Minh had had to enlist the active support of a great percentage of the population. By themselves the city elites could not

decide the struggle for independence. Because the French undertook
a large-scale military reoccupation, the Vietnamese elite depended
upon the people of the countryside, upon the vast reserves of manpower that had lain untouched since the Tay Son rebellion at the
end of the eighteenth century. When the French moved into Hanoi,
the Viet Minh went deep into the countryside like divers, and the villages had closed over them. Attaching themselves to the "net ropes"
of the peasantry, they built a clandestine political organization
large and strong enough to sustain not only the guerrillas but the
regular armies that fought the French on their own ground. In
mobilizing the Vietnamese population to defeat a modern European
army, the Viet Minh proved themselves in a test that few nationalist
movements have undergone and fewer still survived.[37]

The French could not deny the existence of the Democratic
Republic of Vietnam. But they could for the purposes of negotiation
question how much territory it controlled. Even at the peace talks
after their great victory at Dien Bien Phu, the Viet Minh did not
control the cities of Vietnam or the greater proportion of the southern provinces below the 13th parallel (the region of Nha Trang).[38]
The effort of war had been unevenly distributed between north and
south. In the north General Vo Nguyen Giap raised and trained
regular divisions in the mountains to fight with the guerrilla forces
attached to the villages of the Red River Delta. The French armies
could choose either to fight the North Vietnamese regulars in the
mountains or to garrison the populous delta, but they could not do
both at once — and on that dilemma their war efforts foundered.
But the Viet Minh did not so completely mobilize the south. They
raised guerrilla forces adequate to harass the French garrisons, to
contest their control of the population, and to draw their armies
away from the north, but they did not support large units there. In
part this was simply because the Mekong Delta was furthest from
their supply lines into China and its flat plains offered no secure
bases. In part it was because the south did not respond to them as
strongly as did the north. In the Mekong Delta the guerrillas controlled only the peninsula of Ca Mau and the region surrounding
the Plain of Reeds south and west of Saigon. They contested other
parts of the Delta and held most of the thin backbone of central
Vietnam, but they made only limited inroads into the territories
controlled by the sects. Moreover, the southern Viet Minh often did
not measure up in quality to their northern counterparts. Isolated

within the vast horizons of the Delta, they would tend to lose contact with the central command and drift off into inaction or the banditry that characterized most of the political groups in the south — a sin known to the Communists as "mountaintopism." Occasionally the northerners lost patience. In 1951 they executed Nguyen Binh, the chief of all the southern forces, for a series of strategic errors, including the staging of a premature uprising in Saigon.

But in 1954 it did not seem justice or indeed a reality of power that because the Viet Minh had won the war mostly in the north they would therefore have to give up the south. By 1954, after seven years of an expensive and bloody war, the French had renounced their original intention to preserve Vietnam as a part of the French empire. Their main aim at that point was to save the French Expeditionary Corps and extricate themselves from an expensive and ultimately futile conflict. Many French and American officials at the time believed that given the current military situation, any political settlement would have left Ho Chi Minh in control of the entire country.[39] The French and their allies, however, persuaded the Viet Minh to negotiate the whole question of Indochina within an international conference including the great powers — France, Great Britain, the United States, the Soviet Union, and China. At this conference the whole issue of the colonial war was shifted to an entirely different stage and was settled within the context of all the other cold-war conflicts. The agreement there concluded was more favorable to France than many French officials had expected.

Convening in April 1954, the Geneva Conference in three months issued two documents bearing on Vietnam: first, an armistice, signed by the French and DRVN military representatives, that provided for an exchange of prisoners and a regroupment of both combatants to either side of a demilitarized zone at the 17th parallel. The armistice included a provision for the movement of civilian population between the zones within a three-hundred-day period and four articles that prohibited all future foreign military involvement in that country.[40] The second document, the Final Declaration of that conference, repeated the strictures of the armistice and elaborated on the political and administrative arrangements to be made in Vietnam. Most significantly in view of the events to follow, it specified that the demilitarized zone should not constitute a political or territorial boundary, but merely a temporary military demarcation line. Following the period of truce, a political settlement should be made on the basis of "respect for the principles of independence, unity, and territorial integrity" of Vietnam and by means of free general elections to be held in July 1956. In neither of the two documents was there any mention of a second state in Vietnam: it was the French who were to administer their regroupment zone in the south during the period of the armistice. The Viet Minh remained somewhat dissatisfied with the postponement of the political settlement, but, exhausted by the war and under some pressure from Moscow, they finally agreed to sign the declaration. In the future they would be wary of any such political compromise.

The Final Declaration of Geneva was never signed by any of the participants to the conference for the reason that the United States refused even to give its oral consent. Before the conference most U.S. officials had hoped that the negotiations would end in failure; they had hope that France would continue to find the strength to carry on the war against the Viet Minh.[41] By 1954 American officials and politicians of both parties had come to regard Vietnam as vital to U.S. security. Since the victory of Mao Tse-tung five years earlier, American officials judged that China, in alliance with the Soviet Union, constituted the leading threat to American global interests. Whatever these interests were, and whether or not the official line accurately reflected them, the United States had in the early 1950's begun to transfer its European policy of the "containment of Communism" to Asia. With the Korean War and the continued support for Chiang Kai-shek, it had begun to build a wall of anti-Communist American dependencies around China. Vietnam, as the officials saw it, constituted the crucial southern element of that wall: if Vietnam "fell" under Communist domination, then the whole of Southeast Asia would follow after it. In 1950 the United States began to subsidize the French war in Vietnam and by 1954 U.S. military aid covered 80 percent of the French war expenditures.[42] After the Korean War, President Eisenhower contemplated sending tactical nuclear weapons and/or American troops into the conflict. He finally rejected the proposals in his desire not to engage the United States in yet another land war in Asia. When it became clear that the French could no longer carry on the war by themselves, he looked to the Vietnamese government the French had set up in Saigon as a new vehicle for continuing the struggle. Two months after the

Geneva Conference, Secretary of State Dulles set up the Southeast Asia Treaty Organization (SEATO) in a treaty whereby the signatories agreed to assist each other in case of armed aggression from the outside. At the time the organization had only three Asian members, Thailand, Pakistan, and the Philippines — and not Burma, India, and Indonesia, as Dulles would have liked — but a separate protocol covered "the states of Cambodia and Laos and the free territory under the jurisdiction of the State of Vietnam."

In fact the Vietnamese government supported by the French in Saigon had most dubious credentials for statehood. Its very creation had been merely a matter of French convenience — and temporary convenience at that. In 1946, at the very beginning of the war, the French had created a legal fiction called "the Republic of Cochin China" in order to substantiate their claims to the existence of a French union combining the associated states of Indochina. Four years later the French dismantled the "republic" when the exigencies of war demanded that they attempt to provide a rallying point for non-Communist Vietnamese and to demonstrate to American satisfaction that they were fighting an anti-Communist, rather than a colonial, war. The "republic" was clearly inadequate to these purposes, for even the Emperor Bao Dai refused to participate in a government of Cochin China alone. Finally giving in to the principle of a unified Vietnam, the French brought back Bao Dai and on January 1, 1950, installed him as the head of a new "national" government called "the State of Vietnam." But as the French had created the state mainly for public relations purposes, so the state itself remained to a great degree a mere formality. For as long as the French remained in Saigon they continued to control its budget, its external relations, its internal security arrangements, and its jurisdiction over the French in Vietnam. In fact it had only two attributes of a government: first, a small administration composed of old colonial functionaries whose territorial reach extended not far beyond the outskirts of Saigon, and, secondly, an army of some three hundred thousand men split up into small units and commanded by French officers.[43] Taking most accurate stock of his position, Bao Dai removed himself from Saigon to the resort city of Dalat, where he spent the next four years amusing himself with big-game hunting and the distribution of well-paid government appointments. Not until the eve of the Geneva negotiations did the French sign a paper granting the state of Vietnam full independence — a gesture that gave them the means of claiming that they had "handed over" Vietnam not to the Viet Minh, but rather to the Bao Dai government.

The gift, however, seemed of questionable value to anyone. As the period of truce began, the Viet Minh leaders in the north went about consolidating the government they had exercised in fact since the beginning of the French war. In the south only confusion reigned — a confusion not at all alleviated by the Viet Minh's regroupment of some ninety thousand soldiers and cadres (the vast majority of them southerners) to the north. The Viet Minh had not been the only ones to fail at organizing the Mekong Delta. For the course of the war the French had managed, rather than actually governed, the Delta, and partly as a result of their attempt to conciliate all the non-Communist groups, the south had become a political jungle of warlords, sects, bandits, partisan troops, and secret societies. To French observers at the time there seemed to be small chance for the establishment of an administration, much less a nation-state, in the midst of this chaos.

Now in control of the entire western portion of the Delta, the Hoa Hao and the Cao Dai represented a military as well as a political force — or rather, a series of forces, for, since the death of the first Cao Dai grand master and the murder of Huynh Phu So at the hands of the Viet Minh, both sects had split into a number of rival factions. While the Cao Dai remained a church with dissident regional factions and several none-too-cooperative military leaders, the Hoa Hao, without a religious hierarchy, had divided between three different regional warlords. The distinctions between them were, however, small, as the leaders of all the factions looked forward to assuming control of the country or, failing that, control over their own agricultural bases and the rice trade with Saigon. For the sake of freeing their regiments in the north, the French had given military aid and advisers to most of the factions during the course of the war. Though under obligation to the French, the sect factions directed their war efforts almost impartially against the French, the Viet Minh, and each other — depending upon who happened to cross the path directly in front of them. They disliked the Viet Minh, and that was enough for the French in the short term, for they had the power to keep their own territories free of them. The difficulty came only at the end of the war when the sects, with something over two million adherents, refused to allow their troops to be integrated into the national army and refused to permit officials from Saigon to enter their territories. The modicum of control the French had over them came from their manipulation of military aid, and thus it was very much open to question what the sects would do if, and when, the aid ceased and they were left to themselves.

But the affairs of the sects were grand politics next to those of the other French-supported fiefs near Saigon. During the Japanese occupation a man called Le Van Vien, or Bay Vien, had put together a gang of river pirates to collect taxes on the private traffic in and out of the city. In 1948 the French intelligence services had agreed to recognize his gang in return for his submission. A few years later they gave this genial but absolutely ruthless pirate the title of brigadier general in their auxiliary forces as well as the tacit right to control the vast gambling establishment, Le Grand Monde, and to collect taxes from the rich Chinese merchants of Cholon. On his return to Vietnam, Bao Dai gave Bay Vien his support against his own police chief in Saigon — an inexplicable act to those Americans who assumed they knew the difference between the Vietnamese J. Edgar Hoover and the Vietnamese Al Capone.

Counting the army of the State of Vietnam and the various sect forces, the French had supported at least six different non-Communist armies in the Delta. To add to the political and military confusion there were, of course, the Catholics, the Buddhists, the montagnard tribes, and the Khmer and Cham populations — most of which minorities had some means of self-defense and some quite reasonable motive for suspecting the motives of all the rest. As the capital of the south, Saigon was the very hub and essence of this disorder. Its economy lay largely in the hands of the French, the white-suited Vietnamese planters, and the invisible Chinese merchant-profiteers who gave their loyalties to France for as long as she would support the piastre at its current artificial price.[44] Its administration and its police force were composed mainly of the venal and the opportunist. The former emperor, now chief of state, was no exception to this rule. A reasonable man, he saw no reason to risk his own life and fortune to one or another of the bandit groups in exchange for a largely fictional government. He went to France and in the middle of the Geneva Conference abdicated for all practical purposes to a man he rather disliked, his new prime minister, Ngo Dinh Diem.

The American ability to intervene in the affairs of South Vietnam was not, then, at all in question: the southern politicians were ready to accept any foreign power that would feed and protect them. It was the hope of building "a strong, free nation" that was absurd. How should the south build a strong anti-Communist government when most southerners continued to obey the old authorities of the family, the village, and the sect? Communist, anti-Communist, the next war would begin in a language that few of them understood.

3

The Sovereign of Discord

one

Ngo Dinh Diem. The name meant a great deal at one time in Washington as well as Saigon. On a trip to Vietnam in 1961 Lyndon Johnson had called Diem "the Winston Churchill of Asia." Whatever the other points of resemblance between him and that British statesman, the man who undertook the American project of barricading the southern against the northern half of Vietnam certainly provoked hyperbole from Americans. For a period in the mid-1950's Diem was the hero of the American press: this man of "deep religious heart" who, according to *Life,* had "saved his people from [the] agonizing prospect" of a national plebiscite; this "tough miracle man" had built a nation in South Vietnam and halted "the red tide of Communism in Asia." The word "miracle" affixed itself to Diem's name with the adhesion of a Homeric epithet. Diem had performed the "political miracle" of creating a strong government, the "economic miracle" in rebuilding the economy of South Vietnam from the ruins of war. In 1957 Diem traveled to the United States on the American presidential airplane. Welcomed by President Eisenhower at the airport, he addressed a joint session of Congress and visited New York, where Mayor Robert Wagner called him "a man history may yet adjudge as one of the great figures of the twentieth century." Only six years later, Diem was to die in a dark alley of Saigon, denounced by those same periodicals and many of the same politicians as the petty tyrant who had destroyed South Vietnamese society and prejudiced the cause of the Free World in Asia.[1]

But in Saigon in 1966 it was difficult to find a trace of Diem anywhere. The same Vietnamese officers who had overthrown the president only three years earlier celebrated the anniversary of the coup, the National Day, with all the abstracted formality of parades and platitudes. Oddly enough, in view of the political terror campaign the regime had conducted, the officers had taken small revenge upon even the closest confidants of the Ngo family. After three years the heads of the secret police were out of jail, and some of them back in government. Few Americans so much as knew their history. Of course, there were few Americans left in Saigon who recalled the days of Ngo Dinh Diem. With the turnover of American personnel every eighteen months and the endless series of Vietnamese military coups, time in Saigon moved forward like an army, obliterating all it passed over. By 1966 even the scenery of the Diem regime had vanished. Of the presidential palace only the outer garden walls remained, enclosing an acre of grass like the walls of a graveyard from which the graves have been removed.

And yet it was strange that Diem should have disappeared so completely. The round little president and his family had ruled Vietnam for eight years — the entirety of the truce between two wars and the whole history of an unoccupied South Vietnam. The Ngos had not been pale ciphers for the whole American undertaking in that part of the world; on the contrary, any history of the Diem regime would have to be written in vivid, novelesque colors, with the characters of the Ngos quite obscuring those of the Americans. In the first place there was Ngo Dinh Diem himself, the shy, self-righteous Catholic mandarin with his vow of chastity and his ambition to serve as a moral example to his people. There was his brother, the lean, fierce Ngo Dinh Nhu, whose life was a succession of plots, ruses, and metaphysical dogmas. And there was Madame Nhu, the beautiful, outspoken, and wholly outrageous woman whom the American journalists called "the Dragon Lady." For a decade the Ngos had dominated all conversation in Saigon; Americans and Vietnamese alike had spent hours discussing the latest court intrigue or scandal, hours speculating on the intricacies of their philosophy. The Ngos never disappointed them, even in their death. Played out under the gaze of the television cameras, the fall of the Ngos was in its way pure theatre, the denouement of a baroque tragedy.

On June 16, 1963, an elderly bonze named Thich Quang Duc seated himself in a major intersection of downtown Saigon, and amid a gathering crowd, set fire to his gasoline-soaked robes. At that moment the political climate in Saigon changed as if hit by the drop in pressure preceding a hurricane. Vast demonstrations broke out. The city people, who had for years remained passive, terrified before the Diemist police, crowded into the pagodas to kneel and weep, then, following the bonzes, burst forth into the streets calling for the downfall of the Ngos. Schoolchildren, university students, government clerks, now fearlessly confronted the legions of the Ngos' picked troops.

For some months before, Ngo Dinh Nhu had known that a coterie of generals was plotting a military coup. He had no fear of the officers; he had dealt with their shallow intrigues many times before. It was the bonzes who unnerved him, these unarmed, shaven-headed men who until the moment of Quang Duc's death had had no political influence in the cities. The brown-robed monks padded day after day through the streets of the capital to be hauled, screaming, into the police trucks. Early on the morning of August 21, the Vietnamese Special Forces under Nhu's orders surrounded the central pagodas of Saigon, Hue, and other central Vietnamese cities. Shooting at random, they stormed through the sanctuaries, wounding scores of bonzes and hauling the rest off to prison. The next day Nhu claimed that the dissident generals had ordered the massacre. His intention obviously was to destroy the generals and the Buddhists with one *coup de force*, but as he had already divulged his plans for the raid, not even his American supporters could finally accept the story.

For a man who had so long and so successfully manipulated both the generals and the Americans, the whole affair looked oddly irrational. As time went on, Nhu's fury of self-destruction only seemed to increase. When a few American newspapermen reported the truth of the pagoda raids, he and his wife lashed out at the American officials, charging that the CIA chief headed a vast international conspiracy with designs against his life. It was true that a

CIA agent had taken up contact with the dissident generals, but the agent had not given them any encouragement until that point.[2] With the slaughter of the bonzes, and the denunciation of the United States, Nhu effectively forced the Americans to take the difficult step of dissociating themselves from the Diem regime. Still, even with assurances of American support, the generals did not act. A month went by and there were further Buddhist-led demonstrations. In October Nhu ordered thousands of the student demonstrators arrested and many of them tortured. The move seemed designed to provoke the coup so long delayed, for many of the students were the children of his still-wavering officers and officials. In the end Nhu's own troops were refusing to fire on the crowds and even openly encouraging the demonstrators. As one American witness reported, "Saigon, those last days of Diem, was an incredible place. One felt that one was witnessing an entire social structure coming apart at the seams. In horror, Americans helplessly watched Diem tear apart the fabric of Vietnamese society more effectively than the Communists had ever been able to do."[3]

Of course in 1966 the Americans in Saigon never spoke of the Ngos. Their reign had been an unmitigated disaster for American policy in Vietnam. Still engaged in the same policy of fighting the Communists and building up the Saigon government, American officials could not afford to puzzle over their initial setback. For a period of eight years the United States had supported an incompetent dictator. So much had to be dismissed as an error — a tactical error that could be corrected with new Vietnamese leaders, new programs for pacification and administrative reform, new American controls over the Saigon regime. Ngo Dinh Diem, after all, was only one man. In the total context of the American war and the larger social forces at work in Vietnamese society, he could be counted as an insignificant factor.

And yet, perhaps, in passing over the drama of the Ngo family the officials overlooked something essential to the outcome of the entire American effort in Vietnam. Ngo Dinh Diem was only one man; the private psychological drama of Diem and his family was as nothing beside the grand strategies and global concerns of the United States in Vietnam. But, as the French historian, Philippe Devillers, once wrote, "In our age of mass society, where all history seems to be determined by forces so powerful as to negate the individual, the Vietnamese problem has the originality to remain dominated by questions of individuals. Indeed, the problem becomes almost incomprehensible if one transforms men into abstractions."⁴ The notion may sound romantic, but it is not so. In the first place, Vietnam in the days of Diem possessed a very small educated society; most of the prominent men knew each other as well as if they had been the inhabitants of one village. In the second place, the Vietnamese traditionally understood politics not in terms of programs or larger social forces, but in terms of the individual. And their perception was not unscientifically based, for given the size and uniformity of the old society, the life of one man might stand as a model for the life of the society as a whole. If that one man was Ngo Dinh Diem, then the personal drama of the Ngo family with its mysterious and violent denouement described the difficulty of the American project in Vietnam better than would a history of all the counterinsurgency programs or an analysis of all the larger social forces.

The American decision to back Ngo Dinh Diem was not of itself a major policy decision. The policy of supporting a non-Communist Vietnam had been formulated some years earlier, and Diem himself was but one element of the fallback position hastily devised in the wake of the French debacle. It was not until June 15, 1954, that Secretary of State Dulles told the French definitively that the United States would not commit its own troops and planes to the Indochina war. Even after Dien Bien Phu, administration officials did not accept the Viet Minh victory or the principle of a divided Vietnam. During the Geneva Conference their ambitions were not only to build up a government in Saigon, but to undermine Ho Chi Minh's government as well. In June Colonel Edward G. Lansdale was sent out as chief of a Saigon military mission with orders to "beat the Geneva timetable of Communist take-over in the north." By August, during the period of negotiated truce, Lansdale's teams were scattered about the country from Hanoi to the Ca Mau peninsula conducting sabotage operations and what can only be called agitprop work in direct violation of the U.S. government's promise at Geneva to "refrain from the threat or the use of force."⁵ These teams had small success in the Viet Minh–held areas. Their main achievement in the north was to lay the groundwork for the subsequent "flight" of the Catholics to the south. Their tactics were promises and "black propaganda," or the falsification of enemy reports. Many of the rest of their activities were little more than terrorist acts. One team, for instance, managed to contaminate the oil supply in the bus depot of Hanoi in order to wreck the engines of all the city's public transports.[6]

In fact, high American officials could have had very little confidence in the success of Colonel Lansdale's mission in the south or the north. In Saigon the French-sponsored government was in a state of near collapse. Shortly after the Emperor Bao Dai appointed Ngo Dinh Diem as his new premier for the State of Vietnam, President Eisenhower wrote Diem a letter of encouragement that fell short of committing the United States to support Diem. The current national security estimate held out little hope for the prospects of either the French or the Vietnamese establishing a strong government in Saigon. In all probability, the estimate noted, the situation would continue to deteriorate and the Viet Minh would extend their control throughout the south. As the United States directly joined the struggle for Vietnam, American officials weighed the odds against a non-Communist solution and, even more heavily, against the success of the small, retiring mandarin, Ngo Dinh Diem.

In Saigon American pessimism appeared fully justified. Always the home of the entrepreneur and the collaborator, Saigon in the last year of the French war was a very sinkhole of violence, corruption, and intrigue. Its atmosphere of dense marsh heat mixed with diesel fumes and the rotting, vegetable smell of the Saigon river accorded perfectly with its political climate. The French army remained the one force for order. Half of Saigon was controlled by Bay Vien's bandit army, the Binh Xuyen. The countryside belonged largely to the Viet Minh and the sects — the latter no more anxious for a strong government in Saigon than the former. Arriving in Saigon on July 7, Ngo Dinh Diem found himself with hardly a strand of political support. The sects and the Cochin Chinese landlords disliked and suspected him for being a Catholic and a central Vietnamese. The Vietnamese officers and officials regarded him as an interloper, for Diem had left the country four years before in protest against their refusal to hold out for full independence. The French resented him and the whole American undertaking in the south. As for the American military command in Saigon, it retreated into deep diplomatic silence in preparation for backing the strongest candidate that might emerge. When Colonel Lansdale went to visit Diem in the palace of the former governor general, he found the new premier quite alone, abandoned even by his bodyguards.

As a man with a job to do, Lansdale did not share the pessimism of his superiors. Over the next few months he was almost single-handedly to reverse the whole course of events in Saigon. Lansdale was in many respects a remarkable man. Already something of a celebrity among Americans involved with Asia, he had served with the OSS during the war and later helped to rebuild the Filipino army and intelligence service. When the local Communist insurgency movement, the Hukbalahaps, began to gain strength in the Philippines, Lansdale, on special assignment to the Filipino government, counseled the defense secretary, Ramon Magsaysay, on a strategy of social reform and military repression that proved effective in weakening the Huk movement. In the process he became the friend, adviser, and public relations agent to Magsaysay and was instrumental in securing his election to the presidency. In 1954 Lansdale came to Saigon on assignment from Allen Dulles to act as the head of the military mission and then as CIA chief of station for domestic affairs. He met Ngo Dinh Diem just after the premier's arrival in Saigon, liked him, and shifted the weight of the CIA to his support. "To me," he said, "[Diem] was a man with a terrible burden to carry and in need of friends, and I tried to be an honest friend of his."[7]

The remark was typical of Lansdale, a man who never thought in terms of systems or larger social forces. With all his expertise in black propaganda and every other form of unconventional warfare, Lansdale had an artless sincerity. He had faith in his own good motives. No theorist, he was rather an enthusiast, a man who believed that Communism in Asia would crumble before men of goodwill with some concern for "the little guy" and the proper counterinsurgency skills. He had a great talent for practical politics and for personal involvement in what to most Americans would seem the most distinctly foreign of affairs. In Diem he saw another Magsaysay, a man of integrity with a sense of responsibility for his country who might with the proper advice become a hero to his people. While the American command hesitated, he put all of his many talents to work for Diem as he had for Magsaysay. Going to live in the palace, he became a two-way agent: on the one hand, Diem's personal contact man and adviser in the attempt to win over the diverse political elements of the South, and on the other an advocate for Diem within the American mission. In an atmosphere of indecision and uncertainty within and without the mission, his advocacy had a decisive impact.

The first problem for Diem was to assert his delegated powers over the army of the State of Vietnam and, in particular, over its commander in chief, General Nguyen Van Hinh. A young air force officer, Hinh, like most of his colleagues, had vague political ambitions, vaguely nourished by Bao Dai and some of the French in Saigon. Lansdale and his team at first tried to reconcile Hinh and the new premier. When that proved impossible, and Diem fired the commander in chief, Lansdale threatened Hinh with the withdrawal of all American support if he should attempt a military coup.[8] The move was, perhaps, directed as much towards the Americans as it was against General Hinh, for it forced the American military command to choose between Diem and the ranking Vietnamese officers whom they were advising. After a week of hesitation the Americans decided to rechannel the military subsidies through Diem's office and permitted Lansdale to ship Hinh off for a ceremonial visit to the Philippines.[9]

The sects presented Diem with a more formidable challenge, by their very numbers if not by their political strength. From the moment of Diem's arrival in Saigon the various factions of the Hoa Hao, the Cao Dai, and the Binh Xuyen had engaged in a bewildering series of maneuvers to gain power for themselves in Saigon. Had they taken Benjamin Franklin's advice to the representatives of the thirteen American colonies to "hang together," they might possibly have succeeded in unseating Diem. But they were not capable of such grand strategies. Confused, suspicious of each other, and badly in need of funds to replace the French subsidies, they allowed Diem and Lansdale to take advantage of their internal disputes and, almost literally, to hang them separately. According to most historians of the period, Diem's efforts to destroy the sects cost the American government some twelve million dollars in bribes — or subsidies.[10] Lansdale never admitted to having bribed anyone, but it was probably more than a coincidence that the one group that held out in military opposition until March 1955 was the one that enjoyed vast revenues from the gambling houses and protection rackets: the Binh Xuyen. On advice from his brother, Ngo Dinh Nhu, Diem decided to take what seemed to most Saigonese the suicidal step of closing Bay Vien's concessions and bringing about a showdown. As the Binh Xuyen prepared for conflict, Bao Dai, who had formerly supported the Binh Xuyen, cabled his prime minister to return to France. With Lansdale's encouragement, Diem defied the emperor, thereby cutting himself loose from his legal mandate and staking his future on the Americans. At the end of April the Binh Xuyen and units of the regular army joined battle in the center of Saigon; in the course of several days' fighting they managed to destroy an entire district and to plunge the city into chaos and near starvation. Finally the Binh Xuyen retired to the outskirts of the city, allowing the regular army to reoccupy the population centers.

Diem's victory was in fact much more important than the military confrontation indicated. On the eve of the battle Eisenhower's military representative in Saigon, General J. Lawton Collins, flew back to Washington and succeeded in persuading the administration to transfer its support from Diem to another more trustworthy politician. The very day that Secretary of State Dulles was to send out instructions to that effect, Lansdale cabled Washington to say that the regular army had defeated the Binh Xuyen, and that Diem was firmly in control.[11] The American embassy officials rallied to Diem's aid, and the Saigonese politicians, caught off-balance by the *coup de force,* acceded to the Diemist government. With the loss of the city the sect leaders gradually lost faith in the eventual success of their cause. The small warlords retreated into the swamps where, unable to organize a new offensive, they fought a hopeless rearguard action against the well-supplied forces of the regular army. As time went on, administration officials in Washington grew convinced of Lansdale's proposition: in Diem they had found the strong leader they were looking for.

Ngo Dinh Diem was in many respects a curious candidate for the role of American protégé. He came from Hue and, he boasted, from a family of mandarins that since the sixteenth century had held such high rank in government that the peasants of the region thought it good luck to attempt to bury their dead under the cover of night in the Ngo's ancestral graveyard.[12] In fact Diem's ancestors had little or no distinction; Diem simply fabricated high mandarin lineage for himself — and this at a time of general social upheaval. Diem also said that his forebears had been among the first converts to Catholicism in the seventeenth century. This claim, though possibly true, was an odd point for this new "nationalist" leader to insist upon, for the non-Catholic Vietnamese believed with some justification that the Catholics had acted as a fifth column for the French in the period preceding the conquest. Certainly the French had always shown great favoritism towards the Catholics, turning them into a self-conscious elitist minority without necessarily imparting to them a greater degree of French culture. Vietnamese Catholicism was harsh and medieval, a product of the strict patriarchate of the Vietnamese village rather than of the liberal French Church. Its churches stood like fortresses in the center of each Catholic village, manifesting the permanent defensive posture of the Catholics towards all other Vietnamese. A Buddhist mob, so Diem reported, raided the Ngos' village in the period just before the French conquest, killing all of his relatives with the exception of his father, Ngo Dinh Kha.[13] Kha made the fortunes of the family by joining the service of the French-supported emperors. Taking on all the attributes of the traditional mandarins, he rose to be minister of the rites, grand chamberlain, and keeper of the eunuchs to the Emperor Thanh Thai. But when the French exiled that uncooperative monarch to the island of Réunion, Kha, like a model mandarin, retired to his village to live out his life as a farmer and a "notable" of the region.

One out of nine children — the third of Kha's six sons — Diem was born in 1901. A good student, he studied in a small French Catholic school in Hue and then, deciding against the priesthood and a scholarship to France, attended the French college for administration in Hanoi. Graduating first in his class, he went into the mandarinate of Annam (then still under protectorate status) and rose quickly upward through the ranks from district chief to province chief. In 1933 he became minister of the interior. Just two months after his appointment to this most important post in the government, he resigned in protest against the French refusal to allow more Vietnamese participation in the affairs of state. Recalling his decision three decades later, he told Robert Shaplen of the *New Yorker:* "When the French asked me if I were waging a revolution, I told them we had to transform the country in order to fight Communism. Privately, I was convinced that an alarm had to be sounded to make the people feel the need for daring reforms and to make them respond in an energetic and even violent way. I felt it was my responsibility."[14]

The remark looks colored by hindsight, but Diem did in fact recognize the Communists as a potential enemy almost before the

French. In the late 1920's he tracked down some of the earliest Communist cells in his region. At the same time Diem undoubtedly responded to the new currents of nationalist sentiment stirring among educated Vietnamese, and he felt that the correct posture for a man of his rank and estate was one of disengagement from the French authorities.

Upon his resignation from the ministry of the interior, Diem retired to his village, like his father before him, and spent the next decade in the seclusion of his garden, the libraries, and Catholic seminaries. During the years of feverish political activity in the 1930's and 1940's Diem joined no anticolonial organization — he believed in government, not in politics — but he maintained contacts with Phan Boi Chau and other anticolonial leaders of his own background. And he held himself ready to take up what he considered his responsibility towards his country. In the light of the American intervention twenty years later he showed a great deal of prescience. During the Second World War, for instance, he sounded out the Japanese on their willingness to overthrow the French Vichyite regime. When the negotiations came to naught, he dissociated himself from the Japanese and remained obdurate even when in 1945 they offered him the prime ministership of the government they hastily assembled in Hanoi. A few months later Diem was captured by the Viet Minh and brought before the high command. Ho Chi Minh, at that point anxious to have a prestigious Catholic in his first coalition cabinet, asked Diem to serve with him. Diem refused, with the explanation that a Viet Minh guerrilla band had killed his oldest brother.

Pursued by the Viet Minh, Diem went south to live with his clerical brother, Ngo Dinh Thuc, outside of Saigon. For the first few years of the war he made a series of unsuccessful attempts to pressure the French into setting up a Vietnamese government under dominion status. His efforts failed partly for the reason that the Saigonese colonial functionaries and intellectuals, unwilling to renounce their own privileged status, refused to join him in his protests. When the French finally decided to do just as he had suggested, he flew to Hong Kong to ask the Emperor Bao Dai to insist upon a greater degree of autonomy for the new government. Again he was disappointed: the indolent but perhaps realistic emperor refused to hold out for his terms. In 1950 Diem left Vietnam for Rome with the intention of staying on for the Holy Year. En route he changed his mind and went on to the United States.[15] The decision was fortunate for him in that it was in the United States rather than in Vietnam that the political groundwork for his regime had to be laid.

Upon his arrival in the United States Diem was enthusiastically received by a number of dignitaries of the Catholic Church, including Francis Cardinal Spellman. Living for two years at the Maryknoll seminaries in New Jersey and New York, Diem lectured occasionally at American universities and pressed his cause in Washington under the wing of Spellman. Among those who supported his goal of independence for the State of Vietnam were Senator Mike Mansfield and Senator John F. Kennedy. The two senators were later to become charter members of a lobby group called the American Friends of Vietnam, one of whose most influential charter members was Dr. Wesley Fishel, a young academic from Michigan State University with important connections in the Republican administration.[16]

The enthusiasm for Diem on the part of Mansfield and Kennedy could be explained at least partly by the fact that the early fifties was the height of the McCarthy period. In Washington the Catholic senator from Wisconsin had attacked as "traitors" those U.S. State Department officials who had recommended that the United States accept as a fact Mao Tse-tung's victory in China. McCarthy had of course taken the anti-Communist rhetoric employed by Truman and Acheson for their anti-Soviet campaign in Europe and turned it about on itself. Now the "Communists" were inside the American government, plotting with the Kremlin for the expansion of international Communism in Asia. Seeing political benefits in it, the right wing of the Republican Party — Nixon and Senators Bridges and Welker — took up the attack, charging the Democrats with the "loss of China" and "softness on Communism." The campaign was almost entirely rhetorical — no political group advocated putting American troops into mainland China — but it found a sizable audience. Fearing for the loss of their support, the Democratic politicians began to compete with the Republicans for the most staunchly anti-Communist position. Whatever the reason of state involved, it became an axiom to both parties that no administration could possibly survive the "loss of Indochina." By 1956 Senator John F. Kennedy had taken the "domino theory" of the Truman and Eisenhower administrations for his own. At a meeting of the American Friends of Vietnam he called Vietnam "the corner-stone of the Free World in Southeast Asia, the keystone to the arch, the finger in the dike." He maintained that "Burma, Thailand, India, Japan, the Philippines, and obviously Laos and Cambodia are among those whose security would be threatened if the red tide of Communism overflowed into Vietnam." Thus, he added, "The fundamental tenets of this nation's foreign policy . . . depend in considerable measure upon a strong and free Vietnamese nation."[17]

Under the circumstances, therefore, the American government's somewhat haphazard decision to back Ngo Dinh Diem found favor with an influential group of American senators. With respect to the political exigencies of the moment, Diem had all the right qualifications. He was a patriot untainted by service to the Japanese or to the wartime French regime. He had the reputation of a man of integrity and an experienced administrator. Most important of all, he was a Catholic and a strong anti-Communist who had had the foresight to come to the United States for help.

Diem's first act upon arriving in Vietnam was to request American support in transporting and resettling those people who wished to leave the Viet Minh for the French zone of regroupment. The request could not have been more politic from an American point of view, as it permitted U.S. military and civilian welfare services to take up the congenial cause of "saving" Vietnamese from Communism and then from starvation. With the help of the U.S. Seventh Fleet some 860,000 people, the vast majority of them Catholics from the disciplined bishoprics of Phat Diem and Bui Chu, descended upon the south during the three hundred days of the armistice.[18] The arrival of the refugees provided Diem with his first political base in the south — and an important one at that, for the Catholics were the most highly organized of all the non-Communist political groups. Their arrival also provided Diem with a great deal of favorable publicity in the United States, for like their French predecessors in the nineteenth century, the American Catholic missions were anything but reticent about their good works.

By the summer of 1955 Diem and his American advisers felt confident enough about their position in Vietnam and the United States to go about setting up the legal framework for a new government in the south. In October 1955 Diem organized a referendum to determine whether the state should be a monarchy under Bao Dai or a republic with himself as president. As organized by Ngo Dinh

Nhu — and perhaps with excessive efficiency for American tastes —
the vote showed a majority of 99 percent for Diem out of the six
million ballots counted. Already in July Diem had repudiated the
Geneva accords and, specifically, the article proposing a free election between the two regroupment zones. Not content with making
a political division of Vietnam, he proceeded to seal the border
between the two regions with surgical precision, refusing the
DRVN's request for the opening of trade relations and forbidding
even the establishment of a postal exchange — a bitter blow to
those thousands of families whose members the war had scattered
between north and south. A year later, and largely as a result of
international pressure for elections of some sort, he held an election
for a constituent assembly and drafted a constitution for the "Republic of Vietnam."

The United States government expressed its approval of these
measures in the most forceful of terms. By 1956 it was paying the
Diem regime an average of $270 million a year — or more aid per
capita than it spent on any other country in the world except for
Laos and Korea.[19] The U.S. Military Assistance Advisory Group
(MAAG), composed of some eight hundred officers, took on the job
of reorganizing and retraining the Vietnamese army. The U.S.
Operations Mission (USOM) was pumping money into the economy and food for refugee relief into the warehouses of Saigon. The
mission was also providing funds for a land reform program and a
vast project to resettle the northern refugees and the land-hungry
peasants of the center. U.S. officials were lyrical in their reports to
the press and to Congress, asserting that the Diem regime was on
the way to rebuilding the economy and solving the social problems
caused by a decade of war. The American press followed suit in
more colorful terms. The *Saturday Evening Post* called South Vietnam "the Bright Spot in Asia." The blurb for the piece proclaimed,
"Two years ago at Geneva, South Vietnam was virtually sold down
the river to the Communists. Today the spunky little Asian country
is back on its own feet, thanks to a 'mandarin in a sharkskin suit
who's upsetting the Red timetable.' "[20] Other periodicals ran stories
vaunting the "economic miracle" that Diem had performed.

The new U.S. aid program and the public enthusiasm for the
Diem regime were essentially two halves of the same phenomenon — the second reflecting the first almost exclusively without any
reference to South Vietnam. For in truth, few Americans in or out of

Washington knew anything about the country. If Vietnam was "the keystone to the arch, the finger in the dike," it was still a very distant and foreign place, whose major interest to Americans lay in its location to the south of China. Not until the crisis of 1961 did American journalists go in any numbers to investigate this new American dependency. The lacuna had a certain importance, for it meant that for the first six years information about the Diem regime came largely from U.S. government sources.[21]

By far the most prolific of these government sources was the team from Michigan State University led by Diem's earliest supporter, Dr. Wesley Fishel. Under government contract this team, consisting of some fifty scholars and public administration experts, went to Vietnam in 1955 to reorganize the Diemist administration, the police, and the civil guard. In laying the groundwork for the reorganization, groups of social scientists set out to research the economics and sociology of the Vietnamese village as well as every aspect of Vietnamese government operations. By 1963 it would have been difficult to argue that they had any influence on the Diem regime itself. Still, their studies added a new dimension to the art of international public relations. It did not much matter that a number of the social scientists turned into critics of the Diem regime on their return to the United States: it was enough that they should discuss the regime in terms of "developing administrative structures" and "functional integration of value systems." The language alone gave the American project in Vietnam an atmosphere of solidity and respectability. It implied (if the authors did not make the direct assertion) that the United States had certain unimpeachable designs for the development of South Vietnam which with its vast resources of technical expertise it could not fail to achieve. The language also implied (and most reassuringly) that those who did not possess such expertise could not possibly speak with any authority on the subject. As Dr. Fishel himself explained, one had to know the whole history and culture of a country in order to understand its process of political and economic development. As the head of the team, Dr. Fishel himself took over the task of explaining how and in what manner the Diem regime was a democracy.

The idea that the mission of the United States was to build democracy around the world had become a convention of American politics in the 1950's. Among certain circles it was more or less assumed that democracy, that is, electoral democracy combined with private ownership and civil liberties, was what the United States had to offer the Third World. Democracy provided not only the moral basis for American opposition to Communism but the practical method for making that opposition work. Whether American officials actually believed that the Asians and the Africans wanted or needed democracy — and many officials definitely did not — they saw lip service to it as a necessity to selling American overseas commitments to the American people. The American officials and scholars who backed Diem adhered to this convention precisely. During Diem's visit to the United States in 1957, they wrote speeches for him that produced a gush from the *New York Times* over his deep religious feelings, his "firm concept of human rights," and his Jeffersonian stance.[22] They also encouraged Diem to write a constitution that, with its provisions for a president elected by universal suffrage, a unicameral legislature, an independent judiciary, and a wide-ranging bill of rights, looked something like a cross between the constitutions of the United States and the French Fourth Republic. The difficulty was that while Diem agreed with his American advisers completely on issues such as the Catholic refugees and the American aid program, he did not seem to follow them on the issue of democracy.

Diem talked a great deal about democracy, but, as one Vietnamese scholar pointed out, there was a fundamental misunderstanding. What Diem meant by democracy had very little to do with Thomas Jefferson and a great deal to do with the nineteenth-century Vietnamese emperor, Minh Mang. As the reformer of his day, Minh Mang had proposed the creation of a consultative assembly of mandarins to advise him and to give their collective approval to the royal decrees. As Diem once wrote, "Society functions through proper relationships among men at the top." In an article completed before his rise to power, Diem spoke of the function of the sovereign to behave as a father to his people and to uphold the moral values of the country. "A sacred respect," he wrote, "is due to the person of the sovereign. . . . He is the mediator between the people and the Heaven as he celebrates the national cult." And, he continued, "The magistrate in his official capacity must conduct himself as one participating in a religious rite." From the fact that Diem had altars erected about his pictures in the streets and a hymn of praise to him sung along with the national anthem, it could be concluded that Diem, at least in some part of his mind, had assumed the role of the

Confucian emperor.[23] And the emperor required not the support but the obedience of his people; he required not a majority, but unanimity. It was thus with some sense of deception that Diem's American advisers surveyed the results of the elections they had persuaded him to hold and then so carefully publicized in the United States.

For the results of the elections were unequivocal. In the 1955 referendum Diem got 605,025 votes out of a total of 450,000 registered voters in Saigon. According to Bernard Fall, "*Life* in an otherwise wholly laudatory article on Diem remarked innocently . . . that Diem's American advisors had told him that a 60 percent 'success' would have been quite sufficient, 'but Diem insisted on 98 percent.' "[24] In the legislative election of 1959, government candidates won seventy-six out of one hundred and twenty-three seats in the National Assembly. That was the official tally. Actually, of the twenty-two government candidates who lost their races almost all of them lost to other government candidates or to independents who favored the government. (Ngo Dinh Nhu, for example, ran and won his seat under the label of an "independent.") In fact the outcome of the election was never in much doubt, as the Ngos prevented all opposition parties from running and closed down all the newspapers that printed any criticism of the government. One outspoken opposition candidate, the Harvard-educated Dr. Phan Quang Dan, who surprised the government by winning, was refused a seat in the Assembly, and was subsequently jailed and tortured.[25]

While the lack of an opposition gave the Assembly a somewhat lopsided look, the Ngos were more than equal to coping with this cosmetic problem. Quite arbitrarily they divided the Assembly into two groups — a government majority of one hundred and seven, and a "minority" of sixteen, both of which tended to vote with the government. The arrangement did not seem at all unreasonable to the Ngos. As Madame Nhu once told an American university audience, "They [Vietnamese living in the U.S.] ignore the decisions of the Vietnamese people manifested in free elections in order to decree that our executive lacks popular support, and to complain at the same time in the most illogical manner that our legislature is no more than a rubber stamp for the executive." She paused and then continued, "About that question of the rubber stamp argument, I have repeatedly said, but what's wrong to rubber stamp the laws we approve?"[26] Madame Nhu's remark may have had some double meaning, for Diem actually gave the Assembly very few bills to vote on. It was not that he abused his constitutional privilege to rule by executive decree. He simply sent down orders from his office and no one inquired what legal status they held.

The task of extricating American democratic principles from these events was left to Dr. Fishel. And just after the election of 1959 Fishel made a heroic, Houdini-like attempt with an article in the *New Leader* entitled "Vietnam's Democratic One-Man Rule."

Ngo Dinh Diem has all the authority and all the power one needs to op-erate a dictatorship, but he isn't operating one! Here is a leader who speaks the language of democracy, who holds the power of a dictator, who governs a Republic in accordance with the terms of a Constitution. The Constitution was written at his request by a National Assembly which he caused to be elected by the people of the Republic. Ngo Dinh Diem did not *have* to do this. His authority and power at that moment were so absolute.[27]

Dr. Fishel presumably felt that the fact that Diem had so gener-ously adopted a constitution excused him from all obligation to abide by it. Such must have been Fishel's meaning, for in the first five years of his term in office Diem violated every article in the consti-tution, concentrating his attacks most heavily on the bill of rights.

In 1955 the president, against the express prohibition of the Geneva Agreements, launched an Anti-Communist Denunciation Campaign, a program of political re-education aimed at the Viet Minh and their supporters. Ten months later his officials claimed to have obtained the rally of one hundred thousand former Viet Minh to the government and "entirely destroyed the predominant Com-munist influence of the previous nine years."[28] Diem obviously did not consider their efforts adequate. In 1956 he issued an ordinance calling for the arrest and detention of persons deemed dangerous to the state. The order gave legal grounds for the creation of political prison camps throughout the country and the suspension of all habeas corpus laws. In 1959 he issued yet another law establishing military tribunals to deal with "infringements of national secu-rity" — tribunals that permitted the accused no right of defense or appeal and handed out only sentences of life imprisonment or death. This same law abrogated the right of assembly in such a definitive manner as to forbid not only demonstrations but assemblies of over seven people — or most family gatherings. In order to be sure of covering all criminals and all crimes against the state, Diem wrote the laws in the most general of terms, never, for instance, specifying the groups to be considered hostile to the regime or the methods to be used by his officials. In 1956 official estimates put the prison camp population at twenty thousand — a figure that could be correct only to order of magnitude, since no government authority supervised the camps and no outside inspections were permitted. Visiting American congressmen perhaps supposed that all the political prisoners were Communists. The camps in fact contained a wide variety of people, from the leaders of the sects and the smaller political parties to the uncooperative members of the press and the trade unions.[29]

With a few brave exceptions, the Americans in Saigon at that period did not so much as criticize the repressive legislation or even acknowledge the existence of the prison camps. Instead, they concentrated on describing the "positive achievements" of the regime, shifting their emphasis slowly from the theme of democracy to that of "strong leadership." Wolf Ladejinsky, for instance, the land reform expert who went to Vietnam to help Diem with his agrarian programs, argued in the *Reporter:* "The overwhelming majority of the people in South Vietnam are not affected by the regime's authoritarianism. They have probably never enjoyed greater freedom in the conduct of their life and work or benefited in a greater variety of ways. Impatience with the government on the part of those intellectuals who want power for the asking doesn't extend to the peasantry."[30]

Dr. Fishel further explained: "The peoples of Southeast Asia are not, generally speaking, sufficiently sophisticated to understand what we mean by democracy and how they can exercise and protect their own political rights." It was, he continued, naïve to suppose that a "new" state that had no traditions of democracy and no enlightened electorate could immediately adopt a Western-style democratic system. What Vietnam needed for the moment was strong leadership — and strong leadership necessarily implied the concentration of great power. Popular support for the regime could be best assured once the police and security services throughout the country had been adequately developed.[31]

In fact, of course, American officials in Saigon were not at all anxious to see Diem adopt an electoral democracy. Their attitude sprang less from a principle than from a prediction. According to all intelligence estimates, the Communists would win more than a

majority of the votes in a free election. The main objective of the
U.S. officials was to build up the Saigon government to the point
where it could deter the northern regime and suppress the southern
Communists. To that end they were spending some 80 percent of
the entire aid budget each year on the development of the former
French colonial forces and another large slice on the creation of a
civil guard and other security and intelligence services. Rather than
pressure Diem to create a consensus among the political factions, or
find a base of popular support, they urged him to increase his control over the countryside. And Diem was all too willing to oblige.
Within the first two years in office he dispensed with the French
system of village elections and replaced the local village councils
with government officials appointed from the outside — many of
these Catholics. At the same time he issued laws under which his
officials imprisoned members of every political faction along with
some of the active Communist agents in the south. As his official
biographer explained:

> The fundamental fact about Vietnam, and which is not generally well
> understood, is that historically our political system has been based not on
> the concept of the management of the public affairs by the people or
> their representatives, but rather by an enlightened sovereign and an en-
> lightened government. . . .
> The problem that confronts a man like President Ngo Dinh Diem, well
> grounded in traditional administrative principles, but also familiar with
> the Western political systems, is therefore one of giving Vietnam a solid
> moral basis on which to rebuild a strong, healthy democratic State. To
> think of the form before the substance is certainly to run into failure. The
> main concern of President Ngo Dinh Diem is therefore to destroy the
> sources of demoralization, however powerful, before getting down to the
> problem of endowing Vietnam with a democratic apparatus in the West-
> ern sense of the word.[32]

Certain American journalists would later accuse Fishel and U.S.
officials of deliberately deceiving the American public about the
whole nature of the Diem regime and its programs. But the matter
was not quite so simply stated. On the one hand the officials had to
believe in the essential goodness of their policy; on the other hand
they had to believe that Diem shared their goals. If the second was
the natural assumption for Americans to make about their Asian
dependents — many in the Roosevelt administration had believed
the same of Chiang Kai-shek[33] — it was also a necessary assump-

tion for those involved in trying to implement their own policy through a foreigner. Many officials would go so far as to suppress their own awareness of the Diemist repressions, while others would rationalize them on the grounds that such measures were necessary in this moment of crisis. In the future, with American advice, matters would certainly be put to rights.

The result was that the American officials ended by knowing very little about Ngo Dinh Diem or the pressures upon him. Until the NLF forced them to take notice, few of them knew very much more than what Senators Kennedy and Mansfield had known seven years before. They would go on assuming that Diem was jailing Communist agents; they would go on believing that Diem headed a strong, Asian-style government for people not "sophisticated" enough for a full democracy. The Diem regime would, in other words, become a fiction to them, an autonomous creation of the mind. For in reality the Saigon government bore no resemblance whatsoever to a strong, Asian-style government. Indeed, apart from the democratic constitution with which Diem had endowed it, the government resembled nothing so much as an attenuated French colonial regime.

In putting together his "republic" Diem merged the administrations of Cochin China and Annam; he added a few provinces and abolished the elected village councils. Apart from these measures, Diem — for all his talk of the need for "daring reforms" — made no changes in the administration at all. In Saigon the same ministries filled the same colonial office buildings. The civil servants shuffled the same papers their predecessors had filed before them. Many of the civil servants themselves remained the same. By 1959 over a third of them dated their term of service from before the advent of the Bao Dai government.[34] Though Diem disliked and mistrusted these older functionaries for their Francophilia, he made no great effort to replace them. The one civil service academy, the National Institute of Administration, was much too small to meet the need, and in any case trained men more for law careers in France than for any local form of employment. What was most strange was that Diem, this proud nationalist, did not even symbolically dissociate his regime from the government he so despised as a "French puppet." The Republic of Vietnam had the same flag and the same anthem as the Bao Dai government, and Diem himself lived in the governor's palace.[35]

Diem's failure to reorganize the administration had some strange consequences. For lack of judicial reform, for example, the Vietnamese courts followed the French colonial code that adjudicated disputes between persons on the basis of the region from which the parties came. When a dispute involved people from two different regions, the courts had to resort to French international law.[36] Equally disturbing, Diem centralized the government without relocating the powers of the most important French officials, the provincial *résidents*, with the result that power fell to whichever official decided to take it. In many cases power fell into a void, for in six years Diem did not fill many of the posts left open at the time of the French withdrawal; he did not even establish a government presence in certain parts of the country. At the national level Diem neither assumed the powers of the French governor nor redistributed them to others. He had a cabinet, but he held few cabinet meetings, conducted no budget reviews, and prepared no comprehensive economic plan. When one department ran out of funds, it would refer its needs directly to the Americans, and the Americans would make up the deficit without any notion of how, or indeed if, the money would be spent.[37]

As the Diem regime grew older, the administration began to take on more and more of the properties of a sponge. Money, plans, and programs poured into it and nothing came out the other end. This situation was only to be expected, for under the colonial regime the French had exercised the only initiative, the only authority. With their departure the old-line functionaries seemed to lose all powers of forward motion. As one Michigan State University observer noted, their goal seemed to be to put off all decisions until the day after their retirement.[38] In the meantime they guarded their positions by erecting mountains of red tape to bury any program they might have to take responsibility for. Under the French regime the civil servants had looked upon the administration not as a part of a nation-state working for the benefit of the Vietnamese people, but as an exploitative, partially inscrutable, and in any case foreign, concern. They had joined the administration in order to belong to what seemed the most powerful and interesting part of the country, and to take their share of French wealth — as it were, a perfectly reasonable tariff on the foreigners. Early on in his reign, Diem, the puritanical mandarin, issued a law against corruption, recommending the death penalty for all offenders. The difficulty was that few of his officials shared his moral indignation or understood that their long-term interests would best be served by civic probity: the president had not altered their view of the government or filled the vacuum of authority left by the French. For lack of central leadership, private and sectarian politics overwhelmed all national concerns, and corruption abounded in all its forms — from bribery to nepotism to graft to outright embezzlement. Fishel and his associates resolutely defended the corruption on the grounds that all Asian governments were corrupt. Yet Diem had in fact inherited a relatively clean administration. The corruption was increasing, and at least partially as a result of his own efforts. Nepotism, certainly, began at home, and it might well have ended there had the Ngo family been any bigger than it was.

For all Diem's talk of enlightened Confucian governments, the president managed in five years to reduce the administration to a form far more primitive than any Confucian emperor would have countenanced: his own family. To his initial six-man cabinet Diem appointed three of his relatives; two other in-laws served in the most important civil service posts for the bulk of his regime.[39] Madame Nhu's father acted as ambassador to Washington, and Diem's youngest brother, Ngo Dinh Luyen, served as ambassador to Great Britain and other European countries. His three other brothers were by far the most important people in the government, though they held no official posts. Archbishop Ngo Dinh Thuc took no specific authority for the state, but as the senior member of the family he remained close to Diem's councils. (This genial, worldly cleric no doubt found his ambitions best satisfied by the Church, which was, after all, a great deal bigger than Vietnam.)

More directly involved was Ngo Dinh Can. A farouche figure and a bachelor like Diem, Can had lived all of his life with his mother in the family home in Hue. Can had no Western education, and thus very little education at all. With the founding of the Republic he simply assumed power in central Vietnam, and without any official title ruled it as a warlord for the duration of the regime.

The most important of the brothers was, of course, Ngo Dinh Nhu. It was Nhu who had advised Diem to take the dangerous step of attacking the Binh Xuyen — the move that effectively brought Diem to power. Brought to live in the presidential palace after Lansdale's departure in 1956, he assumed the title of political counselor and a power that perhaps exceeded Diem's, for Diem

listened only to him. Nhu was a striking figure. By contrast to the
rotund president he was a lean man with a pale complexion and
piercing eyes. He had spent several years in France at the prestigious but archaic school of paleography, the École des Chartes,
and was thought by Diem to be the intellectual of the family. He
had not in fact the discipline of an intellectual — he merely liked to
speak in sonorous abstractions. He craved power for its own sake
and created a Byzantine labyrinth about Diem through which to
pursue it. His wife, Tran Le Xuan, in no way moderated his craving.
A relative of the emperor, she was a woman of great beauty and
even greater ambition. Living at the palace as the First Lady, she
appropriated to herself much of the public spotlight and the authority over all matters touching upon women and the family. She was
outspoken and fiercely competitive, even with her husband and even
on the subject of Catholicism — a subject about which she knew
nothing until she married Nhu. Possibly, because she was less
complicated, less involved in all the Confucian formalities and the
intellectualizing, she was a stronger character than either of the two
men. With her long red nails and her tight ao dais, she appeared
as a physical force that quite overwhelmed the two pale, dry mandarins. Apart from her there was a kind of sterility about the family,
an empty fervor.

Ngo Dinh Nhu's main contribution to the regime was its governing philosophy. "Personalism" or *Nhan Vi,* as the doctrine was known
in Vietnamese, had its roots in a distorted mirror image of Communism. Ngo Dinh Nhu had lived in Paris in the 1930's when the
French Catholic intellectuals were searching for a doctrine that
held the promise of Communism while remaining conservative —
the era of the *Action Française* and the philosophical slide into
fascism. After the war Nhu had been impressed by the works of
Emmanuel Mounier, the Catholic thinker, and misinterpreted them
as a doctrine of the corporate state in which the alienated masses
would find unity through participating in certain authoritarian social organizations, and through leaders of superior moral fiber.[40]
Always a highly abstract affair that lacked the rigorous analysis of
Marxism, the doctrine in Nhu's hands grew into an incomprehensible hodgepodge having something to do with state power, the
dignity of the Person (as opposed to the individual), and the virtues of humility, renunciation, and sacrifice. Whether or not Nhu
had a clear idea of what he meant by Personalism remained ques-

tionable, for, when once pursued by an American graduate student hot for dissertation material, he said that no written statement on the subject perfectly expressed the true philosophy of the regime. In the end what remained from all the abstractions was a certain tone of voice. As one British adviser noticed, the phrase *Nhan Vi* was a "neologism of Chinese roots suggesting rank and thereby hinting that contentment with one's station might be the quality from the Personalist catalogue the new regime would prize most highly."[41]

In 1955 Ngo Dinh Thuc set up a Personalist school for civil servants in Vinh Long with the intention of persuading them to renounce their egotistical strivings and accept with enthusiasm that enlightened rule of the Ngos. The school did not last long, but the Ngos persisted in their attempt at indoctrination with a series of large-scale political organizations. Founded in 1954, the "National Revolutionary Movement" five years later claimed a million and a half members "grouping in [their] midst revolutionary forces from all classes of the population."[42] Though the number of its members was probably exaggerated, the NRM did have a sizable following for the reason that its leadership was coextensive with the regular administration, and the officials forced the peasants to join. In addition to the NRM the Ngos founded a series of specialized political control groups: the National Revolutionary Civil Servants' League, the Republican Youth Movement, and the Women's Solidarity League — the latter two comprising paramilitary units for the defense of the regime. These organizations were also fairly well subscribed to, membership generally being concomitant with any form of employment in the government.[43] In the case of the Women's Solidarity League the ambition of the members had to be quite overpowering, as Madame Nhu took great pleasure in sitting on a raised dais to watch her women performing judo falls on men or marching to stirring patriotic tunes.

While it was possible to argue that these organizations had their roots in the traditional village community groups or, alternately, that they derived from Communist models, the dominant strain in them was clearly Vichyite. And by no accident. During the period 1940–1945 the French created a number of Vichyite organizations for the Vietnamese — youth groups, sports groups, and so forth — that enjoyed considerable success in Saigon. Nhu admired the Communist organizations and would have liked to imitate them, but the Vichyite groups were the only mass organizations he and his

Catholic officials knew anything about. And he did not understand the function of these. The activity of his "revolutionary" organizations consisted almost entirely of lectures. The NRM officials would lecture the peasants, and the Ngos in their turn would lecture the officials. And it was difficult to say which group suffered the most.

Taken together, the Ngos formed a royal family — a royal family that ruled by fits and starts, in a kind of vacuum. The American officials continued to hope that Diem would finally dispense with some of his relatives and rule through the structure of government. But Diem — much like Chiang Kai-shek — trusted no one else. Apart from those few whom he familiarly "adopted" into his patriarchal clan, he kept his distance from his officials, turning them away with a cold, aristocratic hauteur. Both Diem and Nhu hated to delegate authority. The president would usually work for some sixteen to eighteen hours a day. Each night he would retire with a great stack of papers to sit up into the early hours of the morning in a pathetic attempt to oversee every detail of the administration from the movement of spies to the placement of shrubs about the palace. He did not seem to be able to separate the important from the trivial. For a time he signed all the exit visas for the country himself.

Physically unable to run the entire government, he and Nhu took the next best course of attempting to insure that no cooperation could possibly exist between any two agencies or any two units of the army. The brothers would interfere directly and without warning at all levels of the government, replacing a district chief here, cutting off a credit there, and sending a battalion into operation without the knowledge of its divisional commander. In 1954 Nhu created a secret network of Catholic refugees, whom he placed at strategic points throughout the government to oversee all the rest of the government officials. The Can Lao Nhan Vi Cach Mang Dang, or Revolutionary Personalist Labor Party, as his organization was known, had immense power, if only because all the other government officials assumed its omnipotence. Under the general aegis of his Can Lao chief, Dr. Tran Kim Tuyen, Nhu built up not one, but ten separate secret intelligence agencies, all of which competed to bring him news of traitors, spies, and foreign plots. The political counselor acted as though he knew what all of them were doing, but the amount of intelligence so produced and the necessity for self-protective fabrications on the part of all the agents in fact prevented him from knowing anything of the sort.[44] Officials would occasionally disappear or rise to sudden, unwanted prominence, and that would be that. The inner ring of intelligence agencies, of course, quite neutralized the outer ring, whose job it was to catch Communists. The only consolation for the Diem regime was perhaps that the Communists, who eventually infiltrated both rings in large numbers, were quite as badly informed by the system as everybody else.

All things considered, the Ngo family seemed to have only one great talent, and that was for inducing a state of profound, indeed vertiginous, boredom in almost everyone — a boredom punctured only by moments of terror. As Ho Chi Minh was laconic in formal speeches, the Ngos were voluble. When interviewed by American journalists, Diem would often lecture from four to six hours at a time on his own philosophy of government and the congruence between his own family history and the history of Vietnam. And, unlike Ho Chi Minh, he had not a grain of humor. For his part, Ngo Dinh Nhu would spend hours of his working day composing high-flown sentences for his public speeches. At night he would settle down to lecture American officials on the true nature of Vietnamese society, on the evils of Communism and capitalism, on the mysteries of guerrilla warfare, and the differences between the spiritual East and the materialist West. Certain officials, such as the CIA chief, John Richardson, would listen for hours, awed by the intellectualism, convinced that they were sounding the depths of unfathomable Asia. For others who wished to get something done or to obtain specific answers to specific questions, these sessions were an exquisite torture. On one celebrated occasion when the American embassy forced the Nhus (for their own good) to entertain yet another U.S. congressman for dinner, the Nhus talked from 8 P.M. until four o'clock in the morning, whereupon the congressman, felled by whiskey and jet lag, had to be carried out of the palace.

The alliance of the Ngo family and the United States was, quite obviously, an ill-matched one. The Americans wanted an able administrator, a strong leader, a man of the people — "another Magsaysay," as they put it — and Diem was none of these things. Though the American officials spoke significantly of his experience as an administrator, the president had in fact very little experience, and that in the small, far-off country of the Annamese protectorate. Born a mandarin, he had grown up under the tutelage of that older generation of Catholic mandarins who believed in the resurrection of the traditional state. His sense of patriotism came from the elitist tradition of the mandarinate and the Church, and he was, as the Vietnamese said, by temperament less a priest than a monk. In a time of intense anti-French activity, Diem neither formed nor joined a political party, where the real training for independence might be had. He saw himself as a man of destiny, responsible for the nation by right of birth and superior virtue. His career was a stalagmite of refusals. *Plus royal que le roi,* he held himself aloof from the conflict, waiting for that moment of destiny that God or Fate had already arranged in heaven. And when that moment came, he felt himself justified by it, all his hopes and theories confirmed — never quite understanding that the moment came less as a result of his own virtue than as the result of intervention by a large and interested foreign power. Writing of Diem as he was in 1962, Robert Shaplen perceptively observed that though Diem provoked strong opinions in Saigon,

. . . there was a peculiar impersonal quality to everything that was said about him, as if, despite the urgency of the moment, everyone were talking about a figure in history, already remote and shadowy. The words one heard — "courageous," "proud," "patriotic," "cold," "detached," "uninspiring" — sounded like clichés rather than characteristics of a living, breathing man who held his country's future in his hands. The image was oddly wooden, the portrait unreal, as if there were some doubt as to its authenticity.

When one met Diem, this sense of unreality was borne out. He was a short, broadly built man with a round face and a shock of black hair, who walked and moved jerkily, as if on strings. He always dressed in white and looked as if he were made out of ivory. His self-absorption became apparent as soon as he started to speak. . . . His dark eyes shone, but they seemed to be looking through his listener, through the walls of his palace, through everything, and one experienced an almost eerie sense of listening to a soliloquy delivered in another time and place by a character in an allegorical play.[45]

And perhaps after all those years of isolation Diem did find something unreal about the fact of himself governing a country full of flesh-and-blood people. It was as if he had made an image of himself — an image that was static, two-dimensional, like an icon hung in a museum whose significance has long been forgotten. For Diem was not truly a traditional ruler — he was a reactionary, and like so many reactionaries, he idealized the past and misconceived the present. His whole political outlook was founded in nostalgia — nostalgia for a country that did not exist except in the Confucian texts, where the sovereign governed entirely by ritual and the people looked up to him with a distant, filial respect. Diem realized that Vietnam had changed. But he saw it as his duty to restore the old society and preserve it from the corrupting influences of the West, not by efficient measures but by moral example. "We want," he said, "to re-arm the Vietnamese citizen morally . . . to reinforce the spiritual cohesion . . . which accounts for the capacity to enjoy for many centuries a largely decentralised system without falling into anarchy."[46] Diem's Catholicism, far from opening him up to new ideas, only persuaded him that government by ritual and moral instruction could work, as indeed it seemed to in the ironclad, priest-ridden villages of the north and center. What he did not realize was that such parochial governments could operate merely because the French protected them and organized the administration of the country. His ambition to restore the old society therefore resembled that of the paternalistic French colons who had opposed the reform-ist programs of the metropolitan administrators — the difference being that while the French wished to keep the modern sector for themselves, Diem did not recognize its importance. For him, the modern world was Saigon, that parasite city that fattened from the blood of the countryside and the lucre of the West. Unlike Ho Chi Minh, he saw no distinction between modernization and the corrup-tion that had accompanied foreign rule. The French had protected him from such an insight and left him helpless before their own achievement.

Finally, the Ngo family came from an unfortunate conjunction of worlds. Like so many former colonials, Diem and Nhu were fasci-nated by the West, though they had set themselves up against it: colonialism and Communism were joined in their minds as the two great evils, the two great enemies of Vietnam. At the beginning Diem was influenced by the Americans to the point where he accepted many of their suggestions with eagerness. But he under-stood their general goals no better than he understood Marxism-Leninism. Despite their Western education, he and his brother had absorbed nothing of the scientific, positivist outlook of the West. They knew nothing about management, even less about economics.[47] Diem "thought in a bundle," as the Vietnamese said of those who had not mastered Western systematic thought.[48] As their interests were confined to metaphysics and the sonorous abstractions of French philosophy, their Western education merely confused them, bringing them personalism and Vichyite style, without the substance of the French Vichyite regime. Most Americans looked upon Ngo Dinh Can as the most primitive and backward of the Ngos. But Can, the one brother without any Western education, was in fact the best administrator of them all. Unlike Diem and Nhu, he had a consistency of purpose and a down-to-earth approach to the politics of his region.[49] The other two lived half in one world, half in their own confused perception of another. Unable to reconcile the two, they lived in a constant state of insecurity and defensiveness with regard to both Americans and Vietnamese.

While the Ngo brothers were essentially pathetic figures, their regime was an indissoluble mixture of nightmare and farce. The farce lay generally in the cities, among the people supported by the American aid program and the realms where Madame Nhu could whimsically enforce an anti-divorce law or a ban on dancing.[50] The nightmare lay generally in the countryside, among the rice farmers further impoverished by the American importation of food and the new influx of money to the cities, and where no laws held. The difference was, however, invisible to most Americans.

two

Among those officials and journalists flying in to survey the breaking crisis of 1961 there were very few who understood where the root of the trouble lay. Those who believed that the Saigon government itself was at fault tended to blame the Ngo family itself. Visiting Vietnam on special assignment for President Kennedy, the economist, Eugene Staley, reported that the Diem government would have to carry out wide-ranging reforms in its administration and armed forces before American aid could have any effect. Journalists, such as Robert Shaplen, criticized Diem for alienating the peasants by his oppressive measures, raising a host of secondary questions: Why were the American advisers not having any influence on Diem? Were they giving him the wrong advice? Why did they not insist on a sweeping program of reform? The same questions were to preoccupy for a decade a host of officials and journalists, including such experienced and politically diverse men as Douglas Pike, Chester Bowles, and the British counterinsurgency expert, Sir Robert Thompson.[51] These men saw Diem as the enemy of the anti-Communist project. They wrote history using Diem as the principal actor: "Diem," said Pike, "tore apart the fabric of Vietnamese society." But the United States government had created the Diem regime, and in 1961 the question was whether their creation had any autonomous existence or any roots in the countryside.

A quarter of a billion dollars a year did not, perhaps, seem very much to the Americans, but for the first five years of the Diem regime it covered the whole cost of the Saigon government's armed forces and 80 percent of all other government expenditures. The American aid not only subsidized the government; it paid for the annual trade deficit of $178 million. The American officials initially hoped that the deficit would diminish, but on the contrary it continued to rise owing to the new American expenditures on government services. By 1959 South Vietnam was importing twenty million dollars' worth of food per year under the Food for Peace plan — though food was still its greatest national resource.[52] Except for the settlement of the northern Catholics, all of Diem's agrarian programs were almost unmitigated disasters. In 1955, for instance, Diem undertook a resettlement program designed to establish some land-hungry and politically bothersome central Vietnamese in the formerly uninhabited regions of forest, mountain, and swamp. The Americans provided funds for the program, but the government neglected to prepare most of the new settlement areas adequately or to introduce a crop that could be grown economically in the mountains. With certain exceptions the resettlement camps and the later, much-touted "prosperity centers" and "agrovilles" became little more than squalid banishment camps whose inhabitants slipped away as soon as the government restrictions were relaxed.[53] The land reform program met a similar fate. In 1955 the American ambassador and the French high commissioner proposed a rent reduction and land redistribution law for the double purpose of buying out the French landlords and undermining the appeal of the Viet Minh land program. After a year of hesitation, Diem finally issued a land law that was so poorly designed and so badly implemented that it managed to antagonize both the landlords and their tenants — though very little land actually changed hands.[54] The American and international aid teams managed to perform certain technical feats such as road- and bridge-building, malaria control, and refugee relief. But the Diemist administration had very little hand in these, and by 1960 it would have been difficult to say what else the regime had done in the way of social or economic development. The "economic miracle" of the south was a sleight of hand, having nothing to do with economic growth or increased production. As one disappointed Michigan State University economist wrote in 1961, "In its economic aspect, American aid represents a large-scale relief project more than an economic development program, and because development has not been emphasized, termination of American aid would almost certainly produce both political and economic collapse in Viet-Nam."[55]

The failure of development essentially sprang not from the American aid techniques but from the politics of the Diem regime. Neither Diem nor the responsible American officials dared to put the country on an austerity footing. Through the Commercial Import Program — a fiscal device whereby the Vietnamese importers ordered foreign goods to be paid for in dollars by the U.S. government and put their artificial value in piastres into a counterpart fund for the United States to spend on the Saigon government — they poured money and goods into the cities and into the pockets of these officials and merchants. To pacify the landlords and the businessmen, Diem lowered taxes to almost nothing and put up with the unproductive manorial system of land tenure. The only people who suffered were, of course, the peasants and landless farm laborers: they suffered as they always had under the French from an unjust social system and from the concentration of money in the cities. Neither the Diem regime nor the Americans could alter their plight, for a real program of social and economic reform would have involved a real conflict of interests between the peasants on the one hand and the landlords and the city people on the other. To take the part of the peasants was difficult not merely because the role had been successfully preempted by the Communists, but because it required a concern for the peasants, a fundamental grasp of the problems of the country, ideology, organization, and a will to take risks. And it was precisely those capacities that the Diem regime and its American supporters lacked.

In all the years of his reign Ngo Dinh Diem found only one ally in the countryside, and that was the Catholics, most particularly the northern refugees. From the beginning he staffed his administration heavily with Catholics and favored the Catholic villages over all the rest. The Diemist officials, working closely with the priests, saw to it that the Catholic villages took the bulk of U.S. relief aid, the bulk of the agricultural credit. They gave the Catholics the right to take lumber from the national reserves and monopoly rights over the production of the new cash crops introduced by the American aid technicians. "Turn Catholic and have rice to eat," went the old Vietnamese saying under the French regime. Under Diem the South Vietnamese continued to follow the injunction. In central Vietnam particularly, thousands of people, including in some cases whole villages, turned Catholic in order to escape the government *corvées* or to avoid resettlement — for the benefit of their Catholic neighbors — into some hardship zone of jungle or swamp.[56] To feed the Catholics at the expense of the rest of the population was, of course, a shortsighted policy, but Diem saw no alternative, and the Americans offered him none.

Politically the most enlightened piece of advice the Americans ever offered the Ngos was to "broaden the base" of their government to include other non-Communist groups such as the sects, the urban politicians, and the smaller political parties. What the Americans were asking for — though they did not perhaps conceive of it in that way — was the reinstatement of the French system of group and interest management through a neutral bureaucracy. The idea did not appeal to the Ngos, who saw themselves as creating a government in the full Vietnamese sense of the word — an entire way of life, a uniform society. Throughout their career the Ngos viewed all of the organized political groups as enemies on a par with the Communists. And with some justification, for the Hoa Hao and the VNQDD did not in any way correspond to, say, the American Baptist Church or the Democratic Farmer-Labor Party. They were not just sects or parties. They were, whatever their size, potential states quite as absolutist as Diem's own. Still, had Diem taken the American advice, his position would hardly have been strengthened. The non-Communist sects and factions meant little without the French army. Diem's real political problem was that he did not even control those groups and factions who more or less supported the American-backed government. He did not so much as control his own bureaucracy.

In the period 1955–1959 Diem issued a series of laws that many Americans liked to think were directed against Communist agents actively trying to overthrow the Diem regime. At the time certain French journalists, including Jean Lacouture and Philippe Devillers, reported that the Diem regime was conducting a large-scale campaign of terror against all of the Viet Minh as well as against the leaders of the smaller political factions. Some American and British sources confirmed this report,[57] but neither the American officials nor journalists investigated the matter at the time. Only years later did the next generation of American social scientists designing the next series of counterinsurgency programs discover the full consequences, the reason and cause of the campaign.[58] According to the testimony of the victims — many of whom consequently joined the National Liberation Front — the Diemist officials arrested thousands of people whose only political sin was to have fought for independence against the French before Diem took power. Some of these people they killed on arrest, others they beat and tortured; still others they held for indefinite periods under inhuman conditions in order to extort money or confiscate their land. In certain areas whole hamlets were subjected to such treatment. What most surprised the American researchers was that few of these arrests were ever made in Saigon or in any of the larger cities — a fact that indicated that Diem did not directly order them. In most cases the officials seemed to have acted on their own initiative and for their own personal or sectarian interests. Some of the officials were, after all, former colonial functionaries with blood scores to settle against the Viet Minh. Others were former village notables and landlords who had been driven from their villages by the Viet Minh during the war. Some of them were Catholics fighting their old sectarian battles, and still others were adventurers who joined the new administration in order to make their fortunes. By issuing the anti-treason laws Diem had, in other words, opened a Pandora's box of violence, permitting those Vietnamese who had guns to terrorize those who did not. Even if Diem had understood that the terror campaign worked against the long-term interests of his government, he could have done nothing to stop it. Apart from those people who could use his administration to their own private advantage, he had little support in the country.

The anti–Viet Minh campaign was only one manifestation of the anarchy within the administration and the army. Almost all the

American reporters who came to Saigon in 1961–1962 had tales to tell of army officers gaining promotions through bribery or political influence, of generals running illicit traffic in rice or opium, of intelligence officers refusing to divulge information or lying to conceal a job undone, of officers stealing their men's pay and of soldiers treating the peasants like the members of a conquered race. As one experienced reporter wrote, "Of the thousands of Vietnamese officials I have known, I can think of none who does not more or less hold the Vietnamese people in contempt."[59] There were exceptions, of course, but they remained exceptions. On the whole, the behavior of the officials had a curious uniformity to it. Their misdeeds formed a pattern that transcended the region or social class from which they came. From the tales of the Diem regime as told by the villagers, it would seem that the history of the south was but the history of one village repeated over and over again.

The story as told by villagers throughout the country had its stock characters: the government-appointed village chief; the "haughty," "arrogant" official who took bribes from the local landlords and forced the villagers to work for him; the village security officer — a relative, perhaps, of the district chief — who used his position to take revenge on old enemies or to extort money from the villagers; the government soldiers who, like juvenile delinquents, drank too much, stole food, and raped the village girls; the village self-defense guards, who huddled in their earthwork forts each night and fled when the Liberation Front came in force to the village; the district and provincial officials who, like Kafka's bureaucrats, seemed to inhabit a world impossibly remote from the village. Finally there were the villagers themselves, who complained so little that for years the Americans thought the insurgency would find no root among them. And there was a denouement to the story shocking to Americans of the period: when the Front cadres moved into the village and assassinated one or two of the government officials, the villagers reacted with enthusiasm or indifference.

Dr. Fishel and his colleagues contended that the Diem regime was not the worst government in Asia, and possibly it was not. But the Vietnamese did not make such comparisons — nor did they look upon the corruption and violence of the officials as natural or inevitable, an acceptable reversion to the traditions of the past. The behavior of the officials in fact excited more attention among Vietnamese than it did among Americans. With all the analyses of the American social scientists, it was a North Vietnamese author who compiled the best catalogue of the official failings:

Breaches of the law. Because of personal enmity and rancor, you arrest honest people and confiscate their property, causing them distress. . . .
Sectarianism and connivance. You group your friends and relatives around you and give them positions for which they have no ability. Those who are competent and satisfactory but do not please you, are discarded.
Division. You oppose one section of the people against another. . . .
Arrogance. Abusing your position . . . you become unruly and do things in your own way. . . .
Conceit. Thinking that an official is someone, you look upon the people with contempt. . . .
Localism. [You heed] only the interests of [your] own locality without taking into account the interests of the whole country. . . .
Militarism and bureaucracy. [You] behave like a small king when in charge of a region. . . . [You] belittle [your] superiors and abuse [your] authority and weigh heavily upon [your] subalterns. [You] frighten people by a haughty bearing. . . .
Formalism. Questions are not considered for their practical results or urgency, but only for showing off. . . .
Paper work. Love of red tape.[60]

The author of the catalogue was not a Saigon-based intellectual, but Ho Chi Minh, speaking to the first groups of Viet Minh cadres in 1945 and 1947. The fact is significant, for it indicates that the failings of the Diemist officials arose not out of any one political system, but out of the depths of the society. Ngo Dinh Diem did not create these failings; on the other hand, he could do nothing about them. He could not even analyze them, for although they were not "natural" or traditional, they stemmed from the disintegration of the old society, from a process that he himself did not recognize. And it was this disintegration rather than the larger political or regional divisions that defeated him.

As always, the crux of the matter was the village, the essential community of Vietnam. Traditionally, the villages stood almost isolated in the wheel of their paddies, surviving civil war upon civil war, to protect the cycle of the rice and the Way of the ancestors. But with the coming of the French the villages succumbed — first to the colonial bureaucrats, then to the merchants, and then to the soldiers. Overwhelmed by the new power in Saigon, the southern villages lost their internal structure and the bonds of their community. In 1957 Gerald Hickey observed that in one village south of Saigon, "Most families . . . have no land . . . [their] houses are of perishable thatch, and their graves are mounds of earth."[61] The strict patriarchy, the "natural order" of the Confucian universe, had disintegrated. No longer able to regulate the economy of the village, the old "notables" had lost their positions of authority and had become salaried workers for the state. "The people used to be the servants of the Village Council, now the Village Council is the servant of the people," complained the patriarchs of Hickey's village.[62] In spirit, if not in fact, the fathers had lost their children to the new power in the cities and the armies.

During the 1940's thousands of young Vietnamese volunteered to join the youth corps of the Vichyite French regime in Saigon. Through the crowds of older people the peasant boys strutted in time to the music, carrying their rifles at a precise angle and showing off their new uniforms.[63] Young fascists? Two or three years later the same peasant boys would fall into the first ranks of the Viet Minh and the French partisan army. A generation later, multiplied thousands upon thousands, their sons would volunteer for the National Liberation Front and the armed forces of the Republic of Vietnam. "But why? But why?" the counterinsurgency experts would ask over and over again. And two generations of peasant boys would patiently answer, "I liked the idea of heroism," "I was in debt," "I wanted to free my country," "I always wanted to have an official position and to own a small gun."[64] The pronoun they used was itself an explanation: *toi*. An old word, it had in the 1930's gained currency in the language as a translation for the French first person singular, the neutral, the independent, I, me. In using it the young peasants stood suddenly free of their families and their villages to become, in the older meaning of the word, "subjects of the king."[65]

Released by a similar explosion in the early nineteenth century, the peasant-soldiers of France had marched off to the Napoleonic wars to learn (at the expense of Europe and finally Vietnam), if not the liberty, at least the equality and fraternity of the revolution. But in the service of the Diem regime the young Vietnamese of the 1950's and 1960's marched only as far as the next village — there to confront the same situation they had left at home. From their instructors — reflections of themselves in uniform — they learned only how to fill out a form, how to shoot a gun, and how to parrot a few words — "republic," "Personalism," "nation" — which for all the reference in their experience might have been words in a foreign language. But if they learned nothing, they forgot nothing. Uninstructed, they behaved in keeping not with the organizational charts, but with what they had learned as children in a world still *terra incognita* to the American advisers.

Their world — the Vietnam they continued to respond to — was a world of small, nearly closed systems linked only by the emperor and his mandarins. Within the hedges of the village each person knew his place within the hierarchy of a few families. At birth each child took his place, as it were on an escalator, and held it while moving upwards through the generations. Traditional Vietnam -- Ngo Dinh Diem's Vietnam — was a society of *persons*, not of *roles:* the village elder did not become the village councilor as an American might become President, he *was* the village councilor, his position set in all time by the laws of filial succession, or the "natural order of the universe."[66] Not only was the Vietnamese village a much smaller world than could support a modern nation-state, but its internal structure was such that it would not easily translate into a Western-style army or administration. To employ one useful fiction, the "social contract" of traditional Vietnamese society was the very contrary of Rousseau's free association between equals — the concept on which modern Western constitutions are based. Rather than a bargain made between peers, it was a contract made almost exclusively in vertical between the generations of the patriarchal family.[67] When a group such as the village council gathered, it found its unity by indirection through the relationship of each man to the patriarch. This hierarchical structure was the very foundation of the society itself. As one old Vietnamese proverb goes, "To be without leaders, to obey no one, is unworthy of man: it is to behave like the animals."[68]

As the whole society was modeled on the family, so every relationship, except the rare and precious one of "friend," was analogous to the primary one between father and son. The nature of that primary bond was the heart of the Vietnamese *terra incognita*. Vietnamese society differed considerably from that of the Chinese, but the similarities were great enough for the purposes of contrast with the West. In his study of Chinese psychology Professor

Richard Solomon has provided valuable insights into that father-son relationship and, incidentally, into the character of Ngo Dinh Diem himself and the whole logic of his regime.[69]

> *At the foot of the mountain, thunder:*
> *The image of PROVIDING NOURISHMENT.*
> *Thus the superior man is careful of his words*
> *And temperate in eating and drinking.*
> — *I Ching*[70]

The image of the open mouth, represented in this verse, has a particular poignancy in China and Vietnam, for in both countries it was traditionally the father (the adults) who in times of famine or other disaster had claim to the first available food — even if it meant leaving the children to starve. Westerners might consider such a code of conduct immoral, but it was not so within its proper context. To the same end of propagating a civilization, the traditional, Confucian father built a system of social security radically different from that of his Western contemporary. When a Western father gives his child the "inalienable right" to the first and best food, he is (to put it crudely) bribing the child so that when he reaches manhood and independence the child will remember his debt (and support him in his old age). To the same end the Confucian father used a different method of coercion. Rather than prepare the child for independence by implanting his authority in the form of guilt, the Confucian father kept his child from attaining the same degree of autonomy. Obedient to the dictates of filial piety, the child remained, relatively speaking, a child with respect to his father for the whole of his lifetime. In the Confucian world filial piety was the key to all wisdom and virtue. As Western parents teach their children to "obey all commandments," and to "learn principles," or, in other words, to internalize their authority, the Confucian father taught his child to obey his parents — in other words, to remain dependent upon external authority. In the image of the open mouth the actions of talking and eating are joined, for it was by talking that the father affirmed his authority to demand that the child feed him in old age.

As manifested in the naming process (the ego becomes "your child," "your younger brother," "your humble servant," and so forth), the project of Confucian education was to persuade the child that his very identity depended upon his maintaining a given "place" within the society. While the rites of ancestor worship raised conformity and continuity to sacred powers, the elaborate manners of the Confucian household discouraged self-assertiveness and invention. Traditional Vietnamese children were to be seen and not heard. In school as at home they learned not by questioning but by repetition. Chastened for competing with their elders or scrapping with other children, they learned to hold in their feelings — particularly their hostility and aggressiveness — in the interests of holding their "place" and maintaining the "harmony" of the community as a whole. For the Vietnamese, "sincerity" implied fidelity not to personal feelings but to social norms, to "correct behavior" relative to place in the social hierarchy. One young Vietnamese — I shall call him Huong — gave an American interviewer a revealing account of the upbringing of a twentieth-century Vietnamese child whose father was replaced by a stepfather. He said at one point:

When I was in school, my teacher taught me to be polite to my father and mother and brothers and sisters. Not only in the family, but in society, I was taught to be polite to everyone. I didn't like my stepfather, but he was my mother's husband, it meant that he was higher than my rank in the family. Therefore, I had to respect him.[71]

In the Confucian world the child also had to renounce much of what Westerners would consider his essential personality: his desire to dominate others, to revenge wrongs, his desire for intellectual mastery over tradition. The child's station was to be his identity, his social face, the man. As leverage for this considerable work of repression, the Confucian father sometimes threatened the child not only with punishment but with an actual dissolution of the blood contract. As one American-educated girl told this writer about her very aristocratic Confucian family:

When they found out I wanted to marry an American, they were very angry. They didn't say anything — they hardly talked to me at all. One night when I was out with M., they actually locked me out of the house. A few nights later my father woke me up at two in the morning. I was scared he would throw me out of the house. But he didn't. He was so mad. He talked on and on about the family, saying that it was like a great tree, and we were only leaves on its branches, and I hadn't the right to break it apart.

Such real threats were, of course, reserved for moments of crisis, when the child by showing independence threatened to give up his (or her) essential role in the family. (And the occasion would occur more and more as the modern world opened up new alternatives.) But the threat was often implied, for having brought up the child without "internalized" values, the father feared that the child would otherwise lack the Confucian "self-control" to fulfill his filial obligations. Even in the 1960's young Vietnamese typically described their own fathers as "stern," "cold," and "distant" — men who, unlike their "warm," "easygoing" mothers, refused to show their paternal affection. Kept in constant suspense about the father's loyalty to him, the child came to understand that any challenge to authority might actually prove dangerous. Even in the most Westernized of Vietnamese households childish revolt took the form of self-punishment. If the child believed his parents had done him an injustice, he (or she), rather than cry or argue, would retreat from them and carry on a hunger strike until his parents came to conciliate him.[72] As the father wore the mask of authority, so the son came to wear the mask of deference, the "politeness" that Huong spoke of.

Writing in the 1930's, one French ethnologist described the mandarins of Hue (perhaps the friends and relatives of Ngo Dinh Diem) as looking up to the genii of their ministries "with a touching sense of fear and humility, at the same time of faith and confidence."[73] In the language of the psychologists, the Vietnamese child (civil servant) felt a deep ambivalence about the father (higher authority). On the one hand he feared that his father might lack the "self-control" to fulfill his end of the bargain; on the other hand he saw him to be the only source of security, both physical and intellectual. The relationship between father and son would be deep. It could also be warm when, as under normal circumstances, a mutual trust existed. But when that trust did not exist, as it did not between Huong and his stepfather, then the tension could become acute. Huong said:

Although my family had a good standard of living, I was not happy with it. I felt that my stepfather didn't like me. . . . Once I went out to play with my friends and I quarreled with a friend of mine. When I came home, my stepfather blamed me and would have hit me if my mother hadn't stopped him. He made me feel that, since I was not his son, he could do anything to me he wanted. To me he was a stranger living in my house, enjoying my family's property, and yet he bullied me.[74]

The much desired "social harmony" was in fact very difficult to maintain, and particularly so outside the blood family. Beneath the thin crust of "respect," the relationship between father and son, governor and governed, rested on a delicate balance between the need for "nourishment" and the fear of exploitation. If there were not a deep feeling of confidence between them — such as the mandarins had for their genii and the Saigonese girl had for her father — the relationship would break apart. In a small stable community such as Hue, the traditional village, or the unbroken family, the child or subordinate would have some reason for confidence in his superiors, for his superiors were effectively boxed in. The village patriarch could no more replace his villagers than the father could replace his children. He had no other "place" to go, and thus it was clearly and demonstrably in his long-term interests to fulfill his part of the bargain. If he did not exercise "self-control," if he was not "careful in his words and temperate in eating and drinking," he risked losing his subordinates either by starving them or by driving them away — and, consequently, losing his own position. Authority, therefore, was acceptable on condition that it was insured by the "net ropes" of kinship or long personal association. And in Vietnam the "net ropes" were not very long: in China they sustained cities and embraced provinces, but in northern and central Vietnam they reached only as far as the hedges of the village, in southern Vietnam only to the limits of the hamlet. Despite their Confucian education, the villagers traditionally resented and resisted the mandarins. When a stranger acquired land in one of the enclosed villages, his family would not be accepted into the community for at least a generation: its initial members could not be trusted, for having no "place" in the village, they had no basis for "correct behavior," or, morality.

When I was at home, I loved my mother and she loved me, too. The only person I didn't like was my stepfather. Sometimes he didn't do anything to hurt me, it was just the way he glanced at me. I had the impression that he disliked me. Sometimes he criticized me and I would be angry with him for several days.[75]

In speaking of his stepfather Huong suggested what might be the central dilemma of the Diem regime: the officials appointed from outside the village *were not* the village authorities any more than Huong's stepfather was his father. However they might behave, the villagers would not trust them, and they would need no evidence to support their suspicions. Huong was asked whether the local Diemist officials and soldiers were good men or bad, and he replied:

Some very old officials were good. Sometimes, they stayed in the office to work very late in order to complete the papers for the villagers. But some were bad. When the villagers came to request some papers, they let them sit in the sun for a very long time before they let them come into the office. Moreover, some of the officials received money from the rich landowners in order to take land back from the poor farmers.

But, Huong continued:

I hated the soldiers of the Ngo Dinh Diem regime. . . . I hated them because they were very haughty. The villagers were already very poor, and yet the soldiers commanded them to build roads and bridges. . . . Under Ngo Dinh Diem's regime, people had to pay high taxes. People had to pay all kinds of taxes. A person even had to pay a tax to the government if he wanted to sell a buffalo. Ngo Dinh Diem didn't help people in any way, he made people become poor. And yet, the soldiers carried weapons to protect him and his regime. Therefore, I hated the soldiers.[76]

Huong's complaint about the taxes imposed by the Diem regime was a common one — and in fact Diemist taxes on use and consumption were difficult for the peasants to bear. But they were no higher than the French taxes and they were a great deal lower than the NLF taxes were to become. By failing to explain the taxes (by failing to explain the whole notion of a national tax system), the Diemist officials raised the traditional fears of exploitation by a strange and therefore "undisciplined" authority. Rightly or wrongly, Huong believed that his stepfather would bully him and waste his inheritance. The villagers for their part needed no proof that the Diem regime, through its soldiers and officials, would actually eat up their subsistence. And in many cases their suspicions were fully justified.

During the resistance against the French many rich landowners left the village for the city. The poor, landless farmers farmed the unworked land. After peace returned, the rich landowners returned to the village. . . . The local officials didn't intervene to help the poor, but they helped landowners to get their land back instead. Also, many of the villagers who formerly worked for the Viet Minh had to bribe the officials in order to avoid being arrested.

And further:

Yes, people complained very much about the soldiers' behavior. At night the soldiers used to come to the people's houses to drink wine and eat. After eating, they got drunk and quarreled with each other, and they used their rifles to shoot at each other. If a family had girls, the soldiers came to flirt with them and tease them. Some of the soldiers even wore masks to blackmail the rich people in the village.[77]

Huong's particular story cannot be verified, but there is evidence that the GVN soldiers and officials behaved in a similar manner in many, if not the majority, of the villages of the south. And it was not so surprising. Marriage trapped Huong's stepfather into a relationship he could not manage; similarly, their uniforms imprisoned the soldiers and officials into a position of authority for which neither their upbringing nor their training had prepared them. The soldiers were young peasants like Huong himself, yet they had no more sense of community with the strange villagers than if they had been Martians. Suspect in the eyes of the villagers, they in their turn feared exploitation both by the villagers and by the authorities above them:

I talked to many of them. They told me they didn't want to join the army, but that they were afraid of being drafted. If they were drafted, they would not be able to be with their families. Therefore, they joined the Civil Guards and the Self-Defense Corps in order to be with their families, and they were also able to receive some money to feed their families. This was what they said, but I think many of them were bad. They were very arrogant. They took the villagers as their servants.[78]

The soldiers tried at least once to deny their rank, but they did not persuade Huong of their equality in misfortune. They did not, perhaps, persuade themselves. Taking on the traditional attitudes of authority, they entered the vicious circle of fear and bad faith — or "not a vicious circle, but a downward spiral," as Ho Chi Minh's foreign minister was to remark in a similar context.[79]

It was the course already charted between Huong and his stepfather, and it was to be the course followed by so many of the Diemist officials in the villages of the south.[80] The officials drew back behind their masks of "haughtiness" and "arrogance," and the villagers retreated from them. Hiding their rice from the tax collector and their sons from the army recruiter, they protected themselves as best they could. Rarely — except as a result of NLF instigation — would they make an attempt to bargain with the officials or to complain of their behavior to the higher authorities at district and province level.

"I didn't like my stepfather, but I just hated him in my mind. I never showed my hatred."[81] Huong did not express his anger either to his stepfather or to the soldiers he considered "bad." In the same way the villagers of the south concealed their hatred of the Diemist officials. In Huong's village of Phuoc Khanh there was, after a while, nothing left between the villagers and their officials but the trappings of authority and submission: the villagers' masks of respect, the soldiers' masks of haughtiness. Finally, the soldiers donned real masks and began to make good their threats by bullying the villagers and stealing their food and money. Still the villagers made no outward sign of resistance. Trusting in no authority, they ceased to trust each other to the point where they could not organize to defend themselves. The brittle hierarchy of the village had split apart, and if it were to be put back together again, the initiative would have to come from the outside.

Asked if he had ever quarreled with his stepfather, Huong recalled the time when his stepfather nearly hit him for fighting with another child; following that incident he left home.

But the villagers of the south were unable to leave their land and their houses in order to escape the Diemist officials. Instead, they went into internal emigration. In public they claimed to "know nothing of the government"; even in private they rarely spoke of politics. ("Silence is golden, silence is golden," said one village "notable.") Their resistance took the form of passivity and denial. For two years NLF agents visited the village of Phuoc Khanh to distribute leaflets and recruit young men. They recruited the young man, Huong, and within daily view of the soldiers, he carried on the work of an insurgent, the silence of the villagers a shield of invisibility about him. Gradually they persuaded most of the village officials to stop working for the Diem regime. Those officials who continued to work for Diem had to work and sleep in the military outpost, for some 85 percent of the villagers favored the enemy. Openly by night, invisibly by day, the village belonged to the National Liberation Front. In the old language of Vietnam, the will of Heaven had changed.

Huong did not simply run away from home, he fled to his aunt and then to his paternal uncle. Similarly the villagers went over from the Diem regime to the NLF, substituting one authority for another in the hope that the second would prove better than the first. In villages such as Phuoc Khanh there was very little alternative, for in the sense that the Vietnamese understood government — as a complete order, a complete set of relationships — the Diem regime had been no government at all. Under the guns of the soldiers the village had been reduced to a state of pure anarchy where men did not trust their masters and where no laws held. For those villagers the years of the Diem regime, no less than the war, represented a "time of troubles," an "interregnum" in which the regime could not give the minimum protection and nourishment to its people.

Such periods had come before in Vietnamese history — but never quite in the same way. Traditionally the villagers of the north and center found refuge behind the hedges of the village — the Confucian mask translated into the landscape. In times of trouble they retreated into the maze of interior pathways, as into the circumlocutions of the old-fashioned courtesy, to wait until one or another of the warlords gained full control over the village. Traditionally the emperors, too, had their own defenses. Spaced out across the landscape, their citadels symbolically established their claim to rule over the "mountains and rivers" of the country. But these stern towers of brick and stone also signified the distance between the emperor and his people — a distance that grew with the expansion to the south and the thinning of Confucian culture. When in the nineteenth century the Nguyen emperor Gia Long built a new imperial citadel in Hue, he chose the site for its seclusion according to the laws of geomancy, behind the Perfume River and the mountains called the "Screen of the Kings."[82] With walls over six feet thick, the new citadel was a fortress into which none but the mandarins, the ritually pure, might enter. When the French came to Vietnam in threatening numbers, the Nguyen retreated further and further into their world of rituals until in the end they behaved as though the citadel contained the nation. The walls of Hue never crumbled — at least not until the Tet offensive of 1968 — but, as the French armies moved across the Mekong Delta, the villages broke away from the capital, leaving the last of the Nguyen sacred prisoners without exit from their citadel.

The history of the Diem regime bore a striking resemblance to that of the Nguyen dynasty. Taking his mandate from the Emperor

Bao Dai in 1955, Ngo Dinh Diem, like Gia Long, borrowed foreign arms to use against his own countrymen. Had he managed to design a new political community, many South Vietnamese, including the members of the sects, might have approved his military actions as necessary to the restoration of social harmony. But, like Gia Long, Diem was a traditionalist who looked only backwards into the old stream of Confucian civilization, and he regarded the political movements that grew up out of the south as mere "sources of demoralization" within the country. Initially he tried to pacify the south with moral instruction — it was that, he supposed, that had insured the harmonious working of society in the past. When instruction did not work — and perhaps he had always feared that it would not — he found himself at a loss. The idea that he might consult the people or attempt to win popular support did not occur to him as a possibility. "I know what is best for the people," he would repeat endlessly to his American advisers.[83] Seeing himself as the patriarch, the father of his people, he could not cope with the social disintegration. He scarcely knew what had happened or why. When it became clear that the people would not respond to what many Americans were pleased to call the "traditional government" of the Vietnamese villages, Diem's reaction was to extend his own paternal rule down into the villages with the appointment of officials from the outside. But his administration would not function, and not surprisingly, for a Western-style bureaucracy could not function according to the traditional Way. The old order had rested upon two graduated pyramids, each insulated from the other by custom as well as by the time and space of the old empire. By imposing his own administration upon the villages, Diem broke down the last barriers and exposed the villagers to intolerable pressure. In the end the villagers would break away from him, as they broke away from the Nguyen emperors, leaving him helpless before the foreigners.

In a sense those villagers who, ignorant of bureaucracy, saw their new, government-appointed village chief as Diem's own personal representative to them perceived the true "substance" of the Diem regime more clearly than anyone else. This was not because the Ngo family controlled every official, but because Diem and Nhu resembled those officials. Like the Emperor Ly Thai To, Diem believed that the sovereign exerted a deep influence over the lives of his people — an influence beyond that of cause-and-effect or of simple example. Stripped of its magical overtones, the Confucian notion of "sympathy" between the ruler and the ruled consisted in the bonds of heredity and shared experience between the father and the junior members of the great family of the empire. And more than Ho Chi Minh, more than the bourgeoisie of Saigon, Diem had that sympathy. Like the majority of his people, he grew up in a very small world — Hue in the 1930's was hardly more cosmopolitan than a back-country village. Like them, he watched, uncomprehending, while his world gave way before the strange forces of the West. Suddenly made responsible for a country fashioned by others and altered beyond recognition, he could only react as he had been trained to in his childhood. He *was,* in a sense, the lowliest of his officials, and the history of his reign was the history of Phuoc Khanh village, repeated on a larger scale. Like his officials, he was a man out of tune with his times, a sovereign of discord.

In 1960 a group of eighteen senior Saigonese politicians met with the American press at the Caravelle Hotel to present a list of their grievances against the government. The *Groupe Caravelliste,* as it was called, denounced the regime for driving the peasantry into the hands of the Communists and called for an end to press censorship, to detention without trial, and to the measures that were demoralizing the army — the last an implied criticism of Nhu's secret police. A few months later Colonel Nguyen Chanh Thi undertook an ill-planned and finally abortive military coup against the regime. The Ngo family used the coup as a pretext for intensifying all those measures the Caravellists objected to and slapped several of the politicians in jail.

It was, of course, quite ridiculous for the Americans to expect Ngo Dinh Diem to establish an electoral democracy or to become "another Magsaysay." Diem believed that the Hand of God, or the will of Heaven, supported him.[84] He simply assumed that the people supported, or ought to support, him. The real difficulty was that he could not take the oldest of Confucian advice:

> *The mountain rests on the earth:*
> *The image of SPLITTING APART.*
> *Thus those above can insure their position*
> *Only by giving generously to those below.*
> *— I Ching*[85]

His refusal to "give generously," to "yield" and "conciliate" as a correct sovereign should, resulted perhaps not so much from a quirk in his nature as from a realistic assessment that it would not work. Because he could create no political system, no political constituency apart from his family, his subordinates would have no compunction against behaving like unfilial children: they would try to exploit and finally to replace him.

But Diem could not admit his failure. Given his position — his very identity as president of the republic — he had to believe that the people supported him, and that they had no other choice as long as he held the Mandate of Heaven. Within this circle of logic, closed off by the fact of American support, he could only assimilate the dissension by blaming it upon outside enemy agents — the "colonialists," the "Communists," or the "demoralized elements." These elements could not, so Nhu assured him, be "re-educated" or brought back into the community. Unable to conceive of an alternative, Diem gave way to the ferocity of Nhu and to the attempt to exterminate these "enemies" wherever they were, in the villages and in his own administration. It was here that Diem's alliance with the United States became a disaster for the Vietnamese people. Not only did the Americans give him the power to carry out his repression, but they gave him little alternative to a policy founded on the use of force.

three

Even as late as 1968 many American liberals, including many of the journalists in Saigon, believed the official claims that the United States was at least making an effort to develop South Vietnam and to improve the welfare of the South Vietnamese people. But as a look at the aid budget would show, the claims were, and always had been, false. Even in the period 1954–1960, before the guerrilla war began, the United States spent only a minute fraction of its aid on industrial or agricultural development — two sectors that required heavy investment if South Vietnam were to become an economically independent country. The land reform program of 1956 failed in part because the United States did not allocate capital for the Diem regime or the peasants to buy the land the large proprietors had by law to relinquish. Throughout the Diem era the United States spent approximately 90 percent of its aid on the creation of an army and a military bureaucracy.[86]

This distribution of aid was not arbitrary; nor was it the result of mere shortsightedness on the part of the local American officials. In Washington U.S. officers conceived of their policy not as an attempt to help the Vietnamese, but as an attempt to hold the line at the 17th parallel against the Communists. These officials justified the entire aid and assistance program on the basis of this essentially negative, military goal. When it appeared that the main source of trouble for the Diem regime would come from below the 17th parallel, they made no attempt to change their priorities. All the social scientists notwithstanding, the Americans had no real theory of development, no firm belief that development would reduce the insurgency. And they would make no large-scale appropriations for humanitarian purposes. For the United States government, "security" — or the attempt at a military occupation of the countryside — always came first. The final shape of the Diem regime reflected that concern.

Beginning in 1955, the U.S. Military Assistance Advisory Group under the command of General Samuel T. "Hanging Sam" Williams dismantled the small, mobile units of the French-trained armed forces (the *groupes mobiles*) and replaced them with seven regular divisions armed with American infantry weapons. The reorganization exemplified the usual military obsession with precedent — in this case for the Korean War. The regular divisions were to prove perfectly unsuitable for a domestic guerrilla conflict. But the MAAG, instead of correcting its initial error, merely added to it by forming a new group of units — Marine, Ranger, and paratrooper battalions — from its own repertoire, so that with the addition of a navy and an air force, the armed forces of the Saigon government became a complete scale model of the American army, its soldiers all dressed in American uniforms labeled combat, Asian, men's, large or small. At the same time the civilian side of the American mission, with the help of the Michigan State University teams, built up territorial forces that more or less paralleled the Viet Minh–NLF formations: a self-defense guard (later called the Popular Forces) to patrol the villages, and a fifty-thousand-man civil guard (later, Regional Forces) to provide provincial defense.[87]

The very size of the American military commitment insured that the Vietnamese armed forces would eventually dominate the civil administration. By 1962 village chiefs were installed in most of the villages and military officers assigned to almost all of the crucial territorial posts of province and district chief. The "security" and "control" system was then complete. The village chiefs reported to the military district and province chiefs, the province chiefs to the three (later, four) corps commanders, and the corps commanders to the presidential palace. The whole system brooked no interference from any representative institutions, or indeed from any civilian body whatsoever. The United States had, in other words, made the Saigon government into a military machine whose sole *raison d'être* was to fight the Communists. The only difficulty was that the machine did not work. That the regular army divisions could not effectively cope with the domestic guerrilla warfare was only the superficial aspect of the problem. The real problem was that these divisions bore no relation to Vietnamese politics. From the American point of view, the ARVN appeared to be solid, a group of men in the same uniform trained and ready to do battle against the Communists. But within the Vietnamese context the ARVN was more like a collection of individuals, all of whom happened to be carrying weapons.

In 1961 it became quite clear to the inner circle of the Kennedy administration that the NLF was threatening the very life of the Diem regime. New measures were required if the regime were to survive for long. After a trip to South Vietnam to survey the military situation General Maxwell Taylor recommended to President Kennedy that the United States send eight thousand regular troops to Vietnam for the purpose of raising the morale of the GVN and showing the Communists the seriousness of the American intent to defend South Vietnam. Secretary of Defense Robert McNamara queried the value of a token force, warning, "We would be almost certain to get increasingly mired down in an inconclusive struggle." He recommended that the United States make a clear commitment to the defense of South Vietnam and support that commitment with the introduction of U.S. forces on the "substantial scale" that would be necessary to achieve military victory.[88] President Kennedy did not accept McNamara's recommendation or Taylor's proposal as they stood. But over the next two years he doubled the number of troops Taylor requested, posting sixteen thousand American soldiers as advisers to the ARVN. At the same time he increased military aid to the Saigon government, reinforced the Vietnamese units with squadrons of American helicopters and airplanes, and undertook a CIA-sponsored program of clandestine sabotage operations in Laos and North and South Vietnam, all directed against the DRVN.

As McNamara had predicted, these new measures did not deter the NLF. The success of American policy thus continued to rest on the capacities of the Saigon government. In 1961 American officials presented the Diem regime with a new list of demands for political, economic, and military reform. Possibly they thought that the Diem regime would now meet these demands, for with the increase of military aid the Americans took steps to transform their "advisory" relationship to one of "limited partnership" with the Saigon government.[89] In 1962 the Military Assistance Advisory Group became the Military Assistance Command, Vietnam (MACV) — "something nearer — but not quite — an operational headquarters in a theater of war."[90] Foreign advisers — British and American — were inserted into every part of the GVN bureaucracy with the authority not only to advise but to insist on the adoption of new programs. Within this new arrangement the Diem regime undertook a new pacification plan, designed by Diem's British advisory team and called the Strategic Hamlet program.

The centerpiece of American strategy in Vietnam for the next two years, the Strategic Hamlet program was by far the most ambitious of the Diemist land programs and by far the most destructive. In its very conception the program was a study in misplaced analogy. Sir Robert Thompson, the head of the British team of advisers to Ngo Dinh Diem, proposed to build up a system of fortified villages such as the British had used against the Communist insurgency in Malaya. The difficulty was that while in Malaya the British had fortified Malay villages against Chinese insurgents, in Vietnam the Vietnamese would have to fortify Vietnamese hamlets against other Vietnamese who had grown up in those hamlets. The plan purported not to involve the displacement of the villagers from their homes and fields, as the other failed resettlement programs had done. But it involved precisely that in most regions of the Mekong Delta. Anyone who took an airplane trip across the Delta could have seen that the villagers did not live in concentrated settlements, but in farmhouses scattered through the paddies and along the edges of the dikes. Because the new program made no provision for the allotment of new land to the villagers, many of the peasants who moved into the strategic hamlets ended up with no land at all — five miles being the same as five hundred to those who had to walk to their fields each day and back. The American and British advisers overlooked this basic economic difficulty. The strategic hamlets offered them the military advantage of concentrating people into small, fortified settlements that the armed forces could actually surround. And by 1962 the military situation appeared to be desperate.

The Ngo brothers had from the beginning favored the new program in the expectation that it would give them more direct control over the villages. Once they learned how much money the Americans were willing to commit to the new plan, and the possibility of direct American intervention if they did not concur, they rushed ahead to implement it.[91] Ngo Dinh Nhu took charge of the program himself and insisted that two-thirds of the sixteen thousand hamlets in South Vietnam be fortified within the next fourteen months. His theory — or rather the theory he explained to the Americans — was that with the help of Personalist indoctrination the peasants would be all too glad to defend their own villages against the Communists without any military or financial support. Sir Robert Thompson argued that the program had to proceed more slowly, so that at every stage the government could protect the hamlets from large-scale Viet Cong attacks. But Nhu went ahead with his own plan, whereby the Americans shipped in vast quantities of commodities to enable all the villagers both to construct their own defenses and, as the press releases had it, to build new and better communities for themselves.

By the end of 1962 Diemist officials reported that though they had not quite reached their objective, half of the country's hamlets had been fortified and provided with some means of self-defense. The figure reflected no real achievement but rather the amount of American aid that had gone to the various province chiefs for such a purpose. As one American study later showed, only fifteen hundred, or less than 10 percent, of the hamlets possessed any military security.[92] Actually, even that figure might not have been achieved without the new American commitment of firepower. With artillery, helicopters, and tactical bombers at its disposal, the Allied command declared whole areas outside the strategic hamlet belt "free fire zones," where anything moving might be shot. Inside the belt it permitted the artillery to fire out almost at random every night on suspected Viet Cong concentrations, trails, and staging areas — a tactic known as "harassment and interdiction." All this unguided firing naturally dissuaded many peasants from following what would have been their normal course of slipping away from the crowded, squalid enclosures. At least one American admitted that the NLF were not far wrong in calling these settlements concentration camps.

In those areas where it was actually applied, the strategic hamlet program did give the Saigon government a short-term military advantage. Politically, it proved a disaster. If the American and British officials really envisioned happy and prosperous peasants standing up to defend their villages against the insurgents, their wishful thinking was mighty indeed. Except for the Catholics, the peasants had no possible reason for doing anything of the sort. The amount of American aid that actually trickled down to the villages hardly gave them a motive to support the government — in the Delta it barely permitted them to survive. Armed with Personalist slogans on the virtues of self-sufficiency and self-sacrifice, the officials took the peasants away from their fields and forced them to construct mud and barbed-wire fences that made them liable to NLF attacks and thus put them in some jeopardy. Even those officials who conducted themselves in an exemplary manner induced anxiety among the villagers by their very physical presence. Under constant surveillance and in constant fear of attack, many of the hamlets lost even such unity as they possessed. As one village lawyer said of his hamlet not far from Saigon, "We have no solidarity here, no cooperation. And so if the Viet Cong come, no matter where we are, they can take advantage of us." In his hamlet as in so many others, the circle of artillery and barbed wire enclosed a political void that waited for the NLF.

And from the Plain of Reeds, from the Ca Mau peninsula and the central Vietnamese highlands, the NLF moved slowly in to fill the vacuum. They drove the government forces completely out of many areas. In other places, near heavy troop concentrations, they simply drained away government authority and acted as the government of the nighttime. In the view of the American command, the Viet Cong seemed to have arisen by spontaneous generation. The Americans had not perceived the anarchy of the villages, for to them the first sign of anarchy was unorganized violence, and there was no violence inside the villages until the NLF began to mobilize them in the most compulsively methodical manner. Not until their military offensive of 1962–1963 did the Front persuade at least some Americans that it had extended its influence to over 80 percent of the rural population.[93]

The new American aid commitment bought time for the Saigon regime, but it increased the dangers confronting the Ngo family itself. The larger the military bureaucracy grew, the more it grew to resemble the country itself, its officers no more "pacified" and no more loyal to the Diem regime than the peasants inside the strategic hamlets. Ngo Dinh Diem knew this perfectly well. He as much as told his American advisers that he feared his ministers and generals. But the Americans did not understand his situation. From the very beginning Diem's aim had been not to run the administration but to render it helpless, to bypass it with the help of his brothers. As time went on, his attempt to divide and rule required more and more extreme measures: the sabotaging of military operations, the replacement of the most competent officers by the most venal. The Ngos were not so much running a government as running an opposition within it. Between them they managed to create an underworld of warlords, secret societies, and bandit groups such as had existed in the periods of greatest anarchy between Confucian governments. In order to finance the Can Lao Party and his other subversive intelligence agencies, Nhu engaged in activities similar to those of his old enemy Bay Vien: waterfront piracy, extortion rackets, illicit trading in opium, and exchange manipulation.[94] Ngo Dinh Can ran central Vietnam as his own private business venture: he controlled the local shipping and the cinnamon trade, and with Diem's tacit consent ruled the local officials through adroit manipulation, graft, and extortion.[95] The two brothers jealously guarded their sources of revenue from each other — their agents occasionally killing each other off in an excess of zeal. Madame Nhu had the foresight to amass a fortune in goods that might be quickly translated into European assets. It was later said that, among other things, she owned a large theatre on the Champs Élysées — an odd investment for this most self-advertised of Catholics.

Amazingly, despite all of this illicit traffic, the Ngos maintained an impenetrable façade of self-righteous hauteur. The world, they seemed to be saying, was not good or pure enough for them. After the abortive military coup of 1960 — a daredevil operation mounted by a few paratrooper units under the command of Colonel Nguyen

Chanh Thi and crushed after a day or so — Diem declared that the "hand of God" had sustained him against the rebel assault. And yet the attempted coup had a demonstrable effect on the Ngo family. Ngo Dinh Diem had at one time trusted his relatives, but after 1960 even his family members began to drop away: some were fired, others resigned, still others remained at their posts but no longer had any influence on Diem or Nhu. The extended family narrowed down to the nuclear family of Diem, Can, Thuc, and the Nhus. And even within this inner ring there were fights for power and prestige with Nhu claiming the protocol arrangements for a head of state and Madame Nhu claiming responsibility for her husband's ideas. Only the farouche Can remained constant.

After the coup of 1960 Diem began to withdraw more and more into himself. It was true that he had long been something of a recluse. He was always as Graham Greene so brilliantly pictured him in 1955: "Separated from the people by cardinals and police cars with wailing sirens and foreign advisers droning of global strategy . . . sitting with his blank brown gaze, incorruptible, obstinate, ill-advised, going to his weekly confession, bolstered up by his belief that God is always on the Catholic side, waiting for a miracle."[96] But in the past he had traveled a great deal around the country, visiting those villages where his officials had taken pains to produce elaborate pageants of a thriving, moral, and deeply respectful peasantry.[97] Now he traveled less and appeared at fewer public ceremonies. Each year he celebrated his election as chief of state with a day of parades and speeches. At the anniversary parade of 1962 the *New York Times* reporter, David Halberstam, observed that there were no Vietnamese crowds to be seen anywhere near the route of the parade. The police, on Diem's orders, had erected great barricades to keep the people away, and the parades were held in a vacuum for Diem and his foreign advisers.[98] Now, too, Diem began to talk more and more. In the last year of his life he would lecture for six and sometimes ten hours at a stretch, refusing to be interrupted by questions. Some of the American reporters saw his incessant talking as a sign of defensiveness. The Vietnamese understood it to have a very precise meaning: his talking was the sign that he could no longer exercise the self-control of a true "father," a Confucian gentleman. Diem was frightened of his subordinates, but he had no recourse except to insist on his authority — the image of the open mouth. By his talking he threatened to starve them.

As Diem withdrew into himself, the influence of Ngo Dinh Nhu began to displace the president's as the dark the light of the waning moon. Diem himself possessed many of the puritanical virtues of the true Confucian monarch. Nhu had, and to some degree personified, the complementary vices of arrogance, indiscipline, and brutality. As Diem represented the first sovereign of a dynasty, Nhu represented the last one. Certainly, Nhu came to the end of the "downward spiral" long before 1963. Perhaps anticipating Diem's failure at moral instruction, Nhu had quite early on begun to bully. It was Nhu who defended the special military courts on the grounds that those found guilty must be "wicked people." It was Nhu who organized the internal spy system and who encouraged corruption and factionalism in order to control the bureaucracy. It was Nhu who so divided and demoralized the officer corps that it provided small resistance to the NLF. In the end Diem displayed some of the classical anxieties of a failed Confucian ruler, but Nhu gave signs of insanity. It was Nhu who precipitated the coup of 1963 against his own family.

After a period of quiescence following the failure of the 1960 coup, the army officers once again began to plot against the regime. This time their victory appeared assured. The military collapse persuaded most of the top generals and much of the Saigon bourgeoisie that the existence of the republic required the removal of the Ngo family. And then there were few officers to whom the Ngos had not given excellent reasons for a private vendetta. As one general described the situation in another context — his image recalling the oldest of Confucian metaphors, "While the government deludes itself and its powerful allies by giving the outward impression of authority, those responsive to its authority became fewer and fewer . . . [until it is] balanced like an inverted pyramid and requires only a push from some other self-centered group to topple it from power."[99] In other words, the same process was taking place inside the government as outside it.

But the officers vacillated. Most of them were afraid of Nhu. For eight years Nhu had almost single-handedly prevented them from taking that share of power they always felt was rightly theirs. He had bribed many of them, blackmailed others, and manipulated all of them so successfully that not one of them trusted another. The officers feared that any one among them might inform or lead a counter-coup to place himself in the Ngos' favor. They feared that in the event of a successful coup against the Ngos, one of their number might seize power and oust the rest of them. Dr. Tran Kim Tuyen, Nhu's own security chief, now turned against the Ngos and organized a plot that brought several officers to the point of counting battalions. But still the officers could not bring themselves to act. The Americans controlled the purse strings of the government, and the officers knew they could not count on the rest of the army until they obtained a firm commitment from the embassy. In the spring of 1963 this commitment seemed impossible to come by. Despite the disintegration of the ARVN, Ambassador Frederick Nolting and General Paul Harkins, the MACV commander, remained optimistic about the war and about the capacities of the Ngo family to reform the government under their tutelage. The heads of the mission appeared unable to comprehend the seriousness of the situation inside or outside of the government. Given their faith in the Ngos' own military estimates and their obliviousness to the silent defections within the government, they might, it seemed, have remained ignorant of the situation up until the moment when the NLF took over the government — and then perhaps a little beyond it. Contemplating that end, the officers waited, as if paralyzed.

But then something surprising happened. On May 8, 1963, large crowds of Buddhist priests and laymen surrounded the radio station in Hue to protest Archbishop Ngo Dinh Thuc's order forbidding them to carry the Buddhist flags on the birthday of the Buddha. When the crowds would not disperse before fire hoses, blank shells, and tear gas, the Catholic deputy province chief ordered his troops to fire live ammunition into the crowd, with the result that nine people were killed. The next day the government claimed that the Viet Cong had set off plastic charges in the midst of the crowd — a lie that further antagonized the Buddhists. After weeks of argument, the Americans finally persuaded Diem to meet with the Buddhist leaders and to give in to some of their demands. But the regime never admitted responsibility for the killings, and Nhu ordered the Republican Youth to protest Diem's signing of the agreement.[100] The bonzes demonstrated before the National Assembly building and embarked upon a hunger strike in Hue.

In the second week of June the bonze Thich Quang Duc died by fire, seated in the lotus position in the middle of a busy intersection in Saigon. From that moment on the bonzes went into determined, organized opposition to the Diem regime. Traveling from city to city, the leaders in Hue and Saigon held mass meetings of prayer and political protest; their spokesmen held almost daily conferences for the American press. From that moment on it became increasingly clear that the days of the Diem regime were numbered. Only the details and the timing of their demise remained to be settled.

four

To American journalists in Saigon the whole affair of the Buddhists was puzzling in the extreme. Who were "the Buddhists," after all? Until the May incident the few hundred bonzes who inhabited the city pagodas had never appeared upon American horizons. Few of them spoke Western languages, and with one or two exceptions they seemed naïve about the outside world.[101] It was known, of course, that all nonsectarian Vietnamese were "Buddhists" in some vague sense: they worshiped the image of the Buddha along with the scrolls of their ancestors and the Taoist spirits. But these city bonzes could not be said to represent them, for at least among the peasantry Buddhism had no established tradition, no network of pagodas such as existed in Thailand, Burma, or Japan. The bonzes who initiated the demonstration were men, or the heirs of men, who had gone abroad during the 1930's to draw from the pure, intellectual stream of Mahayana Buddhism and later set up study centers in Hanoi, Hue, and Saigon. At the time of the great nationalist eruption of the 1930's and 1940's they remained politically inconspicuous. Like most of the urban groups, they made their accommodation with the French, never venturing out to seek a following in the countryside, never rivaling the Catholics in organizational strength. By 1962 they had a number of pagodas in Saigon and the central Vietnamese cities and a small following loosely organized into what the Americans always assumed was a "purely religious" group, the Association for the Propagation of the Buddhist Faith.[102] The nominal Buddhists of the countryside had suffered from Catholic persecution since 1954, but the bonzes of the city pagodas never felt the same pressures. In Hue it was said that Ngo Dinh Can had often gone to visit the most important of the Buddhist leaders, Thich Tri Quang, in order to discuss the affairs of the community. It was only when Archbishop Ngo Dinh Thuc, randy for a cardinal's hat, tried to prove his zeal as a defender of the faith that the government issued edicts that impinged upon the Buddhists' religious freedom.[103] But now, suddenly, the bonzes became the leaders of a powerful movement of opposition to Diem. They were energetic, persistent, resourceful — and irreversibly committed to the overthrow of the regime. Most extraordinarily, they seemed to call forth an intense, emotional reaction from the Vietnamese of the cities, and even from those who had never visited their pagodas before. The televised pictures of another monk's death by fire showed people running to the body to fall on their knees and weep. The reaction remained unexplained by the Vietnamese; it was as if the bonzes had touched a chord so profound that it lay beyond explanation.

The logic behind the Buddhist protest was in fact not at all obvious; it lay buried in the depths of Vietnamese history, and it had to do with the particular function that Buddhism had always served in Vietnam. Introduced into the Red River Delta in the second century A.D., Buddhism — Mahayana Buddhism of the school of the Bodhidharma — dominated the intellectual life of Vietnam at the most critical period of its history, the struggle for independence in the tenth century. After the successful conclusion of that struggle the emperors recognized Buddhism as one of the Three Religions, but the Confucian state in its periods of greatest strength suppressed the pagodas and forbade the circulation of Buddhist texts. Buddhism after the eleventh century descended to the intellectual level of the village, where, blending in with the competing strains of Taoism, Confucianism, and animism, it became a part of the popular religion — a tonality, a series of beliefs, rather than a pure, isolated discipline. Buddhism did not reappear again as an intellectual force until the seventeenth century — and then in the worst period of civil wars under the declining Le dynasty. It is said that "the Vietnamese are Confucians in peacetime, Buddhists in times of trouble." The old adage has an historical basis in fact, for the Buddhist pagodas would reappear throughout the country each time the Confucian state went into decline. When the pyramid of Confucian society crumbled, the Buddhist bonzes would return as if to fill the vacuum, to give the country a stable moral and intellectual center apart from the state and the official religion. Even the popular, quasi-Buddhist sects often played the same role. During the decline of dynasties, or the struggle between warlords, "Buddhist" magicians and sorcerers rose up from the underground of the villages to lead small peasant rebellions against the anarchy and violence of a weak ruler. In the period of nationalist resurgence against the French, both forms of Buddhism re-emerged: popular Buddhism in the Hoa Hao and intellectual Buddhism in the city brotherhoods. The scholar of Asian religions, Paul Mus, had indicated just why Buddhism should play such a part in Vietnamese history.[104]

According to Mus, the early brotherhoods that carried Buddhism from India to China and Vietnam had of necessity made a very particular accommodation with Confucian society. Accepting the "universal empire" as a political system and a social structure, they maintained their claims to a greater universality: Confucianism was a social order defined by culture and history; Buddhism was a faith relevant to all times and to all men, no matter what their circumstances. Buddhism lived within the system and beyond it. Not just a civilization, not just a means of living in the world, it was a Way for all men to transcend the limitations of society and the self to reach a higher truth. As Buddhists, all men were brothers in a realm above race and culture. They were not fathers and sons, kings and subjects, but equals in moral responsibility, equals in their capacity for achieving salvation. As incorporated into the Vietnamese folk religion, Buddhism showed a Way out beyond the binding "net ropes" of the Confucian world. In peacetime it offered the Vietnamese an internal life — a soul, a personal identity — outside the conventions of society. In times of tyranny and "splitting apart," it indicated a morality that lay beyond loyalty to existing authorities. The Buddhist "brotherhood" was an alternate form of community that provided a basis for opposition to an oppressive regime. It did not itself incorporate an alternate design for a state or a society-in-the-world, but it provided a means of reconciliation and showed the Way back into Confucian society.

In 1963 the bonzes of the cities gave no such explicit analysis of their goals. But they took on this same moral and political task of their predecessors. Their leaders had certainly pondered the whole course of the regime before that year. They had heard of the secret police, the corruption, the arbitrary arrests, and the terror. They no doubt knew that the Ngo family had managed to alienate even its top officers. The Hue incident only proved to them and to their following that there were no longer any limits to the tyranny of the regime. Though only a small sect, they acted and took on the burden of leading the opposition. In the summer and autumn of 1963 they transcended their sectarian limits to become the conscience of those who continued to support or acquiesce to the regime — the urban Vietnamese and the Americans.

The self-immolation of Thich Quang Duc in June was, of course, the central event of the entire Buddhist protest movement. It shocked the Americans as much as the Vietnamese; it had an important effect on American policy. And yet it remained mysterious. It seemed a barbarous, primitive act, an expression of some atavistic memory, yet it had, so far as anyone knew, no precedent in Vietnamese history. Then too, the publicity the Buddhists gave to it was most incongruously modern. During those endless minutes while the flames leaped up the robes of Quang Duc, obscuring his face, and during the slow fall of the charred body from its upright position, a young bonze with a microphone called out over and over again in Vietnamese and English, "A Buddhist priest burns himself to death. A Buddhist priest becomes a martyr."[105] The bonzes had called the American reporters to witness the scene. Later they would display the heart of Quang Duc in a glass case and insure television coverage of some of the six other self-immolations. Even those reporters who favored the Buddhist cause could not help feeling that the performance was somehow crass and sacrilegious. But the mystery remained.

To those who knew Vietnamese history, Quang Duc's death recalled the suicide of the great mandarins who could not reconcile their loyalty to the emperor with their obedience to the will of Heaven. But those deaths had been quiet, gentlemanly suicides that indicated resignation and inability to resolve a fundamental conflict. Quang Duc's death by fire and loudspeaker had not at all the same tone. As Mus explained, it was not a gesture of resignation, but rather one of protest — an advertisement of the intolerable gap between morality and the reality of the Diem regime. The self-immolation had no precedent in Vietnamese history — but then never before had a Vietnamese regime depended upon the electronic reactions of world opinion. By taking the pose of the Buddha, Quang Duc was indicating to both Vietnamese and Americans a morality and a responsibility for others that lay beyond the divisions of political systems and culture. To the Vietnamese his self-immolation was a call first to reconciliation and then to rebellion. The students of Saigon and Hue responded. Breaking a long tradition of what the Americans called "political noninvolvement," but what was actually political nonresistance to the government, they went en masse to pray in the pagodas and then to join in the demonstrations behind the bonzes. The students, including many of the Catholics, responded by *becoming* Buddhists. They burst through the "net ropes" of Confucian authoritarianism that had paralyzed them with fear and suspicion of one another, and they became for the moment equals. When Douglas Pike wrote that he could see "the whole fabric of Vietnamese society coming apart," what he had in fact observed was the society breaking out from its untenable pyramid of superiors and inferiors to become a brotherhood of trust.

five

On July 11, 1963, Ngo Dinh Nhu called a meeting of all his generals to present them with the veiled threat that they might expect a coup whose participants would be his own dupes.[106] A maneuver worthy of Nhu at his most Machiavellian, the threat proved a brilliant tactical success. The generals, who were on the point of bringing their own plans for a coup to fruition, walked out of the meeting divided and confused.

Nhu was not afraid of his generals, nor was he afraid of the Americans who, he judged correctly, would not withdraw their support until they found a "viable alternative." But the Buddhists, "those miserable unarmed bonzes," as Madame Nhu called them, they were the threat. Day after day they would hold meetings and lead processions through the streets, calling for attention and more attention. Their disingenuousness shocked the Americans, but it was their effrontery that worried the Ngos. The bonzes had dared to step out of place, had dared to stand up in open protest as unfilial sons. Before the autumn passed, six more bonzes followed Quang Duc in self-immolation. "Barbecues," Madame Nhu called them, drawing a psychological curtain before her. Only Ngo Dinh Can urged con-ciliation.[107] The Nhus wanted military action against the Buddhists. To some of their officials they expressed their intention of raid-ing the pagodas on the anniversary of the St. Bartholomew's Eve

Massacre,[108] and it did not seem to matter to them that it would turn world, and more particularly American, opinion against them. President Kennedy's replacement of the sympathetic Ambassador Nolting with Henry Cabot Lodge only made them speed up their plans.

On the morning of August 21, Nhu's own troops surrounded the Xa Loi pagoda, only a few hundred feet from the presidential palace, and shot over thirty bonzes and imprisoned the rest of them. In Hue and other central Vietnamese cities other units perpetrated a similar outrage. The next day Nhu had the telephone lines of the American embassy cut in order to keep the Americans uninformed. He claimed that the army had executed the raids and implied that the troops belonged to one of the last of the officers faithful to him, General Ton That Dinh, the governor general of Saigon. It was a suicidal move, and the Nhus must have known as much, for too many people had heard of their plans. From that time on Nhu went to work with a strange determination. Charging that Diem had been weak in his dealings with the Buddhists, he arrested some four thousand university students and hundreds of high-school students who demonstrated against the raid. His move appeared calculated to alienate those last Saigonese families who might have supported him, as well as the Catholic clergy. But Nhu went further. Assuming that the American press reflected the views of the officials as closely as did his own, he attacked the U.S. government in public and charged the CIA chief, John Richardson, with having formed a plot against his life. He spoke of a vast international conspiracy against the regime and hinted broadly that he had opened negotiations with Hanoi. His rages terrified all those who came close to him. As the Ngos' secretary of state later told Robert Shaplen, "We knew that Nhu was smoking opium in the last year and maybe taking heroin, too, and that this helped create his moods of extremism. . . . You could begin to see madness in his face, a sort of somnambulistic stare, always with that cold smile. . . . It was as if a devil had taken possession of him."[109] In his failure Nhu had withdrawn so far into himself that in the end his face was a mask that no longer opened onto the real world.

Finally the Americans reacted. In August, just after the pagoda raids, the new ambassador, Henry Cabot Lodge, instructed a CIA agent in contact with the generals to tell them that Washington would approve a coup. The generals were suspicious of both

Harkins and Richardson, and demanded further assurances. They allowed the moment to pass. Then in October, after a great deal of internal debate, the Kennedy administration decided to suspend the Commercial Import Program — the source of most of the government funds — and publicly to dissociate itself from the Ngos. Further demonstrations, further assurances, and the plotting of other officers finally impelled the generals to act. When on November 1 the tanks came rolling up to the Norodam Palace, not a single ranking officer remained with his masters inside the iron circle.

But the drama was not quite over. The coup took a whole day to unfold. At 1:30 P.M. army troops took over the central government installations and surrounded the palace with tanks and machine guns. Still the generals did not make a move towards the Ngo family. For hours and hours they waited outside the palace while Diem and Nhu, defended by a few bodyguards, called over the military telephone to the corps and divisional commanders, to the province chiefs, to the heads of the Republican Youth Movement and the Women's Solidarity League. But there was no answer from anyone, not even from the best-rewarded of their favorites. At 4:30 P.M. Diem telephoned Ambassador Lodge to ask what the attitude of the United States was to the rebellion. Lodge replied that he was not well enough informed to say, but reported that he had heard that "those in charge of the current activity" planned to give Diem and Nhu safe conduct out of the country if they would resign. Diem asked Lodge if he had his telephone number, then concluded the conversation, saying that he was trying to re-establish order.[110] A little while later, Diem and Nhu left the palace by an underground escape route, maintaining radio contact with the generals but refusing to disclose their whereabouts. The next morning as they were seeking sanctuary in a Catholic church, the Ngos were discovered, thrown in a van, and killed like commoners by a junior officer.

After the crisis had passed, the people of Saigon rarely spoke of the Diem regime again. There was nothing more to be said. For the city people the fall of the regime was a catharsis played out with full theatrical extravagance. When the news of the two brothers' death went out over the radio, the whole city exploded into rejoicing. On that day there were no more "Diemists" in the city, for the Buddhist demonstrations had already signaled that the regime had fallen in all but title, that the will of Heaven had already changed. In nine years the Diem regime went through the entire life cycle of a dynasty, following the ancient Vietnamese rhythms not of rise, decline, and fall, but of rise, holding, and abrupt descent. There was a finality about it. As the Ngos perhaps recognized, the Vietnamese would commit their regime to that absolute death that comes to a family when it has no heirs, and that comes to a dynasty when the will of Heaven turns against it.

The Diem regime had no issue. Assassinated in secret, the Ngos were buried in unmarked graves. The officers who wrote the original death certificates described Diem not as "Chief of State" but as "Chief of Province" and Nhu as "Chief of the Library Services."[111] By demoting the brothers to the last ranks they had held under the French regime, the officers demonstrated their own similar concern for ritual prestige, rank, and hierarchy. By indirection they reasserted the whole Confucian system that proved the downfall of the Ngos. To change the government required only a rebellion; to change the country, a revolution.*

---

* Ngo Dinh Can was later taken to Saigon, tried in court, and executed by a firing squad in a public square. Madame Nhu was in the United States at the time on a lecture tour, and Archbishop Thuc was in Rome. Neither, needless to say, returned to Vietnam.

4

The National Liberation Front

As the past history of this country shows, there seems to be a national attribute which makes for factionalism and limits the development of a truly national spirit. Whether this tendency is innate or a development growing out of the conditions of political suppression under which successive generations have lived is hard to determine. But it is an inescapable fact that there is no national tendency toward team play or mutual loyalty to be found among many of the leaders and political groups within South Vietnam. Given time, many of these [words illegible] undoubtedly change for the better, but we are unfortunately pressed for time and unhappily perceive no short-term solution for the establishment of a stable and sound government.

The ability of the Viet Cong continuously to rebuild their units and to make good their losses is one of the mysteries of this guerrilla war. . . . Not only do the Viet Cong units have the recuperative powers of the phoenix, but they have an amazing ability to maintain morale. Only in rare cases have we found evidences of bad morale among Viet Cong prisoners or recorded in captured Viet Cong documents.

— General Maxwell Taylor
(From a briefing to principal Washington officials concerned with Vietnam. November 1964)

Introduction

The Americans began by underestimating the Vietnamese guerrillas, but in the end they made them larger than life. During the invasion of Cambodia in 1970, American officials spoke of plans to capture the enemy's command headquarters for the south as if there existed a reverse Pentagon in the jungle complete with Marine guards, generals, and green baize tables. In fact the American generals knew there was no such thing, but in the press and the mind of the public the image kept returning. After all those years of fighting, the NLF and the North Vietnamese had taken on a super-human dimension. Paradoxically, the exaggeration diminished them, for in the dimension of mythology all things are fabulous and unaccountable. By turning their enemy into a mirror image of themselves, the Americans obscured the nature of the Vietnamese accomplishment.

The National Liberation Front, after all, began in a world where men walked behind wooden plows and threshed the rice by beating it with wooden flails. The NLF recruits were largely illiterate or semiliterate, men who spent their life working on one hectare of paddy land, hoping only that one day they might afford a bullock. The NLF taught these men to operate radio sets, to manufacture explosives, to differentiate one type of American bomber from another. It taught them to build small factories, hospitals, and logistical systems that ran the length and breadth of the country without touching a road. With these men the Front cadres shot down helicopters, designed gas masks against American chemicals, and invented small-unit tactics that would add chapters to the history of the art. With them the NLF built a government and an army out of the disordered and intractable society of South Vietnam.

This change, that in most countries takes several generations to perform, the NLF telescoped into five years. The movement was founded in 1960. By the spring of 1965, when the American regular troops entered the war, the Liberation Front had seriously damaged the Saigon government's armed forces and isolated its city outposts from the countryside. With an army of southerners and a supply of weapons largely obtained from their enemy, the NLF was on the point of defeating a state the United States had provided with hundreds of millions of dollars' worth of military assistance, artillery, bombers, and some seventeen thousand American advisers. Five years is a short period in which to make a revolution, but it is a long one in which to fight a major war. Over the next half-decade the NLF with the help of North Vietnamese forces stood up to an American army of over half a million men armed with the most sophisticated array of weaponry the world has ever seen. In 1971 the Liberation forces remained undefeated, and the Front was still the most important political force in the south.

Over the years of war American officials spoke of the NLF as if it were an illustration of some larger principle, some larger menace to the security of the United States. To Walt Rostow the National Liberation Front was but one instance of the "disease of Communism" that affected developing countries around the world. To Robert McNamara it was a test case for the "new" Communist strategy of promoting "wars of national liberation" around the world. To many American military men it was but an example of the threat that guerrillas in general provided to the established governments of the earth. By this attempt at generalization, duplicated in other terms by many Americans on the left, the officials reduced the NLF to the status of a symbol and, again, obscured its achievement.

For the Vietnamese revolution in the south was in many ways unique. If it belonged to a category, then that category was extremely small. Since the period of international turmoil following the Second World War there were only two successful Communist insurgency movements, one in Cuba, the other in Vietnam. In Bolivia Che Guevara brought all his theory and practical experience to bear on the miserable, exploited hinterlands, only to find the Bolivian peasants as unreceptive as stones. In Southeast Asia the Communist movements had an almost complete record of failure. In Burma, the Philippines, and Malaya, they did not succeed in gaining support from the majority of the population. In Indonesia the Party relied upon the magical figure of Sukarno and did not take the necessary steps to seize and hold power.[*] Then, too, since the Second World War only two countries have won their independence after a protracted war with a European power: Algeria and Vietnam. In many respects the Vietnamese war of the 1960's was unprecedented in the history of revolutionary and independence wars. The Chinese Communists and the Viet Minh had, after all, secure base areas within their own country and a relatively weak enemy on their soil. At their greatest strength, the French forces in Vietnam numbered only seventy thousand. The United States by contrast gave the best of its armed forces and two billion dollars a month to the Vietnam War. At one point General Vo Nguyen Giap himself admitted that until the war for the south he knew nothing about "people's war."

During the course of the war Americans wrote a great deal about

---

[*] The Communist insurgencies in Cambodia and Laos have always been inextricably bound up with that in Vietnam.

the military strategy of the NLF and relatively little about its politics. The reason is simple. Most research on Vietnam was official research, and the official American line was that the guerrilla war involved no internal political issues, but that it was merely part of the attempt of the North Vietnamese to conquer the south. As *The Pentagon Papers* showed, many American officials did not believe this line themselves, but it provided them with a convenient method of avoiding crucial and potentially damaging questions, such as what the political problems of South Vietnam were, and how it was that from the same population base the NLF managed to create an organization so much superior to that of the GVN. The result was that even those Americans responsible for the conduct of the war knew relatively little about their enemy, for within the NLF politics was all: it was at the same time the foundation of military strategy and its goal. For the NLF military victories were not only less important than political victories, but strictly meaningless considered in isolation from them. Those few American officials who studied the NLF saw the political focus, but did not understand its significance. Had they understood it, they might have warned that it would be better to send the Saigon regime's army to fight without weapons than to send it to fight without a political strategy, as was the case.

For a non-Vietnamese to write a full account of the NLF is finally an impossible undertaking. It is not that the evidence is lacking. On the contrary. By 1967 the U.S. government possessed more information on the NLF than on any other political phenomenon in Asia. The American mission in Vietnam collected not only "captured documents" — a vast array of reports, orders, laundry lists, tax receipts, soldiers' journals, promotion forms, and propaganda leaflets — but thousands of interviews with defectors and prisoner interrogations that described everything from the movement of battalions to the sensibilities of the individual soldier. By 1970 the collection must have filled entire buildings and, like a section of Borges's Library of Babylon, contained (buried and irretrievable) every written statement the NLF ever made about itself. From this information it is possible to reconstruct the entire scheme of NLF operations and even to some extent the lives of its cadres. The political strategies are clear enough — the NLF itself proclaimed them. But still the task of description remains difficult, for no American can follow the NLF cadres into the world in which they live to see the point where these strategies touch upon the life of the Vietnamese villager. Hypotheses can be made, theories abstracted, but the very essence of the revolution will remain foreign and intractable.

Politics of the Earth

The American soldiers in Vietnam discovered their own ignorance in an immediate way. The NLF guerrillas chose the night and the jungles to fight in, similarly, and they chose to work with that part of the population which was the most obscure to the Americans and to the Saigon government officials. For the Americans to discern the enemy within the world of the Vietnamese village was to attempt to make out figures within a landscape indefinite and vague — underwater, as it were. Landing from helicopters in a village controlled by the NLF, the soldiers would at first see nothing, having no criteria with which to judge what they saw. As they searched the village, they would find only old men, women, and children, a collection of wooden tools whose purpose they did not know, altars with scrolls in Chinese characters, paths that led nowhere: an economy, a geography, an architecture totally alien to them. Searching for booby traps and enemy supplies, they would find only the matting over a root cellar and the great stone jars of rice. Clumsy as astronauts, they would bend under the eaves of the huts, knock over the cooking pots, and poke about at the smooth earth floor with their bayonets. How should they know whether the great stone jars held a year's supply of rice for the family or a week's supply for a company of troops? With experience they would come to adopt a bearing quite foreign to them. They would dig in the root cellars, peer in the wells, and trace the faint paths out of the village — to search the village as the soldiers of the warlords had searched them centuries ago. Only then would they find the entrance to the tunnels, to the enemy's first line of defense.

To the American commanders who listened each day to the statistics on "tunnels destroyed' 'and "caches of rice found," it must have appeared that in Vietnam the whole surface of the earth rested like a thin crust over a vast system of tunnels and underground rooms. The villages of both the "government" and "Viet Cong" zones were pitted with holes, trenches, and bunkers where the people slept at night in fear of the bombing. In the "Viet Cong" zones the holes were simply deeper, the tunnels longer — some of them running for kilometers out of a village to debouch in another village or a secret place in the jungle. Carved just to the size of a Vietnamese body, they were too small for an American to enter and too long to follow and destroy in total. Only when directed by a prisoner or informer could the Americans dig down to discover the underground storerooms.

Within these storerooms lay the whole industry of the guerrilla: sacks of rice, bolts of black cloth, salt fish and fish sauce, small machines made of scrap metal and bound up in sacking. Brown as the earth itself, the cache would look as much like a part of the earth as if it had originated there — the bulbous root of which the palm-leaf huts of the village were the external stem and foliage. And yet, once they were unwrapped, named, and counted, the stores would turn out to be surprisingly sophisticated, including, perhaps, a land mine made with high explosives, a small printing press with leaflets and textbook materials, surgical instruments, Chinese herbal medicines, and the latest antibiotics from Saigon. The industry clearly came from a civilization far more technically advanced than that which had made the external world of thatched huts, straw mats, and wooden plows. And yet there was an intimate relation between the two, for the anonymous artisans of the storerooms had used the materials of the village not only as camouflage but as an integral part of their technology.

In raiding the NLF villages, the American soldiers had actually walked over the political and economic design of the Vietnamese revolution. They had looked at it, but they could not see it, for it was doubly invisible: invisible within the ground and then again invisible within their own perspective as Americans. The revolution could only be seen against the background of the traditional village and in the perspective of Vietnamese history.

In the old ideographic language of Vietnam, the word *xa,* which Westerners translate as "village" or "village community," had as its roots the Chinese characters signifying "land," "people," and "sacred." These three ideas were joined inseparably, for the Vietnamese religion rested at every point on the particular social and economic system of the village. Confucian philosophy taught that the sacred bond of the society lay with the mandarin-genie, the representative of the emperor. But the villagers knew that it lay with the spirits of the particular earth of their village. They believed that if a man moved off his land and out of the gates of the village, he left his soul behind him, buried in the earth with the bones of his ancestors. The belief was no mere superstition, but a reflection of the fact that the land formed a complete picture of the village: all of a man's social and economic relationships appeared there in visual terms, as if inscribed on a map. If a man left his land, he left his own "face," the social position on which his "personality" depended.

In the nineteenth century the French came, and with their abstraction of money they took away men's souls — men's "faces" — and put them in banks.[1] They destituted the villages, and though they thought to develop the economy and to put the landless to work for wages in their factories and plantations, their efforts made no impression upon the villagers. What assets the French actually contributed to the country in the form of capital and industrial plants were quite as invisible to the villagers as the villagers' souls were to the French. At a certain point, therefore, the villagers went into revolt.

Ngo Dinh Diem and his American advisers, however, did not, or could not, learn from the French example. Following the same centralized strategy for modernization, they continued to develop the cities, the army, and the bureaucracy, while leaving the villages to rot. As it merely permitted a few more rural people to come into the modern sector in search of their souls, this new national development constituted little more than a refugee program. For those peasants with enough money and initiative to leave their doomed villages it meant a final, traumatic break with their past. For the nation as a whole it meant the gradual division of the South Vietnamese into two distinct classes or cultures.

Of necessity, the guerrillas began their program of development from the opposite direction. Rather than build an elaborate superstructure of factories and banks (for which they did not have the capital), they built from the base of the country up, beginning among the ruins of the villages and with the dispossessed masses of people. Because the landlords and the soldiers with their foreign airplanes owned the surface of the earth, the guerrillas went underground in both the literal and the metaphorical sense. Settling down among people who lived, like an Orwellian proletariat, outside the sphere of modern technology, they dug tunnels beneath the villages, giving the people a new defensive distance from the powers which reigned outside the village. The earth itself became their protection – the Confucian "face" which the village had lost when, for the last time, its hedges had been torn down. From an economic point of view, their struggle against the Diem regime with its American finances was just as much of an anticolonial war as that fought by the Viet Minh against the French – the difference being that now other Vietnamese had taken up the colonial role.

As an archaeologist might conclude from examination of the NLF's goods and tools, the guerrillas were attempting not to restore the old village but rather to make some connection between the world of the village and that of the cities. The land mine was in itself the synthesis. Made of high explosives and scrap metal – the waste of foreign cities – it could be manufactured by an artisan with the simplest of skills. A technically comprehensible object, it could be used for the absolutely comprehensible purpose of blowing the enemy soldiers off the face of the village earth. Having themselves manufactured a land mine, the villagers had a new source of power – an inner life to their community. In burying it – a machine – into the earth, they infused a new meaning into the old image of their society. The Diem regime had shown a few of them a way out of the village. The NLF had shown all of them a way back in, to remake the village with the techniques of the outside world. "Socialism" – *xa hoi*, as the Viet Minh and the NLF translated it – indicated to the Vietnamese peasantry that the revolution would entail no traumatic break with the past, no abandonment of the village earth and the ancestors. Instead of a leap into the terrifying unknown, it would be a fulfillment of the local village traditions that the foreigners had attempted to destroy.[2]

The Origins of the National Liberation Front

In an attempt to justify the American bombing of North Vietnam and the dispatch of American troops to the south, the U.S. State Department in February 1965 issued a White Paper entitled *Aggression from the North: The Record of North Vietnam's Campaign to Conquer South Vietnam*. In this paper, State Department officials claimed that the NLF was no more than an instrument of North

Vietnam working against the hopes of all the South Vietnamese for peace, independence, prosperity, and freedom. Had these official claims been true, they would have delineated a situation not very different from the civil wars in Nigeria or Pakistan. And a civil war did not, it seemed, always require American intervention — particularly on the weaker side.

But the Vietnam War was not a civil war; it was a revolutionary war that had raged throughout the entire country since 1945. The strength of the revolution had always been in the north, but the Viet Minh had considerable success south of the 17th parallel. In the period of truce following the Geneva Conference the Viet Minh had, in obedience to the military protocols for disengagement, regrouped some ninety thousand soldiers to the north — most of them southerners.[1] Still, below the 17th parallel there remained hundreds of thousands of Viet Minh cadres, local guerrillas, and their sympathizers. The majority of the remaining Viet Minh were not Communists — no more were the majority of the northerners. But many of them had, like the northerners, lived for the years of the war within a political and social system very different from that obtaining in the rest of South Vietnam. In certain areas such as the Ca Mau peninsula, the region west and northwest of Saigon, and northern central Vietnam, villages, often whole districts, belonged to the revolution just as others belonged to the sects.[2] The people of these regions had firmly expected that the end of the war would bring a unified Vietnam under the government of Ho Chi Minh. When six years later the National Liberation Front was formed, the new movement appeared to them only as the logical continuation of the old one. As one village elder told an American in 1964, "The Liberation grew right up from this place. It happened gradually. Another generation started it. Let us say I am now fifty years old, those who are thirty are now going and those who are twenty come to take their place."

And there was a strong element of continuity between the two movements: a continuity of people, of war aims, and of operating methods. The leaders of the NLF worked in close cooperation with the north, even during the years just following the truce, but it was not until the intervention of American combat troops that they became dependent on the north for war materials and for men.[3] In such a situation the notion of "control" becomes ambiguous. (It is difficult, for instance, to imagine that with its own resources and matériel, the NLF had *no* influence in Hanoi.) But even if the NLF had always been "controlled" by Hanoi, the American official conclusion that it was therefore illegitimate as a southern political movement does not by any means follow. The personnel of the NLF was, with few exceptions, southern. Northern troops did not enter the south until the American troops had already arrived. If the north was indeed trying to conquer the south, it was doing so by politics and culture but not by force. But even this case is impossible to make in a clear-cut manner, for there were southerners within the Politburo of Hanoi. The details are incidental.

The National Liberation Front was founded in 1960, but the guerrilla movement in the south began some two or three years earlier. After the Geneva Conference, the active Communist cadres in the south instructed their followers to disband and wait for two years until the national elections were held and a political settlement made. All official Viet Minh activities stopped except for the "legal struggle" for the elections.[4] The NLF leader, Nguyen Huu Tho, later explained this decision of 1954: "There were mixed feelings about the two years' delay over reunification but the general sentiment was that this was a small price to pay for the return to peace and a normal life, free of foreign rule."[5]

Peace did not, however, last very long for most of the southern Viet Minh. In 1955 Ngo Dinh Diem repudiated the Geneva proposals for national elections and began his campaign of terror against the former members of the Resistance. From the accounts of the Viet Minh cadres it appeared that the campaign was largely successful in destroying what remained of the Viet Minh organization and in reducing the villages to subserviency. While some of the Party members fled to Saigon, where they would not be recognized or pursued, others banded together and went into hiding in the jungles and swamps that had served them as base areas during the war.[6] As one cadre remembered, "In those days you could say we were 'based' in the mountains, but these were 'bases' for survival. We had no arms at all and barely the means of existence. . . . Control was so close that it was impossible for us cadres to live among the people. But we came down from the hills at night to try to make contacts."[7]

According to the French historian, Philippe Devillers, the southern cadre at this point pressed for a renewal of the struggle, but the north held back, urging the southerners to give a respite for the consolidation of the DRVN.[8] While Hanoi surely supported the aims of the southern cadre, its judgment on the timing and the policy to be pursued may well have conflicted with that of the southerners. Certainly the northerners then and for several years later limited their aid to the most easily procured commodity of advice. Weapons could be much more easily obtained from the GVN outposts and the Americans than from convoys traveling the long trail down from the north.

In the long run, however, the Diemist repressions only advanced the date of a new armed struggle. They persuaded many of the former Resistance members whose one goal had been to defeat the French that they could not live in physical safety under the Diem regime, that peace was not peace but a continuation of the war. Diemist policy in general threatened the sects and convinced certain intellectuals and rural notables that the new regime would not serve their interests or leave them a hope for future success, as the French and the Bao Daiist administrations once had. A highly trained and dedicated group of soldiers and political instructors, the active Communist cadre in the south went to work on these groups. By 1958 they had established a small network of committees in most of the old Viet Minh strongholds: in the U Minh forest at the southern tip of the Delta, in the jungles west of Saigon and in the west of Quang Nam province. In the next two years they moved out rapidly from their base areas, infiltrating the nearby hamlets, overrunning small GVN outposts to supply themselves with weapons, taking over hamlets, and recruiting again. At the same time they expanded the movement politically, taking in the former Resistance members who did not belong to the hard core and the members of the other political factions alienated by the Diem regime. In December 1960, they formed the National Liberation Front and adopted a ten-point program of "peace, national independence, democratic freedoms, improvement of the people's living conditions, and peaceful national reunification."

Over the next two years the NLF leaders — men who remained for the moment anonymous to the outside world — molded the loose grouping of committees into a close-knit political and military organization. By mid-1961, so American intelligence indicated, its strength had reached fifteen thousand, and half of the guerrillas were fully armed.[9] This military force, known as the People's Self-Defense Forces, developed by a process known to its cadres as "growth and split."[10] A platoon of experienced fighters would split up to train three platoons of new recruits. The company thus formed would split again to train three new companies, and so forth. In the early years these forces remained dispersed in small units, each unit remaining close to the village that formed its own supply base. The plan for expansion included the carefully coordinated activities of propaganda, recruitment, terrorism against the local GVN officials and soldiers, and the establishment of governing committees and mass organizations within the newly liberated villages.

In February 1962, the Front convened a clandestine congress of one hundred delegates and chose a central committee composed of men of every political color, from Communists to Saigonese intellectuals to religious dignitaries from the various sects, including a Catholic priest. Nguyen Huu Tho, the non-Communist Saigonese lawyer whom Diem imprisoned in 1954 for peace activities, was chosen president. While the makeup of this committee opened the way to a coalition in the event that the United States should withdraw support from the Saigon government, the "hard-core" former Resistance fighters formed the only real political party within it — and thus the controlling element. Until 1962 these men, along with their colleagues among the southern regroupees, belonged to the Marxist-Leninist Party of the DRVN, the Lao Dong. At the time of the congress they formed a new and specifically southern party, the People's Revolutionary Party, that called itself the "vanguard" and the "steel frame" of the NLF.[11] When the United States did not withdraw and the Saigon regime did not disintegrate after the fall of the Ngos, the PRP began to expand inside the NLF, absorbing some of the non-Communists and recruiting new members from the villages. As the NLF members recognized, the Marxist-Leninist Party was what gave the Front the strength and discipline to engage in the second and much more difficult phase of the Liberation war.

By 1962 the NLF had reached an important stage in its development. At the battle of Ap Bac it showed a group of unbelieving American advisers that its guerrilla forces could stand up against a multi-battalion ARVN operation supported by U.S. helicopters and artillery. This military achievement was not an isolated phenomenon. It was the visible expression of an underlying political reality. By 1962 the NLF had a presence in some 80 percent of the rural communities of South Vietnam. Not only had it retaken the old Viet

Minh territories, but it had expanded outward from them, and most noticeably into the central regions of the Mekong Delta, where the Viet Minh had never succeeded in raising more than a collection of guerrilla bands. It was obviously not just a regional group or a coalition of special interests, but a national movement with appeal for the great mass of the rural people. The next war would be something more than a repeat of the Viet Minh war in the south.

The last point was significant — and somewhat mysterious because of the very continuity between the Viet Minh and the NLF. The two organizations were more alike than not in organization, program, and technique. The NLF leaders had the advantage of experience, but they had the disadvantage that the nationalist component of their struggle was not at all as obvious as that of the Viet Minh. Apart from racial or cultural opposition, "nationalism" is, after all, a most difficult abstraction. It took a certain amount of political and economic theory to demonstrate that the American role in Vietnam was in many ways equivalent to that of the French — particularly in the early years when there was no American presence in the countryside. As one Front cadre admitted, the peasants did not grasp the national question as well as the city recruits.[12] And yet it was precisely the peasants who were joining the NLF in large numbers. One explanation, and perhaps the only possible one, was that there were new social and political issues at stake — or issues that the peasants had never felt with such acuity before.

A Natural Opposition

It was not the habit of Americans in Saigon to consider the enemy's political program with any seriousness. But there was one issue that the Americans had to confront, over the course of the war, and that issue was land. In 1955 the American ambassador concurred with the French high commissioner that the Viet Minh land reform program posed a significant threat to the future of the Saigon government. That same year the American economist, Wolf Ladejinsky, made a disturbing study of land distribution in the Mekong Delta. According to his survey, 2.5 percent of the people living in the former territory of Cochin China owned fully a half of the cultivated land, while 70 percent of them owned less than 12.5 percent of it. While the pattern of land tenure varied from province to province (the inequality was less severe in such provinces as Binh Duong, Long An, and An Xuyen), two out of three Delta peasants owned no land at all.[1] In 1956 the American mission finally persuaded the Diem regime to adopt a national land reform program. The reform failed to correct the situation, and for various reasons that included fear for the stability of the Saigon government and sheer apathy about the subject, the American officials did not renew their efforts for another fourteen years. Still, the issue remained alive in official circles in Washington. Particularly after the entry of U.S. troops into the war, a combination of liberal journalists, social scientists, and congressmen brought pressure upon the U.S. mission every year to implement a new land law. Their argument was that landlordism constituted the prime social evil of the countryside and that reform was necessary to the victory of the Saigon government over the NLF. As General Edward Lansdale explained to the readers of *Look* magazine in 1969, the "common man" of Vietnam has no interest in ideology: "His one real yearning is to have something of his own, a farm, a small business, and to be left free to make it grow as he wishes." Once the Saigon government gave the people some economic security, the general concluded, the people would have no more interest in the guerrillas.[2]

The difficulty of this argument was that although it seemed to make common sense — the NLF were in fact making political gains with their land reform program — it did not seem to hold as an explanation for the causes of the insurgency. With all their land reform programs the Viet Minh had found their greatest support in those regions of Vietnam — the north and the center — where the land was the most equally distributed. Where they found the least response was in the Mekong Delta, where the greatest inequality lay. With certain variations the NLF seemed to be repeating the same pattern: their strongest base areas lay in the center and in such Delta provinces as Binh Duong, Long An, and An Xuyen, where landlordism was much less prevalent. In apparent contradiction to Lansdale's theory, most of the early NFL recruits (later, the "hard core") tended to be not agricultural laborers or indebted tenant farmers, but small tradesmen, schoolteachers, clerks, and peasants who owned, or could look forward to owning, some land. These facts — quite evident to anyone with a history book and a map — were elaborated in a most tortuous manner in 1967 by a RAND

Corporation economist armed with linear regression analysis and six independent variables. According to this study, the ideal province from the point of view of GVN control would be one where the inequality was the most severe, where there had been no GVN land reform, and where the population density was the highest and communications the poorest.[3]

After the failure of the land reform and all the years of inertia on the issue, American officials in Saigon and Washington naturally seized upon the RAND study as proof that land reform did not matter politically, that, if anything, it was a merely humanistic issue to be settled after the war — along with all the other humanistic issues. The liberals for their part countered by attacking the study as inaccurate and pointing out that the land reform issue was indeed an important source of NLF support.[4]

In point of fact both arguments were much too narrowly drawn to bear upon the causes of the insurgency. In concentrating exclusively on the problem of land tenure, both the liberals and the officials overlooked the more general political and economic problems that had plagued Vietnam since the colonial period: the shift from a subsistence to a market economy, the breakdown of the traditional village government and economy, and the concentration of power and wealth in the hands of a few. The advocates of land reform failed to see that even if the Saigon government did promulgate a land law, the peasants, without access to credit and without political power in Saigon, would remain as chronically indebted and oppressed as ever. The U.S. officials, on the other hand, did not acknowledge that the peasants throughout Vietnam had economic grievances. The difference in response between the landed and the landless peasants merely indicated that economic grievances alone do not determine the course of a revolution. As to the reason for that difference, the suspicion was that it had to do less with economics than with local government.

It is easier to approach the whole issue of the political success of the NLF by looking at it in reverse from the point of view of what opposed it. After 1960 this question became completely mysterious to American officials because they came to believe their own propaganda that the forces of stability and order — as well as "revolutionary" change — reposed in the Saigon government. During the French war, however, the Saigon government had been almost totally ineffective for good or ill; political opposition to the Viet

Minh had been mounted almost exclusively by the local governments and parties. The most obvious of these were the sects — the
Catholics, the Cao Dai, and the Hoa Hao. But there was another
important source of opposition that most European observers overlooked: the landlords.

It was natural for Europeans to think of these landlords simply as
a class. In fact, the Vietnamese landlords were more like a government, for since their first settlement in the south, they had exercised
almost total authority over the people who worked in their domains.
With hardly any regulation from the colonial regime, they possessed
a complete economic hold over two-thirds of the population.[5] They
had the power to assign rents and to sell their tenants' produce to
the city merchants. At the same time, because the French did not
provide any local government, the landlords took over many of the
functions of the old village oligarchies. They arbitrated disputes
among the peasants, assisted them with money for the ceremonies of
birth and death, kept order among them, judged, fined, and pun-
ished them, often with the help of their own private militia forces.
As one landlord described their role in the 1930's:

The landlord acted not only as owner and lessor of land but as an informal administrator, like chief of a small state. . . . The relationship
between the landlord and his tenants was paternalistic. The landlord
considered the tenant as an inferior member of his extended family.
When the tenant's father died, it was the duty of the landlord to give
money to the tenant for the funeral; if his wife was pregnant, the landlord gave money for the birth; if he was in financial ruin, the landlord
gave assistance; therefore the tenant *had* to behave as an inferior member
of the extended family. The landlord enjoyed great prestige *vis-à-vis* the
tenant.[6]

The manorial system of the south did not represent good government, for if surplus labor was available, the landowner could replace his tenant — his "sons" — or drive them into ruin at will. At
the same time it represented *a* government, a *system* of domination
based in economic reality and on the traditional model of government such as did not exist for the small peasant proprietors after the
passing of their communal village institutions.

Since the French Indochina War, however, these local governments — landlord and sect — had been on the decline. As a conscious
political policy, the Viet Minh had assassinated or driven into flight
a great number of the large landlords. The Diem regime in its turn

attacked the Hoa Hao and the Cao Dai, thus crippling the two most powerful non-Communist organizations in the south. The Diemist officials supported the landlords in their attempts to retake their domains, but they could not absolutely restore the old landholding patterns or traditions any more than they could erase all the other socially disruptive effects of the French war. With some foresight, many landlords remained in Paris, Saigon, or the provincial capitals, and hired agents or bribed officials to collect their rents. As this system was not very efficient, land rents never again reached their prewar range in those areas the Viet Minh had controlled.[7] Then, in 1956, the Americans finally pushed through a land reform program limiting all landholdings to one hundred hectares and fixing a rent ceiling at 25 percent of the value of the year's crop. The Diem regime never actually managed to implement either the land law or the rent ordinance, but the very fact that Diem attempted such a reform gave the landlords a renewed sense of their insecurity.[8] Many of the larger landlords now tried to sell out, though it meant prejudicing their position in the community. It was left to the NLF only to deliver the last blow with a really efficient land reform program that directly or indirectly affected some 90 percent of the villages in the Delta.[9]

With the disappearance of the powerful landlords and the sects, the entire political picture of the Delta changed. The effects were noticeable even before the NLF achieved their land reform program and even in those areas that were the most highly garrisoned by the Saigon government.

Harsh as their rule might have been, the landlords had at least some interest in maintaining their authority over the peasants on a basis other than that of coercion. Known, and in a Confucian sense "respected" by their tenants, they constituted a truly conservative force. When the new officials came from the "out there" of Saigon (as opposed to the "in here" of the village), they brought the instability of the national government down to the most parochial of the rural districts. Because they were *not* the established leaders of the village to which they were assigned, the villagers received them much as they might have received proconsuls from a conquering foreign power. The change from the landlords to the bureaucrats demonstrated in concrete terms the change from a subsistence to a mercantile economy, and — or so it seemed from the villagers' reports — brought that awareness of the outside world, that rise in "political consciousness" that the NLF otherwise had to take pains to achieve through political education. In attempting to establish their rule over the villages, the government-appointed village chiefs sometimes gained support from a few of the villagers (often those who hoped to use them and were capable of paying the necessary bribes). But in doing so they almost automatically alienated all of the other villagers. Their very presence in the village touched off a disturbance that spread like the ripples around a flung stone. In telling how he came to join the NLF one young defector described this process perfectly:

In 1956–7 life was pretty easy, villagers had motorcycles. Then came law 10/59. Under this law Diem was given the right [*sic*] to cut off heads of persons suspected of being VC sympathizers. This actually happened in hamlets near mine. Many people were worried. In March 1960 there was a big football game between my team and another team. The two teams fought and were mad with each other. Because the families of some of the boys worked for the government, I really believed they would take revenge on me. I was afraid and tried to hide. I went home. The VC knew that I had won the game, and they came to propagandize me. They said, "Look at you, you have got to hide, but you can't really hide. You have no arms. The people will catch you and hurt you." The VC dug a shelter for me to hide in.[10]

The initial conflict did not have to be all that serious. A game of football would do for those who did not play games except as a matter of life or death, for those who did not indulge in limited conflicts. As one Chinese proverb went, "If the small things are not taken care of, then there will be confusion and great plots." In other words, whatever the Diemist officials did or did not do, their very presence in the village would almost certainly, in the "natural order" of things, create opposition. When the NLF came to a village, they had but to look for a man within this opposition group who could, with training, recruit others. Then the Saigon government would take its turn. Hearing of a "Viet Cong presence" in the village, the province authorities would send more officials and recruit a platoon of "Self-Defense Guards" from that village or one of its neighbors — the result being that the disturbance would spread and a new group of people would become available for recruitment into the NLF. After a while the NLF would assassinate one or two of the Diemist officials or informers, drive away the defense guards, and take over the village. When the government reacted by sending its regular troops to punish the offenders and reassert control, the NLF and their supporters would have the villagers lay punji sticks and snipe at the troops, calling forth GVN fire upon the whole village. By a simple building of action upon reaction, the village would then belong to the NLF.[11]

After the disappearance of the landlords, the process of NLF recruitment was almost mechanical. Even the lowliest of the NLF cadres understood that the more men the Saigon government drafted, the more men would become available to them. In a sense the political success of the NLF did not depend upon the failures and inhumanity of Diemist policy — though Law 10/59 certainly helped — as much as it did upon a simple law of opposition. The NLF was the counterbalance without which the society would not have been complete — the Yang to the Yin of the government — except, of course, that neither force represented stability. In 1961–1962, as the government sent its officials into all parts of the country, the NLF grew from a series of committees, based in the jungles, mountains, and swamps, into a national organization that controlled perhaps a third of the rural population. In 1962–1964, as the GVN developed the Strategic Hamlet Program, the NLF began its shift from a relatively loose political movement into a formal replacement regime. In the succeeding two or three years, while the GVN doubled its armed forces from three hundred thousand to six hundred thousand, the NLF attained the strength that would make the Tet offensive possible. Like the government of India that in the early 1960's built a road through Nepal towards Tibet, the GVN had by all its vast efforts at "nation-building" and "rural construction" succeeded only in building an invasion route for the enemy.

And yet the success of the NLF was not merely a matter of action and reaction. The Diem land program had the negative effect of frightening the landlords and leaving the peasants without any local government. But the NLF program actually worked to the benefit of the landless. Instead of drafting a national law limiting the landholdings and rents, the NLF simply went about making as equitable as possible the distribution of land and rents in every village. Taking account of the extremely varied social and landholding patterns in the different parts of the Delta, they worked not so much to minimize the abuses of the existing system as to maximize the economic position of all the peasantry by every possible means, including that of terror. If a landlord refused to cooperate, or if the NLF felt his

death would serve a political purpose, he would be assassinated —
and usually in public. The use of violence against landlords seems,
however, to have been quite rare — in any case, nothing like that
used against GVN officials. In most cases the very large landlords
had already fled the countryside. As for the smaller owners — those
who worked some of their land and rented the rest out — the NLF
had strict orders to conciliate them. Often in the process of negotiation the small owners were allowed to keep all of their land as long
as they charged "reasonable" rents — in the area of 5 to 15 percent
of the current yield.[12] The NLF did not distribute land titles.
(Probably for two reasons: first, because it had not formally set
itself up as a government; secondly, because the titles would create
unnecessary conflict when the soldiers and the refugees eventually
returned home.) But it did give the peasants in a large part of the
Delta a right to the crops they produced and a sense of their own
bargaining power, their equality vis-à-vis the landlords.

The NLF land reform program had a strong impact upon the
peasantry. At the same time it did not seem to produce the large-
scale shift of support to the NLF that an American working on
humanitarian instincts might have predicted. It made the new
proprietors see the advantage of maintaining an NLF presence
somewhere in the neighborhood, but it did not by itself convince
them of the necessity of an NLF government, nor did it often persuade them to give up their hopes for a quiet, secure life and go out
to fight for the NLF. As the NLF cadres discovered, the peasants
did not initially make the connection between their own economic
situation and the national government. Even after the NLF had
driven the local landlords to flight, the people often remained submissive to the local officials and reluctant to involve themselves in
what they saw as a conflict between outsiders. To turn the villagers
into loyal partisans of the NLF was, in other words, a long project
requiring political education and organization.

The Approach: Children of the People

As the first step in establishing a base and fanning the fires of revolution, the Party began agitation of farmers to seek their own interests —
the right of owning land or reduction of land rent. This struggle, how-

ever, remained sporadic and weak and did not constitute a mass movement. To better meet the enemy, which remained strong in the village, the Party began the elimination of influence of the village notables and local security agents. However, it failed to follow this with the development of a mass base. The cadres thought that efforts to end the authority of the village leaders alone would be enough. The enemy succeeded in maintaining the village administration. In the face of such a situation the Party called for a meeting. We explained to the villagers the evil caused by village notables and security agents. We awoke the people to the fact that if the American-Diem clique succeeded in permanently maintaining the organization of village notables and security, soon Mister H, the cruel landlord, and others would return to the village to seize land and collect back rent. For that reason, we said, the farmers must eliminate the influence of the village notables and sweep away the security agents. At the same time we sought to win the sympathy of the families of the village notables (while we were urging the masses to rise up and eliminate the influence of the notables). It was a good method. After a while certain notables refused to work for the enemy and took the side of the people.

Thus, when our enemies tried to begin projects in the village no one would work for them. The US-Diem clique tried to win back the people by distributing drugs in the village. The offer was flatly rejected. Some of the people even debated openly and strongly with the enemy agents. Finally the Diem clique had to abandon the village, no village council could be maintained there.

— Extract from "Experiences in Turning XB Village in Kien Phong Province into a Combatant Village"; a People's Revolutionary Party document.[1]

To any American reading such a document it would seem that the Front cadre — if he were telling the truth — had left something out. How, after all, could mere propaganda have any effect on these (rightly) cynical and suspicious peasants? As much strangers to the village as the government agents, the cadres had come along and asked the villagers to join them in the desperate task of evicting those people who had always dominated the village, thereby exposing themselves to retaliation by the GVN. Why should the villagers have trusted them any more than they trusted the government officials?

When asked such questions, the villagers throughout South Vietnam tended to give one answer with great consistency: "The Liberation cadres (or, for the benefit of the Americans, "the Viet Cong") were nice to us . . . they behaved politely and nicely to the people . . . they talk to us in a friendly manner . . . they do not thunder at the people like the Government soldiers. . . . The thing that the people don't like about the Government officials is their behavior . . . the Viet Cong treat us well."[2] To the "hardheaded" American analysts of insurgency tactics, the fact that the NLF cadres were "nicer" than the government officials and soldiers hardly seemed an adequate explanation for the success of the NLF. Surely the peasants did not join the guerrillas because the guerrillas were polite. While most analysts agreed that the ARVN could help the war effort by refraining from rape, theft, and pillage, they could not quite see how good manners might translate into the hardware of "population control" and military recruitment figures.

Q. Have you any problems or reasons to be dissatisfied with your life . . . with the GVN cadres?

A. There was nothing for me to be dissatisfied with. Because of VC propaganda I joined the Front.

Q. What did you think were the differences between the Front and the GVN and their policies?

A. This was beyond my understanding.

From such remarks as these the analysts could only conclude that the recruit was concealing something. While it is impossible to ascertain the truth about any young man, it is highly probable that many were telling the whole truth, that the explanation for their desire to join the Front lay squarely within such testimony.

Even in the 1960's many South Vietnamese went through half a lifetime without having any personal contact with a government official.[3] The fact that the NLF cadres had sought them out and spent time talking to them made an impression on them such as Americans must find it difficult to imagine. To such young Vietnamese the NLF cadres were powerful people. They had weapons at their disposal, they brought the exciting air of the outside world with them — and yet they talked to the people of the village as if they cared for them and needed their support. Those young men who had met the GVN officials usually had not had at all the same experience with them. On the contrary, the GVN officials were often "haughty" and "arrogant": they made no effort to establish personal relationships or to show their concern for the people. As one former NLF propaganda cadre, who had covered seven provinces of the Delta, analyzed the GVN propaganda in 1965,

The substance is good but the propaganda cadres don't have an appropriate attitude in dealing with people. They aren't dressed the way the people are; the GVN armed propaganda cadres come to the village and swear and don't know how to gain people's sympathy. Their way of living and their behavior are different from those of the people. They work not as cadres but as officials.[4]

The Americans, who were by then organizing the propaganda campaigns of the GVN, believed in the "substance" of the propaganda. The villagers, by contrast, believed in what they saw with their own eyes: the GVN officials did not care for them. The GVN wanted not to win them over, but merely to rule them.

The GVN officials could not, of course, be blamed for their attitude. Without any form of political instruction (such as the NLF propaganda cadre simply took for granted), they tried to assume the traditional attitude of the mandarins, to become "fathers" to their people, and they did not know what to do when it did not work. Had they been allowed to follow their own inclinations and stay out of such villages, the irritation might not have been so great. But by 1962 the South Vietnamese armed forces had expanded to the point where the GVN was drafting proportionally as many men or more as the governments of such "developed" countries as the United States or Great Britain. The young recruits had perhaps as little allegiance to the Diem regime as to the government of Thailand or Burma. But the military machine kept grinding on, the recruiters filling up their trucks. The American advisers did not see that this recruitment posed a political problem. (Surely, the Americans said, the Vietnamese boys understood they had a duty to defend their country.) Ngo Dinh Diem did not see it as a problem that required a solution. (Did he not possess the Mandate of Heaven?) The two allies were blind to one another and therefore to the effects of their own actions.

The NLF meanwhile, as a matter of conscious policy, took a very different tack. One cadre described the policy in the most vivid of terms: "The soldiers came from the people. They were the children of the villagers. The villagers loved them, protected them, fed them.

They were the people's soldiers. If the soldiers love the people, the people will love the soldiers in return."[5]

Next to Ngo Dinh Diem's own paternalistic thesis about the role of government, the statement of this Front officer is indeed startling, for it sets the whole "family" of the nation upside down. Now, suddenly, it is the people who are the "parents" and the source of all authority, the soldiers who are the "children" and obedient to them. In reversing the whole order of society, the officer turned the Front army and bureaucracy into something much closer to the American military and civil "service" than to the traditional Confucian government. But there is a second message within the statement. Whereas Vietnamese mandarins had always taken the formal, Chinese father-son relationship as the model of statehood, this Front officer now seemed to be offering the Vietnamese mother-child relationship as a substitute. Because to him the soldiers came from the people — as a child comes from its mother's womb — so they should not live in a state of repressed conflict with the people, showing only their "self-control." Rather they should demonstrate their feelings and be nurtured with the permissiveness that characterizes the Vietnamese child's relation to his mother. If they did so, then "government" would come to mean something very different than it had ever meant to the villagers before.

Though the NLF did not always achieve this sort of harmony with the people, its cadres invested a great deal of effort in the attempt, for to the Vietnamese villagers it was not political theory but human behavior that counted. Of the Twelve Points of Discipline for the People's Liberation Army, eight concerned the conduct of the soldiers towards the civilian population: "Be fair and honest in business with the people. . . . Never take even a needle from the people. . . . When staying in civilian houses, maintain it as if it is one's own. . . . Be polite with the people and love the people. . . . Be respected and loved by the people."[6] Every Front member, whether he was a soldier, an officer, or a civilian cadre, had to obey the injunctions to "live together, eat together, and work together" with the people. NLF personnel, both military and civilian, were trained to treat civilians as members of their families, to include them within the circle of their trust and obligation. The cadres who lived for a while in one village would address the people in such familiar terms as *me* (mother), *bac* (uncle), *anh* (elder brother), and so forth, depending on their relative age.[7] To the villagers the very fact that the cadres would speak to them in a familiar manner indicated that they were not unapproachable authorities who might starve or exploit them at will.

Finally, a few Vietnamese-speaking American officials understood. By 1965 they managed to pressure the U.S. mission to pressure the GVN into creating a series of cadre teams to go into the villages and work with the villagers on political and civic action programs.[8] These new GVN cadres were to wear black pajamas, sleep, eat, and live with the people. They were to help the villagers with their tasks of building and harvesting, and get to know them, just as the Front cadres did. In preparation for this task, they had a twelve-week training course in political and social action conducted by a number of former Viet Minh officers who, unlike most of the GVN officers, had some notion of political education and some concern for the lot of the peasants.[9] By 1966 the number of these cadres had grown into the hundreds and, if one were to believe the public speeches of the high GVN and American civilian authorities, constituted the major hope for the pacification program. The Americans and the GVN had, in other words, put all their efforts into creating a line-for-line copy of the NLF teams.

But it did not work. Once out in the villages and away from their instructors, the GVN cadres tended to revert to the old habits of officialdom. They would grow long nails on their right hands — the mark of a man who did not work with his hands; they would strut about the village with their rifles on their shoulders or sit by themselves in the shade watching the villagers come and go from work. The villagers would call them "Mr. Cadre," not even knowing their names, much less using the familiar of "brother" or "sister." There were exceptions, of course, but only exceptions to the rule.

Seen from close at hand, the whole phenomenon was a curious one. The GVN cadres, after all, came from much the same part of the population that had produced the NLF cadres; many of them had brothers in the NLF or would spend some time in it themselves. They had received an equivalent amount of training — and still they could not behave like the Front cadres. The difference between them was completely inexplicable — except for one thing: the NLF cadres alone had the force of necessity behind them. When asked how the NLF treated the people of his village, one defector said with some irritation: "They lived on the people's support, so they had to be nice to the people; otherwise where would they get the supplies for feeding their people?"

The idea that a government depends on the support of the people must appear self-evident to an American, but it was a revolutionary concept for the Vietnamese. Though in theory the traditional empire derived its sovereignty indirectly from the people, it had in practice so little need for revenues as to be in peacetime almost autonomous financially — a ritual state suspended over the villages. As for the French colonial regime and the Diem government, they had been almost wholly supported, armed, and financed from abroad. Of all the political groups in Vietnam, only the Communists had renounced both the Confucian and the French colonial traditions in favor of the European concept of popular sovereignty. Unable to seize power by a simple coup in the capital city, the NLF, like the Viet Minh before them, put their doctrine into practice and relied upon the people for their own survival. It was this necessity that their cadres understood. Conversely, the GVN cadres who went into the villages in black pajamas were merely playing a part, and a part that most of them did not believe in. They were brought up to believe that the people needed them rather than vice versa, and their faith was confirmed by the fact that their job was to dispense American goods to the people and to build hamlet defenses for them that they themselves would never have to rely upon. It did not take very much economic theory for them to see that their superiors, the district and provincial officials, lived on the endless supplies of money and goods from abroad, and that without foreign goods, foreign weapons, and finally foreign soldiers, their cause would be lost. As for the people of the villages, they too understood the situation perfectly. Brought up to suspect all authorities, they could see from the behavior of the officials that the GVN had no compelling reason to treat them well — even though they might actually give them things from time to time. As the former NLF propaganda cadre reported:

People were favorable towards these [GVN assistance] programs, but they doubted they would get much because of official corruption. They did get something, but the VC told them that the GVN tried to gain their sympathy only during wartime. There are a lot of people who still believe the VC. The GVN must improve their way of giving so that the recipients will be more satisfied.[10]

While the GVN officials simply gave without asking, the NLF took the opposite approach — ironically, the same that President Kennedy took to the American people in his inaugural address of 1961. Instead of "giving generously" and showing their "self-control" as "superior men," they asked the people for support and explained that they had an ulterior motive for their good conduct. By reversing their roles with the villagers and becoming the "children of the people," the NLF cadres gave the villagers a position of power such as they had not had even in the days of the empire. Once the cadres had convinced the villagers that they behaved well *out of necessity*, the villagers let down their traditional defenses, trusted them, and tended to believe their propaganda — often despite evidence that belied it.

Q. What has prompted the people to support and join the Front?
A. It is a social problem. The population believes that the GVN does not care for them. For instance, [Vietnamese] physicians treat the villagers with contempt, though they pocket their money. The Front accordingly made propaganda to the effect that those who go to the hospital will die sooner because of the injections they get there. . . . A villager who receives from an American's hand medicine which will cure his illness will believe in the Americans without daring to express it. And later on when the Front puts out some anti-American propaganda, he will no longer believe it.[11]

As if by magic, the Front cadres had undermined the best of the American aid programs. Alchemists, they had transmuted something into nothing, and nothing into something — giving "jam tomorrow" a reality that "jam today" lacked for the villagers. But their alchemy was no mere sleight of hand. They had made a bargain with the villagers, and, as individuals, they paid for it by renouncing all claims to rank and privilege, all rights to feed at the great pipeline of American money and supplies. To become an NLF cadre a Vietnamese had to take what amounted to the oaths of poverty, chastity, and obedience. He had to renounce the city with its bright lights, its wealth, its cosmopolitan interests, and go to live, perhaps until death, in the poor, the boring, and the brutal world of the villagers.

Rebellion: Self-control Is the Root of Exploitation

To the French colons long resident in Indochina, the hesitations of General Leclerc and the new French government of 1946 to take action against the Viet Minh had seemed perfectly inexplicable. Why not attack Ho Chi Minh and end the whole foolish notion of Vietnamese independence once and for all? The idea as advanced by General Leclerc's staff, that there might be some military difficulty involved, that the war might cost France an unacceptable price in money and soldiers, appeared fantastic to them. Not only did Ho Chi Minh have no troops, but he faced the task of recruiting them from among "les Annamites," "les jaunes," from a people utterly lacking in military virtues, completely submissive before their masters, before Fate and *force majeure.* To the colons all that Leclerc had to do was to march a French army into Hanoi, cause a few heads to roll, and that would be the end of the rebellion. The Vietnamese knew their place, didn't they?

By the beginning of the second Indochina War in 1960, such sentiments were, of course, not so common among foreigners in Vietnam. Still, they did crop up occasionally among the American advisers to the ARVN, expressed in such phrases as, "With a division of American troops, what we couldn't do in this country. . . . Just give me one American battalion and this province would turn to the right of Calvin Coolidge." Certainly in 1965 some of the American commanders believed that the NLF and the North Vietnamese would surrender their hopes under the determined application of American airpower.

Such opinions might be dismissed as the product of racism or of the sense of superiority natural to an undefeated army — which in some sense they were. Still, to dismiss them outright would be to neglect certain pieces of evidence that the Westerners — and particularly the French — possessed about the Vietnamese.

For seventy years, from the time of the French conquest until the Second World War, fourteen thousand troops had sufficed to keep all of Vietnam under French rule. The French who had grown up in the colony could hardly have forgotten the Scholars' Revolt in Hue, the Yen Bay mutiny, and the other "nationalist" uprisings that had collapsed almost as soon as the governor called in the troops and showed that he meant business. And then they themselves had watched the tenant farmers crawling to their landlords with presents and obsequious speeches; they had seen the mandarins, who treated their inferiors with such disdain, humbling themselves before their French masters. Few Americans had ever seen the Vietnamese in such a situation — and few knew the Vietnamese as well as the French. Yet many of their in-depth interviews and sociological studies led them to a similar conclusion: that the NLF would disintegrate under stress and the war would be a short one.

Q. Do you know why the other people in your unit became active in the Front?

A. I think that they were like me, they were attracted by the VC propaganda that "The Revolution is ripe and the Front will win over the American imperialists." . . . At first . . . their morale was very high because the GVN troops had left, but . . . then when the GVN troops came often enough to my village, their morale became more and more low.[1]

In 1965 the RAND analyst, Leon Gouré, undertook a study for the American air force of the attitude of the Vietnamese civilian population to the widespread use of American air power in the south. On the basis of just such interviews he concluded that, rather than turning the population against the government, the bombing actually helped to destroy the people's confidence in the NLF. Quite contrary to American expectations, the villagers rarely blamed the GVN or the Americans for the damage. They assigned their sufferings to Fate, or they blamed the NLF for their inability to protect them. Gouré therefore recommended that the bombing be accelerated as planned.[2]

Q. Was your village ever attacked by aircraft?

A. Once . . . the Government troops were conducting an operation in the village. . . . The aircraft were flying very low (over a group of fishing boats). Some of the fishermen were scared and took off their clothes, preparing to dive. The aircraft suspected that they were VC and strafed the boats. . . . Six or seven died either of strafing or drowned.

Q. What did the families of the persons killed say?

A. They did not say anything. They said they had bad luck.[3]

One might question the validity of such interviews on the basis that the villagers were saying what they wanted the Americans to hear. But the NLF confirmed the existence of such attitudes in their own reports.[4] While Mr. Gouré's conclusions were questionable on humanitarian grounds, his analysis had an element of truth to it.

The traditional politics of the Vietnamese villager was that of accommodation. "The essence of small people is that of grass," wrote Confucius. "And when a wind passes over the grass, it cannot choose but bend." In the days of the old empire the people of the villages did their best to avoid participation in the power struggles of their leaders. They preferred to hold themselves impassive, secret, while the warlord armies passed by, and to commit themselves only when the struggle had already been decided in the heavens. As long as the new rulers guaranteed them a minimum of security, the villagers would accept their authority. To resist was to invite destruction, for the conflict, having no rules, could not be settled except by unconditional surrender. Even the high mandarins did not resist implacable force. If unable to "bend" and serve the new sovereign, they would accept the will of Heaven and commit suicide on the battlefield.

Brought up in the traditional manner, the villagers of the 1960's had learned that their very lives depended upon their "self-control," or, in Western terms, their ability to repress those feelings which might bring them into conflict with others. As children they played no contact sports. (When the Westerners brought football to Vietnam, they did not perhaps realize the difficulties the game might provoke.) As adults they took pains to avoid even the smallest argument with their neighbors.[5] Between father and son, superior and inferior, the relationship was even more delicate. When mistreated by his landlord, the tenant, for instance, would tend not to blame the landlord for fear that the conflict might finally break all of the bonds between them. Indeed, his emotion for the landlord might not surface in the conscious mind as anger: he would feel "shame" or "disappointment" that his own behavior or his own fate had brought him to such a low status in the eyes of the landlord. One former Front soldier gave an excellent illustration of this attitude:

Q. Tell me a little about your background.
A. I was the eighth of ten children and we were very poor. We had no

land of our own. I tended ducks for other people. We were moved around a great deal. Once I tried to save money and buy a flock of ducks to raise for myself, but I failed. I never married. Once I fell in love with a village girl, but I was so ashamed of my status that I did not dare declare my love to her.

Q. Were you angry at society because of this?
A. I thought if we were poor it was our own fault. I told myself that probably my poverty was the result of some terrible acts of my ancestors. I was sad but not angry.[6]

Such acquiescence before authority had its place within a stable, family-based community, where custom and community pressure insured a measure of economic and social justice. But within a disordered and unequal society, it hardened the status quo and denied not only the poor peasants but all Vietnamese not actually in power a voice in their country's future. The villagers often resented their government officials, but they made no complaints, for they saw them as instruments of the distant, implacable power of heaven or Fate which they had no means to influence. In the same way, the students of the Saigon university — the sons and daughters of the Diemist officials — made no protest against the Diem regime until the Buddhists led them to it. Like the poorest and most ignorant of the peasants, they simply assumed that they had no power to change the course of events.

Curiously enough, among all the political groups in Vietnam, the Communists alone recognized this political passivity as a *psychological* problem amenable to a psychological solution. One PRP directive made a very precise formulation of it:

Daily the masses are oppressed and exploited by the imperialists and feudalists and therefore are disposed to hate them and their crimes. But their hatred is not focused; it is diffuse. The masses think their lot is determined by fate. They do not see that they have been deprived of their rights. They do not understand the purpose and method of the Revolution. They do not have confidence in us. They swallow [*sic*] their hatred and resentment or resign themselves to enduring oppression and terror, or, if they do struggle, they do so in a weak and sporadic manner. For all these reasons agit-prop work is necessary to stir up the masses, to make them hate the enemy to a high degree, to make them understand their rights and the purpose and method of the Revolution, and to develop confidence in our capability.[7]

The solution of the Viet Minh, like that of the NLF, was the systematic encouragement of hatred. In 1946, just after the French broke off negotiations with the Democratic Republic in Hanoi, Ho Chi Minh began to make a series of speeches that now seem quite uncharacteristic of him. Usually the coolest and least emotional of revolutionaries, he denounced the French not only as colonial oppressors but as perpetrators of the most lurid crimes against women and children. On the battlefields as in the most remote of the villages, his cadres conducted a massive propaganda campaign to call forth the emotion of hatred. Reciting lists of the French crimes (no doubt both real and imaginary), they would produce evidence in the form of artillery shells or corpses and call upon the villagers to describe their sufferings in the hands of the "colonialists" and "feudalists."[8]

Hatred was the beginning of the revolution, for hatred meant a clean break in all the circuits of dependency that had bound the Vietnamese to the Westerners, the landlords, and the old notables.[9] Quite correctly the Party directive equated "hatred of the enemy" with the masses' "understanding of their own rights," for shame is anger turned against self. In calling upon the villagers to blame the "feudalists" and the "American imperialists and their lackeys" for their sufferings, the NLF was making a new map of the world on which the villagers might reroute their lives. The enemy was no longer inside, but outside in the world of objective phenomena; the world moved not according to blind, transcendent forces, but according to the will of the people.[10] In the idea that they might change their lives the villagers possessed a source of power more efficient than a hundred machine guns, for to blame Fate for all injustice was to fire into the air and render any weapon useless. As Ho Chi Minh said to the last of the French emissaries, "I have no army, I have no finances, I have no education system. I have only my *hatred*, and I will not disarm my hatred until I can trust you."[11] Hatred was the key to the vast, secret torrents of energy that lay buried within the Vietnamese people, to a power that to those who possessed it seemed limitless and indestructible. As the interview with one prisoner went:

Q. What about the fact that the GVN has planes, armor and artillery and the Front does not? What difference does that make?

A. It is only a matter of course. The French also had planes and armored cars, but they were defeated. The ARVN has had planes and armored cars for ten years and what have they accomplished? . . . In this war the decisive factor is the people. Weapons are dead things. By themselves they cannot function. It is the people who use the weapons and make them effective.[12]

The Saigon government could not match the NLF, for the systematic encouragement of hatred was a truly revolutionary act. In calling upon the peasants to hate their enemies, the Front cadres were asking them not merely to change their ideas but to disgorge all of the pent-up feelings they had so long held back, to fight what was to them the extension of parental authority and stand up as equal members of the society. To traditional Vietnamese the act was almost unthinkable, for it meant the end of patriarchal society — the end of society as they knew it — and the reversion to that state of bestiality where men have no leaders. Anger itself was a terrifying emotion. Vietnamese society had, after all, rested on the containment of anger, the suppression of conflict. As the Puritans of New England felt that the sexual drive, so long repressed, would prove uncontrollable if let loose in the society, so the Vietnamese regarded anger as a Pandora's box — fascinating and frightening at the same time — that, once opened, would plunge society into a limitless conflict.[13] And, unlike the Puritans, the Vietnamese had actually observed these outbreaks in their history.

After the rebellion of Le Qui Ly in 1400, and during the decline of the Le dynasty in the seventeenth century — indeed in all those periods when there were no strong leaders, no "fathers" to the people — the nation had fragmented. Bands of soldiers had roamed over the countryside, killing, raping, and looting. Like juvenile delinquents, the soldiers had used their energies in an orgy of destruction, wreaking havoc on the very villages that might have provided them with support. During those periods the soldiers had been equals — but equals in anarchy. As to what had happened to them, the PRP directive gave an important clue when it said the masses' "hatred is not focused; it is diffuse." Freed from strong authority, the soldiers had opened the sluice gates of their anger, releasing all the "shame," all the "disappointments" they had felt over a lifetime in their relations with all their superiors, including their own parents. Unchanneled, unregulated, their anger had burst through all of the Confucian restraints and flooded over into anarchic violence.[14]

In 1954, after a period of such anarchy, Ngo Dinh Diem thought to restore peace by reimposing strong leadership and suppressing the anger, the "egotism," and aggressiveness of his people. His was the natural reaction of a traditionalist — or indeed of even the most "Westernized" Vietnamese in Saigon. The difficulty was that patriarchal rule in any form no longer carried the same authority. Under pressure from the West the society had "split apart" to such a degree that many Vietnamese no longer obeyed their fathers, much less their village chiefs or their self-created emperor. Bent merely upon domination, neither Diem nor his officers would succeed in restraining their own soldiers from anarchic violence. The conflicts could no longer be suppressed. The dams had already broken of themselves, and no government could survive if it merely attempted to patch them up again. As Mao Tse-tung once wrote, "The force of the peasantry is comparable to that of raging winds or torrential rain. Its violence grows so rapidly, no power would be able to stop it. The peasantry will rip open all the chains that crush it; it will dash down the road to liberation."[15]

The revolutionary project of the NLF, like that of the Viet Minh and the Chinese Communists, was to use that released aggression as a creative force. The problem — the central problem — for the NLF was to provide a channel for that energy and to prevent it from exploding outward and destroying their own cause. The containment of violence had, of course, always been the problem for Vietnamese governments at war, and traditional Vietnamese had considered it a task of extraordinary difficulty. Confucius once said, "Only when men of the right sort have instructed a people for seven years ought there to be any talk of engaging them in warfare. . . . To lead into battle a people that has not first been instructed is to betray them."[16] To Confucius "instruction" meant not military training, but training in virtue, or, in modern terms, politics. And the principal strategy of the NLF consisted precisely in political instruction.

In the course of their denunciation sessions, for instance, the NLF called upon the villagers to focus their "hatred" and "resentment" upon certain specific objects: the "feudalists" and "the American imperialists and their lackeys," or, alternately, the "wicked tyrants" and "the reactionaries."[17] To most Americans the phrases sounded like nothing more than arid dogmatism: what, after all, could the words "feudalist" and "lackey" signify to villagers innocent of political theory? Nothing at all. And yet that was exactly the point: the words referred only to the people the NLF would later point out as examples of "feudalists" and "lackeys." The words did not — and the distinction was crucial — necessarily indicate the local hamlet chief, the platoon of Popular Forces, or the landowner who lived in the village. They did not even indicate the stray American AID man or district adviser who might come to the village to give out bulgur wheat and cooking oil — unless the NLF cadres said that they did. In other words, while the NLF cadres allowed the villagers to give free, verbal expression to their hatred, they gave them no immediate object for it: certainly not a defenseless minority (such as the Jews in Hitler's Germany) whom the villagers might murder as the scapegoat, the ritual vessel of all evil. And they did not on the other hand indicate an enemy that would appear overwhelmingly powerful to the villagers — an instrument of the will of Heaven. (As the young recruit, Huong, had said, "At first I hated only the Diem regime, then I hated its soldiers." He had begun to hate the soldiers only after he had joined the Front and been persuaded that, as the war extended beyond the borders of his village, he need not be discouraged by the immediate presence of a superior force.) By creating the enemy as an abstraction, the NLF gave itself the time to educate and discipline its recruits: the enemy would appear out of the distance of abstraction only when the recruits had learned to take discipline and to replace their "subjectivism" with a broader perspective on the concerns of the movement as a whole. The force of the NLF's argument was that, unlike the GVN troops, the peasants did not have guns and would not be given them until the instruction was completed.

For the NLF, the energies of "hatred" were to go first not into violence, but into the formation of a disciplined community. The Front's plan was to focus hatred upon an external enemy and thus to create unity among its own members. As the cadres of XB village pointed out, the mere thought of the outside enemy operated to reduce the internal conflicts within the village. To take up once more the story of XB village at the point where the Front had succeeded in evicting both the local landlords and the Diemist village authorities:

The Party unit developed and used this slogan: *"Kill the Land Robbers."* This slogan was welcomed and used by the local people. The farmers now know they have the force to prevent the landowners from retaking their lands and can prevent the US-Diem clique from oppressing the people. Farmers are now free to farm, without paying either land rent or agricultural tax. . . .

Victory came to the farmers and the people then enthusiastically joined the movement and put their confidence in the Party as the leader of the revolution.

However there were some clashes of interest, some discord. There was a dispute between two farmers over a small parcel of land and each threatened to kill the other. The Party stepped in and called a meeting of villagers to hear and solve the problem. A cadre pointed out that:

"Land comes as part of the revolution's achievements and as a result of the people's struggle. Farmers must remain united and share the good and bad. Because the American-Diem clique and the landlords plot to come back, farmers must make concessions to each other to ensure final victory. Only if these conditions are met will the farmers be able to take permanent possession of the land."

Upon hearing this the two farmers became enlightened, embraced each other and wept.[18]

The Front took the same approach to the problem of controlling the behavior of their soldiers towards the civilian population. Front soldiers were instructed not merely to avoid abusing the peasants. They were instructed to love them and to bring them into their own "families" so that the villagers would aid them in defeating the enemy that lay beyond the village. Conflicts had to be restrained because of the larger cooperative enterprise. And the soldiers seemed to understand this necessity. Sir Robert Thompson, the British counterinsurgency expert wrote, "Normally communist behaviour towards the mass of the population is irreproachable and the use of terror is highly selective."[19]

Thompson's statement must come as a surprise to an American audience after the many years of American propaganda about "Viet Cong atrocities," but it would be confirmed by any informed observer of the Vietnam War — particularly one familiar with the ARVN. Whatever the Front leaders felt about the value of human life as a moral absolute, their own self-interest dictated that they impose strict controls on the use of violence. For, unlike the American or the GVN troops, they depended on the goodwill of the villagers. Their task was easier than that of the GVN in some respects, since they had no bombers and their firepower was so limited that their commanders could never be tempted to use it in an indiscriminate fashion. In other respects their task was a great deal more difficult because of the thinness of communications and the demands of an irregular, guerrilla war. Political assassination, after all, formed a basic ingredient of Front strategy in GVN areas, and for the sake of its own security the Front had sometimes to execute men within its own ranks. From the point of view of the Front cadres themselves, this political violence was extremely dangerous in that it opened the way to an anarchic campaign of revenge killings such as the Diem regime had permitted. To preclude such a disaster the Front employed a multitude of institutional controls. In the first place, it used political re-education rather than violence as its principal means of dealing with hostile people. When it used violence, it placed the responsibility for it not with the regular soldiers and cadres but with the specialized and highly professional Security Section. As more than one U.S. government study showed, the Security cadre did not kill indiscriminately, but carefully calculated each of the assassinations for the maximum political effect. The lists of GVN officials to be assassinated or spies to be executed had to undergo long bureaucratic scrutiny before they could be put to use. The killings were then carried out in a cold-blooded manner by specially trained Armed Reconnaissance Teams. The NLF generally proscribed torture and preferred the bullet to any other means of dispensing death.[20] In its political violence as in its military operations the Front generally employed the principle of economy of force. Only once did it perpetrate political violence on a massive scale, and that was in Hue during the bloody battles during the Tet offensive of 1968. In the month that they occupied Hue the Front and the North Vietnamese forces murdered some three thousand civilians, including not only government officials, but hundreds of Catholics and members of other anti-Communist political parties and sects. It was this incident that gave President Nixon the major grounds for his prediction that the NLF would carry out a large-scale massacre of Vietnamese civilians if the Americans "abandoned" the GVN. But the attempt to generalize about Front policy from this incident was a dubious undertaking at best. The NLF high command undoubtedly planned to kill a number of GVN officials and other political enemies during its occupation of the city, but there is no clear evidence that it planned the mass slaughter that occurred. The manner in which the killings were performed indicated that in the confusion of the offensive the Security Section lost control and the NLF and the North Vietnamese military units operated without their usual discipline.* In any case, as even the RAND study used by Nixon pointed out, the incident offered a contradiction to normal Front practices over all the previous years of war and to Front behavior in the other cities and towns it occupied during the Tet offensive.[21] On the whole the Front maintained discipline even under the extraordinary test of the American war and even during its full-scale attack against the cities. The achievement testified to the strength of its organization.

* In the wake of the Tet offensive in Hue the GVN estimated that a total of 5,800 people were dead or missing. The vast majority of those deaths certainly occurred as the result of the Allied bombing of the city and the bloody battles between the U.S. Marines and the entrenched North Vietnamese divisions. The GVN authorities, however, later discovered 1,200 bodies buried in shallow mass graves within the city — a half of which, according to official reports, showed signs of deliberate execution: hands bound behind the back, and so forth. Later on the GVN discovered two more mass graves a long way from the city — one almost at the other end of the province — containing something over 1,200 bodies. Three NFL defectors reported witnessing the execution of about four hundred of these people. By piecing various bits of evidence together Douglas Pike concluded that the NLF cadres had taken these four hundred people — most of them Catholics — from their sanctuary in a church and had marched them out of the city. One NLF unit then executed twenty of them as a public example and slated the rest of them for a program of political re-education. Another unit then took charge of the prisoners, and, after wandering about the countryside with them for several days, killed them all. Pike believes this unit wished to dispose of the witnesses to the previous crimes, but it seems more than likely that in fleeing the American forces the unit saw the prisoners as an impediment to its progress and a threat to the local organization.

According to other evidence, the assassination of certain GVN officials, VNQDD leaders, and former Can Lao Party members was performed under orders from the NLF Security Section. The other killings do not appear to have been planned at all. A report from the Front Security Section in Quang Tri province indicated that many of the security cadres questioned the mass execution of those who had already "surrendered" to the troops on the grounds that this was inconsistent with NLF policy. Other reports indicated that the responsible units did not execute the right people in the city. The Tet offensive clearly created intense confusion and terror on all sides. Members of the NLF local forces and hangers-on, as well as members of other political groups, may have used the period of confusion as a chance to revenge themselves on old enemies. Since the days of Diem, Hue had, after all, been hot with political passions — so much so that it seemed to be the prism for all of the political conflicts throughout the country.

Organization: The Liberated Village, the NLF Command Structure, and the PRP

> Prior to the seizure of power, and in order to seize power, the sole weapon of the revolution and the masses is organization. The salient feature of the revolutionary movement led by the proletarian class lies in its sophisticated organization. All activities aimed at leading the masses to advance step-by-step toward the uprising to overthrow the ruling clique can be summed up as organization, organization and organization.
>
> — Le Duan, February 1970[1]

Apart from military strategy, the one aspect of the NLF that the American counterinsurgency scholars investigated in any detail was its organization, both civil and military. Among others, Douglas Pike, Michael Charles Conley, and W. P. Davison of the RAND Corporation[2] wrote exhaustive studies of the organization of the combat villages, the Liberation Army, the NLF command structure, and the Communist Party within the NLF. Pike, for one, justified this special concern by arguing that organization was the most important component of the revolution. As he wrote in the preface to his study: "If the essence of the Chinese revolution was *strategy* and the essence of the Viet Minh was *spirit*, the essence of the third-generation revolutionary guerrilla warfare in South Vietnam was *organization*." And then later, "The Communists in Vietnam developed a sociopolitical technique and carried it to heights beyond anything yet demonstrated by the West working with developing nations. The National Liberation Front was a Sputnik in the political sphere of the Cold War."[3]

The subject of NLF organization was clearly of great interest to the U.S. government. At the same time it had a more general interest, for, under the circumstances — that is, the necessity to fight both a domestic enemy and a vast foreign power within a very small space — the success of the NLF rested heavily on its ability to mobilize the population into a disciplined and coherent force. As Pike himself showed most convincingly, the task of organization for the NLF involved not merely the creation of a command structure but the transformation of the life of the villages.

With such a fruitful subject in hand, Pike and his colleagues ought to have had some interesting insights into the whole problem of government and society in Vietnam. But their conclusions are curiously underdeveloped. Indeed, insofar as they draw any conclusions at all, they tend merely to support the claims of State Department propagandists that the NLF used foreign methods of organization in order to coerce a passive and generally apolitical peasantry. The same charge, however, might just as well be leveled against the GVN, and it begs the question of what made the NLF, by contrast to the GVN, such a powerful political and military force. The conclusion is inadequate; at the same time it is foregone by the nature of the materials used to reach it. Pike and his colleagues conducted their analyses in a void without reference to the nature of Vietnamese society or to the problems besetting it in the twentieth century. Thus their analyses are wholly misleading. In the absence of any information to the contrary, South Vietnam in their work appears to possess a stable, thriving traditional society and an adequate government. Against this background the NLF emerges as a sinister, disruptive force that has no local basis in legitimacy, and that quite possibly is the arm of a larger and more sinister power trying to impress similar methods of organization upon all nations throughout the world.

To look at the organization of the NLF within the context of Vietnamese society in the 1960's is to charge the same group of facts presented by Pike and his colleagues with an entirely different meaning. It is to see that the NLF strategies constituted not an arbitrary system of domination but, in many respects, solutions to problems that neither the GVN nor the indigenous political groups had been able to solve.

One of the central problems, of course, was the disintegration of village society. The traditional Vietnamese village was in a special sense a collective enterprise. Though each family owned its own land, the village operated as a unit to a great degree. The village council was responsible for the upkeep of the local dike system, for the collection of taxes, for the management of communal lands, for the administration of charity and emergency relief, and for the arbitration of disputes. The family heads usually gave a certain proportion of their crop to the village council for storage in case of a general emergency and banded together in mutual-aid societies for the defraying of certain large, irregular expenses, such as house-building and the ceremonies of marriage and death. The extended families, a handful of which made up the village, also owned land whose produce would be used for the perpetuation of the rites and for the general welfare. This intensive form of cooperation among individuals within the extended family and the village existed in a particular social and psychological landscape radically different from that of, let us say, a New England township. Vietnamese villagers identified themselves not as individual "souls" but as members and dependents of the collectivity. A villager might have said with Paul Valéry, "Every man here feels that he is both son and father . . . and is aware of being held fast by the people around him and the dead below him and the people to come, like a brick in a brick wall. He holds. Every man here knows that he is nothing apart from this composite earth."[4]

The disintegration of the traditional villages under the French regime brought disaster for the individual Vietnamese farmer. By the 1930's the numbers of beggars, paupers, and prostitutes had increased to the point where even the French administration noticed it.[5] The villages no longer provided any social welfare system, any sanction against glaring inequalities in the distribution of land, or any institution of cooperative work. The villagers lived at the mercy of the weather, their neighbors, merchants, and, most important, the nation-state. After the worldwide depression of the 1930's the rice consumption of the poor peasants in the "rice bowl" of Cochin China dipped below subsistence level.[6] In 1945 a million North Vietnamese peasants died because the French and Japanese administrations had neglected to fill the emergency rice granaries in the north and the war prevented any shipments of rice from the south. Even for those who did not suffer starvation or penury the psychological consequences of the breakdown of the village were severe, for the collectivity, that "brick wall," had been the very *raison d'être* of individual existence. Without it, the individual descended into a kind of chaos, separated not only from society but, as it were, from his own soul. It was not so much anticolonialism as the need to re-establish some form of community that led the peasants of the north and the south to join the sects and the Viet Minh at the period of the Indochina war. Anticolonialism was, in fact, only a means to the end of this new community.

In the south after the war the Ngo family had in a confused manner attempted to revive the old collectivity. The attempt was doomed to failure, for the old authorities of the family had been quite superseded by the new economy and the new state. Working at cross-purposes to the Ngos, the American AID representatives had, during the Diem regime and later, made certain small attempts to reform the villages along new lines with farming cooperatives, self-help projects, and finally, in 1966, with the institution of village elections in the "secure" areas. But their efforts were largely abortive. The self-help projects fell away into inertia, the cooperatives disintegrated into factional feuds, and the elected village chiefs proved hardly more effective in solving village problems than their appointed predecessors. The villagers did not trust each other, much less the government above them. To organize them to work together involved not merely the demonstration of the economic feasibility of a project but the changing of their whole perspective on the functioning of society. The West had undermined the authority of the patriarch: but the program of the ancestors remained nonetheless as an invisible obstruction, preventing the villagers from organizing as equals and from accepting the authority of the government. The American AID representatives had success only when they worked with one villager at a time or when they worked in conjunction with the Hoa Hao or the Catholics, the only two non-Communist groups that by the mid-1960's had extensive organization in the rural areas. The plight of the nonsectarian villagers was all the more pathetic by comparison. In 1967 one of the Mekong tributaries flooded through several provinces of the western Delta, destroying vast areas of paddy land and burying whole villages under layers of mud. Even before the river had subsided, the Hoa Hao leaders were demanding aid from the government, organizing rescue teams and doling out food to the stranded villagers. In the space of a few weeks they had organized a labor force from among the sect members in two provinces to rebuild the villages and dig new irrigation canals. Their villages slowly recovered, but the nonsectarian villagers in the area continued to suffer from disease and near starvation despite the American attempts to deliver aid from Saigon.

Within their limited areas the sects had for a time managed to solve some of the problems of the village. But the extent of their authority was limited, and they depended on foreign assistance for their very survival. The problems of the village were, finally, national problems, and the NLF alone among the southern political groups offered a solution on a national scale. Its methods were indeed "foreign"; they were derived from the Leninist tradition as elaborated by Stalin, Mao Tse-tung, and finally, Ho Chi Minh. But they proved more successful in dealing with the particular, local situation than the equally foreign methods of the GVN.

In most cases the NLF had to begin their work of organization by undermining and finally expelling government authority. Thus it is interesting to take a close look at the whole process of how the insurgents took over a village and established their control. The take-over of Ich Thien village provides a good case study, not because Ich Thien was a typical village but because politically there was every reason to suppose the NLF would not be successful there. It had no Viet Minh tradition and for three years it was one of the model settlements of the Diem regime. (And then the narrator of the story of Ich Thien is an NLF defector who had small love for the Front after its cadres fired him from his position as head of their administrative committee.)[7]

Not many miles from the resort town of Dalat, Ich Thien village comprised one of the few successful land development centers the Diem regime had built for non-Catholics. In 1961, two hundred and twenty-five families from the coastal plains of the center had come to settle there in the highlands and to farm the land the government had cleared for cultivation. Allotted a small acreage, they were given enough money to tide them over until the first harvest and the rights to all the jungle land they could clear and till for their own use. After three years of good harvests, the farmers — most of them former landless laborers — had achieved a degree of prosperity they had never known before: they built substantial houses, bought buffaloes for the plowing, and new clothes for the women and children. To them the land development center had every virtue but one. As one farmer — I shall call him Mr. Buu — described the source of the trouble:

An official from the Office of the General Commissioner for Land Development was . . . in full charge of the area. . . . The area chief (as he was called) could distribute money and materials to whichever family he wanted and refuse to give it to whoever he wanted. It was the area chief who ordered that family records and identification cards be made. He could refuse to give these extremely necessary papers to whichever family he disliked and that family would have no place to turn. The people's fate lay in the hands of the area chief.

The area chief . . . was a very wise man. Outwardly, he seemed very nice, gentle with everyone, but inwardly he was corrupted and siphoned off aid such as flour, penicillin and milk and so on.

Besides growing rubber trees in the land they had been given, the villagers cleared more land to grow corn, potatoes, manioc, etc. They went to the jungle to gather firewood, bamboo shoots, and honey. The people were forced to sell all these products to the area chief at a very low price. The area chiefs in turn sold these products to the dealers at high prices. The people knew about this, but there was no way they could stop this exploitation.

The other officials . . . were no better. They often caused trouble to the people, such as each time someone wanted to leave the Land Development Center, he had to obtain a certified statement of his absence. The absent person couldn't receive his food money for the day he was absent . . . but he still had to sign the paper to certify that he had received his food money for that day so that the officials could pocket the money. And so the people couldn't like these officials. They were afraid of them because their lives were directly related to the officials of the office of the General Commissioner for Land Development."[8]

Beginning in 1963 the NLF cadres began to come to the center occasionally at night to talk to the families in the hamlets nearest the forest. Before a year had passed, they were coming every two or three nights. From time to time the guerrilla units would surround one of the hamlets so that the cadres, with the help of their newly recruited supporters in the village, could hold a general meeting to explain Front policies. By the end of 1964 the GVN officials, including the area chief, no longer dared to spend the night at the center. The twenty government defense guards hid in their outpost every time the NLF appeared. Finally in February 1965 a large number of Front troops came to surround the entire center. The defense guards hid their weapons and fled. The next morning the guerrillas deployed themselves around the center, leaving only a few armed cadres inside. These cadres then called the people together and proclaimed the dissolution of the "illegal local government of Ich Thien village" and raised the Front flag on a pole.

In Ich Thien village the Front had no need to employ violence against the government authorities. Its cadres had already prepared the way carefully, making friends among the villagers and gathering intelligence and explaining their policies — making the kind of contact with the villagers that the government officials had never bothered to make. But for the Front there was no question of "rooting out the infrastructure" of government. The GVN officials had never had any roots in the village.

Once their military forces had taken control of the village, the Front cadres took steps to sever the last political and administrative ties the village had with the GVN. In the first week they collected the villagers' government identification cards and classified all of the villagers according to the extent of their former contacts with the GVN officials. The hamlet and interfamily group chiefs were compelled to attend "re-education" courses for a period of a week to a month. At the same time they kept close watch over the villagers' movements to and from the village.

These security measures were, of course, much the same as those the GVN took. By themselves, however, they were of little use, for the Front did not maintain full military control of the area. After a few days the regular forces departed, leaving only a few guerrillas behind, who hid when the regular GVN forces appeared to make sweeps through the village. Militarily, in other words, the Front was in precisely the same situation as the GVN when it had controlled the village a month or so before. The difference was in the attitude of the villagers. When the GVN troops searched the village, they found nothing but an occasional empty combat trench. The villagers protected the Front cadres because, as Mr. Buu said simply, they trusted them. But Mr. Buu's explanation was perhaps too simple.

After the meeting at which they declared the "illegal government" dissolved, the Front cadres called another meeting and asked the villagers to choose a man who was "talented, virtuous, clean, and capable," to act as chairman of an administrative committee to manage the affairs of the village. Under Front direction the villagers unanimously elected Mr. Buu and approved the appointment of Front cadres to a council to take charge of security, finance, education, and propaganda in the village. Not long afterwards they called yet another meeting to ask the villagers to join a series of associations: one association was for farmers, another for youth, a third for women, and a fourth for old people. Over the next two months the Farmers' Association became an active force in the life of the village. Organized into cells of seven to nine people, the farmers took turns doing the farm labor that required a collective effort and helped each other to increase the harvest.

At the same time the Front cadres gave great attention to political instruction. During the frequent association and hamlet meetings and in the course of the collective activities, they explained that the people of the village "belonged to the Very Poor Class and so they should stand up to lead the proletariat class to struggle against the governing capitalist class, which was the Americans, and their lackeys who called themselves Nationalists."[9] When Mr. Buu was asked whether the people of the village understood the doctrine of the class struggle, he replied that he did not know, but that since the cadres used appealing words and supported their arguments with concrete facts, the people liked to listen to them: they remembered how corrupt the area chief had been and they began to feel hatred for the class that oppressed both them and the landless peasants all over South Vietnam.

The propaganda campaign and the activities of the Farmers' Association bore tangible fruit when the Front cadres began to exact "contributions" in food from the villagers to feed their troops. Most of the villagers did not make the contributions with enthusiasm, but they at least understood, as few of their compatriots had ever understood of the government taxes, that there was a reason for the exactions. Moreover, they could not suspect favoritism or injustice in the collections. Thanks to the rotation of duties within the Farmers' Association, most of the farmers knew exactly how much food each family produced, and they saw that the Front cadres levied it from each family in fair proportion.

Within the space of three months the Front cadres had — despite the comings and goings of the government troops — managed to bind the villagers to them by a series of fairly strong ties. Rather than substitute one bureaucracy for another, they set up an organization that brought the villagers into a new relationship with government authority and with each other. Through their constant meetings, their private talks with the villagers, and their organization of collective work, they had established a network of personal contacts much more dense than the village had ever known. If only because they dared not break the balance of intelligence, the villagers protected both the Front cadres and each other from the government troops. To the extent that they kept this trust, they increasingly boxed themselves into a series of obligations, one of which led to another. They voted in the Front elections, worked on the Front's projects, and made contributions to the upkeep of the Front troops. They might not have wholeheartedly supported the Front, but they were at least committed to it by occupation. Mr.

Buu and others served on the administrative committee, and some of the young men helped the local guerrillas. Who then was a "member of the Front" and who was not?

Certainly the government authorities could not make the distinction. After three months of running fruitless operations through the village, the Allied command sent out a group of helicopters to strafe one of the hamlets where, as it happened, there were no Front guerrillas. In twenty minutes the pilots managed to burn down thirty-five houses and kill nine of the villagers, including two children and three old people. When the Front organized a committee from among the villagers to go to district headquarters and demand reparations for the damages, the delegation was turned away by the district chief. Six months later a large force of government troops swept through the village and took all of the remaining families away with them to a government-controlled area. The GVN had removed the villagers in order to remove the NLF.

The Front controlled Ich Thien village for only a few months, but there were many scores of villages in Vietnam where it maintained control for over a period of years. The development of these villages followed essentially the same lines that the cadres had drawn in Ich Thien village. The end product of this development was a complex, specialized organization capable both of defending itself and of supporting the weight of a regime at war.

For the ordinary people of the village, Front control meant a gradual change in the patterns of daily life. Before the focus of life had been the family; now it was the hamlet and the village. In villages more secure than Ich Thien, every person over the age of seven would belong to a community organization and participate in community projects. Each household belonged to an interfamily group and a hamlet association; each individual belonged to a Liberation Association. Of these last, the Farmers' Association continued to be the most important. Its members organized the collective work of digging irrigation ditches or constructing the village defenses. They also arbitrated land disputes and assessed taxes on rice crops. The Women's Association took care of the Front soldiers who passed through the village and helped those families whose sons had joined the regular forces. Certain young women were specially trained to proselyte the young men of the village and the local GVN troops. Members of the Youth Association — many of whom would later join the Front forces — carried messages and acted as guides to the regular Front troops. Where the defense of the village or the hamlet was concerned, men, women, and children participated either by collecting intelligence on the local GVN troops or laying out primitive defenses such as punji sticks and nailed boards. Each hamlet had a squad or more of self-defense forces and each village an armed militia.[10] In addition, the village would probably have a small factory or workshop for the production of Front uniforms, medicines, or small arms.

The Front village was a cooperative agricultural center and military base. It was also a training camp for the new members of the revolution. In every village the cadres formed schools, classes for illiterates, and centers for the dissemination of news and propaganda. In most of them they would begin small theatrical and singing groups or bring in groups of entertainers from the outside to enliven the continual round of political education meetings. The secure Front village would usually possess its own mimeograph newspaper or information center to relay the news of the war and to bring the villagers into contact with the outside world. In these villages the Women's Association would organize health education classes and set up small maternities and medical dispensaries. The youth groups would engage in sports programs and train their members to enter the regular guerrilla forces.

The government of the villages remained in the hands of Front cadres — most of whom were, after 1964, members of the People's Revolutionary Party. In the beginning, these cadres would retain strict control over the administrative committee and in particular over the security, finance, and propaganda sections. The government of the village was unquestionably authoritarian, but it worked in a very different manner from the government of the GVN villages. While the GVN village chiefs pursued their impossible task of ruling the villages as they were, the Front attempted to remake them so that they might rule themselves.

As was the case in Ich Thien village, the first act of the cadres in taking over a village was usually to call a meeting and have the villagers elect one of their number as chairman of the administrative committee. These elections were not free, for the cadres chose the candidates. At the same time, the cadres took care to choose people whom the villagers respected. The cadres continued to control the committee and to initiate policy, but they would gradually train local men to take over the day-to-day work of administration. At first they would train farmers for the simple tasks of gathering villagers for a meeting or handing out propaganda leaflets. After a while they would turn over to them the more complicated tasks of collecting taxes, making speeches, recruiting new partisans, and administering the informal welfare program. As the villagers proved themselves competent to perform these tasks, the cadres retreated further and further into the background. For the NLF, the creation of a local administrative staff served an important function. It slowed, if it did not stop, the whole chain reaction of fear and hostility that the presence of any one bureaucrat would have set off in the village. The Front cadres *were not* the hereditary village chiefs, any more than were the Diemist officials, but they at least did not take on the position of supreme paternal authority. Partly concealed behind the administrative staff, they intervened in village affairs only indirectly — to initiate programs and policies, to direct the education and propaganda work, to see to village security, and to arbitrate disputes that could not be resolved by the villagers. By holding themselves above the relationship between the villagers and their "elected" officials, they could arbitrate between both parties while continuing to develop the Front organization in the village.

The obvious question of whether or not the villagers "liked" the Front government is impossible to answer directly. The villagers under Front control were engaging in an extremely complicated process, the end of which they themselves could not visualize. More importantly, the question did not pose itself to them in abstract terms. When asked whether they liked the Front, the low-level defectors and prisoners would usually reply in terms of whether or not the war had gone badly for them. Many peasants, for instance, objected to the Front taxes, which became increasingly high after the arrival of the American troops. Others objected to having their time taken by labor on the tunnel and fortifications. Still others objected to the Front government because of their concern that the GVN or the Americans would reoccupy the village, and a great many objected to having their houses bombed or shelled by the Americans. These same people, however, welcomed the Front when it appeared to be winning. Beyond them were the loyalists who looked upon the Front as the only true system. Because of this diversity of opinion, it is perhaps more useful to look at what internal changes the Front made in village life.

American officials and scholars have always emphasized the coercive aspects of the Front government. And the Front was in many
respects coercive. When the Front cadres came into the village, they
gave the villagers very little choice in the matter of whether or not
they would join Front organizations and accept their authority.
With the sanction of armed force behind them, these highly trained
political cadres could, and often did, put pressure on recalcitrant
individuals by keeping them under surveillance, by threatening
them with "re-education," or some other form of isolation from the
community. Often the Front would assassinate a GVN official as an
"example" to the villagers of what might happen if they decided to
work for the government. Violence, and the threat of violence, was,
however, most frequently employed when Front control was weak:
that is to say, when the Front took over a new village or when a
contested village came under heavy attack and the villagers threatened to leave for a more secure area. In these situations the villagers
could, and often did, protest to the cadre in a way that they never
would have dared to protest to a government village or district
chief. In the end, though, they had only the resort of collective
noncooperation and passive resistance. With the Front this tactic
often worked, as it did not with the GVN officials when they had
sufficient military support.[11]

But American charges of coercion reached beyond the war policies of the Front and extended to the system of government itself.
American officials spoke of the lack of freedom in Front elections,
the secret control of the Front cadres responsible to higher echelons,
and the oppressive nature of the collective institutions. Much of this
talk was sheer propaganda deduced from the official premise that all
South Vietnamese hated the Communists, and that the Front operated by terror alone. (The question of who was to terrorize the
terrorizers made this premise illogical as well as inexact.) Still, not
all of the talk was propaganda. Much of it was the result of American attempts to assess the Front system in American terms without
reference to Vietnamese values. Many American officials simply
assumed that the Vietnamese would oppose the Front system because it was "not democratic," that is, because it did not operate by
majority rule. But if they had looked about them, they would have
noticed that no Vietnamese government or political party had ever
operated by majority rule. To most Vietnamese of the twentieth
century the idea that a government ought to give the people a

choice on its very makeup appeared quite absurd. If a government did not know what it was and what it wanted, then it was no government at all. Of course, if it made the wrong choices, then it would be a bad government, but majority rule meant nothing more than chaos and "confusion."

With all of its political education programs and its organizational work, the Front was attempting to create the conditions for a new unanimity — and a unanimity not of passive acceptance but of active participation. In a sense the anonymity of the Front apparatus in the village was less of a deception than an explanation of what the Front was trying to do. Rather than take the villages for their own personal fiefs, the cadres were creating a system that operated by a set of impersonal standards. The aim of their work in the village was to train local people and to educate local sentiment to the point where the villagers could govern themselves, and they, the teachers, could actually leave the village. The "election" of the administrative committee chairman demonstrated that intention to the villagers from the very beginning. To the villages the Front offered not majority rule, but an equal opportunity for advancement by merit — or what the Confucian sovereigns had offered only the mandarin class. Besides that, they offered all of the villagers a system of predictable rewards and punishments that applied to everyone equally, including themselves. And many villagers understood that. While they referred to the GVN officials by their names or titles, they usually spoke of the Front cadres as an organization ("the Front cadres," "the Liberation men," "the Viet Cong"), the implication being that *whoever* the cadres were, they would treat the villagers impartially, that the village would be run not by private whim but by public policy. (As one government-sponsored study showed, the villagers, when they criticized the Front, would usually criticize Front policy rather than the cadres themselves, whereas the reverse was true of their criticisms of the GVN.)[12]

As for the Front's mass organizations and its demands for political conformity, an American might well find these oppressive — though not perhaps to the extent imagined, if he were fighting for the life of his country. But many of these same demands had been made upon the Vietnamese by the traditional village and family collective. One of the aims of the Front was to restore some of the old powers of the village council. The mature Liberation village would possess its own treasury and tax collection agency, a council for the arbitration of land and other disputes, and its organizations for social welfare and collective work. But the Front was not merely trying to restore the old villages. It was attempting to create a community of individuals rather than of families. In the Liberation Associations men, women, and children had to work with their peers. In the beginning the villagers often felt some anxiety about working with people who after all did not belong to their families — but under peaceful conditions these difficulties did not seem to last long. As a result of the system of rotation in the working groups, a large number of villagers finally had the opportunity to take on responsibility and learn basic management skills. At the same time they learned the bureaucratic — and democratic — concept of interchangeable parts; the idea that power resides not in the man himself but in the job he temporarily fills. The idea, or rather the sense of the idea, was an important one in that it led on one hand to the capacity to work with strangers and on the other to the basic and revolutionary notion of human equality. The cadres of the new generation might finally understand and accept the fact that they were not the "fathers" but the "children" and the "servants" of the collectivity.

The project of the Front was not merely to reorganize the village but to broaden the villagers' horizons so that they, even if they remained confined to a certain place, took part in the life of the nation. The undertaking was a revolutionary one and it required — particularly in time of war — the kind of intervention in daily existence to which the villagers were not at all accustomed. While the GVN contented itself with broadcasting messages about the horrors of Communism and the wonders of "freedom," the Front cadres took every opportunity to talk to the people about the political struggle and to make the connection between their own activities of building roads or hamlet defenses and the future of the country as a whole. Depending on the quality of the cadres involved, all of this talk and activity could confer a sense of excitement and importance to life within the village — or it could be a terrible bore. In either case, however, it was not a matter of empty words, for though the villagers remained where they were, they were not as far from the city as they once had been. The villages were not merely the agricultural bases but the cities for the NLF.

As an authoritarian and a revolutionary organization, the Front quite clearly depended to a great extent on the quality of its cadres. If a cadre spoke harshly to the villagers, if he concealed information, if he stole food and money, or otherwise acted like so many of the GVN officials, he might actually lose the village for the Front, for at the beginning the Front could offer nothing but hope — and a hope founded in the good behavior of its cadres. The problem of insuring that this would not happen was, however, an enormous one. It involved not *finding* competent men, but *creating* them out of a generation brought up within the traditions of the Confucian family. The behavior of the GVN officials was after all, quite "natural." It simply did not fit within the new situation.

Looked at from a distance, the task of creating good cadres was identical to that of making the entire Front organization work — problems of organization being always and finally problems of men. The American counterinsurgents never fully appreciated that the NLF faced destruction at every turn from the same chain reaction of fear and hostility that sprang up between superior and inferior within the GVN. Had it not found some means of arresting this "natural" impulse, the Front too would have undergone the same process of disintegration: first atrophy in the channels of communication, then corruption, loss of initiative in the lower echelons, isolation from reality at the top, and finally a breaking up of the whole system. Certain symptoms of this disintegration did appear from time to time within parts of the Front organization, but the high command usually managed to suppress them. The organization as a whole remained intact even under the great pressure of the American war. Its main instrument of self-control was political education, but political education did not by itself suffice, for even among the best-indoctrinated there remained a potential for reversion to type. In addition, therefore, the Front created a series of organizational checks and balances. These may be thought of as control devices for the benefit of leadership but they may also be thought of as measures to assist the individual cadre and to insure justice for the people under his administration.

The basic unit of the Front was the cell. Every responsible member of the NLF from the highest Party cadres to the members of the Liberation Associations belonged to a cell composed of some three to ten people of the same rank and the same general occupation. Among the ranks of the cadres one member of a cell would also belong to a cell at the next highest level: one member of the village committee cell would also belong to the district committee cell, and so forth. Orders from above and reports from below were transmitted through that link member. In theory, the lower cell elected its representative to the higher cell but in practice the reverse seems generally to have been the case — and necessarily so in the beginning, as the higher body had actually to create the lower one. American scholars of the subject have tended merely to profess outrage at this "undemocratic" practice, neglecting the benefits the cell system conferred.

The cell, particularly among Party cadres, was an extremely close-knit group that met perhaps every week to review activities and to plan for the future. Ideally the cell acted as a substitute family — a group to which the cadres could come to speak freely of their problems and receive advice or reassurance from their comrades. Doubtless all cells did not function in such a harmonious manner, but the cell system did tend to encourage close working relationships and to alleviate some of the anxiety of the superior-inferior relationship. With the constant meetings, the link cadre would come to recognize the problems of the lower group much better than if he issued orders from afar. Similarly the lower group might come to understand the problems of the higher echelon and to trust its representative. Psychologically, the cell system tended to drive away the cadres' concern for loss of "face" and to remove the sense of isolation and alienation that affected so many of the GVN officials and soldiers. Practically, it discouraged those abuses that so often resulted from that sense of alienation: the corruption, the dishonesty in reporting, and the refusal to take responsibility. If a cadre made an error in judgment, his colleagues would have a chance to take him to task for it as equals in the cell meeting without reporting him to the higher authorities. The danger, of course, remained that two or more cadres might combine to tyrannize the others, but that danger exists within any form of bureaucratic organization. Because the cell system shifted the emphasis of command and control from a hierarchical to a collective basis, it tended to reduce the threat of irreconcilable conflict and "splitting apart" so prevalent within the GVN. It also reduced the vulnerability of the organization as a whole. The death or defection of one cadre would not, for instance, bring with it the "confusion" that usually attended the death of a single, strong leader.[13] A man might die, but the system would nonetheless survive to reproduce itself.

The cell system existed at every level of the Front command. So too did the principle — if not in every case the fact — of collective leadership. At the head of the NLF was a central committee of sixty-four members, theoretically elected by a congress of delegates chosen at district level. The executive powers of this national organization were vested in a presidium, responsible for foreign and military affairs, and a secretariat, responsible for domestic civil and political affairs, each composed of seven or more members of the central committee. At the next level of the organization lay the inter-zone commands. (The inter-zones roughly corresponded to the GVN corps areas, only there were three of them: a) southern central Vietnam, the coastal plains below the DMZ; b) the Western Highlands; and c) Nam bo or the Mekong Delta area.) There was also a special zone for Saigon and the surrounding provinces. Below the inter-zone were the zone and finally the provincial headquarters. The zone commands seem to have been little more than communications centers. The inter-zone and provincial commands followed along much the same organizational lines as the central body: a legislative committee and an executive body responsible to it that directed the local military forces and coordinated their operations with the civilian agencies for finance, supply, communications, propaganda, and mass organization. Below province level the Front organization varied, depending on the amount of population under Front control. In certain areas, such as the highlands and the sect-controlled portion of the western Delta, it was an informal network of guerrilla units. In others, it was an elaborate administration with district and village committees whose organization paralleled that of the provincial body.[14]

American diagrams of the NLF command structure tend to show a hierarchical organization in which the lines of authority run solidly from top to bottom — as was the case within the GVN. In fact, the operations of the Front presented an almost antithetical picture to that of the GVN, in part for the excellent reason that its supply of men, goods, and intelligence came from the bottom up rather than from the top down. The GVN combined an almost total lack of central planning with a highly centralized administration. The Front combined a complete central planning system with a highly decentralized administration.[15] At least until 1966, when the American armed forces began to depopulate the countryside and to drive the NLF to dependence on the North Vietnamese, the Front's developed village, district, and provincial organizations were almost entirely self-sufficient. Each village, for instance, supported its own militia and its own intelligence, education, and welfare services, and its own public works projects. The village committees could survive in logistical isolation for long periods of time. This decentralization gave an enormous flexibility. It also enforced cooperation between the civil and military authorities and between the higher and lower levels of the bureaucracy. The provincial and national battalions depended on the district and village committees for intelligence, if not for some part of their supplies, and thus their commanders had to take directives from the civilians — even those in the lower echelons of the bureaucracy. Brought into the military councils, the village cadres could, for their part, coordinate all of the local government activities. They could prepare propaganda campaigns in conjunction with military operations and they could (unlike the GVN village and district chiefs) work with the peasants without fear that their efforts would be brought to naught by an ill-timed movement of troops. This system insured a degree of local influence over national affairs that did not begin to exist within the GVN. The NLF village leaders had to accept policy from above. But with their own militia, and their own local supply lines and intelligence services, they had a great deal more power vis-à-vis the central command than any GVN village council — appointed or elected.

The NLF leaders instructed their cadres in this distribution of power by the very style in which they lived. Even the highest of the Front cadres showed no outward sign of rank. The highest of them dressed in the black pajamas of the peasants and held titles no more impressive than that of "chairman," "secretary," or "cadre." Unlike the regular North Vietnamese army, the People's Liberation Army of the south conferred no permanent titles at all. An officer would be designated "commander of the *n*th battalion" or "the *n*th regiment," never Colonel X or General Y. This anonymity served as a security precaution, but it also served to reinforce the idea that rank was not a ritual station gained by long tenure or ritual actions. Rank was a responsibility earned and held by continuing positive achievement.

In fact, all diagrams of the NLF tend to be confusing and to some degree deceptive, for in addition to its vertical chain of command the Front possessed a strong lateral element in the form of the People's Revolutionary Party. PRP cadres participated in all of the Front organizations from the village level up, but their chain of command ran parallel to, and to some extent independently of, the

NLF itself. To visualize the NLF it is necessary to imagine not a diagram but a three-dimensional cone with a core of denser material corresponding to the PRP. The role of the PRP was much the same as that of the Communist parties in China and the Soviet Union. Its function was to provide political education and "correct" political leadership at all levels of the bureaucracy. In the villages the Party cadres created and directed all of the Front organizations from their positions within the administrative committees. In the military units and in the district and provincial headquarters they acted as "generalists" amid specialists, coordinating the military, administrative, and logistical machinery so that it served the overall political aims of the Front. The Party cadres held veto power over all military activities and authority over all aspects of the political struggle. The Party, in sum, was the government of the NLF.

Government, as it were from the inside out rather than strictly from the top down, presented certain practical advantages to the NLF in its conduct of the political struggle and the guerrilla war. As most American analysts recognized, the presence of Party cadres at all levels of the command helped to prevent ideological splits and bureaucratic snafus in a struggle where all forms of communication had to be kept to the minimum. The Party was in fact the key to the ability of the NLF to provide centralized policy control with a decentralized administration. Less obvious to American analysts was the fact that government by the Party constituted a part of the solution to the problem of mandarinism that plagued the GVN. Within the GVN an official would look upon promotion as a movement upwards, a gain in power, wealth, and prestige. Because of the PRP, however, the NLF presented a very different picture even to its newest recruits. A guerrilla fighter could, he knew, rise upwards through the ranks to control more men, but he could not gain real power until he joined the Party. And to join the Party was to move not upwards but *inwards;* it was a promotion but it was also a demotion in the sense that it meant no rise in wealth or outward status, but, on the contrary, obedience to a discipline much more severe than that exacted from the ordinary NLF member. The Party cadre had to serve as an example of courage, discipline, and abstemiousness. He had, in other words, to descend to the status of a model "servant of the people."

The egalitarianism of the Party operated not only as a psychological corrective, but as a force for social change. What distinguished the PRP from the elite of the GVN was its effort to remain as close to the people as possible. As one Party directive put it, "The Party is like a plant. The people are like the soil that nourishes the plant. . . . If the roots of the plant go deeply and firmly into the ground, only then will the plant grow well and steadily."[16] Whether or not the Party served the interest of the people in other respects, its members lived in the villages and recruited directly out of them. An NLF soldier, technician, or member of the village administrative committee, could join the Party at any time provided he had the proper qualifications. The Party tended to favor those with lower-class backgrounds, even though it needed men with education. By 1965 the NLF was what it never would have become without its Marxist-Leninist core, an organization of peasants.

Over the years American counterinsurgency scholars have given a great deal of effort to arguing that the NLF with its program of moderate reform was no more than a deception, a façade that camouflaged the Communist Party with its doctrinaire Marxist program. But the issue is not quite so clear-cut. Even at its inception the NLF was not a true coalition of "front" in the sense of uniting a number of strong political parties. Its national and provincial committees included a number of people from the sects and the small urban political parties, but these people did not bring their organizations with them. Presumably the PRP would have used these people and the moderate NLF program as the basis for a coalition had the United States withdrawn from the war during the period when the sects remained a potent political force. In that case, however, the Party would have had to enter a coalition and test its strength against all the other political groups that believed just as strongly as it did that their particular political line would eventually triumph. When the United States did not withdraw and the coalition did not take form, the NLF became during the years of war an almost single-minded organization. Growing up among people who had no previous political affiliation, it evolved into a movement whose members differed politically only in the degree of indoctrination in Marxism-Leninism. The Party did, of course, infiltrate certain non-Communist organizations in the cities, and it did create certain cover organizations to enlist the support of urban intellectuals or rural religious dignitaries. But in most cases the difference between Party infiltration and NLF infiltration was nonexistent. In perhaps 90 percent of the villages there was no political distinction between the Party cadres and the Front committees, and the peasants did not differentiate between the PRP and the leadership of the Front as a whole. The Party cadres were simply "the Front cadres" who created and directed the government of the villages.[17] The Party maintained the Front and its program as a means of obtaining a coalition and a national reconciliation after an American withdrawal.

Americans, and particularly American liberals, find it difficult to understand how an elite, disciplined party could be an acceptable form of government for any people in the world. But the Vietnamese have always believed that some people know how to govern better than others. This belief may change – it may already be changing – but for the moment the question for the Vietnamese is simply to know who those people are. Traditionally, those people the Vietnamese assumed to be best qualified were those who had studied government as a science and a system of morality. Whatever the virtues or vices of its policies, the PRP has laid strong claim to this tradition – its important modification being that it opened the opportunity for such study to the poorest members of the society. Oddly enough, from the American point of view, the very anonymity of the PRP constituted an element in its favor for many Vietnamese. For the traditional Vietnamese peasant, power, like wisdom and virtue, lies (and ought to lie) at the core of things. A man of real power is not one who makes a brazen display of his might, but one who speaks softly and maintains his reserve. The NLF worked to destroy this ideal by bringing certain kinds of conflicts out into the open and by exposing themselves directly to the people. But the ideal has powerful roots. In Western terms Vietnamese peasants have always identified with the fox rather than with the lion. Believing that ruse and cunning will (and should) prevail over brute force, they disdain the displays of prowess so much admired by the hunter. The Oriental science of judo – literally, "the easy way" – opposes knowledge and the inner force of concentration to brawn and weaponry. For many Vietnamese the PRP was attractive just because of its qualities of innerness.

The Making of a Revolutionary

Force binds for a time, education enchains forever.
— A Vietnamese proverb

Even in 1966 the American Military Assistance Command —
General Westmoreland's apparatus for dealing with the Vietnamese — was still very much in the business of producing studies on
"morale" and "motivation" within the ARVN. These studies had
their own scientific curiosity since, like perpetual motion machines,
they had a perfectly circular logic as well as a perfect record for
circulating around and across a hundred desks and back into the
same filing cabinet without the slightest coefficient of friction. The
problem of morale (the officers argued) was a problem of training,
which was a problem of leadership, and the problem of leadership
was a problem of promotions, which was a problem of corruption,
which was a problem of motivation.

The American civilians, who for their part were not wedded to
the structure of the regular army, took a much less spiritual view of
the same group of "problems." According to the studies produced by
their analysts, a reform of the Vietnamese government depended
upon its reorganization, to wit: the success of the pacification program depended upon the reorganization of the cadre teams, whose
success depended upon the reorganization of the ARVN, and so
forth. Those Americans who recognized the NLF as a part of the
scheme of things tended to agree, as in their view the success of the
Viet Cong depended on the superiority of their organization.

All of which was absolutely true and absolutely not true at the
same time. The reason that few GVN bureaucrats proved effective
administrators, that few ARVN soldiers patrolled regularly at night,
was that their entire education in society had not prepared them for
such tasks. Brought up in the traditional Way, most Vietnamese
had, as children, taken their place within a society that confined
most forms of communication to the vertical transmission of authority and obedience. Restricted to this single, exclusive system of
relationships, they had found it difficult to establish any community
with those outside their own blood families. To recognize a stranger

was automatically to bring him into the most intimate circle of obligation and to give him a place as "father," "younger brother," or "uncle." It was either to recognize his authority or to insist upon his recognition of one's own. Such a relationship was dangerous, for it demanded the unconditional surrender of one party to the other. The inferior had to depend upon his superior as a child depends upon his father — only without those guarantees implicit in the family relationship. The peasant could not risk a relationship with an official; similarly, the under-minister could not risk submitting to the authority of his minister except as a matter of form. Underneath the mask of form, of "face," mutual suspicions would grow until the most trivial of problems became insoluble. Given a title, an office, and the job of running some seemingly straightforward logistical operation, the under-minister would spend his time knotting and unknotting the web of intrigue around him: Was the minister losing his influence with General X, and if so, who would be blamed for the disappearance of that million piastres? Why had the section chief told his American adviser that the warehouse to be built with that money would not be built for six months? In the same way, the simple GVN squad leader, given ten men, a radio, and a mission to patrol the outskirts of a hamlet, would spend his night in the outpost because headquarters had not delivered two rifles and he feared that his second-in-command might want his job badly enough to report the squad movements to the local guerrillas.

To many Americans these small intrigues appeared to be a series of day-to-day frustrations, insignificant problems that could be overcome with time and training. They were in fact symptoms of a profound condition within the society. The GVN struggled to survive, but it lived on like the dinosaur whose nervous system can no longer adequately transmit information from its mind to the ends of its great body. To operate such Western organizations as a city government, a factory, or a battalion without American help, the GVN required a much more flexible and specialized order of communications. It required a system of relationships that included not only "father" and "younger brother," but "colleague," "expert," "buddy," and "citizen": a system that allowed communication to flow evenly throughout the society. The under-minister had to be able to question his minister without fear of a final break in their relations. The squad leader had to be able to persuade his deputy of their common interests and to take the initiative to procure what arms were necessary for the security of the hamlet. A sociologist might well conceive of the inadequacy of the GVN as a structural problem. It was also, as the NLF insisted, a political or ideological problem, for in its very essence, a modern army or bureaucracy implies a certain freedom of communication, a certain equality between men. From this perspective the success of the NLF depended largely on its ability to give the Vietnamese a new identity, a new sense of their own society and its purposes. In some sense its organizations were but shells for men, and its program of political instruction the essence of the revolution.

The NLF organizations were not purely functional military or administrative units; they were also training camps where the new men and the new society would be formed. Entering into a guerrilla unit or a village association, the young peasant boy would step into a new medium of talk and activity which grew denser with time and increasingly shut out the world beyond it. Under Front aegis he would learn that the world had a very different set of dimensions than the one he had imagined. He would also learn that to achieve his ends he must behave in a different manner from that he had thought desirable. For him, to join the NLF was to embark on a process something like that of growing up from childhood again: it was to begin a "re-education."

When I got to my unit, we shook hands all around saying, "Now that we have come from various directions to this place, we should treat each other as members of a big family." They seemed to be happy to have me with them. . . . [They] addressed me as "comrade." . . . Their enthusiasm remained the same throughout.[1]

In a sense, the major task of the Front consisted in breaking down the traditional barriers of fear and giving the peasants or soldiers some sense of their community with each other. When they joined their units, few of the young men had any sense of the coordination — both physical and mental — with which a modern society must operate. Unfamiliar with clocks, with school or factory routines, with large machines or precision instruments, they lived in rhythms of time and space too extended for the needs of a modern army. According to several of the squad leaders, their major disciplinary problem was the soldiers' habit of walking away from their unit and forgetting to return on schedule. Having never, or rarely, played team sports, the soldiers had little experience of a common endeavor requiring immediate group response. They could not depend on each other. Like the ARVN soldiers, the young recruits tended to neglect their weapons, to sleep during guard duty, and to scatter or freeze when attacked. But then, when the ARVN training stopped, the NLF training began.

Joining their units after a bare two or three weeks of preliminary training, the Front recruits would learn the real stuff of war from the experienced fighters seeded among them. Unless the situation demanded desperate measures, their commanders would initially send them into battle only as a controlled exercise, retiring them later for basic training. Usually an NLF main force unit would go into action only once a month; the rest of the time was spent in education for the illiterate, in political instruction, in military training and retraining. On his visit to the Liberated zone in 1964 the Australian journalist, Wilfred Burchett, watched a People's Liberation Army battalion rehearse an assault on a government installation, using first a sandpit model and then a full-scale wooden mockup of the blockhouse. Like the cast of some Hollywood spectacular on set, the recruits went through the operation over and over again until their commanders were completely satisfied with their performance.[2] Those American advisers who found this painstaking attention to detail almost comical did not perhaps consider that to change a Vietnamese peasant into a soldier, a radio operator, or a gunnery or demolition expert, was to change the entire pattern of his life.

As a radio operator, my job was to listen to the GVN radio communication. I had a little 3-band Philip short-wave transistor radio and a GRC-9 — confiscated from the GVN — with which I could listen to all GVN communications in the area. . . . I must say the GVN people were lousy as far as radio communication was concerned. They were lazy, irresponsible and careless. Their conventions were never changed and were the same everywhere. For example, "banana bud" was "shell" and "eagle" was "aircraft." Once in a while a telegram was sent from one post to another in coded morse, but a few minutes later the receiving operator would cry out, "Come on, buddy, use the ordinary language, I'm tired of decoding." Thus the other would continue the telegram in plain morse. . . . When there was no official communication, the men would talk shop or would exchange gossip. So that it was easy for us to know their exact location, their units and even their names.[3]

This young radio operator, a defector from the NLF, manages to convey a great deal of the difference in atmosphere between the two armies.[4] The GVN operators knew how to tap out the Morse code, but they had very little sense of their own importance and the consequence of their actions on the lives of hundreds of men. They were irresponsible because they could not see the connection between their own welfare and that of their fellow soldiers.

The Front's political training might be thought of as the verbal counterpart to the physical, or military, training, for it was "political" in the most extended sense of the word. Brought up within the small, enclosed world of the family, most of the young recruits found it natural to trust each other, to share their food and their complaints, to discuss and to compromise the interests of group action. On a broader scale, they had very little conception of "public property" or "public service." Like the ARVN soldiers, they did not see why they should not intrigue against their superiors or steal food from the villagers. The Front cadres had to spell out everything in detail and show them little by little how their own actions related to the goals of the larger community.

An hour before any big operation, such as an attack on a GVN post, the battalion political officer would call a meeting of all the men and urge them to keep their spirit up and do their duty properly. If there was a larger scale operation, the Military Section of the province would send some men down to explain the importance of the operation to the men. For example, they would say that this particular operation was designed to destroy some enemy setups, and politically to liberate the people in that area. They would mention the advantages and disadvantages of the VC, but of course the advantages always outweighed the disadvantages. They talked about the duty and responsibilities of the Liberation fighters. They said that the people needed them badly this particular time, and that if any of the men were killed in action, they could be sure their sacrifice was not a waste, and that their families and the people would benefit from it. The group members and Party leaders were called upon to set an example for the others.[5]

In the regular squad, platoon, and company meetings, the unit leaders would review their activities in public and give the fighters a chance to question or criticize their performance. At the same time the Party cadres (there were usually three to each battalion, one to each company) would discuss the overall political and military situation and instruct the fighters in the general aims of the revolution. Because most of the soldiers had no previous experience of political discussion, the cadres would start off with simple slogans, songs, riddles, and jokes that illustrated such abstractions as "the class struggle" in terms the fighters could understand. In between meetings they would engage the men in friendly conversation and encourage them to question the points of doctrine and express their feelings about life in the army either directly or by writing poems, articles, or stories for the "wall newspaper." Instead of lecturing the fighters, the cadre attempted to draw them out, to deal with their complaints in the open, and finally to coerce the stragglers by means of collective rather than authoritarian pressure.

This particular form of political education — that of a dialogue between the ranks — had an underlying force to it. The young recruits had little intellectual reason for observing the soldierly disciplines. They had at the same time a strong emotional bias against doing so, for, as they saw it, to cooperate with their superiors was to expose themselves to exploitation. By talking with the soldiers the cadres were not only educating them in their duties, but on some deeper level assuring them that they would not abandon them and (literally as well as figuratively) keep all the food for themselves. "Talking was the best we could do," explained one of the squad leaders. "We would have a private talk with a man whose spirits were particularly low. I don't know if the talks were any good, but we believed that the men might feel better if they could talk about their troubles." The cadres did not expect to keep all of their men from defecting, but they felt — and correctly — that the constant pressure of their attention acted as some counterweight to the hunger and cold, to the jungle leeches and the bombing. As one defector testified, "The Front's political cadres are very dangerous. Nothing can escape them. When they see a combatant looking sad, they don't hesitate to comfort him."[6]

Rather than simply asserting command over their soldiers, the cadres first established the legitimacy of their authority by gaining the fighters' confidence and participation. To some degree their efforts amounted to an attempt to transfer the soldiers' attachments from their real families to the great "family" of the Liberation.

Unlike the ARVN soldiers, who usually settled their families near their fixed bases or in an accessible town, the Front fighters rarely saw their families more than once or twice a year. Removed from their villages, they entered into a society entirely composed of their peers — a society isolated and thrown back upon itself by the external walls of danger. The cadres did not attack the soldiers' filial ties directly; rather they played them down in a number of important ways. By performing the ceremonies of marriage and burial, by promising to support the crippled soldiers, to help the families of the dead and the wounded, and to pay special attention to those of the fighters' families who lived in the Liberated areas, they relieved the soldiers of their most pressing economic worries. For many of the fighters a sense of obligation was the strongest attachment they had to their families. The transfer of responsibility thus helped them to rationalize the breach of filial piety that they had made in the very act of joining the NLF. "How can you help your families," the cadres asked, "if the nation is in such trouble? The best thing you can do for your families is to fight for the Liberation." In all of their talks with the fighters the cadres praised the "masculine" virtues of aggressiveness, courage, and comradeship as against the "feminine" qualities of sentimentality, cleverness, and guile. Given their solidarity and strength of purpose, the soldiers had, so the cadres said, the power to overcome all hardships, including that of long separation from their families.

As soon as the soldiers began to talk to each other more freely and to rely on each other in combat, they naturally began to look upon their fellows as a source of security and affection. And they began to regard themselves as an elite: in contrast to the GVN soldiers who were "lazy," "ill-trained," and "corrupt," they were virile, disciplined, and capable of sacrifice. At the beginning they interpreted all their privations as a sign of the Front's weakness and inability to succor them, but later on they began to look upon the same hardships as a continual proof of their strength and virtue. As American statistics showed, the more time they spent with the NLF, the higher their morale rose and the lower went their rate of defections.

Though in the light of hindsight much of the NLF training program must seem to be little more than a thoroughgoing civics course, there was one aspect of it that went beyond all the boundaries which Westerners customarily draw around the concept "education." This was the institution of *khiem thao*, "criticism" or "self-criticism" (the words mean "to verify" and "to discuss"). Used previously by the Chinese Communists and the Viet Minh, *khiem thao* was a "truth game" in which every member of the organization from the lowliest soldier to the highest cadre had to participate. In the "criticism sessions," held on a regular basis as a part of the daily activities, each NLF member had to admit his own failings and given his honest opinion about the conduct of all the other members of the group. Within the sessions he did not have to fear punishment for his own errors other than the most devastating one of concerted group criticism. Only if he refused to participate would he incur the final penalty of expulsion by the group.

Khiem thao was a game in which the rules of life were suspended, but it was a game designed to reach back into life and change its players. When the NLF recruits came into the army or the administration, they arrived almost totally insulated from their fellow men by their masks of "politeness." Suspicious of both their commanders and their peers, they remained *attentistes*, always watching for a sign of trouble, always on the point of defection. The *khiem thao* sessions forced them to participate, forced them to break down all the defenses which they had built up around them in childhood. For the newcomer "criticism" was a terrifying experience. "When they were being criticized," reported one squad leader, "their manner was correct and humble, but when the *khiem thao* was over, some would leave the unit to go home or to rally to the GVN, while others would swear and then forget all about it. We lost a lot of men because of those criticism sessions. After all, every man has his self-respect, and when his short-comings were brought up publically, he was hurt."[7]

But to the extent that *khiem thao* was painful, so it was perhaps necessary to the functioning of the entire organization. If the recruits could not strip themselves of their anxieties about each other and the power of the group, they could not begin to work together or to commit themselves to a common cause. Without a real psychological readjustment, their loyalties to any organization, other than that of their own families, would remain only surface deep. Given the newcomer's ambivalence between fear of the group and desire to belong to it, the cadres had to strike a delicate balance in their disciplinary measures. As one Party manual warned:

The criticism must be made in a spirit of mutual, comradely affection, helping each other to reform. But criticism in a hostile spirit does harm, causes loss of face, goes too far, etc. Criticism of this kind really causes divisions and prejudices in the Party. It is not useful for helping each other to correct defects, in a spirit of compassion, to advance together.[8]

In practice the Party cadres attempted to restrain the low-level guerrilla fighters from discussing more than the details of the day-to-day work. (Burchett, for instance, observed several of these tactical *khiem thao* sessions going on in the intervals between the practice attacks on the GVN blockhouse.) Discussion of more profound and difficult matters was reserved for those who had already developed strong attachments to the Front — and was used primarily as a corrective. If a supply system broke down or a battalion performed badly in a fight, not only the top-ranking officers, but the entire group of cadres who bore some responsibility for the operation would meet for a period of perhaps two or three weeks to discuss their technical errors and the obstacles in their communication with each other. No one but the NLF cadres themselves know what went on at these sessions, and thus it is possible only to imagine the process in a rather distant and abstract manner.

Given a safe forum in which to express his own grievances, the cadre came to see that he did not depend directly on any one member of the group. He could put his case on the table with some assurance that it would be judged on its own merits rather than on a personal basis. When, as must frequently have happened, two members quarreled, the group would not dissolve itself until the matter was settled by mutual agreement. With some experience at *khiem thao* the cadre would grow less and less afraid to disagree with another member, for he would realize that by initiating a verbal conflict he did not risk his entire career in the Front, or indeed his life. By the same token, he would come to understand that when others criticized him for mishandling a situation, they were not doing it from motives other than that of desire to get the job done better the next time. The knowledge came as a revelation — though one perhaps gradually arrived at; and if he allowed it to, that revelation could change his life. What mattered now was not the maintenance of "face," but the competence to deal with the "objective" problems that confronted the entire group.

By forcing the cadres into conflict and limiting the damage done by it, the *khiem thao* sessions opened up entirely new channels of communication within the NLF. From the outside it is impossible to match cause exactly with result. But it takes only a small stretch of the imagination to see that in melting down the whole hierarchical structure of relationships the *khiem thao* gave the NLF a strength that could be measured in battalions. If, for instance, a number of soldiers from one company died or deserted, the local Front commander would have an excellent chance of hearing about his losses and taking measures to deal with them. His counterpart in the ARVN, by contrast, rarely knew how many men he commanded. The ARVN company, battalion, and regimental commanders made it a general practice to conceal their losses in the hopes of disguising their own failures or of collecting the pay due to the missing men. (According to American analysts, most ARVN units remained at 70 to 80 percent of their reported strength for the duration of the war.) The ARVN generals thus courted military disaster when they committed anything but an overwhelming force into action.

The Front propaganda reports did not always reflect reality, but the reports they circulated among themselves were almost unique in their realism. Unlike either the Saigon officials or many members of the American mission, Front cadres were actually able to report bad news. So good was their intelligence and security system, indeed, that they were able to prevent much of the intrigue, corruption, graft, and blackmail which had effectively paralyzed the ARVN.

Q. How many party members were there in your company?
A. There were eight or nine of them.

Q. How did these men become party members?
A. They had excellent performance records, and were ready to sacrifice anything that was asked of them. They were virtuous and enthusiastic. They were the outstanding members of the unit.[9]

The above remarks came from a young man the NLF had refused to promote. Instead of assuming that his rivals had gained their position by influence and intrigue, he felt, as did most of his fellow soldiers, that he had an equal opportunity to compete. Unlike the ARVN soldiers, the Liberation Army's rank-and-file members usually trusted their commanders. In the *khiem thao* sessions they had a chance to criticize their superiors and to find out for themselves that the promotion system was in no way arbitrary.

Khiem thao helped to prevent the Front organization from splitting apart into a network of self-protective cliques. Also — and by extension — it opened the gates to the villages and allowed the cadres to have some communication with the peasants, who since the beginning of time had resisted officialdom with all their vast inert strength. "In administering the rural area," wrote the cadre from XB village, the Party seeks to settle contradictions between people, teach the people Party policy, urge the people to have spite for the Americans and Diem and seek to unite all groups and social classes in the village. If a Party member or cadre makes a mistake he will be freely subjected to the criticism of the people. When the people can boldly criticize Party members they will then be ready to forgive them.[10]

With some experience in *khiem thao*, the cadres were better prepared to go to the people without fear of "loss of face," without the inner need to keep their distance from the people and turn the mask of authority towards them.

By accepting criticism from the people, they could show them that a commitment to the NLF did not imply an unconditional surrender to authority. The Front cadres, they suggested, were not trying to be the "fathers of the people"; on the contrary, they were confirming the people in their own rights and powers.

The leaders of the NLF, and of the Viet Minh before them, had the ability, unique among Vietnamese politicians, to make alliances with other political groups and to make compromises in negotiation. This capacity, too, may have owed to *khiem thao*. Certainly it came from an assessment of their place in society similar to that *khiem thao* awoke in the individual. The NLF leaders hoped to become the sole government of the people, but they, unlike the Ngos or the sect leaders, knew that they *were not* – at least not for the moment. They believed the victory of the revolution to be inevitable. But they also knew that making compromises and temporarily sharing their claim to power with other real powers might be sometimes necessary, sometimes advantageous. In the period 1954–1960 they did not destroy themselves, as did the sects – and later the Diem regime itself – through inflexibility and futile military resistance. They did not have to take Ngo Dinh Diem's passive, all-or-nothing attitude, and so they had the freedom to be truly Machiavellian, taking their advantages where they saw them and giving in on issues that they could not win immediately by direct confrontation. Here, within an attitude, a psychological set, lay clues to those mysteries known as the NLF's "superior organization" and "superior leadership."

For a Westerner it is tempting to equate *khiem thao* with the new American practice of encounter group therapy and sensitivity training. A parallel between the two exists, but it is not a direct one: the similarity lies buried beneath an acute difference in psychological perspective. In theory at least, the goal of the American encounter group is to free the individual, to permit him to understand himself and express his personality as fully as possible. The goal of *khiem thao* — and of the NLF's political training in general — was, on the other hand, to free the individual from old social constraints only to impose new ones. By its own admission the PRP was interested in far-reaching control over the individual. In a study entitled "How Should Party Members Promote Revolutionary Virtue?" the Party outlined the requirements for its members:

The comrades we want are revolutionaries who are determined, hard-ened, who are well-forged, who have discarded individualism. . . . They have a steady, firm, impartial spirit, absolutely loyal to the Party. They will work either morning or evening, are tested in battle, in daily work. They always think in terms of controlling their thoughts, their attitudes, their expressions in a sincere way. They always ask the question: are we doing this right, are we thinking correctly? Is this useful or harm-ful for the revolution? When we act and think that way, are we serving the interests of the revolution or individual interests? . . . If we see clearly, see there are still shortcomings, such as individualistic thoughts, we must try to overcome them. We must bravely carry on self-criticism, point out where we are wrong, where we are right in our work and in our thought.[11]

Rather than opening the cadres to themselves, the Party was, on the contrary, demanding that they repress their inmost thoughts and feelings and conform to the narrow, exacting standards of the group — or rather, of the Party cadres who controlled the group. If a cadre showed no enthusiasm, if he deviated from the Party line or put his own interests ahead of those of the Party, he would be criticized and finally expelled if he did not correct himself. Beyond the freedom of their cadres to criticize each other, the Party seemed to want authoritarian order and unanimity. *Khiem thao* and the Front's political education in general was what Westerners called "thought control" or "brainwashing."

Of all the aspects of the Vietnamese revolution, it was this domi-nation of the individual by the state which Americans — even those most opposed to their government's policy in Vietnam — found most difficult to come to terms with. On their trips to Hanoi in 1968 the writers Mary McCarthy and Susan Sontag discovered to their dismay that the North Vietnamese they met seemed to speak entirely in Communist jargon. "Everything is on one level here," complained Miss Sontag to her journal. "All the words belong to the same vocabulary: struggle, bombings, friend, aggressor, imperialist, patriot. . . . I can't help experiencing them as elements of an *official* language."[12] Had Miss Sontag been any less sympathetic to the North Vietnamese, she might have simply concluded that they were "brainwashed victims of Communist tyranny" — though they did not seem to be, for there was not a heavy atmosphere of Stalinism about them. On the contrary, they seemed to take a lucid, almost childlike pride in their government. In Eastern Europe many intellectuals had made it plain to Miss McCarthy that the official language was an oppressive weight upon their normal speech, but the North Vietnamese seemed to possess no other kind of rhetoric. Neither of the writers could dispute the truth of their hosts' words (the Americans were indeed, they felt, "imperialists" in Vietnam), but they could not help feeling that the North Vietnamese were in some way children, or, as they were not children, people who lacked a dimension of sensibility. Without any rebelliousness, indeed with a kind of joy in their achievement, the North Vietnamese seemed to have suppressed their private lives, their very personalities, in order to act out the cardboard role of "patriotic citizens."

Miss McCarthy and Miss Sontag saw in North Vietnam what no American official had ever prepared them for: the very foreignness of the Vietnamese. The familiarity of the Communist language was in many ways a deception, for the Vietnamese were not like the Russians or the East Europeans. As Miss Sontag rightly concluded, the Communist ideology was not responsible for the social discipline of the Vietnamese. Rather, the impetus to such discipline rose out of traditional Vietnamese society.

Traditionally, the Vietnamese notion of society was not that of an aggregate, a collection of people, but that of a complete organism. The whole of society was much greater than the sum of its parts because it reflected and duplicated the overall design of the universe. Within his society the individual had no separate existence. His sense of personal identity came from his sense of participation in the society and in the universe. The moral problem for the individual was to discover not what he himself thought or wanted, but what the society required of him. The goal of speech was less to express the individuality of the ego than to arrive at a harmonious relationship with others and with the laws of the universe. "Truth" was* not a conquest of reality, but an attempt to harmonize with it — an ethical as well as a scientific goal.

The French invasion effectively destroyed the Confucian design for society and the universe. It did not, however, change the impulse to a social and ideological coherency. For the Vietnamese "freedom" in the Western sense meant the disjunction of the ego from the superego. A disintegration of the personality, it led only to social chaos and the exploitation of the weak by the strong. As one PRP directive explained:

A Party member must forge for himself a spirit of heart and soul serving the people, serving the Party. When the Party [member] joins in work, he must bring all of his mind and thoughts, all of his efforts to try to work as well as possible. He must try to struggle at first to overcome individual difficulties. Generally speaking, people affected with individualism cannot serve the revolution well when they perform a given task if they are thinking more of themselves, thinking about social position, thinking about reputation, thinking about personal gain. The sickness of individualism is the original source of the sickness of negativism, dissatisfaction, corruption. . . . Bad, old, degenerate habits [such as] bureaucracy; petty authoritarian practices; showing one's power with the people; not thinking of the interests and aspirations of the people — these are the forms of individualism.[13]

"Individualism" had much the same connotation for the Communists that "egotism" or "selfishness" had for the non-Communist Vietnamese: it was immoral behavior and the very expression of anarchy. For traditionalists and Communists alike, virtue consisted of the sustained effort to reduce the gap between the individual will and the will of the community that itself expressed the objective laws of the universe. However else they differed, all the Vietnamese sects and political groups of the 1930's and 1960's directed their efforts towards creating a conformity of opinions, values, and life-styles, towards creating a community that would once again give the individual his "place" and *raison d'être*. As a Buddhist bonze once said, "You Westerners believe that you can destroy an idea by killing the man who holds it; we, on the other hand, believe that you must change men's ideas."

In some sense, however, it is impossible to compare the Front with all the other political groups of the south. The Front, with its "steel frame" of the Party, was a revolutionary group engaged in a new independence war, and the demands it made upon its cadres were of a different order than those made by the sects. The spirit of "heart and soul serving the people, serving the Party" was not to be found elsewhere, except perhaps among a few Catholic communities. For both the northerners and the southern Party cadres, the discipline did operate as a reduction in the scope of life. The "hardcore" Party cadres did speak in slogans and did abandon their private thoughts and feelings to the cause as no other political leadership did. But that discipline was for many a fulfillment, rather than a suppression, of the personality.

The necessary perspective on the NLF is not contemporary but historical. Traditionally, the rise of an energetic new dynasty never coincided with a period of literary or artistic flowering. The Vietnamese, who looked for the political "virtue" of the regime in a whole man, regarded a time of revolution as a time of austerity in all things. During periods of reformism or revolutionary change the "superior man" threw aside private concerns and, as it were, reduced himself to his role as a member of the society. In such periods the powerful Confucian sovereigns banned the Buddhist literature and shamed their mandarins into avoiding the Taoist temples and giving up their private, "egotistical" pursuits of poetry, painting, and feasting. Austerity in culture went along with austerity in material things. Too many words were like too many dishes on the table — a luxury, a waste, and a distraction. For the Confucians the reduction — even to the burning of books — was not a sign of authoritarian sterility and constriction, but a sign of moral clarity, order, and self-control. The NLF participated in this tradition, but its undertaking was much more radical than that of the Confucian reformers. Instead of merely trying to renew an elitist system, it was attempting to change that system and to bring the common people, the "children," to participate in the affairs of state. Its reduction was correspondingly severe. The Front cadres dressed in the black clothes of the poor peasants, and, similarly, they confined themselves to slogans so simple that the poor peasants could understand and use them. Only when the revolution was completed, when the round water displaced the thin flame, only then would there be time for the expansion of the self and the indulgence in material plenty and the private pursuits of the intellect. Until then the Party would attempt to keep its cadres thin.

Marxism-Leninism in the Vietnamese Landscape

Driving through the Mekong Delta in the swollen heat of the monsoon rains, Westerners, even those familiar with Vietnam, must find it difficult to imagine how Marxism-Leninism found resonance in that land. Where was the meeting ground between these peasants with their ancient magic, their rituals of the rice planting, and that small German who lived by cold analysis amid the soot of the great black factories and the mildew of books in the British Museum? What had Marx with his treatise on European capitalism to say to those peasants who prized their bullocks and their ancestral tombs above all things? Like their colonial masters, he had considered them "backward people" whom European influence could only improve. Why then had Marxism come to be their standard for an anticolonial revolt? And why was it the dominant influence on all Vietnamese nationalist parties?[1]

As a young man living in Paris, working "now as a retoucher at a photographer's, now as a painter of 'Chinese antiquities' (made in France!)," Ho Chi Minh joined the Socialist Party. He had read no Lenin. As a child he had learned from his French teachers the beautiful words "liberty, equality, fraternity" and learned at the same time that they did not apply to Vietnamese. He had no ideology apart from that, but the "ladies and gentlemen" of the Socialist Party (as he called them then) had shown sympathy to him and to his cause. During the debates on whether the Party should join the Second or the Third International, one of these "gentlemen" gave him Lenin's *Thesis on the National and Colonial Questions* in which the Russian leader argued that socialists ought to support the struggles of the colonial peoples for national independence. Ho Chi Minh became a Leninist on that day. "There were," he wrote,

political terms difficult to understand in this thesis. But by dint of reading it again and again, finally I could grasp the main part of it. What emotion, enthusiasm, clear-sightedness, and confidence it instilled into me! I was overjoyed to tears. Though sitting alone in my room, I shouted aloud as if addressing large crowds: "Dead martyrs, compatriots! This is what we need, this is the path to our liberation!"[2]

As a true internationalist, Lenin was the first European leader to extend his philosophy to the peoples of Asia and to support national revolutions against the Europeans. Later, in his appeal to the peoples of the East, he called upon the revolutionaries to apply the theory and practice of Communism to local conditions, where the peasants formed the basic masses, and the task was to struggle not against capitalism but against vestiges of the medieval past.[3] Marxism was not, Lenin argued, a utopian socialism, but a dialectical theory of history in which each new movement originates in the concrete condition of the society. The nature of each revolution is determined by the nature of the system of oppression. The task of the Europeans was to wage an anti-capitalist revolution. The task of the Easterners was to wage a nationalist revolution against the colonialists and the native reactionaries in league with them. Lenin saw no contradiction in the Marxist direction of an anticolonial struggle, since, if Marxist theory was correct, the Marxists knew better than anyone else what direction the society ought to take in the future.[4]

Lenin opened the doors of Marxism to Ho Chi Minh. In going through those doors Ho found international support for his own particular rebellion. But he also found what he could not have foreseen: an economic analysis that could be brought to bear on the conditions of Vietnam and a set of values that, as it happened, coincided to a great degree with those of the Vietnamese peasants.

To support his argument for economic equality, Marx had, after all, attributed all surplus wealth to the exploitation of human labor. In Europe his analysis was a conclusion reached only after long examination of the complex tissue of society — government, industry, and the capital market — but in Vietnam it was a truism that even the smallest peasant understood: wealth was a product of labor in the rice lands. An agricultural country with a single technology, few precious metals, and little national or international trade, traditional Vietnam possessed almost no surplus wealth. Compared with their rivals in China or Cambodia, the Vietnamese emperors did not accumulate great fortunes. When the French came to build their plantations, their roads, and their cities, they built them only by direct taxation of human labor. The traditional economy was both simple and inelastic: to acquire wealth within a village meant to deprive others of it. For the sake of their own survival, the villagers had to maintain a relative equality between their members. A man gained prestige not by increasing and maintaining his wealth, but by giving it away. Within the villages, as within the empire of the north and center, the accumulation of private wealth was a sign of anarchy — a sign that the great family of the village or empire had broken apart to such an extent that some of its members threatened the others with starvation.

In Vietnam equality of wealth always bore a direct relation to the order and harmony of the society. The southerners of the 1960's had never lived in an equal society, but many of them still assumed that it was desirable. As the young recruit, Huong, had said:

I, personally, don't want to be rich while others have to suffer misery. I want to have the same living standard that most of the people have. . . . If the people are not happy because they have miserable lives, I could never enjoy life. . . . I never want to have a high position in government and to be rich while many other people are poor. I simply want to have enough to eat and for all the people in the society to have equality.[5]

This desire for equality was no mere altruism. On the contrary. Many Vietnamese of the twentieth century sought wealth as a form of social security, but this search had meant an unbridled competition of the sort that terrified them. Inequality meant division and conflict in the once uniform society.

The Marxist notion that economic equality could be gained by a nationalization of the means of production was not at all unfamiliar to the Vietnamese. By Confucian law the emperor acted as a trustee of all the rice lands, reserving the right to redistribute them among the people. The strong emperors exercised this right either to rid themselves of the independent barons or to improve productivity and the lot of the peasants. The powerful Confucian emperors prevented their own mandarins from establishing large estates on the principle that as senior members of the great family, they had no need for food: the people would feed them of their own free will. At a lower level of government, the village councils and the heads of the extended families acted as guardians against glaring economic injustice. In their role as administrators of state rituals and upholders of state values, they mobilized individual labor and individual resources for the benefit of the collectivity. To some degree, then, the land had already been collectivized and nationalized before the coming of the Marxists.

The French changed the economy of Vietnam, but they did not succeed in persuading the Vietnamese to accept the notion of private enterprise, or even of "private property" in the Western sense of the word. Many Vietnamese landlords of the Delta, the one large group with any considerable assets, often regarded the transferable value of their land as relatively unimportant. To them, the wealth was the land itself and not the price of it, a physical presence within a small community. The ownership of land meant the establishment of a family and a government over the people. Ngo Dinh Diem protected these landlords for reasons of political weakness, but he persistently opposed the American attempts to establish private industry in South Vietnam. Diem regarded private industry much as the Confucian sovereigns had regarded the vast "feudal" estates of the warlords. In his view, the establishment of private industries would create a series of irreconcilable rival powers; it would undermine the state and the "natural laws" of the universe, and it would lead finally to anarchy. The Vietnamese Marxists differed from him only in that they put their theoretical emphasis on the people rather than the state. To them capitalism was "egotism" or "individualism" unbridled. Because it was morally unjust, it would, they believed, lead to popular discontent and rebellion. And in a society where "individualism" is looked upon as immoral, they might well have been right.

The socialization of the means of production, the centralization of power in the state — so much of the Marxist program did not present at all the same difficulties of application in Vietnam, as it would in Europe or the United States. By contrast to almost all Western countries, Vietnam traditionally possessed no institutions independent of the state — neither guilds nor corporations nor churches nor feudal fiefs that recognized, and cooperated with, the state. The "feudalism" of the warlords and, later, the landlords, was no more than an ad hoc system of exploitation — pervasive, but by all Confucian standards illegitimate.

Overlooking this background, certain American experts — particularly George Carver of the CIA — began to argue after the fall of the Diem regime that the Communist attempt to unify the country and to centralize power ran counter to Vietnamese political traditions. Vietnam, they argued, was a country of autarchic villages, a country so long divided by regional and religious feuds that the peasantry, by and large, felt very little loyalty to the nation-state. The South Vietnamese, they concluded, would resist all attempts at centralization, and therefore the GVN could defeat the Communists by turning itself into a federal state. The argument, however, ran counter both to the grain of Vietnamese politics and to the course of Vietnamese history. In the eighteenth and nineteenth centuries the Vietnamese monarchy was not as strong or well developed as the national governments of Europe at that period. On the other hand, the state was all that existed above the villages. After the French destroyed the village system, there grew up not a group of intermediate institutions — guilds, churches, and so forth — but a group of competing states. From the Hoa Hao to the Communist Party, all the political groups claimed sovereignty over the entire country — at the expense of all the rest. In the eighteenth century Vietnam had sustained two separate, antagonistic states, the Nguyen and the Trinh monarchies, for a long period of time. In the twentieth century, however, the "states" of South Vietnam could not survive independent economic enterprises. If Vietnam were to be independent, it would have to be unified — north and south. And it would not be unified under a federal system because the Vietnamese, whatever their political outlook, believed in uniformity, not in agreement to disagree. While the Americans were trying to teach the Vietnamese to live with their differences, the Vietnamese were only interested in erasing them. And Marxism-Leninism provided them with one method.

It was not apparent to many Americans, but the coincidence between the Confucian and Communist ideas of the state intrigued many non-Communist Vietnamese intellectuals. Communism held a peculiar fascination for the Catholic Ngo brothers: the attraction of opposites, perhaps, but opposites within a single class. For a Communist as for a Confucian *plus royaliste que le roi*, the state was monolithic. It did not represent the people, it *was* the people in symbolic form. For Communists and Confucians the society was embarked upon a way that never ended but that led towards a condition of social harmony so perfect that the state did not have to function at all: for the Taoist mystics, the "emperor who rules by non-doing," for the Marxists, the "withering away of the state." Confucianism, like Marxism, focused not on the individual, but on the society as a whole. Because there was no separation between religion and state — "religion" in the sense of a private search for the absolute, "state" in the sense of a social order — there was no liberal tradition in Vietnam. As Confucians, the Vietnamese had never been interested in diversity or originality for its own sake. From their intellectuals they required only what was "morally enlightening," or in Communist language, "socially useful." The writing of lyric poetry, along with gambling and worshiping of Taoist goddesses, they consigned to an area of free play outside the moral and intellectual world. The duty of the intellectual was to keep society on the correct path. (This tradition did not necessarily imply in the twentieth century the banning of all criticism, or the construction of art and science to the corridors indicated by Stalin. The Confucian sovereign had never subscribed to such restrictions any more than did Lenin.)

Like Confucianism, Marxism was a social morality. Like Confucianism, it was also a science that described the progress of society through history. In blaming the demise of the early nationalist parties on their failure to perceive and follow the "objective" laws of social development, Ho's theorist, Truong Chinh, was saying something quite similar to the Emperor Ly Thai To when the emperor blamed the three-year drought on his neglect of the rituals. As far as the authors were concerned, their statements were true, and that truth lent an absolute authority to their own political systems. Because the system was "true" or "natural," it could, if properly handled, guarantee success to the state that employed it correctly. The mandarins studied the Confucian texts in order to learn how to govern; similarly, the Communist Party cadres studied Marxism-Leninism, not merely because it was more important than technical knowledge, but because in their minds it permitted the state to function. The proof of the system was that it worked inside history. If at a certain point it ceased to work — as had been the case with Confucianism — then, as they saw it, it should be abandoned without further ado.

The legitimacy of a Confucian or a Marxist government rested directly on its faithfulness to a science. It rested indirectly, but nonetheless absolutely, on the will of the people. As to what the community was and how its will ought to be expressed, there Confucianism and Marxism diverged sharply. In the Confucian world the ancestors constituted the source of all wisdom and power. The state was the interpreter of the wishes of the people, and the people were consulted only in exceptional moments when the state dissolved and left them as the only transmitters of tradition. According to Marxism-Leninism, however, power and wisdom lay with the people of present and future generations. As Truong Chinh put it, "The people's intelligence and experience are infinitely rich and their force immensely great." The people had to be consulted by the state at all times because "every policy we put forward has direct repercussions on the people's interests."[6] In theory, popular opinion would support the proper application of the historical sciences. But just how and by whom these laws ought to be interpreted remained open to question, for Marxism gave no precise set of instructions. As guides, there remained only the practice of other socialist countries — just as for the Vietnamese emperors there remained the practice of the Chinese. Like the Confucian monarchs, the Vietnamese Party leaders saw it as their duty to set a course between "dogmatism" or slavish imitation of precedent on one hand and "revisionism," or localism, and the dilution of the universal truth on the other. In sum, even the dilemma of nationalism and internationalism remained the same.

While Marxism-Leninism accorded to a surprising degree with traditional Vietnamese notions of government and society, there were elements within Vietnamese Marxism that appeared completely unfamiliar to Westerners. As scholars such as Pike and Zasloff of the RAND Corporation pointed out, the northern as well as the southern Party cadres seemed to know very little about Marxist doctrine. Few of them could explain the class struggle of the international proletariat against world capitalism or describe what their future society would look like. Even middle-level cadres tended to describe the programs of the Party in such vague terms as "land to the tillers" and "the abolition of classes." Furthermore, there was a strangely moralistic tone to all of their pronouncements. Eager to show that Communism was essentially un-Vietnamese, Pike, for one, concluded that the People's Revolutionary Party was not Marxist-Leninist in any philosophical sense at all.[7]

To draw such a conclusion is, however, to misunderstand the place of ideology in a society. Like religion, ideology must rest upon a base of cultural, social, and economic conditions. Many Americans tend to identify Communism as the practice of the Soviet leadership. To do so is to ignore not only important ideological questions but the difference between theory and practice, life and literature. What is "pure Communism"? Which among the Jesuits, the Copts, and the Holy Rollers represents "true Christianity"? In their awe of the French, some of the early Marxists clung to the debates and conventions of the European parties and ended by communicating as much to the Vietnamese as actors speaking in Shakespearian accents would to a twentieth-century audience. As Lenin and Ho Chi Minh understood, Marxism was not a dead language or a precise set of instructions; it was a theory that required translation into life. The work of Ho Chi Minh was to make that translation for the Vietnamese.

The introduction of Marxism into Vietnam and the development of a Marxist movement were attended by a series of far-reaching debates on revolutionary strategy. At various points in the 1920's and 1930's there were three Leninist parties and four Trotskyite factions in Vietnam, all of which took slightly different positions on the issues of the class struggle, of nationalism versus internationalism, and on the problems of alliance with the Soviet Comintern, the Chinese Kuomintang, and the French Communist Party. The Trotskyites in general took a "purist" line, opposing the Comintern and its allies in the Kuomintang, opposing an alliance of the Vietnamese proletariat with the peasants and the national bourgeoisie. For them the proletariat constituted the one true revolutionary class. The industrial workers alone were to participate in the Communist organization.[8] The curiosity of this line was that the Trotskyite parties were based primarily in Saigon, where there was no urban proletariat to speak of. The Trotskyites disliked French colonialism as much as anyone, but their very exclusiveness drove them to legal activities and finally to dependence on the undependable French left wing. By contrast, Ho Chi Minh's organization — finally, a coalition of three regional groups called the Indochinese Communist Party — stood for the Leninist program of a two-stage revolution: the first stage a national rebellion uniting the peasants and the bourgeoisie under the leadership of the proletariat, and the second the proletarian, socialist revolution. Allied with the Comintern and in certain periods, the Chinese Kuomintang, the ICP took what advantages the French Stalinist party could offer it during the period of the Popular Front. At the same time it continued to build, where it could, a popular base among all classes of Vietnamese. When the moment of opportunity came in 1945, Ho Chi Minh resolved this last tactical ambiguity. (And without cost to himself, since the French Communist Party did not contest the government over the issue of decolonization.) Abandoning the "Indochinese Communist Party," the Dong Duong Cong San Dang, the name that spoke of French colonialism and a political unreality, he formed the Viet Minh (Viet Nam Doc Lap Dong Minh Hoi), the Vietnam Independence League. At one stroke he rid himself of French influence and class bias. His movement would be nationalist, but it would be nonetheless orthodox from a Marxist-Leninist point of view. The Viet Minh would carry out the first stage of the revolution — a stage that had no fixed duration, but that depended on the development of the various social classes within it.

Upon bringing the name "Vietnam" into the name of his party, Ho Chi Minh took the concomitant step of changing the phrase indicating "socialism" and his future social policy. For *cong san,* a phrase of Chinese roots suggesting a secular aggregate of individuals, he substituted *xa hoi,* a Vietnamese phrase linking the future distribution of wealth with the sacred communal traditions of the old village.[9] (*Xa Hoi Dang* was the name of the socialist party within the Viet Minh.) The second alteration might also seem to be opportunist — was not Marx an atheist? But for Marx revolution meant not a complete break with the past, but rather the fulfillment of what was already taking place within a society. Ho Chi Minh's new formulation merely reflected the fact that in Vietnam the proletariat remained a small minority. The first stage of the Vietnamese revolution would take place not within a secularly organized industrial society, but within an agrarian community that visualized itself in sacred terms.*

The elimination of class bias from the Viet Minh and the NLF had very different consequences in Vietnam from those such a policy would have had in the West. In Vietnam, and particularly in the south, where there was no industry to speak of, the urban workers did not constitute a true proletariat, nor the urban businessmen a true bourgeoisie. Both belonged to a service economy that depended on foreign capital, if not a foreign presence in the country.[10] When Americans, such as Douglas Pike, claimed that the Vietnamese did not understand the class struggle, that they were more interested in nationalism and land reform, they ignored the

---

* Americans, informed that "Viet Cong" means "Vietnamese Communist," have always wondered why the term was not acceptable to the NLF. The explanation lies not only in the fact that the NLF was not an exclusively Communist front, but in the translation of "Communism." "Viet Cong" was a term invented by the Diem regime to connect the NLF with the secular, proletarian-based revolution that Ho Chi Minh had specifically rejected.

fact that in the Vietnamese context the class struggle and the war of national liberation were almost identical. To rid the country of the foreigners was, in a sense, to rid it of every class enemy with the possible exception of the landlords, Lenin's "medieval vestiges." With the inclusion of a land reform program, the nationalist rebellion was also a struggle for a classless society.

But national liberation was only the first goal of the revolution. The second goal was the transformation of Vietnamese society. To Westerners it was this project that appeared by far the most problematic in Marxist terms, for it involved not merely capturing the means of production, but creating them. Like the Chinese, the Vietnamese believed that this creation could not be accomplished without a change in human nature itself. To many Westerners, including Soviet scholars and non-Communist Americans alike, this formulation implied a revision, if not a rejection, of Marxist causality that puts economic development before the development of political consciousness. According to classical Marxist theory, the elimination of social classes would of itself provide the condition for a solution to the problems of government and the economy. Optimistically, Marx believed that once social oppression had been removed, human nature would gradually improve of itself to the point where even the state would become unnecessary. This optimism was, however, premised on the existence of a proletariat quite as capable (so much went without saying) of managing the factories as the classes it served. In Vietnam and China, however, this essential condition did not obtain. There, classless society — while relatively easy to achieve — meant a society largely composed of peasants and generally ill-adapted to managing any form of modern organization. There the problem of the revolution was not merely to raise the consciousness of the workers, but to change the consciousness of peasants. In Vietnam, as in China, the fact that an official came from a peasant background did not insure that he would behave like one of the people. Whatever background he came from, he would not be immunized against the familiar "diseases" of "authoritarianism," "cliquishness," "love of red tape," and so forth. The society suffered not so much from "the mandarins" as from *mandarinism* — that is, not from a social but a psychological problem rooted in the very structure of the Confucian family. The problem was not necessarily a consequence of the fact that the Chinese and Vietnamese had "skipped" the capitalist "phase of develop-

ment"; it was quite possibly a consequence of any attempt to indus-
trialize and modernize these particular societies at this stage in
world history. The same problem perhaps existed elsewhere in
different forms, but the Vietnamese and the Chinese Communists
recognized and attempted to deal with it as such.

This attempt had one immediate, and to Westerners somewhat
strange, consequence for the Vietnamese definition of the "class
struggle." While the Party cadres often used class categories in the
"scientific" or economic sense, they also used them as moral categories. A man could, for instance, become a "feudalist" if he behaved like one. Conversely, a man with bourgeois antecedents could
lose his designation of "class enemy" if he changed his ideas and
joined the revolution. The historical dialectic was carried out, then,
not just between one part of the society and the other, but between
the conflicting tendencies in each man. "Re-education" was thus
essential to the revolution, and the possibility of it accorded very
well with the traditional Vietnamese understanding of revolution as
an atmospheric change that comes over the whole society at once.

The project of "re-education," of changing human nature, went
far beyond what Marx and Lenin had envisioned as the role of the
socialist state, but it was not so unfamiliar to the Vietnamese. The
Confucian state had, after all, attempted to instruct the society in
personal, as well as in broadly social, morality. Confucianism was
not merely a political system but Tao, a whole way of life. The idea
of an official morality must seem threatening to Westerners, but it
was natural to the Vietnamese: indeed, it was *the* way in which they
understood a political system. Western Marxism with its emphasis
on doctrines, theories, and programs would have been not merely
antipathetic but actually incomprehensible to those brought up in
the Confucian Way.

For the Vietnamese Party cadre Marxism-Leninism was no more a
set of doctrines than was Confucianism, but rather a Tao, or, as the
Marxists put it, a "style of work," "a style of leadership." The Confucian son learned to imitate his father; similarly, the cadre learned
to emulate the revolutionary models of conduct. To him policies and
programs were of secondary importance. He believed that if all
members of the Party behaved "sincerely," they would automatically come up with the correct policies and programs. The low-level
PRP prisoners could not give their American interviewers a theoreti-

cal analysis of Marxism nor describe what their future society would look like any better than they could understand the concept of probability. For them, the heart of Marxism-Leninism was the practice of their Party. As Ho Chi Minh once said, "Our Party is as great as the immense sea, the high mountain. . . . Our Party is virtue, civilization, unity, independence, a peaceful and comfortable life."[11] No Party chairman in Eastern Europe would have made the same claim, for its scope is Confucian — only now the Party instead of the emperor elides with the ideas of "land" and "civilization."

As a matter of practical politics during the years of the war, the Vietnamese Communist parties in the north and the south attempted to follow the middle course between "dogmatism" and "revisionism" by means of mass organization, the parallel hierarchies of the state and the Party, and the principle of collective leadership. To a great extent both succeeded. But the problem with that system was that of all authoritarian systems: its final success in moral as well as power-political terms rested on the wisdom of its top leadership. And that wisdom could not be institutionalized. In 1956 the DRVN undertook a land reform program that proved a total disaster for the state, perhaps, as well as for the people involved. On the advice of Chinese experts, the Vietnamese Party incited the poor peasants to arrest, try, and sentence the "landlords" and "traitors to the revolution" in their villages. The result was an anarchic campaign of terror much like that waged by the Diem regime in 1955–1958 in which, by conservative estimate, some fifty thousand people of all economic stations were killed and the lower ranks of the Party badly damaged. Too late to stop a rebellion in his own native Nghe An province, Ho Chi Minh stepped in to halt the campaign, demoting or firing the officials involved and declaring the program an "error" that required rectification.

The true reason and cause behind the land reform remains problematical. Did the Party initially benefit from the terror? Or did the architect of the program, the theoretician, Truong Chinh, blindly follow Chinese advice without realizing what consequence it might have for the Vietnamese villages? Whatever the reason, the terror pointed up in a lurid manner the kinds of conflicts the revolution created in Vietnamese society, and the moral discrepancy, so common to violent revolutions, between means and end. Were those thousands of people sacrificed for the good of the Party, or was the whole program a disaster from beginning to end? In either case, the exercise of great power in the north for a time exacted the same price in suffering that the Diemist anarchy had demanded in the south.

Still, whatever the damage done during the land reform, the "Rectification of Errors" campaign was a remarkable achievement for the North Vietnamese Party and Ho Chi Minh. It may have been the only occasion when a Communist Party leader has publicly declared himself and his own Party chiefs in error over such a major issue. The term "error" must sound Orwellian to Westerners, but for a Party and a people who believe in the confluence of virtue with the laws of the universe, scientifically understood, it has profound, even cosmic, moral implications. The equivalent in the West would be for a president or prime minister to confess that he committed treason against the nation. Ho Chi Minh was able to do it in part because of his tenacity to the principle of collective leadership.

This tenacity distinguished the Vietnamese Party, for in so many other Communist countries the top leadership itself destroyed the Marxist-Leninist collectivity. In the Soviet Union, for instance, Stalin, after Lenin's death, elevated himself to the position of supreme leader with powers of infallibility. Every program he undertook had therefore to be infallibly correct. Ho Chi Minh, by contrast, enforced Party discipline even upon himself, thus endowing his government with a great degree of flexibility.[12] After 1954, when the Democratic Republic was firmly established in Hanoi, Ho gave up responsibility for the administration of state to act as the symbol of national unity and, upon occasion, as the arbiter between the political factions. From this position he was able to resolve crises when they arose without damaging the unity of the Party. As Paul Mus once put it, he promoted himself out of the political sphere to become the revered "ancestor" of the revolution within his lifetime. The advantage of the semi-abdication was that while he remained as charismatic a figure to his own countrymen as Mao was to the Chinese, he was able to limit the "cult of personality" and provide for his own succession. When he died in 1969, he left his power and prestige to the same close associates that had been transacting the affairs of state for over a decade.

Given the personal view that the Vietnamese take of politics, the stance and personality of Ho Chi Minh had a significance for the political system as a whole that escapes Western political science "concepts." For the Vietnamese, Ho Chi Minh was not only "the George Washington of his country," as an American senator once put it. He was the personification of the revolution — the representative of the new community to itself. For that reason the study of Ho Chi Minh is perhaps more important to an understanding of the Vietnamese revolution than an analysis of all the ideological debates. For Ho was perfectly conscious of his role. He orchestrated his own public gestures just as carefully as the emperors had performed the rites in order to *show* the Vietnamese what had to be done. His reticence was in itself a demonstration.

Quite consciously, Ho Chi Minh forswore the grand patriarchal tradition of the Confucian emperors. Consciously he created an "image" of himself as "Uncle Ho" — the gentle, bachelor relative who has only disinterested affection for the children who are *not* his own sons. As a warrior and a politician he acted ruthlessly upon occasion, but in public and as head of state he took pains to promote that family feeling which Vietnamese have often had for their leaders, and which he felt was the proper relationship between the people and their government. "Our Party," he said, "is great because it covers the whole country and is at the same time close to the heart of every compatriot. . . . It has won so much love in thirty years of struggle and success."[13] Whether in giving sweets to children or in asking the peasants what they received of the hog that was killed for the cadre's birthday, he evoked the world of the old village, where strict patriarchal rule was mitigated by the egalitarian pressure of the small community. The affairs of small nations, he seemed to suggest, are qualitatively different from those of large ones: Vietnam would need none of the great powers' grandiose illusions — or their grandiose brutalities. The Vietnamese style should be that of simplicity combined with inner strength and resiliency. Ho Chi Minh, with his wispy figure, his shorts and sandals, had the sense of irony and understatement so common among Vietnamese. When asked by a European why he had never written a book of his own "Thoughts," he answered with perfect ambiguity that Mao Tse-tung had written all there was to say, hadn't he? In his last will and testament to the Vietnamese people Ho made no claims to singularity. He merely hoped that Vietnam would make a "worthy contribution" to world revolution; he hoped, too, that he would not be given a great funeral lest it "waste the time and money of the people."

Just days before the Tet offensive of 1968, the NLF cadres from the battalions that were to assault Saigon took their men — or so it was reported — to a certain place in the forest to give them their last instructions and words of encouragement. There, where the underbrush had been cleared away for acres, they showed them the hundreds of coffins they had built for the soldiers who would be killed in battle. When they had seen the coffins, the soldiers, it seemed, felt happier and less afraid to die.

As Paul Mus once said, the Vietnamese know a great deal better than we do that society is largely made up of its dead. For the Vietnamese, life is but a moment of transition in the unbroken skein of other lives stretching from the past into the future. Death in the absolute sense comes only when there is a break in the society that carries life on through the generations. Such a break had come in the life of the Ngo family; it had by the 1960's occurred to most Vietnamese families of the south. It was not just that so many had lost their sons and their ancestral lands in the war; it was that even before the war so few of the young people had practiced the rites of ancestor worship. They had not practiced the rites because they were, as the young said, "not practical." But the NLF had offered them a new kind of family, a new form of social security. The sight of the coffins reassured the soldiers because it showed them not only that the Front cared about their future, but that it could fulfill its promises. The provision of the coffins was, after all, a logistical triumph and, as such, a sign that the Front had the power to re-weave the society and restore its continuity through past, present, and future. The weaver of that unity was Ho Chi Minh.

Upon his return to Vietnam in the 1940's, Ho Chi Minh set up his headquarters in a cave in the northern mountains above a swiftly rushing river. He renamed that mountain Marx and the river Lenin, making a symbolic connection between the ancient Vietnamese image that defined the country and the new history in which that country would live. His method was traditional — the rectification of names. Ho Chi Minh's life made the same connection. As a child he lived in the countryside with his mandarin father, who had engaged in the last resistance of the traditional Confucians to the West. As a young man he had gone West — to Paris, to Moscow, and then back to Vietnam by way of China. As a mature man he had made the synthesis, turning Western theories and methods to use against the Western occupation of his country. Through Marxism-Leninism he provided the Vietnamese with a new way to perceive their society and the means to knit it up into the skein of history. He showed them the way back to many of the traditional values and a way forward to the optimism of the West — to the belief in change as progress and the power of the small people. Through Marxism-Leninism he indicated the road to economic development, to a greater social mobility and a greater interaction between the masses of the people and their government. He reformed the villages, linked them together, and created a nation. Whether or not the system could stand up to the full force of the American war, whether it would last a thousand years, whether it would in the end prove only destructive to Vietnam and the rest of Southeast Asia, it was, nonetheless, a way to national unity and independence, and, by the end of the American war, still the only way the Vietnamese knew.

II

The Americans and the
Saigon Government

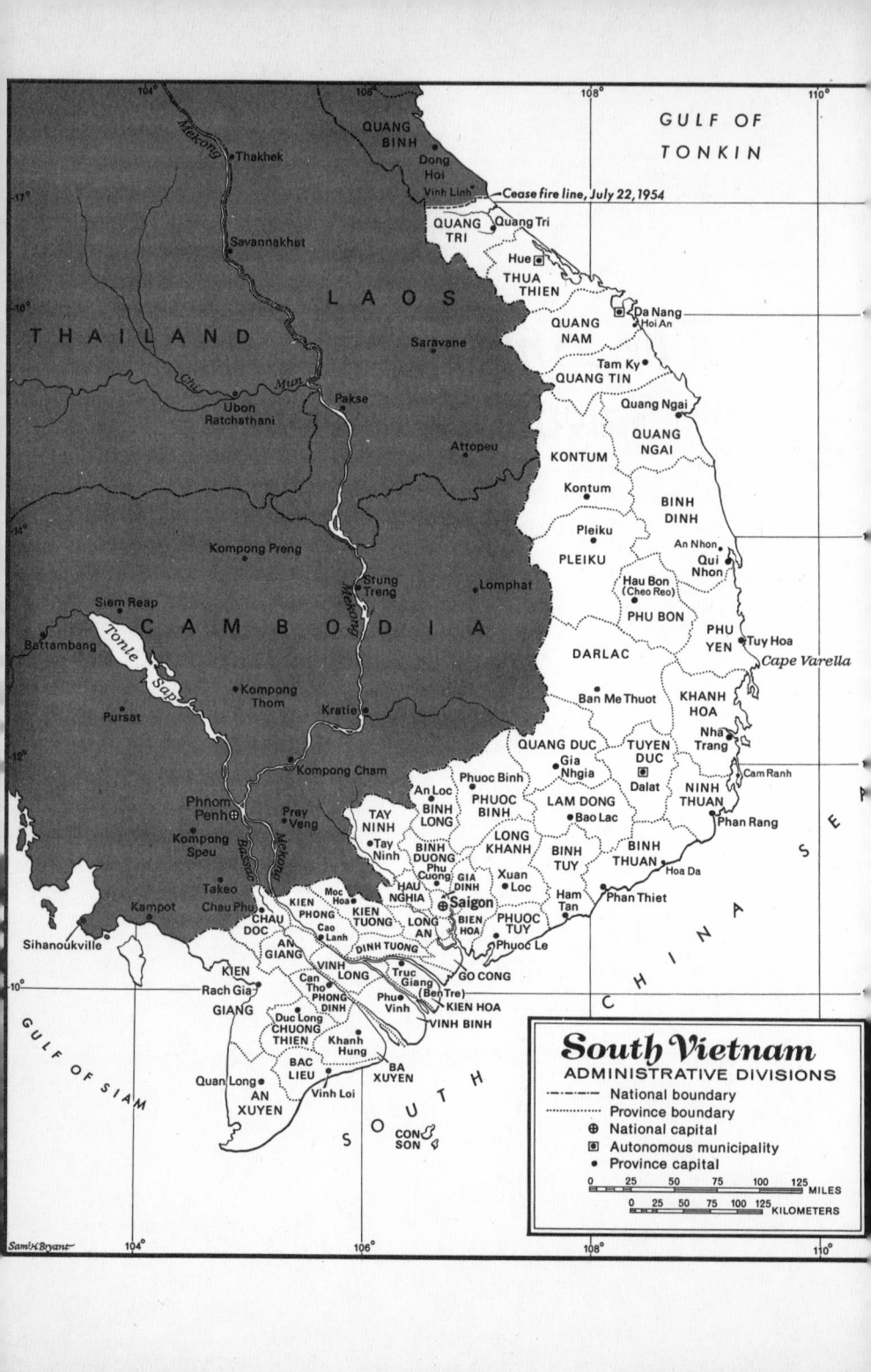

South Vietnam
ADMINISTRATIVE DIVISIONS

—·—·—	National boundary
··········	Province boundary
⊕	National capital
⊡	Autonomous municipality
•	Province capital

0 25 50 75 100 125 MILES

0 25 50 75 100 125 KILOMETERS

GULF OF TONKIN

LAOS

THAILAND

CAMBODIA

GULF OF SIAM

SOUTH CHINA SEA

Thakhek

Savannakhet

QUANG BINH

Dong Hoi

Vinh Linh

Cease fire line, July 22, 1954

QUANG TRI

Quang Tri

Hue

THUA THIEN

Da Nang

Hoi An

QUANG NAM

Saravane

Tam Ky

QUANG TIN

Quang Ngai

QUANG NGAI

Ubon Ratchathani

Pakse

KONTUM

Kontum

BINH DINH

Attopeu

Pleiku

PLEIKU

An Nhon

Qui Nhon

Kompong Preng

Lomphat

Stung Treng

Hau Bon (Cheo Reo)

PHU BON

PHU YEN

Tuy Hoa

Cape Varella

Siem Reap

DARLAC

Battambang

Tonle Sap

Pursat

KHANH HOA

Kompong Thom

Ban Me Thuot

Kratie

Mekong

QUANG DUC

Gia Nhgia

TUYEN DUC

Nha Trang

NINH THUAN

Cam Ranh

Kompong Cham

Phuoc Binh

Dalat

An Loc

BINH LONG

PHUOC BINH

LAM DONG

Phan Rang

Phnom Penh

Prey Veng

TAY NINH

Bao Loc

BINH TUY

BINH THUAN

Kompong Speu

Tay Ninh

LONG KHANH

Hoa Da

Takeo

Chau Phu

Moc Hoa

BINH DUONG

Phu Cuong

GIA DINH

HAU NGHIA

Xuan Loc

Ham Tan

Phan Thiet

Kampot

KIEN PHONG

Cao Lanh

KIEN TUONG

Saigon

BIEN HOA

PHUOC TUY

CHAU DOC

AN GIANG

LONG AN

Phuoc Le

Sihanoukville

Can Tho

VINH LONG

DINH TUONG

Truc Giang (Ben Tre)

GO CONG

Rach Gia

KIEN GIANG

PHONG DINH

Phu Vinh

KIEN HOA

Duc Long

CHUONG THIEN

Khanh Hung

VINH BINH

Quan Long

BAC LIEU

BA XUYEN

AN XUYEN

Vinh Loi

CON SON

Sam H. Bryant

5

Mise en scène

This war, like most wars, is filled with terrible irony. For what do the people of North Vietnam want? They want what their neighbors also desire: food for their hunger, health for their bodies and a chance to learn, progress for their country, and an end to the bondage of material misery. And they would find all these things far more readily in peaceful association with others than in the endless course of battle.

These countries of Southeast Asia are homes for millions of impoverished people. Each day these people rise at dawn and struggle through until the night to wrest existence from the soil. They are often wracked by disease, plagued by hunger, and death comes at the early age of forty.

Stability and peace do not come easily in such a land. Neither independence nor human dignity will ever be won by arms alone. It also requires the works of peace. The American people have helped generously in times past in these works. Now there must be a much more massive effort to improve the life of man in that conflict-torn corner of our world.

> Lyndon Johnson,
> Speech at Johns Hopkins University
> (April 7, 1965)[1]

In the forties and fifties we took our stand in Europe to protect the freedom of those threatened by aggression. . . . Now the center of attention has shifted to another part of the world where aggression is on the march and the enslavement of free men is its goal. . . .

If we allow the Communists to win in Vietnam, it will become easier and more appetizing for them to take over other countries in other parts of the world. We will have to fight again some place else — at what cost no one knows. That is why it is vitally important to every American family that we stop the Communists in South Vietnam.

> Lyndon Johnson
> at Honolulu
> (February 6, 1966)[2]

On February 6, 1966, the President of the United States met with the premier and chief of state of the Republic of South Vietnam for the first time in over a decade. The meeting, held in Honolulu, was one of those symbolic gestures that statesmen make from time to time in order to underscore a decision — gestures that in this age of television and wire photos become instant portraits, showing, or purporting to show, what is going on behind closed doors. In this case, however, the gesture marked no solution to a crisis, no real change in policy. The American troops had landed in Vietnam almost a year before. If it marked any event at all, it marked the change in Johnson's temper. Over the past few days the President had had his patience severely tried by, among others, the members of the Senate Foreign Relations Committee who were conducting an investigation into what had become a major war in Vietnam.

Johnson later confessed that he could never understand why Senator Fulbright had questioned his constitutional right to commit American troops to Vietnam when the Tonkin Gulf Resolution so clearly permitted him to "take all necessary steps including the use of force to assist any member or protocol state of the Southeast Asia Collective Defense Treaty requesting assistance in defense of its freedom." Senator Fulbright, however, contended that the President ought to have brought a declaration of war before the Senate. The legal argument was important, but the heart of the matter was that Fulbright, with the support of liberals in and out of the universities, had begun to challenge the entire Vietnam policy. In the first month of 1966 Johnson realized that he would have to fight for his war. And thus the Honolulu Conference.

The decision to call the conference was a typically Johnsonian gesture, combined of vanity, shrewdness, and overbearing energy. On February 4, the President, like a Tartar chieftain, suddenly instructed most of the cabinet, the chairman of the Joint Chiefs of Staff, several generals, ranks of assorted diplomats and technical advisers, the heads of mission in Saigon, and the Vietnamese government officials, to convene in Honolulu in two days' time. "We are here," he announced upon arrival, "to talk especially of the works of peace. We will leave here determined not only to achieve victory over aggression but to win victory over hunger, disease, and despair. We are making a reality out of the hopes of the common people."

It was the great justification. The United States was not going into Vietnam merely for crass power objectives, but for the salvation of the Vietnamese, who, like the majority of mankind, lived in poverty and ignorance. The fight against Communism demanded

not only military power and determination, but all the prowess of an
advanced industrial society and the generosity of a nation that led
the world in its search for peace, prosperity, and freedom. One
section of the final declaration read, "The United States is pledged
to the principle of the self-determination of peoples and of government by the consent of the governed. . . . We have helped and we
will help [the Vietnamese] to stabilize the economy, to increase the
production of goods, to spread the light of education and stamp out
disease."

Surely the leader of no other nation would have made such a
pledge in the midst of a war. No other leader would have expected
his countrymen to take it as anything but a cynical gesture. But
Johnson was not cynical, and he did not see himself as straining the
limits of American credibility. His rhetoric was, after all, familiar,
even traditional, to American diplomacy. Woodrow Wilson wanted
to "make the world safe for democracy," Franklin Roosevelt, Eisenhower, Stevenson, and Kennedy had in their turn pledged the nation
to fight against oppression, hunger, ignorance, and disease around
the world. Confidence in American power and virtue suffused the
American view of the world. In proclaiming the Open Door policy
for China, in conquering the Philippines and supporting Chiang Kai-
shek during the Second World War, American statesmen had confidence that their own actions were in the best interests of the countries concerned. This faith, this shrewd innocence, they guarded
with a ferocity.

Lyndon Johnson preserved and guarded it perhaps better than
any of his predecessors. Brought up in the small towns of Texas, he
began his career as a populist of the old school, a defender of the
small farmer and businessman against the vast industrial interests of
the East. As a congressman under Roosevelt in the 1930's and 1940's
he saw the countryside change rapidly as a result of government
intervention. He identified with Roosevelt, with government power,
and with the notion of a strong presidency. And he believed in the
essential goodness of the United States and its almost infinite capacity for righting the wrongs of mankind. "We must move the country
forward," Kennedy said, but Johnson saw Kennedy as the phrase-
maker and himself as the instrument of that progress. At home he
intended to fulfill Roosevelt's New Deal legislation with his own
"Great Society" program, and abroad . . . One of the Vietnamese
officers understood the implication exactly. "Mr. Johnson," he said,

"we are a small country and we don't have pretensions to building a Great Society. We just want to have a better society." But the irony was lost on Johnson. Even more than Roosevelt, who claimed to understand China because of his family connections with it, Johnson tended to see the world as an extension of his own person. In April 1965 he offered the North Vietnamese the opportunity to participate in a billion-dollar American development project for Southeast Asia, centering on a vast TVA-like development of the Mekong River. It would have been the greatest piece of pork-barrel legislation in history — except that the Mekong River does not run through North Vietnam. But perhaps that could be fixed, too. The idea that the United States could not master the problems of a country as small and underdeveloped as Vietnam did not occur to Johnson as a possibility.

Nor did it occur to many other Americans at the time of Honolulu. The Americans who sat with Johnson at the conference table made a picture of that confidence — a heroic frieze portraying the weight and substance behind the Vietnam policy. Beside the President sat Secretary of State Dean Rusk, Secretary of Defense Robert McNamara, Secretary of Agriculture Orville Freeman; Secretary of Health, Education and Welfare, John Gardner; Assistant Defense Secretary John McNaughton; McGeorge Bundy, the President's chief foreign policy adviser; General Maxwell Taylor; Admiral U. S. Grant Sharp; General Earle Wheeler, the chairman of the Joint Chiefs of Staff; the Honorable Averell Harriman, Ambassador Leonard Unger, Governor John Burns of Hawaii, General William C. Westmoreland, and Ambassador Henry Cabot Lodge. If not each of them individually, then all of them taken together gave a fair representation of the power and dominion of the United States. Some of them were brilliant men, and all of them had long and distinguished careers in the high offices of government, of big business, and the universities. They were the essence of professional Washington, the men who had made or influenced policy over the course of several administrations. Though some of them would not have put the matter in quite the same terms as Johnson, all of them believed in the willingness and capacity of the United States to achieve the program of Honolulu in Vietnam. They were powerful men, after all, and, being powerful, they were self-confident.

Too self-confident, perhaps, to notice that the conference, seen as a frieze, had a curious lopsided look to it. On the other side of the table from the Americans were three Vietnamese; in the center, Air Vice-Marshal Nguyen Cao Ky. Ky was not wearing his pearl-handled revolver and his black flying suit with the purple silk handkerchief tied around his neck, but this catlike figure with his rakish moustache still provided some contrast to the gentlemen sitting opposite. For the past eight months the thirty-five-year-old bomber pilot had been acting premier of the Republic of Vietnam. Beside him at the table sat General Nguyen Van Thieu, the chief of state and chairman of the Armed Forces Council. Five years older than Ky, he had a more solid look about him. Reportedly the brains of the junta, he had been Ky's closest associate in the series of coups that brought them to power, but he remained an unknown quantity even to those Americans arriving from Saigon. On Ky's other side sat the defense minister, General Nguyen Huu Co, with his strange snake's head, the yellow skin stretched tight across his small, high cheekbones. Despite his looks, Co was an affable man with a taste for French champagne and pretty women. He had, it was said, made certain investments in Vietnamese real estate soon to be acquired by the Americans.

"The Vietnamese chiefs of state today pledged their country to 'the work of the social revolution, the goal of free self-government, the attack on ignorance and disease.'"

The *New York Times* was undoubtedly correct, but somehow its prose failed to convey the quality of the statement, or the extravagance of the gesture that President Johnson had made in calling such a conference. The frieze was there. It accurately recorded the events that were to come, but those men who sat for their portraits did not realize what it signified.

6

Politicians and Generals

Lullaby
There were many nights
Many, many nights
When I nursed and whispered to my child:
Sleep tight my child
Then when you grow up
When you grow up
You will sell your country to become a mandarin.
— A popular song in Saigon, 1969,
by Mien Duc Thang.

one

The fall of the Diem regime had come like the breaking of a great river dam, the political energy of the cities overflowing and using itself up in the act of destruction. Having cleared away the barrier of the regime, the rebels seemed to have no positive ideas, no energy for the task of building a government. Rather than organizing and pressuring the generals for reforms, they indulgently returned to their private pursuits: the intellectuals to their endless discussions, the students to their jazz music and their university elections, the Buddhists to the obscure world from which they had come. Hastily assembled from among the most prestigious of the generals, the new military junta barricaded itself into the general staff headquarters on the outskirts of town and occupied its time with bickering over the distribution of army posts.[1]

There was an air of relief, of celebration. The political prisoners returned from Poulo Condore, the bars and nightclubs reopened, and the bar girls came back like painted swallows to settle in the bars of Tu Do Street. At the same time there was an air of uncertainty and fear for the future. Who, after all, did the "revolution" belong to? A truly popular uprising, it had no single leader and no political dynamic except that of revulsion for the ineffectual tyranny of Diem. The generals had executed the plot, but their coup came as a distinct anticlimax to the outburst of popular demonstrations. The most prestigious of the generals joined the coup only at the thirteenth hour. General Tran Thien Khiem, for instance, had been engaged in another officers' plot; General Ton That Dinh, a Catholic and a distant member of the royal family, had until the day before the coup appeared to be working for a phony coup planned by Ngo Dinh Nhu himself.[2] Because almost every general had been involved in one or more of the officers' plots, it was only a matter of chance that the Don-Minh coup succeeded and the others failed. No one was more conscious of this than the junta members themselves. While they made hopeful proclamations of national unity, they took care to post the most powerful of their brother officers to distant parts of the country.

Their difficulty, however, lay not so much in smothering the opposition as in creating a government. The bluff professional soldier, General Duong Van Minh, inspired some trust among the Buddhists, students, and intellectuals — but less, it seemed, for what he did than for what he did not do. He was the chairman of the junta, and yet he refused to appear in public — to give the Vietnamese a picture of the new regime — or to set about reorganizing the government. Undecided about setting themselves up as the state authority, he and his fellow junta members did little to create a framework of civilian institutions through which a political authority might emerge. In all the months of plotting they seemed to have thought little beyond the coup itself.

The government was leaderless — and perhaps predictably so, for, insofar as the coup represented more than a change of personalities, it represented a victory for the southerners against the northerners and centrists, a victory for the landlords against the mandarins. Like many of the Saigon students and intellectuals, the generals came mostly from the Cochin Chinese bourgeoisie. They were people who lacked any tradition of self-government and who, as men from the rich provinces, considered government more a threat or a nuisance than a way of life.[3] Still, as Vietnamese, they could not conceive of government as a federal system. For years they had relied on the French to provide the authority for a system they could not themselves manage. After twelve years of Diem they both feared a strong central government that would forceably reduce the complexities of southern politics, and feared the anarchy that would result from its absence.

But the choice could not be made in the abstract. And in the winter of 1963 there was no one in the cities who possessed that revolutionary legitimacy that the Vietnamese knew as the Mandate of Heaven. Lacking such authority, the generals could do little but wait and watch the slowly shifting colors of the political landscape. The Americans — officials and reporters — attributed their inaction to personal weakness, or worse, to their "neutralist sympathies," but the generals exercised only realism by refusing to push forward with some arbitrary plan. For the Vietnamese there either was a "correct solution" or there was no solution at all. And in that winter the prospects for a national anti-Communist movement arising did not look bright.

In the countryside the non-Communist political groups had grown considerably weaker since 1954. Between them, the NLF and the Diem regime had managed to disable, if not to destroy, most of the local governments that had resisted the Viet Minh — the one exception being the Catholics. The landlords were gone from much of the Delta. Some continued to collect rents through the GVN officials, but the vast majority had lost their exclusive hold over the peasants. The Hoa Hao and the Cao Dai had survived the Diemist repressions, but their area of influence had contracted to a few provinces along the Cambodian border: An Giang, Chau Doc, and Tay Ninh. Because their greatest desire was to avoid occupation by either of the large armies, no government in Saigon could count on them for active military support. In central Vietnam the old Vietnamese Kuomintang, the VNQDD, held onto a few thousand adherents in the villages and the cities. Led by a group of rather tired old men, it remained totally autarchic — anti-Communist, anti-Buddhist, and anti whatever part of the Saigon government challenged its rule over the villages.

Unlike the French, the Diem regime had paid very little attention to conciliating the non-Vietnamese minorities: the Cambodians of the western Delta, the Cham of central Vietnam, the montagnard tribes, and the urban Chinese. The last two were of particular importance — the montagnards because they inhabited the strategic Central Highlands, the Chinese because they controlled virtually all the trade and commerce of the country. Over the years the Ngos

had attempted to reduce these groups' importance by settling Vietnamese in the Highlands (on montagnard land) and by insisting
that the Chinese accept Vietnamese citizenship and Vietnamese
government control. They had succeeded only in alienating both
groups. By 1963 the montagnards were divided between tribes that
supported the NLF and tribes that, largely because of the work of
the American Special Forces and the CIA, claimed their independence from all Vietnamese authorities. The Chinese, for their part
dependent on the trade through Saigon, held themselves aloof from
political commitment and, in general, from Vietnamese society.

This patchwork of sects and ethnic minorities was further complicated by factionalism within each group. The Chinese were divided
into a number of societies, the montagnards into numerous language
groups. The VNQDD had three factions, the Hoa Hao at least four,
and the Cao Dai a masterful eight, none of which agreed even on
the terms of disagreement with each other, and all of whom opposed
any intrusion by the central government.

In the cities alone could an American-backed government expect
to find mass support. As an economic enterprise, Saigon was, as
always, a capon tied to the strings of the international market.
During periods of war it lived off foreign aid instead of foreign trade
and grew more and more dependent. The political repression of the
intellectuals aside, Saigon profited under the Diem regime, and
could expect to do so as long as its armies kept the NLF out of the
city itself and American support continued. The French arrangement, in other words, continued to work in the cities as it did not in
the countryside. The one difficulty with this arrangement was that it
did not operate as anything more than a negative political force.

In Saigon and Hue the fall of the Diem regime called forth a mass
of new political parties and newspapers and a whirlwind of rhetoric
consisting of denunciations of the old regime and proposals for and
criticisms of the new. The debates came as a welcome change after
the uniformity of the Diemist press, but they revealed all too clearly
the absence of any coherent political force. Such "parties" as existed
were fragmentary and generally unstable coalitions formed around
one or two intellectuals or civil servants. In Saigon, it was said, two
men constituted a party, three men a party and a faction. The
largest of these parties, the Dai Viet (of which there were three
factions) was little more than a network of useful contacts for
prominent officers and civil servants. And none of these parties had

a plan, a program, even an ambition to organize in the countryside or among the poor of the cities.

The smallness and incoherence of the urban parties had been a hallmark of Vietnamese politics since the colonial period. During the years of French liberalism in the 1930's, Saigon had supported dozens of such parties from the Constitutionalists to the Trotskyites. Since that time none of them had grown to any size or penetrated beyond the suburbs. French, and later American, analysts provided complicated cultural explanations for this phenomenon, but the most convincing explanation is economic. The group of intellectuals and civil servants from which these parties came constituted a privileged elite — an elite such as exists only in colonized countries, an elite that sustains itself not on any local base of production but on the work of the foreigners. Frantz Fanon has argued with regard to African countries that the role of this elite is to serve as an intermediary between the foreigners and the natives of the interior. In periods of colonial liberalism it forms parties not to organize the people against the foreigners but to manipulate the foreigners for its own ends, using the threat of the discontented masses as its means of leverage. It demands independence for the country, but it cannot produce it, for its interests lie not in building a nation but in assuming exclusive control over what the foreigners have created.[4] Granted independence, it will attempt to continue to act as an intermediary with the foreigners and to defend its own exclusive entrée into the trade market, the higher educational system, and the government bureaucracy. The Saigon intelligentsia was such a group under the Americans as under the French. By virtue of its success as an intermediary, it became a group of people with a very different culture from the rest of the Vietnamese.

Even after a decade of independence, most of the prominent Saigon politicians and high-ranking intellectuals were being educated abroad. (This in striking contrast to the NLF leaders.)[5] Many of them were the very people, or the descendants of the people, who had served the French and acted as their loyal opposition. They lived in the luxurious walled villas of French Saigon and worked in the yellow- or pink-stuccoed office buildings with their ceiling fans and their air of colonial decay. Now after ten years of the Diem regime there were simply more of them than there were before, and some spoke English instead of French. Among them there were a number of intelligent and hard-working men, such as the northern populist, Dr. Phan Quang Dan, the newspaper publisher, Dr. Dan Van Sung, and somewhat further to the left, the lawyer Tran Van Tuyen and the economists Vu Van Thai and Au Truong Thanh. These men provided some cogent criticisms of American policies in Vietnam, and yet they have had no real influence and provide no political alternative. Like Ngo Dinh Diem, many of them were confused men who could find no meeting point between their own education and interests and the demands of their countrymen. Fanon described their dilemma perfectly.

The colonialist bourgeoisie, in its narcissistic dialogue, expounded by the members of its universities, had in fact deeply implanted in the minds of the colonised intellectual that the essential qualities remain eternal in spite of all the blunders men may make: the essential qualities of the West, of course. The native intellectual accepted the cogency of these ideas, and deep down in his brain you could always find a vigilant sentinel ready to defend the Greco-Latin pedestal. Now it so happens that during the struggle for liberation, at the moment that the native intellectual comes into touch again with his people, this artificial sentinel is turned into dust. All the Mediterranean values . . . become lifeless. . . . Individualism is the first to disappear.[6]

That moment had arrived for Nguyen Huu Tho and the other Saigonese leaders of the NLF, but it never did for those who remained behind in the cities. The Saigon politicians and intellectuals would continue to tinker with legislatures and constitutions that did not begin to touch upon the lives of the peasants or even the poor of the cities.

One proof of the impotence of these intellectuals was their failure to provide leadership during the last few months of the Diem regime. In an age of increasing secularism the students of Saigon and Hue looked to the religious groups for guidance at the moment of crisis. Curiously enough, the student conspiracy against Diem began within the Catholic Student Union — the only student organization permitted to exist. When the Buddhist rebellion broke out, the Catholic dissidents allied with the nominally Buddhist students to support the bonzes. After the November coup, the alliance fell apart, leaving the various student activists to form their own small, intransigent movements and to engage in a bewildering series of factional fights that paralleled those of their elders. In the morass of city politics only the religious groups, that drew the city people back to the values that predated colonial rule, managed to sustain any organized vitality.

Because of the nature of the coup, the Catholic organizations did not suffer as much as might have been expected from the fall of the Diem regime. Some of the members of Nhu's Can Lao Party went to jail and the Buddhists challenged the Catholic dominion over Hue, but the majority of the reprisals were personal vendettas that had little effect upon the Church as a whole. With a communion of at least two million members and the strict discipline imposed by its priestly hierarchy, the Catholics remained the most powerful group in non-Communist South Vietnam. Catholicism was a force which had to be reckoned with by every government — and yet, like the Hoa Hao and the Cao Dai, it was a syncretic sect and not a nationalist movement. If the fact had to be demonstrated (and it did not, for the Catholics did not make the same claim as the Buddhists to representing "the whole mass of the people"), the fall of Diem did that. As a revealed religion with a precise doctrine and a Western form of social organization, it was both too narrow and too closely associated with the French regime to have appeal for the great mass of the Vietnamese. Under the Diem regime a few ambitious young men, such as Nguyen Van Thieu, converted to Catholicism for much the same reason as their predecessors had under the French, but the Catholic population remained essentially stable: one either was a Catholic or one was not depending on one's family background. Furthermore, one was either a northern or a southern Catholic — the distinction being as hard and fast as any in Vietnamese politics.[7]

The Catholics formed the most stable and predictable of the southern political groups; the Buddhists, by contrast, constituted the most fluid and ill-disciplined of them all.[8] The Buddhists set the standard of rebellion against Diem, but they had, as yet, no coherent political organization and no support in the countryside. Their advantages lay in their leadership and in the resonance of Buddhism in the historical memories of the Vietnamese. Unlike the Catholics, they could claim to speak for "the whole mass of the Vietnamese people" and to feel some common cause even with those Vietnamese who supported the NLF. In a speech to the crowds gathered at the new headquarters, a vast barnlike pagoda in the slums of Saigon, the elderly Thich Tam Chau, now head of the Institute for the Propagation of the Buddhist Faith, could recall the time when a Buddhist monarch ruled Vietnam and when during the years of war and political chaos, Buddhism sustained the inner life of the country. A northerner and a political moderate in Saigonese terms, Tam Chau began to gather followers from among the straight-laced bourgeoisie of Saigon that rejected Catholicism and Communism alike as foreign-influence doctrines. He and his associates worked closely with the rest of the bonzes during the events of 1963, but as time went on it became apparent that the unity of the bonzes could not survive the release of pressure. On goals as well as on questions of tactics Tam Chau split with the High Clerical Council (the spiritual, as opposed to the secular, authority of the Unified Buddhist Church) and the brilliant central Vietnamese, Thich Tri Quang.

The divisions among the bonzes must have run deep, for in many ways Tri Quang was the most able and inspired of all the non-Communist political leaders. An intense and fiercely independent man in his early forties, Tri Quang had spent some time with the Viet Minh during the early part of the French Indochina War. Breaking with the Communists in the early 1950's, he had returned to the pagoda and directed his enormous energies to forming a Buddhist movement in Hue. As one of the prime movers in the conspiracy against Diem, he had, in flight from Diemist police, taken refuge for several weeks in the American embassy, an asylum for which he professed a debt of gratitude to the United States. After the November coup, he set himself to the task of establishing contact between the Mahayana organizations of the cities and the Theravada bonzes of the Delta. When, like most attempts to organize the Delta, his initiative more or less failed, he began to concentrate his energies upon Hue and the surrounding villages, setting up family and youth associations formed partly on traditional models, partly on those of the Viet Minh.[9]

A fiery speaker and at the same time an introspective intellectual, Tri Quang belonged to the tradition of religiously inspired Vietnamese leaders. His looks commanded attention — the high forehead, the large brilliant eyes, and the small body expressing the cerebral intensity of the man. As was not true of most of the Saigon bonzes, including his own supporters, Thich Thien Minh and Thich Ho Giac, he lived the correct, ascetic life of a bonze, fasting on the proper days, sleeping in a bare cell, and spending hours of each day in meditation. Like Ho Chi Minh, he lived in a "sincere" manner, and, like him, he had the capacity to inspire trust in all kinds of people from the poor cyclo drivers of Hue to the most sophisticated intellectuals. In Hue he tended to avoid foreigners and to refuse to speak anything but Vietnamese. To Americans, therefore, he was something of an enigma, someone to be watched and mistrusted, a man who professed anti-Communism and yet refused to make an unconditional commitment to the war or to the Saigon government.

But in the winter of 1963–1964 it was not at all clear what the Buddhist movement might become. The American journalists were bewildered by the relation of these bonzes to Vietnamese Buddhism, and understandably so, for no one, including the bonzes, knew who might finally respond to the call of those who claimed to express the wishes of all "Buddhists." Tri Quang and Tam Chau would not explain that their strength depended upon the extent to which they could reconcile the diverse interests of those who had joined the anti-Diemist demonstrations and mold the formless impulse of rejection into a disciplined force. Nor would they explain that beyond the problem of organizing the urban bourgeoisie lay that of organizing the poor and the people of the countryside, who, though nominally "Buddhist," obeyed no religious authority. Would "Buddhism" disintegrate, would it harden into a small autarchic sect, like all of the other religious groups, or would it develop and take on the dimensions of a nationalism? The question was an important one for the future — that is, if non-Communist Vietnam had a future — for Buddhism was the only new political movement in the cities and the only one that seemed to have any potential for growth.

It was, in a way, pathetic, this call for unity on the part of the junta. Now, after eight years of the Diem regime, non-Communist Vietnam was less united than ever. To the Delta there remained only a handful of landed families and the miraculous sects; to central Vietnam, the towns and villages in which the Catholics, Buddhists, and old-fashioned political parties continued their fierce blood feuds. Saigon itself remained much as it was when French legionnaires, bitter and exhausted, watched the French empire collapse, revealing unfathomable depths of corruption and chaos.

The generals of the Minh junta themselves represented the last and best dream of France — the success of its *mission civilisatrice* and its policy of assimilation. General Tran Van Don had been born in the Gironde, and many of the others had spent the better part of their youth in France. General Minh — "Big Minh," as this tall and robust officer was affectionately known — had been a star student at the École de Chartres; General Le Van Kim had trained to be a film maker in Paris and was, it was said, working on a film with René Clair when the first Indochina War broke out.[10] All of them had joined the army to fight for a French-influenced Vietnam — to preserve what there was of Paris in Saigon — and they had failed to understand that France had never penetrated the villages. The rise of Ngo Dinh Diem put them in a dilemma, for though they were "nationalists" (all Vietnamese were "nationalists" in the sense that they wished for a government by Vietnamese), they found themselves fighting for a Vietnam they did not believe in. Finally, and almost fortuitously, taking power, they found they had nothing to offer the people of the villages and the city streets. Of more immediate consequence, they found that the war was being lost.

During the two months following the November coup, the NLF moved into the Delta provinces just south of Saigon, confining the GVN troops to the province capitals and inflicting upon them their highest casualties of the war. The new Front victories were not precisely the fault of the generals: the Front merely seized the opportunities laid open to them in the interval of change and uncertainty. But as two and then three months passed, the generals seemed to be making slight progress at imposing order within the army and the administration.

Washington was anxious. Shortly before the coup, Attorney General Robert F. Kennedy had urged that the National Security Council consider disengaging the United States from Vietnam if the war appeared unwinnable by any successor to the Diem regime. President Kennedy at the time dismissed the option of withdrawal and decided to encourage a coup in the hopes that the new government would be more capable of pursuing the war than the last. In giving its support to the military junta, the Kennedy administration passed an important checkpoint in its involvement in the war and its commitment to the Saigon regime. American officials simply assumed that the responsibility they were taking on would lead to a new degree of American influence, or control, over the Saigon government. But in attempting to direct the Minh junta, the Americans might as well have been trying to sculpt in Silly Putty. There were so many generals, so many ambitious young officers, that the embassy could hardly keep track of them, much less exert any pressure. General Minh claimed to be making the decisions for the junta, but he clearly held small authority: the commander of the vital Saigon region did not even make a pretense of doing his job. In December 1963, on the first of what was to be a series of trips to Vietnam over the coming months, Secretary McNamara reported to Johnson that the situation was "very disturbing" and that the generals seemed almost to have given up fighting the war in favor of their internal political squabbling. He lectured the generals on the need for leadership, programs, action.[11] The generals respectfully agreed and went back to their squabbling.

Were the generals anti-Communist? Even that was difficult to determine. Certainly they were not as religiously anti-Communist as Ngo Dinh Diem had been. They were soldiers, anti-Communist by social background and economic interest. But above all they were Cochin Chinese who believed in the politics of arrangement. And, American support notwithstanding, the time for an arrangement seemed to be approaching. In December President Charles de Gaulle proposed a plan for the neutralization of all the former states of Indochina in pursuance of the Geneva accords. The Americans worried that the generals might look favorably on his proposals. In his New Year's message to the Republic of Vietnam, President Johnson wrote to the Minh junta:

Neutralization of South Vietnam would only be another name for a Communist take-over. . . . The United States will continue to furnish you and your people with the fullest measure of support in this bitter fight. . . . We shall maintain in Vietnam American personnel and material as needed to assist you in achieving victory.[12]

Many Americans in Saigon blamed the junta for its inability to reconstitute a military offensive — assuming, perhaps, that the generals had some authority over their subordinates, or perhaps that they could create a government and an army out of the void. But the American assurance of support and expressions of dissatisfaction only had the effect of exciting the ambitions of those generals who did not belong to the junta and pushing the junta members to look for new alternatives. In December a rumor spread quickly around Saigon that three of the junta members, Generals Don, Kim, and Xuan, were involved in a French plot to neutralize the country. The rumor may or may not have been true — Saigon at the time was thick with agents dealing in every sort of currency — but it was enough that some of the Saigonese believed it. Throughout late December and early January there were student demonstrations in the city and wage strikes involving some violence. On January 29, 1964, General Nguyen Khanh, the commander of the First Corps, executed the plot he had prepared since November with the Catholic General Khiem and the general who headed the other major officers' conspiracy against Diem. Moving their combined troops into the city, Khanh seized the general staff headquarters, arrested several of the junta members on charges of treason, and proclaimed himself chairman of the Military Revolutionary Council.[13]

The second coup did not come as any real surprise to the Americans or the Saigonese. Any battalion commander might well have predicted something of the sort, for as far as the Vietnamese army was concerned, the first junta had no more right to power than any other group of generals. The generals all proclaimed their commitment to the "unity of the army," but they trusted each other no better than they ever had in the days of Ngo Dinh Diem. As there were forty-eight generals, so there were forty-eight reasons for upsetting the status quo and at least twelve plans in motion for doing so. General Khanh merely carried out his plan. It made little difference that the first junta had expressed fairly well the division and uncertainty of the non-Communist population, that it had been the first government of southerners in the south: it had failed to mobilize the political support necessary to dampen the ambitions of the other generals. Such support was extremely difficult to come by.

Khanh's move was nothing but a coup, plain and simple. Still, it signaled the one significant change that had occurred within Saigonese politics since 1954: the development of the Vietnamese army as the preponderant political force. This development owed entirely to the American aid program. In the first five years of the Diem regime the United States contributed three-quarters of its aid budget to the armed forces of South Vietnam. Over the course of ten years it provided thousands of Vietnamese officers with trips to Fort Bragg and other American training camps. With the steadily growing stream of American advisers, it educated an entire generation within the Vietnamese army. By mid-1964 the U.S. Military Assistance Advisory Group (soon to be "upgraded" to the Military Assistance Command, Vietnam, or MACV) consisted of some sixteen thousand men with a budget of over half a billion dollars — the equivalent of twice the budget of the city of Washington, D.C. As the MAAG grew to overwhelm the civilian branch of the U.S. mission in Saigon — and to exert pressure for further American military intervention — the Vietnamese armed forces similarly outgrew all the civilian institutions of non-Communist Vietnam. Except for his control over American aid, Diem possessed little leverage against the army. Forced to give his officers control over the entire rural administration, he took the expedient of shifting them around so frequently that they did not have time to build up a stable power base. It was a tactic that could not work forever, and when the Buddhist demonstrations momentarily healed the divisions within the army, the generals simply seized power. The generals were now no more united than the civilians, but they at least had guns, and they commanded the entire flow of American aid.

It was the same thing that had happened in so many underdeveloped countries. In Egypt, the Congo, Ghana, in most of Latin America and the Arab world, the army seized power by virtue of its weight alone, by virtue of the fact that (with the occasional exception of the Communist Party) it was the only large, modern organization in a traditional world. In most of the decolonized countries the colonial power was responsible for this imbalance. At a certain point it had built up an indigenous army in order to defend the colony's borders or to keep one part of its population under control. Once the country was decolonized, the former colonial army reigned supreme in a void of those organizations — industrial concerns, trade unions, and political parties — that maintained civilian power in the metropolis. As opposition it had only the traditional leaders and the ineffectual colonial bourgeoisie. This consequence did not concern the colonial regimes, which, after all, intended to rule the countries themselves, but it ought, perhaps, to have been of some interest to the Americans allotting aid to Vietnam. Given the American preoccupation with the Communist "invasion from the north," however, the aid apportionment never came under serious debate under the Eisenhower, the Kennedy, or the Johnson administrations. By 1964 most Americans concerned in the war planning either refused to admit the consequences or accepted them as a fact of life about which they could do nothing. And then, of course, many American officials, including Henry Cabot Lodge and Robert McNamara, positively welcomed the prospect of military rule. In their view, the Republic required a strong military leader to stop the alarming succession of defeats and to halt the general demoralization of the army. In their view the Vietnamese ought to wait until the Communist threat had passed before they indulged, as Lodge said, in the "luxury" of politics.

To the eternally optimistic General Paul D. Harkins, commander of the MAAG since 1962, General Nguyen Khanh appeared to be the strong man that the country required. A northerner by birth and reportedly one of the ablest field commanders in the ARVN, Khanh became deputy chief of staff in the early years of the Diem regime. He had — or so he claimed — begun to oppose Diem in 1960, and though somewhat younger than the other top generals of the first junta, he then began to think of himself as the potential leader of his country. Outmaneuvered in the first coup and shunted off to the command most distant from Saigon, he made efforts to ingratiate himself with Harkins as well as with the other dissident generals.[14] The military precision with which he performed the coup seemed above all intended to impress General Harkins. It certainly had that effect. When, shortly after the coup, Khanh agreed to the American suggestions for a reform of the administration and the Strategic Hamlet program, the enthusiasm of the American mission for the general rose to new heights.

American hopes for the new regime were founded not merely in General Khanh, but in the new group of officers who followed him to power. The Khanh coup, as it happened, marked a generational change in the army leadership. Though only a few years younger than the generals of the first junta, Generals Nguyen Khanh, Nguyen Chanh Thi, Nguyen Huu Co, Nguyen Cao Ky, and Nguyen Van Thieu came from a very different conjunction of Vietnam and the West — the difference manifesting itself in their personal style as well as in their views on the war and the role of the army. The generals of the first junta typically came from the small French-educated elite. General Don, for instance, was training to be an economist, General Chieu to be a doctor, and General Xuan was serving in the high echelons of the French police when the French Indochina War broke out.[15] The new group of generals came from much more modest backgrounds. General Khanh's mother had owned a bar for French soldiers in Dalat, while his stepmother had been a renowned Vietnamese torch singer. General Ky came from a family of low-level civil servants in a province just south of Hanoi. Men from central Vietnam, Generals Thieu, Co, and Thi came from similar petit bourgeois families. Most of them went straight into the army after leaving high school, and they did not take on important rank until after Vietnamese independence in 1954.[16] After that, they rose rocket-like to power. At the age of thirty, Khanh was a general, Ky the head of the Tan Son Nhut air base outside of Saigon, and Thieu a division commander. Unlike the generals of the first junta, these men had no real loyalty to France. Many of them indeed claimed to hate the French, preferring to speak English, even if it were the pidgin dialect they had picked up at Fort Bragg, to the "language of colonialism." The adaptation pleased their American advisers who, convinced that the French had ruined Vietnam, were equally convinced that they would succeed where the French had failed. Under the Diem regime these advisers had found it uncomfortable to be snubbed by Vietnamese for not speaking French grammatically.

A second point in their favor, in the eyes of the American advisers, was that these officers were professional soldiers. Most of them had combat experience, and some of them, such as Khanh, Thi, and Ky, who commanded the elite units, had great physical courage and a mastery of all the techniques Fort Bragg had to offer. Ky was an ace pilot and Thi commanded the paratroopers in their daredevil attempt to bring down the Diem regime in 1960. No intellectuals, the younger generals picked up some of the soldierly camaraderie of the French and American officers. They liked a good joke, and when they did not feel the weight of rank upon them they went to the extent of slapping their knees and indulging in belly laughs. At the same time, as their advisers noted with some paternal pride, the young officers had dignity and were generally respected by the men under their command. The officers appeared to like the Americans and to be firmly dedicated to the war against Communism. Instead of turning a cold shoulder to the suggestions of their advisers, they would often agree with them, earnestly admitting that there was a great deal to be done and that they must work harder for their country. With their aggressiveness and their democratic manners, the officers appeared to many Americans to be the young modern leadership that was necessary to usurp the corrupt traditionalists who had ruled the south. "If General Minh is the Naguib of Vietnam," the Americans said, "then General Khanh is the Nasser." Similarly, when they came to power under Khanh, Generals Ky, Thi, Co, and Khang were known as the "Young Turks." The analogy was farfetched — too farfetched, perhaps, to describe the realities of Vietnam. True, the younger officers did not possess the most obvious of Diem's failings, but the question was what they had to offer their country. Certainly the officers had no education to speak of. For the administration of the state they would have to depend upon the civilians whom the French and the Americans had trained in those disciplines normally useful to rulers — economics, diplomacy, management, public health, political theory, and so forth. And these civilians, whose families had for generations dominated the bureaucracy of Saigon, despised the young officers as ignorant upstarts. A militant Catholic and anti-Communist professor once remarked, "The generals are so stupid you wonder how they manage to make those coups all by themselves."[17] There was a certain amount of social snobbery, if not class antagonism, in such an attitude, but the civilians had a point: while the professional military officers remained at the head of state there would be an almost total divorce between knowledge and power.

To many Americans, however, the generals' lack of education seemed in many respects a virtue. Education had, after all, meant isolation for the Saigonese elite. Without any local nationalist tradition the intellectuals learned their patriotism in French classrooms that excluded the mass of the Vietnamese people. Even despite themselves, they belonged to France rather than to Vietnam; they were not at home in their own countryside. To many American officials who were offended by the Vietnamese upper-class attitudes, the army officers seemed to offer some hope for a more socially responsible leadership. Because the younger generals had no French education, they would be closer to the people, more "Vietnamese." In an article in *Foreign Affairs* of April 1965, George Carver, the leading CIA expert on South Vietnam, claimed that for these reasons the rise of the Buddhists and the younger army officers constituted "a fundamental shift in the locus of urban political power and a basic realignment of political forces — in short, a revolution."[18]

Carver's conclusion stands today as a sublime example of American official scholarship. The accession of the younger officers was no more of a revolution than the succession of George Carver to the role of Wesley Fishel. It was a change of men. And not, perhaps, a change for the better.

Considered in another way, the young officers had the worst of both worlds. Unlike the older officers, they had no formal education;

unlike Ngo Dinh Diem and the Buddhists, they had no nationalist credentials whatever. They served the French for the duration of a colonial war — and in the most menial of capacities. True, they had no loyalty to the French, but then they had very little loyalty to anything. They regarded the French war not as a national political struggle, but as an unlooked-for boost to their otherwise unpromising careers. Nguyen Khanh, for instance, joined the Viet Minh after leaving high school. After fifteen months of rather desultory activity he and his comrades were fired by the Viet Minh for "tiredness" and lack of discipline. Khanh then returned to Saigon to pursue his military career under less arduous circumstances at the military school that the French had just opened for the training of Vietnamese officers. He rose through the ranks to become an officer in the elite French-commanded *gardes mobiles*.[19] As for General Nguyen Cao Ky, he joined the French forces as soon as he came of age, and spent the last years of the war training as a bomber pilot in France and North Africa. He married a Frenchwoman, had four children, and divorced his wife not long after independence, divesting himself of what had probably been a striving — conscious or unconscious — to become a Frenchman. Like Ky, most of these younger officers turned against the French, but only after the French stopped paying their salaries. Their change of heart neither cleared their reputations with other Vietnamese nor gave them another kind of education. The French had not taught them Descartes or Pascal, but instead had occupied their formative years with instruction on how to serve a European army fighting a European war. The French trained them — trained them badly. And the Americans took up where the French left off.

Had Carver and the American advisers read, or understood, Ho Chi Minh, they might have realized that Ngo Dinh Diem's "mandarinism" had very little to do with an accident of birth. General Khanh and the "Young Turks" had none of Diem's aristocratic pretensions, but they felt most of the same terrors that had incapacitated him politically. They distrusted their fellow officers, disdained the civilians, and had no more idea of how to "go to the people" than Diem himself. The generals began their lives much closer to the peasantry than Diem or the older Cochin Chinese generals, but, by concerted effort, they successfully overcame their initial advantage. Petit bourgeois who aspired to the status of the haute bourgeoisie, they were, if possible, more jealous of their positions and more anxious to close the doors of opportunity behind them than their predecessors. The older officers had at least the security of wealth and a civilian education; the younger officers had only the army as a vehicle to enter the privileged upper class. Probity, a desire for social justice and equal opportunity for all — such virtues might more reasonably be expected in the heads of a Mafia ring than in those generals who had spent their formative years struggling to the top of the corrupt, inefficient, and demoralized army of the Diem regime.

two

Today the government of General Khanh is vigorously rebuilding the machinery of administration and reshaping plans to carry the war to the Viet-Cong. He is an able and energetic leader. He has demonstrated his grasp of the basic elements — political, economic and psychological, as well as military — required to defeat the Viet-Cong. He is planning a program of economic and social advances for the welfare of his people. He has brought into support of the government representatives of key groups previously excluded. He and his colleagues have developed plans for systematic liberation of areas now submissive to Viet-Cong duress and for mobilization of all available Vietnamese resources in defense of the homeland.

Secretary of Defense Robert McNamara
March 26, 1964[1]

"The fighting is going on in four fronts: the government versus the generals, the Buddhists versus the government, the generals versus the ambassador, and, I hope, the generals versus the VC."

General Maxwell Taylor to a dozen American correspondents in Saigon, 1965[2]

It was in a way most fitting that General Maxwell Taylor should have served as ambassador to Saigon during the bewildering year that followed General Khanh's accession to power. With his report to Kennedy in 1961 and his subsequent chairmanship of the Joint Chiefs of Staff, Taylor had done as much as anyone in the American government to lay the groundwork for the American commitment to Vietnam. Previously he had never cared much about GVN politics, but on becoming ambassador he was to place more importance on the creation of representative bodies and the establishment of civilian rule than either McNamara or Cabot Lodge. As a soldier, he was perhaps rather less impressed by soldiers than many American civilian officials. And he believed in the power of the United States to influence the Vietnamese government to reform.

In March 1964, Secretary McNamara reported that since the preceding November, "the political control structure extending from Saigon down into the hamlets virtually disappeared. Of the forty-one incumbent province chiefs of November 1 [1963], thirty-five were replaced. Nine provinces had three chiefs in three months; one province had four. . . . Almost all major military commands changed hands twice."[3] McNamara looked upon this situation as an abnormality that Khanh might, with some firmness, correct. But the convulsion was merely the visible expression of what had been going on within the army for all the years of the Diem regime. The lid was now off, and the conflicts so long suppressed were now openly fought. And the conflicts did not end with the army. Since the fall of Diem liberated all of the various political groups in the cities to make their bids for power, the political struggle was taking place not only within the army or between the army and the civilians, but between various unstable factions of both, the army officers acting sometimes as the leaders, sometimes as the led. In the resulting chaos it became very difficult to tell where the government began and ended and where the realm of ideological and religious conflict met that of factional and personal ambition.

Almost before General Khanh patched together a government, he began to discover signs of dissension within its topmost ranks. General Minh, whom the Americans insisted be retained as chief of state, attacked Khanh for having arrested his fellow officers, Generals Don, Kim, Dinh, and Xuan. The Dai Viet leaders, whom Khanh appointed to his cabinet, complained that he was using them as figureheads for an army-controlled government, while the militant Catholics accused him of "fomenting religious discrimination."[4] By mid-July of 1964, a group of politicians, including Khanh's own vice-premier and a number of high military officers, had worked out all the details of a coup against the new regime.

One prime mover in this struggle was the organized Catholic minority. Concerned with the dismissal of a number of Catholics from the administration, the priests and leading laymen in Hue and Saigon began to incite demonstrations and to proselyte within the army so as to build up a secure base of opposition against Khanh. The non-Catholics, with some reason, accused them of having political ambitions. But it was also true that they were frightened — frightened not by the regime itself so much as by the Pandora's box of animosities that the junta let loose. And they saw no alternative to constituting themselves into a protective association. But for every action there is an opposite reaction, and as the Catholics were by far the most powerful of the city parties, their maneuverings had the effect of polarizing the struggle and creating an anti-Catholic constituency where none had existed before. As the second most powerful group, the Buddhists naturally became the focus of this opposition.

Now thrust into the bread-and-butter issues of local politics, the Buddhists began to develop and harden the outlines of their organization. In Hue, where the death of Ngo Dinh Can left a vacuum of power, Tri Quang began to develop political contacts among a great variety of people, ranging from the local civil servants to the trade unionists to the students and left-wing intellectuals who ran the socialist paper, *Vietnam-Vietnam.* In Saigon Tam Chau began to build his constituency among the non-Catholic civil servants and businessmen who, though not very far from the southern Catholics politically, wished to develop their own protective associations, their own educational and social services. With money extorted from the Khanh government (there is no other verb for the transaction, but it must be recognized that there was no "better" or more legal way to obtain money from the government), they set up the Vanh Hanh University, a small college in the Xa Loi pagoda dedicated to the teaching of Buddhist studies by contemporary (Western) methods, a number of orphanages, schools, and a Buddhist Youth Center under the leadership of Tri Quang's deputy in Saigon, Thich Thien Minh.

The Catholics naturally felt challenged by the growth of these new Buddhist associations and by the ability of the Buddhists to compete for administrative posts. There were demonstrations and counterdemonstrations and an occasional revenge-killing in the provinces. And yet there was no clearly defined political issue between them. The Americans, with their tendency to see a struggle as having only two sides, pitted "the Buddhists" against "the Catholics" in their own minds, but the situation was in reality far more complicated. For one thing, the Buddhists and the Catholics were divided among themselves, and for another, they had, as civilians, some common interest in restoring civilian rule and their own hold over the American aid program. After five months of the Khanh regime, the Buddhists, some of the Catholics, and a number of the senior politicians proposed a complete reorganization of the government that would exclude the Military Revolutionary Council from all but military affairs.

Not surprisingly, General Khanh objected to this proposal. Under pressure from Ambassador Taylor, he agreed to have a series of civilian committees draft a constitutional charter, but after the politicians wrote several drafts, he tore up all of them and issued his own somewhat ill-written draft, giving him virtually dictatorial powers over the whole government.[5]

The Buddhists reacted suddenly. On August 21, Tri Quang's organizers moved into action in the midst of a disorderly student demonstration in Saigon, forcing what might have been but a fitful gesture of protest into a full-scale governmental crisis. The student demonstrations grew in size and spread to Hue and Da Nang. While the Catholics marched in counterdemonstration, NLF organizers (or so it was thought) incited both demonstrating groups against each other. Unknown agitators set off bombs in various places in Saigon. In Hue Tri Quang's organization showed its full strength for the first time. From among the student and civil service demonstrators there appeared a group called the People's Revolutionary Committee that demanded radical changes in the structure of the government and — as some interpreted it — autonomy for the administration of central Vietnam. The demonstrations in Hue remained orderly, but the Buddhists appeared to lose control of those in Saigon. Before the week was out the high school and university students were joined by gangs of young toughs who seemed to answer to no one. Without warning mobs would appear in the streets, overturning cars, burning, looting, and killing with clubs and chains whoever stood in their way. To American reporters the spectacle was deeply shocking; it was as though the civilization had suddenly disintegrated, leaving people to fight like rats in an overcrowded cage.[6]

Never his best in moments of crisis, General Khanh retired to Dalat and announced his resignation as president — though not as prime minister. Having made his bid for dictatorial powers, he now seemed not even to possess the authority to call out the police. One day during the crisis the students rode him around through the streets on the top of a tank and forced him to shout, "Down with military power, down with dictatorships, down with the army!"[7] With his round face and his little pointed beard, he now appeared a complete figure of fun.

Had the army not been so divided, General Khanh's reign would, no doubt, have ended there and then. As it was, none of the officers could so much as agree on the terms of their common desire to depose their humiliated commander, and Khanh floated like a cork on the whirlpool of their disputes. On September 1, one group of coup plotters marched into the city with their battalions only to be met by another group that, although not exactly loyal to Khanh, was determined to keep the first group from seizing power. Less than two weeks later a new group of officers, headed by a former member of Khanh's cabinet and the commander of the Fourth Corps, due to be deposed, staged another completely inadequate attempt at a coup. Air Vice-Marshal Ky bore the main responsibility for its defeat. Supposedly sympathetic to the plotters, he himself flew his air wing over Saigon, counted the troops on the road in from the Delta, found them wanting, and instead of threatening to bomb Khanh's defenders as planned, threatened to bomb his opponents.[8]

Over the next few months Saigon politics took on the pace and style of a Marx Brothers movie. Under pressure from Ambassador Taylor, Khanh surprised everybody by making good his promises to establish a civilian government. Under his aegis the High National Council — a body of men so ancient that it became known as the High National Museum — wrote a constitution in record time (a month) and picked two civilians as head of state and prime minister, thereby depriving Generals Khiem and Minh of their jobs and at the same time taking the heat off Khanh. Innocuous as the new government seemed (the chief of state, Dr. Pham Khac Suu, was in his nineties and the prime minister, Tran Van Huong, was an elderly Cochin Chinese schoolteacher who made his reputation by opposing Diem), it pleased no one. When, rather than involve himself in a religious feud, Huong consulted neither the Buddhists nor the Catholics on appointments, he succeeded in driving both sects into the opposition and himself into the hands of the military council, the strongest faction of which did not want a civilian government at all. There followed a demi-coup against the High National Council led by the "Young Turks," Generals Ky, Thieu, Thi, and Khang.

This last coup drove Ambassador Taylor to the end of his patience. Calling the generals together to protest what he saw as the government's last shred of legitimacy, he opened the meeting by asking:

"Do all of you understand English?" (Vietnamese officers indicated they did, although the understanding of General Thi was known to be weak.) "I told you all clearly at General Westmoreland's dinner we Americans were tired of coups. Apparently I wasted my words. Maybe this is because something is wrong with my French because you evidently didn't understand. I made it clear that all the military plans which I know you would like to carry out are dependent on governmental stability. Now you have made a real mess."[9]

Taylor was, once again, wasting his words, for the generals refused to reinstate the High National Council, and Premier Huong, unable to resist their pressure, asked Generals Ky and Thieu to join his government. The Buddhists then mounted a series of anti-Huong, anti-American demonstrations during which a mob of students sacked and burned the USIS library in Hue. Fearing to be outflanked by the "Young Turks," General Khanh joined his erstwhile enemies, the Buddhists, and pressured the Armed Forces Council into ousting the Huong government. By January 27, 1965, the civilian government that Taylor had so carefully constructed collapsed like a house of cards.[10]

With thirty thousand American advisers in Vietnam and the bombing of the north under consideration, the American officials naturally took the Saigonese conflicts with extreme seriousness. George Carver and others wrote long analyses of the regional and cultural differences, the religious and ideological feuds that created these imponderable controversies. In fact, like any farce, the Saigonese conflict had a simple, mechanical logic to it. The first principle of it was that the "outs," whatever their party, hated the "ins," whatever theirs. This universal principle of party politics was, of course, complicated by the shale-like consistency of each party. If General Khanh appointed a Buddhist, a Hoa Hao, or a Dai Viet leader to government office, the new official would usually find that his party had deserted him on the assumption (usually justified) that once in a position to make his own fortune, he would abandon his original loyalties. As the Buddhist Tri Quang once said, "Experience shows that each time a government was set up, Buddhists were betrayed even though there were Buddhists in it, and sometimes Buddhists betrayed us more than anyone else." Like Ngo Dinh Diem, the generals discovered that to rule meant to divide. Those divisions which the Americans attributed to ancient regional feuds actually resulted from the second principle, that the "ins" exerted a centripetal force and the "outs" a centrifugal one. Clearly it was in the interests of those who dominated Saigon to back the American project of "building a strong government." Clearly too, it was in the interests of those who held power in the provinces to engage in the contrary attempt to assure that the central government held as little power as possible. Because they were at the end of the American supply line, the people in the provinces furthest from Saigon tended naturally to be the most "anti-government" and "anti-American." Once taken into the establishment, however, they tended to modify their line and make extremists out of the former establishment.[11] With their base in Saigon the Catholics normally remained the strongest supporters of the government and the Buddhists of Hue the greatest single source of trouble for it. The generals, particularly the corps commanders, would change their viewpoint and their methods whenever they were moved from place to place — those in Saigon engaged in underground battles for influence, those in the First Corps going to the point of open insurrection. These dynamics naturally had the most surreal effect on American policy. Assuming that the disputes had something to do with support for, or opposition to, the war, the officials tended to back whichever group held power in Saigon and to oppose those who ruled the provinces.

It was thus that, five months after he had been publicly humiliated by the Buddhists, General Khanh returned to power with the support of the Buddhists. In the process, however, Khanh infuriated the Catholics and the Americans. In February 1965 a group of Catholic officers attempted their own coup under the leadership of a mysterious figure called Colonel Pham Ngoc Thao, who managed to be at once a former Viet Minh officer, a friend of the departed Archbishop Ngo Dinh Thuc, and a great favorite of the Americans. The coup failed mainly because Thao's troops did not succeed in capturing the air base fast enough, and for the second time in five months General Ky, high up in the air over Saigon, threatened to bomb the rival units of his own army. Ky desisted only when it was pointed out to him that there were American troops as well as Vietnamese at the air base. The coup was stalemated for three days during which time General Khanh toured the Delta provinces in search of support. When he returned, he discovered to his surprise that Colonel Thao had been defeated, but that the generals who had apparently rushed to save him were now voting to depose him as president and chief of the Armed Forces Council. On February 21, General Khanh accepted an appointment as ambassador-at-large and joined the other two ousted heads of state, Generals Minh and Khiem, in exile.

The end of the Khanh regime left the political situation more confused than it had ever been. The Armed Forces Council, having succeeded in all its objectives, now could not decide who its leaders were nor whether it ought to dissolve itself in favor of a civilian government. At this point the Buddhist-Catholic conflict broke out again — the struggle duplicated and complicated by the personal rivalries between General Thi and Colonel Thao on the one hand and the civilian chief of state and his new premier, Dr. Phan Huy Quat, on the other. In the end — that is, after some five months of disputation — these rivals knocked each other out, leaving the field clear for the younger generals to seize power. On June 12, 1965, Generals Thieu, Ky, and Co proclaimed the establishment of a National Leadership Council. The triumvirate later expanded to ten members and, to Ambassador Taylor's dismay, appointed General Ky as chief of the executive council charged with the day-to-day administration of the country.[12] About two weeks later President Johnson announced that he was sending a contingent of fifty-three thousand regular combat troops into action beside those of the Saigon government.

The arrival of the American regulars in Vietnam was a demonstration, if such was necessary, of the failure of a decade of American policy in Vietnam. The Johnson administration did its best to represent the intervention as a response to "aggression from the north" and, indeed, an "invasion" of North Vietnamese troops, but by February 1965 there was little more than a regiment of North Vietnamese troops below the 17th parallel, and there were already thirty thousand American soldiers in Vietnam openly supporting the ARVN in offensive action. In March American airplanes began bombing targets in both North and South Vietnam. The fact was that the GVN was succumbing to the NLF even though it had over three times as many regular troops and an overwhelming superiority of firepower. By late spring the GVN was losing one battalion and one district capital a week to the NLF;[13] its cities and provincial capitals were largely isolated from the countryside. More ominous still, the GVN was deteriorating from within. The desertion rate had risen dramatically throughout 1964. The increase gave only a super-ficial indication of the lowered morale, as in many units soldiers did not even have to desert in order to stop fighting the war. No keener than the enlisted men to fight a battle they knew they were losing, the officers forsook operations in order to concentrate on the scramble for power in Saigon and the making of arrangements with the Liberation Front.

In analyzing the debacle, those American officials and journalists who saw it as such returned to much the same set of arguments that their predecessors had made about the declining Diem regime. On the one hand they blamed the sects for their continual agitation and disruption of government efforts. (Was not the government working on their behalf to defeat the Communists?) On the other hand they blamed the politicians and the ARVN officers for their fractiousness, their failure to compromise with the sects, and their disregard for the general welfare of the country. Certain long-established journal-ists such as Robert Shaplen also blamed the American embassy for its failure to pressure the Vietnamese officers to make compromises and "meaningful" reforms. The irony was that only three and a half years before, Ambassador Maxwell Taylor, with the advice of State Department officials, had in his 1961 report implicitly criticized his predecessor, Frederick Nolting, recommending that the United States pressure the Diem regime to make a similar set of reforms. The repetition of history perhaps ought to have raised some suspi-cion that there was some larger issue at stake that they had thus far failed to identify.

In looking for a Vietnamese leader, American officials such as McNamara, Taylor, and Cabot Lodge looked merely for a general or prime minister with administrative skills and the political acumen to deal with the sects. They looked for a manager to run an organiza-tion already functioning. In their eyes the army and the civil service were functioning institutions. But they were deceived by their own creation, for army and administration were no more than shells: artificial, foreign-made shells encasing people who had not made them and who could not use them. What the American officials could or would not realize was that the sects were less a part of the problem than an attempt at a solution — an inadequate one, perhaps, but nonetheless an attempt to deal with the chaos caused by the collapse of a traditional society.

The problem for the Vietnamese soldiers and politicians was, then, not simply to rule but to create a system through which to create power and to begin ruling. The inability of the young officers to do anything of the sort owed not to their bad characters but to their background, their training, and to the situation in which they found themselves. Generals Khanh, Ky, and Thieu were, after all, professional soldiers. During the first Indochina War they had worked within a foreign army and served foreign ends. They were trained to fight, not to consider the issue of war as an extension of politics or diplomacy. Catapulted to power as a result of their capacity for petty infighting, they did not so much as understand the nature of their problem. Like their American advisers, they saw the war as a series of military engagements. By contrast, Vo Nguyen Giap, a teacher and a political journalist by training, based all his militery strategy on an analysis of the political issues. Traditionally the Vietnamese feared and disdained professional soldiers, not out of any class or caste distinction, but out of the suspicion that they had not the moral or political authority to build up a government behind them. Occasionally the old warlords had managed to transform themselves into emperors or mandarins, but they had the traditional Confucian system to fall back upon. The Saigon generals faced the task of creating an entirely new way of life, a new civilization for the Vietnamese. Trained and for so long dominated by foreigners, they had perhaps less capacity to undertake it than anyone in Vietnam. They had some desire to defeat the Communists, but their desire did not constitute a political system. Unlike Ngo Dinh Diem, they had not even an unworkable system in mind; their anti-Communism was founded in a simple ambition to hold onto what they had, rather than give it up to the NLF.

For those Americans who associated the word "strong" with the words "military leadership," the government of the Saigon generals would be almost impossible to comprehend. If the generals were ruthless, theirs was the ruthlessness of adolescents who see themselves in terms of fanciful clichés and think no further than tomorrow. Since 1960 General Khanh believed he had a role to play in Vietnamese history, and yet, though nurtured for more than four years, his schemes had no substance. He and the other generals had

simply no idea of what Vietnam was or ought to be. Even their
conflicts were insubstantial. Preceded by a few titillating moments
of suspense, their coups were habitually followed by the double
ceremonies of weeping and breast-beating on the part of the losers,
declarations of unity and harmony on the part of the winners. While
the sects with their cosmic concerns murdered each other's members, the generals did very little damage within their own ranks.
Apart from the case of the unfortunate Colonel Thao, fingered by
General Thieu, and mysteriously disposed of, there were no killings
and not a single suicide among the coup leaders. The deposed generals were either named ambassador-at-large or exiled to play endless
games of tennis with the American military attachés in Washington
or Bangkok — a fate no worse, perhaps, than that of Anthony Last
in Evelyn Waugh's *A Handful of Dust*, trapped in a South American
jungle and forced by his keeper to read aloud the entire work of
Charles Dickens.

Seen under the great klieg lights of international politics and the
war that was to overwhelm their country, the Saigon generals
looked quite simply out of proportion — ordinary men who otherwise would have lived ordinary lives. General Khanh made an
excellent staff officer under the French regime, Generals Thi, Ky,
and Thieu, excellent subalterns, but, as the American military command repeated monotonously for a decade, the "problem" of the
ARVN was not its lack of training but its lack of leadership. Those
Americans who held the Ngo family responsible for the loss of
battles and the alienation of the peasantry were to find that the fall
of the Ngos meant not a social revolution but a replacement of bad
leadership by no leadership at all. The generals stepped into a
vacuum of power they could not fill, and their reign over Saigon fit
the classical Vietnamese definition of the "interregnum," the period
of warlordism and anarchy following the decline of a Confucian
regime.

7

The United States Enters the War

Before the dry season of 1965 ended, the Johnson administration had taken those steps necessary to transform a holding action against the NLF into a major war involving North and South Vietnam. The American intervention in force did not rest on any single decision, nor was it the reaction to any unforeseen circumstance. As early as 1961 General Taylor and Secretary McNamara had predicted that United States troops would be needed to preserve the Saigon government. President Kennedy resisted that final commitment, but from 1961 on the American buildup in Vietnam proceeded steadily with a series of incremental decisions. In February 1964, a few months after the fall of Diem, the Johnson administration began the covert bombing of Laos near the North Vietnamese border and increased its program of secret intelligence and sabotage missions inside North Vietnam. It was in response to an amphibious sabotage raid by GVN forces that North Vietnamese PT boats attacked the U.S. destroyer *Maddox*, mistaking it for one of the belligerent South Vietnamese vessels. The administration portrayed this incident as an example of North Vietnamese aggression and in July 1964 sent Congress a resolution authorizing the use of American force in Southeast Asia — a resolution American officials had drafted two months earlier.[1] By September 1964, during the presidential campaign in which Johnson ran as the candidate who opposed an enlargement of the war, administration officials came to what the Pentagon historians called a "general consensus" on the bombing of North Vietnam.[2] The bombing began in March 1965, and in March the first U.S. regular troops were landed in Da Nang.

In their history of American decision-making during this period the Pentagon analysts have shown that, apart from George Ball, no high administration official came out against the general policy of intervention to save the Saigon government. The issues debated within the administration were merely those of strategy and timing. Certain officials — principally the Joint Chiefs of Staff — urged that the President pursue a rapid schedule of escalation. Those whose views prevailed advised a slow and carefully orchestrated campaign combining a gradual increase of force with diplomatic initiatives that would signal to the North Vietnamese the strength of American resolve to go as far as was necessary. Interestingly enough, few, if any, of the proponents of the gradualist approach had confidence that such a strategy would deter the North Vietnamese from (in Dean Rusk's phrase) "doing what they are doing." The CIA estimates were uniformly pessimistic, and at no point were the high officials deceived about the results of their actions. By the beginning of 1965 virtually all the high administration officials had faced the prospect of a commitment of U.S. ground troops.[3] Throughout this period Johnson gave cryptic indications of his plans, but concealed the official doubts about their effectiveness. The picture of Johnson the Pentagon history presents is that of a President constantly pressed forward by the tempo of events in Vietnam and constantly hanging back from the final commitment out of domestic political considerations. Politically, Johnson faced a dilemma. On the one hand he, like his predecessors, judged the "loss" of Vietnam to be irreconcilable with U.S. security interests and unacceptable to the American public. On the other hand he had no certainty of immediate success for his policy and felt that the American public would be reluctant to support another ground war in Asia. His political strategy was therefore to conceal his doubts about the outcome of the policy while attempting to convince the U.S. public of the necessity for the war.[4]

The commitment of American troops in no way removed the desire of the administration for concealment. Even with the bombing of the north and the prospect of U.S. ground combat operations, the CIA intelligence analysts remained pessimistic. In July 1965, Johnson authorized the deployment of forty-four maneuver battalions charged with the mission to search out and destroy the enemy units in the south. The implication of this order was that the administration officials had relinquished hope that the very presence of the American troops would deter the North Vietnamese and the NLF. The high officials had no confidence that the ARVN would recover in the near future or that the enemy would respond to anything less than the destruction of its main forces. Given their estimates on enemy strength, Johnson's advisers were — the Pentagon analysts concluded — preparing for a long and costly war.[5]

In the spring of 1965 the U.S. commander in Vietnam, General William C. Westmoreland, judged the military situation so critical as to require deploying the American troops even before an adequate supply or logistics system could be constructed. In March a Marine Expeditionary Force arrived in Da Nang with the mission of defending the airport against enemy attack. Over the next few months Westmoreland reinforced this contingent, bringing it up to more than division strength, and sent it into combat with the ARVN. In September the First Cavalry Division set up base in the area of Pleiku and soon afterwards engaged three North Vietnamese regiments in the bloody battle of the Ia Drang valley. The concentration of troops in central Vietnam was a product of Westmoreland's theory that the enemy's intentions were to "cut the country in half" at a latitude close to Pleiku. What this phrase meant was difficult to say, as the NLF had already "cut the country in half" in the sense that it controlled most of the central Vietnamese countryside and had confined the GVN to air traffic between the province capitals. On the other hand, a military occupation of the northernmost cities did not seem a likely strategy for the NLF, given the weight of American air power. Apparently even Westmoreland did not entirely believe his own theory, for in the fall of 1965 he judged the enemy threat to Saigon great enough to warrant the deployment of the First Infantry and elements of the Fourth Infantry to Binh Duong province, just north of the city. By the end of 1965 American troop strength had reached 184,000 men, and, with the addition of a few Korean units, five combat divisions.[6]

The American military achievements in 1965 promised anything but a quick end to the war. What progress there was could be

discovered only from a negative point of view. Westmoreland himself later claimed merely that his troops had "defeated a concentrated
North Vietnamese effort to cut the country in two."[7] Rather more
concretely, it could be said that the First Cavalry had repulsed a
North Vietnamese attack on a Special Forces camp in the jungle
region of the Laotian border, and that the very presence of the U.S.
troops with their air and artillery support had reduced the chances
for an enemy occupation of the major South Vietnamese cities. The
American troops fought well, but apart from two large-scale battles
their activities were confined to small-unit patrolling supported by
artillery and tactical bombing, as well as by "strategic bombing" in
the south by B-52s stationed in Guam. It was not until the next year,
when U.S. troop strength rose to well over 200,000, that Westmoreland took the offensive with a series of "search and destroy" missions
against enemy units and base camps. At that point enemy strength
in the south was far more formidable than it had ever been, for with
all the bombing of the north and all the enemy deaths recorded by
American troops, the North Vietnamese and the NLF main forces in
the south had grown to 221,000.[8]

Still, despite their less than decisive performance of the first year,
the American troops brought a surge of optimism to the American
mission in Saigon. The embassy officials and military advisers were
not, after all, concerned with the long-range goals of U.S. policy, but
rather with their own appointed task of saving the Saigon government. As they looked at it, the President had finally recognized their
plight and given them the wherewithal to get the job done. They
could not imagine that the administration would take on something
that it could not finish. The Vietnamese officials seemed to have the
same confidence. The Americans who weathered 1964–1965 saw a
startling change come over their Vietnamese allies. The morale of
the ARVN rose appreciably, and the city bourgeoisie no longer
seemed to fear the prospect of an NLF victory. There was a sense
among Vietnamese and Americans in Saigon that a crisis had been
passed.

As if to underscore the change in the war, Washington sent a new
group of American officials to Saigon. In place of Maxwell Taylor,
with his distressing experience of coups, riots, and military defeats,
there came Henry Cabot Lodge, the handsome, imperturbable Bostonian. Having left Vietnam in June 1964 to take part in the
Republican political campaign, Lodge missed the teenage mobs and

the sectarian murders. But then he seemed a man who would never have contact with such unpleasantness. Charming and bland in an upper-class Bostonian way, he ignored the routine desperation of his officials, took naps, and spent an hour or more at lunchtime every day swimming laps in the pool at the Cercle Sportif. Whatever the crisis, he and his wife would attend services every Sunday at the small Episcopalian church in the center of town. To be near Lodge was to forget that such things as misery, deceit, corruption, and brutality existed in the world. Brought up at a military school, Lodge looked upon the military profession as a noble calling. He saw no reason to exert strict civilian control over U.S. military operations and, though he held veto power in the mission council, he rarely, if ever, used it. The aggressive, almost high-handed manner with which he had treated General Harkins during the Diemist crisis was no longer in evidence. Curiously enough, he, as a politician, had much less interest than General Maxwell Taylor in a civilian government for the Vietnamese. With his air of benign disinterestedness he managed to develop a friendly, almost paternal, relationship with the new military leaders.

Lodge's second-in-command at the embassy was Deputy Ambassador William J. Porter. A career diplomat of some distinction but without previous experience in Vietnam, Porter took over the job of reorganizing the civilian operations and putting together a new pacification program. His task of reorganization was an enormous one, for, as the American troop commitment increased, the civilian mission grew with it into a replica of Washington, D.C., a small satellite state of bureaucrats on the other side of the Pacific. By the beginning of 1966, USAID and JUSPAO (the Joint U.S. Public Affairs Office) alone included hundreds of people ranging from agricultural experts to hospital administrators, film makers, sociologists, artificial limb manufacturers, and water pollution experts. Where before there were but a few voices there was now a cacophony in which each specialist, seizing upon the Vietnam problem, a sphere of unknown proportions, proposed to move it from the particular angle of his own expertise. The attendant bureaucratic power struggles were therefore acute and never-ending: reformers of the GVN police fought with reformers and expanders of the RF-PF program, advocates of industrialization fought with those of agricultural development. Land reform, education, "motivational research" — every possible "solution" turned up at least once in the roulette wheel of priorities. The result was that most of the top mission officials, such as William Porter and the shrewd, articulate head of JUSPAO, Barry Zorthian, spent most of their time working on administrative problems and dealing with other Americans. This preoccupation put a certain distance between them and the Vietnamese reality.

One exception to this rule of bureaucracy was to be General Edward Lansdale. Again at the behest of the CIA, Lansdale returned to Vietnam at the end of 1965 with a team of enthusiastic young men and the general mission of injecting some new ideas into the counterinsurgency program. This vague definition of role did not serve him as it once had. Lansdale's zeal for political conversion and his disapproval of the very scale on which the American operations were now conducted made him an uncomfortable neighbor for the "regulars" at the mission. In a series of careful jurisdictional maneuvers, the bureaucrats narrowed his "area of responsibility" to the point where they had effectively cut him off from the mission command and from all work except that of a symbolic nature. For the next few years Lansdale would spend most of his time in talk with Vietnamese intellectuals, a few ex–Viet Minh officers, and his own American devotees. Living in his grand villa, isolated from the press, he would become an American counterpart to the elusive Vietnamese "Third Force," a hero to idealistic young American officials who saw the failure of American policy as a failure of tactics.

Lansdale's bureaucratic defeat was only an indication of the general shift in emphasis of American policy. With the commitment of American troops Washington began to look upon the war as an American affair. The Vietnamese seemed to recede into the background, and along with them those Americans who had spent years in Vietnam and believed in the regeneration of a non-Communist nationalism. The romantic warriors, such as Frank Scotton and Jean Sauvageot, who, like Lansdale, spoke and thought Vietnamese, who loved the exoticism of the villages and believed with fervor in a non-Communist liberation front — they were to remain merely the "characters" in a generally faceless enterprise. With all the civilian infighting, the talk of political strategies and "winning the hearts and minds of the Vietnamese people," the American war was to be a conventional military operation. As commander of the U.S. forces in

Vietnam and head of the advisory and assistance mission, General William C. Westmoreland was to exercise the primary influence and bear the primary responsibility for it.

In his *Antimémoires,* André Malraux wrote that he found it instructive when dealing with generals mentally to strip them of military uniform and reclothe them in civilian dress. In the case of Westmoreland the mental disrobing would have been most useful, for Americans in Vietnam tended to regard him as a man above praise or censure, the commander *par excellence.* With his square, jutting jaw and his ramrod bearing, Westmoreland certainly looked like the essence of general. And to a great extent he was the model representative of the post–Second World War American army. A Southerner and the son of a textile manufacturer in South Carolina (the contrast is nice with his civilian counterpart, Cabot Lodge), he had in conformity with family loyalties gone to West Point, where he had succeeded not so much by intellectual achievement as by that mysterious quality that army officers and corporate managers know as "leadership." During the Second World War he saw action as an artillery officer in North Africa and Sicily, ending up as chief of staff of the Ninth Division. Afterwards he moved quickly up through the ranks by way of Maxwell Taylor's General Staff, the 101st Airborne — the elite helicopter-mobile unit that Taylor and later Kennedy saw as the advance guard of the entire army — and finally West Point again, where at the age of forty-six he held the august position of superintendent. An innovator in artillery and helicopter assault tactics and an administrator who had learned McNamara's cost-effective approach to large organizations at the Harvard Business School, Westmoreland possessed those credentials that the modern army required. His personality seemed to suit his experience. He lacked the brilliance and eccentricity of the great Second World War generals, but he also lacked the towering ego and political ambition of a man such as Douglas MacArthur. So much was invaluable to Johnson in this particular war. He worked well in committees, maintained excellent relations with superiors, and was liked rather than feared by his troops. The French commanders in Vietnam had been counts and cardinals in military dress; Westmoreland was a clean-living, upright, corporate vice-president, his professionalism tempered by decency and good manners. In all, he made a perfect representative of the United States in Vietnam —

with the perfectly representative blind spot that he neither understood, nor particularly cared for, the Vietnamese.[9]

Westmoreland arrived in Vietnam at the beginning of 1964 to
serve for a few months as deputy commander before taking up his
new post. During his first year — a year of chaos within the GVN —
he undertook a large-scale program for the pacification of the
guerrilla-held provinces around Saigon. The theory behind the program was that the GVN troops would move outward from Saigon,
clearing and securing the adjacent ring of hamlets and then moving
outwards again while the GVN established its administration behind the troop shield. This so-called "oil slick" theory had a long
ancestry tracing back to the French concept of *quadrillage* — the
pacification of small squares of the countryside at a time — and to
Sir Robert Thompson's ideas for the Strategic Hamlet program.
Westmoreland's program (known as HOP TAC) worked no better
than its predecessors, for the undertaking was something like that of
trying to stop a brush fire with rotten sticks. As even Westmoreland
admitted, HOP TAC was a disaster. Moved precipitously down
from its old territorial base in the Second Corps area, the ARVN
Twenty-fifth Division fell apart; its soldiers deserted in droves to
escape their enemy or to rejoin their families in Second Corps.[10]
The police hid from the experienced NLF political cadres, and the
Vietnamese ministries failed to deliver the American supplies that
were to show the peasantry the desirability of life in the GVN-held
areas. The experience removed whatever illusions Westmoreland
had had about the Saigon government. After 1965 he concentrated
his attentions almost exclusively on the American troops — a nar-
rowing of perspective that was to explain much of his later reporting. Like most American officials, he believed that if only the Saigon
government would cease their interminable wrangling, the U.S.
forces could accomplish the task the President had set for them.

The expansion of the war brought a proportional expansion in the
American press corps in Saigon. By the beginning of 1966 some five
hundred journalists were accredited with MACV — the television
crews and administrators far outnumbering the reporters. The news
corps included senior editors from New York, cub reporters from
home-town papers, Ivy League graduates, crime reporters with two-
syllable vocabularies, spaced-out young photographers, combat veterans of Korea and the Second World War — everything, in fact,

except a determined opponent of the war. But such was the sense of the country at the time. With the commitment of American troops the old, and perhaps natural, reaction to support the troops and believe in the wisdom of the President once again triumphed — though there was no great enthusiasm for the war. The reporters would express doubts and make criticisms of American tactics, but almost all of them, including the old Vietnam hands — Robert Shaplen of the *New Yorker,* Sol Sanders of *U.S. News and World Report,* François Sully of *Newsweek,* and Takashi Oka of the *Christian Science Monitor* — accepted the broad lines of American policy. The important question for them was whether or not the United States could win in an acceptable amount of time. And the arrival of the American troops brought a new confidence on this score. The conflict that these experienced reporters had been watching for years now seemed to have changed in character.

Certainly the atmosphere of the war had changed substantially. The two hundred thousand U.S. troops made a profound impression on the cities. The troops carried with them the businesslike atmosphere of a country where the telephones worked, where schedules are kept and teamwork is assumed. They carried with them the sense that Americans long in Vietnam tended to lose, of the disproportion between Vietnamese politics and American power. Arriving in their starched summer uniforms from Honolulu, Wake, and Guam, the GIs seemed to overawe the small stucco terminal with its public flowers and its damp, tropical smell. The stiff, square carriage of their shoulders set them apart from the limber Vietnamese. Physically, Saigon seemed to change in their direction, the rectilinear shapes of the new American office buildings, billets, and hotels towering above the sloping red-tiled roofs of the French and Vietnamese city. Having established such a visible presence, the United States would surely do what was necessary to maintain it. It seemed only natural that the United States should take control of the war.

To the reporters recently arrived in Saigon, American control over the GVN was already an assumption. How should it be otherwise? The assumption was to be reinforced by the type of experience they were to have in Vietnam. Unlike the old Vietnam hands, who spent their time attempting to understand Vietnamese politics, these new reporters thought of themselves primarily as war correspondents attached to the U.S. armed forces. The American war filled their horizons. Every day at five they would gather in the windowless theatre in the JUSPAO building to watch colonels pointing out the sites of American actions on four-color overlay charts and toting up the figures of "structures destroyed," "enemy dead," and missions flown against "targets" in the north. Few of them went to the seedy room across the street where the Vietnamese held their briefings, and, as the American officers refused to report on ARVN operations, these operations and their results — or lack of them — were generally ignored. With the insatiable demands for combat coverage from their home offices, the television and newspaper correspondents spent most of their time with American units, visiting aircraft carriers, and watching demonstrations of new weaponry. Though it was difficult to find the battles and to write the kind of stories that came out of the Korean War, the new American presence appeared to have a certain solidity to it. Besides, there had been no political activity to speak of in Saigon for several months. By the beginning of 1966 the Ky junta was the longest-lived government since the Diem regime.

The stability of the Ky government took most American officials by surprise — a not very pleasant surprise at that. Gloom had, after all, reigned in the American embassy that preceding June when the Armed Forces Council had announced the formation of a new triumvirate. On principle, Maxwell Taylor had opposed the dissolution of the civilian government. To him the new junta seemed merely a middle term in an endless progression: each junta being ousted by a coup, each coup skimming off a new layer of generals and promoting a new group of colonels, majors, and captains, onward ad infinitum through the ranks of the army. The new National Leadership Council was certainly the youngest and least experienced of all the juntas yet formed. Most of the generals were under forty; they had risen to power by virtue of the fact that they controlled the air force, paratrooper, and Marine battalions stationed near the Armed Forces Headquarters in Saigon. In particular, General Ky — or Air Vice-Marshal Ky, as this commander of a handful of Skyraiders and training aircraft entitled himself — seemed to have very few qualifications for the job of government. Among Americans he had achieved a certain notoriety for threatening to bomb Hanoi with his own aircraft a good six months before it was American policy to do so; and then, when he was permitted to fly north, for leading his squadron to bomb the wrong target.[11] He had also twice threatened to bomb Saigon. Apart from these exploits, his political experience was confined to one coup, two demicoups, and a counter-coup. Upon hearing of his nomination to the role of acting premier, Taylor tried to block the appointment out of fear that he would prove both insensitive to American policy and unacceptable to the Vietnamese. Taylor thought Ky positively dangerous.

Taylor perhaps exaggerated the differences between Ky and the other Vietnamese generals. Still, it was true that Ky did not resemble any leader the Vietnamese had ever had before. He was thirty-four years old, a slight, rather elegant, figure who, as one writer put it, suggested a tango instructor rather than a general. His tastes ran in somewhat the same vein, from nightclubs to cockfighting to fast cars. His new wife, a beautiful stewardess from Air Vietnam, was to accompany him on trips throughout the country dressed, like him, in a black flying suit and batting her long lashes over newly doctored, "Westernized" eyelids. General Ky was a pilot at heart as well as by training. He played the part well, and his troops adored him for his mastery of these important American machines. As his chief of staff, General Cao Van Vien, once said of him, "He can fly so well bombers, helicopters, fighters — anything. You should see him. He is . . ." Vien paused, searching for a suitable epithet. "He is Superman!" Outspoken to the point of rashness, Ky had all those qualities that usually go into the making of a successful juvenile gang leader. That Ambassador Taylor tried and failed to prevent the gang from electing him as its chief did not increase his modesty or his sense of responsibility to the Americans.

Much to the ambassador's chagrin, Ky not only became premier, but then refused to follow his predecessors into the obscurity they no doubt deserved. Despite his seeming lack of qualifications for office, the young general showed an extraordinary capacity for survival. Two months, three months, and then six months passed without a single coup attempt. The American officials gradually began to reconcile themselves to him. When Henry Cabot Lodge replaced Taylor as ambassador, the adjectives surrounding Ky's name began a slow migration over from "immature" and "irresponsible" to "informal," "colorful," and "charming." After seven months passed without a single coup, embassy officials began to speak of "that young man who is maturing so rapidly in office." The phrase "transitional regime" no longer passed their lips. In February 1966, even Maxwell Taylor made his peace with the Ky government, testifying before a Senate Foreign Relations Subcommittee that "this is the first government which is solidly backed by the armed forces; and as long as they are behind this government in the present sense, it is not going to be overturned by some noisy minority as some governments were overturned in the previous years. So I do feel there is some encouragement, indicators of growing stability in the political scene."[12]

The Honolulu Conference in February 1966 came as the final confirmation of this new American view of the Ky government. President Johnson's decision to meet with Generals Ky, Co, and Thieu signified that the United States would support the junta in a way they had supported no government since the Diem regime. As most reporters recognized, of course, Johnson looked upon the conference as having more relation to American than to Vietnamese politics. His primary concern was perfectly expressed by a remark he made to Barry Zorthian, his chief information officer in Saigon. "Barry," the President said, "Barry, every time I see a picture of a battle in the papers, I want to see a picture of a hog." But with all his interest in putting a good face on the war by means of public relations, Johnson no doubt did believe in the efficacy of his new alliance. That is not to say that he and his aides attributed any extraordinary virtues to this new junta. They simply believed in the power of the United States to put the Saigon government on the right track. From their perspective, all the Vietnamese generals had to do was to deliver a stable government and an effective pacification program — the United States would do the rest. And in the opinion of most high American officials the generals were well on their way to the first objective. In Saigon, embassy officials sagely concluded that the generals had worked out their political differences and were settling down to the real work of the war. The new reporters nodded sagely back at them. It seemed only natural that the generals should do so. It was their responsibility to the American troops. The whole two-year history of coups and riots was forgotten as if it had never existed.

8

The Buddhist Crisis

In April 1966, just two months after the Honolulu Conference, two American journalists were wandering through the Vietnamese military headquarters inside the old imperial city of Hue. They were wandering in the vague hope of finding someone — a general, a flack for the ARVN First Division, anyone whom they might quote on the position of the government in this crisis. But the offices were empty. Doors banged, and their steps echoed hollowly on the stairs. After a while they began to debate whether or not they should give up the attempt and join the student demonstrators in the street. They turned a corner, opened another door and finally, to their surprise, came upon an official who looked as if he were of some importance. In the succeeding interview they managed to establish that this personage was the chief of police for Hue. Just what he was doing in this empty office, just what he had been doing for the past few weeks of near civil war, and which government he now represented — these questions remained unanswered. Quite clearly the chief of police had come to that office with the express purpose of avoiding anyone with such inquiries. For the last few weeks he had been pretending with some success that he did not exist at all.

For the American journalists new to Saigon the Buddhist crisis began in Robbe-Grillet fashion from middle to beginning and proceeded in a series of apparently disconnected events. On March 10, 1966, Premier Nguyen Cao Ky announced that the First Corps commander, General Nguyen Chanh Thi, had tendered his resignation because of a sinus condition and was en route to the United States for treatment of his nasal passages. The U.S. military briefers could give no clarification of this report, not considering the matter within their jurisdiction. When pressed for an explanation, the chief civilian information officer, Barry Zorthian, said that Ky had fired Thi with the full approval of Ambassador Lodge as the first step towards strengthening the powers of the central government. The next day, however, the United Buddhist Church issued an obliquely worded communiqué demanding that the junta hold elections for a civil government. Advised by their more experienced colleagues that the two events were probably related, the newly arrived journalists dutifully reported that the Buddhists were protesting the dismissal of General Thi. The Buddhists, however, claimed that this was not true. The next day a series of demonstrations broke out in the capitals of the First Corps — Hue, Da Nang, and Hoi An — and cloth banners appeared in the streets of Hue demanding the resignation of Generals Ky, Co, and Thieu.

As the week went on, the demonstrations grew larger. Or so it seemed, but even the most experienced officials and journalists in Saigon found it difficult to tell, for the communications with the First Corps appeared to be breaking down. For what reason no one knew. On March 16, a thousand people appeared at a large intersection in Saigon calling for a return to civilian government. When a band of young toughs broke through the crowds and began swinging clubs and setting fire to automobiles, the police did little to stop them. Why? There were rumors everywhere, but nothing the journalists could fasten upon as printable news. During the next week, the Ides of March, the demonstrations once again spread from their starting point in Hue, down through all the coastal cities of the center — Da Nang, Hoi An, Qui Nhon, Dalat, and Nha Trang — and back into Saigon. What most alarmed the resident American officials was that neither the police nor the army moved against the demonstrators in any city except Nha Trang. In Da Nang, the headquarters of the First Corps, thousands of soldiers and civil servants marched with the dock workers shouting anti-government and occasionally anti-American slogans. Most of the regular army operations

stopped and the port of Da Nang closed down. The entire government appeared to be falling — to be replaced by no one. The
Buddhist bonzes, the only visible leaders of the revolt, continued to
disclaim all responsibility for the violence in Saigon and to insist
that they had no interest in the generals' quarrels, but only in the
future of Vietnam in this time of crisis. As for General Thi, he
remained in Saigon under house arrest claiming that he had refused
American bribes to go to the United States and that his sinus infec-
tion had come from "the stink of corruption in Saigon." Going to
visit Thi, a few of the old hands among the journalists found him in
his villa entertaining the Saigon chief of police who, they knew, was
an old friend of his. Whether the chief was guarding Thi from Ky or
Ky from Thi they could not be certain; nor could they explain why
Ky had chosen at this moment to fire his old political crony and the
only one among the corps commanders who was not noticeably
venal. The chief Vietnamese public information officer himself
could give no explanation. Upon hearing the news from an American reporter, he said, "If this is true, it means I know nothing about
Vietnamese politics."

A few weeks later, a high U.S. embassy official called a meeting of
the more "responsible" journalists in Saigon to inform them discreetly that the ambassador had nothing to do with the firing of
General Thi, that the U.S. information officer had spoken hastily
and without sufficient information, that General Ky had in fact fired
Thi in a sudden fit of pique and told the ambassador afterwards.
Clearly the embassy officials had until that moment thought that the
affair would blow over.

By the second week of demonstrations the journalists newer to
Vietnam were beginning to register the full shock of the political
crisis. Led to expect some organized gratitude on the part of the
Vietnamese for all the sacrifices of the American troops — the image
was, perhaps, of crowds of native girls throwing leis over the necks
of the incoming U.S. soldiers — they found only hostile crowds and
officials who seemed to be growing more uncooperative every day.
What was more, the American officials themselves could not give
them a straight answer as to what was happening. The "bastion of
the Free World" that the military officials had talked about seemed
to be disintegrating into a chaos of generals with interchangeable
names. In the cafés and corridors their more experienced colleagues
rushed about trading rumors as to whether General Thi would oust

Ky or vice versa, whether the whole affair had to do with General Thi's ex-mistress in Cambodia (allegedly a Communist) or whether Generals Co, Thieu, Bao Tri, Vinh Loc, and Quang would take sides. When asked their opinion, most of the Vietnamese politicians would explain that it was all the fault of President Johnson.

As usual, the Vietnamese were right — only in a somewhat oblique manner. As the events of the past eight months were later reconstructed, the Ky junta had remained in power as a result not of its own virtues but of the hundreds of thousands of American troops in Vietnam. Pressured by the Americans to form a "stable government," the generals of the ARVN had come to a meeting of minds and agreed on a careful division of power: General Thi ran the First Corps, General Vinh Loc the Second, General Bao Tri the Third, and General Dan Van Quang the Fourth; the other generals and colonels either claimed their due from the corps commanders or divided up the non-territorial services between them. As titular head of this collection of autarchic baronies, the generals chose the man who seemed to have the least ability or ambition to interfere with their arrangements and who, fortunately enough, got along with the American ambassador. The Americans expected that a stable regime would bring the ARVN some measure of unity and coherence, but the generals saw to it that the opposite would happen. In dividing up the country they carefully removed all power from the central government so that the very stability of the Ky regime was no more than a function of its weakness. A vain but not a stupid man, Ky understood his position perfectly well. To an American reporter he once described his government as "a very delicate matter, in which many things must be kept balanced. The way we work is that my colleagues decide what they want done and then I try to carry it out."[1]

Regulated by arrangements normal to the Delta, as opposed to central Vietnam, the Ky government had in its own way functioned quite harmoniously until the Honolulu Conference. And then it foundered, for, like almost every other Vietnamese, Ky interpreted the meeting with Johnson as a demonstration of U.S. support and a mandate for him to attempt to consolidate power in his own hands. His dismissal of General Thi was the old Diemist tactic of weakening the territorial commands in order to rule them — except that Ky's problem was not to maintain control but to achieve it.[2]

During the week of March 18, it became quite clear that the

political crisis ran a great deal deeper than the quarrel between the generals. The dismissal of General Thi was no more than a trip wire setting off the explosion of long-suppressed anger against the regime and all it stood for. Despite the skepticism of the Americans, the Buddhists meant exactly what they said: they had no interest in a power play for one of the general's cliques. When on the eve of Thi's departure for the United States the American embassy persuaded Thi to return to Hue and help quiet the students, Thi went docilely but could do nothing. Without official position, he was of no use to the Buddhists. In the weeks that followed he took to sulking in his small villa, going out occasionally to lurk on the fringes of the crowds assembled to hear the impassioned voice of Thich Tri Quang.

In Saigon the demonstrations became an almost daily occurrence. Beginning in the heart of the French city, in Cholon, or in outlying slums, they started up quickly and without warning, as if from a spontaneous combustion of the noise, the dirt, the traffic, and the crowds. One day it was a gang of fierce slum boys running through the streets, breaking windows, overturning buses and American jeeps and burning them. Another day it was a thousand people squatting in the dust before the Vinh Hoa Dao pagoda, listening patiently to hours of speeches; another day, a parade of students chanting slogans followed by crowds of people wheeling their bicycles and Hondas and turning the streets into rivers of tear gas and exhaust fumes. The bonzes themselves marched only in peaceful demonstrations, but the threat of violence was always there, even in the faces of the white-shirted bourgeois boys of the Buddhist Youth Movement. An American walking through the hot streets knew that he could not trust the police to save him.

In Hue, by contrast, the demonstrations were most often orderly affairs. Led by bonzes or university students, they would move down the long tree-lined avenues between the pagodas and the government and university buildings without disturbing a stone. At night, crossing the bridge over the Perfume River in torchlight procession, they would look like a Chinese festival of lights. In Hue lay the real strength of the Buddhist "struggle movement." On March 22, the students took over the radio station and closed the university. A large proportion of the soldiers and civil servants in the city went over to their side while the rest guarded an uneasy neutralism. The American advisers simply woke up one morning to find their "counterparts" at war with what they considered the Vietnamese government. When on April 1 General Ky sent his gentle northern colleague, General Pham Xuan Chieu, up to negotiate with the local army officers, the students, shouting and jeering, put Chieu in a pedicab, wheeled him around the city, then sent him ignominiously home. The top generals of the First Corps remained in radio contact with Saigon, but their American advisers could not predict from moment to moment what they would do. In Da Nang the civilian mayor, Dr. Nguyen Van Man, openly went over to the side of the dissidents and was to be seen in the front of the government offices encouraging the soldiers and civil servants to oppose the regime. In Qui Nhon the province chief, a notoriously venal man, barricaded himself into his house to protect himself from the hundreds of angry, heckling high-school students, and refused to perform his duties.

To experienced observers the struggle movement was assuming the shape of the first attack on the Khanh government in the summer of 1964: on the one hand a regional separatist movement in Vietnam, on the other a revolt of the civilian parties — including the Catholics — against military rule. These two major vectors were complicated by a student protest against corruption in government, a nascent peace movement, and a growing anti-American sentiment among student groups, left-wing intellectuals, and some of the trade unions. As always, the Buddhists provided a focus for the movement, but the bonzes remained as divided as ever. Tam Chau, the cautious old northerner, made his peace with the Catholics and the Americans, and counseled moderation. The radicals, Thich Thien Minh and Thich Ho Giac, sped around Saigon in their black limousines and called for action. Thich Tri Quang, as always, remained the controlling influence over the whole struggle movement in central Vietnam. Only now, as befitted the gravity of the war, the proportions of the Buddhist movement were a great deal larger than they had been in 1964.

To American journalists new to Vietnam the whole situation had become hallucinatory. For the past six months the American generals had been congratulating themselves on their great victory in preventing the Viet Cong from "cutting the country in half" and now the opposite had happened: the GVN had cut itself in half and all the American troops in Vietnam could do nothing about it. Where now was the "government" that the United States claimed to be supporting? The GVN officials in the First Corps remained conciliatory, but the demonstrations revealed a great reservoir of anti-American feeling among the urban population. And a deep hostility to the Saigon generals.

On April 4, Air Vice-Marshal Ky announced that Da Nang was an "enemy-held city" and that he intended to liberate it from the Communists. General Wallace M. Greene, the U.S. Marine commandant visiting Da Nang, took strong exception to Ky's statement — as far as he was concerned, the U.S. Marines were still holding Da Nang — but the American embassy in Saigon appeared to agree with Ky's view, for on the same day Ambassador Lodge declared that "the government" was justified in attempting to reestablish its control over Da Nang and Hue by all means, including the use of force. A week of chaos followed.

On April 5, Premier Ky and Defense Minister Nguyen Huu Co arrived at the Da Nang air base with fifteen hundred Vietnamese Marines and two companies of national police in six U.S. troop transports piloted by Americans.[3] On arrival they discovered that their writ extended no further than the end of the runway — indeed not that far, as the Da Nang air base was controlled by the Americans. Learning that the local dissident troops had set up roadblocks and machine gun positions on the road to the city, the American commander thought it advisable to close the airport gates. After a day spent at the airport — a day spent watching the irate citizens of Da Nang cursing and throwing bottles at his troops — Ky flew back to Saigon with the surprising announcement that what he faced was a "political problem."

Ky's inept little demarche left the junta in a much weaker position than before, for now its troops had been counted and found wanting. The commanders of the Second and Fourth Corps, Generals Vinh Loc and Quang, began to absent themselves from meetings of the Armed Forces Council with curt excuses about pressing appointments. The demonstrations blossomed once more in Saigon and throughout the cities held by the First Corps. The Da Nang incident forced the Buddhists to take a much harder stand. Having backed the use of force, the Americans now tried the diplomatic threat of removing all American civilians from Hue and Da Nang — with the result that the demonstrations took on an even more anti-American tone. In Hue there were street signs reading DOWN WITH THE CIA, END THE FOREIGN DOMINATION OF OUR COUNTRY, and END THE OPPRES-

SION OF THE YELLOW RACE. Sent to relieve General Thi's replacement
(the first government appointee ended by defecting to the Buddhists), General Ton That Dinh found that he had no troops to
carry out the junta's orders. Against all instructions he began to
meet with the Buddhist leaders, to calm the fears of the Catholics
and the VNQDD, and to restore some order to the city.[4] His was the
only intelligent move made by a government official for the duration
of the crisis, for by April 10 it was clear that the Buddhist struggle
movement controlled central Vietnam, and that the three generals
of the junta would have to negotiate — on their own.

On April 10, American transports removed the Vietnamese
Marines from Da Nang, and the next day President Thieu convened
a National Political Congress made up of representatives from all
political parties, including the Buddhists, to work out a transfer of
power to the civilians. Two days later, ignoring Ky's threatening
movement of paratroopers in and out of the airports of Saigon and
Da Nang, Thieu signed a decree promising elections for a constitutional assembly within three to six months. The document was
vaguely worded, but it was interpreted as a total capitulation to the
Buddhists.

The irony of the American position was now complete. Calculated
to impress the Vietnamese with the need for stability and political
harmony, the Honolulu Conference had done the opposite. Instead
of pressuring Ky into more cooperation with the United States, it
boxed the Americans into supporting the general in whatever self-
serving or impolitic schemes he might undertake. With the Buddhist
revolt, the United States found itself backing three generals (now
quarreling among themselves) against the biggest popular movement ever to arise out of the Vietnamese cities, and opposing what
they had more or less favored all along — elections and a constitutional civilian government. What was more, they had counseled the
use of force against a civilian population. What was more, they
lost.

What could account for such a policy? In part it had to do with
the strange rigidity of State Department thinking. After six months
of "stability," the military junta in Saigon had in the eyes of American officials become a government on a par with that of West Germany or Great Britain. The fact that the Ky regime had little
support in its own country, and the idea that purely as a matter of
realpolitik it might not be the best government with which to fight a

war, did not seem to weigh as considerations. The Ky junta was the government and therefore the Buddhists were the illegal insurgents.

Behind the legalistic habit of mind, however, was the fact that the United States had made a heavy investment in the Vietnamese army and none in the civilian parties. The commitment of two hundred and fifty thousand American troops in 1966 was a commitment not so much to a government or to a political process as to the thirty thousand American soldiers and the millions of dollars the United States had *already* invested in Vietnam. Only two junior officers in the entire State Department staff at the embassy were employed to pay some attention to the civilian parties; the rest were formally required not to have any contact with the opposition – an order which under the Ky regime effectively prevented them from seeing any civilian politicians at all. At the outset of the crisis the U.S. embassy had almost no contact with the Buddhists. In the entire American establishment in Vietnam – a matter of some thousands of people apart from the regular combat troops – only a handful of young men, volunteer workers for the nongovernmental International Voluntary Service, had any notion of the extent of the Buddhist and central Vietnamese resentment against the Ky regime.

Still, U.S. policy did not seem to be entirely a function of unconditional American support for the junta. As the crisis wore on, U.S. officials in both Saigon and Washington seemed to grow more and more convinced that the Buddhist movement would be, if it were not already, dominated by the Communists. Just after Ky's debacle in Da Nang, Johnson's chief adviser, McGeorge Bundy, attacked Tri Quang in a public speech, charging that he intended to seize power and then make a coalition with the Communists.[5] A few days later the *New York Times* columnist, Cyrus L. Sulzberger, who was at the time staying at Deputy Ambassador Porter's house in Saigon, wrote a series of editorials describing the Viet Cong infiltration of the Buddhist movement and predicting a Communist take-over of Hue and Da Nang if the Buddhists were not stopped.[6] The truth of these allegations was extremely questionable. There were, to be sure, NLF agents within the Buddhist movement, but at the time no American official could have ascertained that there were more of them in that movement than, say, in the ARVN headquarters of the General Staff or in the American employ. Given the previous American ignorance of Buddhist politics, the speed with which the officials came to such a drastic conclusion revealed less about the

Communist leanings of the Buddhists than about the suspicion and hostility existing between the Buddhists and the Americans.

A few American officials — notably the intellectuals, such as Douglas Pike and George Carver — had been sympathetic to the Buddhist struggles in the past, but relations between the embassy and the Buddhist leadership had never been good. Except at the time of the 1963 coup, the Buddhists avoided close contact with the Americans, and the Americans made small effort to accommodate themselves. The result was an impasse — a void filled by fantasy from both sides. To many Americans the bonzes with their bare feet, their shaven skulls, and their curious aged-child bodies appeared to come from some mysterious Asian past where the rules of "civilized" conduct did not hold. Watching Tri Quang speak — the huge eyes of the bonze glittering in the light of the television cameras — one English correspondent said to a colleague, "Yul Brynner playing Dracula."[7] The joke revealed the obscure fear he felt for a man whose ambition it was to imitate Gandhi. Such remarks were fairly common among those journalists who had seen thousands of people following the Buddhist banners, who had seen the panic as the police attacked, and heard the high-pitched screams of the bonzes. If they had not witnessed it, Americans in Vietnam imagined the leap of flame, the smell of burning flesh, and the slow fall and disintegration of Thich Quang Duc. Some perhaps tried to talk to the bonzes, but found them "too moralistic, too devious." For American journalists and officials alike, the Buddhists, perhaps even more than the NLF, conjured up the old racial clichés of "the yellow masses" and the "inscrutable Orient." Among the journalists only Takashi Oka, the Japanese-American correspondent for the *Christian Science Monitor*, had over the years continued to visit Thich Tri Quang. As one non-Buddhist Vietnamese explained dryly, "The Americans don't like the Buddhists for the same reason they did not like Ngo Dinh Diem. The Buddhists are too Vietnamese for them."

The remark had more than a superficial truth to it. Under the Diem regime Ngo Dinh Can, the president's tough, peasant-shrewd brother, who ruled the First Corps, spent long hours with Tri Quang discussing the affairs of Hue and of the nation. Until the last year of the regime, when the president's brother, Archbishop Ngo Dinh Thuc, hungry for a cardinal's hat, legislated against the Buddhist, Can had kept the tensions between the two sects to a minimum. It had perhaps not been that difficult a task, for the two central Vietnamese sects had more in common with each other than with anyone else in Vietnam.

Living in that impoverished land, the last outpost of the Nguyen empire, the central Vietnamese were traditionalists whatever their adopted faith. Catholics or Buddhists, they believed in the same old customs, the old morality of the patriarchal empire. Halfway between Hanoi and Saigon, they clung to a nationalism that opposed Vietnam to the West and to Western innovation. As Harvard-trained Dr. Phan Quang Dan once exclaimed during the Buddhist crisis, "Tri Quang on the cover of *Time!* He's just a witch doctor people go to until modern medicine comes along."[8] His remark was not the disparagement that he meant it to be, for the fact was that Tri Quang's ideas were much closer to the traditionalist peasantry than Dan's could ever be, despite the doctor's good intentions. Neglected by the Americans as well as by the French, Hue was the countryside compared to Saigon.[9] As a centrist, Tri Quang, perhaps more than Thien Minh or Tam Chau, saw Buddhism as the spiritual force that united all Vietnamese. "The Communists," he told Takashi Oka, "are against us because our religion is tied to the Vietnamese nation — because it has always had a nationalist character. The Communists always want to be a mass organization, but Buddhism *is* the mass — and that makes it more difficult for the Communists as well as for us." For him Buddhism was the "Middle Way," that is, both the "Way of the Ancestors" and the Way that united the Yin and the Yang, the two opposing principles of the universe. Certain of the intellectuals that surrounded Tri Quang called themselves socialists, but they believed, as he did, that the real enemy, the real deviation from the Middle Way, was superficial Westernization. Like Ngo Dinh Diem and like so many of the "old-fashioned" people of the country, they saw the difficulty the country people had in coping with Western wealth and Western ideas. To them Saigon was a city of prostitutes, beggars, corrupt generals, and juvenile delinquents — a new Shanghai that had capitulated to the foreigners and isolated itself from the rest of the country. As the American officials pointed out, they expressed their animosity towards the American troops in much the same language that the NLF used. But then so did the Catholics, the Hoa Hao, and the Cao Dai. The NLF had not converted the Buddhists to anti-Americanism, rather the Communists had learned xenophobia from the central Vietnamese mandarins and the people of the countryside.

And it was this that the Americans could not acknowledge, if they understood it, for it meant that in opposing the Buddhists they were opposing the voice of Vietnamese traditionalism.

The Americans erred in their analysis of the Buddhists, but they were perhaps correct in their conclusions: if the Buddhists were forced to choose between the Americans and the NLF, was it not likely that they would choose their own countrymen? In the middle of April 1966, the U.S. Embassy looked from the small safe island of the Ky government down into a vast abyss of people who did not want them in Vietnam.

Still, in that month of April the Buddhist leaders gave no signs of opposition to the war. Indeed, in their relations with the Americans they behaved in a much more reasonable and conciliatory manner than the generals themselves. Once the promise of elections was made, Tri Quang toured the northern provinces, calling on rebellious soldiers and officials to return to their posts and asking for a restoration of order. Had he been in any way beholden to the Communists, such an appeal would have been difficult for him to make, for it meant effectively restoring the foundation for the entire war effort in central Vietnam. As it was, he had to resist a good deal of pressure from the local GVN officials demanding the immediate resignation of the junta. To overcome their fears of retaliation, he gave them his personal assurance that Ky and Thieu would retire after the election and that their jobs would be secure.[10]

Slowly calm returned to the cities and with it a silence indicating that all of the political factions had retired from the public stage to make their arrangements for the forthcoming elections. The Catholics voiced some fear that the Buddhists would dominate the new assembly, but only the American embassy appeared to be positively unhappy with the prospect of elections. In a televised interview Ambassador Lodge spoke darkly about the possibilities for voter intimidation, fraud, and Viet Cong infiltration of the electoral system.[11] What undoubtedly disturbed Lodge about the entire situation was the fact that he had no control over it.

On May 6, after a month of quiet and order, Premier Ky announced quite casually to a group of American newsmen that the junta had agreed to elections for a constituent assembly, not a legislative body, and that he intended to stay in power for at least another year. The next day U.S. Secretary of State Dean Rusk said on national television that he believed the press must have misquoted Ky: the Vietnamese premier had made it quite clear that he intended to resign his powers to the new assembly. Rusk was wrong. The young general had not been misquoted and he meant exactly what he said.

On May 14, a thousand Vietnamese Marines, supported by Ky's wing of fighter-bombers, landed in Da Nang and seized the radio station, the corps headquarters, and other key installations throughout the city. The move came as a total surprise to everyone, including the American advisers to the Marine battalions who, until the moment of landing in Da Nang, believed they were engaged in an operation against the Viet Cong. Caught off guard, Ky's own corps commander, General Ton That Dinh, fled to Hue in a helicopter lent to him by the local U.S. Marine commander. Once safe in the First Division Headquarters, he refused — or so he later testified — the junta's offers of cabinet posts and ambassadorships abroad as the price for saying he had "invited" the Saigon troops in. The commander of the ARVN First Division refused to receive Ky's emissary, and the mayor of Da Nang, Dr. Man, disappeared.[12] In Saigon fifty thousand trade union workers struck in protest against the junta's action.

Washington was in an uproar. Without consulting the American ambassador, Ky had provoked a crisis that looked as if it might turn into a civil war within the Vietnamese army. Which portion of the army should the U.S. troops support? Already the First Corps troops had begun to launch shells at the American base, where Ky's Marines were stationed, and the Buddhists of Da Nang had taken steps to barricade themselves into their pagodas. Appalled by the prospect of so much bloodshed, the new corps commander, sent up to replace General Ton That Dinh, refused to obey an order to clear the dissidents out of the pagodas. On May 16, Tri Quang sent an urgent appeal to President Johnson asking him to intervene on behalf of the Buddhists. The President did not himself reply. Secretary of State Dean Rusk, however, responded that he could not pass judgment on Ky's use of force and that he hoped that all the Vietnamese would settle their "lesser differences" and concentrate on pursuing the war against the Viet Cong.[13]

No doubt emboldened by this American reaction, the Ky junta proceeded to fire the new corps commander and to hand over command of the Da Nang operation to Colonel Nguyen Ngoc Loan, the northern-born paratrooper colonel whom two years later an AP photographer was to catch summarily executing a Viet Cong suspect with his revolver. Colonel Loan had few scruples. With reinforcements from the tank corps and the airborne division, he began to move on the pagodas and in a wild series of gun battles, managed to kill approximately a hundred civilians and to wound hundreds of others. On May 22 he forced the last Da Nang pagoda to surrender and completed his preparations for the capture of Hue. The junta initially lacked troops and transport to take Hue as well as Da Nang by surprise, and so it began by laying siege to the city, cutting off all but essential food supplies.

Within the city of Hue the dissidents began to feel the pressure of want and to hear gruesome reports of the atrocities committed by government troops in Da Nang. Blaming himself for the fate of the Da Nang Buddhists — it was he, after all, who advised them to cease their resistance — Tri Quang (according to one report) shut himself up in his cell for several days, crying out and beating his head with his fists.[14] On May 26, a group of students and young workers burned down the USIS library in Hue; the city fire trucks, called in to stop the blaze, made no attempt to put the fire out. In retaliation the U.S. officials withdrew the remaining American personnel from the city. At the same time they attempted to bring the generals to a compromise. Once again their initiative failed completely, for General Thi, their one pawn, now refused to treat with the junta. The Buddhists of Hue were desperate. The same day of the USIS fire one hundred and twenty-five bonzes and nuns began a hunger strike in the U.S. consulate and some six thousand people marched in demonstration; the next day the Buddhist nun Thich Nu Thanh Quang set her gas-soaked robes alight and burned herself to death before one of the central pagodas in Hue. She left a note addressed to President Johnson in which she condemned the irresponsibility of American support for the junta and asked that the United States continue to be the friend and ally of the Vietnamese people. Her death inspired a demonstration of some twenty thousand people in Saigon and a series of eight other self-immolations by Buddhist bonzes and nuns throughout the major cities of Vietnam. Within the week there were more suicides by fire than there had been during the entire Buddhist campaign against Diem. President Johnson called the suicides "tragic and unnecessary" and said that they obstructed progress towards holding the elections for a constituent assembly. On May 31, a group of students and Buddhist youths burned down the U.S. consulate in Hue.[15]

Simultaneously with the Da Nang raids Colonel Loan's police broke into the Buddhist Youth Headquarters in Saigon and arrested twenty students, setting off a new series of demonstrations. This time, however, the police counterattacked with tear gas and bayonets. Thich Thien Minh, a supporter of Tri Quang and the only important Buddhist leader left in Saigon (the wily Tam Chau left the country on an official tour), attempted to negotiate with the junta, but his support was slipping away from him. The southern sects and other political factions that had backed the Buddhists on the issue of elections had come to fear that the Buddhists would dominate the assembly. They turned against them now that it was safe to do so. Despite the daily demonstrations in the city, the junta would give Thien Minh no more than the token concession of enlarging the Armed Forces Council with a few unaffiliated civilians.

Slowly and steadily the siege began to tell on Hue. Realizing that no help could be expected from the Americans, the commander of the dissident Vietnamese First Division sent a secret message to Saigon through his wife, professing his loyalty to the junta.[16] A short time later the mayor of Hue, Lieutenant Colonel Pham Van Khoa, openly declared his change of heart and moved out of the city with the thousand troops at his disposal, leaving Hue defenseless before the government battalions. Most eager to dissociate themselves from the violence against American property, the other city officials and officers of the First Division went along with the decision. When the GVN invasion finally came on June 8, only the unarmed citizenry of Hue offered any resistance; families put their household altars out on the streets and groups of students formed human roadblocks across the avenues leading into the city. Wishing to avoid further bloodshed, Tri Quang ordered the people of Hue to remove their altars from the streets and to allow the GVN troops to enter the city in peace.[17] That day he began a hunger strike that was to last for several months and bring him to the point of death.

Colonel Loan's clearing operations dragged on. It was a full month after the attack on Da Nang before Hue surrendered completely. With a certain consideration for the feelings of the Americans and the rich Buddhists in Saigon, the junta determined not to imprison the senior bonzes of Hue, but merely to put Tri Quang under house arrest in a Saigon clinic. The Saigon generals were similarly careful with the ranking First Corps officers, many of whom had close relations with their American advisers. Arresting General Thi, General Ton That Dinh, and the commander of the First Division, they took them to Saigon and kept them there under house arrest before exiling them abroad. But they showed no mercy to the student leaders, the trade unionists, and the other lay members of the struggle movement. Imprisoning many of them in their foulest political camps, they left the rest no alternative but to join the NLF. The Buddhist struggle movement was never to recover.

9

Prospero, Caliban, and Ariel

CALIBAN: This island's mine by Sycorax my mother,
Which thou tak'st from me. When thou cam'st first,
Thou strok'dst me and made much of me, wouldst give me
Water with berries in't; and teach me how
To name the bigger light, and how the less,
That burn by day and night; and then I loved thee
And showed thee all the qualities o' th' isle,
The fresh springs, brine-pits, barren place and fertile.
Cursed be I that did so! All the charms
Of Sycorax — toads, beetles, bats, light on you!
For I am all the subjects that you have,
Which first was mine own king; and here you sty me
In this hard rock, whiles you do keep from me
The rest o' th' island.

William Shakespeare,
The Tempest, act 1, scene 2

In the fall of 1966 the Buddhist crisis passed into history. It had disrupted the war effort for some months and disabled the Vietnamese government in the critical area of the First Corps for the rest of the year. Still, the war continued and the Ky junta remained in power. The importance of the crisis lay not so much in what it did as in what it showed about the relationship between the United States and its non-Communist Vietnamese "allies."

The Buddhist crisis, first of all, forced U.S. officials to clarify and substantiate their policy towards the Saigon government. During the course of the crisis they made clear that the United States would support the military junta against all opposition, whatever its political weight. In effect they were giving the Vietnamese the choice between the generals and the NLF. The Buddhists had, of course, suspected that from the time of the Honolulu Conference. They created the struggle movement to show how repulsive that choice was to the urban Vietnamese. And they successfully demonstrated that fact. The curiosity was that they finally went down to defeat. While many Americans simply assumed that they could not prevail against U.S. opposition, the serious American journalists were impressed by the lack of influence the United States appeared to have over its "allies." Despite its subvention of the regime, despite the two hundred thousand American troops in Vietnam, the embassy failed to control the three generals it supported, much less the Buddhists and other political groups. Granted, it managed to maintain the junta in power and to continue the war on the same terms, but that was all. Except for the resignation of General Thi, all of the American initiatives, diplomatic and otherwise, ended in failure. For the past three months the world had watched the ludicrous spectacle of the largest power on earth occupying one of the smallest and hopelessly trying to unknot a civil war inside a revolution.

The reason for this failure the journalists found difficult to fathom — and particularly difficult if they talked to the Vietnamese. For the Vietnamese seemed to see the crisis in a completely strange light. According to many of the politicians concerned, the United States had planned and orchestrated the whole sequence of events in order to further its own interests. Sometime in the weeks between the Honolulu Conference and the first Da Nang assault, one student leader (a man in his thirties) wrote a strongly worded manifesto charging that the U.S. embassy had deliberately and selectively cut off the electricity in various portions of Saigon in order to undermine the Vietnamese government, Vietnamese sovereignty, and the aspirations of the Vietnamese people. At the time the American reporters (who suffered from the lack of electricity a good deal more than the Vietnamese) simply laughed, but the student's complaint began to seem less and less out of the ordinary as the Buddhist crisis progressed. More outspoken and possibly more courageous than their elders, many of whom echoed the same sentiments sotto voce, the student leaders would regularly stand up and accuse the embassy or the CIA of responsibility for every event that displeased them, from the activities of the Ky junta to the corruption of the provincial officials. Some of their complaints were justifiable — the United States was indeed supporting the Ky junta, despite all its claims of neutrality in "internal Vietnamese affairs" — but others were simply inexplicable. Just after the promulgation of the election decree, for example, the militant Catholics (probably inspired by the junta) demonstrated before the American embassy with signs charging that Ambassador Lodge had supported the Buddhists against the junta in their bid for power. When asked why they held such an opinion after all the evidence to the contrary, they merely answered that the Buddhists could not have succeeded in doing what they did without the help of the Americans.

It was not something that an American could argue — or rather, he could argue it for hours only to have his Vietnamese friends agree completely while continuing to regard him with eyes shuttered by disbelief. The Vietnamese of the cities seemed to take a miraculous view of the Americans. It was not that they overestimated the ultimate power of the United States, but that they misjudged the American desire and capacity to use it in the small, personal world of GVN politics. On the one hand the Vietnamese believed the United States had an absolute power over the actions of their enemies; on the other hand all of them, even the generals, behaved in such a way as to demonstrate that the United States had no influence at all. On that paradox rested the whole surreal course of the Buddhist crisis — and perhaps of the whole future of U.S. relations with the Saigon government.

In coming to Vietnam with their advisers and troops, the Americans assumed a particular kind of relationship with the Vietnamese: they had expected the Vietnamese to trust them, to take their advice with gratitude, and to cooperate in their mutual enterprise of defeating the Communists. The Buddhist crisis came as a terrible shock, for it showed that a good proportion of the urban Vietnamese had no confidence in American policies. Not only the Buddhists, but General Ky and Colonel Nguyen Ngoc Loan seemed to resent American interference. The crisis exposed the contradiction between the Americans' desire to put the GVN on its own feet and their desire to maintain some control over GVN politics. The Vietnamese recognized that contradiction, but they reacted to it in a way that Americans could not understand. Did their view of the United States as a ruthless, omnipotent force have something to do with their long history of colonial rule? If so, could the Americans, whatever their intentions, cope with these suspicions any better than the French in Saigon? The questions were crucial ones, for if the GVN officials continued to regard the Americans in this light there could be no possible basis for cooperation between the two governments or between the Vietnamese government and the rest of the non-Communist groups in Vietnam.

The whole notion of an overwhelming power was, of course, an important theme in Vietnamese life. As anyone with a knowledge of Freud might suspect, it had something to do with the relationship of the Vietnamese child to his father, with the idea, conceived in early childhood, that the father, and behind him the ancestors, have far-reaching control over the child. As men tend to see the world according to their earliest and strongest impression of it, the Vietnamese had transferred this image of childhood to the relationship between two different nations. In his study, *Prospero and Caliban,* the French ethnologist and psychologist, Otare Mannoni, gives an interesting insight into this process. His subject is colonial society in Madagascar, but much of his analysis seems to fit Vietnam, and understandably so, for the Madagascans, like the Vietnamese, were ancestor worshipers.[1]

When the French first arrived in Madagascar, so Mannoni reports, the natives received them not with hostility but with fear and then a kind of elation. A popular Malagasy song of the period describes the French as almost supernatural creatures and tells how they frightened the king and queen and then brought peace and order to the country. What impressed the Malagasy was not so much the French military power (there were in fact few French soldiers involved in the pacification, and few battles fought) as their readiness to take command and the freedom with which they violated all of the traditional Malagasy customs. Instead of looking upon the French as simply foreigners with different customs, the Malagasy placed them within their own context and concluded that the French had superhuman powers. Because their ancestors were also superhumans, they by analogy accorded the French a position similar to that of their ancestors. The French became their masters, protectors, and scapegoats, all in one.

Obscurely, the French understood that their rule over Madagascar depended not so much on their superior weapons as on the psychological power they held over the Malagasy. Whenever a disturbance arose, they would show panic by taking spectacularly violent actions that, if transferred to Europe, would seem quite irrational as political or military strategy. In their view, once the Malagasy showed any sign of independence, all was lost. And they were right in a certain respect. What they could not understand, however, was that their power did not derive from the Madagascans' humiliating sense of their own inferiority, but from their acceptance of a dependent relationship. To the Malagasy, the French were not "better" than themselves, they were simply people who (for obscure reasons of their own) wished to take on the responsibility for their country.

The French conquest of Vietnam had certain startling similarities. As in Madagascar, the French troops met small resistance, partly because the state had already been undermined by Catholicism and by the emperor's dependence on foreign weapons. Some of the mandarins gathered guerrilla armies around them and fought to the end, but the imperial armies disintegrated quickly under direct assault, and the French succeeded in pacifying all but the northern mountains with a very few men. For almost sixty years they ruled Vietnam with only fourteen thousand troops in the country. A few of the old mandarins never gave up their resistance, but others acquiesced to the French in fascination with the strange sciences, the strange customs. While educated Vietnamese felt that the French would eventually leave Vietnam, they, by their acquiescence, accorded them the mantle of legitimacy that had always been known as the Mandate of Heaven, the collective power of the ancestors over their national life.

The French in Vietnam, like the French in Madagascar, accepted the position that the Vietnamese offered them as their just due. In the opinion of the old colons, all the Vietnamese needed was a firm authority (in that phrase lay all the echoes of the British in India and Africa, the Germans, Spanish, and Portuguese in their colonies). "Behave in the royal manner" towards the Vietnamese, the French ethnologists, Huard and Durand, counseled their countrymen. In Saigon in the 1960's an old French doctor who had lived in Vietnam most of his life continued to follow the same principle. Looking at his two neat, competent nurses, he said, "The Vietnamese are excellent people as long as they are kept in second place. But you Americans do not understand them. You have not given them the proper authority, and you have corrupted them." His remark was interesting in that it implied he knew his treatment of the Vietnamese was a manipulation. But he did not know why it worked. To him and his compatriots, *les Annamites, les jaunes,* were inferior beings. They might be "bestial," "childish," or "good-natured" and "receptive to improvement," but they did not belong in the same category as Frenchmen.

Unable to understand the natives, the French colonialists of the nineteenth century, along with their American and European counterparts in the rest of Asia, invented all the racist clichés that have passed down into the mythology of the American soldier: that Orientals are lazy, dirty, untrustworthy, and ignorant of the value of human life. The persistence of these clichés, despite all evidence to the contrary, suggests that they have derived not from observation but from a fantasy. Just what did the American soldiers mean when they called the Vietnamese "gooks"? Again, Mannoni is of help. The colonialist is, he says, by nature a Robinson Crusoe; he is a man who has chosen to escape the society of men and to build an empire for himself in a world that will unquestioningly accept his dominion. The natives to him do not constitute human society, but an extension of the world of nature. In a sense, then, it is the colonial and not the native who is a "child," for his desire to escape rises out of the sense of insecurity and inferiority he felt within his own culture. In the native he finds a fulfillment of his childish dreams of domination and an object (for the native is to him an object) upon which to project all his repressed desires. In calling the native "dirty," "bloodthirsty," or "cruel," he relieves himself of his own guilt. The "colonialist," according to Mannoni, is a distinct type who selects himself out of his society for the role. The colonial impulse is nonetheless present in varying degrees within most Westerners and will tend to emerge when the situation permits it.

In Mannoni's judgment the best portrayal of the relations between colonial and native lies in Shakespeare's *The Tempest*. On the one hand there is Prospero, the European, who, unable to get along in his own society (his brother, he says, has betrayed him), has invented a world that he with his "magical powers" can dominate. In Caliban, the "bestial" native of the island, he sees everything he detests in himself — including a desire for incestual relations with his daughter Miranda. On the other hand there is Caliban himself, the native who hates his master not because Prospero dominates him but because he treats him so badly. As Mannoni points out, Caliban remembers a time when his master loved him and treated him kindly. He looks forward not to independence, but to finding a new and better master. This temporal sequence is in fact a representation of his own ambivalence towards authority: on the one hand he desires it, on the other hand he feels it will harm him. (The temporal succession is also curiously representative of the Vietnamese view of life, where it is hoped that the "golden age" of childhood will return once again in old age.) Ariel, the third character in the drama, combines features of both of the others. An important figure in colonial society, he is the houseboy, the intermediary between the colonial and the native Calibans. He desires independence, but he cannot take it for himself, for in exchange for his master's "magical powers," he has relinquished his independence of spirit and bound himself in servitude. (Prospero keeps insisting on the debt Ariel owes him for having "saved" him from the curse of Caliban's mother. Prospero is here the missionary who "saves" his houseboys from the "darkness," "misery," and "paganism" of native life — but who will not let his houseboys go.)

As *The Tempest* indicates, the relationship between colonial and native must eventually end, for while there is some superficial correspondence, the attitudes of both colonial and native are based on false, and finally contradictory, assumptions.

During the 1920's and 1930's the character of colonial society in Vietnam changed appreciably with the influx of men from the metropolis — professional civil servants, journalists, and party organizers — who in demanding liberal reforms, shook the very foundations of the paternalistic colonial authority. The colonial type did not disappear (indeed it often cropped up among those who came out to destroy it), but the reforms indicated to the Vietnamese that the French were no longer sure of themselves. Because they were no longer sure of their right to power, the Vietnamese intelligentsia began to conclude that they had no right to rule.[2] On their own many Vietnamese had, like Caliban, concluded that the French were not their patrons but tyrants who treated them as inferiors. During the 1930's Hanoi and Saigon were riddled with subversive groups, all of which wanted to drive the French out of Saigon. (Their cause was later aided by the Japanese invasion and coup d'etat that demonstrated to the people of the villages that the Westerners no longer had heaven's will behind them.) Among the subversive parties the Viet Minh alone succeeded in their object, not because they hated the French any more than the others, but because they managed to create a real alternative to French rule, a state with sufficient authority to mobilize the peasantry and direct their long-suppressed anger against the French to the achievement of national independence. But the resistance war was a political revolution and not a transformation of the Vietnamese personality. Through the Viet Minh the Vietnamese merely found a new "master," and it was themselves.

In the north the drama was ended, but in the south it merely passed into a new phase. The peasants, even those who once belonged to the Viet Minh, looked upon the Americans much as they had looked at the French. Afraid of the Americans, afraid of their own anger, they tended to avoid the confrontation by blaming the sufferings caused by the American bombs and soldiers on Fate. One major effort of the NLF went into convincing the southern peasants, so long dominated by foreigners and landlords, that they had a real and vulnerable enemy in the regime created and supported by the Americans. While they taught their cadres to hate the Americans, they taught them also not to overestimate them — that is, not to attribute to them all the hostile forces of Fate or Nature. In the 1947 rebellion in Madagascar the peasants charged the French guns uttering incantations that would, so the witch doctor assured them, turn the French bullets to water.[3] The NLF propaganda was not so contrary to science, but it served somewhat the same function, at once demystifying the Americans and creating a bond between the fighters that attached indirectly (through the structure of Vietnamese society) to the Americans. To the well-indoctrinated cadre, the contest appeared to be more or less equal: the Americans had powerful bombers and artillery, but the NLF had the strength of the Vietnamese people behind them.

The attitude of those who lived under the aegis of the GVN was, however, very different. Those who supported the Bao Dai government and later the Diem regime were the "Ariels" of Vietnam — the people that grew rich and powerful under the French and who could not maintain their status without them. When the French gave them their independence, they found a willing new master in the Americans. And they and their successors made the same transference. They assumed the Americans were endowed with an invincible power, an omnipotent intelligence and a ruthless desire to control them. But their assumption was more wish fulfillment than fact: they wanted the Americans to feed them and take responsibility for them. An incident this writer witnessed illustrates this attitude perfectly. In Washington a young Vietnamese girl of a "good family" who had come to teach Vietnamese to American foreign service officers was invited to a party at the house of a high official in the U.S. government. When introduced to the official, she, without a word of prologue, asked him whether he would help her find a small diamond ring that she had lost in a washbasin at the Foreign Service Institute. The official, greatly taken aback, mumbled some excuse about having nothing to do with the Foreign Service Institute and moved away. What the girl could not explain was that she had only a marginal interest in finding the ring: she wanted a protector — and the more powerful the better — among the Americans.

But the Vietnamese view of the Americans as ruthless and invincible also carried within it a terror that quite contradicted this desire for protection. Their image of the United States was in fact the expression of an ambivalence similar to that the young man, Huong, had faced in relation to his stepfather. They wanted the Americans to save them from their own people; but as the Americans were *not* their own people, they sought to preserve their autonomy from a power that was by definition untrustworthy. During the Buddhist crisis one student committee issued a manifesto calling for the United States to increase its military and economic aid to the GVN and at the same time to stop interfering in Vietnamese politics. The generals, the Saigon politicians, and the Buddhists echoed both of these sentiments alternately. That the Americans were already interfering in Vietnamese politics was a connection that neither they nor the Americans were willing to make. This contradiction between desire for, and hostility to, the American presence was to govern the whole history of the relationship between the Americans and the Vietnamese under the GVN aegis. In their struggle movement the Buddhists gave this contradiction its most violent and dramatic expression.

In beginning their protest against the Ky government, the Buddhists had much the same division of purpose that plagued all the other non-Communist parties. On the one hand, they were merely attempting to redistribute the power and wealth of the GVN. On the other hand, Tri Quang saw this attempt as a step towards the final goal of creating a community strong enough to unite the nation and banish both the Americans and Communism from Vietnam. The difficulty was that to separate tactics from strategy Tri Quang required a much more disciplined organization than he had in hand. In initiating the anti-government protests he ended by breaking down the Confucian restraints and unleashing the deep-running rivers of resentment against the new authority, the Americans. He had not meant to, for while he believed with an absolute religious conviction that Buddhism would one day unite the Vietnamese, he knew perfectly well that for the moment his organization was divided, weak, and finally as much dependent upon the Americans as the generals.[4] But he failed in his attempt to control the outburst. The Americans turned against him, and the movement could not survive their opposition, for even in their anger the Buddhists remained divided between resentment of the American presence in Vietnam and fury that the Americans did not support them against the junta.

Nearly half a century earlier the French ethnologists, Huard and Durand, wrote of the Vietnamese:

The rupture of dependency has . . . provoked violent feelings of inferiority [*sic*] with their habitual successions of manic and depressed activity . . . [leading among a minority] to a fierce will to destruction, a desire for the holocaust and an aesthetic of oblivion, which in turn leads, collectively, to a scorched earth policy and, individually, to suicide.[5]

Just three days after the junta, with American consent, began the siege of Hue, one hundred and twenty-five bonzes and bonzesses went on a hunger strike in the compound of the U.S. consulate. It was not a tactic the NLF would have used. By refusing food the bonzes were in effect pleading for the Americans to feed them.[6] When it became clear that the Americans would not do so, Tri Quang despaired. On June 8 he began a hunger strike that, prolonged for over a month, weakened him to the point where he could no longer give leadership. Rather than live with defeat and begin again, he chose a form of suicide and abandoned his followers to the full revenge of the junta. His hunger strike was a sign that the Buddhist movement was finished. In the same period eight bonzes and bonzesses from different parts of the country committed suicide by fire in an attempt to repeat the experience of 1963. Because the Americans did not respond, their self-immolation was not an effective act of protest but merely suicide. Simultaneously, the Buddhist students of Hue began what amounted to a scorched earth policy, burning the empty USIS library and the empty U.S. consulate, which buildings remained their only symbolic link to the Americans.

A vain and desperate gesture, it stripped them of their last possible defense against the junta — an appeal to the American press — and left them with only the choice of imprisonment or flight to the NLF.

The Buddhist movement was never to recover. Buddhism failed because it was not a Middle Way between the Communists and the Americans, but a last-ditch stand of the Vietnamese traditionalists against the West. Writing to a young American friend, one Buddhist student described the desperation he and his companions felt as they saw the two walls of the war close in upon them. The letter is a fitting epitaph to the whole Buddhist struggle movement:

> Maybe this is the last letter I send you — because I must make the choice, the choice of my life. I am pushing to the wall. To choose this side or the other side — and not the middle way!
>
> I can no more use my mouth, my voice, my heart, my hands for useful things. All the people here have to choose to manipulate guns — and they have to point straightly in face of each other. One side the Vietnamese city people and Americans, another side Vietnamese rural people and Communists and Leftist minded people.
>
> What have I to choose?
>
> But all things are relative now — I can't side even with Americans or Communists. But you have no choice. Or this side or the other side — With Americans, you are accused of valets of Imperialism, of pure Colonialism — You are in the side of foreigners, of the people who kill your people, who bomb your country, with the eternal foreigners who always wanted to subjugate you for thousands of years . . .
>
> No, it's a desperate situation. I want so desperately to be still in jail —[7]

For the Buddhists and for those who felt themselves rejected or ill-treated by the Americans, the ambivalence took open expression in the attempt at flight, in the search for oblivion, and in the death reflex that appears the one possible means of escape from an intolerable situation.[8] For those who did not feel rejected it took quite another form. It would involve constant duplicity, and constant effort at deception and self-deception, but it would eventually lead to much the same destruction.

10

Bad Puppets

Seen from the viewpoint of General Westmoreland, the events of the Buddhist crisis and the civil war within the GVN were but ripples in the steadily building tide of the American war. By Westmoreland's account, the year 1966 was the year of the Allied offensive against the Communists. Before the year was out, the United States had nearly four hundred thousand troops in Vietnam, its soldiers outnumbering the ARVN and the enemy forces in the south. In one year American spending on the war leaped from one hundred and five million dollars to two billion dollars a month — a sum whose equivalent would have paid every South Vietnamese more than a hundred dollars a year. The American military engineers and a group of U.S. construction firms went to work building roads, bridges, barracks, and ports, and completed construction of fifty-nine new airfields. By the end of the year the quantity of American supplies arriving in Vietnam reached six hundred thousand tons a month.[1] In 1966 the U.S. forces launched over six major search-and-destroy operations against large enemy units and base camps. Their main efforts were concentrated just below the DMZ and in the middle tier of central Vietnamese provinces.

Now developed into action, Westmoreland's strategy consisted of a defense against what he considered a renewed attempt by the North Vietnamese to "cut the country in half" and an offense of attrition — that is, the attempt to cut down the enemy's main forces to the point where they could no longer carry on the war. In terms of these goals Westmoreland counted the year a success. Reporting to the President in the spring of 1967, he said that the American troops had "spoiled" four enemy offensives, prevented the North Vietnamese from taking over the northern provinces of the First Corps (that is, the northern capitals of the First Corps) and raised the enemy death toll from four to eight thousand a month.[2]

From one perspective the American officials seemed to have excellent reasons for optimism about the war. Whether or not Westmoreland correctly calculated North Vietnamese intentions, the American troops successfully engaged the enemy main forces and killed a great number of their troops. The statistics, even if they were only approximate, meant a great deal for a country the size of Vietnam. In Operation Masher/White Wing alone — a multiregimental sweep through the north of Binh Dinh province — the Allied forces, by the estimates, destroyed an entire enemy division. In the process they left hundreds of civilians dead and wounded and "generated" so many refugees as almost to depopulate the fertile An Lao valley. In military terms the very scale of the war promised victory. Even in its first year the American war dwarfed the former struggles of the French and of the Saigon government. It seemed to dwarf Vietnam itself, reducing Vietnamese politics to the microscopic dimension of struggles between rotifers and paramecia. What army, after all, could take so many casualties and continue to fight with only the prospect of more destruction in sight? Ridiculous to talk of protracted warfare when the American forces killed eight times the number of men the enemy killed each month.

But oddly enough, these statistics — and the destruction they more or less represented — did not seem to have any immediate consequence for the war. Despite all of the bloody battles that year, the enemy actually increased its strength in the south. The Front forces maintained their numbers with a strenuous effort at recruitment, and the North Vietnamese, taking the brunt of the large-scale war in the northern provinces, continued to replace their losses through infiltration. While the American troops opened roads and "cleared" great stretches of territory, the Front guerrillas came back into every area except those heavily garrisoned by U.S. troops. By the end of 1966 the NLF continued to govern the An Lao valley as well as the suburbs of Da Nang, Hue, Nha Trang, and Saigon. If the war was being won, then it was not being won quickly; indeed, it was taking a great deal longer than administration officials had suggested the year before. With four hundred thousand troops in Vietnam, Westmoreland continued to request thousands more every two or three months. The generals remained optimistic, but in a way that by no means encouraged the President. As one general said, "We can knock this off in a year or two at the most if we intensify and accelerate the war. We could use several more divisions. . . . We could bomb North Vietnam more effectively, and really cripple their lines of communication and war-supporting industry. My guess is that with between 500,000 and 700,000 men, we could break the back of the Communist main forces by 1968–69."[3] Westmoreland wanted to invade the enemy "sanctuaries" in Laos and Cambodia; and there was talk of a "requirement" for the invasion of the southern provinces of North Vietnam and the "necessity" for an American presence in Vietnam for the next fifteen years.

In March 1967, just a year after the Honolulu meeting and the beginning of the Buddhist crisis, President Johnson and his advisers met once again with the members of the Vietnamese junta, Generals Ky and Thieu. (Only General Nguyen Huu Co was missing. While Co was off on one of his many "goodwill" trips to European and American capitals, Ky simply wired him not to return to Vietnam.) Johnson hoped for a strategy review session with the American field command alone. But the Vietnamese leaders offered the U.S. mission a completed draft of the constitution in return for an invitation to the conference. Their offer accepted, they wasted very little time on diplomatic modesty. "The first time we talked about building democracy at Honolulu," Ky told the assembled journalists, "everyone talked about the so-called military junta and just laughed. So it's now a pleasure to be able to be here and tell the Americans about the progress we have made." This time it was Ky and not Johnson who turned the conference into a public relations display. In contrast to Ky's confident talk about military victories, Johnson spoke of Vietnam as a "serious, long-drawn-out, agonizing problem that we do not yet have the answer for," and McNamara said that the Communists were "by no means beaten."[4]

There was, it appeared to the public, some miscalculation. In the first place, it seemed, Washington had underestimated the effort the

North Vietnamese were willing to give to the south and overestimated the damaging effect the bombing would have on that effort. In the second place, the Pentagon had not taken into account the potency of the old and very well known strategy of "people's war." The North Vietnamese regulars had drawn off the American troops from the populated regions of the south, allowing the local Front guerrillas to harass the enemy bases and build up their strength among the civilian population. So long as the Front controlled the villages, its strength would remain far greater than the sum of its combat troops. To win the war, the Allies would have simultaneously to destroy the main forces and to secure the countryside, and with the present number of troops they did not seem able to do both at once.

Whether the Pentagon had erred in its estimates of the enemy or in its estimates of the President's willingness to expand the war, the generals in the field took pains to impress their version of the source of the difficulty upon the journalists. In their view the American troops with reinforcements and an accelerated bombing program could halt the infiltration and destroy the regular Front forces within an acceptable amount of time. The real difficulty lay with the pacification program. As the Marine commander, General Lewis W. Walt so vividly put it, "Breaking the back of the VC main force won't take that long, but rooting out the VC guerrilla is a long-term task."[5] To put the matter thus was, of course, to make a false distinction between the political and the military aspects of the war — but it was to pinpoint the blame for the slowness of progress. During 1966 the ARVN, under some American pressure, almost relinquished the large-scale war to the Americans to concentrate on the task of "clearing" the populated areas. The generals' implication was thus that the Saigon government bore the responsibility for holding up the war effort.

The explanation seemed to come as a revelation to a large section of the American press corps. Here, at last, was the reason for the discrepancy between expectations and actual progress. Bursting through the solid front of coverage on American operations, *Time*, *Newsweek*, and some of the television networks began all of a sudden to stress the importance of pacification and "the other war." The same publications that had stoutly defended the Saigon government for thirteen years began to run articles describing the poor combat performance of the ARVN and hinting at corruption and inefficiency within the top ranks of the GVN. These articles generally concluded with a suggestion that the Saigon regime might well improve with political stability and American training programs, but on the other hand that might take a long time. The tone was one of innocent surprise. Who, after all, could have predicted two years before that the Saigon government might not live up to its responsibilities as an American ally?

To certain experienced reporters such articles appeared to be a kind of madness. Returning to Vietnam after three years' absence, David Halberstam found that his strongest impression was not that of the change wrought by the American buildup, but his sense of *déjà vu*.[6] Around the great American operations that were the exclusive concern of briefing officers in Saigon and the focus of Westmoreland's strategy, the old war continued much as it had in the days of Diem. The Saigon government had changed no more than the war itself.

The improvement in ARVN morale, so carefully catalogued by Robert Komer and George Carver the year before, meant little more than an improved sense of security — a realistic assessment that with the American troops in the country the NLF would not win that year. The ARVN fought no better than it had in 1962. Relegated to the tedious duty of standing guard over the villages, the strike force battalions collapsed into lethargy and indiscipline. They refused to go out at night, to patrol in small units, or to use the local intelligence sources to engage the guerrillas. There were the same horror stories as there had been in the days of the Strategic Hamlet program. Just ten miles or so out of Saigon on Route 4 to My Tho, the U.S. congressmen visiting the Delta might have seen the encampment of one ARVN battalion and, five hundred yards down the road, the charred ruins of a village that the Front forces had burned to the ground while the battalion stood by without firing a shot. In one province, a "priority area" for the American command, an ARVN regiment had butchered the livestock of an entire village and raped so many women that the men of the village had cut their trigger fingers off as a protest against the government.[7] If the "problem" of the ARVN was a problem of leadership, as the MACV officials insisted, then it was only one in the most extended sense of the word. When Halberstam, interviewing enemy defectors, asked a North Vietnamese major what he could do if given command of an ARVN battalion, the major replied, "I could command a division in

North Vietnam. I have the ability to do that. But a platoon here, even a squad, I could not do that. What can you do? They have no purpose."[8]

The GVN administration remained almost precisely as it was in the days of Diem. In the yellowed colonial buildings where the ceiling fans plowed through the damp heat, the officials leafed slowly through their piles of papers, affixing stamps to forms, signatures to documents, and turning them over again. There were a few new faces, but none to break the routine. The vast expansion of the bureaucracy merely meant that it was somewhat less exclusive, somewhat less wieldy and less competent than before. With the army officers holding the key posts in the provincial administration, the sole GVN authority in a district was often a young man with a year's experience of dress drills. In theory the military administration coordinated civilian programs with military strategy, but in practice the regular army, the civilian ministries, and the military administration worked in almost total isolation from one another. The officers had a purpose — only it was not quite the same as that of the Americans. Orders, truckloads of supplies, even whole units would appear out of — or disappear into — nowhere. As usual, the chain of command had little to do with the organization charts.

As always there were new "concepts," new hopes for the GVN within the American mission. In 1967 it was the Revolutionary Development program, heralded as a "coordinated approach to rooting out the Viet Cong infrastructure and rooting in the government." From an administrative point of view, the goal of the program was to eliminate all the red tape that resulted from having several Vietnamese ministries and several U.S. agencies all involved in the pacification program. The achievement of the new program was in the nature of a compromise: the United States created a vast new ministry while continuing to maintain all the others. The duplication of efforts and the departmental fights therefore continued while the new ministry itself became a paradigm of the whole governmental and U.S. advisory system. In Saigon ambitious bureaucrats quit their jobs in the ministries of agriculture and social welfare to offer their services to the new program; in the provinces military officials turned their attention from juggling the budgets of the old ministries to juggling the budgets of the new; within the American mission the various agencies sharpened their bureaucratic teeth to fight over this vast new establishment. Instead of cutting

through the bureaucratic morass, the Revolutionary Development
ministry was absorbed by it as molasses in a solution of molasses.

The central feature of the ministry (known more modestly in
Vietnamese as "Rural Reconstruction") was the creation of fifty-
nine-man cadre teams to do the complete work of pacification in the
hamlets. The "concept" for these teams had an extremely long history in the GVN, beginning with Diem's Catholic rural workers and
proceeding through the Political Action and Census Grievance
teams developed by Frank Scotton in 1964–1965. None of those
teams had any spectacular success, but they were nonetheless
bathed in a certain Special Forces mystique, the principle behind
which was that the Americans could win the war if they imitated
enemy tactics. The training program for the new cadre teams
involved instruction by former Viet Minh officers under CIA aegis in
everything from "self-criticism" to interrogation techniques to the
art of living among villagers without stealing their food or their
women. Graduating from the Vung Tao school with torchlight
processions, patriotic songs, and speeches by Nguyen Cao Ky on the
social revolution, these new cadres were then sent into the "cleared"
hamlets to perform one hundred and ten tasks, beginning with the
"rooting out of the Viet Cong infrastructure," proceeding through
the "elimination of wicked village notables," and ending with the
supervision of hamlet and village elections. The obstacles to their
performing all these tasks were, as always, insurmountable. Placed
under the jurisdiction of the district chiefs, many of the teams went
to insecure villages and were threatened or killed by the NLF;
others, switched about from village to village each week like common soldiers, had hardly the time to perform the first ten of their
appointed tasks. Those teams that actually got to the point of
investigating the political situation of the village usually discovered
that the "wicked village notables" were in fact relatives or financial
supporters of the local GVN officials. Retreating to the more innocuous tasks of building wells or maternities, they would find themselves without concrete or tin roofing so that all their efforts slipped
back into the mud. As usual, the major difficulty was that only the
exceptional men among them had any notion of how or why they
should go about working with the peasants. With no cooperation
either from the villagers or from the GVN officials, many grew
discouraged. During the first year of the program one in four RD
cadres deserted — most of them no doubt for the bright lights of a

town. The majority, largely innocent of any desire to improve the government or the lot of the villagers, accepted their fate and became an addition to the GVN's local defense system, an ill-rewarded and ineffectual and occasionally brutal occupation force.

If it was true, as Robert Komer said, that the NLF in 1967 controlled 24 percent of the population, it did not therefore follow that the GVN controlled the rest. As designed by the "regulars" and the GVN officials, the pacification program meant little more than military control and a few welfare programs. As in the days of Diem, the only people who had a political commitment to something other than the Front were the members of the sects and political factions. And they, perhaps less than the others, were "under the control" of the government. Under American pressure General Khanh had ended the repressive Diemist policy towards the sects and granted them a measure of autonomy and government support, but he had succeeded only in reinstating something like the status quo ante of the French regime. The Hoa Hao and Cao Dai did not make common cause with the NLF, but they supported the military junta on condition that it did not interfere in their local affairs. When in moments of crisis the generals would try to pull the sects into the arena of Saigon politics to act as a conservative force, they would cooperate to the extent of protecting only their own investment in a weak and accommodating government. They favored a civilian government because they felt it might give them a greater share of power and preserve the barter politics of the Delta against the self-righteous *étatisme* of the centrists and northerners. But they were not willing to fight for it: Saigon politics, they felt, was not really their concern. Indeed, they looked upon the succession of coups and counter-coups with a certain *Schadenfreude*. The governmental chaos only confirmed their view that Vietnam was passing through an interregnum preceding the coming of their respective saviors. With respect to this final goal, a strong Saigon government was as much of a danger to them as the NLF.[9]

The GVN could perhaps claim the status of referee between the various rural political factions, but it could claim only the role of oppressor with regard to the various non-Vietnamese minorities. Under an organization called FULRO (*Front Unifié pour la Lutte des Races Opprimées*) many of the montagnard tribes had for years lived in a state of open revolt from the GVN. When the American

Special Forces armed and fed the tribesmen with a view to keeping them out of the NLF, the GVN officials repaid their efforts by accusing them of favoritism and subversion of GVN authority. In 1966 the anthropologist, Gerald Hickey, managed after months of labor to arrange a treaty whereby the Vietnamese government would recognize the montagnard tribal rights and property. Just a few weeks after the ceremonial accord, a few Vietnamese officers, finding it convenient to sacrifice a montagnard village for the sake of their own safety, wrecked the agreement and drove the montagnards back into their old resistance.[10]

The GVN officials had not quite the same racist disdain for the other minorities — the Chams, the Khmers, and the Chinese — but they (in sharp contrast to the NLF) systematically excluded them from all but the lower ranks of the army and administration. This discrimination naturally insured that none of these important groups would give their loyalties to the government. As the Tet offensive showed, the GVN failed to pacify even the Chinese enclave of Cholon. But then, if by "pacified" the Americans meant anything more than "non-Communist," it was questionable whether the ruling junta itself was "pacified."

After the trying four months of the Buddhist crisis, the Vietnamese Armed Forces Council settled down to business as usual. Having promised the Americans and the various political groups a constitutional assembly, the generals went about preparing for elections and restaffing the First Corps with their own political cronies. Now in debt to the three southern corps commanders, Generals Ky and Thieu left them to consolidate their positions and make the arrangements — personal, financial, and logistical — necessary to support a new and more stable system of corruption. As befitted the nature of the government, the system was perfectly decentralized: General Dan Van Quang, the Fourth Corps commander, ran a brisk trade in rice and opium; General Vinh Loc of the Second Corps and General Hoang Xuan Lam of the First Corps dealt in military preferments and American commodities. While still minister of defense, General Nguyen Huu Co held extensive real estate concerns. His purchases may have seemed arbitrary at the time of negotiation, but the various seaside villas and barren tracts of land turned out with monotonous regularity to be the choice of the U.S. military procurement office for the sites of new American installations. Though General

Thieu did not engage in such transactions, his wife managed the family finances and, judging from the grape-size diamond she wore to everyday functions, she managed them most efficiently.

Of all the top generals, only Nguyen Cao Ky did not noticeably derive any financial gain from his job. Living in a spare bungalow within the protective confines of Tan Son Nhut airport, he diverted the incidental tax receipts he might have spent on the beautiful Madame Ky to the purchase of province officials and to the organization of his own gang of street toughs. (His Anti-Fraud and Corruption League was later disbanded by General Thieu on well-founded charges of fraud and corruption.) General Ky's goal for the moment was not money but power. The Saigonese laughed cynically at his speeches against corruption, but Ky was no doubt sincere in his opposition to it. He would have preferred to run an honest government than a corrupt one. The only difficulty was that his power depended upon corruption, both directly — his mainstay and mastermind, the Colonel, now General, Nguyen Ngoc Loan, had all but cornered the extortion racket in Saigon — as well as institutionally. During his great anti-corruption drive in the fall and winter of 1965–1966 Ky arrested only one man, a Chinese businessman whom the Chinese community reportedly delivered up to Ky as a scapegoat (no doubt for his refusal to pay their own local protection racket). And a scapegoat in the ritual sense of the word, for Ky had the unfortunate Mr. Ta Vinh shot by a firing squad in the central market of Saigon.

Unequal to the task of "rooting out corruption," Ky had virtually no power to implement any of the other reforms the Americans pressed upon him. He could not fire the bad officials because they had bought their jobs; he could not promote the good officials because they had not. With a power base in the nonterritorial commands — the Marines, the air force, and the paratroopers — Ky could not change a district chief or divert a truckload of supplies unless he convinced the corps commander that it might be in his interests to convince the province chief that it was in his interests to execute the order. "In a way," mused one Vietnamese minister, "it is the most democratic government we've ever had."

Boxed in on all sides, Ky managed to take his aggression out on the people who could not protect themselves — the French who remained in Vietnam, the newspaper publishers who criticized him (he banned their newspapers from time to time, or simply took the newsprint out of circulation), the Buddhists, and the student leaders. It was not much, perhaps, but it was a good indication of what would have happened had he possessed more power.

The returning reporters could see little change in the Saigon government since the days of Diem; the American embassy officials also seemed to perceive none. In the face of corruption, apathy, and military defeat for the ARVN, Ambassador Henry Cabot Lodge, Deputy Ambassador Porter, Robert Komer, and the AID officials maintained, at least in public, the traditional sangfroid. The Revolutionary Development program was going forward with an "integrated management system in sight"; nine hundred and sixty-six more hamlet classrooms were built, 10,134 sewing kits were distributed, temporary shelter was provided for almost two hundred and eighty thousand refugees, and twelve thousand Viet Cong voluntarily left the jungles and swamps to return to the government. Premier Ky was doing a good job under difficult conditions and the Vietnamese people were building a nation in the midst of war. At the top of a tower of statistics and progress reports, the embassy officials hardly seemed aware of the disorder around them. General Westmoreland avoided the subject altogether by focusing his attentions on the American operations and insisting that the embassy deal with all "political" matters. His august position gave him the dizzying breadth of perspective to speak of progress in the war and the improvement of the ARVN while asking the President for more American troops.

And yet with all the official optimism, the American mission lacked its old unity of tone. During the summer of 1963 only a few officials had broken the serenity of the mission; now there were at least as many malcontents as there were optimists in the middle and lower ranks — the phenomenon less a result of change in the Saigon government than of the new numbers of Americans in Vietnam. In 1966–1967 thousands of Americans, in addition to the regular combat troops, took up posts throughout the country as agricultural experts, military advisers, nurses, refugee coordinators, and logistics experts. Largely unprepared for what they would face, many of them could not help remarking on the general disorder of the Vietnamese government. Among them were men like Dr. Goodhope. A physician from a rich suburb in California, Dr. Goodhope sacrificed two months' vacation in order to treat napalm burns and gangrenous bullet wounds as well as cases of plague, typhoid, and cholera at a

Vietnamese civilian hospital. Arriving in Qui Nhon, he found the hospital, recently rebuilt by AID, a bare, excrement-covered shell of a building: the lighting and toilet fixtures had been torn out of the walls, the kitchen had been dismantled, and a pair of dogs came daily to dig for the amputated limbs buried in the hospital yard. With seven hundred beds and two to three patients in each bed, the hospital barely accommodated the numbers of war-wounded civilians coming in from the countryside, but Dr. Goodhope and two doctors from New Zealand constituted the entire hospital staff. As Goodhope was to discover, the Vietnamese doctors preferred their private practices to working at the hospital; the nurses allowed the patients to die of thirst and filth; the procurement officer stole the hospital funds and (perhaps with Viet Cong help) the shipments of essential drugs from Saigon. After a month and a half in Qui Nhon, Dr. Goodhope hated the Vietnamese — all Vietnamese — and demanded that the United States take over the country. He did not ask himself who had created the casualties and put the Vietnamese in such a situation.

Hardly more sanguine than Dr. Goodhope was Colonel William R. Corson, the somewhat eccentric Ph.D., Oriental linguist, ex-CIA agent and Marine officer who, among other things, commanded a battalion in the First Corps. Though a believer in the universal value of American capitalism, Colonel Corson did not approve of the initiative the local Vietnamese division commander took in setting up all of the eleven laundries used by the U.S. Marines in that area. More understandably, he did not condone the local district chief's habit of presenting him with the bodies of dead Vietnamese tied up in a sack to claim the reward for dead Viet Cong (particularly when the same dead bodies were presented to him more than once). Both as the commander of a battalion and the head of the Marine Combined Action Program, he did his best to carry out the unspoken Marine policy of avoiding the GVN administration as far as possible and working directly with the peasants. In the book that he wrote upon quitting Vietnam and the Marine Corps, Corson concluded that the United States could not win the war if it maintained a purely "advisory" relationship to the GVN.[11]

Americans everywhere had stories to tell: this Vietnamese was corrupt, this one incompetent, and the other, treacherous or cowardly. The soldiers complained openly that the Vietnamese units in their laziness or inefficiency had cost the lives of many of their buddies. The American generals did not complain in public, but they too seethed for all the enemy cadres that escaped through faulty intelligence, all the operations ruined through military snafus. Their anger transmitted itself quickly enough to the journalists. After a few weeks' tour of Vietnam, William Lederer, the author of *The Ugly American,* wrote a book "exposing" the "scandal" of the war effort — the corruption, the military lethargy, and so forth. He indignantly accused the Americans of permitting themselves to be exploited by the Vietnamese, while at the same time he defended the basic goals of the war.[12] For many Americans such as Lederer (and perhaps particularly for those who had a similarly superficial knowledge of the country), the "answer to the whole problem" was a disengagement of the American war effort from the GVN. This formula, of course, implied disengagement only in the sense that apartheid implies separation; it meant an abrogation of Vietnamese sovereignty, if not an American take-over of the whole Vietnamese government. In justification of what was essentially a colonialist position, the sophisticated Colonel Corson argued that the United States had a responsibility to save the Vietnamese people from the Vietnamese government. This, of course, in addition to saving them from Communism.

As might have been expected, these attacks on the Vietnamese angered the embassy officials in charge of maintaining the status quo more than they angered anyone else. And yet there was a certain irony to the situation. When the opponents of the war combined with its most avid proponents in attacking the GVN, only the embassy officials remained to defend the Vietnamese from what took on the coloring of a racist attack against them. By virtue of their interest in the current U.S. policy, it was the young mission officers such as Paul Hare, Frank Wisner, and Frank Scotton, and not the more "dovish" journalists who best understood the difficulties that the American war presented to the Vietnamese of the GVN. In answer to men like Lederer and Corson the young officials would point out that the Vietnamese soldier faced not a year but a lifetime of war — and war on their own soil. Living on fixed salaries, the soldiers and civil servants suffered badly from the American-induced inflation. While the artificial war economy lasted, there was bound to be corruption because they could not otherwise support their families. As for the advisory system, if that did not work well, it was at least partly because the advisers themselves were incompetent to deal with Vietnamese problems. They simply did not know enough, and with only a year or a year and a half in Vietnam, could not know enough, even to interpret what was happening. An experienced Vietnamese officer on his fifth or sixth American adviser probably had excellent reason for disregarding all advice. Neither incompetent nor cowardly, he might be simply trying to deal with things as they were. To increase American "control" over Vietnamese government activities would make the jobs of the officials even more difficult. As the young embassy officers put it most bluntly, the idea that the Americans ought to take over the GVN was a position taken by men who had no sympathy with the Vietnamese and furthermore no grasp of what the war was about.

These young officials were right — at least as far as they went. The difficulty was, of course, that their own advocacy of the war drove them back to the official embassy position that the United States was helping the Vietnamese people — despite all evidence to the contrary. Their critique thus lacked any systematic basis. In order to account for the failings of the GVN both before and after the American intervention, they had to criticize individual Vietnamese, individual Americans, and the defects of almost every individual program ever perpetrated by the Americans in Vietnam. Brought to an extreme, their position was not unlike that of Robert Shaplen, the *New Yorker* correspondent, who in his cautious, reasoned analysis for nine years attributed the demise of every pacification program and of every attempt to create a stable, constitutional government to the failure of American officials to give more constructive advice at the right time. The young embassy officials would have rejected the comparison — their position was far more complicated, and would become more complicated still the longer they stayed in Vietnam — but there was an inescapable logic to it. Those who supported the war — that is, all of the officials and most of the journalists — had to line up behind one of two general positions: the first, the conventional diplomatic position that the Saigon government was not so bad and would improve with American help; and the second, the position held by many within the regular military forces (which were, after all, suffering the consequences), that the GVN would never reform itself until the Americans took stricter control over it. In fact the two positions were more like each other than not, for neither acknowledged that the United States was in fact the cause of the problems within the GVN.

Created, financed, and defended by Americans, the Saigon regime
was less a government than an act of the American will — an artificial military bureaucracy that since the beginning of the Diem
regime had governed no one and represented no one except upon
occasion the northern Catholics. The U.S. attempt to polarize the
Vietnamese between Communists and non-Communists made as
much sense as an attempt to polarize the American people between
Southerners and Catholics: the two groups were not in any way
equivalent. Indeed, there were not two sides at all. The period from
1963 to the spring of 1965 demonstrated clearly enough that American-supported governments corresponded to no internal political
forces. After a dozen coups and counter-coups, the Ky junta was not
even the leadership of the army, but a group of officers who
happened to be occupying the Armed Forces Headquarters at the
time of the American military intervention: a directory of hostile
generals, ministries full of tangled and struggling civil servants and
a rabble of soldiers in American-made uniforms, caught and held by
the glacial flow of American troops. The American mission had the
option to depose Ky, but as Jean Lacouture once pointed out, if the
names of all the generals were put into a hat and Vy or Thi pulled
out, the results would have been much the same. What the Americans did not see was that this constituted a stable situation — and
one that resulted directly from the stability of American policy in
Vietnam.

Since the days of the Diem regime, the Americans had assumed
that technical changes such as a retraining program, an increase in
aid, a change of priorities or province chiefs, would change the
nature of the GVN and start it on the road to improvement. But year
after year those administrative reforms were attempted, if not
achieved, and they made no difference at all. The ARVN soldiers
fought badly not so much because they were badly trained as
because they had nothing to fight for (the proof of this being that
they often fought bravely and well when cornered or when defending their own villages). Those soldiers who allowed the Front forces
to burn the hamlet on Route 4 and those that in 1967 permitted the
destruction of seventy-five million dollars' worth of American airplanes in Da Nang[13] obviously saw no connection between that
hamlet, those airplanes, and the welfare of their own families. Had
they risked their lives for that hamlet, those airplanes, they would
have gained neither the immediate reward of a promotion nor the

long-term reward of knowing they had brought the goal of a just society nearer. The same was true of the bureaucrats, the police, and all the various groups of cadre. The CIA trained them to use many of the NLF techniques, but the cadres saw no reason to use them. Unlike the NLF they did not depend on the support of the villagers for their lives and they did not feel that their efforts would be rewarded by those in authority. And they were correct in that assumption.

The injustice and the anarchy were not, however, the responsibility of the Saigon generals. As the Front leaders perceived most clearly, the generals were themselves as much victims as their subordinates. When they stole from the government or mistreated their own men, they did so out of much the same motives as their subordinates. Without any larger system of social security, they obeyed only the morality of the kitchen — the commitment to feed themselves and their families. Exiled by General Ky after the Buddhist crisis, the defense minister, General Nguyen Huu Co, wrote to a former colleague from Hong Kong:

My family of 12 children is now fine. My oldest child, nineteen years old, passed the first exam and is still studying at the Lycée Yersin, Dalat. The other children are also in school and I don't have to worry much about my family. Luckily, while General Khanh hated me, I took my cue and constructed a house in Nha Trang on government land which the Americans rent for three million [piastres] per year. After annual taxes and maintenance, I still have half that for myself, enough to raise my 12 children. If it weren't for that, I don't know what I would do for a living. In our career as generals, and once we are turned to pasture, it is very difficult to change profession.[14]

General Co was perhaps too modest. One of the biggest profiteers of the period, he continued after his exile — or so the story went — to make a comfortable living by acting as financial liaison for the generals remaining in power. Still, his letter shows the reason and the necessity for much of the profiteering. What is more striking, it shows that General Co had a real sense of virtue about his undertakings: he had fulfilled his social obligations; he had in fact fulfilled them a great deal better than had those many honest and improvident officers who were fired for similarly arbitrary reasons. Evidently Co, like so many of the generals, felt himself isolated and (in the most precise sense of the word) alienated from his fellow officers, from the Americans, and from the state to which he belonged. Even while in office he did not think of himself as the defense minister, but rather as an obscure officer who for a moment held that title in a disorderly, Malthusian world.

In 1963 the Buddhists had protested against a small-time tyrant, but in 1966 they had protested this anarchy, this Shanghai-ism emanating from Saigon. The most sophisticated of them saw the irony of it: the Americans who despised the corruption had collectively visited it upon the Vietnamese. From the bar girls with their PX transistors to General Ky with his helicopter and his silver jet, the Saigonese were engaged in little more than a scramble for their own selfish interests. And the Americans could do nothing to stop it, for by their very presence they made the city people into prostitutes, parasites. Saigon was the first to go, for, so recently a dependency of the French, it was not strong enough to stand up to the Americans. Nor had it really wished to. As the perpetual middlemen, the servants and translators for the foreigners, the Saigonese wished for a new master to replace the French and to defend them against their own countryside. Now once again feeding in safety on the foreigners, they gave up their own independence of spirit, their own will to reform themselves.[15]

In his first major speech of the 1968 campaign, Senator Robert F. Kennedy cited the corruption and the general frailty of the Saigon government as reasons for a withdrawal of American troops from Vietnam. It was a conclusion that did not seem at all just to many urban Vietnamese, even those who had long and staunchly opposed the military regime. At a meeting at the American Council of Foreign Relations Senator Tran Ngoc Chau, a former Viet Minh officer soon to become the foremost Vietnamese proponent of a negotiated settlement, replied with restrained anger: "As a politician, I understand him very well. But as a Vietnamese I must be angry with him. We are to blame for the Government's failure, but so are you Americans. When you took over the war, you took on a responsibility towards us, and you must recognize that responsibility."

Chau's remark had a double edge to it. He was speaking of the morality of the "objective" situation, but he could also have been speaking of the psychological effects of the American occupation on the Vietnamese leaders. As the generals saw it, the United States had taken on total responsibility for their country. After his fall from power Ky called the Americans "colonialists," though he himself had requested American money and air and troop support. Despite their fierce struggles for position and power, he and the other generals felt themselves to be no more the government of their country than when they were subalterns under the French regime. How should they resist the overwhelming power of the United States? Where were the terms of equality? Now that the United States had come to Vietnam in force, it would, so the generals assumed, do what it had set out to do with or without their participation. The ARVN officers took an aggressive nationalist stance in public, but they expressed other feelings in their actions. In 1966 the American command discovered that only one Vietnamese field grade officer had been wounded in action since 1954 (this by contrast to the NLF, the North Vietnamese, and the American forces, whose officer corps took many casualties), and out of the hundreds of officers graduating from the military academy in the past few years, only two or three cadets had requested assignments outside of Saigon. The American military briefers spoke of the ARVN officers' "tiredness," but the condition was more like that of apathy and a sense of impotence. Why should they expose themselves to danger in a war that was not theirs? What possible function would it serve? Ironically, their passivity only convinced the Americans that the Vietnamese were not capable of running their own country.

In an interview with Pham Van Dong, one American asked the North Vietnamese foreign minister how he could call the Saigon government an "American puppet" when it acted with such consistency against American interests. "Ah," replied the minister, "it's a puppet, all right. It's just a bad puppet."

The paradox explained the situation perfectly, for with regard to the United States, the generals, like the Buddhists, stood at the crossroads of two contrary emotions, one of which was a real desire for American protection. Like the Emperor Dong Khanh, who first submitted to the French, they made a bargain with the foreigners, abdicating their legitimacy in return for the attributes of foreign power. Since the beginning of the Indochina War the generals had been the Ariels *par excellence* of Vietnam — and appropriately enough, for it was in the army that the believers in a superhuman power, whether magic or technology, found each other. They were therefore "puppets" in the sense that until the Americans broke with them, they would not overstep the limits and risk the withdrawal of American support. Presented with reports of American massacres or the damage done by nine years of American defoliation in South Vietnam, they would not defend their own people; they would ban the subject from the newspapers. On the other hand they, like the Buddhists, feared domination by what they saw as a vast and implacable power. Angered by journalists' questions, Premier Ky once said, "There is no reason you or other people should impose on us to surrender or accept domination from the Communists. Now we want to be free men. We are willing to fight."[16] His statement said two things at once: "we do not want you to abandon us" and "we are afraid of losing our independence to you." Ky expressed his hostility to American domination — a sentiment that he, like most Vietnamese, sincerely felt — but it was clear that he could do little to create a counterforce, and that his only power lay in his ability to manipulate the Americans.

In this enterprise the generals, unlike the Buddhists, were largely successful. Appearing at conferences with the American brass to pledge "the work of the social revolution" and "the attack on hunger, ignorance, and disease," they would return home to their speculations in American goods and their anti-American intrigues. In late 1966 General Nguyen Ngoc Loan, then the Saigon chief of police, arrested a man whom he described to the newspapers as a "Viet Cong spy on his way to the American embassy with peace proposals." Whether or not such a man existed, and whether or not the embassy knew anything about him, Loan's little public relations job was carefully calculated to fan the suspicions of the Saigonese that the Americans would sell them out in secret — were it not for the vigilance of the Ky government.[17] The American embassy could do nothing to counteract his move. As the Buddhist crisis showed, they had only one lever of influence over the Ky regime, and that they would not use, for to withdraw support from the Ky regime would, they calculated, be far too great a risk to take in the middle of the war. The situation was therefore a most curious one: the Americans dominated the GVN but could not make it work for them.

Beyond this central conundrum, the difficulty for the Americans was that not only the Communists, but all Vietnamese in the opposition — a category that by 1966–1967 included most politically conscious Vietnamese — considered the Ky regime to be an "American puppet." In a realm that lay beyond the reach of argument, even such men as Dr. Dan Van Sung, the most pro-American of Vietnamese, believed that the Ky regime was corrupt, inefficient, and unjust because the Americans wanted it that way. If they had not wanted it that way (so the logic went), they would have done something about it. As a solution to the dilemma, the editor of a Saigon English-language newspaper, the Jesuitical Ton That Thien, quite seriously suggested that the Americans depose Ky and find themselves a good puppet who would stamp out corruption and carry out their reform program. Thien himself knew that the Ky government did not obey American wishes (his implication was that everyone else believed it did), but he believed that the Americans had the power to change it for the better. His argument revealed a strange parallel between Vietnamese and American thinking: even in the most sophisticated circles, both peoples believed that the United States could control the Vietnamese government — a belief that, while wholly misplaced, was comforting to both parties. As Lieutenant General Stanley "Swede" Larson once said, "What's wrong with those Americans down in Saigon? Why can't they produce a decent civil government to match the military effort?"[18] Clearly the Ariels had found their Prosperos.

11

Elections

My birthday is in late August. The greatest birthday present
you could give me is a national election.
— President Johnson to Generals Ky and
Thieu at Guam, March 1967[1]

You journalists make things so complicated. Elections are really
quite simple. You can't expect most voters to know who is good
and who is bad. Either they don't bother to come and vote, or
else they choose their candidates at random. Far better to let
us choose the candidates for them.
— a Vietnamese district chief[2]

Candidates are like birds without feathers. We, the voters, give
a candidate his feathers — each vote being another feather.
When he has enough feathers, off he flies — and we never see
him again.
— a Vietnamese villager[3]

A month or so after the bloody end of the Buddhist crisis, the
public relations machinery of the U.S. mission went into high gear
on the subject of the elections scheduled for early fall. The press
corps was alerted; ranks of distinguished Americans were invited to
watch the balloting for a constitutional assembly that would in the
succeeding months write a constitution for South Vietnam. To the
mission, at least, the elections appeared a momentous event in Vietnamese history. The Vietnamese, said Ambassador Lodge, "never
had elections on a national basis and a national question. It's never
happened in their whole history." As Bernard Fall pointed out, the
ambassador had not got his facts quite straight: the South Vietnamese had participated in something like twelve elections, the last
two of them financed by the Americans under the Diem regime. The
last election had taken place just a few months before Cabot
Lodge's arrival as ambassador.[4] But then historical memory was
never the forte of Americans in Vietnam.

In the United States the liberal social scientists who favored the war delivered themselves of a torrent of Latinisms on the subject of "consensus-making bodies in a fractionalized political system" and "viable institutions for power-sharing which would gradually lead to the legitimization of the entire governmental framework." While expressing some hesitation about the usefulness of a constitution, Professor I. Milton Sacks, a teacher at the Saigon and Hue universities and a consultant to the American mission, concluded that the elections would at least produce "spokesmen who can claim legitimacy through popular mandate and speak with authority on the issues of war and peace for their constituency."[5] While in private the American officials expressed anxiety about the possibility of election fraud and Viet Cong terrorism, in public they claimed the election as the crowning achievement of the Vietnamese government: the GVN would be a real democracy with a real constitution. The message, as received by the American public, was that the United States was generously bringing all the virtues of its own political system to this underdeveloped country, that it was creating a democracy to win the Vietnamese people away from Communist totalitarianism. So clear was the message that none of the distinguished Americans arriving to view the elections remembered that the embassy and the Ky government agreed to elections in the first place only under the threat of defection of the entire northern half of the country and total anarchy in Saigon. Within the new embassy perspective, the near civil war had become a minor incident and the Buddhist militants non-persons. According to the officials, the Ky government was holding the elections merely to redeem the pledge it made at Honolulu — a pledge most gratifying to Americans. "Of course," said one embassy official blandly, "the embassy has always been in favor of elections for a civilian government. Look, we've had these elections on our agenda for the past three years." His argument was incontrovertible: the project of elections had been on the American agenda for the past three years.

The American buildup of the elections was quite typical of the attitude of embassy officials in all their dealings with the GVN. While they patronized the Vietnamese and consciously deceived the American public, they managed at the same time to maintain a perfectly pristine faith in the efficacy of their endeavors. Even those who spoke cynically of the public relations campaign in the United States believed that the elections might help to knit up the snarl of political factions into a few stable, non-clandestine parties and legitimate the government in the eyes of many Vietnamese. They believed it despite all the evidence of history and the opinions of all politically minded Vietnamese.

For the Vietnamese view of the elections offered a rather sharp contrast to the American serendipity. From the Buddhists on one side to the generals on the other, the spectrum of opinion seemed to range from indignation to indifference. Charging "American interference in Vietnamese affairs," the same Buddhist leaders who three months before had packed the squares of six cities with crowds shouting for elections, now announced that they would organize a boycott against the balloting. Though hostile to the Buddhists, the southern politicians and sect leaders did not give out the expected air of triumph. Dutifully going about the task of selecting candidates and combining them into slates, they displayed as little interest in the elections as they might have in the organization of a new National Day. The GVN officials expressed a weary annoyance about the prospect. "I've had to put off everything," complained one Delta province chief, "budget revisions, tax schedules, military operations, building programs. I've wasted a whole month on voter registration and there will be another month gone on the election campaigns. But it can't be helped. It's orders from Saigon — highest priority. They want all of the people to vote." From the way the province chief pronounced the last phrase, it was not difficult to see why he felt the whole enterprise a waste of time. Still, he had some reason to feel put upon. As usual, the district and province chiefs bore the brunt of the work. Under heavy pressure from Saigon, they had to vet all the candidates for "Communist" or "neutralist" sympathies and interpret the voting laws, which, perhaps for a purpose, were more complicated than any ever devised by the ingenious politicians of the French Fourth Republic. Moreover, they had to register a number of voters proportionate to that part of the population they had previously declared "pacified."

It was clear why the GVN officials resented the elections, but it was less clear why they had no interest at all in the results. Questioned about the candidates and their programs, the Delta province chief answered politely, "Oh, yes, there are four slates. We've eliminated another two for technical reasons. No, I have no idea who will win. No, I don't really know if there are any issues except personalities." While the Americans spoke darkly about the difficulties of holding an election in the midst of a war, the GVN officials faced the prospect with a bored tolerance, as though despite the livid antagonisms of their constituents, the elections were just another tedious bureaucratic routine.

Their confidence was, it seemed, justified. American fears to the contrary, there was very little evidence of direct NLF or government intimidation of the voters and no substantial case of election fraud. An astonishing number of people registered, a figure that, if the population estimates could be trusted, represented two-thirds of the adult population of South Vietnam. Of that number, 81 percent voted in the election — in other words, a far higher proportion than ever turns out for presidential elections in the United States. The South Vietnamese went to the polls with the docility of lambs to the dip. Furthermore, they elected an assembly that quite fairly represented the strength of all the various political groups and minority populations within the GVN, with the striking exception of the militant Buddhists. Among the one hundred and seventeen elected delegates, there were twelve Hoa Hao and five Cao Dai representatives, nine members of the various Dai Viets, twenty military officers, nineteen members of the various VNQDD factions, three Chinese, and nine montagnards (the montagnard deputies were chosen indirectly by their tribal councils). The Catholics were somewhat overrepresented with thirty-two delegates, but the number testified quite accurately to the discipline of their communities and the normal weight of their influence over the GVN. Most of the well-known older politicians, such as Dr. Pham Khac Suu, won their races, but so too did a number of younger men who lived and worked in the districts they represented. In public the Americans were gratified; in private they were as ecstatic as a bureaucracy can get: their distinguished American visitors had seen democracy working at "the rice roots."

The Constituent Assembly convened in October 1966 with a great flourish of military ceremony. The delegates from the provinces looked awed and somewhat embarrassed by the proceedings. As Richard Critchfield noticed, "One delegation from Quang Ngai Province turned up in matching white Palm Beach suits that all looked as though they had been cut from the same bolt of cloth and probably were. They were mortified to see that the rest of the deputies wore dark suits."[6] They had not realized, in other words,

that white suits belonged to the old days of French colonialism and
that the Americans wore gray. Still, the deputies seemed proud of
themselves and excited by the prospects that lay before them. Once
installed in the Assembly building, in the hall that had once held the
Saigon opera, they began to make passionate speeches about the
reform of the government, their determination to stand up against
the Communists, the moral duties of the state, the plight of their
nation, the price of rice in Long Xuyen or Vinh Long, and their own
rights as deputies. It was as though they had just been released from
a seven-year vow of silence. Day after day, week after week, a
torrent of words poured out of the Assembly building and fell upon
deafer and deafer ears. After all the fuss they had made about the
elections, the American embassy officials paid no attention to the
speeches. Once they had run a check on their deputies' backgrounds, they seemed to lose all interest in them. As for the Ky
government, it made quite clear what it thought of them by small
indelicate gestures, such as that of refusing to pay the delegates'
promised *per diem*. On October 22, a number of the poor provincial delegates were evicted from their sleazy downtown hotels
because they were unable to pay the inflationary Saigon rate. Ky
finally agreed to "loan" them the money, but he did not cease to
make obvious his desire to be rid of them as soon as possible. The
delegates did not, however, seem willing to oblige. Week after week,
they continued to make speeches on every conceivable subject
without coming to any kind of resolution. Sitting in the eye of a war
and a revolution, the deputies acted like political science professors
attending a university-sponsored conference on some imponderable
subject. While many of them had special interests to defend, the
political factions that formed and reformed in the course of the
debate proved neither large nor stable enough to merit the name
"party." The delegates seemed unable to find an issue around which
to organize. As Dr. Sung rather pathetically explained, "I ran for the
Assembly in order to oppose the government, and now I find there is
nothing to oppose."

Eventually, under some pressure from both the Americans and
General Ky, who wished to attend the Guam Conference, the delegates settled down to the job of writing a constitution. With no
apparent zeal for the enterprise, they turned out a most professional
document — so professional, indeed, that John Roche, the "constitutional expert" whom the U.S. government rather tactlessly ap-

pointed as "adviser" to the proceedings, found that he had no advice to give. And not surprisingly, for while Roche had never written a national constitution in his life, many of the members of the Assembly had written at least three. Finally completed in March 1967, in the nick of time for the Guam Conference, the document included a bill of rights, an article on land reform, a provision for the encouragement of labor unions, and a provision supporting an improvement in the general welfare of the peasantry. According to the document, the governmental system was to be a cross between the American presidential system and the French Fifth Republic: on the one hand, a president with wide powers, and on the other, a prime minister and a cabinet responsible to a bicameral legislature. The Assembly made concessions to the junta — notably, the vague determination of presidential powers and the fixing of the age requirement for presidential office at thirty-five instead of forty (a provision that allowed Air Vice-Marshal Ky to qualify), but it showed a certain independence in turning down several of the junta's specific requests. The U.S. embassy was once again gratified. Unlike the Diemist assemblies, this one could not possibly be accused of being a "rubber stamp" congress. At Guam, President Johnson said that he looked at the constitution "just as proudly as I looked at Lynda, my first baby."[7]

For Western journalists the whole enterprise from the elections to the writing of the constitution remained puzzling. Great numbers of Vietnamese voted; the constitution was an admirable document — and yet there was an air of inconsequence to the proceedings. It was as though the whole thing had been performed on stage as a graceful and empty gesture. In an atmosphere of total indifference the peasants had turned out in astonishing numbers to vote for the same sort of men as those who had such trouble "pacifying" them. Even by stretching a point, the left-wing European journalists could not explain it away on the basis of electoral fraud or government intimidation of the voters. They had a stronger argument in claiming that the electoral lists were too complicated for anyone to understand, and that the province chiefs in charge of making up the lists had excluded not only "neutralists" and Communists, but everyone that did not meet with GVN approval. To put it simply, the peasants had been free to choose between one landlord and another. But why then had they bothered to vote at all?

The question was finally a more complicated one than could be explained in the columns of a newspaper, for, as was true of so many events in Vietnam, the elections could not be fully understood from one perspective alone. Like a mirror, they reflected only what the onlookers brought to them, and the American and the Vietnamese perspective had very little in common. Looking at the elections, both peoples could find different lessons to be drawn, different victims and different oppressors.

Brought up in a tradition that prescribes free elections as the proper solution for most political conflicts, the Americans had come to look upon them as the moral foundations of a state. If a nation had free elections, it belonged to the "free world"; if it did not, it belonged to those moral nether regions inhabited by Communists, Fascists, and backward people. The embassy officials did not consider it an immediate moral necessity to press for elections in Vietnam, but even the most cynical of them supposed that elections and a constitution would somehow make the GVN a better government. Their faith was a perfect example of synecdoche, the poetic device that substitutes a part for the whole. "Free elections" implied to the Americans an entire political edifice — a belief in individual freedom, in majority rule and the compromise of individual interests — a skyscraper, as it were, of ideals, principles, and organization, in which the elections were no more than the elevator. Largely unconscious of this edifice, they did not realize that when the Vietnamese used the elections they had an entirely different building in mind — a building founded on the community rather than the individual, fashioned out of uniformity instead of diversity, and operating not on a set of principles, but on an appreciation of the whole man, an entire way of life. Like the Americans, the Vietnamese assumed the architecture of their building, and therefore found no occasion to describe it or to show how the elevator worked within it. When asked what he thought of the 1966 elections, one former hamlet schoolteacher said, "I cannot tell you whether the elections will be good or bad. If the candidates are good men who will work for the people, then they will be good, for the Assembly will bring peace." In other words, the teacher was not interested in his right to vote, but the duty to register his approval. And with half a million American troops in Vietnam, it was a duty that he could not afford to neglect. Every adult was supposed to have a card showing that he had voted, and the GVN officials checked these along with identification cards in their search for "Viet Cong suspects."

"So it was not a free election," one American reporter concluded. "The government coerced the peasants into voting." But the conclusion was not quite just, though the GVN had made known its wishes to the peasants in no uncertain terms. The essence of the matter was not that the officials were oppressing the peasantry, but that both shared certain assumptions about the nature of government. The peasants, like the officials, saw no reason why the government should ask their advice. Presented with a ballot sheet, their attitude was, "If the program is bound to succeed, the Americans or the French, our counselors, would involve themselves and take credit for its success. If they 'pass the baby' to us, if they want us to vote on those issues about which we know so little, it's because it will fail and once it has failed, they will tell us, 'Well, you asked for it.' "[8] That the peasants were absolutely right in this case was, in a sense, beside the point, for the logic was based not so much on experience with elections as upon a profound set of convictions about all forms of authority. The idea that their vote might actually help change the government was an almost impermissible one, for it implied that there was no authority above them. And if there was no authority, then there was nothing but chaos and "confusion." To be given a choice by means of a vote was therefore to be handed an instrument of terror — an unthinkable one.

The Vietnamese governments of the north and the south had used the device of elections many times before 1966, but they had used it for their own purposes and in such a way that it fitted in with the whole architecture of their political life. In 1946 Ho Chi Minh held elections for a legislature in both northern and southern Vietnam. His Viet Minh candidates gained an overwhelming percentage of the vote even in those places where the polling was done secretly in the shadow of the French garrisons. Ngo Dinh Diem held a plebiscite a few years later, and took 98 percent of the vote from the very same areas of the south. Quite clearly in these cases neither Diem nor Ho Chi Minh was interested in giving the voters a choice of alternatives. They used the elections not as a means of settling a political conflict, but as a means of showing the Westerners — and perhaps their own people — that the conflict was already settled. To the Vietnamese people an election used in this way was perfectly acceptable as long as they agreed that the settlement had in fact been accomplished. If it had not been accomplished — as certainly was the case during the Diemist plebiscite — then the elections would be coercive and fraudulent. The election results (though not the real political results) would in any case be the same: the party that held the elections would win. With this understanding the GVN had and would continue to refuse elections with Communist participation. With this understanding, the Buddhists decided in the summer of 1966 to boycott the elections that they had demonstrated for all spring. It was not that they had changed their minds on the principle of elections, but merely that they had predicted the results under two different sets of circumstances.

The 1966 election was then, like all those before it, a redundancy. Once the real issue of power was settled, the South Vietnamese, choosing from a group of names presented to them by the province chiefs, elected a group of delegates from all the racial, religious, and political groups that already exerted influence on the GVN. In all important respects the Assembly was no more than a larger model of the GVN. The Americans congratulated themselves on the establishment of a new institution for sharing power and reconciling diversity, but the Vietnamese saw in the Assembly only a confirmation that Vietnam was passing through a period of interregnum and "confusion." The generals desired unanimity, but in contrast to Ho, Diem, and Tri Quang, they had no idea of what it might consist. Dr. Sung's surprise at finding "nothing to oppose" was occasioned by the contradiction of his private belief that there *had* to be some clear intelligence behind all those ranks of soldiers, all that tonnage of machinery.

Ambassador Lodge's opinion to the contrary, the election of 1966 was traditional — the Cochin Chinese tradition being the colonial one. As Bernard Fall pointed out, the French municipal and regional councils had been filled with bitter critics of the colonial regime.[9] The new assembly was rather less radical in its constituents (the French had, after all, permitted Trotskyites to run in the 1930's), but the members felt equally free to criticize the government on matters of policy. How, indeed, should they act as a rubber stamp if the generals had no clear policy? They were free, that is, to criticize up to the point of discussing an alternate government or negotiations with the NLF. For as long as the Americans continued to support the GVN, they would be just as dependent on the Americans as the generals. Like the French before them, the Americans felt that all the talk was an encouraging sign: it meant (so they imagined) that the urban bourgeoisie now had a chance to let off steam, and that the Vietnamese would learn to form cohesive parties and majorities for the eventual goal of self-government. The French had been ready to make concessions to these "legally constituted" bodies; the Americans hoped that the generals would do the same. But all the talk led nowhere, nowhere at all, because it did not touch the fundamental issue of power. In the elections the Vietnamese had a choice, but only a choice between one abstraction and another. However they voted, whatever they said, the generals and the Americans would continue to rule the country. Rather than "train them in democracy," the elections of 1966–1967 convinced the Vietnamese that elections were useless as a means of settling political conflicts.

What did the Americans want? That was the question of the 1967 election, when "the Vietnamese people" would be called upon to vote not simply for a legislature, but for the head of state, for the government itself. For the urban politicians, the need to answer the question seemed to be a matter of life or death. What did the Americans want? Rather than announce their position, the American embassy officials, in their devious Occidental manner, continued to insist that they wanted "free elections." But that meant nothing. It was rather as if a customer in a restaurant, when asked what he wanted for dinner, kept insisting that he liked to read the menu, but that he would leave the choice to them. To the Vietnamese it was quite evident that the customer did care what he ate, but that he preferred to keep it a secret, so that at any moment he might get up, blame the management for the poor service, and leave without paying his bill. The fear of abandonment by the United States was never far from their minds. To them the American silence was infuriating — and furthermore hypocritical, for, as they saw it, the elections would impose a responsibility upon them without really giving them a choice: the United States was already supporting the regime of Nguyen Cao Ky. Until it ceased to do so, there would be no chance for a civilian candidate to win.

Like the generals, the civilian politicians gave the Americans too much credit for purposefulness. It was true that the mission heads more or less favored the continuance of military government. But their inclination owed at least partly to the fact that they saw no alternative — having themselves precluded the formation of one. Had the Assembly agreed to make it impossible for Ky to run, and united behind a single candidate, they would have had a much more difficult decision to make. But after a year of the Assembly, the civilian parties were as divided as ever and, as a result, submissive to the generals. Instead of putting up one candidate, they put up twelve, most of whom had no serious political differences. Under some pressure from above, the Assembly voted by a large majority to invalidate the candidacies of the only two men who looked as if they might run a serious opposition campaign. Au Truong Thanh, the capable former minister of economics under Ky and a former favorite of the Americans who now openly advocated a cease-fire, it eliminated on the grounds that he was a "neutralist." The once popular General Duong Van Minh, now living in exile, it eliminated on the technicality that he was residing out of the country.

Taking advantage of the civilian disarray, General Ky tightened up on press censorship and limited the forthcoming election campaign to one month, thereby granting himself the exclusive right to press his suit for all the intervening months. To make sure the voters understood the situation, he announced that he would make a coup d'etat if they elected a civilian whose policies he disagreed with. "In any democratic country you have the right to disagree with the views of others," he explained. But the necessity seemed unlikely to arise, for between them, the Americans, the Assembly, and the generals had succeeded in reducing the element of choice or "confusion" as far as the formal trappings of the elections would permit.

But then something happened that destroyed all of these careful preparations. In May, General Nguyen Van Thieu announced that he would run for president. The generals were shocked, and quite understandably, for having once fulfilled and assimilated the unreasonable demands of the Americans, they now faced the terrifying prospect of a real political conflict between two equal contenders for the office of chief of state. Now the worst was bound to happen: the army would split, the electorate would divide, and — who knew? — in the general anarchy a civilian candidate might actually win. Interestingly enough, the Americans appeared to share their fears. Above all, the mission did not want a divided army. Suspecting that Thieu had used the announcement as a feint towards some other objective, the embassy appealed to him to withdraw, doubtless with some other offer in hand. But Thieu would have none of it. He agreed that the army should not be divided, but he refused to withdraw unless Ky, too, declared his retirement. For him, so he said, it had become an affair of honor.

The embassy was, as one reporter put it, "deeply disquieted." For the past two years the officials had taken for granted that Thieu was no more than a figurehead in a stable Ky government (a peculiar assumption in that respectability is the usual qualification for figureheads); now they had to admit that Ky's power was limited, and that in Thieu the premier had not a submissive partner but a bitter rival. What was worse, the embassy seemed to have no power over either of them. Having failed to persuade Thieu to withdraw, the officials found Ky, their own favorite, equally deaf to their diplomacy. Outraged at the insult to him, and no doubt well aware of what might happen to him if Thieu won, Ky refused to withdraw.

To resolve this unbearable crisis, the defense minister and chief of staff, General Cao Van Vien, called a meeting of all the general officers in the armed forces of the Republic. The meeting lasted for three days — a three days during which, according to Robert Shaplen's fascinating account, the generals went through the full histrionic range from patriotic outbursts to threats on self and others, to cool fury, to embarrassed silence and tears. On the first day they accused each other of corruption, and debated the suggestions that they should, a) allow a civilian to win the election, or b) tear up the constitution and keep on ruling without it. Generals Thieu and Ky made affecting speeches offering to withdraw their candidacies. The next day General Thieu came to the meeting with a determination that apparently belonged at least in part to his most powerful wife. Instead of keeping to the usual vaguely worded denunciations of the general corruption, he cited facts and figures describing the horrible corruption of the national police. As the police were run by General Nguyen Ngoc Loan, and as General Loan ran Nguyen Cao Ky, the direction of his attack was not difficult to follow. In embarrassment General Loan walked out of the room, and three of the four corps commanders tore off their stars and vowed not to return to their commands until the confrontation was ended. The intolerable moment was relieved by everyone bursting into tears. Thieu wept and thanked everyone for listening to him. Ky wept and offered once more to resign. Finally, as if exhausted by the proceedings, the generals accepted Ky's withdrawal and prevailed upon him to run for the vice-presidency on Thieu's ticket in return for certain compensatory arrangements and guarantees.[10]

Once the military crisis was settled, the electoral campaign could proceed in its normal Alice-in-Wonderland manner. Without any transportation of their own, the ten civilian candidates accepted by the Assembly were forced to travel around the country together in an airplane loaned them by the military junta. This mode of travel had its disadvantages. If the candidates organized a meeting in Quang Tri, the airplane would tend to fly them to Dong Ha or some other provincial town where no one was expecting them and where they would face the totally unacceptable alternatives of taking a lift from the Americans or braving a bus ride on the Front-controlled highways. When General Thieu made his rare appearances on the same platform with them, he would insist on speaking in ninth place — nine being the lucky number for the Vietnamese. He did not, of course, need such stratagems, for, even in his civilian clothes, he was the only recognizable figure on the platform. Of the ten civilian candidates, only three had any political reputation — and that almost exclusively in the cities: the ancient Dr. Pham Khac Suu, the former chief of state and president of the Constituent Assembly; Tran Van Huong, the former premier, who, reportedly, had strong support among provincial notables in certain parts of the Delta; and Dr. Phan Quang Dan, the renegade of the Diemist assembly, who had been elected to the Constituent Assembly by an overwhelming vote from the working-class neighborhood of Saigon where he practiced medicine. Though all three were honest men with few political differences, none of them would agree to withdraw to give the others more of a chance. They did not like each other, and that was that. Unable to compromise, unable to reach the mass of the voters by airplane, radio, or newspaper, they and the other civilian candidates took to complaining about the junta to the foreign press — a tactic that was the logical one both because the generals were holding the election to help Johnson win his own political battle with the American public, and because the Vietnamese, by and large, remained as indifferent to the second election as they had been to the first.

When the ballots were counted on September 3, very few people in Vietnam were surprised to learn that the Thieu-Ky ticket had won. What was astounding was the smallness of its victory. Out of the five million votes cast, the generals won only 1,649,561, or 35 percent — their strongest support coming from the isolated military districts, where the local commanders kept close watch over the voting, and the Americans did not.[11] In the more politically sophisticated and less militarily controlled urban districts the generals made such a poor showing that at the end of the day their managers, panicky at the low count, stuffed the ballot boxes with thousands of extra votes. Had they thought in advance that it might be necessary to rig the election, they undoubtedly would have shown more ingenuity; as it was, even the Americans could attest to the fact that in Gia Dinh province (the province surrounding Saigon) twenty-two thousand votes appeared very suddenly on the tally just before the polls closed.[12] But the returns came as a surprise to everyone, to the civilian candidates no less than the generals. As runner-up to Thieu came not one of the establishment politicians, but an almost unknown figure called Truong Dinh Dzu. A Buddhist layman with no political background and a rather shady reputation as a lawyer, Dzu waited until the Assembly passed on his candidacy before declaring that he favored recognizing the NLF and engaging in peace negotiations as soon as possible. Under the justifiable impression that Dzu was no political leader, the generals had not bothered to remove him from the ballot, contenting themselves by attacking him personally as (among other things) "a dog that should be put in a cage." They made an error, for while very few of the Saigonese politicians took him seriously, Dzu with the dove of peace as his ballot symbol, wound up with some 817,120 votes, a large percentage of which came from those parts of the Delta that the generals had conceded to the southerner, Tran Van Huong.[13] To many observers it appeared that the Front had taken advantage of the regime's own elections to discredit the regime.

Conceived by the Americans to "legitimize" the Saigon government and implemented by the junta to "legitimize" President Johnson's war to the American people, the election ended as a fiasco of noble proportions for both responsible parties. A few days after the election, eight of the civilian candidates joined with twenty-seven of the candidates defeated in the senatorial elections to form a committee which openly — and, of course, plausibly — accused the junta of fraud and called upon the Assembly to invalidate the elections. Under pressure (real or imagined) from the generals and the Americans, the Assembly refused to order a new election. The committee then denounced the U.S. embassy for its "interference in Vietnamese domestic affairs" and warned that such interference would "force the Vietnamese people to consider the United States as an imperialist power, plotting colonialism in Vietnam and in underdeveloped countries."[14] (Their language, as Shaplen remarked, bore a striking similarity to that of the NLF. But so much was only to be expected as NLF language was the only one the Vietnamese had to express total hostility to the foreigners.) Many of the southern "moderates" of Tran Van Huong's persuasion felt that with the elections went their last chance to gain influence over the American-supported government by conciliation. In their view the Americans had backed the northerners to defeat them. The generals felt no less put upon, even though their candidate won. Ky felt the Americans had wished to depose him. General Thieu was of the opinion that the U.S. embassy set up the entire election, in full knowledge of the results, in order to discredit him personally and to make him more amenable to embassy directives.[15]

General Thieu misinterpreted the embassy's intentions, but the fact remained that the elections did considerable damage to what small measure of credibility he had as a head of state. The American press worried about his "lack of popularity," but the Vietnamese were more interested by his lack of authority. How could a government that possessed every resource for propaganda, voter intimidation, and election fraud fail to gain even a simple majority of the votes? A government that could not create unanimity was no government at all. The fact that the generals' minions made a last-minute attempt to stuff the ballot boxes and failed to get away with it made the generals seem merely laughable. As one Vietnamese student said to an American reporter, "Thieu and Ky are the black humor of Vietnamese history."[16] The student might well have said the same about the American mission in Saigon. Having attempted this "exercise in democracy" with somewhat questionable motives, the U.S. government found itself in the position of having to support what was perhaps the only government in the world that had come close to losing an election at least partially rigged by itself.

The election had its ludicrous aspects, but it did not end as a comedy for many Vietnamese. Not long after the balloting for the lower house was finished, President Thieu slapped a number of the defeated candidates and their supporters into jail. As the greatest source of his humiliation, Truong Dinh Dzu was the first to go; after him went Thich Thien Minh, the only bonze who remained politically active, and Vo Van Thai, one of the top leaders of the Vietnamese Confederation of Labor, and finally some twenty other political, religious, and labor leaders who, during the campaign, had expressed some doubts about the continuation of the war. When the American AFL-CIO and some civil liberties groups protested these arrests, the State Department replied that it had no control over General Thieu's actions. As always, it had only one lever of influence — and that it was not ready to use. What the civil liberties and labor leaders did not realize was that the elections themselves were responsible. The elections brought all the latent conflicts out into the open. Vietnamese politics being an all-or-nothing game, General Thieu had either to persuade his opponents to join him or to silence them. And he was unable to do the former. The Vietnamese might be able to deal with their own problems but not also with those imposed by the United States.[17]

12

The Downward Spiral

The elections took their toll, but, like most governmental changes, they affected only a small group of Saigon politicians and passed over the countryside unnoticed. Before the elections many South Vietnamese did not know the name of General Ky; after the elections they remained similarly unconscious of General Thieu and their constitutional rights to form unions and to own the land they tilled. The year of 1967 was for them not the year of the elections but the year of the war. In January the year began with a bombing halt over North Vietnam and a flurry of peace rumors in Saigon. But that was a false start. There was to be no change in the war. No change at all despite the bright new crop of Americans in the provinces — the AID representatives with their scrubbed faces and short-sleeved shirts and the young captains in their starched fatigues. "Now here we're plugging in three more RD teams, and if we can divert some of the budget allocations from district C and get the ARVN to cordon off the east bank of the river, we can give the settlements here, here, and here the status of New Life Hamlets."

There was a timeless quality to the American effort — which is not to say that it was static but that it was constantly moving over the same ground. Each year the new young men, so full of vague notions of "development," so certain of their own capacity to solve "problems," so anxious to "communicate" with the Vietnamese, eagerly took their places in this old, old war. "Last year's program fell short of its goal, but this year for the first time we've got some coordination between the ARVN, the RF-PF, and the RD. The hamlet chief here is sleeping in his hamlet. And Major Trinh, an outstanding guy, is giving us his full cooperation." Only the faces of the young men and the numbers of the hamlets changed year after year. For those who stayed in Vietnam long enough, it was like standing on the ground and watching a carousel revolve.

Nineteen sixty-seven was the year of the "oil spot" approach to pacification, the approach that General Westmoreland had attempted in 1964–1965, and the year of the *Ap Doi Moi,* the "Really New Life Hamlets." In parts of the country one could see fences of the *Ap Doi Moi* standing over the ruins of the New Life Hamlets, which in turn stood on the ruins of the Strategic Hamlets. There was an archaeology of pacification going back ten, sometimes twenty years. Many of the PF outposts, those pathetic mud-walled forts circled with barbed wire, had been built by the French for the fathers of those same peasant soldiers.

Of course there were always new approaches, new "concepts" in pacification. This year it was a "rethinking" of the Revolutionary Development program. After the failures of 1966, the CIA decided to call back the RD cadre to give them a month more of retraining: a month more, but this time, so the officials said, the program would succeed. To measure that success more accurately, Robert Komer, now chief of the entire RD program, developed, with the help of McNamara's staff a new evaluation system using computers and multiple choice questionnaires. After explaining with logic and clarity how the Hamlet Evaluation System worked, he said modestly that it was not a perfect system, but that it was an improvement over its predecessors. And he was undoubtedly correct: the only uncertainty was what was being measured. And Komer in his clear and logical exposition apparently did not find it necessary to decide. "Some," he said, "call this [pacification, revolutionary development, or rural reconstruction] chiefly a matter of providing protection or continuous local security in the countryside. Others call it the process of winning hearts and minds. For my money both descriptions are pretty good."[1] It was enough, perhaps, that the new system convinced the American public that 67 percent of the Vietnamese population lived under government control, and that that figure represented a gain of 4.8 percent over the year before.[2]

If the figures were not convincing, then a tour of Vietnam almost always was. Year after year delegations of high officials, congressmen, and other dignitaries would arrive in Saigon and, still dizzy from the trip, would receive massive, two- or three-hour briefings from colonels with seven-overlay charts, then dine with the ambassador or the commanding general, those tall, noble Anglo-Saxons who emanated all the confidence of surgeons to their patients. The next day they would be issued green fatigues and flown around by daredevil helicopter pilots to spend (but for the air trip) an unutterably boring day visiting hamlets with pig farms, maternity clinics, "miracle rice" plots, and children washed, scrubbed, and smiling, lining the streets and waving GVN flags. Boredom and all, the tours were almost exact replicas of those that Ngo Dinh Diem used to take, and for which he was so criticized by his American advisers. Only the Potemkin hamlets had changed, for Diem's tours were four pacification programs and four priority areas ago.

The VIPs would return to announce that progress was being made. How could they deny it? The confidence of the mission officials was so pure. Faced with the contradiction between the ambassador's untarnished faith and a mortar attack on the Tan Son Nhut airbase the day of their arrival, the distinguished Americans would have to find that faith somehow more solid and convincing. "I was down in An Giang province just yesterday — and in the Delta," Robert Komer said, "and it's amazing how much of a difference there is down there in the course of a year." An Giang province — the very name reduced a decade of American briefings into a single palimpsest. "Why don't you go down to An Giang province and see for yourself . . ." But there had never been any NLF in An Giang, for the Hoa Hao controlled the province, and they had long ago made their accommodation with the Front. The generations of VIPs who had gone down to An Giang without knowing that! Even the "dove" congressmen and the serious journalists found it difficult to resist this surreal dialogue with the mission. When Ambassadors Porter or Komer announced that *x* percent of the population was pacified, the *New York Times* reporter might sagely argue that the figure was probably closer to two-thirds or five-eighths of *x*, never once asking what "pacification" meant or whether indeed it was the right thing for the United States to be doing in Vietnam. The dialogue of Saigon turned around on its own axis, giving no exit onto reality.

The dialogue was, of course, not entirely without issue, for though American policy had not changed, the American effort had increased by orders of magnitude. By the fall of 1967 there were half a million American troops in Vietnam — and that partly a result of the mission's confidence. "We are winning," the argument went. "We can win with a little more support." Every two or three months Westmoreland asked for thousands more troops, and after some debate the President acceded, though giving him each time something less than he asked for. Finally, Johnson put a "troop ceiling" at 525,000 men, or close to the number the U.S. military could send without calling up the reserves. The figure was arbitrary with regard to Vietnam. But then any figure would have been arbitrary, for no one knew how many troops or how long a fight would be necessary to "stop the North Vietnamese from doing what they are doing." The dilemma was that the figure of half a million represented not enough and too much at the same time.

In 1967 the "Free World Forces" in Vietnam — Americans, Vietnamese, and Koreans, with additional small contingents of Australians, Thais, and Filipinos — had reached a combined total of 1,300,000 men: one soldier for every fifteen people in South Vietnam. With two thousand tactical jet aircraft and the B-52s of the Strategic Air Command at his disposal, Westmoreland "for the first time" had what Komer described as "marginally adequate resources" to take the offensive.[3] The year began with operations against the oldest and most secure enemy base areas in the south: War Zone D, or the "Iron Triangle" north of Saigon, and War Zone C, the jungle region of Tay Ninh near the Cambodian border. It proceeded with a series of bloody set-piece battles against North Vietnamese regulars in the Central Highlands near the Lao border and in the mountainous country just below the DMZ: Dak To, Con Thien, the "Rockpile," Khe Sanh — all of these battles ended with hundreds of Americans and thousands of North Vietnamese dead. Westmoreland counted all of them victories — and they were victories in the sense that with the support of saturation bombing the "kill ratio" always ran in the favor of the United States. From another perspective they were defeats, for the United States seemed to have gained nothing by them — neither the control of territory nor any reduction of the enemy's effectives. The North Vietnamese managed once again to maintain their numbers in the south while drawing an important section of the U.S. combat forces away from the populated areas. The American casualty figures combined with the apparent lack of progress towards the termination of the war had a most depressing effect on the popularity of the war in the United States.

Westmoreland's strategy had always been to use the American troops as a "shield behind which" the GVN forces could move in to establish government security. The commanding general never quite came to terms with the fact that the war was being fought at points rather than along lines. With the support or even the neutrality of the population, the enemy forces could break up into small units and go anywhere in the countryside circumnavigating the "Free World" outposts. Westmoreland was trying to play chess while his enemy was playing Go. The result was that he kept having to make moves which in no way conformed to his strategy. From the very beginning the American troops were forced to engage in the small-unit patrolling and the "holding" operations that were supposed to be the tasks of the ARVN and the local security forces. As their numbers increased, the U.S. forces took on more and more responsibility for pacification in the critical areas around Saigon and in the First Corps. In 1966 the U.S. Marines had some three divisions engaged in "clearing and holding" the narrow coastal strip of Quang Nam province; two Korean divisions and other Marine units were settled into the villages of Binh Dinh and Quang Ngai, while by 1967 three U.S. army divisions sat astride the routes into Saigon. The difficulty, however, remained that the American forces could not be everywhere at once, and that military occupation did not constitute pacification. A different approach had to be found.

Two years before — that is, two years too early — Westmoreland had outlined his new strategy for "pacification." "Until now," he said in 1965,

the war has been characterized by a substantial majority of the population remaining neutral. . . . In the past year we have seen an escalation to a higher level of intensity in the war. This will bring about a moment of decision for the peasant farmer. He will have to choose if he stays alive. Until now the peasant farmer has had three alternatives: he could stay put and follow his natural instinct to stay close to the land, living beside the graves of his ancestors. He could move to an area under government control. Or he could join the VC. . . . Now if he stays put there are additional dangers. The VC can't patch up wounds. If the peasant becomes a refugee, he does get shelter, food, and security, job opportunities and is given a hope to possibly return to his land. The third alternative is life with the VC. The VC have not made good on their promises; they no longer have secure areas. There are B-52 bombings, the VC tax demands are increasing; they want more recruits at the point of a gun, forced labor to move supplies. The battle is being carried more and more to the enemy.

"Doesn't that give the villager only the choice of becoming a refugee?" one journalist inquired. "I expect a tremendous increase in the number of refugees," answered Westmoreland.[4]

Westmoreland's statement was significant, for it meant that with the arrival of the American troops the U.S. command had largely given up hope for the conventional pacification schemes, the aim of which was to drive the NLF out of the villages and to secure the villagers' loyalty to the government. The new attempt would be to destroy the villages and, as it were, dry up the "water" where the "fish" of the Liberation forces swam in their element. As Robert Komer put it in American terms, "Well, if we can attrit the population base of the Viet Cong, it'll accelerate the process of degrading the VC."[5] The logic was impeccable. Given the American war objectives and the political impotence of the GVN, the strategy was to be the only one available. Furthermore, it would have worked had the Vietnam War been a war for control of territory.

In Operation Cedar Falls — the operation chronicled by Jonathan Schell in his book *The Village of Ben Suc* — the U.S. armed forces in effect drove a steamroller over the densely populated area of the Iron Triangle, flattening the villages with five-hundred-pound bombs, bulldozing the miles of tunnels, and destroying the jungle cover with herbicides. This operation "generated" (in the impersonal military phrase) seven thousand refugees and rendered the area uninhabitable by anyone except the Front troops. By Westmoreland's own estimate, it put the Front headquarters out of action for a mere six months.[6] In the region of the large-scale war in the Central Highlands and around the DMZ, the U.S. forces moved a total of seventeen thousand people and resettled them in barrack-like camps, where without any independent means of survival most had to depend on the irregular handouts of supplies from the Saigon government. In other provinces of Vietnam, when the resettlement was not so well organized, the refugees swarmed to the government outposts and the cities of their own accord to avoid the bombing and the military sweeps. The coastal regions of central Vietnam were particularly hard hit. Having failed to "pacify" Quang Nam province even by a battalion-sized occupation of each district, the Marines simply tore down the villages, sending thousands of people into Da Nang, where not even the Americans were able to feed them. In the same year U.S. forces expended tons of herbicides, which ultimately stripped an area the size of Massachusetts of crops and vegetation. The American command claimed that the aim of the "resources control program" was to deny food to the Front troops. The crop destruction, however, affected the civilians almost exclusively. For while the troops, being mobile, could find other sources of supply, the civilians, particularly the women and children, could not.[7]

In early 1967 Westmoreland gave a most complicated and interesting explanation for the rationale behind the President's "ceiling" on the number of American troops. "If," he said, "you crowd in too many termite killers, each using a screwdriver to kill the termites, you risk collapsing the floors or the foundation. In this war we're using screwdrivers to kill termites because it's a guerrilla war and we cannot use bigger weapons. We have to get the right balance of termite killers to get rid of the termites without wrecking the house."[8] To continue this extraordinary metaphor, the American force had managed to wreck the house without killing the termites; they had, further, managed to make the house uninhabitable for anyone except termites. In a different manner they had made the GVN "house" unlivable as well.

With the influx of refugees from the countryside, the cities and towns overflowed with people. Two million in 1966, three million or more by 1967 — the numbers were impossible to estimate, as most refugees, if they came to the government camps to begin with, did not stay in them for fear of exposure or starvation. But the number was surely more than the 4.8 percent of the population that Komer claimed came "under government control" that year. The swamps of Saigon and the dunes seaward of Da Nang, Hoi An, Qui Nhon, and the other capitals of the center now supported small cities of tin shacks. Many of the neat towns of the Delta almost disappeared beneath a tide of *bidonvilles*. These settlements survived because of the American presence; they survived as dependencies of the American bases. The American aid went not into the improvement of these American-created slums, but, as always, into the countryside for the purposes of counterinsurgency.[9]

At the Guam conference President Johnson took the long-awaited step of putting all civilian operations under the command of General Westmoreland. His move signified that Washington no longer gave even symbolic importance to the notion of a "political" war waged by the Vietnamese government. The reign of the U.S. military had begun, and with it the strategy of quantity in civilian as well as military affairs.

As an assistant to Westmoreland, Robert Komer had something of the general's notion of scale. After all the history of failed aid programs, he believed that the only hope for success lay in saturation. The Vietnamese officials might rake off 25 percent and 25 percent more might go to waste, but the rest of the American aid would reach its destination. The U.S. government had no choice but to force its supplies upon the Vietnamese people: thousands of tons of bulgur wheat, thousands of gallons of cooking oil, tons of pharmaceuticals, enough seed to plant New Jersey with miracle rice, enough fertilizer for the same, light bulbs, garbage trucks, an atomic reactor, enough concrete to pave a province, enough corrugated tin to roof it, enough barbed wire to circle it seventeen times, dentists' drills, soybean seedlings, sewing kits, mortars, machine tools, toothbrushes, plumbing, and land mines.

In part, of course, this aid was absolutely necessary, for the U.S. military was at the same time bombing, defoliating, and moving villages at such a rate that all the aid the United States could ship would not have been excessive as refugee relief. The difficulty was that the Americans had to distribute the supplies through the Vietnamese government — a vessel which, even despite its spongelike properties, could not dispose of all the commodities. The U.S. aid had grown beyond the point of absorption.

Partly to solve this "technical" problem of GVN efficiency, the United States sent in more American advisers. At the beginning of 1966 the mission had three or four civilians in every province capital; by the end of 1967 it had a small bureaucracy in each, comprising pig experts, rice experts, market and gardening experts, AID administrators, International Voluntary Service workers, English teachers, city planners, accountants, doctors, police inspectors, welfare workers, handicraft consultants, "psychological warfare" and counterinsurgency experts. (One man who, in the early 1960's, was sent out to study underground water levels remained in Vietnam unnoticed until the late 1960's when a secretary happened to come across his dossier in the back of an old filing cabinet.) After a few months "in country," the advisers and experts usually came to the conclusion that the United States was not sending enough commodities for them to do their job properly. Most of them came to that conclusion in a most reasonable manner — the advisers discovering that few of the commodities had reached their province capitals, much less the villages they wished to develop; the experts suggesting that, while progress was being made, a new approach might be more fruitful. So the U.S. government sent them more commodities and better transportation, utilization of which required more advisers and experts such as refugee relief coordinators, underwater engineers, warehouse architects, port overseers, labor leaders, sanitation engineers, and systems analysts, who in their turn discovered new "requirements for" and "shortages of" new and different types of commodities: television sets, plastic limbs, chicken feed, mosquito repellent, air conditioners, Bourbon, paper clips, prefabricated houses, rubber bands, and athlete's foot powder.

The Vietnamese government had developed the Midas touch — in much the same manner as the king himself, and with much the same results. Having once requested American support, the officials could not seem to stop it. Inefficiency, military defeats, rape, pillage, and coup d'etats made no difference. Everything they touched turned to commodities — commodities that were, like Midas's gold, quite useless for the purpose of government. The pigs, the barbed wire, and the tin roofing sheets that actually arrived at their destinations remained pigs, barbed wire, and tin roofing — things with no political significance. Where the NLF remained strong, the GVN officials could not even use the commodities as bribes, for the peasants did not consider pigs an adequate inducement to take up arms against the Front. Where the American troops had gone with artillery and bulldozer, the commodities could not compensate the peasants for the loss of their rice fields and their ancestral homes.

But the American aid to the Saigon government was not merely useless. In the days of the Diem regime the desire for profit persuaded at least some of the officials to try to keep the peasants alive, productive, and only moderately discontented, but now they could forget the peasants entirely and concentrate on filling out forms. The aid program had, in other words, relieved them even of their desire to exploit the peasants. If the farmers starved, died, or moved into the provincial capitals, the GVN officials had merely to change their requisitions from agricultural extension to refugee relief. It was the culmination of a logical development: the more money the GVN had, the less attention it had to pay to the peasants. Under the Diem regime the paternalistic landlords were replaced by officials; under the Ky and Thieu regimes, the officials themselves began to disappear from the peasants' horizons. And as the "problem" for the Americans was even further from solution, General Westmoreland began to discover new "requirements for" and "shortages of" American troops and advisers.

By 1967 the U.S. presence in Vietnam had reached the critical mass where Vietnamese officials, down to the level of district chief, spent most of their time dealing with Americans. On days when there were no visiting congressmen, no intelligence analysts, no AID supervisors, charity representatives, or journalists to see, the province and district chiefs would meet with their two sets of advisers and coordinate their operations with the local U.S. military command. The Vietnamese government, like the Vietnamese economy, had become little more than a service to the Americans. As it was not always a very efficient service, the Americans in some cases managed to dispense with it almost entirely. In the First Corps, for instance, the U.S. Marines carried out their own "civic action" programs on a scale that quite overwhelmed the government aid. (Granted, of course, they were doing a more than equivalent amount of destruction: even in 1966 fully a quarter of the population of Quang Nam province turned refugee.) Many of their commanders were indeed convinced that only the Vietnamese government kept them from driving out the Communists and pacifying the population. The goal of Colonel Corson's scheme to turn one hamlet into a bastion of capitalism was not, as the colonel explained, "the official one of 'paving the way for the GVN to assert its control over Phong Bac and to engender the support of the people for the GVN' but rather to make Phong Bac strong enough to resist the encroachments of *both* the GVN and the Vietcong against the rights of the people."[10]

What did it matter now that the Vietnamese province chiefs were corrupt and the peasants had no affection for the government of General Thieu? The Americans had not taken over the Saigon government, as many would have liked, but they were now in occupation of large parts of the countryside — only the lower Delta remained exclusively policed by Vietnamese. And they had changed the entire life of the cities. Into a country that even under the French lived close to the economy of barter, the Americans poured hundreds of millions of dollars. The actual amount was impossible to compute, for it included not only the direct military and civilian aid to the GVN, but the value of the Vietnamese labor in all the construction projects and the private spending over the years of occupation by more than half a million Americans. The cities were flooded with piastres. Between January 1965 and the end of 1967 the cost of living in the cities by conservative estimate rose 170 percent; the price of rice and the supply of money rose by 200 percent. The inflation had been kept to the minimum by the issuance of scrip instead of dollars to the American GIs and by the Commercial Import Program. But these devices, too, exacted their toll on the Vietnamese economy. The black market flourished near every American base on dollars, scrip, and PX goods. The CIP, designed on the model of the Marshall Plan to deliver aid in the useful and uninflationary form of production equipment, did something altogether different in Vietnam from what it had done in Europe. Rather than buying tractors or industrial machinery with their dollars, the Vietnamese importers bought what could be sold to that proportion of the population that made the most money from the Americans. The result was a vast influx of luxury goods, including watches, refrigerators, radios, Hondas, television sets, sewing machines, and motorcycles. With the decline of rice production (owing to the bombing and the defoliation), the United States had also to import millions of tons of rice to Vietnam to keep the price somewhere near the means of the huge city populations. The peasantry therefore did not enjoy any of the profits: the Commercial Import Program maintained the two entirely separate economies, the barter economy of the country and the inflated economy of the cities. In addition it destroyed all nonagricultural types of production. Most of the cottage industry and such larger industries that the Vietnamese possessed — the textile mills around Saigon and the small mining concerns — went down before the flood of American goods. But it could not be helped: the country's economy was simply not strong enough to support the vast American military presence.

There were, of course, people who profited: the hotel owners, for instance, the licensed importers, the brothel keepers, pharmacists, real estate dealers, diamond merchants, and distributors of American luxury goods. The big businessmen knew the value of a dollar; many of them had made similar profits during the last war when the French drained *their* gold reserves to support the piastre. As the only people in Vietnam who profited enough by the war to hope it would go on forever and to take what steps needed to be taken vis-à-vis the GVN officials to see that it did, these people held an absolute veto over the existence of the Republic of Vietnam. (Not that they would ever use it as long as the supply of dollars continued.) Behind them — indeed invisible both in the streets and in the pages of any economic analysis — were a number of non-Vietnamese: the Chinese merchants, who dealt in rice and war materials between Saigon and Hong Kong, Paris, Singapore, and perhaps finally Peking; the Indian merchants, money traders, and black marketeers. These men leeched from the Americans as they had once leeched from the French. Servicing them or stealing from them — it made little difference, as few of them had any commitment to the aims of the American war.

These men had some experience at their trade, but they could not initially have imagined the magnitude of the current transaction. In the single year of 1968 an estimated two hundred and fifty million dollars went into the black market traffic in currency. Whereas only a small elite had profited by the first war, now a considerable sector of the urban population was involved: the restaurant owners who put up their prices to New York rates, the hotel managers who demanded a sizable bribe to rent a room, the PX clerks who stole from the commissaries (with or without the help of U.S. supply sergeants), government clerks who demanded ransoms for exit visas and other necessary papers. Finally there were the bar girls and prostitutes of Tu Do Street, those lovely girls in their floating *au dais*, who told the soldiers sad stories about their widowed mothers, took their money, and invested it in another bar in Nha Trang or Da Nang. There were professional beggars, pimps, drug dealers, and thieves — a Brechtian cast of characters in the midst of a new Thirty Years' War.

Saigon had a long and well-integrated tradition of corruption that only a revolutionary upsurge could have rejected. Now that corruption took on a new dimension. In the fall of 1967 a young American embassy officer told David Halberstam that he had recently listened to the wife of the chief of staff, General Cao Van Vien, giving orders to a group of provincial officials on the distribution of San Miguel beer. "What was so amazing," he said, "was not the extent of her financial interest, which was very considerable, but the *flagrancy* of it — the absolute indifference to what we thought. She knew I spoke Vietnamese and she simply did not give a damn."[11] A few months before, General Nguyen Ngoc Loan's police arrested a leading member of the French community and the head of all the beer and soft-drink concerns in the country, alleging that he was giving payoffs to the Viet Cong. The gentleman in question had granted distributorships to the wives of four generals and his company had been paying NLF road taxes almost openly for years; it was therefore not hard to imagine just why he had gone to jail and just how he had managed to walk out of jail a week later with no more questions asked.

Under the Diem regime the corruption was covert and restrained by the barriers of practicality and good form; it was now unlimited, all-pervasive and naked of hypocrisy. The mayor of Quinhon, for instance, turned his official residence into a "massage parlor" for American soldiers, and the American officials could not persuade his superiors to order him to get the girls out. When AID imported forty garbage trucks to clean the fetid streets of Saigon, the GVN ministry concerned left them at the docks for a few days. Upon going down to check on them, an American official found some of them missing and the rest empty shells from which all the movable parts had been taken. On a rather grander scale, the head of the Saigon city council, La Thanh Nghe, took thousands of dollars every year in kickbacks from American drug companies for his pharmaceutical business. According to Halberstam, the corps commanders sold the job of district chief for a going rate of a million piastres (somewhere around ten thousand dollars, depending on the rate of exchange), and that of province chief for three million.[12] Given the total size of the American war budget, the price of a Vietnamese official was not, perhaps, excessive — if thereby the job was done. But there are two types of corruption in this world — the first, which permits an ill-made system to function; the second, which becomes the *raison d'être* of the system — and the corruption of the GVN was of the second type.

"Saigon has become an American brothel," said Senator William Fulbright in 1967. And he was right. A Tokyo or a Berlin could perhaps accommodate an American occupation and survive with some of its privacy intact, some of its leaders uncorrupted. But Saigon was a small and terrified city, and though money could not kill, the vast influx of American dollars had almost as much influence on it as the bombing had on the countryside. It turned the society of Saigon inside out. Almost every night a young man stood on his Honda at the end of Tu Do Street, waiting to take the American soldiers from the bars and brothels back to their bases: the young man was an under-secretary in the ministry of revolutionary development. The French war had sustained the old professions of land ownership and government service, but this war profited only those who served the Americans. In the new economy a prostitute earned more than a GVN minister, a secretary working for USAID more than a full colonel, a taxi owner who spoke a few words of English more than a university professor. Small wonder, then, that many GVN officials were corrupt and that the students, so criticized by the Americans for their refusal to "participate" and "take responsibility," put off taking their final exams year after year. The old rich of Saigon had opposed the Communists as a threat to their position in society; they found that the Americans took away that position in a much quicker and more decisive fashion — and with it, what was left of the underpinning of Vietnamese values. As one soldier complained ironically, "We people in this society curse the Communists because we live in a free society. Thus, crooks, cheats, thieves, and prostitutes are free to climb the ladder of values."[13] For many Vietnamese the life of the cities had become a carnival-like existence, a permanent *Fasching;* Generals Ky and Thieu reigned as the Lords of Misrule over a country where all laws were suspended, all license permitted.

Just before his departure for a two-week tour of Vietnam in 1967, the defense analyst, Herman Kahn, listened to an American businessman give a detailed account of the economic situation in South Vietnam. At the end of the talk — an argument for reducing the war — Kahn said, "I see what you mean. We have corrupted the cities. Now, perhaps we can corrupt the countryside as well." It was not a joke. Kahn was thinking in terms of a counterinsurgency program: the United States would win the war by making all Vietnamese economically dependent upon it. In 1967 his program was already becoming a reality, for the corruption reached even to the lowest levels of Vietnamese society. Around the American bases from An Khe to Nha Trang, Cu Chi, and Chu Lai, there had grown up entire towns made of packing cases and waste tin from the canning factories — entire towns advertising Schlitz, Coca-Cola, or Pepsi Cola a thousand times over. The "food," "shelter," and "job opportunities" that Westmoreland had promised came to this: a series of packing-case towns with exactly three kinds of industry — the taking in of American laundry, the selling of American cold drinks to American soldiers, and prostitution for the benefit of the Americans. But to Robert Komer and General Westmoreland these towns meant only more Vietnamese under "government control." They had become obsessed, these important people from Johnson to McNamara to the patrician Cabot Lodge, with the eradication of a few thousand Front troops and cadres. In their pursuit of "pacification" it did not seem to matter how much the United States spent, how many soldiers it took, or what happened to the millions of other Vietnamese. Nor could they build the Vietnamese government to stand on its own; at least, if that were their intention, they were coming no closer to their goal. In fact, quite the contrary.

In the spring of 1967 Westmoreland authorized the 199th U.S. Light Infantry Brigade to integrate its operations with those of the Vietnamese Fifth Ranger Group, placing all of the troops, from squad to battalion, under the joint command of an American and a Vietnamese officer. In November the brigade's commander, Brigadier General Robert C. Forbes, decided to terminate what he then called an "experiment." "Quite frankly," he said, "integrated operations are relatively good if they don't go on too long. . . . Six to eight months is enough. Other than that, you're going to get involved in a situation where the underdeveloped forces are going to become totally dependent on the developed forces. That's not the name of the game here."[14] The general, it appeared, was somewhat understating the case. According to his subordinates, the Vietnamese officers were already dependent on the Americans to the point where they sometimes forsook their commands in the field, leaving the Americans with two companies instead of one to command. "They became dependent on us for rations, for medical supplies, for calling in air strikes, even for leadership," said one American officer. "Well, they're not supposed to be mercenaries, they're supposed to be an independent fighting group." The truth was that all the other Vietnamese units, to the degree that they received U.S. aid and support, were becoming similarly dependent on the Americans.

By 1967 the Vietnamese officers had begun to look at the war from an entirely new perspective. General Phan Truong Chinh, for instance, the commander of the Twenty-fifth Division and the stalwart of generals Khang and Ky, apparently ceased to think of himself as conducting a military operation. In that year more of his men were killed in traffic accidents than in combat. The fact that he was a poet, and a good one by Saigon standards, may have had something to do with it, but he seemed preoccupied by the presence of three American divisions within a fifty-mile radius of his division headquarters. In November of 1966 he had put the Long An province chief under house arrest for going beyond his authority and requesting helicopters from the U.S. First Division for hot pursuit of the Viet Cong. This and other uncooperative acts (the general had managed to stop three American operations in the ten days before that incident; he had also caused the current American hope, Colonel Sam Wilson, to leave his pacification project for operations in the trackless Plain of Reeds) led the general's adviser to send out a secret report on him to General Westmoreland. Within a few days Chinh acquired a copy of the report and issued an order forbidding all his officers from speaking to their American advisers. For Chinh, as for many other GVN officials, the main concern now seemed to be not the Communists but the Americans.

The attitude of the Vietnamese officials towards the Americans was a complicated one. The sense and tone of it are perhaps best explained in the famous parable by the Greek poet, Cavafy. In that poem the people of a fictional city are waiting for the approach of a barbarian horde. Having decided not to resist, they wait in the public square to welcome the barbarians. The emperor sits passive on his throne, the senators stop passing laws, and the orators are quiet so as to make the best impression on the barbarians. After they have waited all day, the people hear that the barbarians have turned away from the city. And they are strangely disappointed, for as they say, "Those people were a kind of a solution." The Vietnamese officials waited in the same manner for the Americans — only the Americans did not turn away, did not leave them with the problem of how to cope with their own freedom. They entered the city and did what they wanted with it. The officials never grew to like them — in a sense there was no question of "liking," for communication was impossible — but they nonetheless grew to depend upon them. Whatever happened in the city, the barbarians were responsible. The barbarian horde committed outrages upon the citizens from time to time, but the situation was generally satisfactory. The Vietnamese officials no longer had to worry about their own survival, and they felt no obligation towards their masters. The barbarians were all-powerful; they did what they liked, and therefore the Vietnamese were free to do anything they liked. In a sense, life was more difficult for the barbarians than for the people of the city.

In 1967 an experienced American adviser told the *New York Times* correspondent, R. W. Apple, that recently his "counterpart," a battalion commander in the Vietnamese Twenty-fifth Division, had disappeared during one ferocious all-night battle. Assuming that the officer was dead, the adviser took command of the battalion and led it through the fight. The next morning, however, the commander emerged from the foxhole where he had spent the night, shook himself, and ordered his men to move out. When the adviser suggested that he deploy his men in a less bunched-up formation, the officer coldly ignored him and marched his men back to base as they were.[15]

The officer was an exception — an exception, that is, among thousands of exceptions — but the story is an excellent illustration of what, in a wider sense, U.S. military "support" did for the Vietnamese government. Instead of helping the officials to govern, it alienated them from their own position as leaders. Such officers did not act like "puppets," but they saw themselves as puppets or mercenaries with respect to their public duties. Mistrustful of the Americans, the Vietnamese attempted to box them into accepting the total responsibility for a situation that was, as the Vietnamese saw it, of American making. General Chinh, Mme. Cao Van Vien, Lederer's famous Major Hao, General Thieu himself — all of them watched the Americans as a prisoner watches his jailer until finally they could make a defiant gesture showing the imprisonment of the guard and the freedom of the prisoner. They felt what they did was in no way immoral, but merely a matter of self-protection.

In many ways the most tragic figures of the war were those Vietnamese who trusted the Americans and believed in their own responsibility for all those fine words written at the Honolulu Conference. In Dinh Tuong province a young half-Chinese official, the protégé of a fatherly American AID adviser, had dedicated himself to the thankless task of trying to persuade the villagers to organize and build schools for their children with government aid. When his American protector departed the province, the local police chief threw the young man in jail on trumped-up charges and demanded all of his wife's jewelry as a ransom. Because the official was honest and had friends among the Americans, he was seen as a threat to the whole provincial system of corruption. Similarly, Major Nguyen Be, a former Viet Minh officer and one of the few men in the GVN with any political concern for the peasantry, became, as the deputy province chief of Binh Dinh, the focus of all American hopes for the pacification program in early 1966. While in Binh Dinh he told (or was thought to have told) his American friends too much about the workings of the local bureaucracy. Unable to remove him by any other means, the province chief, a cousin of the corps commander, General Vinh Loc, one day sent his agents out to assassinate him. Alerted just in time, Be escaped the city in a jeep and, thanks to his Viet Minh training, managed to hide out in the nearby villages for a week without being caught by either the GVN officials or the Front cadre.

Be escaped and managed to get a job training the RD cadre for the CIA in Vung Tau. But his colleague, another former Viet Minh officer, Colonel Tran Ngoc Chau, elected to the Assembly in 1967, was later jailed by General Thieu against all the laws of the constitution and the protests of high officials in the mission. Chau's error was to have complained publicly of a certain businessman who, as Thieu's bagman, had a great deal to do with passing Thieu's bills through the Assembly. Many of the deputies at first supported Chau against the official charge that he had negotiated with his brother, an officer in the NLF, but many of them and much of the Saigon press turned against him when, in his defense, Chau admitted that he had told the CIA all about his meetings with his brother. Thieu emerged from the encounter (like Nguyen Ngoc Loan before him) as the protector of Vietnamese sovereignty. The Catholic scholar, Nguyen Van Trung, expressed the feelings of many Saigonese when he wrote:

The countries belonging to what is called the free world revere democracy and equality, yet in fact they are only democratic and egalitarian within their own countries. . . . With regard to small countries . . . their policy is still the policy of domination. . . . Only this domination is not overt and crude as under the forms of the old-model colonialism, but is rather very discreet, subtle, and scientific. . . . Because it does not directly control and govern, the masses of people do not resent it. Furthermore, it not only does not produce feelings of nationalism but makes those feelings disappear. Even those revolutionaries who fought against the old colonialism, because they now hold power, receive the aid of "advisers" and enjoy it. For precisely this reason, the new-model policy of intervention is more dangerous than the old colonialism, because the new style does not create conditions which give rise to opposition.[16]

The argument had a great measure of truth to it. The Americans were in control of South Vietnam, and any claims they made for the independence of the Saigon government were hypocritical given that fact. But the argument was also in some sense a rationalization. The "masses of people" resented the French no more and no less than they resented the Americans: it was the Viet Minh who focused that resentment, and there was no such group within the Saigon government. The fact was that many Vietnamese of the cities had wanted the Americans to intervene — wanted them not only for practical reasons but for the psychological ones suggested by Cavafy. They wanted the Americans to be the all-powerful barbarians, to take responsibility for the war — at the same time that they feared American domination. By one of those strange reverses that the mind makes for the sake of self-consistency, both the desire and the fear merged in an expression of fear that the Americans would leave them. The constant demands — the demands of the Fifth Ranger Group for more supplies, the demands of the Thieu government for more American aid[17] — were demands for reassurance that the Americans were "sincere" and would continue to feed them whatever the cost. The demands were insatiable — far in excess of the need — for the reassurance could never be obtained: the Americans *were not* their leaders and thus could never be trusted. Paradoxically, of course, the American attempts to assure the Vietnamese that they were not colonialists, and that they would one day leave Vietnam, only heightened the Vietnamese anxiety about their good faith. How could they enter into a relationship they knew would not last? The Americans who demanded that the United States take over the Saigon government were responding to this anxiety in a classical colonial fashion. Here again, however, the Americans could not win because the expressed fear was only an aspect of the real one: the Vietnamese were afraid of their own dependence.

While the young American advisers went on trusting in the future, the "communication" and "cooperation" they expected with the Vietnamese would never materialize. Both peoples — individually and collectively — were making conflicting demands which neither could satisfy. Furthermore, both had a wholly different idea of the relationship. One incident — an incident among many — that happened to a Marine doctor in Quang Nam province described these contrasting images.

As part of the Marine "civic action" program the doctor, so he explained, spent the whole of one very hot day in a hamlet going from door to door, examining patients and dispensing medicines without charge. At the last house — a shop, as it happened, where the women sold cold drinks — he treated four members of the family for various minor illnesses. When he had finished his work, he asked the woman politely if he could have a cold beer. The woman refused. She demanded that he pay for it — and at American rates. Later, as he recounted the story, the Marine officer was once again puzzled and angry. "Those Vietnamese," he said finally, "they just aren't . . . they have no *gratitude*."

The Marine would seem to have been justified in his anger. But, as Otare Mannoni has pointed out, gratitude is a strange emotion in that it is made up of two seemingly contradictory expressions: first, that the individual is deeply indebted to his benefactor, and second, that he is not indebted at all. Gratitude is, in effect, a compromise, and one made almost uniquely by Westerners, to reconcile the demand for obligation with the need to maintain personal independence. In asking for gratitude the Marine had not been quite as altruistic as he imagined, for, while he asked for no monetary payment, he asked for a deeper acknowledgment of his services — an emotional quid pro quo.

In a sense, the American mission was making the same kind of complicated demand upon the Vietnamese. The officials asked the Saigon government both to maintain its independence and at the same time to oblige them by following their advice. They regarded their commitment to the GVN as being in the nature of a business deal — a loan of funds and management consultants such as a large company may make to a smaller one that is threatened by bankruptcy. As they were to have no return on their investment except that of foiling the schemes of their rival consortium, they assumed they had the right to some thanks, if not to obedience.

Like the seller of cold drinks, the Vietnamese officials did not take the same view at all. They saw the relationship not as a business transaction but as a long-term personal engagement between superior and inferior — between master and slave when there is only one master and one slave in the market. Even those Vietnamese intellectuals who opposed the regime objected to American demands for a quid pro quo. Writing in 1969, at least five years after the Americans had last threatened to cut off any aid to the GVN, one intellectual complained:

In going to help us, you always placed your own interests above personal relationships and against the moral spirit of East Asia; why should so many people not feel irritated? Every time you felt your own interests being chipped away, you did not hesitate to use every method to apply pressure against us, and the nut and the bolt of the whole matter has always been the question of money. Your special cardsharping trick [lit., your professional fingers] was always "aid and the cutting of aid."[18]

As the Vietnamese reasoned, the Americans had no right to exact anything from them; on the contrary, the Americans owed them something for the use of their soil to fight a war that was really directed against China and the Soviet Union. The fact that so many American soldiers thought of themselves as giving their lives to save the lives of a lot of "ungrateful" Vietnamese officials did not change their point of view. Like Caliban in *The Tempest*, they believed the Americans had already broken their trust and relieved them of the necessity to show their obligation. They were free to work against the Americans up to the point at which the Americans would abandon them.

The more Americans spent their best efforts and their lives in Vietnam, the less influence the United States had for reform upon the GVN. With both men and material resources, the Americans were enforcing corruption and destroying the tissue of Vietnamese society. Further, they were tearing the GVN officials further and further away from their own people. The thousands of dead ARVN soldiers, the bombed-out villages, and the refugees, all attested to the alienation. The officials continued to speak of "the Vietnamese nation" and the "Vietnamese people," but they had lost whatever residual solidarity they once had with the villagers. The Saigon government had turned over on its back to feed upon the Americans.

13

Prospero

PROSPERO: (*aside*) I had forgot that foul conspiracy
Of the beast Caliban and his confederates
Against my life: the minute of their plot
Is almost come. . . .

FERDINAND: This is strange. Your father's in some passion
That works him strongly.

MIRANDA: Never till this day
Saw I him touched with anger, so distempered.

PROSPERO: A devil, a born devil, on whose nature
Nurture can never stick: on whom my pains,
Humanely taken, all, all lost, quite lost!
And as with age his body uglier grows,
So his mind cankers. I will plague them all,
Even to roaring.

William Shakespeare,
The Tempest, act 4, scene 1

In September 1967, four staff members from the International Voluntary Service in Vietnam resigned from their posts and with forty-nine of their colleagues wrote a letter to President Johnson condemning the American war. These young volunteers had come to Vietnam with the intention of helping to carry out the "war against hunger, ignorance and disease" described in the Honolulu program, and the mission had judged their contribution valuable.[1] Two of the staff members, Don Luce and John Sommer, had spent a total of thirteen years in Vietnam; they had been working with the montagnards, students, and poor farmers long before the arrival of the American troops, and they had a commitment to the whole notion of aid to underdeveloped countries and, in particular, to the success of the American aid program in Vietnam. Thus they resigned reluctantly, and they did so not because they had just decided that the aid program was a failure (this Luce and Sommer

had known for some years) but because they had come to realize
that the main efforts of the United States in Vietnam were destructive rather than constructive. "We do not accuse anyone of deliberate cruelty," the IVSers wrote. "Perhaps if you accept the war, all
can be justified — the free strike zones, the refugees, the spraying of
herbicide on crops, the napalm. But the Vietnam war is in itself an
overwhelming atrocity. Its every victim — the dead, the bereaved,
the deprived — is a victim of this atrocity."[2] It was from the beginning an error for the young men to project their own idealism onto
the United States policy in Vietnam, but at least they realized their
mistake and acted upon their convictions. And in this the young
men were unique, for no other American official in Vietnam resigned
publicly for reasons of conscience.

For the rest of the American officials, nothing seemed to have
changed. In the air-conditioned offices of Saigon, the mission "regulars" pored over plans for the dredging of a long canal through
NLF territory — a project that would employ the labors of some
eight or nine thousand people for months in order to bring the Delta
rice two days closer to Saigon. In his villa not far away, General
Lansdale entertained a select company with talk about the motivation of the cadre teams and the spirit of democracy in Asia. The
confidence of the Americans was something quite extraordinary —
indeed it was probably incredible to those who had not spent time
in Vietnam. After thirteen years of failed programs and fallen
governments, the officials were still planning new approaches not
only to winning the war, but to building a prosperous, independent
nation out of the shreds of non-Communist Vietnam. "Democratic
elections . . . rooting out corruption . . . rooting in the government . . . land reform . . . rural electrification . . . revolutionary development" — the phrases had become so familiar that it was
difficult now to grasp the magnitude of the changes they implied, or
to sort out the intellectual confusion. In Da Nang one might find (as
one writer did) a Marine colonel distributing carpentry sets paid for
by Marine Reserve officers in the United States and saying, "Of
course we try to make what we do seem as though it comes from the
government, not us. We want the villagers to think their own people
are looking after them and not Uncle Sam. We're trying to get some
other kind of training for people. Maybe in ten or fifteen years
there'll be some ground to build democracy on here."[3]

Confusion of goals and motives extended not only to the soldiers and the junior AID officials. By 1967 Vietnam was inundated with social scientists working under contract to the Defense Department.[4] Herman Kahn and his colleagues at the Hudson Institute briefed colonels on increasing "security" by means of substituting German shepherd dogs for Vietnamese soldiers on night patrols and building a moat all the way around Saigon. At a conference in 1968, Professor Ithiel de Sola Pool of MIT and the Simulmatics Corporation[5] spoke about the great success of the Vietnamese elections and the drive against corruption, proposing that the United States "build a bridge" between the new legislature and the elected village councils so as to reduce and finally eliminate the autonomy of the Vietnamese military bureaucracy. Dr. Pool, in other words, proposed that the U.S. mission destroy the whole infrastructure of the war and deliver power to a group of unarmed legislators, whom the Vietnamese generals tolerated as creatures of an American whim.[6]

In this third year of a major war that had made the Vietnamese civilians into survivors and refugees, the mission had an air of freshness and newness about it. Young men from RAND and Simulmatics bounded about the countryside in Land Rovers studying "upward mobility among village elites" or "the interrelationship of land reform with peasant political motivation." "Of course," they would say with a slight swagger as they emptied the clips from their Swedish K submachine guns, "if the GVN realized the RF-PF potential, the lower-level Viet Cong village hierarchies would disappear in a matter of weeks." The old-timers would scoff at their naïveté. In the embassy weary State Department officials would look up from their desks to describe the disasters that had occurred to the RF-PF in Quang Ngai, Quang Tin, and Quang Nam provinces. "So the program isn't working," a journalist might conclude. "Not working?" They would look up, startled. "Why, just look at An Giang province. The GVN is really pulling itself together this year."

Many American newspaper readers had come to regard such statements as propaganda, but they were nothing of the sort. The time for such propaganda had long since passed, and the officials were sincere, sometimes painfully so. In 1956, even in 1962, this sincerity could be thought of as no more than a product of native American optimism and a misunderstanding of the Vietnamese. Many officials in Vietnam believed, with most Americans, that they faced an enemy who ruled by force and terror alone. They believed they could give the Vietnamese material prosperity and political reform. At the time it took a great deal of sophistication to see why U.S. ambitions might be unrealistic. But now in this third year of the war, after the U.S. mission had set up a weak military dictatorship and dismantled the economy, after the American troops had killed countless thousands of Vietnamese, had burned their villages and destroyed their crops, all the talk of "social revolution" and nation-building evidenced an extreme removal from reality.

In many respects this distance was institutional. The high officials of the mission had created a system by which they could receive no bad news. Under the reign of Lodge and Porter, for instance, all civilian province officials filled out a single report every month describing not what the situation was but what the "Free World Forces" had done in their province for the past month. The aim of this report was patent, as its title was "Progress Report." And it did indeed show progress up to the point of a perfect tautology. What went in one end of the pipeline came out the other: a hundred bags of bulgur distributed, two villages cleared, and so forth. As a perfectly closed system, it did not even contain a space where the province representative might write that the NLF had gone back into the two villages or that the refugees who did not receive the bulgur had starved. The equivalent accounting system in the military was the description of all U.S. actions undertaken, followed by an enumeration of enemy deaths and enemy "structures" destroyed. Most Americans in Vietnam automatically discounted the ARVN "body counts" as fabrications, but they were not so willing to admit that the American tallies often reflected no more than Vietnamese dead and Vietnamese houses ruined — if that. The system put pressure on *all* military men to exaggerate or falsify statistics.[7] Furthermore, as the only "indicator of progress," it suggested that death and destruction had some absolute value in terms of winning the war. That the enemy might continue to recruit, rearm, and rebuild (often with the help of people enraged by the American destruction) did not seem to enter into the calculations.

Another even more obvious form of error arose from the way in which the high officials arranged the already questionable figures they received. Robert Komer, for instance, included the number of refugees within the total of the "increase of people living in secure areas," thereby leaving the impression that the entire increase, as opposed to a small percentage of it, owed to his own pacification teams and the expansion of the GVN into the countryside. (Komer's

Hamlet Evaluation Survey, a most sophisticated system that classified hamlets into five categories of GVN control according to eighteen political, economic, and military criteria, had similar built-in
deceptions, and in any case proved much too complicated for any
American with a one-year tour to use.) The U.S. military intelligence, for its part, estimated the enemy effectives by counting only
those fighting in the main force units and ignoring the number
employed as cadres or village guerrillas, thereby overlooking the
NLF's entire base of recruitment and supply. (After what was
undoubtedly a long interservice battle, the CIA managed to make
the larger view prevail. The result was that after all the military
claims of enemy killed during the Tet offensive, the estimates of
enemy strength shot up from 245,000 to 600,000.)[8]

The neophyte journalists naturally assumed that these estimates
were solely for their own benefit, but this was not the case. The
officials made those figures for themselves. Each layer of officials
added a new distortion with the result that the higher the official,
the less he usually knew about the situation on the ground. President Johnson, perhaps, knew the least of all. Upon replacing Robert
McNamara as secretary of defense in 1968, Clark Clifford quite
quickly came to the conclusion that the President was being mis-
informed by the ambassador and others in Saigon. He realized soon
afterwards that this misinformation was only a part of the problem.
In his meetings with the President he would occasionally read the
passages he considered significant from the reports of the CIA chief
of station and the U.S. commander in Vietnam. Instead of objecting
to those passages, the President would say, in effect, "Where did
that come from? Why didn't anyone show me that before?" But the
President had read those same reports already; he had merely overlooked those passages.

The reason for this failure of vision was not hard to locate. Before
the United States committed troops to Vietnam, the American intelligence estimates were with some exceptions extremely accurate.
They continued to be accurate throughout the war in those sections
of the bureaucracy (notably the intelligence, as distinct from the
operations, divisions of the CIA) that had no responsibility for
carrying American policy to success. But by 1968 there were very
few such groups in Vietnam or among those concerned with Vietnam in Washington. In 1968 the job of the American ambassador, the military command, the heads of the aid programs, the CIA

operations groups, and their counterparts in Washington, was not to discover if the American effort was morally wrong or doomed to failure, but to make that war effort a success. Each individual bureaucrat wished to prove himself a member of a successful enterprise. Each official believed (wished to believe) in his own wisdom and "effectiveness." He believed (wished to believe) in U.S. policy and the war in Vietnam. This credo could be read from front to back or back to front and one tenet would still follow the other as night the day. To admit that the war was excessively destructive or that it was not being won was to admit to personal as well as institutional failure — an admission difficult for anyone to make. The higher the official, the more he was publicly identified with the war policy, and the greater was his temptation to look only for an optimistic interpretation of events. (Facing an electorate that received the war largely with indifference or hostility, the President himself had very little latitude to alter his public stance and little interest in discovering the gloomy truths.) The circle of self-interest created a complete circle of self-deception that began and ended in the office of the President of the United States.

In 1966 Senator George Aiken of Vermont suggested that the United States government simply announce that it had won the war and then withdraw its troops from Vietnam. In refusing to take this plausible alternative of ignoring reality altogether, Johnson condemned his officials who worked on Vietnam to the excruciating mental task of holding reality and the official version of reality together as they moved farther and farther apart. For many officials the attempt entailed a total self-contradiction. In 1966, for example, Vice-President Hubert Humphrey went to Vietnam on Johnson's bidding to congratulate the Saigon government on the progress it had made in the area of Revolutionary Development. In the course of a ritual visit to the RD training camp in Vung Tao, he heard the chief instructor of the program, Major Nguyen Be, assert that the program was not working because the entire Saigon government was corrupt. The Vice-President, who had made his political fortunes in Minneapolis as a muck-raking reformer, found himself in the position of defending a government he must have known was corrupt against a Vietnamese reformer.

The incident only illustrated in a public way what happened in private to many American officials who had to deal with the Saigon government. The aim of the American advisory program was, after all, to help the Vietnamese officials; in practice this meant to help them with whatever they wanted. Few American advisers dared to criticize their "counterparts" for fear of limiting their "effectiveness" in the future; few dared to send in pessimistic reports for fear of damaging their own careers.[9] Even if their "counterparts" were corrupt or otherwise incapable, they would send in glowing reports, recommending that the mission send them more aid, more arms, more men, in order to make up for a deficiency that remained invisible to their superior officers. The result was that the necessity for false reporting would increase — along with the fortunes of their "counterparts." As men with access to the source of supply, the advisers became active participants in the Vietnamese network of corruption. The penalty for doing otherwise was too severe. In 1967 William Lederer discovered that a district chief in Quang Nam province (the same official who so enraged Colonel Corson) was stealing the rations of his own PF soldiers, thus causing the PF to desert and to leave the U.S. Marine pacification teams unprotected. When he took that story to the American adviser to the First Corps commander, Lieutenant General Hoang Xuan Lam, the U.S. army colonel refused even to hear him out. As a Marine officer later explained to Lederer, the adviser was caught in an impossible situation: if he cut the district chief out of the supply line, General Lam (from whom the district chief had undoubtedly bought his job) would complain to the Saigon junta; a member of the junta would then tell the American command that the adviser was unable to get along with the Vietnamese; the adviser would then be removed (losing his chance for promotion) and the district chief would continue to steal the supplies.

To the end of "helping" the Vietnamese government, American officials not only concealed Vietnamese corruption but suppressed information about the extortion rackets, rape, pillage, and outright military atrocities. For at least two years, the generals of Westmoreland's staff refused to let even the analysts on contract to the Defense Department investigate the wholesale slaughter of civilians by the Korean troops in the course of their "pacification" program. And it was not until 1970 that members of a congressional committee stumbled across a concealed group of "tiger cages" on Con Son Island, where for years the Vietnamese military, with the knowledge of American advisers, had kept political prisoners — that is, Buddhist students — under conditions that hardly bore description.[10]

The information first revealed by Don Luce came to general public attention only because one member of the committee staff decided to give the story to the newspapers; the camp situation had not been discussed in the later congressional report. A few days later a doctor working for the American Friends Service in Quang Ngai province reported that she had treated "political prisoners" after they were tortured in a Vietnamese interrogation center, with the knowledge of American officers, by Vietnamese officers, who were carrying on a thriving extortion racket through the center.[11]

To suppress information of this kind required the cooperation not only of a few colonels bucking for general but by the heads of the American mission in Saigon.

That the mission heads were capable of tolerating such abuses should not, perhaps, have been surprising. In 1966 Henry Cabot Lodge had, after all, condoned Colonel Nguyen Ngoc Loan's slaughter of more than a hundred Buddhist civilians in Da Nang. In 1967 Ambassador Ellsworth Bunker, the distinguished career diplomat who succeeded Lodge, applauded a rigged election and condoned the imprisonment of a large number of opposition political and labor leaders on false charges.[12] In the name of freedom and democracy, the ambassadors did nothing while the Saigon officials arrested or murdered whomever they liked without fear of reprisal from the rest of the population.

Rather than reform the Vietnamese, these distinguished men, who operated with a perfectly clear conscience as to their own integrity and patriotism, presided over a system that corrupted both Vietnamese and Americans. Further, in deceiving themselves into a belief in "progress," they worked against the interests of the government and the country they served.

The effort of trying to hold reality and the official version of reality together finally took its toll on the Americans in Vietnam. When added to all the other strains of war, it produced an almost intolerable tension that expressed itself not in a criticism of American policy so much as in a fierce resentment against the Vietnamese. The logic of that anger was a simple one, combined of guilt and illusions destroyed. The nature of those illusions was even less apparent to Americans than it had been to the French, but the illusions were nonetheless powerful. At the Senate Foreign Relations Committee hearings in 1965, General Maxwell Taylor, just returned from the ambassadorship in Saigon, said in describing the pacification program: "We have always been able to move in the areas where the security was good enough. But I have often said it is very hard to plant the corn outside the stockade when the Indians are still around. We have to get the Indians farther away in many of the provinces to make good progress."[13] In Vietnam American officers liked to call the area outside GVN control "Indian country." It was a joke, of course, no more than a figure of speech, but it put the Vietnam War into a definite historical and mythological perspective: the Americans were once again embarked upon a heroic and (for themselves) almost painless conquest of an inferior race. To the American settlers the defeat of the Indians had seemed not just a nationalist victory, but an achievement made in the name of humanity — the triumph of light over darkness, of good over evil, and of civilization over brutish nature. Quite unconsciously, the American officers and officials used a similar language to describe their war against the NLF. According to the official rhetoric, the Viet Cong did not live in places, they "infested areas"; to "clean them out" the American forces went on "sweep and clear" operations or moved all the villagers into refugee camps in order to "sanitize the area." Westmoreland spoke of the NLF as "termites." The implications of this language rarely came to consciousness (some of the American field commanders actually admired the Front as a fighting force), but they were nonetheless there. The Americans were white men in Asia, and they could not conceive that they might fail in their enterprise, could not conceive that they could be morally wrong.

Beyond all the bureaucratic and strategic interests in the war, it was this "can do" attitude, this sense of righteous mission that had led the U.S. government deeper and deeper into Vietnam. Moral infallibility, military invincibility — the two went together and were not to be differentiated, not in Vietnam, in any case, where the enemy was not only Communist but small, yellow, and poor.[14] The difficulty was that the "allies" of the United States belonged within almost the same category — the same category with the one term of Communism removed. The distinction — Communist, non-Communist — so obvious in theory, became an elusive one in practice when juxtaposed with the much greater contrast between Americans and Vietnamese.

In coming to Vietnam, most American advisers, for instance, expected their "counterparts" to render them their due as members of a more "advanced" society. The expectation was not, after all, unreasonable, since the U.S. government sent them out to advise the Vietnamese. But the advisers tended to see themselves in the roles of teacher and older brother, and when the Vietnamese did not respond to them in the expected manner — when they did not even take their advice — few succeeded in reconstructing the truth of the matter. Few saw that the Vietnamese were not the pupils of the Americans, but people with a very different view of the world and with interests that only occasionally coincided with their own. For those few who succeeded there were an equal number of others (men such as the Marine colonel with his carpentry set) who took an extreme parochial view, looking upon the Vietnamese as savages or children with empty heads into which they would pour instruction. Covered with righteous platitudes, theirs was an essentially colonialist vision, born out of the same insecurity and desire for domination that had motivated many of the French. When their "counterparts" did not take their instruction, these advisers treated the Vietnamese like bad pupils, accusing them of corruption or laziness, and attempted to impose authority over them. And when the attempt at coercion failed, they retreated from the Vietnamese entirely, barricading themselves in behind American weapons and American PX goods, behind the assumption of American superiority and the assumption that the Vietnamese were not quite human like themselves.

"Don't you realize," exploded one young embassy officer, "don't you realize that everything the Americans do in Vietnam is founded on a hatred of the Vietnamese?" His outburst was shocking, for he, of all Americans in Vietnam, had managed to preserve a sense of balance. He understood the point of view of the Vietnamese officials as well as the Americans, and because of his own success at reconciling the two, he had believed that the best in both would prevail. Two years earlier he had confidence that the two could find some common ground for cooperation against the NLF. But he, the diplomat *par excellence,* had seen his compatriots turn into spineless bureaucrats and frustrated proconsuls. And into murderers.

In 1969 an incident came to the attention of the U.S. Congress that had occurred a year and a half before in the wake of the Tet offensive. On a routine search and destroy operation a company from the America Division had walked into the village of My Lai and without provocation had gunned down three hundred and forty-seven civilians, most of them women and children. A photographer had taken pictures of screaming women, dead babies, and a mass of bodies piled up in a ditch. Even once substantiated, the story seemed incredible to many people. How could American soldiers have committed such an atrocity? The congressional subcommittee investigating the incident wrote much later, "What obviously happened at My Lai was wrong. In fact it was so wrong and so foreign to the normal character and actions of our military forces as to immediately raise a question as to the legal sanity at the time of those men involved."[15] But as teams of psychiatrists were later to show, Lieutenant William Calley and the other men involved were at the time quite as "sane" as the members of the congressional committee who investigated them. The incident was not exceptional to the American war.

Young men from the small towns of America, the GIs who came to Vietnam found themselves in a place halfway round the earth among people with whom they could make no human contact. Like an Orwellian army, they knew everything about military tactics, but nothing about where they were or who the enemy was. And they found themselves not attacking fixed positions but walking through the jungle or through villages among small yellow people, as strange and exposed among them as if they were Martians. Their buddies were killed by land mines, sniper fire, and mortar attacks, but the enemy remained invisible, not only in the jungle but among the people of the villages — an almost metaphysical enemy who inflicted upon them heat, boredom, terror, and death, and gave them nothing to show for it — no territory taken, no visible sign of progress except the bodies of small yellow men.[16] And they passed around stories: you couldn't trust anyone in this country, not the laundresses or the prostitutes or the boys of six years old. The enemy would not stand up and fight, but he had agents everywhere, among the villagers, even among the ARVN officers. The Vietnamese soldiers were lazy and the officials corrupt — they were all out to get you one way or another. They were all "gooks," after all. Just look how they lived in the shacks and the filth; they'd steal the watch off your arm.

And the stories of combat were embellished: about how the enemy attacked Alpha Company one night and hundreds of them were killed, but they kept on coming in "human waves," screaming like banshees. It didn't matter how many you killed because they were fanatics who didn't know the value of human life. In boot camp or in the barracks late at night, an experienced sergeant would tell about how the VC killed women and children and tortured their prisoners, cutting off the ears of their victims, or their genitals. And how the ARVN soldiers did the same when their American advisers weren't around.

There was terror in these stories, but also a kind of release, since if the Vietnamese did not act like human beings, then they did not have to be treated as such. All the laws of civilization were suspended. "And when you shot someone you didn't think you were shooting at a human. They were a gook or a Commie and it was okay, 'cause, like, they [the American officers] would tell you they'd do it to you if they had the chance."[17] The expressiveness of the soldiers' language made even more explicit the fact that these stories were largely fantasies — and fantasies of exactly the same sort that the Americans had created about the Indians and Prospero about Caliban. Like the French soldiers before them, GIs mentally stripped the Vietnamese of their humanity in order to deliver themselves of their own guilty desires. The war brought out their latent sadism, as perhaps all wars between races (and particularly guerrilla wars) have brought it out of all armies. The Americans were no different — that was the shock. "You'll look at your enemy and these people that you're sort of a visitor to. You'll look at them as animals and at the same time you're just turning yourself into an animal, too."[18]

The American soldiers were, perhaps, no different from other soldiers; certainly they were no different from other Americans at home. It was just that the Vietnam War had given them an opportunity to carry their fantasies out. And some of them had taken that opportunity. Some, but not all, of the soldiers at My Lai took it; so too did a number of others, including a number of officers. As the experienced war correspondents knew, many soldiers used to carry around in their wallets pictures they had taken of Vietnamese men and women in obscene positions, obscenely wounded. Another all too familiar spectacle was the beating and crude torture of "Viet Cong suspects" by men from combat units on their way in from an operation. But the officers tended to restrain their men when the press was around. In early 1971 a hundred honorably discharged veterans testified in Detroit and then again before the Senate Foreign Relations Committee of the atrocities they had witnessed or participated in since 1965. Some had seen prisoners thrown out of helicopters; one had seen two platoons set fire to a hamlet where they found no enemy troops and then shoot down the escaping women and children with high-caliber machine guns. Several others had seen Americans rape, torture, and mutilate Vietnamese women. At least one of them confirmed previous reports that American Special Forces and intelligence officers practiced sophisticated methods of torture on their prisoners in the interrogation centers.[19] (In this case the officers presumably justified their methods by the importance of the intelligence thus received. The irony was that while most Americans in Vietnam believed that only the ARVN interrogators tortured their prisoners, those ARVN officers who were interested in information rather than in the torture itself used psychological means — isolation, ridicule, and humiliation — as a much more effective way of dealing with Vietnamese prisoners. Had the American officers really been interested in exacting information, they would have figured that out.)

Once investigated, the My Lai report and others that followed led to the courts-martial of five soldiers — among them Lieutenant William Calley. In making a case for the accused, some of the defense attorneys considered the advantage of raising the question of the legitimacy of the war and the responsibility of the higher political and military authorities. The military courts naturally refused to touch such an explosive political issue, but the very fact that the issue had been raised allowed Calley and others to take a moral position that proved sympathetic to thousands of Americans all over the country: Calley had committed no crime, he was just doing his job as a soldier in killing Vietnamese — civilians though they were. The argument did not, of course, take account of the principle of individual responsibility established at the Nuremberg trials of Nazi war criminals, nor did it take account of those thousands of American soldiers who did not see killing civilians as in the line of their duty. Still, there was a certain sense in which it could be said that the responsibility belonged to American policy in Vietnam.

According to the State Department's justification of the war in international law, the American soldiers had been sent to Vietnam to defend the South Vietnamese against an "invasion from the North." In this the State Department had, of course, deceived the soldiers, for when they arrived in Vietnam, the GIs found that they had also to fight the South Vietnamese. This deception did not, however, surprise them, for the administration officials and their superior officers had as much as told them that the legal grounds in international law were no more than a fiction, that they were going to Vietnam not so much to defend territory as to defend the "Free World allies" of the United States against totalitarian Communism. But it was in this purpose that they would feel themselves most bitterly deceived, for upon arriving in Vietnam, they found not a nation of Communists and democrats, but a nation of "gooks." To say that one "gook" was a Communist whereas another was not was to make what seemed to be a purely metaphysical distinction which, if wrongly made, might cost you your life. As Calley said after his trial, "When my troops were getting massacred and mauled by an enemy I couldn't see, I couldn't feel and I couldn't touch — that nobody in the military system ever described them as anything other than Communism. They didn't give it a race, they didn't give it a sex, they didn't give it an age. They never let me believe it was just a philosophy in a man's mind. That was my enemy out there."[20] Thus in the My Lai massacre the soldiers abandoned the unrealistic war aims of Dean Rusk and drew their mistaken but nonetheless understandable conclusion: since all Communists in Vietnam are Vietnamese, and since the only good Communist is a dead one, then all Vietnamese had to be killed.

Of course, the syllogism was faulty, and the defenders of Calley were being disingenuous in describing the cold-blooded murder of babies and old women as necessary to the safety of his troops.[21] The logic would not hold for him. But there were many other cases in which the moral issue was much less clear. When, as happened frequently, a unit received enemy fire from a village, the officer in charge would have the choice of flattening the village with artillery or ordering his troops to go in and search it. If he chose the first alternative, he might discover that the village contained only one or two snipers and a large number of civilians — many of them now dead. If he chose the second, he might find it contained an enemy company, and that he had (unnecessarily?) forfeited the lives of his own men. His dilemma pointed to the more fundamental dilemma of the highly mechanized American armed forces fighting a "people's war" in a foreign country. The basic problem was, of course, that the U.S. official picture of "the Viet Cong" as an army and a coercive administration fighting over an apolitical peasantry was simply a misrepresentation of facts. In many regions — and those where the greatest U.S. military effort was made — the unarmed peasants actively and voluntarily cooperated with the Front troops, giving information, carrying supplies, laying booby traps. Where, then, was the distinction between "soldiers" and "civilians"? In many regions "the Viet Cong" were simply the villagers themselves; to "eliminate the Viet Cong" meant to eliminate the villages, if not the villagers themselves, an entire social structure and a way of life. It is in this context that charges of war crimes against the American civilian and military authorities who directed the war have a certain validity. In the first place, by the very act of sending American soldiers to Vietnam the U.S. command was denying many of its soldiers and field officers the very power of choice over killing civilians. It was making some civilian deaths inevitable. In the second place the U.S. command's decision to use certain weapons and certain strategies insured that the number of civilian deaths would be sizable.

From 1954 to 1968 the entire American effort in Vietnam went through many of the same changes that occurred in the most insecure and domineering of the American advisers. The central aim of the United States in Vietnam had never been to develop the economy and reform the Saigon government, but to "stop Communism" in Southeast Asia. When the military aid together with the attempts at reform and development failed as one means to that end, the United States adopted two additional strategies: the bombing of the north and the commitment of American combat troops. The second strategy the officials had hoped to avoid for the reason that it cost American lives and raised political difficulties at home. The first was much less "expensive." In 1965 they began to prosecute the air war on a large scale and for reasons that were of dubious rationality.

Though enclosed in "tough-minded" analytical terms, such as "graduated escalation" and "limited war," the American bombing of North Vietnam made little military sense. As Clark Clifford pointed out when he came to the Defense Department, it did not constitute a strategy for winning the war or even for gaining the administration's "limited objectives." During the Second World War the Allies had — it was arguable — contributed to the defeat of Nazi Germany by bombing its industrial plant and thus impairing its capacity for war-making. The Americans could not, however, hope to defeat North Vietnam in the same way because that country could continue to obtain munitions from the outside, from noncombatant powers. In August 1967, Robert McNamara himself took pains to show a Senate committee that the bombing had not significantly reduced infiltration or affected North Vietnam's war-making capability. In his opinion it was not the air war that limited the infiltration but "the ability of the Viet Cong and the North Vietnamese, operating, by the way, without, for all practical purposes, a single wheeled vehicle in all of South Vietnam, to accept the men and matériel from the North."[22] In answer to his objections, the U.S. Joint Chiefs had only psychological theories about "punishing" the North Vietnamese and "destroying their morale." But a man does not "punish" an equal; he punishes someone over whom he has some legal or moral superiority. In thinking they might destroy North Vietnamese morale by the bombing, the generals had to assume the North Vietnamese to be psychologically inferior to the British under the German air raids of the Second World War, or indeed to themselves.

The administration's theory proved false. The North Vietnamese refused to acknowledge the legitimacy of American "punishment" and insisted upon being treated as an equal, an enemy. At that point the administration, if it were to pursue its objectives, had very little choice but the strategy of attrition. And because of the very nature of the war, that strategy meant the attrition not only of enemy troops and military supplies but of all Vietnamese. No one in the American government consciously planned a policy of genocide. The American military commanders would have been shocked or angered by such a charge, but in fact their policy had no other military logic, and their course of action was indistinguishable from it. By 1969 South Vietnam had become one of the three most heavily bombed countries in history — the other two being Laos and North Vietnam. South Vietnam was certainly the most heavily bombarded by artillery.

American commanders, of course, liked to interpret their whole military policy as nothing more than an impersonal exercise of their military machine. But as applied in Vietnam, the policy of "harassment and interdiction," the creation of "free fire zones," the use of artillery to replace ground patrolling in populated areas — these and other bombing and artillery practices would have been unthinkable for U.S. commanders in occupied France or Italy during the Second World War. In Europe the Americans rejected the use of chemical warfare, but in Vietnam they used napalm, phosphorus, tear gas, and various kinds of defoliants as a general practice and in such quantities as to render certain parts of the country uninhabitable. The use of a "body count" as an index of progress was also unique to the Vietnam War. Besides all of these unconventional military tactics, and to some extent the guiding forces behind them, was the Westmoreland-Komer strategy for pacification: to remove from the countryside all those people who could not be put under military occupation. The ARVN commanders had no great record of humanitarian concern for civilians, but even they would never by themselves have gone to the lengths of removing entire villages to refugee camps for the sake of eliminating the NLF from a certain piece of real estate. Humanitarian concerns aside, the strategy did not even bring the Americans any closer to winning the war: it merely postponed the losing of it for some time while it strained the resources of South Vietnam beyond its limits. (In the First Corps it even stretched the American resources beyond their limits. In 1967 the AID representatives in the First Corps asked the U.S. military command to stop "generating" refugees because they had neither the food nor the logistical capacity to feed the people already removed from their land. The military command agreed, but rather than stop its bombing raids or its search-and-destroy operations, it merely stopped warning the civilians that their villages would be destroyed. The omission of the warning system was a change the American commanders had wanted to make for some time because they suspected, and with reason, that the enemy units were the first to take notice of the warnings.)[23]

But by the beginning of 1968 it was precisely time that mattered to the American government in its attempt to save itself from something that might look like a defeat. Whether or not Johnson ever had any greater ambitions, it now became clear that the original war aims as explained to the American public no longer held. What had looked like an attempt to "save Vietnam from Communism" was rather an attempt to save American "prestige" around the world. But the time for that had already passed by. The leaders of other nations had already seen what a small and determined group of people could do to the United States and were in the process of drawing their conclusions. The American war effort had, then, become almost entirely solipsistic: the U.S. government was trying

to save "American prestige" for Americans alone, to convince itself
of American superiority.

At the same time, the war was putting the American officials and
politicians who favored the anti-Communist struggle in an increasingly difficult moral position. As the IVS letter to President Johnson
predicted, they had either to withdraw their support from the war
or to look upon its brutality as a necessary and acceptable means to
an end. As few wished to do either, the majority attempted to avoid
the dilemma altogether by taking the refuge of the ostrich. As
Richard Nixon's closest adviser, Dr. Henry Kissinger, pointed out
with some interest, a poll taken in St. Louis at the time of the My
Lai disclosure showed that only 12 percent of those who had heard
the story said they believed it to be true. Such a refusal of belief
was, perhaps, excusable for Americans many thousands of miles
removed from the scene of action, who had learned to discredit
much that they heard about Vietnam; but it was the same stance
taken over similar issues by Americans in Vietnam whose job it was to
know the results of American actions. Asked in 1967 whether the U.S.
bombing of the north did not produce as many civilian casualties as
Viet Cong terrorism in the south, one American spokesman replied:

There is no possible comparison.

We use the most sophisticated electronic measures known to keep from
killing civilians with our bombs. Our gear cross-check and double-check
everything an airplane does up North.

Here in the South, Charlie [the Viet Cong] is out to get any and all he
can, without regard to political affiliation, nationality or anything else.
The point is to prove to the people that Charlie can call his shots without
any regard to the thousands of Government soldiers.

We haven't even take into consideration some little guy's well, or the
pagoda that the residents of an entire village might have put all their
money into, a pagoda that the Viet Cong leveled.

Any figures you get won't take into consideration the tons of groceries
that never got to market, the produce that will rot where the bridge or
foot bridge is blown out, of the plants that will shrivel up and die in the
field because the fruit can't be gotten to market because of the Viet Cong.[24]

What was interesting about the statement was the discrepancy
between the impersonal, bureaucratic language the official used to
describe the American actions and the vivid, almost poetic, description he lavished upon those of the NLF. Douglas Pike similarly
distorted the facts in his widely circulated monograph, "The Viet

Cong Strategy of Terror." In his extended study, *Viet Cong*, published in 1966, Pike went to some length to show that the success of the Viet Cong came not so much from their use of violence and terror (as many Americans assumed) but from their organizational methods. By 1970 he had given the subject a new emphasis. "Terror," he said, "is an essential ingredient of nearly all [the Viet Cong's] programs."[25] And he went ahead to show his own colors:

A frank word is required here about "terror" on the other side, by the Government and Allied forces fighting in Viet-Nam. No one with any experience in Vietnam denies that troops, police and others commanding physical power, have committed excesses that are, by our working definition, acts of terror. . . .

But there is an essential difference in such acts between the two sides, one of outcome or result. To the communist, terror has a utility and is beneficial to his cause, while to the other side the identical act is self-defeating. This is not because one side is made up of heroes and the other of villains. It is because, as noted above, terror is integral in all the communist tactics and programs and communists could not rid themselves of it even if they wanted to. Meanwhile, the other side firmly believes, even though its members do not always behave accordingly, that there is a vested interest in abstaining from such acts.[26]

Interestingly, Pike's "working definition" of terror was the "systematic use of death, pain, fear and anxiety among the population (either civilian or military) for the deliberate purpose of coercing, manipulating, intimidating, punishing or simply frightening the helpless into submission."[27] And by that definition the entire American bombing policy in Vietnam, North and South, was a strategy of terror. Even within the narrower definition of "terror" as an unconventional, clandestine act of violence — an assassination or a satchel-charge bombing — the Allies had been using terror deliberately for a number of years through professionally trained paramilitary units such as the Special Forces and the Provincial Reconnaissance Units. As head of the Psychological Warfare section, Pike knew this as well as anyone in Vietnam. Only he, like many Americans who backed the Vietnam War, ascribed the best of motives to the Americans and their allies, while laying all the evil at the door of the enemy. It was the same kind of bad faith and bad conscience that in 1967 inspired all the American rhetoric about "revolutionary development" and "building democracy" in Vietnam. It was the same kind of rhetoric that inspired the unrestricted use of violence upon the Vietnamese.

14

Guerrillas

MIRANDA: Abhorred slave,
Which any print of goodness wilt not take,
Being capable of all ill! I pitied thee,
Took pains to make thee speak, taught thee each hour
One thing or other: when thou didst not, savage,
Know thine own meaning, but wouldst gabble like
A thing most brutish, I endowed thy purposes
With words that made them known. But thy vile
    race,
Though thou didst learn, had that in't which good
    natures
Could not abide to be with; therefore wast thou
Deservedly confined into this rock, who hadst
Deserved more than a prison.

CALIBAN: You taught me language, and my profit on't
Is, I know how to curse. The red plague rid you
For learning me your language!
                                        William Shakespeare,
                                        The Tempest, act 1, scene 2

And the Vietnamese? Were the GVN officials and politicians, for instance, immune to this rage directed against them and to the destruction of their country by the Americans? Judging by appearances, one would have to say yes, for in 1967 there were no coups, no demonstrations, no protests of any kind against the war or the increasingly difficult economic situation. While the legislators bickered over small matters, General Thieu went about putting together a cabinet with one or two of Ky's protégés, one or two intellectuals, an army officer, and several technicians: a cabinet that, as usual, pleased no one. But it did not seem to matter that year. After the elections, a political calm descended over the cities, such as had not been seen since the days of the Diem regime. The Buddhists, the ironic politicians, and the brash young army officers seemed engrossed in their own petty affairs and unconcerned with the larger issues of war and peace. The American officials seemed finally to have what they had wanted for so long: stability and the acquiescence of the non-Communist groups to working with the Americans. A foreigner, in any case, might have assumed that to be true if he did not know the rhythms of Vietnamese political life, those periods of quiet that, like the damming up of a riverbed and the inevitable rise of the level of the river, led only to catastrophe.

The French in their day preserved this state of quiescence for years. Early in the century Paul Mus, as a boy, was present when a North Vietnamese mandarin came to visit his father, the director of the first French lycée in Hanoi to accept Vietnamese students. Mus and his father knew perfectly well that the mandarin hated the school for giving his son foreign ideas along with the technical instruction, but the mandarin merely bowed, thanked the director for having educated his son so well, and walked stiffly out.

"To show anger is to imitate the conduct of the barbarian," said Confucius. But manners are the expression — often contradictory — of the civilization itself. The mandarin's exquisite irony betrayed a fear of showing anger, a fear that the anger would become uncontrollable and that the interview would end in irreconcilable conflict. Except for the NLF, no Vietnamese political party had decided upon the course of conflict; and thus in moment of crisis the rest did not show their anger against the Americans. And yet the anger was there. It was merely repressed or transferred to some other object. The peasants blamed Fate for their sufferings and abused their children after the passage of an ARVN unit through their village; similarly the Buddhists of Hue took their anger out upon themselves in hunger strikes and self-immolation.

In his observation of the African and Arab peoples on the eve of decolonization, Frantz Fanon had seen much the same phenomena, including the belief in Fate and the symbolic killing of self, which he called "the behavior patterns of avoidance." But he had also seen other patterns that seemed equally well to fit the Vietnamese of the GVN: the sudden crime waves that spread through the cities, the tribal warfare, and the fierce, irrational feuding of the native sects. As he explained them,

Tribal feuds only serve to perpetuate old grudges deep buried in the memory. By throwing himself with all his force into the *vendetta*, the native tries to persuade himself that colonialism does not exist, that everything is going on as before, that history continues. . . . It is as if plunging into a fraternal blood-bath allowed them to ignore the obstacle, and to put off till later the choice, nevertheless inevitable, which opens up the question of armed resistance to colonialism.[1]

For years American officials had urged the Vietnamese politicians to stop their feuding and to unite against the Viet Cong — but to no avail. The same fierce internal quarrels had been going on since the 1930's, claiming all the energies of every political group except the Viet Minh and the NLF. From this distance in history it is not to strain the limits of belief to accept Fanon's explanation of them: the Vietnamese of the cities were by their feuds expressing their anger against France and the United States, their hatred of their own dependence. The vast American presence merely tore those feuding groups into smaller and smaller pieces, and the calm of 1967 was a result of that diminution of scale. The feuds were now only the innumerable conflicts of splinter groups and individuals.

The political infighting was one form of displaced aggression; the egregious profiteering was perhaps another, more direct one. The primary motives of the GVN officials were, of course, need or greed for money and security in an uncertain world. But the corruption was so often exaggerated, the stealing so far in excess of the needs of the officials and so clearly harmful to the purposes of the United States and the GVN that it was difficult to believe there was not a double motive at work. While the Vietnamese sometimes liked to think of the Americans as being too rich and powerful to be vulnerable to them, they also liked to think of Americans as large dumb creatures continually outwitted by the small, clever Vietnamese. When the tough little slum kids stole from the American soldiers, they knew very well that they were hurting them; in the same way the district chief must have known — though perhaps obscurely — that to steal the food supplies of the PF soldiers and to cause desertions was to endanger the local American troops and to hurt the entire war effort. To believe that he and his colleagues did not understand that is to believe they were something less than human.

And then there were other forms of sabotage that could even less easily be accounted for by self-interest: the shirking of responsibility, for example. And the slowness. For an American in South Vietnam the simplest of chores often turned into endless and painful ordeals. To register a car, to move a truckload of goods from one place to another, often required weeks, if not months, of concentrated attention — of negotiation, of explanation, of filling out of forms, of argument in which the non sequiturs seemed to have very little to do with the language barrier. An American in Saigon could not help thinking bitterly of Kipling's epitaph for the colonial civil servant, "A Fool lies here who tried to hustle the East." Like Kipling, many Americans, particularly the "old Asia hands," believed that slowness, lethargy, and corruption were native to the Vietnamese, and that they, as Europeans, were simply beating themselves to death against the torpid masses of Asia. But had they ever witnessed an NLF operation or watched the GVN officials smuggling American goods out of the port, they would have had to change their minds. And perhaps they would have found Kipling's explanation less plausible than that of Frantz Fanon: the slowness of the native is not natural to him, but merely a manifestation of his resistance to his colonial master — a resistance that he often does not dare to admit to himself.

That the GVN officials shared this resistance with the Viet Cong was not at all surprising, for, metaphorically speaking, every Vietnamese is brought up to be a guerrilla. Taught to observe the dictates of filial piety, the Vietnamese child learns to hide his aggressiveness and the demands of his ego behind an impenetrable mask of humility and obedience. As the guerrilla feeds off the land without owning it, so the child, without right to property or person, feeds off his family until his father dies. Unable to leave his family, unable to give open challenge to his superiors, he carries on an endless underground battle for survival that is well described by General Giap's famous dictum: "When the enemy attacks, retreat, when he retreats, harass him . . ." Not only the Viet Minh and the NLF, but all Vietnamese political parties have been underground parties with subversive intentions. Given this tradition of self-protection and concealed hostility between inferior and superior, it would be difficult to imagine how the GVN officials could avoid resenting the Americans, who, after all, were *not* their leaders. By their slowness, their profiteering, and their intractability, they were carrying on their own guerrilla war against the Americans.

But though there is only one kind of child — the child that grows up to take his father's place — there are two kinds of guerrillas. One kind expects to grow in strength until his movement becomes the majority and the government of the country. (To a Marxist who believes in the historical dialectic, this process is as natural and inevitable as the child's replacement of his father.) The second kind will never give an open challenge to the government, and expects to retain his status of guerrilla forever, feeding off the land without taking responsibility for its government. As the country *par excellence* of the guerrilla, Vietnam had a long tradition of both. But since the French occupation, only two groups have fit into the first category — the Viet Minh and the NLF. Dependent on the foreigners for their very existence, the other nationalist parties remained unable to assert their autonomy, feeding on the French and then the Americans while at the same time trying to sabotage their interests.

An American reporter, experienced in Vietnam, once said to me, "I finally realized we'd never win this war when I noticed that all of the streets in Saigon were named after Vietnamese heroes who fought against foreign invaders."

The street names were in a sense the perfect metaphor for the resistance of Saigon. Though written in Roman letters and used every day by Americans, they were perfectly incomprehensible to those who did not know a great deal about Vietnamese history. The xenophobia of Saigon was hidden in plain sight. And yet the street names also deceived the Vietnamese — they were both deception and self-deception — for Saigon could never make good on its claim to the tradition of Le Loi, Tran Hung Dao, and Phan Dinh Phung, or of the street called Tu Do (Independence). Like Generals Thieu and Ky, the Saigonese fought the foreigners only from within their own service — a war they never hoped to win.

The Americans did not understand this war of the city people against the foreigners. But for them it was in a sense more destructive than the war fought by the enemy. While the Communists were attempting by relatively straightforward means to get the Americans out of the country, the Saigon government was attempting (and succeeding in the attempt) to draw the Americans further and further into Vietnam. The strategy of the generals was something like that of General Kutuzov when he retreated across the plains of Russia before Napoleon's armies. It was a scorched earth policy with the difference that the Saigon generals never expected to retake the land they had lost. Their harassment would be constant, their retreat never-ending; they would leave behind them a wasteland whose people would be killed or prostituted by the foreigners.

The toll that their forces had already taken on the Americans and on the civilian population gave certain plausibility to the rumor among southerners that Premier Ky was the agent of Hanoi. And yet even that notion was too farfetched, for if the North Vietnamese were planning to take over the south, they would not have wished such devastation upon their future inheritance. Dependent upon the Americans, the GVN was, like a parasite attacking its host, engaged in a pure act of self-destruction. The corruption, the endless factional disputes, the civil war of 1966, the bombing and terrorization of the peasantry — all of them were acts of violence against the very population that might have sustained it. They were suicidal acts by a government that had not even the power to kill itself.

But the violence was only one side of this urge to self-destruction. On the other side there was a strange passivity, an inertia that was the image of social death. The Buddhists had been the first of the urban groups to fall into this state. After the 1966 invasion of Hue and Da Nang, they had abandoned three years of intense political activity for cynical, apathetic silence. Now unreservedly anti-American, Tri Quang waited in the An Quang pagoda in Saigon, making no further effort to organize or to mount demonstrations. (The junta, however, liked him none the better for it. During the Tet offensive the GVN troops leveled the An Quang pagoda, where the NLF had set up a post, killing a score of bonzes. Tri Quang was lucky to escape with his life.) The American mission was pleased by the lack of Buddhist "disturbances," but the silence of the bonzes was only a signal of what was to follow for the rest of the urban population. As Nguyen Van Trung wrote:

Truly it is difficult to make a clear-cut decision in favor of either one of the two formal positions of today. . . .

If the Southern Liberation Front truly was merely resisting "American imperialist aggression," then why up until now has it not yet been able to stimulate . . . an ardent uprising among all the people as in the 1945 period against the French colonialists? If a policy of opposing Communism has truly only been called into existence because of the aggression of the northern Communists, why has it not been able to stimulate a positive attitude of self-defense, why do we have indifference, desertions from the army, collaboration, escapes to the enemy army?

Trung then went on almost to paraphrase the letter written by the Buddhist student after the invasion of Da Nang:

We cannot make a clear-cut choice, but we have not yet found another way out. We are being closed in, our situation is like being in a bag. The problem is how to enable all of us to avoid the plight of having to choose.[2]

A paralysis had descended over the urban Vietnamese. In Saigon there were in 1967 some four hundred places — not establishments but simple rooms — where the students went to smoke opium. Opium had never been a habit even for the rich, but between 1967 and 1970 those rooms multiplied until there were some three thousand of them.[3] An American journalist visiting Hue just after the Tet offensive was shocked to find the students sitting back and cracking jokes about the corruption of the Thieu government. Even after their city had been ruined they refused to take sides. The journalist could not get over it, but then he could not imagine their situation. For them to join the NLF meant to leave the Westernized Vietnam they had been brought up in, to enter a strange and possibly hostile world; while to join the GVN meant to join a mercenary army that was likely to have no future after the Americans left. The idea that they might change the GVN (no doubt what the journalist had in mind) was to them absurd. As one Vietnamese intellectual said, "The young people feel impotent before the corruption; they don't know what to attach themselves to, and that's why their revolt leads to suicide. They don't have the means of confronting the situation and finding the responsible parties. They find themselves lost."[4] In this case their Confucian attitudes agreed perfectly with Marxist logic: the GVN could not be changed by attempts at gradual reform, but only by a change in the whole state of society. Without that change they saw only suicide in all directions.

The government and "opposition" spokesmen called endlessly for movements of "national unity," but it was becoming more and more plain that even they did not believe in it as a possibility. The American military successes had divided the Vietnamese even more thoroughly than the ARVN defeats. They had given them the sense that though they might survive as individuals, their society would not: it had changed beyond recognition. In 1967 Thieu's first premier, Nguyen Van Loc, told a meeting of the new national congress: "The scale of values of our society has led to an erosion of our society with the psychological result that everyone has become discontented and cynical." The premier was referring not only to the intellectuals and the students, but to most of the political "moderates" — the Cochin Chinese bourgeoisie, the Catholics, and many of the deputies and the ARVN officers. And the psychological result was something more than cynicism — it was despair. "People today," wrote Nguyen Van Trung,

> have become abstract people rather than concrete people. Every man among us can no longer be regarded as he himself wants to think of himself, but instead as "that person" or, even more, as an "imaginary enemy," against whom one must defend oneself. And so we divide ourselves up into categories, and claw each other, because we have labelled each other imaginary enemies. And finally, these errors and ugly deeds always arise because of others, while we ourselves are without sin.[5]

Brought up within a society whose very language implies that man is a function of the people around him, the Vietnamese experienced the division of their society as the alienation of will from action. As one official American report on "Vietnamese attitudes" noted, "The hope for peace, when expressed, often reflected a dim conception of external forces beyond one's control. . . . Thus from Binh Thuan in the Second Corps area it was reported that the people believed the Americans will send more troops to Vietnam next year to end the war sooner and help the campaign of President Johnson for re-election to the Presidency."[6]

But the war actually was out of the control of the Vietnamese. The Vietnamese of the GVN had no choice. At the same time (and this was the meaning of what they told the U.S. official), they had no commitment to the future that was being decided for them. As they saw it, the only course of action that lay open to them was a refusal of choice, a passive resistance to all demands made upon them. According to the same official report, when a new mobilization law went before the congress, one legislator insisted that the law was merely an attempt to calm American public opinion. Another asked, "Why should our young men be drafted to serve U.S. interests?" In the provinces a rumor circulated that the Americans had forced the Thieu government to accept the new law in order better to carry out their real intentions of killing as many Vietnamese as possible; another rumor was that the Americans were attempting to prolong the war in order to maintain a market for their surplus production. The second rumor was an answer to what for many Vietnamese was the most puzzling question of all: why, with all its great power, had the United States not won the war already?

"To counter this with the argument that it's a Vietnamese war," the American report continued, "falls on deaf ears, as many of these people feel it's now a war between the US and the Communists."[7]

It was into this atmosphere of American overconfidence, Vietnamese apathy and despair, that the NLF launched the Tet offensive of 1968.

15

The Tet Offensive

We begin '68 in a better position than we have ever been before, but we've still got problems of bureaucratic inefficiency. There are still leadership difficulties that will degrade performance. There is a requirement for tackling corruption in the countryside. We've got to cut down more on the RD team attrition. There's a crying need for better province and district chiefs, which the GVN itself has recognized.

Robert Komer
(Press Conference, Saigon,
January 24, 1968)

At three o'clock in the morning on the first night of the Vietnamese New Year, nineteen NLF commandos blasted their way through the outer walls of the American embassy in Saigon. They entered the compound, killed two of the U.S. military police on duty, and attacked the heavy doors of the embassy with antitank rockets. Failing to break down the doors, they took cover in the compound, pinning down the "reaction force" of six Marine guards, and held off a helicopter assault by U.S. paratroopers until daylight. Not until nine in the morning did the U.S. troops regain control of the embassy. By the time embassy officials came to work, all nineteen of the young commandos lay dead, their bodies twisted over the ornamental shrubbery and their blood pooling in the white gravel rocks of the embassy garden. The battle for the cities had begun.

In the early morning of January 31, NLF troops attacked almost every important American base, every town and city of South Vietnam. The combined force of eighty-four thousand men simultaneously moved in to five out of the six cities, thirty-six out of the forty provincial capitals, and sixty-four district capitals. During the same night of the raid on the embassy, elements of eleven NLF battalions entered Saigon. One unit penetrated the grounds of the presidential palace, four blocks to the south; another took over the government radio station and a third assaulted the Tan Son Nhut air base, breaking through the heavily guarded perimeter to blow up aircraft and engage in gun battles with the American troops. In the Delta, Front forces moved into the most "secure" of the province capitals — Can Tho, My Tho, Vinh Long, Rach Gia, and Ben Tre — entrenched themselves in the poorer quarters, and drove the ARVN units to the defense of their headquarters. In the Second Corps area the NLF attacked the very center of Allied operations in Nha Trang, Qui Nhon, and Tuy Hoa and the great American base at Cam Ranh bay. Dalat, the resort town for Vietnamese generals and the site of the ARVN military academy, came under attack by six NLF battalions. But it was in the First Corps, where North Vietnamese troops joined the battle, that the offensive was by far the fiercest. From a hamlet outside of Da Nang the Front troops lobbed rocket and mortar shells into the American air base, closing down the field from which most of the tactical air strikes were run. Simultaneously, other units moved in on the American bases at Chu Lai and Phu Bai as well as the Korean headquarters down the coast, destroying scores of American airplanes and forcing the American troops to defend their positions while they overran all five of the provincial capitals. In Quang Ngai city and elsewhere they opened the jails and released thousands of prisoners. In Hue battalions of local NLF troops supported by North Vietnamese regulars overcame the ARVN defense forces and marched straight into the center of the city, occupying the university, the provincial headquarters, the central marketplace, and the imperial citadel.

The offensive came as an almost total surprise to the Allied military command. Nearly half of the ARVN soldiers in the country had left their units for the New Year holiday. Few American troops were stationed in and around the cities, for General Westmoreland had a long-standing policy of leaving the ARVN troops to stand guard over the cities and the heavily populated districts. Lieutenant General Frederick C. Weyand, the commander of American forces in the Third Corps, had put all his troops on maximum alert the night before the attack, but still there were only three hundred American troops ready for immediate action in Saigon.[1] The timing of the Allied response therefore varied throughout the countryside. In certain places the large American units repulsed the attacks on their bases sufficiently quickly to aid the beleaguered ARVN units within one or two days. In other places, where the attacks were heavier, it took two or three days to open the airfields and mobilize the scattered troops.

The battle for Saigon claimed the first attentions of the Allied command. Forced to fight on their own terrain, the American and GVN commanders committed tanks, helicopter gunships, and bombers to the counteroffensive. By the end of that day they had burned the radio station to the ground, and bombed into ruins the model cotton mill outside the city and the single low-income housing project ever built by the municipality. But the NLF were not so easily dislodged. Holing up in Cholon and around the Phu Tho racetrack, they held out for two weeks, alternately disappearing and reappearing to direct sniper fire against the ARVN troops. The city was in chaos. Those American soldiers and civilians who lived outside the barracks and the center of town were forced to hide in their houses and defend themselves with small arms. A half-mile from the American embassy many of them witnessed NLF political cadres going from house to house declaring the complete victory of the Liberation and holding street "trials" for their prisoners. There were fire fights in the market squares between ARVN soldiers and NLF troops wearing ARVN uniforms. Tank units thundered through the city, demolishing whole buildings in their advance. Fires spread, and whole districts of thatched huts and jerry-built houses burned to the ground, leaving thousands without food or shelter. Crowds of civilians, panicked by the troops and bombers, flooded through the streets carrying their dead and wounded with them on bicycles or pedicabs.

Elsewhere the battle was equally intense. In Dalat, for instance, the NLF battalions entrenched themselves in the central marketplace and held out for weeks against a disorderly counteroffensive. In My Tho and Ben Tre, the ARVN battalions, caught off guard, barricaded themselves into their compounds, leaving the NLF to set up positions in the streets and fly their flags over the poorer quarters. Heavy fighting continued for some time in Kontum City and Ban Me Thuot. The vast montagnard refugee camps established by the GVN on their outskirts came under attack from both sides, and thousands of montagnards fled back into the jungles. In Hue, where the aftermath of the Buddhist crisis had permanently alienated large sections of the populace from the GVN, the ARVN disintegrated, allowing the NLF to take full control of the central city.

The shock of the Tet offensive carried through the United States as well as Vietnam. Over the past year Westmoreland, Bunker, and Komer had given the impression that the enemy threat had receded, that the American troops had pushed the main force units out of the populated areas into the jungles of the border. Now there were pictures of the mission coordinator, George Jacobson, leaning out of the chancellery window with a pistol, and televised reports of fighting in the center of Saigon. It was incomprehensible. The Americans had seemed so firmly in control — and yet they had allowed the enemy to launch a coordinated counteroffensive with eighty-four thousand men against all the cities and towns from the base of the Ca Mau peninsula to the DMZ. The fact that the American command had been unprepared for such a gross movement raised doubts about the quality of American intelligence and wisdom of American military strategy over the past two years.

In his official report on the war published a year later, General Westmoreland claimed that he had anticipated a major enemy offensive against the populated areas around the time of Tet, and that he had prepared for it by modifying his offensive plans and moving several units up to the area of the DMZ. Actually, Westmoreland had not taken the previous intelligence reports that seriously. General Weyand and certain civilians at the mission, who were more closely in touch with the situation, had pressured him to cancel some of his offensive operations in the border areas and bring some of his troops back into the area of Saigon. They had not, however, made him change his plans for deployment in the northern provinces, and particularly in the area of Hue.

In mid-January a North Vietnamese division had begun to maneuver around the American base at Dak To in the far reaches of the central highlands. Westmoreland reinforced the post and drove back the enemy units. At the same time a number of North Vietnamese divisions crossed the DMZ and surrounded the U.S. Marine outpost at Khe Sanh. Westmoreland was certain that the enemy wanted to overrun the base and create another Dien Bien Phu.[2] At that point he (like General Navarre before him) had the choice of extricating the Marines or of reinforcing them while bad weather made bombing support and resupply by air problematical. He chose the latter course, just as he had chosen it at all the other large-scale border engagements in late 1967. By mid-January he had lifted six thousand Marines onto the barren plateau of Khe Sanh and moved several other brigades north of Hue for a total of forty thousand supporting troops. The North Vietnamese did not move. Though they far outnumbered the Marines at the base, they simply waited, transforming the siege into a war of nerves that quite preoccupied the American command as well as much of the American press. It preoccupied the U.S. military to the extent that a week after the Tet offensive had begun, Brigadier General Robert N. Ginsburgh, attached to the Joint Chiefs of Staff, was still talking of the enemy's intentions to make Khe Sanh "another Dien Bien Phu."[3] What the American command had somehow neglected was the possibility that during the weeks of the siege other North Vietnamese and NLF units might simply walk around the blockade of American troops and into Hue itself. This they did, capturing a defenseless city. The American inattention to this move was all the more surprising since just four months earlier, by Westmoreland's account, General Giap had announced that the Liberation Forces would draw the American forces out to the border areas and then attack the population centers. He would, in other words, reverse the strategy he had used against the French. By his own account, Westmoreland had simply not believed that the enemy would undertake such a venture in the face of overwhelming American and GVN force. He thought that he had enough troops to stop an enemy offensive in both the border regions and the populated areas. And he was correct — that is, if the Tet offensive could be considered as a purely military engagement between two opposing armies.[4]

Once they collected themselves, the U.S. and the ARVN forces responded to the attack with the fury of a blinded giant. Forced to fight in the cities, they bombed, shelled, and strafed the most populous districts as if they saw no distinction between them and the jungle. By the fourth day of the battle, Allied planes had flattened large sections of Cholon and Gia Dinh, the extensions of Saigon. Even harder hit were those cities where the ARVN forces had not reacted at all. In the course of a week, American troops and planes bombed out parts of Kontum City, Can Tho, and Vinh Long, and reduced to rubble a third of My Tho, that rich Delta capital, and a half of Ben Tre. Hue suffered the worst of all. There the ARVN troops made so small an advance against the enemy that the North Vietnamese were able to reinforce the original assault battalions. After a few days, Westmoreland committed U.S. Marine units to fight a bloody house-to-house battle for the left bank of the

Perfume River, where the university, the government office buildings, and the American consulate stood. As the North Vietnamese
retreated slowly across the river and set up positions inside the
heavy walls of the imperial citadel, he brought the troop strength
up to three U.S. Marine Corps and eleven Vietnamese battalions.[5]
The American air force struck the poor quarters of the city. The
GVN was left to bomb and shell the palace that was the last archi-
tectural monument of precolonial Vietnam. Still, it took a month to
drive the enemy troops out of the citadel, and by that time the city
lay in ruins.

Surveying the corpses and shattered buildings of Ben Tre, one
American officer told an AP reporter, "We had to destroy it in order
to save it." His explanation was the only one the Americans could
give for the damage they had wrought. The NLF had taken many
civilian lives in attacking the cities, but the Americans alone had the
firepower to destroy the sanctuaries they had created. By the end of
three weeks the Allied command estimated the toll of civilian dead
at around 165,000, and the number of new refugees at two million.
Five hundred Americans died in the battles. But that was not the
end of it, for the damage to Hue had not yet been calculated, and
the fighting continued in many other regions of the countryside.

On retreating from the cities, the NLF entered the rings of
formerly "secure" hamlets around their circumferences and stayed
there to lob mortar shells back at the GVN and American bases.
Instead of sending soldiers to drive the scattered Front troops out of
the hamlets, the Americans stood back and bombed the villages of
their own Vietnamese "allies." As one American official in Binh Dinh
province argued, "What the Viet Cong did was occupy the hamlets
we pacified just for the purpose of having the allies move in and
bomb them out. By their presence the hamlets were destroyed."[6]
Whether or not the NLF had predicted the American response, the
American official certainly could not imagine an alternate strategy.
The destruction of those places occupied by the NLF — whether
jungle, paddy, or village — had become standard operating procedure for the U.S. forces in Vietnam. The destruction of the
Vietnamese cities and towns during the Tet offensive was merely a
logical extension of that procedure.

The Tet offensive had an electric effect on popular opinion in the
United States. The banner headlines and the television reports of
fighting in the cities brought the shock of reality to what was still

for many Americans a distant and incomprehensible war. The pictures of corpses in the garden of the American embassy cut through the haze of argument and counterargument, giving flat contradiction to the official optimism about the slow but steady progress of the war. Those who had long held doubts and reservations now felt their doubts confirmed. For the first time the major news magazines, *Time, Life,* and *Newsweek,* began to criticize the war policy overtly; television commentators such as Walter Cronkite, who had always backed the administration, now questioned whether or not the war could be won. In spite of the President's attempts to reassure the public and to reduce the offensive to the dimensions of an incident, the opinion polls showed that public confidence in the President's handling of the war had dropped to a new low of 35 percent. Even the most "hawkish" of the congressmen registered this disenchantment, as did the President's close advisers, particularly Dean Acheson, McGeorge Bundy, and the new Secretary of Defense, Clark Clifford. In Chicago Robert F. Kennedy made a major speech on the war, saying quite bluntly that the United States was not winning it and should no longer attempt to do so. "Our enemy," he said, ". . . has finally shattered the mask of official illusion with which we have concealed our true circumstances, even from ourselves. . . . [They] have demonstrated that no part or person of South Vietnam is secure from their attacks."[7] In New Hampshire Senator Eugene McCarthy's student-run campaign for the presidential nomination took on a sudden life, speeding up the train of events that was to lead a month later to Johnson's decision to curb the bombing of North Vietnam and to withdraw his candidacy for the 1968 election.

The curious aspect of the American public reaction to the Tet offensive was that it reflected neither the judgment of the American officials in Saigon nor the true change in the military situation in South Vietnam. "The whole campaign was a go-for-broke proposition," declared General Westmoreland shortly after the initial assault;[8] later he would conclude that the offensive was a major defeat for the enemy. In backing up this judgment U.S. officials pointed out that the Viet Cong never took control of any city but Hue. The General Uprising promised by the Viet Cong cadres did not occur, and in most places the enemy could not sustain momentum after the initial onslaught. In a sense the enemy had delivered himself into the hands of the Allied troops. During the first week of the fighting the U.S. and GVN forces killed an estimated fifteen thousand enemy soldiers. The statistics were to increase as the weeks went by and to multiply once again during the May-June offensive — a renewed attack upon Saigon and other GVN strongpoints throughout the country. As the succeeding year was to show, the Tet offensive seriously depleted the NLF main force units and wiped out a sizable proportion of its most experienced cadres, driving the southern movement for the first time into almost total dependency on the north. By all the indices available to the American military, the Tet offensive was a major defeat for the enemy.

Victory or defeat — the very question seemed senseless in Saigon. To the Vietnamese of the cities the Tet offensive brought neither hope nor militance against the war, but merely a reinforcement of all the old attitudes. It came as a shock but not as a surprise. It was the Armageddon so long awaited, that confirmed to them their own ruin and their own helplessness before the blind forces of Fate. American officials told the press that the attack would bring a new unity and a new determination to the GVN. The GVN officials for their part debated whether or not the Americans had planned the offensive with malice aforethought or whether they had simply allowed it to happen in an attempt to frighten them into action. (Their suspicions were to some extent prompted by the claims of the American generals that they had expected an attack around that date.)[9] The people of the cities did not rise up to help the Front during Tet, as many NLF cadres had expected, but they did not rise up to support the government either, even though most assumed that the Americans would eventually drive the Front troops out. The scope and timing of the NLF attacks showed not only that the GVN was riddled with NLF agents, but that the people within the "secure" areas had no real interest in supporting the government. The NLF and the North Vietnamese, after all, spent months putting together an operation involving an immense logistical effort in all regions of the country. They clandestinely introduced five battalions into Saigon alone. During the previous week their soldiers simply walked or rode on Hondas down the main roads into the city which were patrolled by at least three ARVN divisions as well as local security guards. They imported their weapons by the same routes in flower trucks and coffins. And not one citizen informed. The people of the cities had themselves opened the invasion route and passively awaited their destruction.

The physical damage was, of course, immense — more than a small country could possibly deal with on its own. The rebuilding would have taken months under the best of circumstances, but the Saigon government seemed to have fallen apart as completely as its architecture. As usual, those towns furthest from the source of American supplies suffered the most severely. Three weeks after the offensive, officials in the Delta capital of Can Tho had not so much as assessed the damage to the smaller capitals. Even in that city they had not begun to build shelters for the refugees because the money from Saigon had not arrived, and the merchants refused to extend credit to the government.[10] Six weeks after the offensive the GVN had not provided a single brick or bag of cement for the people of Ben Tre. The high-school students and local Cao Dai officials pitched in to repair some of the buildings, but the government officials were nowhere in evidence. "In six weeks here," said one American official, "we have seen that the Government cannot protect the people, or control them, or administer them or help them recover."[11] President Thieu was initially more concerned about the possibility of a coup, and later about explaining the disaster. About half of the ARVN forces in the Saigon area were on leave during the offensive, and no one knew how many of them later returned to their duties. Reportedly, all units were under strength, and only half of the Revolutionary Development teams returned to their posts in the Delta. The American command seriously contemplated taking the South Vietnamese "out of the business of pacification."[12] "One way or another," wrote the columnist Flora Lewis, "Americans here talk about the war with passion and bitterness. Few Vietnamese do. They speak with the dull tones of hopelessness, of tragedy beyond response or, anyway, beyond any response but the dogged effort to stay alive."[13]

Hue was a particular nightmare. At the beginning of March the U.S. troops were still bombing and shelling the outlying villages, while the people of the city searched for the bodies of their relatives in the ruins. Some ten thousand soldiers and civilians died in the battle; whole quarters were leveled by North Vietnamese rockets and by five-hundred-pound to seven-hundred-pound American bombs. The streets stank of decomposing corpses.[14] As soon as the fighting began, all of the Vietnamese doctors moved into the university refugee center, appropriated rice and medical supplies, and refused to come out of their rooms to treat the hundreds of patients

streaming in from the embattled portions of the city. When the
American troops appeared, some of them attempted to flee, leaving
scores of patients behind them dying of gangrene. As one American
doctor said, "Their whole little world was torn down and they just
withdrew. Instead of giving when they were most needed, they gave
up. They totally insulated themselves. Astonishing."[15]

As for the GVN itself, it had ceased to exist in Hue. The province
chief, the same Colonel Pham Van Khoa who had moved his troops
out of the city during the Buddhist crisis, spent the first six days of
the Tet offensive hiding in the rafters of the hospital and the rest of
the time organizing his friends to steal the emergency shipments of
rice sent in to avert starvation in the refugee camps. Charged with
having been informed of the offensive two days in advance by the
NLF, he said, in his defense, that he had allowed the Communists to
come into the city so that they would be trapped there.[16] Led by
his example, the ARVN soldiers defending the city (one thousand of
whom had gone on leave for Tet) found their way to the refugee
center and stayed there for three weeks behind the U.S. Marines,
making no effort to regroup. "A full colonel walked out of there,"
one American reported. "He hadn't done a damn thing but hide for
three weeks."[17] When the fighting stopped, the same soldiers went
about brazenly and systematically looting every house that still
stood; not for seventeen days did Colonel Khoa issue orders that all
looters would be shot. "By then," said an American official, "everything had already been stolen, sometimes twice."[18] As for the civilian officials, most of those that survived the enemy onslaught and
remained in Hue concentrated their energies on cornering what
they could of the relief supplies and complaining to the Americans.
Frank Kelly, one of the most experienced Americans in Vietnam,
told Robert Shaplen, "I walked through the refugee centers and was
accosted by colonels out of uniform, high-society ladies, university
professors and others who begged me to help them escape. No one
ever really smiled at the United States here before, but I haven't
met anyone who is mad at the Communists and what they did."[19]
To many Americans in the field, the Tet offensive appeared to
complete the demoralization of the Saigon government and its
supporters.

The same was by no means true for the high American officials in
Saigon. Throughout the weeks of fighting and desperation in the
cities Ambassador Bunker and General Westmoreland maintained

their seamless façade of optimism, never once expressing regret for the damages the Americans had wrought or fear for the political consequences. In a CBS interview Ambassador Bunker said that the South Vietnamese armed forces had "demonstrated their ability" in fighting the Communists and "gained confidence in themselves." And he added, "I think the people have gained confidence in them. There is an indication, I think, that the government has probably a wider support today than it had before the Tet offensive. The fact that the government has handled this situation, has moved in quickly to restore the damage, to take recovery measures has demonstrated to the people that the government is capable of acting."[20] He was never to change his opinion; no more was General Westmoreland, who some months later wrote in his report on the war, "The *Tet* offensive had the effect of a 'Pearl Harbor'; the South Vietnamese government was intact and stronger; the armed forces were larger, more effective, and more confident; the people had rejected the idea of a general uprising; and enemy forces, particularly those of the Viet Cong, were much weaker."[21]

Westmoreland was in some sense correct. The ARVN was not routed; the GVN did not fall, and as a year would show, the Tet offensive had weakened the Front and forced the GVN to recruit the troops necessary to support the American operations and occupy much greater areas of the countryside. Only the real question remained, and that was whether these changes made any fundamental difference to the war. What Westmoreland and Bunker could not see, could not appreciate, was that the Tet offensive had simultaneously revealed and answered this question for much of the American people.

On March 10, just two weeks after the U.S. Marines had driven the last North Vietnamese units from Hue, a story was leaked to the press that General Westmoreland had asked for 206,000 more American troops to be sent to Vietnam. The press and the public naturally assumed that the request was made out of desperation about the American military position in Vietnam. But such was not the case at all. Westmoreland really meant what he said. He wanted additional troops to cut the Ho Chi Minh trail, to invade the enemy sanctuaries in Cambodia, and to carry out an "Inchon-type" landing in North Vietnam, encircling the enemy troops at the DMZ. It was the strategy he had been recommending all along; the Tet offensive, he imagined, would make his strategy suddenly acceptable in Washington. His lack of political perspicacity in this matter was matched only by that of General Earle Wheeler and the Joint Chiefs of Staff. Concerned not so much for Vietnam as for the depletion of American strategic reserve forces around the world, Wheeler visited Westmoreland in Saigon and made an agreement to give him 100,000 of the 206,000 troops he would request. Wheeler, who knew perfectly well that Johnson would not accept Westmoreland's plan, reversed the whole tenor of Westmoreland's report to him and asked the President for the troops on the grounds that the United States needed them to recover from the heavy blow of the Tet offensive. The new commitment would, however, have forced Johnson to call out the inactive reserves, and that was the last thing the President wished to do after the domestic political debacle of Tet. Appointing a task force to review the request, Johnson handed over the responsibility to Clark Clifford, who, though formerly one of the most hawkish of Johnson's advisers, ended up recommending not only that the request be denied, but that an attempt be made to open negotiations with a bombing halt.[22]

Johnson's decision did not reflect a "failure of nerve" among the American people, as certain U.S. officers would later claim. It reflected the American judgment on the administration's original war aims. And that judgment was much the same as the one the French had made on their own war aims in Vietnam some fifteen years previously. "The French people," wrote Michel Debré at the end of 1953, "feel that the war is out of their control and in the hands of destiny. . . . They have the impression that France does not know what she wants and that we are fighting aimlessly without a clear objective. What is painful is not so much the fact of fighting and accepting the sacrifices, it is that we are apparently fighting without any goal."[23] Only those responsible for the conduct of the war in Vietnam — those who had witnessed the devastation of the cities, the bodies piled on the streets and the crowds of refugees — did not appear to reflect upon these larger questions.

Returning to Saigon in the fall of 1968, the *Washington Post* correspondent, Ward Just, found the American officials in much the same frame of mind that they had been in the year before: self-confident and generally satisfied with the progress being made. The pacification program was going forward, the war was being won. "It is so remote," he reported,

One had forgotten how thoroughly caught up one had been, how thoroughly a part of the war's odd, mad logic. So when you asked about the effect here of the Tet offensive, you were not prepared for the bizarre analysis. The feeling is almost universal that the attacks were a good thing, almost beneficial, because they made clear to both the Vietnamese and the Americans in the cities that the war was real; the Saigonese could no longer fiddle while Rome burned. The analysis offered by most Americans in Saigon was turned on its head, topsy-turvy: the effect of Tet was something of a psychological triumph for the reason that it woke up the Americans and badly frightened the Vietnamese and their fragile government.

"We had people here after Tet who actually volunteered to go into the ARVN," said one official. "And if that isn't progress, I don't know what is."

Baffled, one tried to explain that if a single moment could be marked as a turning point in the support of the war in America it was the moment that the Vietcong occupied the American Embassy, and later the pictures in *Life* magazine of George Jacobson leaning out of his bedroom window with an automatic pistol in his hand. *The Communists have occupied the Embassy!* Well, that may be the way it looks to you in Washington, they say here, but it is not the reality in South Vietnam.[24]

To many American officials in Saigon, Tet was not an end but a beginning.

Conclusion

III

16

Nixon's War

The war must stop being a French war supported by Vietnam
and become a Vietnamese war supported by France.
Paul Reynaud,
vice-premier of France, 1953

By the fall of 1968 much of the American public felt that the issue
of the war had been settled. With the withdrawal of President
Johnson from the presidential election the American peace movement had, as one analyst said, come as close to overthrowing the
government as can happen within the American system. During the
primary campaigns of Eugene McCarthy and Robert Kennedy it
seemed on the verge of becoming a majority. Even after the assassination of Kennedy and the victory in the nominating conventions of
two long-term hawks, Vice-President Hubert Humphrey and
Richard Nixon, the pressure for peace remained constant. Just
before the election President Johnson took the important steps of
establishing a negotiating table in Paris and stopping the bombing
of the north. The train of events seemed irreversible. Nixon came
to the presidency with a promise to end the war, and most Americans believed that he would end it, if only because it was for
nothing.

But the war did not end. It expanded and grew bloodier. In the
first three years of Nixon's administration fifteen thousand Americans were killed. In that same period the GVN armed forces lost
more men than they had lost in the three previous years and more

than the total of American dead in Vietnam. In those three years there were more civilian casualties than there had ever been before — that is, Laotians and Cambodians as well as Vietnamese civilians. In 1970, two years after the start of the peace talks in Paris, the Vietnam War became the Indochina War with major battles in three countries. By 1971 the governments of Indochina had more than two million men under arms; the political and social geography of Laos, Cambodia, and South Vietnam had changed more radically than it had changed in all the years of the Johnson administration.

How was it possible? It was possible because the American government did not want to face the consequences of peace. It was, after all, one thing to wish for an end to the war and quite another to confront the issues upon which the war had begun. President Johnson had wanted to end the war; so, too, had President Kennedy. But to end the war and not to lose it: the distinction was crucial, and particularly crucial after all the American lives that had been spent and all the political rhetoric expended. Nixon, perhaps even more than his predecessors, felt that he could not take the responsibility for "losing the war." "Johnson got us into the war quietly, now we are trying to get out of it quietly," said Henry Kissinger. But the time for Senator Aiken's solution had long since passed: the issues were all too clearly formulated. To withdraw support from Saigon and allow the Thieu government to fall would be, by Nixon's definition, to "lose the war." There remained the hope of winning it, and failing that, of not losing it until sometime after an American withdrawal from Vietnam.

Politically unable to recharge the war to meet the specifications of the Joint Chiefs for a quick military victory, Nixon adopted a policy of scaling down the participation of American ground troops while increasing every other form of military pressure on the enemy. His aim was still to force Hanoi to accept an American-supported government in Saigon, and his strategy was still that of attrition. In fact his policy involved little more than a change of tactics — and a change that originated not with him but with President Johnson in the summer of 1968.

The centerpiece of this policy was "Vietnamization," the ironic name for the slow withdrawal of American ground troops and the buildup of Vietnamese armed forces to fight an American-directed war in their stead. It was, of course, the same strategy the French officials had attempted in 1950, when the war began to seem too expensive and too politically divisive for their country. And it was the same strategy that led to the situation the United States took over in 1954. Still, as was not the case with the French, the Americans dominated South Vietnam militarily. At the height of their strength in 1968–1969, they had the troops, the air power, and the money to maintain the Saigon goverment over a number of years, even with a schedule of troop pullouts. Most important of all, Nixon found a measure of support for his policy in the United States. As was calculated, the American troop withdrawals cut the middle-of-the-road "doves" off from the peace movement, for it indicated to them that Nixon intended to end the war. At the same time Nixon's assurance that he would not abandon the South Vietnamese convinced many "hawks" that he had found a way to win the war without using American ground troops. Nixon's campaign promise to "end the war and win the peace" was perfectly ambiguous.

For the first sixteen months events played in Nixon's favor. Nineteen sixty-nine was a year of military success for the Allies in South Vietnam. The North Vietnamese units remained relatively inactive while the NLF showed an appreciable decline in strength following the bloody campaigns of 1968. Seizing the initiative, General Creighton Abrams, the successor to Westmoreland, diverted the American forces from the large-scale border battles to an all-out attempt to destroy enemy base areas and supply lines in the south and to put as much South Vietnamese territory as possible under GVN control. Under the so-called Accelerated Pacification Campaign the U.S. Ninth Division almost literally "cleaned out" the Front-held regions of the northern Mekong Delta, bombing villages, defoliating crops, and forcing the peasants to leave their land. The Korean forces, the U.S. Marines, and the Americal Division wrought similar destruction upon large parts of central Vietnam. The results of these operations and of the overall pacification campaign were spectacular by contrast to those of earlier years. Front units still operated through central Vietnam, but the Delta slipped away from them with an abruptness that surprised experienced American observers. In the spring and summer of 1969 ARVN soldiers walked through villages formerly held by the Front without receiving a single sniper round. Setting up their outposts and an occupation force of RD cadres, they discovered either that the Front "infrastructure" did not exist, or that it operated in parody form, with sixteen-year-old boys running village or district committees.[1] American civilians drove unarmed down roads that had been defended by NLF battalions since 1962. The guerrilla units that remained in action were heavily seeded with North Vietnamese soldiers, and captured documents described a return to the small-scale tactics of the early stages of the war. For the first time, the eternal pessimists of the American mission, Frank Scotton, John Paul Vann, and others, reported that the situation had changed and that the tide of the war was running against the enemy. The NLF, they said, was now finding it difficult to recruit and to maintain the support of the population.

Under these favorable conditions the program of "Vietnamization" proceeded in an apparently satisfactory manner. In the wake of the renewed Front attacks in May 1968, General Thieu, by various persuasions, managed to have the legislature authorize the general mobilization that the Americans had for so long urged. The mobilization law allowed the GVN to induct all men from eighteen to thirty-eight into military service and to order seventeen-year-olds and men from thirty-nine to forty-three into the newly formed self-defense forces for the protection of the villages.[2] By the end of 1970 the GVN had added some 400,000 men to its armed forces, bringing the total up to 1,100,000. The number itself was staggering, for, if it were anywhere near correct, it meant that the GVN had mobilized about a half of the able-bodied male population of the country into the armed forces. Counting the militia, the civil service, and the 110,000-man police force, the United States was arming and, in one way or another, supporting most of the male population of Vietnam — and for the duration of the war.[3]

At the same time the United States began to arm the Vietnamese with a generosity unknown in the days of General Westmoreland. For the first time it issued the infantry with the powerful M-16 automatic rifles, the grenade launchers, and machine guns that the Americans used. It imported helicopters, patrol boats, tanks, APCs, artillery pieces, air transports, and squadrons of F-5s, the reliable tactical jet bomber.[4] New advanced military training courses were set up in South Vietnam, and one hundred Vietnamese soldiers a week went to the United States for six to eighteen months of technical training. The greatest benefit to the Vietnamese was not, however, in the area of sophisticated armament, but in that of conventional infantry weapons. For the first time the ARVN battalions had more firepower than the North Vietnamese ground troops; the territorial forces, once ragged groups of men with old carbines, now far outgunned the Front forces and possessed access to the massive air and artillery screens that covered the country. In the fall of 1969 an American officer working on the "Vietnamization" program said, "I think we are at the point now where we are giving them enough training and equipment so that if they lose this war, they can only blame themselves."[5] His statement characterized the moral ambiguity of a policy designed to save American lives while continuing the war.

In effect the result of the "Vietnamization" program was that a half of the Vietnamese population, armed and trained by the United States, sat in military occupation over the other half. By 1970 regional, popular, and police forces swarmed through almost every village, every hamlet in the country. The upkeep of these security forces was extremely expensive, but it did not begin to compare with the cost of keeping American troops in Vietnam. Though the system could not have been erected before the commitment of American troops, it was in certain respects a much more efficient system of control. Where before the American troops had occupied the Vietnamese, now all, or most, of the Vietnamese were swept up into the American war machine. "Vietnamization" preempted the manpower base of the country and brought it into a state of dependency on the American economy. And the results were spectacular. The major roads were open to traffic; the cities flourished on American money and goods; those peasant families that remained in the fertile areas of the Delta grew rich on bumper crops of "miracle" rice. The country was more "pacified" than it had ever been before.

To many Americans in Vietnam it seemed that the progress in pacification might continue indefinitely, with the territorial forces slowly "cleaning out" the local guerrillas and the countryside opening up to the city economy. The difficulty was that the process depended on something more than the continuation of American aid. With all their new weapons and with all the American air power that continued to support and supply them, the ARVN divisions were still no match for their North Vietnamese counterparts. Certain optimists in the American mission claimed that the North Vietnamese were "hurting" and near the end of their capacity to make war. But from the amount of supplies coming down the Ho Chi Minh trail it was clear that they were "hurting" no more than they had been under the bombing. Quite possibly they were experimenting to see whether the slowdown of their offensive might not bring the United States to a negotiated withdrawal and a political settlement. Failing that, they were simply waiting for more American troops to leave. As the Tet offensive had shown, they had more dedication to their war aims than the American people had to those of the Nixon administration, and they remained militarily capable of disputing the American presence in the south. And then the root of the problem lay elsewhere. As one former GVN premier put it, "The problem is not the North Vietnamese, it is the Saigon government." Whenever Thieu repeated that a coalition with the NLF would be a "disguise for surrender," he was admitting that the GVN could not compete politically with the Front. After all these years of war, the Saigon government remained a network of cliques held together by American subsidies, a group of people without a coherent political orientation, bent on their own separate survival. By building up the ARVN the Americans were merely enlarging this artificial tissue without injecting any life into it. The NLF had lost strength, but it was difficult to believe that it could not recover as the Americans moved out for the simple reason that the GVN did not constitute a "side" within the domestic political struggle. Thieu's own maneuvers in 1968–1969 demonstrated this point well enough.

Just after the Tet offensive Thieu, with some American prodding, attempted to put together a "national congress" of all the non-Communist political splinter groups, including the moderate Buddhists. The Americans applauded the attempt as an effort to "broaden the base" of the GVN, but Thieu contradicted them by giving the congress no share in governmental power. Just why Thieu acceded to American pressure and convened the congress at all remains a matter of doubt, but, quite plausibly, he wished to distribute the blame for the Tet disaster on as many different people as possible. In any case, the congress collapsed a few months later in much the same manner as had all the American-sponsored congresses and councils of 1964–1965, leaving little more to Thieu's own "political coalition" than a number of men susceptible to bribery by Thieu's businessman friend, Nguyen Cao Thang. In the fall of 1969, the president dismissed his conciliatory post-Tet cabinet (composed of such men as the former premier, Tran Van Huong) and replaced it with a cabinet composed almost exclusively of his old military cronies and former members of Ngo Dinh Nhu's

Can Lao Party. The American officials went into high reverse gear
on the subject of "broadening the base of the GVN," discovering
extraordinary virtues in these old political toughs, but they could
not explain Thieu's reasons for so obviously rejecting their advice.
They could not have explained them, had they understood them, for
to have done so would have been to admit that Thieu was trying to
gain what he was already supposed to have: some control over his
own administration. In the attempt a sharp sword was more useful
to him than the unmatched parts of a blunderbuss. Thieu would
need that sword shortly in order to deal with the political effects of
the American troop withdrawals.

Nixon's announcement of the "Vietnamization" policy signaled
much the same thing to the Saigonese as it did to the American
middle-of-the-road doves. When Nixon ordered a withdrawal of ten
thousand American troops per month, the Saigonese politicians, reasonably enough, came to the conclusion that he intended to end the
war in the near future. Alarmed by the intransigence of their own
government at the Paris negotiating table, a certain number began
to seek alternate routes to a political settlement before the American
troops departed. Deputy Tran Ngoc Chau proposed that a group of
Saigonese legislators visit the north in order to talk with their opposite numbers in Hanoi. Students and intellectuals formed committees and put out manifestos attacking the U.S.-GVN conditions for
peace negotiations. The Saigonese had, unfortunately, misjudged
Nixon, and Thieu for his own protection had to silence them. In
March Thieu, overriding the constitutional provision for legislative
immunity, had a military court sentence Chau to ten years' hard
labor. A month or so later he arrested the heads of the newly formed
student opposition group.

From these events many Americans concluded that Thieu, personally, held the extreme right-wing position in the Vietnamese
political spectrum. As usual, however, the situation was not so
ideologically linear as it seemed.

In the fall of 1969 American intelligence in Saigon discovered an
NLF ring consisting of some one hundred members, many of them
placed in high positions throughout the GVN. When arrested by the
Americans, one member revealed that he had had dealings with
President Thieu's own political adviser, a man called Huynh Van
Trung. While the Americans were congratulating themselves on
having removed a viper from the breast of the GVN, many Saigon-

ese were laughing at the joke on both General Thieu and the Americans. General Thieu's adviser, after all, had a well-known history as a Viet Minh informer during the first Indochina war. Recently, and perhaps as a result of his wife's infidelity, he had been going around Saigon complaining about the corruption of Vietnamese society. When Thieu's military court gave the man a sentence of only two years in jail, the suspicions of the Saigonese seemed confirmed: Thieu had known about the man all along and had been using him as a liaison with the NLF. (The fact that this man was of such a dubious background suggested that both parties had left him in an exposed place as a cover for their better-protected liaisons.)

Had the affair never reached the press, many Saigonese would have nonetheless assumed that Thieu possessed such a contact. It was only reasonable — and besides, the war had gone on for so long that its history could only be repetitious. In 1963, at the moment when the United States threatened to withdraw its support from the Diem regime, Ngo Dinh Nhu attempted to enter into relations with the North Vietnamese while still hotly professing his anti-Communism. The present situation differed only in that now the Americans appeared to be threatening to withdraw their support from the entire Saigon regime. To the Saigonese the only illegitimate aspect of these contacts was their secrecy. Had there been any unity or responsibility within the GVN, General Thieu would have attempted to make the accommodation in public — as Chau intended — and to show the way of least resistance to the people who depended upon him. But, as even the highest officials of the GVN did not trust each other, Thieu, like many others, was doing his best to see that he did not hang separately. It was this attempt at self-preservation that led, as it always had in the past, to a political repression in the cities. Thieu would use the leverage of American support to suppress those who challenged his personal position and his own contacts with the NLF.

Finally, after a year of accommodating the Nixon administration, Senator Fulbright and other members of the Senate Foreign Relations Committee held hearings to argue the fact that the new American effort was having very little effect on the GVN: the ARVN remained ineffective, the Saigon government unable to meet the political challenge, and so forth. The discussion could have been put together from old newspaper clippings. But in some sense the situation was a new one and the issue was not joined.

In his foreign policy message to Congress in January 1970, President Nixon revealed what was to be his prime moral justification for the continuation of the war through the "Vietnamization" policy. "When," he said, "we assumed the burden of helping South Vietnam, millions of South Vietnamese men and women placed their trust in us. To abandon them would risk a massacre that would shock and dismay everyone in the world who values human life."[6] Many American doves disputed this argument on the basis that the American military had already done more damage in Vietnam than any Vietnamese group (presumably Nixon meant the Communists) could possibly do. The United States had a moral responsibility for its own actions and not for the (hypothetical) actions of every foreign political party towards its own people. So much the "doves" could say without any knowledge of Vietnam, but from the perspective of Vietnamese politics there was something more to be said. The experience of the war had shown that the buildup of the ARVN was not only ineffective as a means of "stopping the Communists" but actually destructive to the South Vietnamese people. To continue this buildup in the context of an American withdrawal was both to compound the errors of the past and to increase the chances of those "massacres" that Nixon said he hoped to avoid. As one illustration will suffice to show, "Vietnamization" was the tactic most likely to produce present and future violence against the civilian population.

Just six months before the Tet offensive, the United States finally succeeded in pressuring the GVN to adopt its latest-model counterinsurgency scheme for "rooting out the Viet Cong infrastructure." The Phoenix program, as the plan was known, consisted of the centralization of all intelligence data and counterespionage operations in the person of an army or police officer at each level of the bureaucracy. The aim of the program was to eliminate the rivalries between the various army units and the police which had so long prevented the Americans and the GVN from identifying, much less capturing, the political agents of the Front. In addition the GVN revived the old detention law whereby without the delay and uncertainty of trial by jury a provincial security committee could condemn a suspect to up to two years in prison. As with the Revolutionary Development program, however, the Americans managed to clear away mountains of red tape only to build another mountain. They created an efficient system of counterinsurgency in a void of any efficient agencies to carry it out. The results were predictable. In 1969 the United States set a goal for the Phoenix program to "neutralize" twenty thousand NLF agents during the year, and at the end of the year GVN authorities reported 19,534 agents "neutralized." The figure was unsettling in that there had been no corresponding decline in American estimates of NLF agents at large.[7] Who, then, were the 19,534 people, and what had become of them? As only 20 percent of those arrested were actually sentenced — and then only for periods of a few months — the American officials concluded that a large percentage of the "neutralized agents" were simply people whom the Phoenix agents herded in and out of the police stations in order to fill their quotas. American advisers on the spot complained of GVN inefficiency and collusion with the NLF.[8] Their complaints were undoubtedly justified, but the matter was more serious than that. Despite the fact that the law provided only for the arrest and detention of the suspects, one-third of the "neutralized agents" were reported dead.[9] Then, too, the survivors had stories to tell. In one village in An Giang province a woman had come to the Phoenix officials with a story that her brother-in-law had tried to persuade her husband to pay taxes to the NLF. As was later discovered, the brother-in-law was an old man with heart disease against whom the woman held a long-standing grudge. But the discovery came too late. Within the week the Phoenix agent had the old man arrested and tortured as a "Viet Cong tax collector." In another village a conscientious village chief discovered the local Phoenix agent was extorting gold and jewelry from the people of the village on the threat of arresting them as "Viet Cong agents." When the village chief attempted to tell the district chief about the racket, the Phoenix agent had him fingered as a "Viet Cong suspect."[10]

With the Phoenix program the United States succeeded in fashioning much the same instrument of civilian terror that the Diemist laws for the suppression of Communism had created in 1957–1958. The only difference was that given the numbers of American and GVN troops and the participation of statistics-hungry U.S. intelligence services, the terror was a great deal more widespread than it had been before. The program in effect eliminated the cumbersome category of "civilian"; it gave the GVN, and initially the American troops as well, license and justification for the arrest, torture, or killing of anyone in the country, whether or not the person was carrying a gun. And many officials took advantage of that license. Some of the district and province chiefs engaged in systematic extortion rackets, arresting the rich of their districts twice and three times a year. Other officers settled their old scores or terrorized their fellow officers. The Phoenix program permitted them to indulge in all the practices classical to an irresponsible secret police. But the corruption of individual officers was not the worst of it. The true destructiveness of the program came from the very structure of the program itself. Like any stranger to the village, the district intelligence officer, were he a model of probity, would of necessity have some difficulty distinguishing between the "hard-core" Front cadres, the marginal Front supporters, and the people who went along with the NLF for the sake of survival. Inclined by the nature of his position to arrest anyone with Front contacts, he would tend to act like the Americans when they came into a "Viet Cong-held area." He would introduce legalistic notions of justice into what ought to have been a family affair, filling his quota and his prisons with anonymous people who had lived under the Front aegis. Rather than eliminate the "hard-core" cadres (who were, after all, the best protected and concealed), he would actually create new ones, for, as during the Diem regime, the peasants had to accept what protection they could get from such arbitrary justice. By its very nature the Phoenix program tended once again to polarize the villages and to destroy what order and accumulation existed, thus involving a new portion of the population in the life-or-death struggle.[11]

The Phoenix program was in a sense a model for the entire Vietnamization program. The armed forces of the GVN everywhere contained underpaid and badly led soldiers who terrorized rather than pacified the civilian population. To augment this force meant to increase the number of bandits at large in the country — and bandits that were now supplied with modern American weapons. But again, there was another issue at stake. As American-made institutions, the armed forces of the Saigon government were structurally incapable of dealing with the political struggle. By fitting out more Vietnamese with rifles and uniforms, Nixon was merely forcing them into a conflict they could not possibly win even if there were no Front soldiers left in the south. With American support the top-heavy bureaucracy of the ARVN tended merely to crush those people at its base; without American support it threatened to topple over, crushing everyone including its own officers. In the anarchy that would ensue from such an event there was a high probability that the massacres and revenge-killings would become general: the ARVN units would turn to banditry, and the NLF would have to respond with violence. In any case the potential for domestic violence increased with the drafting of each new soldier.

The "Vietnamization" program was, like so many American policies in Vietnam, a solution to an American rather than to a Vietnamese problem. While it permitted Nixon to claim that the United States was "saving" the South Vietnamese, it was in effect creating a social upheaval and exposing more Vietnamese to those very dangers he claimed to be saving them from.

"Vietnamization" was not, however, Nixon's only strategy for the expansion of the war. In April 1970, the administration sent a large force of American and South Vietnamese troops to destroy the North Vietnamese base areas across the Cambodian border. It was the initiative that the Joint Chiefs had for so long requested; only now with the overthrow of Prince Norodom Sihanouk by a general of Thieu's political complexion, the administration had no fear of opposition by the Cambodian government. Nixon presented the invasion as a necessary step to prevent a North Vietnamese buildup and an eventual attack on the dwindling numbers of American troops. Despite the flimsiness of this pretext (the North Vietnamese had by then offered to refrain from attacking American troops if the United States set a withdrawal date), he was, it appeared, surprised by the force of the reaction in the United States. The American public would tolerate the buildup of the Saigon regime's army, but it would not, it seemed, stand for the invasion of another country by American troops. There were demonstrations and student strikes throughout the country, their numbers and intensity growing after the incident at Kent State University in which National Guard troops shot and killed four white students. Spurred on by this public outcry, Senate doves invoked the constitutional issue of the right to declare war and passed an amendment calling for the prohibition of American troops and air support from Cambodia after July of that year.

From a purely military point of view, the advantage the Cambodian invasion gave the United States and the GVN was important but temporary. It was one thing for the Joint Chiefs to recommend such a strategy in the context of an American buildup in 1966 or 1967, but it was quite another for an administration to implement it during a period of American troop withdrawal. In their two months in Cambodia the U.S. troops destroyed thousands of tons of North Vietnamese equipment and supplies, but they killed very few enemy troops. The greatest achievement of the operation was indirect: it permitted the new Cambodian regime to close the port of Sihanoukville to the Front and the North Vietnamese, thereby cutting sharply into the flow of munitions and other supplies to the southern guerrillas. Still, by most Pentagon estimates the operation set back the North Vietnamese offensive by no more than a year. Before the operation — and in anticipation of such an event — the North Vietnamese troops drove west to occupy the northern provinces of Cambodia and to set up a new (and indestructible) supply route along the Mekong river. At the same time they began to build up a local insurgency movement, the FUNK (Front Uni National de Kampuchea), and to menace Phnom Penh itself with guerrilla units. With the removal of the American forces from Cambodia in July 1970, Nixon put himself in the position of having to defend yet another government that could not protect itself and of leaving the ARVN with a new responsibility that it could not fulfill.

A second border of Indochina was crossed the next year with the ARVN invasion of Laos — an operation that had much less happy results even in the short term than the Cambodian initiative. In February 1971, sixteen thousand ARVN troops, supported by American aircraft and helicopters, marched across the DMZ with the mission of cutting the Ho Chi Minh trail that ran from North Vietnam into Cambodia. The American commanders who planned the operation in Saigon saw it as a decisive blow to enemy supply lines: the North Vietnamese would either fall back and abandon their communication centers and storage depots, as they had in Cambodia, or they would fight a last-ditch battle for control of the trail, which would be their Waterloo. The American command had, however, greatly underestimated North Vietnamese strength in the region and the problems of operating in such terrain. In order to cut enemy lines it is first necessary to surround them, and in Laos it was the ARVN units who walked along a line and the North Vietnamese who surrounded them. For days there was no action to speak of. The ARVN columns moved slowly forward down the long narrow valleys, while American helicopters lifted in battalions to set up fire bases overlooking the vast network of camouflaged roadways the North Vietnamese had built through the mountains. Then, suddenly, just as the advance units reached the center of the trail, the North Vietnamese attacked with tanks, heavy rockets, and four of their best divisions. Most of the ARVN units stood up to the assault, and American aircraft killed thousands — perhaps ten thousand — North Vietnamese with close-in bombing near the ARVN positions.[12] But the North Vietnamese were on their own territory and they clearly outclassed the ARVN units, which still depended upon American air power and upon their now absent American advisers to call it in with precision. The ARVN casualties mounted and the positions of their units weakened so that certain battalion commanders had to request orders for a withdrawal. Their requests were refused. The American command and the White House had claimed that the ARVN would stay in Laos and occupy the trail until the end of the dry season in May, and the ranking ARVN officers did not dare contradict the Americans. It was not until some of the commanders on the ground threatened to take the troops out and the retreat had already begun that the order for withdrawal was formally given. By the end of the forty-five day campaign the ARVN reportedly suffered about 50 percent casualties: 3,800 killed, 5,200 wounded, and eight battalions put out of action.[13] Three months later U.S. intelligence sources reported that the traffic on the Ho Chi Minh trail had, if anything, increased during the spring.

The Laos operation was a military failure in terms of the objectives the American command had set for it; it was a political failure as well. During the initial stages of "Lam Son 719" President Nixon said that this operation, like its predecessor in Cambodia, was designed to save the lives of American troops in Vietnam. Whether or not his announcement made any impression on the skeptical American public, it certainly had a powerful effect on the ARVN troops, who with some justification blamed their casualties on the failure of American intelligence and American air power. Lam Son 719 showed the South Vietnamese that "Vietnamization" meant increased Vietnamese deaths in pursuit of the American policy objective to extricate the American troops from Vietnam without peace negotiations. In Lam Son 719 the Americans had actually risked an ARVN defeat in pursuit of this short-term goal. And their maneuver had not worked.

As Daniel Ellsberg, a former Pentagon consultant, suggested, the operations in Laos and Cambodia were designed not only for their military utility but for their importance as a signal to the North

Vietnamese.[14] The signal was that Nixon was willing to remove the constraints that Johnson had observed; he was willing to use whatever force he had at his disposal in order to maintain the American position in South Vietnam. Just how far Nixon was actually willing to go remained a matter of doubt. He would not reintroduce American troops into Vietnam or take any action that was likely to bring the Chinese into the war. But short of that he had a number of options, all of which — or so the signal indicated — he was willing to use. In the first week or so of the Laos operation Vice-President Nguyen Cao Ky had threatened a ground incursion by the ARVN into North Vietnam. The announcement was, no doubt, an attempt at a bluff. But had the Laos operation been a success, the North Vietnamese would have had to live with the threat of a future invasion by the ARVN. As it was, Nixon now had to rely on his air power alone.

Even before Laos the U.S. air force had taken on the main burden of the war. The Johnson administration had intended that it should do so in 1964, but the strong ground position of the NLF inside South Vietnam forced the President into a commitment of American ground troops. Because after 1968 the main military threat came from the north, such a strategy was now feasible as a temporary measure. From 1969 on, Nixon expanded and intensified the air war, doubling the total tonnage of bombs dropped, so that after two years and a few months of his administration the United States had dropped more bombs on Indochina than it had in both the European and the Pacific theatres during World War II.[15] The tactical strikes in South Vietnam continued while the B-52s expanded their operations in northern Laos, turning a large percentage of the Lao population and most of the montagnard tribes into refugees.[16] U.S. air operations over Cambodia finished the job the troops had taken on, killing thousands of people and displacing millions.[17] The administration also renewed the bombing of North Vietnam with what American officials called "protective reaction strikes against antiaircraft positions." This hail of bombing did not substantially affect North Vietnamese military strength, but, perhaps, it was not even designed for such a purpose. Nixon could only claim in a vague manner that the strikes were made to protect American lives. Had he been interested in saving American lives, he would have negotiated a withdrawal and a political settlement. The raids were providing

Nixon with the means to maintain the Thieu regime and the American presence in Saigon for a certain length of time at the cost of the lives and property of millions of Indochinese.

The strategy would work for a while, but it would not work indefinitely, for the withdrawal of the American troops was removing the underpinning of the war. In May 1971, the U.S. and the GVN command announced a new drive into Laos through the Ashau valley with several thousand ARVN troops. The troops stalled in the valley while the ARVN generals demanded more American bombers and helicopter support. After two weeks, news of the operation receded from the newspapers, and, after three, it was possible to determine that the ARVN remained in place only because a North Vietnamese unit attacked a forward patrol. The ARVN would not go into Laos again that year, and, after a bloody battle near the Cambodian town of Snoul, certain divisions would be most reluctant to return to Cambodia.[18] In 1970, during the first Cambodian operation, the desertion rate rose from its normal level of eight thousand a month to twelve thousand; after the Laos operation it was questionable how many battalions remained combat-effective. In the fall of 1970 the CIA reported that there were some thirty thousand people inside the Saigon government who more or less cooperated with the NLF, and that soon their numbers might reach fifty thousand, or 5 percent of the GVN armed forces.[19] To change the Saigon government in the future, the Front would hardly require an introduction of any new personnel. The following year the resurgence of the political apparatus of the NLF began to manifest itself in a decline in GVN security in the countryside. The history of the insurgency, going back to 1961, had begun to repeat itself. At the end of the process, time would once again run out for the U.S. government. If the President did not make a settlement, he would be faced with the same dilemma with which the war had begun.

The history of the war was repeating itself, only now the tide was running in the opposite direction. The Vietnamese of the cities understood and registered that shift. With the announcement of the bombing halt and the negotiations in Paris, the mood of Saigon changed. The vocal political groups now expressed open resentment against the Americans. The head of one Saigon student committee described to an American reporter how the change came over him. As a high-school student in central Vietnam the young man had, he said, admired the American soldiers. "They seemed so carefree, so strong, I was moved to think they would have come from so far away to die for something other than their own country." But later he began to look at them more critically. "I saw how they interfered at all levels in Vietnamese society. I read about the massacre of Vietnamese civilians in Mylai. I saw myself how the lives of city people were disrupted by the American presence. I began to feel that the American presence itself is the reason why the Communists continue the war." And, his friend continued, "We students take note of the fact that on this side we have half a million foreign troops, while on the other side there are none."[20]

It was not only the students who criticized the Americans. For the first time in years, the Saigon newspapers, even those that supported the Thieu regime, began to attack the United States and expose stories of new military atrocities.[21] The politicians who had been the strongest supporters of the United States now spoke of the Americans as they used to speak of the French in Vietnam. Just before his arrest, Deputy Tran Ngoc Chau issued a statement regretting his own cooperation with the United States and warning General Thieu and his associates of the "schemes of the U.S. officials" to keep the GVN weak and unrepresentative — in effect, a puppet to their will. At a meeting of "retired" generals, including the former chiefs of state, Generals Duong Van Minh and Tran Van Don — the nucleus of a new opposition group — General Ky ironically called the American ambassador "Governor General Bunker," after the French authority in Indochina. Elsewhere, even more plainly, he spoke of the Americans as "colonialists."[22]

Rather than allay the resentment of the politicians, the slow process of "Vietnamization" only increased it. As time went on and the Americans hesitantly pulled at the fabric they had created, every slight tear seemed to remind the Vietnamese of the inevitable. The central and most sensitive issue was the economy. Resistant to all attempts at public relations camouflage, the value of the piastre registered with an almost mathematical precision the amount of U.S. aid to South Vietnam and Vietnamese confidence in the continuation of the war. As the U.S. troops withdrew and the flow of dollars diminished, the black-market rate shot up to new heights and the inflation, once "stabilized" at 30 percent a year, rose dangerously.[23] The political temperature rose with it. When the Americans urged Thieu to impose higher taxes and devalue the piastre, the

Vietnamese politicians warned him against complying with American "schemes" to impoverish all Vietnamese. There were fistfights in the legislature when Thieu presented a bill requesting dictatorial powers over the economy for the next several months. In 1970 there were demonstrations of veterans and war widows calling for reparations. Thieu met these complaints with stopgap measures, but he could not raise the salaries of the armed forces enough to compensate for the rise in prices. And it was the soldiers upon whom the regime depended.[24]

During 1970 and 1971 the attacks against the regime and the American presence remained largely rhetorical. The soldiers, the city people, and the non-Communist groups disliked the regime and resented the Americans as much as they ever had, but they depended — and more heavily than before — upon the flow of American aid. Just after the Cambodian invasion, on June 11, 1970, the anniversary of Quang Duc's death, a seventy-four-year-old bonze burned himself to death in a Saigon pagoda. A spokesman for the Buddhists said that while the Buddhists would never encourage self-immolations, they regarded the act as a sign of growing aspirations for peace.[25] The statement was a good deal more ambiguous than the act itself, for while the Buddhists, like all Vietnamese, wished for peace, they knew that for the moment it would be quite futile to oppose American policy and the American-supported government. For the moment they, like most of the non-Communist "opposition" groups, aspired only to replace the Thieu government and take control of the American aid. As a result, the "opposition" remained as divided as ever and as incapable as ever of formulating any long-term strategies for creating a non-Communist movement or negotiating with the Front. After the Cambodian invasion it was thus only the students who demonstrated — some of them calling for the overthrow of the Thieu government and others, more significantly, for the withdrawal of American troops. Thieu's response was to throw the demonstrating students in jail and to raid the central pagoda of Saigon. Still the students continued to protest, and in 1971 they were joined by a number of young Catholic priests, who openly advocated a political settlement with the Front. The defection of these young priests was significant in that it pointed towards a political shift within the Catholic Church as a whole and a weakening of the last solid moral support for the regime.

The elections of 1971 offered some hope both to those who hoped

for peace and to those who hoped for the maintenance of American
policy and a substitution of men. But the moment of hope was short-
lived. Well before the presidential election it became clear that
Thieu would do what was necessary to keep himself in power and
that the Americans would support him. The Americans did not want
a change of policy, and though they wanted a contested election —
a façade of electoral democracy — they judged a change of men too
dangerous at that moment in history. They assumed, and quite
correctly, that after four years of the Thieu government a change of
president would have meant a shake-up of government personnel
throughout the country and a situation like that succeeding the fall
of Diem. The difficulty was that their stance was quite apparent to
the two potential opposition candidates, General Nguyen Cao Ky
and General Duong Van Minh. When Thieu unsuccessfully attempted to get Ky out of the race, Minh withdrew his candidacy and
Ky refused to act as a substitute for him. To the great dismay of the
Americans Thieu finally ran the election as a referendum for himself
and collected an impossible 94 percent of the vote. It was, as Tri
Quang said apropos of Thieu's police actions against the Buddhists,
much like the last days of the Diem regime. Only now Catholics and
non-Catholics alike began to compare Thieu unfavorably with
Diem.

It was like 1963, only now the power in question was that of the
Americans rather than that of any particular government in Saigon.
General Thieu did not matter. He himself announced that he would
quit the government if and when the Americans decided to withdraw their aid from the GVN. For the moment he controlled the
police, but the more he had to use them against opposition groups,
the more his power declined. For the moment he controlled the top
army officers and province officials. But he trusted no one — not
even his own premier — and he appointed only those particularly
indebted to him as commanders of the provinces controlling the
roads into Saigon. The regime was closing in on itself, just as Diem's
had done. The opposition in Saigon waited for a change of American
policy, but as the American troops withdrew and the economic situation worsened, the signs of disintegration began to gather. The
armed forces increased their financial exactions upon the civilians,
and incidents of theft, hooliganism, and even fighting between whole
units were reported throughout the countryside. In the strategic
Central Highlands the montagnard troops, once the protégés of the

American Special Forces and now incorporated into the regular Vietnamese army, began to defect en masse from their Vietnamese officers. In these and other border areas the junior Vietnamese officers complained that they were being sacrificed to the interests of their senior officers and the Americans. The people of the central Vietnamese cities, still the last on the supply lines and the closest to the fighting, gave signs of turning against Saigon once again in reaction to the American withdrawals. Except for certain isolated incidents, such as the students' burning of American vehicles before the presidential election, Saigon was quiet, betraying as little of itself as it had in the early spring of 1963. Once again the Saigonese were withdrawing from political life and waiting for that crisis — economic, military, or diplomatic — that they felt sure would fall upon the regime. When it came, they would respond, breaking through the surface of order and orderly repression and putting an end to American power in Saigon.

Though Nixon took no initiative to end the war, the U.S. government had used up its credit with the American as well as the Vietnamese people for the pursuit of its war aims. Vice-President Agnew liked to make a distinction between the "hippies" and "subversives" who opposed the war at home and the young patriots who nobly served their country in Vietnam. But by 1971 there was no political distinction between young Americans in and out of the armed forces. The army, once dominated by career men and volunteers, was now filled with draftees who did not want to die in Vietnam for a cause they felt had already been abandoned. Many opposed the American war aims; others merely resented their own condition. It was a white man's war being fought by blacks, a rich man's war being fought by the poor, an old man's war being fought by the young. While Agnew talked of patriotism, the soldiers grew more and more sensitive to these antagonisms. The American command made it practically impossible for the soldiers to demonstrate, write, or petition against the war, and thus the overt opposition to it was confined to the wearing of peace symbols, an occasional letter or petition, and the antiwar movement of the Vietnam veterans. These were the healthy signs. In general the soldiers expressed their sense of alienation in a manner reminiscent of the ARVN, turning their suppressed, and often unfocused, anger against themselves or their superiors. There were more reports of atrocities against Vietnamese civilians, and then, quite suddenly, there was a rash of "fragging" incidents in which enlisted men killed or wounded their officers. These incidents remained scattered, but many officers took the threat seriously and grew less and less willing to compel their men to carry out orders. The well-known Vietnamese practice of passive resistance and avoidance became almost standard. Combat units would shirk patrols and routine security duties, leaving their positions open to enemy attack.[26] Many — perhaps the majority — of the soldiers in Vietnam smoked the cheap, locally grown marihuana on and off duty. In the spring of 1971 the U.S. command itself estimated that 10 percent of the troops in Vietnam were taking heroin, and that 5 percent were addicts.

The traffic in heroin was the final, and perhaps the blackest, irony of the war. The heroin came largely from Burma and Laos. Much of it was processed in or near Vientiane by those people for whose sake (it was to be supposed) the U.S. government was demolishing the rest of Laos. It came to Vietnam either by air drop from Vietnamese or Lao military planes, paid for by the U.S. government, or through the customs at Tan Son Nhut airfield. The Vietnamese customs inspectors earned several dozen times as much for not inspecting the bags and bundles as for inspecting them. When the American customs advisers attempted to crack down on their "counterparts," they discovered that the two key customs posts were held by the brothers of Thieu's premier, General Tran Thien Khiem.[27] General Khiem was one of the three men the NLF said they could not include in a coalition government. American officials refused to consider dropping their support for Khiem because, they said, he belonged to the "freely elected government of the South Vietnamese people." As this "freely elected government" would not prosecute the customs officials (heroin, the Vietnamese said, was "an American problem"), the heroin continued to enter the country unimpeded. Once in Vietnam it was sold openly in the streets and around the American bases by young war widows and children orphaned by the American war. Finally, the heroin, unlike anything else the Vietnamese sold the American soldiers, was of excellent quality — white as ivory and of such purity that it would cost a small fortune to support a habit of it on the illicit market of the United States. Such was the revenge of the Indochinese who, Nixon had claimed, "trusted in" the Americans. And such was the reward of the U.S. government to the soldiers who served its cause in Vietnam.

The United States might leave Vietnam, but the Vietnam War

would now never leave the United States. The soldiers would bring it back with them like an addiction. The civilians may neglect or try to ignore it, but those who have seen combat must find a reason for that killing; they must put it in some relation to their normal experience and to their role as citizens. The usual agent for this reintegration is not the psychiatrist, but the politician. In this case, however, the politicians could give no satisfactory answer to many of those who had killed or watched their comrades being killed. In 1971 the soldiers had before them the knowledge that President Johnson had deceived them about the war during his election campaign. All his cryptic signals to the contrary, he had indicated that there would be no American war in Vietnam, while he was in fact making plans for entering that war. They had before them the spectacle of a new President, Richard M. Nixon, who with one hand engaged in peaceful negotiations with the Soviet Union and the People's Republic of China and with the other condemned thousands of Americans and Indochinese to die for the principle of anti-Communism. To those who had for so long believed that the United States was different, that it possessed a fundamental innocence, generosity, and disinterestedness, these facts were shocking. No longer was it possible to say, as so many Americans and French had, that Vietnam was the "quagmire," the *"pays pourri"* that had enmired and corrupted the United States. It was the other way around. The U.S. officials had enmired Vietnam. They had corrupted the Vietnamese and, by extension, the American soldiers who had to fight amongst the Vietnamese in their service. By involving the United States in a fruitless and immoral war, they had also corrupted themselves.

17

Fire in the Lake

I hammer the pain of separateness
into a statue to stand in the park.
Below it I carve a horizontal inscription
that reads: Soul of the Twentieth Century.
— Tru Vu[1]

Before entering Saigon, the military traffic from Tan Son Nhut
airfield slows in a choking blanket of its own exhaust. Where it
crawls along to the narrow bridge in a frenzy of bicycles, pedicabs,
and tri-Lambrettas, two piles of garbage mark the entrance to a new
quarter of the city. Every evening a girl on spindle heels picks her
way over the barrier of rotting fruit and onto the sidewalk. Trium-
phant, she smiles at the boys who lounge at the soft-drink stand, and
with a toss of her long earrings, climbs into a waiting Buick.

Behind her, the alleyway carpeted with mud winds back past the
façade of the new houses into a maze of thatched huts and tin-
roofed shacks called Bui Phat. One of the oldest of the refugee
quarters,[2] Bui Phat lies just across the river from the generous villas
and tree-lined streets of French Saigon. On its tangle of footpaths,
white-shirted boys push their Vespas past laborers in black pajamas
and women carrying water on coolie poles. After twelve years and
recurrent tides of new refugees, Bui Phat is less an urban quarter
than a compost of villages where peasants live with their city children. The children run thick underfoot. The police, it is said, rarely
enter this quarter for fear of a gang of teen-age boys, whose leader,
a young army deserter, reigns over Bui Phat.

Most of Bui Phat lives beyond the law, the electricity lines, and the water system, but it has its secret fortunes. Here and there amid the chaos of shacks and alleyways, new concrete buildings rear up in a splendor of pastel-faced walls, neon lights, and plastic garden furniture. In one of them there is a half-naked American who suns himself on a porch under a clothesline draped with military uniforms. He does not know, and probably never will know, that the house just down the alleyway is owned and inhabited by an agent of the NLF.

Bui Phat and its likenesses are what the American war has brought to Vietnam. In the countryside there is only an absence: the bare brown fields, the weeds growing in the charred earth of the village, the jungle that has swept back over the cleared land. The grandest ruins are those of the American tanks, for the Vietnamese no longer build fine stone tombs as did their ancestors. The U.S. First Infantry Division has carved its divisional insignia with defoliants in a stretch of jungle — a giant, poisonous graffito — but the Vietnamese have left nothing to mark the passage of their armies and an entire generation of young men. In many places death is not even a physical absence. The villages that once again take root in the rich soil of the Delta fill up with children as quickly as the holes made by the five-hundred-pound and thousand-pound bombs fill up with paddy silt. The desire for survival has been greater than the war itself, for there are approximately two million more people in the south today than there were before the war. But the balance of the nation has changed, and Saigon is no longer the village, it is Bui Phat.

From Dong Ha in the north to Rach Gia, the slow port at the base of the Delta, these new slums, these crushed villages, spread through all of the cities and garrisoned towns. They are everywhere, plastered against sandbag forts, piled up under the guns of the provincial capitals, overwhelming what is left of the Delta's yellow stucco towns. Seaward of Da Nang the tin huts of the refugee settlements lie between the ammunition and the garbage dumps, indistinguishable from either. These huts have been rebuilt many times during the war, for every year there is some kind of disaster — an airplane crash or an explosion in the ammunition depot — that wipes out whole hamlets. Around Qui Nhon, Bien Hoa, and Cam Ranh bay, where the Americans have built jetports and military installations to last through the twentieth century, the thatched huts crowd so closely that a single neglected cigarette or a spark from a charcoal brazier suffices to burn the settlements down. On the streets of tin shacks that run straight as a surrealist's line past the runways and into the sand, babies play naked in the dust and rows of green combat fatigues hang over the barbed wire like dead soldiers.

Out of a population of seventeen million there are now five million refugees. Perhaps 40 or 50 percent of the population, as opposed to the 15 percent before the war, live in and around the cities and towns. The distribution is that of a highly industrialized country, but there is almost no industry in South Vietnam. And the word "city" and even "town" is misleading. What was even in 1965 a nation of villages and landed estates is now a nation of *bidonvilles,* refugee camps, and army bases. South Vietnam is a country shattered so that no two pieces fit together.

In Saigon alone more than three million people live on swampy ground between river and canal in a space made to accommodate a quarter of a million. Saigon now has one of the most dense populations in the world, although few houses rise above two stories, for in the monsoon season whole quarters of the city sink into the marsh. Some districts are little more than gigantic sewers, lakes of filth, above which thatched huts rise on stilts, connected only by rotting boards. In other quarters where the refugees have not had time to build stilts, the sewage inundated even the houses. But there is nowhere else for these people to go. The squatters have already filled up all the free space; their shacks elbow across the main thoroughfares.

In the spring of 1970 crowds of disabled veterans came to the presidential palace to demonstrate against the plan of the Saigon municipality to tear down the squatters' shacks. The scene of these veterans — the blind, the tubercular, the double and triple amputees — advancing on the palace on crutches and wheely boards might have come straight from a Goya illustration of *The Disasters of War.* The first expression of the ignored and hugely silent masses of the city, the veterans marched upon the newly built palace and the American embassy like a nemesis.

At least there is for the moment employment and food in the cities. Westmoreland predicted that correctly. In the cities the women can become prostitutes or cleaning women; they can hawk gelatine or sit on the street corners with their trays of stolen PX goods. The men can push cyclos or break stones in the American construction projects; they can also steal or work at the docks stealing for others. Of course, their jobs will disappear slowly as the American troops move out, but in the meantime they are better off in the cities than in the free fire zones or a refugee camp. The Americans were correct there.

In one camp just south of Da Nang, the refugees from a nearby hamlet have lived for three months in shelters that would adequately house pigs or chickens. Their hamlet has been burned to the ground by the U.S. Marines, and they do not know when, if ever, they can go back to rebuild it. The district chief lives only one hundred yards away, but he has not come to visit them at all this month, no doubt because it was he who appropriated the supplies of cooking oil and bulgur designated for the camp, and the people are near starvation. A funeral procession makes its way through the camp — two women carrying the covered body of a child on a makeshift stretcher. The other villagers hardly look up to watch it pass. "The children die so quickly here," says one woman. "But perhaps it is better that way."

The physical suffering of South Vietnam is difficult to comprehend, even in statistics. The official numbers — 859,641 "enemy," over 165,268 ARVN soldiers and about 380,000 civilians killed — only begin to tell the toll of death this war has taken. Proportionately, it is as though twenty million Americans died in the war instead of the forty-five thousand to date. But there are more to come. In the refugee camps and isolated villages people die of malnutrition and the children are deformed. In the cities, where there is no sanitation and rarely any running water, the adults die of cholera, typhoid, smallpox, leprosy, bubonic plague, and their children die of the common diseases of dirt, such as scabies and sores. South Vietnam knows nothing like the suffering of India or Bangladesh. Comparatively speaking, it has always been a rich country, and the American aid has provided many people with the means of survival. But its one source of wealth is agriculture, and the American war has wreaked havoc upon its forest and paddy lands. It has given great fortunes to the few while endangering the country's future and forcing the many to live in the kind of "poverty, ignorance, and disease" that South Vietnam never knew before.

Still, the physical destruction is not, perhaps, the worst of it. The destruction of an entire society — "That is, above all, what the

Vietnamese blame the Americans for," said one Vietnamese scholar. "Willfully or not, they have tended to destroy what is most precious to us: family, friendship, our manner of expressing ourselves."[3] For all these years, the columns in the Saigon newspapers denouncing Americans for destroying "Vietnamese culture" have sounded somehow fatuous and inadequate to those Americans who witnessed the U.S. bombing raids. But the Vietnamese kept their sights on what is permanent and irreparable. Physical death is everywhere, but it is the social death caused by destruction of the family that is of overriding importance.

The French colonial presence and the first Indochina war swept away the Vietnamese state and the order of the village, but it left the family. And the family was the essence, the cell, as it were, that contained the design for the whole society. To the traditional Vietnamese the nation consisted of a landscape, "our mountains and our rivers," and the past of the family, "our ancestors." The land and the family were the two sources of national as well as personal identity. The Americans have destroyed these sources for many Vietnamese, not merely by killing people but by forcibly separating them, by removing the people from the land and depositing them in the vast swamp-cities.

In a camp on the Da Nang sand-flats a woman sits nursing her baby and staring apathetically at the gang of small children who run through the crowded rows of shacks, wheeling and screaming like a flock of sea gulls after a ship's refuse. "It is hard to do anything with the children," she says. Her husband is at first ashamed to talk to the visitors because of his torn and dirty clothes. He has tried, he says, to get a job at the docks, but the Vietnamese interpreter for the Americans demanded a price he could not pay for putting his name on the list. Nowadays he rarely goes out of the barbed-wire enclosure. His hands hang stiffly down, as if paralyzed by their idleness.

An American in Vietnam observes only the most superficial results of this sudden shift of population: the disease, the filth, the stealing, the air of disorientation about the people of the camps and the towns. What he cannot see are the connections within the mind and spirit that have been broken to create this human swamp. The connections between the society and its product, between one man and another, between the nation and its own history — these are lost for these refugees. Land had been the basis of the social contract — the transmission belt of life that carried the generations of the family from the past into the future. Ancestor worshipers, the Vietnamese saw themselves as more than separate egos, as a part of this continuum of life. As they took life from the earth and from the ancestors, so they would find immortality in their children, who in their turn would take their place on the earth. To leave the land and the family forever was therefore to lose their place in the universe and to suffer a permanent, collective death. In one Saigon newspaper story, a young ARVN officer described returning to his home village after many years to find his family gone and the site of his father's house a patch of thorns revealing no trace of human habitation. He felt, he said, "like someone who has lost his soul."[4]

The soul is, of course, not a purely metaphysical concept, for it signifies a personal identity in life as well as death. For the Vietnamese to leave the land was to leave a part of the personality. When in 1962 the Diem regime forced the peasants to move behind the barbed wire of the strategic hamlets, the peasants found that they no longer trusted each other. And for an excellent reason. Once landowners or tenants, they became overnight improvidents and drifters who depended for their survival on what they could beg or take from others. Their behavior became unpredictable even to those who knew them.

The American war only completed the process the Diem regime had begun, moving peasants out of the villages and into the refugee camps and the cities, the real strategic hamlets of the war. For these farmers, as for their distant ancestors, to leave the hamlet was to step off the brink of the known world. Brought up as the sons of Mr. X or Mr. Y, the inhabitants of such a place, they suddenly found themselves nameless people in a nameless mass where no laws held. They survived, and as the war went on outside their control, they brought up their children in this anarchic crowd.

It was not, of course, the cities themselves that were at fault. To leave the village for the towns was for many Vietnamese far from a personal tragedy. In the 1940's and 1950's the enterprising young men left their villages voluntarily to join the armies or to find some employment in the towns. The balance of village life had long ago been destroyed, and, in any case, who was to say that the constant toil and small entertainment of a peasant's life was preferable even to the harshest of existences in a city? To join the army was in fact to see the world; to move to a town was to leave a life of inevitability for one of possibility. Though, or perhaps because, the hold of the family and the land was so strong, it contained also its contradiction — the desire for escape, for the death of the father and the end of all the burdensome family obligations. But it was one thing to escape into the new but ordered life of the NLF and quite another to escape to the anarchy of the American-occupied cities.

They are not like village children, these fierce, bored urchins who inhabit the shacks and alleyways of Saigon. When a Westerner visits these slums, the women look out shyly from behind their doorways, but the children run out, shoving and scratching at each other for a better view. They scream with hysterical laughter when one of their number falls off the planking and into the sewage. In a few moments they are a mob, clawing at the strangers as if they were animals to be teased and tortured. The anger comes up quickly behind the curiosity. A pebble sails out and falls gently on the stranger's back, and it is followed by a hail of stones.

There are street gangs now in every quarter of Saigon. Led by army deserters and recruited from among the mobs of smaller children, they roam like wolf packs, never sleeping in the same place twice, scavenging or stealing what they need to live on. Many of their numbers are orphans; the rest are as good as orphans, for their parents remain helpless peasants in the city. As a result, these boys are different from other Vietnamese. In a society of strong parental authority and family dependence, they have grown up with almost no discipline at all. Like the old street gangs of Harlem and Chicago, they have special manners, special codes. It is as though they were trying to create an entire society for themselves — a project in which they cannot succeed.

"In an absentminded way," wrote Professor Samuel Huntington in 1968,

> the United States in Vietnam may well have stumbled upon the answer to "wars of national liberation." The effective response lies neither in the quest for a conventional military victory, nor in esoteric doctrines and gimmicks of counter-insurgency warfare. It is instead forced-draft urbanization and modernization which rapidly brings the country in question out of the phase in which a rural revolutionary movement can [succeed.][5]

But there was nothing absentminded about the manner in which the U.S. armed forces went about their program of "forced-draft urbanization." Nor was it a simple oversight that they neglected the corollary of "modernization." Since 1954 — indeed since 1950 with the American sponsorship of the French war in Indochina — the United States has had only one concern and that was the war to destroy the revolutionary movement. It has not won that war and it has not destroyed the revolution, but it has changed Vietnam to the point where it is unrecognizable to the Vietnamese.

In 1966 the ministry of social welfare in Saigon wrote in preamble to its program: "With respect to this nation, this Ministry intends to stir up by all ways and means people's patriotic and traditional virtues with a view to shoring up our national ethics [which are] on the verge of ruin." Such a statement would have been perfectly appropriate coming from the priest of a rural Catholic village, but issued by the "government" of a country where numbers of prostitutes, beggars, orphans, juvenile delinquents, war wounded, and the otherwise infirm comprised an important percentage of the population, it seemed a kind of insanity. And in some sense it was, for over the years of war the GVN officials and bourgeoisie of the cities lost their grip on external reality. Cloistered within the high garden walls of their city houses, they looked back through the city, as if it were a transparency, to their old life of the family, the village, and the landed estate. They were dependent on the Americans for plans and programs as well as for the machinery to carry them out, and they lived intellectually in a state of suspended animation. They expected that the Americans would protect them in their sheltered existences, as the French had before them. But instead of protecting them, the Americans drove the peasantry into the cities with them. They created a mass where none had existed, and then they threatened to abandon their protégés.

In April 1968, just after Johnson's announcement of the bombing halt and his withdrawal from the presidential race, a young GVN official sat talking with an American reporter in a café in Tu Do Street. Asked his opinion of the speech, he blurted out suddenly, "You Americans can leave, you can leave whenever you wish. We cannot leave Vietnam. We have little choice." He leaned forward across the table. "Everything here is a theater. Everything is part of the play, even this table is a prop. We are just pawns. We have no say. But we are to be blamed. We have always been pawns."[6]

In a moment of crisis, or seeming crisis, the young official had without thinking confirmed the NLF analysis of the relationship between the Americans and those Vietnamese who cooperated with them. Instead of helping the Saigon government to stand on its own, the Americans made it more and more dependent upon them, economically, politically, militarily. And now the Americans were threatening to withdraw their support, leaving their "allies" as helpless as puppets to control their own destiny.

The American war did not so paralyze the revolutionary movement, but it removed much of its original base and changed the terms under which it operated. The NLF had, after all, pursued a peasant revolution designed to take power from the hands of the foreigners and the few Vietnamese — landlords and officials — who profited from their rule. The Russian, the Chinese, and the North Vietnamese revolutions were also in varying degrees peasant-based, but on a continuum of the four the NLF lay at the extreme end, for there was no industry in the south, and the bourgeoisie, preempted from the trade market by the Chinese, did not constitute a true class. The peasantry was all that existed as a productive force in South Vietnam, and the Front leaders based their program of development upon them. The Stalinist program of bleeding agriculture for the sake of industry was in fact useless to them, for the south had no mineral resources, and the country as a whole no potential to compete in the world market with heavy industry. Out of economic as well as military necessity, the NLF program consisted of agricultural development and the building of small, almost cottage, industries throughout the countryside. Now, after years of exile from the cities, they had to confront a social and economic situation completely new to them.

The economic problem of South Vietnam is not, however, primarily intellectual. It is easy enough to construct theories of development, but not so easy to deal with the chaos that the American war has left. In 1954 South Vietnam held great promise as an economic enterprise. Unlike so many countries, it could feed its population and, with some agricultural development, produce enough raw materials to create foreign exchange. Its rich farmland perfectly complemented the mineral resources and the industry of the north. Given a modicum of outside aid, the Vietnamese with their relatively skilled population might have succeeded in breaking through that cycle of poverty and underdevelopment that affects so many countries of the world. But the American war has undermined those possibilities — by the side effects of its own military presence as much as by the bombing. The phenomenon is a curious one. The

United States has had no direct economic interest in Vietnam. Over the years of the war it has not taken money out of Vietnam, but has put large amounts in. And yet it has produced much the same effects as the most exploitative of colonial regimes. The reason is that the overwhelming proportion of American funds has gone not into agricultural or industrial development but into the creation of services for the Americans — the greatest service being the Saigon government's army. As a whole, American wealth has gone into creating and supporting a group of people — refugees, soldiers, prostitutes, secretaries, translators, maids, and shoeshine boys — who do not engage in any form of production. Consequently, instead of having no capital, as it had at the moment of the French conquest, South Vietnam has an immense capital debt, for a great percentage of its population depends on the continued influx of American aid. The same was true to a lesser degree in 1954, and Saigon experienced an acute depression in the months between the French withdrawal and the first direct American commitment of aid. But now the balance of the population has changed so that the agriculture of the country scarcely suffices to feed its population, much less to create foreign exchange.

To be sure, as the American troops depart and the supply of dollars declines along with the shooting, many of the refugees will return to their villages and to agriculture. But for many the return will not be so easy. It is not merely that the population has grown and some of the arable land has been permanently destroyed. It is a social problem. Some millions of Vietnamese have now lived in the cities for five, ten years, or more; a half a generation of their children has grown up without ever watching a rice plant harvested. A certain number are used to the luxuries of the West and the freedoms of a Western-dominated city. The life of the peasantry is almost as foreign to them as it is to Americans, and yet they lack the very foundation upon which American society rests. These new city people have no capital — most of the money the United States invested in Vietnamese officials and businessmen has flown to safer investments abroad — and they have no industrial skills. They are not producers, but go-betweens who have engaged in nothing but marketing and services. The American war has altered them and rendered them helpless.

In considering the future of Vietnam, American officials have naturally tended to see these social and economic problems as amenable to American solutions. In 1969 David Lilienthal and a team of economists under commission from AID prepared a plan for the postwar development of the south. The plan, indeed the very fact of its commission, was perhaps the ultimate expression of American hubris. The officials of AID obviously believed even then that the United States could win the war and "modernize" the country to the point where it would pass the "phase" for a "rural insurgency movement." They had, it appeared, learned nothing and forgotten nothing from all those thousands of plans and programs, all those studies produced by MSU professors, the RAND Corporation, and other consultancy firms. They had not learned that economic development does not exist in a void. A political matter in all countries, it is most essentially political in a society that is not organized to make that development possible. AID itself demonstrated this truism in Vietnam. The politics of development were visible even in the landscape.

On the roads outside of Tay Ninh, Dalat, and Bien Hoa, an American visitor could for years see the same constellation of three hamlets. In each case the central hamlet, nominally Buddhist, consisted of no more than a group of palm-leaf hovels where one or two chickens scratched in the dust. The two surrounding Catholic hamlets might have belonged to another country, for they had ample concrete houses, herds of pigs and water buffaloes, and a church — nearly a cathedral — made of USAID cement and embellished with stucco and plaster statuary. For years the local AID advisers tried to bring the Buddhist hamlets up to the status of their Catholic neighbors, but they found it impossible to reverse the order of favoritism. The Catholic communities alone had the organization to demand GVN aid and to put that aid to use.

In many respects the GVN was a larger replica of that nominally Buddhist hamlet. When it received aid, it could not channel it into constructive purposes, nor could it even follow American plans to put it to work. This inability to organize was not "natural" to the GVN leaders, but rather the result of years of dependence on the French and the Americans. With the influx of people into the cities and into the American economy, the disorganization now extended down from the small elite to the very base of the population.

There are no counterparts to the Catholic hamlets in the cities. Though initially Catholic in population, Bui Phat never responded to Catholic leadership as did the villages. The political cadres of the

Buddhists and the NLF tried for years to organize in the slums of Saigon, but they never succeeded in forming long-lived, disciplined movements. Their failure owed in part to the difficulty of reaching people who did not belong to any other form of organization — a village or a factory — and who had few interests in common. More profoundly, however, it owed to the fact that the city people did have one thing in common: they depended on the foreigners for their livelihood. When a nationalist political party aimed to assert Vietnamese power, Vietnamese independence, it aimed also to destroy the subsistence of the city people. Beyond the threat of American military power, it was this economic dependency that prevented the city people from rising up to support the NLF during the Tet offensive. And it will be for this reason of dependency that the cities will remain corrupt, anarchic, and miserable so long as the United States continues to dominate the economic life of the country.

If the Lilienthal plan proposed to reconstruct Vietnam through the Saigon government, then it was a contradiction in terms. Like all other aid plans and programs that preceded it, it was designed for a hypothetical country that did not, and furthermore could not, exist while the Americans continued to make plans and programs for it. The United States could, of course, build factories and introduce agricultural extension programs that would benefit a few Vietnamese. It could suppress city politics and maintain the current state of anarchy for many years. But it could not (Professor Huntington to the contrary) build an independent government and move the society beyond its revolutionary "phase." The solution to Vietnamese problems would have to be Vietnamese — and all attempts at such a solution would be suspended for as long as the United States maintained the anti-Communist struggle.

In looking beyond the American withdrawal to a Vietnam governed by Vietnamese, American officials have generally seen nothing but disaster ahead. They have predicted a long period of armed struggle culminating in a severe political repression and the massacre of thousands of their "allies." Many of these predictions have been no more than self-serving propaganda designed to camouflage the destruction the United States itself is perpetrating in Indochina. Others have been sincere expressions of doubt that the Vietnamese can recover from the war without further upheavals and violence. The officials may be right in their predictions. The Vietnamese, after all, have to deal with over a million soldiers and a vast disorganized mass of refugees as well as with the personal and political hostilities that have grown up over the years of war. The difficulty of this task will only increase for as long as the United States continues to fight the war by proxy and to give the Vietnamese no latitude to make a political settlement. In the future the possibility exists that the ARVN will disintegrate into banditry and the NLF and North Vietnamese will repeat their performance in Hue, slaughtering thousands of anti-Communist partisans in an attempt to take control. The American war has devastated the economy while at the same time it has broken down the political power — sectarian as well as Communist — that is necessary to restore it. If no group, or coalition of groups, has the authority to govern by rule of law, the chances are that there will be a severe political repression followed by a draconian attempt to force the urban masses back into some form of production. Such organized violence may in its turn lead to a disorganized reign of terror such as succeeded the North Vietnamese land reform of 1956. But these disasters may well not occur — or at least not on a scale that would make them significant beside the past horrors of war. It is a notable fact that with all the new Vietnamese troops the level of violence has decreased wherever the American troops have pulled out. It is also notable that the Vietnamese who depended economically upon the Americans have survived their withdrawal without any form of community organization or government help. South Vietnam is still a rich country. The withdrawal of all foreign aid would bring a serious economic crisis, but not starvation for thousands of people. Then, too, the American officials, who have witnessed only the division and paralysis their presence has created among their own "allies," tend to underestimate the capacities of the Vietnamese. The American war has created a social and economic chaos, but it has not stripped the Vietnamese of their vitality and powers of resistance. The Vietnamese survived the invasions of the Mongol hordes, and they may similarly survive the American war.

The first source of strength in the south is the National Liberation Front. With North Vietnamese help the NLF has fought the United States for over a decade and remained undefeated. Standing in the place of all Vietnamese, it has carried on the tradition of Le Loi and those other Vietnamese heroes who waged the millennium-long struggle against foreign domination. Unlike the Nguyen emperors, the NLF never compromised their struggle by seeking the military assistance of a foreign power that would come to dominate their own efforts. They fought the war in a traditional manner by unleashing the vast resources of power within the Vietnamese villages. Their victory would not be the victory of one foreign power over another but the victory of the Vietnamese people — northerners and southerners alike. Far from being a civil war, the struggle of the NLF was an assertion of the principle of national unity that the Saigon government has endorsed and betrayed. With the North Vietnamese the Front leaders faced up to the threats, the promises, and finally the overwhelming military power of the United States. They held out against a country that could never be defeated by force of arms, and they provided an example of courage and endurance that measures with any in modern history.

Viewed in the abstract, it is possible that success might cause the revolutionary movement to disintegrate, just as it all but dissolved the Liberation Front in Algeria. But it seems unlikely. The Viet Minh did not disintegrate after the French war, and the NLF has an even firmer foundation in domestic politics than did its predecessor. In the countryside its success rested primarily on its revolutionary strategy, secondarily on its nationalist position. Land reform and a broad program of economic and social justice — these are the policies that gave it appeal to the rural people. If and when foreign governments cease to dominate the economy of the cities, the NLF program will seem equally attractive to many Vietnamese. The NLF has always been extremely flexible and politic in the planning and implementation of its social policies — thus it has left itself the latitude to adapt its plans to the postwar conditions of Vietnam. By contrast, its organization has been tight and disciplined. An organization that could survive the offensive of 1968 and the prospect of military defeat may eventually be able to cope with the huge tasks of resettlement, development, and rehabilitation necessary to its country.

Throughout the years of war GVN officials, like Americans, have always maintained that a coalition government would be a "disguise for surrender" to the Communists. At the time they were perfectly correct — though it was questionable, once the GVN were dissolved, how many people would have seen that dissolution as a "surrender." Men like Tran Ngoc Chau, and the imprisoned students and priests, no longer make such predictions. It is not that they deceive themselves, it is that they have come to regard the issues of war and peace in a new perspective. In late 1970 representatives from Buddhist groups, women's groups, youth councils, and trade unions, constituted themselves into the Popular Front for the Defense of Peace and issued a manifesto calling for the departure of all American troops as "a first necessary step to end the fighting" — a demand much more uncompromising than that the NLF was making. The political program of the Popular Front with its paragraphs on independence, democracy, and social and economic reform closely resembled the program the NLF had written a decade earlier.[7] This program did not represent a "surrender" to the NLF, but rather an assertion of the common ground among Vietnamese.° The American officials argued that programs meant little, and that the important question was who ended up in control of the country. But even the distribution of political strength was not quite so clear as it once was. The demands for peace showed that many Saigonese — far more than risked loss of income, imprisonment, and torture to make such demands — had reached the end of a process begun in 1968. At first there was only fear and uncertainty about the prospects of an American withdrawal. These feelings persisted because of the continuing ambiguity of American policy, but along with that uncertainty there was now anger against the Americans. Though still economically dependent on the Americans and thus unable to express their anger in public, many Saigonese cut through the knot of conflicting emotions and looked with clear eyes at the situation in which the Americans were leaving them. That anger, that clarity, gave them the promise of a force far greater than that of all the military equipment with which the Americans had provided them. It promised all those who had for so long depended on the Americans the capacity to break that dependency and to transform themselves from passive victims of their fate into strong and active citizens. It promised an end to the constant internal feuds and the beginning of a new community.

° American officials might also assert that this and other such peace groups were in fact directed by the NLF. In many cases they would be correct. But that fact would not alter the contention. It is only reasonable that a group, once it reached an NLF position, should have contact with the NLF and even welcome NLF direction. The point was that these city people had arrived at an NLF position.

Such groups as the Popular Front tended to have no permanent organization for the excellent reason that the Thieu regime would not permit them to survive as public associations.

"It is beyond imagination," wrote Professor Kissinger just before joining the Nixon administration, "that parties that have been murdering and betraying each other for twenty-one years could work together as a team, giving joint instructions to the country."[8] It may be beyond the imagination of American officials, but it is not necessarily beyond that of the Vietnamese who have come to hold the Americans responsible for those murders and betrayals. It is true that there will never be a permanent coalition in which each party joins in an amicable agreement to disagree. The Vietnamese way is not that of a balance of power, but that of accommodation leading to unanimity. The majority of Vietnamese, in any case, do not belong to parties and have no interest in dividing themselves up to continue the fratricidal struggle. For them a coalition government would be the Middle Way so long desired that could modulate the differences between the political groups and lead to a national reconciliation.

But this reconciliation may be difficult to achieve. The Nixon administration is, after all, determined to prevent it. It is determined for the sake of what its officials imagine to be American prestige to force the Saigon government to go on fighting for as long as possible after an American troop withdrawal. At a time when all Vietnamese political parties have been shattered by the war and a half of the population depends on the United States, American economic aid and firepower will have a great deal of influence on the Vietnamese. If the force of the American peace movement has expended itself on obtaining American troop withdrawals, then Nixon may well succeed in compelling Vietnamese to kill each other for some time to come. His prediction of massacres may thus be a self-fulfilling prophecy.

Whatever strategy the American government uses to carry on the war, it will only be delaying the inevitable. It is not just that the North Vietnamese and the NLF will refuse to surrender; it is that after all these years of war the Vietnamese have an immense desire for peace. And peace not merely as an end to violence, but peace as unity: the unity of north and south, the unity of a way of life and the continuity of Vietnamese history from the past into the future. Over the years, Americans have grown so used to a divided Vietnam that they have come to imagine these divisions as natural and permanent, but they are not so. In 1954 it was possible to imagine that the foreign powers could maintain the barriers between north and south, as they had maintained similar barriers in Germany and Korea. But the Vietnamese did not accept the division, and now after a decade of war the maintenance of it appears impossible even in the abstract. The Americans have destroyed the economic base of that region they hoped to preserve as a separate country. Furthermore, they have, instead of ending the drive for reunification, destroyed the regional political groups that held out in resistance against it. They have uprooted the sect populations and flattened the local ethnic, religious, and cultural peculiarities beneath a uniform, national disaster. If Vietnam is to be independent, it must now have a national government.

For the Vietnamese, domestic peace implies not merely the cessation of hostilities, but the victory of a single political system and way of life. In the past, "peace" meant the rule of that Confucian monarchy that certified the traditional way of life in the Vietnamese villages. Today, however, peace implies revolution — a complete change in the order of society. The NLF has been engaged in this project from its very beginning, but it is not alone; the southern sects have also worked for a social revolution in their own various ways. Even in 1946 revolution meant not so much the overthrow of an established order as the adjustment of society to those changes that had already taken place within it: the imposition of order upon disorder. In Vietnam the scope of the revolution ranged from the redistribution of wealth and power down to the relationship of the individual to his fellow men. Just what shape the new society should take has been a matter of debate, but there has been no debate on the necessity for a comprehensive new order. The American war with its "forced-draft urbanization" policies has only sharpened this need to the point where it is felt by the majority.

The slum children and the juvenile gangs are only the most visible manifestations of the disorder and the unease that underlies much of southern Vietnamese society. The cities, the army bases, and the refugee camps are filled with people who get along in one way or another, who cause no trouble and survive. Only the meaning of their lives has gone. Brought up to regard themselves as part of a larger enterprise — brought up in a world that would seem oppressive to most Westerners — they experience the life of the cities as a profound alienation, a division of self. "Even the bar girl," said one Vietnamese intellectual, "even the bar girl who now has money, who lives in the city and no longer wants to return to the country, who is accustomed to independence and gets along very well, even she feels guilty. At bottom she does not feel easy with herself, even after five or ten years of such work. She feels there is something missing. To find it she will give up her independence and all the advantages she now possesses."⁹

Personally, socially, politically, the disorder of the cities is a highly unstable condition — a vacuum that craves the oxygen of organized society. The Americans might force the Vietnamese to accept the disorder for years, but behind the dam of American troops and American money the pressure is building towards one of those sudden historical shifts when "individualism" and its attendant corruption gives way to the discipline of the revolutionary community. When this shift takes place, the American officials will find it difficult to recognize their former protégés. They may well conclude that the "hard-core Communists" have brainwashed and terrorized them into submission, but they will be wrong. It will simply mean that the moment has arrived for the narrow flame of revolution to cleanse the lake of Vietnamese society from the corruption and disorder of the American war. The effort will have to be greater than any other the Vietnamese have undertaken, but it will have to come, for it is the only way the Vietnamese of the south can restore their country and their history to themselves.

Afterword

I finished writing *Fire in the Lake* in 1971, four years before the war ended, and though I returned to Vietnam several times in those years, I never wanted to update it. Books have a certain structure, and when they're finished, they are, for better or worse, finished. Also, they are the product of a particular time in history and in the life of their author, and the time can't be recaptured. The light changes, the landscape alters, and so does one's state of knowledge and state of mind. Now, more than thirty years later, I have no intention of reflecting back on the war or trying to fill the subsequent history of Vietnam in just a few pages. But what I discovered on recent trips to Vietnam seems to me worth recording as kind of a coda to the book.

Driving across the Red River Delta in northern Vietnam a couple of years ago, Mary Cross, an American photographer, and I stopped at a cemetery with several handsome old tombs and a group of new earthen graves on mounds above the paddy land. In the distance we could see a procession coming down the lane from a nearby village to the sound of stringed instruments, gongs, and drums. In the lead were people with banners and flags from the local pagoda, and after them two lines of elderly women in brown and purple tunics carrying unlit straw torches and a long scroll with Buddhist iconography. Next came four men carrying a shrine with a photograph of the deceased — a patriarch in his seventies — an incense burner, and offerings of fruit and flowers. The musicians followed. Then, amid a crowd of family members in white headbands, six men rolled an ornate hearse with a double roof turned up, pagoda-style, at the corners. A middle-aged man, apparently the eldest son, walked backward in front of the hearse in filial deference. When the procession reached the cemetery, the coffin was lifted from its carriage and brought to the grave; incense sticks were lit, prayers were said, and the family wailed as the coffin was lowered into the ground. What we were witnessing, I realized, was a ceremony from precolonial times.

It was early March in the year 2000, just a month before the twenty-fifth anniversary of the end of the war. While exploring the countryside around Hanoi, I often came upon processions of people in brightly colored silk robes marching to the music of flutes and drums, with parasols overhead and the young men carrying a palanquin with the gilded red-and-gold throne of the tutelary spirit of the village. In central

Vietnam, on the road between Hue and Danang, Mary saw a fisherman launching a decorated paper boat into a lagoon as an offering to the sea spirits. On an island in the Perfume River near Hue, the two of us watched a mother and daughter in red and yellow robes dance before an outdoor altar to thank a favorite goddess for lifting a spell that had made the mother ill. All over the country the Buddhist pagodas we visited were filled with Vietnamese pilgrims and tourists.

Watching such ceremonies, I sometimes imagined that all the upheavals of the past century, from the French conquest to revolution and two major wars, had been no more than a parenthesis in Vietnamese history. This is hardly the case. Vietnam has been profoundly marked by all of these events. Still, there has been an astonishing revival of traditional social and religious practices throughout the country in the past few years. What is more, the revival is most pronounced in the north — in the region that most enthusiastically supported the revolution and in which there has been a Communist government for half a century. But then the north is by far the oldest part of Vietnam and the wellspring of its traditional culture.

On my first postwar visit to Vietnam in 1993, I went with a group from an American foundation to see a new handicraft project in a village some twenty miles from Hanoi. Surrounded by a thick hedge of bamboo and thorny plants, the village was invisible from the road. Within the hedge was a labyrinth of narrow dirt lanes flanked by hedges and brick walls. Walking along the lanes and looking through the gates in the walls, we could see houses with tiled roofs and open fronts giving onto brick courtyards and tiny gardens. The village was a honeycomb in which each household maintained its privacy. Near the center of the village was a big rectangular primary school, built in the 1960s, with sports fields around it. But on the hillside above it was the village *dinh*, built in the old style with heavy wooden pillars supporting a red-tiled roof. Shaded by a huge old banyan tree, the *dinh* faced south, overlooking a pond.

The school aside, the village looked to me much like the traditional northern villages described by French scholars such as Paul Mus and Pierre Gourou. I had never expected to see one this physically intact. In the 1960s the DRV had collectivized the family farms, merged the villages into larger administrative units, and organized the farmers into specialized production brigades. The government had also modernized the irrigation systems and rationalized the division of the rice lands, creating straight lines where none had existed before. In 1986, after the collectivization program failed, creating a near-famine in parts of the north, the government dismantled the communes and reinstituted private enterprise and family farming. In the meantime, however, the population of the country had grown almost exponentially, spilling millions of people into cities, towns, and roadside settlements.

By 2000, the major roads out of Hanoi had become corridors so built up with houses, shops, and small businesses that it was difficult to catch a glimpse of the landscape beyond. But farther out in the countryside we could see from the heights of a dike the old-style settlements commanding their rice fields like fortresses. Physically and politically, these villages are hardly as they were in precolonial times. Still, some institutions of village life have not changed, and a surprising number of others have been revived since 1986.

From medieval times on, most villages had their own particular handicraft industry — and they do today. Driving in the countryside, we could see the raw materials stacked up by the roads: plywood near villages that made toothpicks or matches, bundles of reeds and straw by those that wove baskets or mats. Some villages continue to produce the same handicrafts they did centuries ago. Bat Trang, for example, just outside of Hanoi, has long been famous for its blue-and-white pottery, Chuong in Ha Tay province for the *nom* leaf covering for conical hats. In the village I visited in 1993, a young woman, a mother of three small children, had contracted with a Japanese company to make baskets of a traditional design, giving employment to dozens of households. Elsewhere, villagers had used their entrepreneurial skills to take advantage of the new demands of the Vietnamese market. In Duong Ho in Hai Duong province, a village known for its traditional woodblock prints, most families, we discovered, had turned their talents to making paper offerings for the ancestors. Officially the government still frowned on the practice of burning paper imitations of luxury goods people wanted their ancestors to have in the afterlife, but after the economic reforms of 1986, it had given up trying to stop the practice. In tune with the times, villagers of Duong Ho were turning out not just paper shoes, umbrellas, and dress shirts, as in the old days, but paper motorcycles and cell phones as well.

In Dong Ky in Bac Ninh province, a village that has used its ancient woodworking skills to produce inlaid furniture for the international market, I talked with the manager of one family business, a young man with an executive air, about how he had coped with the Asian economic crisis of 1997 and what he was doing to fill the needs of an expanding Taiwanese market. Later he took us back to the family compound, where a tent was still up from a big family wedding held there the day before. His father, a Mr. Vu, gave us tea in the main house in front of the ancestral altar and discoursed on various subjects, including his service in the Viet Minh and the continuing relevance of Confucian values. A man in his seventies, Mr. Vu, we gathered, was the patriarch of a subclan, or extended family. He told us that the clan, which had seven branches in the village, kept genealogical records going back for centuries, and that everyone in the village knew his or her place in the patrilineage. Apparently neither revolution nor war nor business success had altered the family structure of Dong Ky.

As we were leaving the village, we stopped to watch a wrestling match in an open-air stadium. High school athletes were competing with wrestlers from a neighboring village, and the crowd was cheering and groaning with the fortunes of the local boys. It was a completely modern scene, but the tournament, we learned, was a part of the spring festival celebrating the patron genie of the village.

I happened upon several such festivals that March. The first was in Quang Ba, beyond the West Lake of Hanoi, a village that used to grow flowers but that has been built over and transformed into a residential neighborhood where many foreigners live. The *dinh*, a fine example of traditional architecture, just recently restored, had a lacquered and gilded altar decorated with flowers and miniature orange trees. One of the chief organizers, Mr. Vu Hoa My, welcomed me in rusty French and told me that the guardian spirit was Phuong Hung, an eighth-century king who had led an uprising against the Chinese. Mr. My was, it turned out, a retired government and Communist Party official who, he told me, had made money in real estate. He had given generously to the restoration of the *dinh*. I arrived just as the procession returned with the throne of the genie, pennants flying, musicians making a great noise, and a beautiful cloth dragon billowing out overhead. The procession, Mr. My said, had gone to the village pagoda to collect pure water — the dew of the morning. A couple of hundred people, the women in *ao dais*, the men in Western dress, had gathered to greet its return. After the throne had been ceremonially replaced in the *dinh*, a group of elderly men in blue Chinese-style robes said prayers before the altar. Families came forward out of the crowd with trays piled high with rice, vegetables, fruits, and cooked chickens. Leaving symbolic morsels on the altar, they asked the patron spirit to bless their meals and went outside to have their holiday photographs taken.

Afterward, amid a genial hubbub, the entertainment began. The village chess masters set up a human chess game in the courtyard with high school students dressed in robes representing kings, queens, knights, and pawns; the students sat on chairs and moved from square to square as directed. The play was fast, but one of the queens, who was hardly moved at all, got bored and read a movie magazine through most of it. Meanwhile, a flock of ducks was let loose in the pond and little boys competed to capture the ducks with long-handled nets — or simply by diving in and grabbing them. In a field behind the *dinh,* men huddled around rings in which spurless fighting cocks struggled more or less energetically to force their opponents out of the ring.

At a simple luncheon Quang Ba held for visitors from neighboring villages and a few other guests, Mr. My told me that for many years the *dinh* festivals had not been celebrated in this way. But now, he said, the government favors the ceremonies and traditional games because they remind people of their history and help to create strong communities. Listening to him, I began to think that the festivals were some kind of government effort to resurrect "tradition" for state purposes. Later I discovered that it was the villagers who had insisted on reviving their festivals — along with their other religious practices.

Northern Vietnam never had a cultural revolution, but in the period of "building socialism" from 1954 to 1986, the government curbed the old rites and banned the expensive feasts that often accompanied them. The elaborate family ceremonies, the cult of the village genie, and other spirit cults were variously denounced as wasteful, superstitious, and "feudalistic." By the mid-seventies even ancestor worship seemed to be on the wane. But then came the failure of collectivization and the economic reforms. Villagers immediately began to put more time and resources into their family rituals, and when they had some money, they refurbished their *dinhs* and began to celebrate the festivals. According to anthropologists, the villagers were readjusting to the return of family farming and the need for voluntary cooperation among households. The family and village ceremonies helped this process along.

In the early 1990s, the government gave the historic *dinhs* landmark status and helped to restore them. It also gave its blessing to the festivals. "When we collectivized, we said the festival was feudalistic. Now we bring the festival back and call it traditional," one villager told an American development expert with some irony. Apparently, in the wake of the economic disaster caused by its own "scientific" methods, the government had decided to relegitimate itself on traditional grounds.

Central Vietnam was the region hardest hit by the American war. Driving from Danang to Hue on my first trip back, I somehow expected to see the rusting bodies of tanks, the tin shacks of the refugee encampments, and scars from the bombing and shelling on the hillsides. But the wounds of war had disappeared from the countryside, and in Hue the citadel and the palaces and tombs of the Nguyen emperors had been so completely rebuilt and restored that it was hard to imagine that the sanguinary battle for the city in 1968 had ever occurred. Along Route 1, the landscape looked much the same as when I first saw it in early 1966 — except for one thing. Here and there by the roadside were cemeteries with enormous new family tombs freshly plastered and painted in pastel colors.

When I returned seven years later, Route 1 outside of Hue had become a bustling commercial highway lined with stores, repair shops, and houses. New houses had sprung up in the villages as well, some with highly decorated spirit screens in front of them. But the *dinhs*, even those the Ministry of Culture had designated as historical monuments, lay in various states of disrepair. "It's hard to raise money for the *dinhs*," an elderly guardian of one of them told me. "People take care of their clan houses, but the *dinhs* are lost in these large communities."

In central Vietnam — at least south of the seventeenth parallel — the villages do not have the cohesiveness they do in the north. Whether this is a recent or a historical development, they are today little more than administrative units. But all the people we talked with knew exactly how many clans and subclans there were in their villages, and, as the *dinh* guardian suggested, the most impressive buildings were the houses that people had built or repaired in honor of their ancestors. Walking around one village — as it happened the home village of

Le Duc Anh, the president of Vietnam in the early nineties — we found a splendid new house, completely unoccupied, that the members of a clan had built for the ancestral altar and for family gatherings on the death anniversaries of their forebears.

On a road just north of Hue, we came across a lineage hall: a shrine built in the 1990s by a branch of the imperial Nguyen family containing the family's ancestral tablets and a genealogical chart tracing the family back fifteen generations. Lineage halls were, I knew, a feature of traditional society, but I had never seen one in the sixties and seventies. Just opposite the Nguyen hall was another one, also of recent construction, this one honoring a branch of the Do family. The caretaker of this shrine, Mr. Do Van Le, showed us a book, privately printed in 1998, that traced the family back twelve generations to the ancestor who had come here from Thanh Hoa province in the north five hundred years ago. In 1977, by his account, a member of the family had found a record of the first seven generations compiled by a Confucian scholar in 1875. He had the text translated from Chinese characters and added information about the succeeding generations. Subsequently the family had appointed a board of editors to do the remaining work.

According to Mr. Le, most of the Do family had lived in this district until the American war, when there had been a partial diaspora. Some members now lived in Hue, some in Ho Chi Minh City, some in the United States. Mr. Le told us that his elder brother had joined the NLF and been killed in the U Minh forest, but he spoke of the war as if it were ancient history. What pleased him, he said, was that as many as two hundred fifty members of the family came back for reunions, including a number from California.

Listening to Mr. Le, I remembered a family feast a colleague and I had stumbled upon in 1973 in a hamlet not far from Danang. The village had been razed in the sixties, but the rice was growing again, and people had put up thatched huts on the old brick foundations and terraces. On one of the terraces some forty people — old men, women, and children — were gathered around a long wooden table laden with dishes of fish, chicken, vegetables, and fruit. The elders at the gathering gave us to know that the village had supported the revolution through the French and the American wars. They were telling us obliquely of their own exploits in the resistance when an ARVN major in dress uniform pulled up on a motorbike. The patriarch acknowledged his arrival and motioned him to a place at the table. The old men went right on talking about what they had done to help the NLF. The major was, after all, a member of the family.

That family feast had seemed to me a natural resumption of tradition — a simple exhalation of breath after all those years of war. But the appearance of clan houses and lineage halls in the 1990s seemed to require some explanation. Families such as the Do and the Nguyen had not simply renewed their local ties after a decade of collectivization. Rather, they had gone to considerable scholarly effort — one they had not made since the French arrived in the nineteenth century — to discover their roots in the distant past. In doing so, they had created clans that encompassed large numbers of people, some of them living as far away as California. But perhaps that was just it. Central Vietnamese families had been torn apart by two wars and geographically dispersed. The effort to put them back together was so great as to seem artificial, but it was proportionate to the trauma of the deaths and the separations.

In the Mekong Delta, where the bonds of the village have never been strong, and where families worship their ancestors only to the third generation, the *dinhs* are, as always, neglected, and it's difficult to find a clan house like those in central Vietnam. But the local religious practices are back, and so, in big way, is Buddhism. All the hamlets I visited in the central delta had small pagodas, and a number had private prayer houses built by well-to-do families. In My Tho, the beautiful Vinh Trang pagoda, built in 1849, has become a major pilgrimage center for the delta. On the fifteenth day of every lunar month, thousands of visitors come to admire the temple's exuberantly colorful facade and to worship in its sanctuaries. The pagoda has a school of Buddhist studies, and it helps to support many of the smaller Mahayana pagodas in the province.

Possibly the most remarkable development in Vietnamese cultural life since 1986 is the revival of Buddhism throughout the country. In southern and central Vietnam the revival came after a hiatus of only ten years, but they were years in which the government regarded the monasteries as potentially subversive, and people were afraid to visit the pagodas. In the north it followed upon almost a half century of quiescence: decades of war, revolution, and "building socialism" in which the priests left the villages and many of the pagodas and shrines fell into disrepair. Yet after the economic reforms, people all over the country flocked to their local pagodas and petitioned the government to help preserve those of historic importance. The government acquiesced, and beginning in 1989 it gave many pagodas, north and south, the equivalent of landmark status. At the same time, it lifted many of the restrictions it had put on the monasteries and on Buddhist folk practices. During the nineties the monasteries came to life again, and priests returned to celebrate the rites at village temples and shrines, and at least a dozen pagodas became major pilgrimage sites and tourist attractions for the Vietnamese.

One of the most popular pagodas in the north is Ba Chua Kho in Ha Bac province, dedicated to the eleventh-century empress who provisioned her husband's troops for war against the Chinese. Neglected during the fifties, it became part of an army base and was virtually destroyed in the war. In the nineties the Ministry of Culture rebuilt it almost from the ground up, justifying the expenditure on the grounds that it was a national historical monument. But, for its visitors, the main attraction is the provident empress's reputation for conferring prosperity and good fortune upon her devotees.

Arriving at Ba Chua Kho at 10 A.M. on a Friday morning, I found the parking lot already filling up with buses and cars. In the booths in front of the pagoda steps, scribes were writing out prayers in Chinese characters for their customers, and vendors of fruit, sticky rice, joss sticks, and paper offerings were doing good business. At one of the booths a woman from the Ministry of Health in Binh Dinh province, who had been called to Hanoi for a meeting on malaria control, was ordering a tray piled high with an arrangement of fruit, flowers, and gilded paper offerings to take to the goddess on behalf of herself and some of her coworkers. She was, she said, building a house and needed help with the financing.

The main sanctuary of the pagoda was crowded with people and with the trays of offerings they had left before the altar. Going in through a side door, I found myself pressed against a wall next to a young woman in jeans and a fashionable black leather jacket. On the wall a government poster enjoined people to practice religion and eschew superstition, a distinction the author did not even try to define. In front of us a group of men were handing around a cup with three antique coins and taking turns throwing the coins: heads you got your wish, tails you didn't. After some conversation, the young woman told me she had come to the pagoda because she wanted a boyfriend. Sure, she said, she was making an effort, but a little good fortune always helped.

Ba Chua Kho is one of those eclectic pagodas in which Buddhism has melded with folk traditions, Taoism, and the worship of a national hero. What's happening there is fairly easy to understand. With the economic reforms of the late 1980s, the government essentially told its citizens: the system isn't working, so we're breaking it up and you're pretty much on your own. That meant that people had to take economic risks — a novelty for most in the north. In temples such as Ba Chua Khoa, the Vietnamese are taking out the spiritual equivalent of insurance policies on their houses and businesses — or their potential for finding husbands or having children.

At the orthodox Mahayana temples, some of great age and beauty, the atmosphere is more subdued and the quest of the visitors not so obvious. In the north, the ancient Thay pagoda in Ha Tay province, built into the lee of a limestone mountain, and the nearby Tay Phuong pagoda are both very popular. On weekdays, most of the visitors are women from Buddhist associations traveling together on buses from one temple to the next. Quiet and serious, they listen as the local guide explains the history and the religious significance of the sculptures, carvings, and musical instruments. Some ask questions about the iconography, and at the main altar they stop to light joss sticks and pray. On weekends, the crowds swell with family groups, busloads of civil servants and factory workers, and groups of young people from the cities in a holiday spirit. Clearly these people are exploring their country — a luxury the Vietnamese have never had before — and watching them examine the shrines and grottos, I could imagine them simply as museum-goers, except that some of them stop to pray.

With the reforms of the eighties the government did something more than open up the economy, for in the Vietnamese context Marxism-Leninism was more than an economic system and an ideology. Like Confucianism, it was a social system grounded in a claim to an immutable, scientific understanding of human nature and the laws of history; it was also a set of ethics, and the ethics, or "revolutionary virtues," taught by Ho Chi Minh closely resembled those of

Confucianism. In abandoning the command economy, the government was withdrawing from its claim to know how the larger laws of history worked and its claim to represent a complete moral and social system — or a complete replacement for the Confucian regime.

In fact, the system had already broken down by 1986, and everyone knew it. In the villages of the north, people — including Communist Party members — worked to rebuild their communities along traditional lines. In central Vietnam, people reconstructed their family ties to include those who had fought on both sides in the war. But Vietnamese farmers, along with city people, live in a larger society as well. In many countries in certain periods of history, multitudes of people made pilgrimages to shrines long distances away. Whatever the pilgrims hoped to accomplish, they saw something of the larger world and developed a sense of spiritual community with their fellows: a community that transcended local boundaries and regional differences. Then, too, in Vietnam the traditional pattern was that Buddhism flourished in times of trouble, when the Confucian state weakened. In this case, of course, the "trouble" is the market economy and the old order reasserting itself to deal with what Westerners blithely call modernization.

Back Notes

1: States of Mind

1. Viet Hoai, "The Old Man in the Free Fire Zone," in *Between Two Fires: The Unheard Voices of Vietnam*, ed. Ly Qui Chung, pp. 102–105.
2. Léopold Cadière, *Croyances et pratiques religieuses des viêtnamiens*, vol. 2, p. 308.
3. Nghiem Dang, *Viet-Nam: Politics and Public Administration*, p. 53.
4. Confucius, *The Analects of Confucius*, p. 127.
5. Conversation with Paul Mus.
6. Confucius, *Analects*, p. 104. According to Waley, "The saying can be paraphrased as follows: If I and my followers are right in saying that countries can be governed solely by correct carrying out of ritual and its basic principle of 'giving way to others,' there is obviously no case to be made out for any other form of government. If on the other hand we are wrong, then ritual is useless. To say, as people often do, that ritual is all very well so long as it is not used as an instrument of government, is wholly to misunderstand the purpose of ritual."
7. Charles Gosselin, *L'Empire d'Annam*, p. 149.
8. Truong Buu Lam, *Patterns of Vietnamese Response to Foreign Intervention: 1858–1900*, p. 77. From an anonymous appeal to resist the French (1864).
9. Paul Mus, "Les Religions de l'Indochine," in *Indochine*, ed. Sylvain Lévi, p. 132.
10. There were also handicraft guilds and Buddhist and Taoist priesthoods, but these are details. The generalization in true enough for the purposes of contrast.
11. For the French, the emperor's persecution of French Catholic missionaries (though there were relatively few cases) served as a pretext for intervention in Vietnam. But to the French emperors conversion to Catholicism signified not just a religious apostasy, but alienation from the state itself.
12. The Gia Long code, promulgated by the early-nineteenth-century founder of the Nguyen dynasty, was a much more exact copy of the Chinese codes than the Le code that governed Vietnam from the fifteenth to the nineteenth centuries.

13. Le Thanh Khoi, *Le Viêt-Nam*. According to the French historian, Henri Maspero, the land did not belong to the emperor, but to the people, whose will was expressed by the mouth of the sovereign. This reflexive relation between the people and the sovereign is typical of the Vietnamese political philosophy derived from Mencius.
14. Truong Chinh, *President Ho Chi Minh*, p. 68.
15. In the seventeenth century a French missionary, Alexandre de Rhodes, transcribed the Vietnamese language into the Roman alphabet, using diacritical marks to indicate the different tones. His aim was to render the Bible and other Christian texts into Vietnamese. The first people to use *quoc ngu*, as his system was called, were therefore the Vietnamese Catholics. The Latin alphabet came into general use only after the French conquest.
16. A hypothesis: the spoken language with its five tones may also be more concrete (more allusive, less abstract) than Western languages because of the element of music in it. In the way that people recall particular situations and particular people from the sound of a familiar tune, so the Vietnamese may associate words more directly with particular events than do Westerners. Cf. A. R. Luria, *The Mind of a Mnemonist* (New York: Basic Books, 1968).
17. Gosselin, *Empire*, p. 27.
18. Douglas Pike, *Viet Cong*, pp. 379, 383.
19. *New York Times*, 8 October 1970.
20. Nguyen Truong To, "Memorials on Reform," in *Patterns of Response*, ed. Truong Buu Lam, p. 98.
21. If the Buddhists were, for instance, to be proved wrong in the end, then their statement would be both untrue and useless.
22. Phan Thi Dac, *Situation de la personne au Viet-Nam*, pp. 137–156.
23. Phan Thanh Gian, "Letter on His Surrender," in *Patterns of Response*, ed. Truong Buu Lam, pp. 87–88.
24. Ibid., p. 88. Phan Thanh Gian may have been wrong in his assessment of the military situation. Other mandarins had behaved differently, many of them resisting the French to the last. Given his assessment, however, there was little else for him to do.
25. Confucius, *Analects*, p. 168.
26. Paul Mus, "Cultural Backgrounds of Present Problems," p. 13. In the *Analects* the Master recounts this story about one of the divine sages of the past.
27. Ho Chi Minh, *Ho Chi Minh on Revolution*, p. 145.
28. *I Ching*, p. 190.
29. John T. McAlister, Jr., *Vietnam: The Origins of Revolution*, pp. 186–188.
30. Jean Lacouture, *Ho Chi Minh*, p. 179.
31. In the Sino-Vietnamese world, dates were not reckoned from a single point (such as the birth of Jesus Christ) but from the beginning of each new dynasty or each new emperor's reign. Thus even the numbers of the years repeat themselves.
32. *I Ching*, p. 190.
33. Ibid., p. 189.

2: Nations and Empires

1. This secret society was the northern branch of the Dai Viet Party (see below for further details). Far from being an arm of the Lao Dong Party, it was the group that General Edward Lansdale used in some of his intelligence and sabotage missions in North Vietnam just after the French war. Cf. "Lansdale Team's Report on Covert Saigon Mission in '54 and '55," in Neil Sheehan et al., *The Pentagon Papers*, pp. 53–66.
2. Ly Thuong Kiet, "The Principle of Identity," in *Patterns of Vietnamese Response to Foreign Intervention: 1858–1900*, ed. Truong Buu Lam, p. 47.

3. Nguyen Trai, "A Great Proclamation upon the Pacification of Wu" (1428), in *Patterns of Response,* ed. Truong Buu Lam, p. 56.

4. Ho Chi Minh, "Speech Opening the First Theoretical Course of the Nguyen Ai Quoc School" (7 September 1957), in *Ho Chi Minh on Revolution,* ed. Bernard B. Fall, p. 321.

5. In 1945–1946 Ho Chi Minh had even courted American support. He quoted from the American Declaration of Independence in his own independence declaration and he wrote a series of letters to the American government asking for diplomatic aid.

   American scholars and scientists who visited the DRVN during the American war were always surprised by the interest and knowledge the North Vietnamese showed in the United States and their particular scholarly disciplines.

   The Vietnamese desire for outside contacts was not by any means confined to the non-Communist world.

6. Cynthia Frederick, "Cambodia: Operation Total Victory No. 43," p. 9.

7. Paul Mus, *Viêt-Nam: Sociologie d'une guerre.* Chapter 1 is an extensive discussion of the role of the village in traditional Vietnamese life and in guerrilla warfare.

8. John T. McAlister, Jr., and Paul Mus, *The Vietnamese and Their Revolution.* This book is to a great extent a translation and condensation of Mus's earlier *Sociologie d'une guerre.* I have used citations from this rather than from the original because the translation is good and because it is more available to American readers.

   Mus wrote: "In these plains of irrigated rice there are no natural sanctuaries in which one may hide: no woods, no marshland or moors. If a man wants to take cover and disappear, he can only do so behind man. Consequently, this type of disappearance is a solution only for those people native to the region. But with that reservation the populous masses are an effective shelter against any adversary of a different language, or more especially, of a different skin.

   "When a man creeps in among his own people, how can he be found? In the last analysis it is the villages that have the answer." (Mus, *Viêt-Nam,* pp. 51–52.)

9. Truong Buu Lam, *Patterns of Response,* p. 3.

10. Some of the colonizing villages were military or penal colonies sent out by the state, but they, too, tended to follow the same pattern of behavior.

11. Léopold Cadière, *Croyances et pratiques religieuses des viêtnamiens,* vol. 2, pp. 13–14.

12. Gerald C. Hickey, *A Village in Vietnam,* p. 82.

13. "Interviews Concerning the National Liberation Front of South Vietnam," RAND Corporation File AG-533, pp. 22–23.

14. One of the main streets in Saigon was named after independence for the most brilliant of the Tay-Son commanders, Nguyen Hue.

15. Joseph Buttinger, *The Smaller Dragon,* p. 176.

16. A. B. Woodside, "Some Features of the Vietnamese Bureaucracy Under the Early Nguyen Dynasty," p. 18.

17. The force consisted of 3,500 men.

   Le Thanh Khoi, *Le Viêt-nam,* p. 176. The number was small compared to that the Tay Son and the Nguyen fielded against each other.

18. For a more complete account of the French occupation of Vietnam, see Buttinger, *Smaller Dragon,* chapter 4 ("Missionaries, Merchants and Conquerors") and chapter 6 ("The Conquest of French Indochina").

19. The name "Indochina" was coined by a Danish geographer in 1852. The French adopted it, perhaps, as rhetorical consolation for having failed to conquer either India or China.

20. Eric R. Wolf, *Peasant Wars in the Twentieth Century,* p. 170.

21. Paul Mus, "Viet Nam: A Nation Off Balance," and Wolf, *Peasant Wars,* p. 167.

22. Bernard B. Fall, "The Political-Religious Sects of Viet-Nam," pp. 235–239.

23. McAlister and Mus, *Vietnamese and Their Revolution,* pp. 90–92.

24. Fall, "Sects of Viet-Nam," p. 243.

25. Ibid., pp. 245–247.

26. Ibid., p. 245. The Trotskyites made contact with So during his stay in Saigon and had some political influence on him. Neither the alliance nor the influence upon the Hoa Hao survived his death.

27. In certain areas the workmen customarily received one cent for an entire day's work. The average annual income of a peasant family of eleven was thirty-two piastres. Of that the French took six piastres in direct taxation alone. McAlister and Mus, *Vietnamese and Their Revolution*, p. 76.

28. Out of the 6,530 landowners in Indochina to own more than 125 acres of land by 1930, 6,300 were located in southern Vietnam. (John T. McAlister, Jr., *Vietnam: The Origins of Revolution*, p. 70.) And of the 8,600 Vietnamese who received an annual income of more than six thousand piastres in 1931 (or, the wealthy in Vietnam), eight thousand were residents of the south, whereas 45 percent of the middle-income receivers lived in the north. (Ibid., p. 72.)

29. Ibid., p. 80. In 1931 a little more than thirty-nine thousand Vietnamese had received five years of primary education. A little more than four thousand had received nine years of that education, and a few hundred had gone on to more advanced studies.

30. Ibid., pp. 87–91. In 1929 they undertook a militant campaign against the French with the assassination of one prominent labor recruiter and a small troop uprising at Yen Bay. The perpetrators of both attempts were eventually caught by the police.

31. It is said that Ho Chi Minh opposed the uprising, but he did not at the time have the power to stop it. Ibid., p. 94.

32. Ibid., p. 194. Ho Chi Minh's speech as quoted from the *Documents* of the Democratic Republic of Vietnam.

33. Paul Mus, *Le Viêt-Nam chez lui*, contains an account of his experience in the villages making his escape from Hanoi.

34. McAlister, *Vietnam*, pp. 191–192. The emperor himself then said: "You could understand even better if you were able to see what is happening here, if you were able to sense the desire for independence that has been smoldering in the bottom of all hearts and which no human force can any longer hold back. Even if you were to arrive to re-establish a French administration here, it would no longer be obeyed; each village would be a nest of resistance, every former friend an enemy, and your officials and colonials themselves would ask to depart from this unbreathable atmosphere."

35. It was at this point that Ho Chi Minh sent a series of notes to the U.S. government asking for diplomatic support. The Truman administration did not reply. Sheehan, *Pentagon Papers*, pp. 4–5, 26–27.

36. McAlister, *Vietnam*, p. 300.

37. According to American and British information, the Viet Minh received no aid from the People's Republic of China until 1950, and very little the next year. Chinese deliveries of supplies of all sorts went from twenty tons a month in 1951 to four thousand tons a month in 1954. Dennis J. Duncanson, *Government and Revolution in Vietnam*, p. 177.

38. Jean Lacouture and Philippe Devillers, *La Fin d'une guerre*, p. 278. See also George McTurnan Kahin and John W. Lewis, *The United States in Vietnam*, p. 34 (General Navarre's map).

39. Kahin and Lewis, *United States in Vietnam*, pp. 103–104.

40. Article 16 banned the introduction into Vietnam of "any troop reinforcements and additional military personnel" from the outside.

    Article 17 banned the "introduction into Vietnam of any reinforcements in the form of all types of arms, munitions and other war matériel, such as combat aircraft, naval craft, pieces of ordnance, jet engines and jet weapons and armoured vehicles."

    Article 18 forbade "the establishment of new military bases."

    Article 19 stated: "[No] military base under the control of a foreign State may be established in the re-grouping zone of either party; the two parties shall ensure that the zones assigned to them do not adhere to any military alliance and are not used for the resumption of military hostilities or to further an aggressive policy." (Kahin and Lewis, *United States in Vietnam,* p. 50.)

41. Lacouture and Devillers, *Fin d'une guerre,* pp. 103–104.

    The United States did, however, make a statement promising to refrain from any threat or use of force that might undermine the Geneva Agreements. The statement also said that, "In the case of nations now divided against their will, we shall continue to seek to achieve unity through free elections supervised by the United Nations to insure that they are conducted fairly." Sheehan, *Pentagon Papers,* p. 52.

42. Kahin and Lewis, *United States in Vietnam,* p. 32. The United States increased its aid to the French war effort from $150 million a year in 1950 to $1.33 billion in 1954.

43. Duncanson, *Government and Revolution,* p. 193.

44. See Lucien Bodard, *The Quicksand War,* for a colorful account of this period.

3: *The Sovereign of Discord*

1. Robert Scheer, *How the United States Got Involved in Vietnam,* pp. 38–40. Original quotations are from the *New York Times* and *Life* magazine.

    Eisenhower met only one other man at the airport — King Saud of Saudi Arabia.

2. Neil Sheehan et al., *The Pentagon Papers,* p. 166–172.

3. Douglas Pike, *Viet Cong,* p. 73.

4. Philippe Devillers, *Histoire du Viêt-Nam de 1940 à 1952,* p. 469.

5. Sheehan, *Pentagon Papers,* p. 52.

    In its statement on the Geneva accords the U.S. delegation said that the United States would "view any renewal of aggression in violation of the aforesaid agreements with grave concern and as seriously threatening international peace and security."

6. "Lansdale Team's Report on Covert Saigon Mission in '54 and '55," in Sheehan, *Pentagon Papers,* pp. 53–66. Many of Lansdale's Vietnamese agents who went north ended by defecting to the Viet Minh.

7. Robert Shaplen, *The Lost Revolution,* p. 104.

8. "Lansdale Team's Report," in Sheehan, *Pentagon Papers,* pp. 53–66. Lansdale at first tried to approach Hinh through his mistress, whom the Lansdale team was carefully cultivating, along with the mistresses of several other important Vietnamese, by means of classes in English.

9. Ibid. Hinh was later to return to Vietnam to fight for a while with the sects. When the sects were defeated, he retired to France to become a general in the French air force — leaving the Vietnamese air command open to younger officers, such as Nguyen Cao Ky.

10. Lansdale personally persuaded one of the dissident Cao Dai generals, Trinh Minh The, to rally to Diem for only the price of his troops' salaries. This incident forms the basis for Graham Greene's excellent novel of Vietnam between the two wars, *The Quiet American.* General The was killed during the battle with the Binh Xuyen.

11. Shaplen, *Lost Revolution,* p. 124.

12. Ibid., p. 105.

13. Ibid.

14. Ibid., p. 108.

15. Ibid., pp. 109–112.

16. George McTurnan Kahin and John W. Lewis, *The United States in Vietnam,* p. 77.

17. Frank N. Trager, *Why Vietnam?,* pp. 110–111, quotes Kennedy.

18. Bernard B. Fall, *The Two Vietnams,* pp. 153–154. Also Scheer, *How the United*

States Got Involved, p. 26, says that two hundred thousand – or almost all of the remainder – were dependents of the State of Vietnam's soldiers and officials based in the north.

19. Robert Scigliano, *South Vietnam: Nation Under Stress,* p. 112. This comparison continued to hold true throughout the war and for most statistics, including the tonnage of bombs dropped.

20. David Halberstam, *The Making of a Quagmire,* p. 42.

21. The one exception was the naturalized American citizen, Bernard B. Fall. Fall, a Frenchman by birth, had been in Indochina during the French war and had written a doctoral thesis on the government of the Viet Minh. Though Fall supported the American aims in Vietnam, he knew too much about Vietnam and the French official attitudes towards it to be taken in by the optimism of the local American officials.

22. Scheer, *How the United States Got Involved,* p. 39.

23. Nguyen Thai, "The Government of Men in the Republic of Vietnam," pp. 100–118.

24. Bernard B. Fall, *Last Reflections on a War,* p. 167.

25. Dennis J. Duncanson, *Government and Revolution in Vietnam,* p. 227, and Scigliano, *South Vietnam,* p. 95. The remaining seats were held by montagnard deputies, selected by co-optation.

26. Transcript of Madame Nhu's televised speech at Fordham University, 11 October 1963.

27. Wesley R. Fishel, "Vietnam's Democratic One-Man Rule."

28. Scigliano, *South Vietnam,* p. 168.

29. Duncanson, *Government and Revolution,* p. 257, and Scigliano, *South Vietnam,* p. 171. In any case, twenty thousand prisoners represented better than a thousandth of the population of the south.

30. Scheer, *How the United States Got Involved,* p. 41.

31. Fishel, "Vietnam's Democratic One-Man Rule." Also "Problems of Democratic Growth" in *Problems of Freedom,* ed. Wesley R. Fishel, pp. 9–29.

32. Dennis Warner, *The Last Confucian,* p. 91.

33. The parallel is almost exact, for in China the Americans had to overlook the fact that Chiang was concentrating almost all of his attentions on defeating his own internal enemy, the Chinese Communists, instead of America's enemy, the Japanese.

34. Scigliano, *South Vietnam,* p. 49.

35. Ibid., p. 63.

36. Ibid., p. 35.

37. Duncanson, *Government and Revolution,* pp. 228–229.

38. Scigliano, *South Vietnam,* p. 58.

39. One was secretary of state at the presidency and the other the assistant secretary of state for national defense. Diem himself was the secretary of defense.

40. Duncanson, *Government and Revolution,* pp. 215–216.

41. Ibid., p. 217.

42. Scigliano, *South Vietnam,* p. 77.

43. Ibid., p. 173.

44. Duncanson, *Government and Revolution,* pp. 255–256.

45. Shaplen, *Lost Revolution,* p. 104.

46. Anthony T. Bouscaren, *The Last of the Mandarins,* p. 82.

47. Duncanson, *Government and Revolution,* p. 215.

48. Nguyen Thai, "Government of Men," p. 213.

49. Ibid., pp. 228–235.

50. This Catholic law must have seemed very odd to most Vietnamese, for in this quasi-Buddhist country it was often the custom for men to take a second or third wife without the legal formality of a divorce.

51. A perfect example of this logic appears in an article by Chester Bowles:
    In July, 1954, when the Geneva Agreements were signed, there was some basis for

hope that a stable peace might be assured by the free elections which the agreements called for to determine the future governments of North and South Vietnam [sic]. But South Vietnam's President Ngo Dinh Diem, on one pretext or another, refused to cooperate, and, without connivance (the United States never actually signed the accords), the elections were never held.

When the Ho Chi Minh Government in Hanoi, bitter over what it considered to be a deliberate violation of the Geneva election agreement, launched a new campaign of terrorism against the Diem Government, Diem promptly sought our assistance.

In retrospect, this was a turning point. If we had learned our lessons from the failure of Chiang Kai Shek in China and the French in Indochina, and insisted as a condition for our economic assistance, on a sweeping program of domestic reform and development in South Vietnam — a more equitable tax system, increased rural credit, irrigation, schools and roads, and above all a sweeping land reform program that would have assured each rural family in South Vietnam ten or fifteen acres of their own — I believe the political and economic situation still might have been stabilized.

At first Diem demonstrated a heartening degree of courage and understanding, but gradually, like most recipients of American military aid in the underdeveloped world, he slipped under the control of the great landlords and the other right-wing elements who were determined at any cost of blood and suffering to maintain the political status quo.

Rejecting what he (correctly, I think) believed to be a half-hearted urging from the United States, Diem refused to place a ceiling on land holdings (as he had promised to do), to clear up corruption in the villages and cities and to grant even minimal local powers in a society long accustomed to strong political institutions in the villages.

(Chester Bowles, excerpts from testimony to the Joint Economic Committee of Congress, *Boston Sunday Globe,* 14 February 1971.)

52. Fall, *Two Vietnams,* pp. 294–295. Though, as the Americans pointed out, rice production had regained its prewar level, the country had half again as much population as it had in 1938.

53. Duncanson, *Government and Revolution,* p. 247.

54. See fuller discussion of land reform in the next chapter. The French government bought out its own nationals who owned rice land, and the Diem regime allowed those who owned rubber plantations or other industries to remain.

55. Milton C. Taylor, "South Viet-Nam: Lavish Aid, Limited Progress," p. 243.

56. Shaplen, *Lost Revolution,* pp. 191–192.

57. Scigliano, *South Vietnam,* p. 171, cites the hawkish British historian, P. J. Honey.

58. J. J. Zasloff, "Origins of the Insurgency in South Vietnam, 1954–1960." See also the RAND interviews cited elsewhere.

59. Joseph Buttinger, *Vietnam: A Dragon Embattled,* vol. 2, pp. 950–951, cites Malcolm Browne.

60. Ho Chi Minh, *Ho Chi Minh on Revolution,* pp. 150–152 ("To the People's Executive Committees at All Levels," October 1945), and pp. 180–184 ("Letter to Comrades in North Viet-Nam," 1 March 1947).

61. Gerald C. Hickey, *Village in Vietnam,* p. 90.

62. Ibid., p. 185.

63. Conversation with Paul Mus.

64. The quotations come from RAND Corporation "Interviews Concerning the National Liberation Front of South Vietnam."

65. Phan Thi Dac, *Situation de la personne au Viet-Nam,* p. 143.

66. Of course, in a Vietnamese village the position of a village councilor was not *entirely* determined by birth. But the sense of stability is the same in a society so small that almost everyone knows everyone else.

67. By means of language the ego adopts extra-family members into the patriarchal clan: the wife becomes, familiarly, "my younger sister," the schoolteacher "my master" (father).

68. Charles Gosselin, *L'Empire d'Annam,* p. 45.

69. Richard Solomon, "Mao's Revolution and the Chinese Political Culture." Phan Thi Dac, Dr. Walter Sloate, and other anthropologists and psychologists working on Vietnam have indicated that Vietnamese behavior, at least from the point of

view of comparison with that of the West, contains many of the elements Dr. Solomon describes with reference to the Chinese.

70. *I Ching*, p. 521. This is the image of PROVIDING NOURISHMENT.
71. "Interviews," RAND Corporation File FD2A, p. 6.
72. Phan Thi Dac, *Situation de la personne*, pp. 126–127.
73. Léopold Cadière, *Croyances et pratiques religieuses des viêtnamiens*, vol. 2, p. 313.
74. "Interviews," RAND Corporation File FD2A, pp. 5–6.
75. Ibid.
76. Ibid., pp. 7–8.
77. Ibid., p. 8.
78. Ibid.
79. Halberstam, *Ho*, p. 110.
80. The strong sect villages — Catholic, Hoa Hao, or Cao Dai — would tend to organize and contain this form of behavior.
81. "Interviews," RAND Corporation File FD2A, p. 6.
82. Cadière, *Croyances*, vol. 2, on the construction of Hue.
83. Fall, *Two Vietnams*, p. 236.
84. Pike, *Viet Cong*, p. 60. After the abortive coup of 1960, Diem said that the "hand of God had reached down" to protect him. Though Diem used the Catholic language, his idea is here not of mercy from an anthropomorphic God, but justification from an impersonal heaven.
85. *I Ching*, p. 501.
86. Scigliano, *South Vietnam*, pp. 114–115. In the first five years of the Diem regime, the United States spent 78 percent of its aid to Saigon on the development of the armed forces. To that sum the Department of Defense added eighty-five million dollars a year in direct military assistance — mostly military equipment. Of the remaining 22 percent of the aid budget, the United States spent 40 percent a year on transportation, and most of that on road-building. The Vietnamese officials hoped the roads would serve commerce, but the Americans gave priority to those roads which would serve strategic military interests. (The twenty-mile stretch of superhighway designed to carry heavy military traffic between Bien Hoa and Saigon cost more money than the United States provided for all labor, community development, social welfare, housing, health, and education projects in Vietnam during the entire period from 1954 to 1962.) The second most important percentage of the nonmilitary budget went for food and the third for public administration — that is, primarily for the building of the civil guard, the police, and other security services.
87. The RF and PF were known as the "Ruff-Puffs" to many Americans in Vietnam.
88. See McNamara memorandum on Taylor's cable to Kennedy in Sheehan, *Pentagon Papers*, p. 48.
89. Taylor and others used the phrases. See Sheehan, *Pentagon Papers*, pp. 146–147, and Ralph Stavins, "Kennedy's Private War." The political recommendations, drawn up by State Department officials, appeared in the official "Taylor report."
90. The quotation is from General Maxwell Taylor's report (3 November 1961) on his mission to South Vietnam, in Sheehan, *Pentagon Papers*, p. 147.
91. Duncanson, *Government and Revolution*, p. 316. The minister of the interior spoke of the Strategic Hamlet program as the last chance for Vietnam to preserve her independence, indicating that the Vietnamese government had heard of the proposal to send American troops.
92. Bernard B. Fall, *Viet-Nam Witness*, pp. 197–198.
93. Ibid., p. 283. He cites Robert Scigliano in *Asian Survey*, January 1963.
94. Warner, *Last Confucian*, p. 116.
95. Scigliano, *South Vietnam*, p. 61.
96. Halberstam, *Making of a Quagmire*, p. 41, cites Graham Greene in the *New Republic*, 16 May 1955.

97. These pageants took some pains to produce, as Diem in his role of emperor wished to see only people with clean hands and clean clothes. As one peasant reported his visit: "In early 1962 when he came to visit the agricultural center in Duc Hue district, I don't know whether or not he realized that the people in several villages had spent almost two months preparing his walk way. Just imagine! Many people had to work day and night to cut all the bamboo trees in the villages to put on a ten-kilometer muddy road for the President to walk during his one-hour visit to the center. . . . At the time, all of the villagers disliked Ngo Dinh Diem, but no one dared say anything against him." ("Interviews," RAND Corporation File FD1A, p. 14.)
98. Halberstam, *Making of a Quagmire*, p. 46.
99. Duong Van Minh, "Vietnam: A Question of Confidence," p. 85.
100. Shaplen, *Lost Revolution*, p. 193, describes Nhu's instigation of the RYM.
101. Halberstam, *Making of a Quagmire*, p. 205.
102. Though there were a number of Theravada bonzes in the Delta and in Saigon, they were never very active politically. Tri Quang and others never quite succeeded in recruiting them.
103. Georg W. Alsheimer, *Vietnamesische Lehrjahre*, p. 133.
104. Paul Mus, "The Buddhist Background to the Crises in Vietnamese Politics." The foregoing comes essentially from this work.
105. Halberstam, *Making of a Quagmire*, p. 211.
106. Shaplen, *Lost Revolution*, p. 199.
107. Halberstam, *Making of a Quagmire*, pp. 206–207.
108. Warner, *Last Confucian*, pp. 231–232.
109. Shaplen, *Lost Revolution*, p. 189.
110. Sheehan, *Pentagon Papers*, p. 232.
111. Shaplen, *Lost Revolution*, p. 210.

4: The National Liberation Front

Politics of the Earth

1. John T. McAlister, Jr., and Paul Mus, *The Vietnamese and Their Revolution*, p. 90.
2. Ibid., p. 117. See further discussion of this below.

The Origins of the National Liberation Front

1. The figure of ninety thousand is the U.S. official estimate. Other sources differ somewhat. Bernard Fall gives the figure of eighty thousand in "Viet-Cong — The Unseen Enemy in Viet-Nam," in *The Viet-Nam Reader*, ed. Marcus G. Raskin and Bernard B. Fall, p. 252. Other historians say one hundred thousand.
2. Gerald Hickey gives a description of the differences between Viet Minh and other villages in the period from 1955 to 1956 in "Accommodation and Coalition in South Vietnam," pp. 38–39.
3. After the publication of the White Paper, I. F. Stone gave a convincing rebuttal of the U.S. argument that the NLF was supplied from the north and manned by northerners, using only the internal evidence of the paper. The "infiltrators" the paper spoke of were in fact the southern regroupees who after 1959 began to reinfiltrate the south to join their own liberation movement. I. F. Stone, "A Reply to the White Paper," in *Viet-Nam Reader*, ed. Raskin and Fall, pp. 155–162.

In 1964 U.S. official estimates in Saigon were that the NLF obtained a maximum of 10 percent and perhaps only 2 percent of their weapons from the north. (Malcolm W. Browne, *The New Face of War*, p. 24.) Even this estimate may be high, as most of the weapons suspected to have come from the north were Soviet or Czech, and these could have been bought anywhere by the NLF itself.

4. J. J. Zasloff, "Origins of the Insurgency in South Vietnam, 1954–1960," p. 1.
5. Fall, "Viet-Cong," in *Viet-Nam Reader*, ed. Raskin and Fall, p. 254.
6. Zasloff, "Origins of Insurgency," pp. 11, 17. Douglas Pike points out that the Diem regime did not even have a physical presence in many parts of the country-side and thus hazards that the repression could not have been so great as the NLF leaders made out. The apparent contradiction is, however, resolved by the fact that the anti–Viet Minh campaign was not merely the work of the government but of various *revanchiste* political groups, and this particularly in the Viet Minh areas of the center. The NLF leaders naturally do not like to admit this any more than the Saigon government officials.
7. Wilfred G. Burchett, *Vietnam Will Win!*, p. 49.
8. Philippe Devillers, "The Struggle for the Unification of Vietnam," p. 15. Quoted by Douglas Pike, *Viet Cong*, pp. 75–76.
9. Fall, "Viet-Cong," in *Viet-Nam Reader*, ed. Raskin and Fall, p. 258.
10. Burchett, *Vietnam Will Win!*, p. 24, describes this process in more detail.
11. Pike, *Viet Cong*, p. 137.
12. Burchett, *Vietnam Will Win!*, p. 14.

A Natural Opposition

1. Wolf I. Ladejinsky, "Agrarian Reform in the Republic of Vietnam," in *Problems of Freedom*, ed. Wesley R. Fishel, p. 155.
2. Edward G. Lansdale, "Two Steps to Get Us out of Vietnam," p. 64.
3. Edward J. Mitchell, "Inequality and Insurgency." The counterargument is brought by Robert L. Sansom in *The Economics of Insurgency in the Mekong Delta of Vietnam*, pp. 230–232.
4. See Sansom, *Economics of Insurgency*, for this argument.
5. John T. McAlister, Jr., *Vietnam: The Origins of Revolution*, p. 70. In 1930 there were 6,300 landlords with over 125 acres in the south as opposed to 230 in the rest of Vietnam. Some of these southern landlords also belonged to the sects.
6. Sansom, *Economics of Insurgency*, pp. 29–30. The whole quotation is as follows:
    In the past, the relationship between the landlord and his tenants was paternalistic. The landlord considered the tenant as an inferior member of his extended family. When the tenant's father died, it was the duty of the landlord to give money to the tenant for the funeral; if his wife was pregnant, the landlord gave money for the birth; if he was in financial ruin, the landlord gave assistance; therefore the tenant *had* to behave as an inferior member of the extended family. The landlord enjoyed great prestige *vis-à-vis* the tenant. For this reason a tenant who proposed to purchase land would have risked *condemnation* by the "father." . . .
    The landlord acted not only as owner and lessor of land but as an informal administrator, like the chief of a small state. All disputes between tenants were judged first by the landlord. Only if the landlord failed to resolve such a dispute did the parties go to the government — the village council. There was an unwritten code administered by the landlord; it applied first. For example, if there was a case between tenants involving violence or animosity, the landlord would come down to their houses with twenty or thirty armed followers to settle the dispute. Occasionally there were difficult cases. At such times the landlord would gather the eldest tenants and set up a committee, serve them a meal and obtain their advice. The landlord would enforce his own type of discipline, including corporal punishment for the men and detention for the women. Often the guilty party would be beaten with three, seven or ten strokes. The tenants considered their landlord as their protector and as a good father; they would not dare to ask to purchase land.
    (From an interview on 18 August 1967 with Mr. Truong Binh Huy of Bac Lieu city. The respondent is a landlord describing the conditions in the 1930's.)
7. Ibid., p. 56.
8. Ibid., p. 58. See also Ladejinsky, "Agrarian Reform," in *Problems of Freedom*, ed. Fishel, p. 164. The Diemist law was actually less radical than that promulgated but never implemented by the Bao Dai government during the war. Sansom, *Economics of Insurgency*, p. 57: "The major land reform decree issued by the Diem government was Ordinance 57 of October 22, 1956. It limited an

owner's holding to 100 hectares for the family's cult or ancestor worship land, and additional 30 hectares if the farmer cultivated it himself. By February 28, 1957, under this law, 2,600 owners had declared themselves the owners of 1,075,000 hectares. From this amount approximately 740,000 hectares, roughly 30 percent of the rice land in South Vietnam, were available for redistribution. But by 1965, only 440,678 hectares had been expropriated and only 247,760 hectares redistributed to 115,912 farmers. This left approximately 818,000 tenants (87.5 percent) who did not benefit from Ordinance 57."

9. Sansom, *Economics of Insurgency*, p. 59.
10. Samuel L. Popkin, "The Myth of the Village," p. 57.
11. "Experiences in Turning XB Village in Kien Phong Province into a Combatant Village," in Michael Charles Conley, *The Communist Insurgent Infrastructure in South Vietnam*, p. 348ff. This NLF report gives a perfect example of this process.
12. Douglas Pike, *Viet Cong*, pp. 276–279.

The Approach: Children of the People

1. "Experiences in Turning XB Village in Kien Phong Province into a Combatant Village," in Michael Charles Conley, *The Communist Insurgent Infrastructure in South Vietnam*, p. 349.
2. Samuel L. Popkin, "The Myth of the Village." See also RAND Corporation "Interviews Concerning the National Liberation Front of South Vietnam."
3. Q. How much contact did the local GVN officials have with the villagers?
   A. They appeared when they came to collect taxes. They rarely met the people and talked to them.

   Q. Did the GVN ever send people to the village to talk to the people the way the VC did?
   A. The GVN have never done that.

   Q. Were there any . . . units of ARVN passing through your village?
   A. Yes. . . . They treated us correctly. They did not organize meetings and did not say anything.
   (Nathan Leites, "The Viet Cong Style of Politics," p. 252.)
4. "Interviews," RAND Corporation File AG-346, p. 22. This man is a defector, and in such an interview might be expected to say nothing against the GVN.
5. "Interviews," RAND Corporation File G-5, p. 4.
6. Conley, *Communist Insurgent Infrastructure*, p. 369. The soldiers' "Eight Points for Attention" also run in the same vein.
7. Leites, "Viet Cong Style," p. 111.
8. Those Vietnamese-speaking Americans, such as Frank Scotton, who initiated the idea of the cadre programs, never expected it to reach such a size. They had begun one small program that worked while it remained small and filled with dedicated people.
9. Major Mei, Major Nguyen Be, and Colonel Tran Ngoc Chau were the principal instructors. (See next chapter for further discussion of the program.)
10. Ibid., File AG-346, p. 24.
11. Ibid., File AG-68, p. 11.

Rebellion

1. "Interviews Concerning the National Liberation Front of South Vietnam," RAND Corporation File AG-239, p. 13.
2. The story of the Gouré study is an excellent illustration of the importance the U.S. military attached to such social science reports.

   When the U.S. Air Force first contemplated extensive bombing in the south, it commissioned Gouré to study the possible effects. Some months later, an air force general arrived to collect the results, but Gouré had hardly begun his research. The setting up of offices in Saigon and the preparation of interviews, data sheets, and control groups, after all, took quite some time. But the air force had not that amount of time to spare. The report finally appeared some months after the bombing had already begun.

It is, of course, possible that the general had anticipated the results — the RAND Corporation being three-quarters financed by the air force.

3. "Interviews," RAND Corporation File AG-278, pp. 14–15.
4. The evidence, both direct and indirect, is too great to be dismissed as the error of a pollster in Vietnam. It crops up in all forms from the personal experience of the Front soldiers ("Each time my unit defeated the GVN forces, the people slaughtered pigs and cattle and prepared a big feast for us. But when we were defeated . . . they didn't like us one bit." Nathan Leites, "The Viet Cong Style of Politics," p. 3) to the instructions from NLF agencies ("We will educate these people and inculcate in them the idea that the Revolution will surely win the final victory so that they may become good people." Ibid., p. 2). One of the most interesting accounts is from an NLF defector who said that he used to know when a village was hostile or frightened because the people, though they didn't dare ask the soldiers to leave, showed their dissatisfaction by beating or insulting their children. The displacement of anger was visible.
5. See Gerald C. Hickey's *Village in Vietnam* for an account of the stratagems used to avoid conflict when a dispute cropped up between two villagers.
6. David Halberstam, "Voices of the Vietcong," p. 45.
7. Douglas Pike, *Viet Cong*, p. 122.
8. Joseph R. Starobin's *Eyewitness in Indochina* contains a fairly detailed account of one of these denunciation sessions. The technique was also used by Mao Tse-tung.
9. One recruit actually used — manipulated — the emotion of hatred to free himself from his new bonds of dependency on the NLF.

> A. I didn't want to stay in the Front, so I had to build up my hatred in order to have enough determination to leave the Front.
>
> Q. Why did you have to build up your hatred towards the Front in order to defect?
> A. I thought if I didn't hate them, I would never be able to steal their weapons or kill some of them in order to escape. If I didn't hate them, I would always feel attached to them and I could never make up my mind to leave them.
>
> (Leites, "Viet Cong Style," p. 187.)

10. One village youth leader testified:

> After the Vietcong came, the people in our village worshiped less at the shrine and the pagoda than ever before. In the past the rich and the bourgeois used to tell us that the poor were simply those not blessed by heaven. But the Vietcong worked very hard to change this. They said the people were poor because they didn't have any land to till; heaven had nothing to do with economics. So the people listened and decided that if heaven did not affect their economic life they did not have to go to the shrine and pray for a better life, and they stopped going. They began to change their traditions and paid less attention to their ancestors' graves. They used to put their best food on the altars as offerings to the landowners and the rich people so these people would be well disposed toward them. But after the Front came, the people were no longer in constant fear of the rich and no longer offered them their best food.
>
> (Halberstam, "Voices," p. 48.)

11. Paul Mus quotes this remark in the documentary film by Emile de Antonio, *The Year of the Pig*.
12. "Interviews," RAND Corporation File G-5, p. 24.
13. Many of the NLF and GVN reports of violence by the other side seem to contain the kind of fantasy that Westerners usually connect with obscenity. One Front soldier, for instance, wrote that the "lackey troops," trained by the Americans, had raped and beaten a pregnant woman until she aborted and had forced one of their men to eat a soup made of human heads. (Pike, *Viet Cong*, p. 438.) The first story is quite possibly true — such things did happen — but the second seems somewhat too elaborate to be the truth. The point is that some fantasies were executed, some remained pure fantasy.
14. Paul Mus has compared the mental landscape of the Vietnamese to that of the physical world that encloses them. "The rivers have a seasonal exuberance and

must be dammed; the dams that are built up also raise — through an inevitable physical effect — the river bed; they must therefore be made a bit higher. Pushed to the limit this picture becomes one of catastrophe. Perhaps the same may be said of Vietnamese formalism." (John T. McAlister, Jr., and Paul Mus, *The Vietnamese and Their Revolution*, pp. 96–97.)

15. Ibid., p. 119.
16. Confucius, *The Analects of Confucius*, pp. 178–179.
17. There was, of course, some variation in these phrases — "the U.S.-Diem clique," for instance — but the abstraction remained the same.
18. Michael Charles Conley, *The Communist Insurgent Infrastructure in South Vietnam*, p. 350.
19. Sir Robert Thompson, *No Exit from Vietnam*, p. 40.
20. Stephen T. Hosmer, "Viet Cong Repression and Its Implications for the Future," pp. 95, 108.
21. Ibid., p. 76.

Organization: The Liberated Village, the NLF Command Structure, and the PRP

1. Le Duan, "Under the Glorious Party Banner," p. 25.
2. Douglas Pike's *Viet Cong* is to date the only published American work on the NLF. Michael Charles Conley's *The Communist Insurgent Infrastructure in South Vietnam* is a report written for the Department of the Army and the American University's Center for Research in Social Systems. The RAND Corporation has done a great deal of work on the NLF for the U.S. Air Force and other defense agencies.
3. Pike, *Viet Cong*, pp. ix, 111.
4. Paul Valéry, extract from *History and Politics No. 10*. Valéry here invents a discourse by a Chinese mandarin.
5. See Virginia Thompson, *French Indochina*, for a discussion of the economic and social conditions of Vietnam in the 1930's.
6. Robert L. Sansom, *The Economics of Insurgency in the Mekong Delta of Vietnam*, pp. 35–39.
7. The story that follows comes from "Interviews Concerning the National Liberation Front of South Vietnam," RAND Corporation File AG-545.
8. Ibid., pp. 3–4, 9–10.
9. Ibid., p. 10.
10. See W. P. Davison, "Some Observations on Viet Cong Operations in the Villages," and Pike, *Viet Cong*, pp. 166–194, for further information on the activities of the Liberation Associations.
11. Davison, "Some Observations," pp. 149–153.
12. Samuel L. Popkin, "The Myth of the Village," p. 86.
13. A recent example of this process occurred in the early spring of 1971. General Do Cao Tri, the energetic commander of the Saigon government's operations in Cambodia, died in a helicopter accident. Even though Tri had left battle plans for the operation, his successor was unable to put the operation back together again for several months.
14. See Pike, *Viet Cong*, pp. 210–232, for a more detailed description of the NLF command structure.
15. This fact is admitted by most American analysts of the subject, but none draw the conclusion that power thereby devolved upon the lower echelons. Only Jeffrey Race makes this argument effectively, in "How They Won."
16. Conley, *Communist Insurgent Infrastructure*, pp. 321–322.
17. Davison, "Some Observations," p. 49.

The Making of a Revolutionary

1. "Interviews Concerning the National Liberation Front of South Vietnam," RAND Corporation File AG-572, pp. 6–8.

2. Wilfred G. Burchett, *Vietnam Will Win!*, pp. 35–39.
3. "Interviews," RAND Corporation File AG-121, p. 15.
4. Ibid., File G-7, p. 14.
   Q. What did you do between operations?
   A. Between operations we have cultural training. Those who do not know how to read and write learn to read and write. The Front is very serious about that. It wants to raise the level of education of its members. Not like the GVN soldiers between operations; they go out and drink, gamble or do other nonsense things. Besides cultural training, there is also military training for those with less experience. Sometimes the soldiers go into the villages and make friends with the villagers.
5. "Interviews," RAND Corporation File AG-121, p. 58.
6. Ibid., File AG-68, p. 4.
7. Ibid., File AG-121, p. 59.
8. Michael Charles Conley, *The Communist Insurgent Infrastructure in South Vietnam*, p. 332.
9. "Interviews," RAND Corporation File AG-572, p. 30.
10. Conley, *Communist Insurgent Infrastructure*, p. 350.
11. Ibid., p. 331.
12. Susan Sontag, *Trip to Hanoi*, pp. 16–18. See also Mary McCarthy, *Hanoi*.
13. Conley, *Communist Insurgent Infrastructure*, pp. 330–331.

Marxism-Leninism in the Vietnamese Landscape

1. Whether because of the intellectual influence of Marxism or the political influence of Marxist parties themselves, many Vietnamese of the 1960's used Marxist terminology even though they did not belong to the NLF.
2. Ho Chi Minh, *Ho Chi Minh on Revolution*, p. 6.
3. Ho Chi Minh quotes this doctrine in an article reprinted in *Pravda* on Lenin in 1955. Ibid., p. 257.
4. See John T. McAlister, Jr., and Paul Mus, *The Vietnamese and Their Revolution*, chapter 8 ("The Marxist World View and Revolutions in Modernizing Countries") for further discussion.
5. "Interviews Concerning the National Liberation Front of South Vietnam," RAND Corporation File FD-2A, p. 5.
6. Truong Chinh, *President Ho Chin Minh*, p. 73.
7. Douglas Pike, *Viet Cong*, p. 381. Pike also notes that Vietnamese Communism was "characterized by great moralism and was far more moral than ideological" (p. 379). See also J. J. Zasloff, "Political Motivation of the Viet Cong and the Vietminh Regroupees," pp. 115–118.
8. I. Milton Sacks, "Marxism in Viet-Nam," in *Marxism in Southeast Asia*, ed. Frank N. Trager, pp. 128–129. Sacks discusses the program of the Trotskyites.
9. McAlister and Mus, *Vietnamese and Their Revolution*, chapter 7 ("Marxism and Traditionalism in Vietnam"). On this issue Ho Chi Minh's own party, in alliance with the Soviet Comintern, had differed with the Trotskyites (of which there was an articulate group in Saigon) as far back as the 1930's. The Trotskyites insisted on a proletarian revolution; the Indochinese Communist Party looked for an alliance with the peasants and the national bourgeoisie. (See Sacks, "Marxism," in *Marxism in Southeast Asia*, ed. Trager, pp. 102–170, for further details of this ideological debate.) In September 1945, Ho Chi Minh's agents in the south assassinated six Trotskyite leaders and effectively destroyed that party in Vietnam. Just what influence the Trotskyites might have had had they survived remains unknown, but, as McAlister notes (*Vietnam: Origins of the Revolution*, p. 208), the fact that Ho was able to eliminate them so easily indicates that their party, like all the other urban political parties, had no mass base and no strong organizational structure. The suspicion is that the Trotskyites were just another group of urban intellectuals who in the last analysis depended upon France.
10. See Frantz Fanon, *The Wretched of the Earth*, pp. 121–126, for a discussion of the dependence of the colonial proletariat and the bourgeoisie.

11. Ho Chi Minh, *Ho Chi Minh,* p. 341.
12. The North Vietnamese newspapers, *Nhan Dan,* printed severe critiques of Party programs — so severe, in fact, that American analysts, comparing it with other Communist newspapers, tended to overestimate the seriousness of the political or economic difficulty it discussed. The paper did not, of course, represent an independent editorial position, but rather the Party's critique of itself.
13. Ho Chi Minh, *Ho Chi Minh,* pp. 340–341.

5: *Mise en scène*

1. Marcus G. Raskin and Bernard B. Fall, eds., *The Viet-Nam Reader,* p. 347.
2. *New York Times,* 7 February 1966.

6: *Politicians and Generals*

one

1. Jean Lacouture, *Vietnam: Between Two Truces,* pp. 99–102.
2. Robert Shaplen, *The Lost Revolution,* p. 206.
3. Lacouture, *Vietnam,* p. 122, gives this atmosphere.
4. Frantz Fanon, *The Wretched of the Earth,* p. 122ff., gives an excellent description of this class.
5. David Wurfel, "The Saigon Political Elite," p. 530. "An analysis of forty ministers in six cabinets since 1962 indicates that little more than one-third had all their advanced training in Vietnam."
6. Fanon, *Wretched of the Earth,* pp. 37–38.
7. The southern Catholics leaned towards the support of the anti-Communist regimes, but they were not so intransigent as to support the war indefinitely at the expense of the entire southern population. In January 1968, just before the Tet offensive, the archdiocese of Saigon issued a statement calling for peace and a halt to the bombing of North Vietnam. The northerners tended to be more politically "reliable." At least until 1970 the military regimes could count on the refugee settlements around Saigon to provide truckloads of demonstrators for them on command.
8. The Catholic organizations were the only ones whose numbers could be estimated with any degree of accuracy. In the summer of 1967, *Time* magazine spoke of Tri Quang's one million followers. But there the editors had performed a statistical miracle equivalent to that of determining the number of angels that can fit on the head of a pin. (What kind of pin? is the first objection.)
9. Shaplen, *Lost Revolution,* p. 247. The Americans suspected Tri Quang because of his Communist-inspired methods (his propaganda techniques, according to Shaplen) but they themselves were to hire former Viet Minh officers to head all of their various pacification programs.
10. Lacouture, *Vietnam,* p. 121.
11. McNamara report to President Johnson on the Vietnam situation, 21 December 1963, in Neil Sheehan et al., *The Pentagon Papers,* pp. 271–274.
12. George McTurnan Kahin and John W. Lewis, *The United States in Vietnam,* p. 152.
13. Shaplen, *Lost Revolution,* pp. 232–234.
14. Ibid., pp. 227–234.
15. Lacouture, *Vietnam,* p. 121.
16. Shaplen, *Lost Revolution,* p. 228.
17. But of course they did not. The coup against Diem was conceived by a civilian, the shrewd security officer, Dr. Tran Kim Tuyen, and made possible by the self-immolations of several others.

18. George Carver, "The Real Revolution in South Vietnam," p. 404.
19. Shaplen, *Lost Revolution*, p. 228.

two

1. Marcus G. Raskin and Bernard B. Fall, eds., *The Viet-Nam Reader*, p. 201.
2. Richard Critchfield, *The Long Charade*, p. 96.
3. Raskin and Fall, *Viet-Nam Reader*, p. 200.
4. Robert Shaplen, *The Lost Revolution*, p. 246.
5. Ibid., p. 270.
6. Ibid., p. 277.
7. Jean Lacouture, *Vietnam: Between Two Truces*, p. 135.
8. Ibid., pp. 136–137.
9. Excerpts from Saigon airgram to the State Department, 24 December 1964, in Neil Sheehan et al., *The Pentagon Papers*, pp. 379–381. Taylor may not even have been sure to whom he was speaking. He asked at one point who the spokesman for the group was.
10. Shaplen, *Lost Revolution*, pp. 297–301.
11. A later example of this same mechanical logic was General Ky's behavior during the Cambodian invasion in 1970. Very much excited by the idea of ARVN troops going into someone else's country, Ky asked to head the expedition. When Thieu allowed him to conduct the negotiations but refused him a military role, Ky began to give quiet support to the disabled veterans' and students' protest against it. (*New York Times*, 12 June 1970.)
12. Shaplen, *Lost Revolution*, pp. 342–346.
13. William C. Westmoreland, *Report on the War in Vietnam*, p. 98.

7: The United States Enters the War

1. Neil Sheehan et al., *The Pentagon Papers*, p. 257.
2. Ibid., pp. 307, 313–314, 323.
3. Ibid., pp. 341–343.
4. Ibid., pp. 382–386, and Daniel Ellsberg, "Escalating in a Quagmire."
5. Ibid., pp. 462–474.
6. William C. Westmoreland, *Report on the War in Vietnam*, p. 100.
7. Ibid. From Westmoreland's account it is impossible to discover what form this "concerted effort" actually took.
8. Ibid. MACV estimated that thirty-five thousand enemy troops were killed that year.
9. Blair Clark, "Westmoreland Appraised," pp. 96–101.
10. Westmoreland apparently did not realize how attached these ARVN divisions were to their own territories — his sense of scale being somewhat different to that of the Vietnamese. In fact the Twenty-fifth did not recover from its displacement. Years later the ARVN commander-in-chief, General Cao Van Vien, was to call it, "not only the worst division in the Vietnamese army, but the worst division in any army in the world."
11. Sheehan, *Pentagon Papers*, p. 391.
12. *The Vietnam Hearings*, p. 183.

8: The Buddhist Crisis

1. *Time* magazine, 18 February 1966.
2. Zorthian had assumed that Ky had chosen to fire Thi because he was the strongest of the corps commanders. After Thi was fired, so the logic went, he could get

rid of the other corrupt officers more easily. The theory, however, depended on what was meant by "strong." Thi's honesty and devotion to duty had made him popular with many of the officers and civil servants in his own corps area, but it had at the same time isolated him from Saigon and the rest of the country. The other three corps commanders, by contrast, presided like huge spiders over a countrywide network of intrigue and corruption. An attack on one of them would have meant an attack on all of them.

3. *New York Times,* 5 April 1966.
4. Takashi Oka, "Buddhism as a Political Force. No. 5: Danang and Afterwards," p. 3.
5. *New York Times,* 9 April 1966.
6. Ibid., 14 April 1966.
7. Richard Critchfield, *The Long Charade,* p. 64.
8. Ibid., p. 293.
9. That the Americans had carefully kept their troops out of Hue only increased the contrast between it and Saigon, it and all other Vietnamese cities.
10. Oka, "Buddhism," p. 4.
11. *New York Times,* 23 April 1966.
12. Ibid., 15 May 1966.
13. Ibid., 17 May 1966.
14. Oka, "Buddhism," p. 10.
15. *New York Times,* 1 June 1966.
16. Oka, "Buddhism," p. 10.
17. Ibid., p. 14.

9: *Prospero, Caliban, and Ariel*

1. Otare Mannoni, *Prospero and Caliban.*
   Frantz Fanon has attacked this work in *Black Skin, White Masks,* but he does not convincingly refute the foregoing. His argument is that the reactions and behavior patterns of the native to the European colonizer had nothing to do with a pre-existing set. "If, for instance," he says, "Martians undertook to colonize the earthmen — not to initiate them into Martian culture but to *colonize* them — we should be doubtful of the persistence of any earth personality" (p. 95). The argument that colonialism (as opposed to any other form of disaster) negates personality itself cannot accord with a Freudian point of view. If Freud is correct, then men always react to new situations according to patterns set in their childhood. In *The Wretched of the Earth* Fanon actually corroborates many of the observations made by Mannoni, only he looks at them from a slightly different point of view.
2. Paul Mus has spoken of this period and what to French liberals seemed to be the paradoxical reaction of the Vietnamese in his *Viêt-Nam: Sociologie d'une guerre.*
3. Mannoni, *Prospero,* p. 59.
4. The movement, as Tri Quang told Takashi Oka, "did not begin as an anti-American movement. It was not even really opposed to Ky. We had only one plea — elections as a means of establishing a legitimate government." (Takashi Oka, "Buddhism as a Political Force," p. 11.)
   The Americans never believed him sincere, but Tri Quang knew well that only the Americans could insure Buddhist success — and the elections were the only way they might be brought into making a redistribution of power.
   Later on, alarmed by the anti-American tone of the demonstrations, Tam Chau had pressured Tri Quang to defuse the struggle movement and restore order to the First Corps. Once the promise of elections had been given, Tri Quang had acceded, even though he realized leaving the junta in power might be a strategic error.

5. Pierre Huard and Maurice Durand, *Connaissance du Viêt-Nam*, p. 87. The original text is as follows: "La rupture de la dépendance a, sous l'influence de troubles extérieurs ou intérieurs, provoqué des sentiments d'infériorité violants avec leurs successions habituelles de defoulement et de refoulements. L'angoisse de la conscience nationale essayant de se créer un sur-moi a base de compensations s'est alors traduite dans une minorité agissante par une volonté de destruction farouche, une volupté de perir dans l'effondrement total, une esthétique du néant qui pousse, collectivement, à la politique du terre brûlée et, individuellement, au suicide."
It is the observation rather than the analysis that is interesting here.

6. According to the Vietnamese sociologist, Phan Thi Dac, the hunger strike is one of the ways in which the Vietnamese child registers discontent with the strictures of his parents. In the case of particularly strong-willed children these hunger strikes last two or three days. In general, says Miss Dac, "the parents try to find a way of getting out of the difficulty that will leave everyone's honor intact, because the child who has recourse to this procedure is profoundly wounded, because whether or not it is true, he believes himself the victim of an injustice (correction or reprimand). If he obstinately refuses all attempts at conciliation, all diversionary maneuvers, and remains deaf to all appeals, the parents send him discreetly to an aunt or a cousin for a short visit so that, away from the 'guilty' parent, he can forget his misadventure and feed himself again without too much loss of pride."
(Interestingly enough, the other method of opposition, and the one most feared by parents, is simple inertia. The child does not complain, he does not avoid punishments, but he continues to repeat his past conduct. In this case the parents take what seems to be their only recourse and send the child away to relatives or friends for a while.)
(Phan Thi Dac, *Situation de la personne au Viet-Nam*, pp. 126–127.)
In other words, far from revolting against the Americans, the Buddhists were behaving towards them as child to parent. They were trying to force the Americans to make a correction in their behavior by inflicting suffering upon themselves. The difficulty — which Tri Quang certainly realized — was that the Americans *were not* their parental rulers.

7. Don Luce and John Sommer, *Viet Nam: The Unheard Voices*, p. 279.

8. Fanon, *Wretched of the Earth*, p. 43.

10: Bad Puppets

1. William C. Westmoreland, *Report on the War in Vietnam*, p. 114.

2. *Newsweek*, 27 March 1967.

3. Ibid.

4. *Time*, 31 March 1967.

5. *Newsweek*, 27 March 1967.

6. David Halberstam, "Return to Vietnam," p. 52.

7. Samuel L. Popkin, "The Myth of the Village," pp. 169–172.

8. Halberstam, "Return to Vietnam."

9. This attitude, largely shared by the central Vietnamese factions, posed a most perfect dilemma for the GVN that on the one hand needed to establish its legitimacy and, on the other hand, needed all the help it could get against the NLF. When in 1967 a fraction of the VNQDD began to infiltrate the pacification program in central Vietnam, the Americans, like the French before them, tended to support the party because it was disciplined and passionately anti-Communist. The GVN officials, however, resisted the VNQDD because they knew they would have little more influence over the villages thus pacified than over those in the grip of the NLF.

10. On 6 January 1971, the *New York Times* reported that Mme. Nguyen Cao Ky had claimed the right to more than five square miles of montagnard land in the Cen-

tral Highlands as a public domained concession. The land had been under the control of the Front for the past several years, she argued, so it ought to be declared a public domain. Naturally the Vietnamese officials were not disposed to recognize the montagnards' ancestral rights over the claim of the vice-president's wife, but a public scandal was made. Madame Ky had by this time come a long way from her pretty stewardess days, under the competitive influence of Mesdames Co and Thieu.

11. William R. Corson, *The Betrayal.*
12. William J. Lederer, *Our Own Worst Enemy.*
13. Corson, *Betrayal,* p. 86. The Regional Forces outside Da Nang neglected to lay their ambushes that night, and the NLF mortared the air base.
14. Don Luce and John Sommer, *Viet Nam: The Unheard Voices,* pp. 97–98.
15. Frantz Fanon never went to Vietnam, but much of what he says about the colonized bourgeoisie in Africa is peculiarly appropriate to that of Saigon. For instance:

> The national middle-class which takes over power at the end of the colonial regime is an under-developed middle-class. It has practically no economic power, and in any case it is in no way commensurate with the bourgeoisie of the mother country which it hopes to replace. . . . [It] is not engaged in production, nor in invention, nor building, nor labour; it is completely canalised into activities of the intermediary type. . . . In its wilful narcissism, the national middle-class is easily convinced that it can advantageously replace the middle-class of the mother country. But that same independence which literally drives it into a corner will give rise within its ranks to catastrophic reactions, and will oblige it to send out frenzied appeals for help to the former mother country. . . .
>
> The national middle-class discovers its historic mission: that of intermediary. . . . [It] identifies itself with the Western bourgeoisie from whom it has learnt its lessons. It follows the Western bourgeoisie along its path of negation and decadence without ever having emulated it in its first stages of exploration and invention. . . . It is already senile before it has come to know the petulance, the fearlessness or the will to succeed of youth.
>
> The national bourgeoisie will be greatly helped on its way towards decadence by the Western bourgeoisies, whom come to it as tourists avid for the exotic. . . . It will in practice set up its country as the brothel of Europe."
>
> (Frantz Fanon, *The Wretched of the Earth,* pp. 122–125.)

16. *Washington Post,* 21 March 1967.
17. General Thieu would repeat the same maneuver in 1970 with the trial of Colonel Tran Ngoc Chau, now the deputy elected by the largest number of votes to the lower house of the legislature. When accused of having secret contact with his brother, an NLF officer, Chau claimed to have done so only with the full knowledge of the CIA. That was his mistake. After his confession a large number of opposition deputies, newspapermen, etc., supported Thieu's unconstitutional attempt to put him in jail on the grounds that he was selling them out by establishing a link between the Americans and the Viet Cong.
18. Richard Critchfield, *The Long Charade,* p. 157.

11: *Elections*

1. *Newsweek,* 3 April 1967.
2. Takashi Oka, in the *New York Times,* 15 July 1970.
3. Ibid.
4. Bernard B. Fall, *Last Reflections on a War,* p. 163.
5. I. Milton Sacks, "Restructuring Government in South Vietnam," p. 526.
6. Richard Critchfield, *The Long Charade,* p. 309.
7. *Newsweek,* 3 April 1967.
8. Paul Mus, "Cultural Backgrounds of Present Problems," p. 12.
9. Fall, *Last Reflections,* p. 164.

10. Robert Shaplen, "Letter from Saigon," *New Yorker,* 7 October 1967, pp. 152–153.

The meeting had its own interest. Had the same confrontation taken place in 1964, it almost certainly would have been resolved by a military coup. The meeting was, then, a substitute for a coup under conditions that made even a show of force impossible. From the American perspective, it looked something like a cross between an encounter group and a meeting of ward bosses. From the Vietnamese perspective, it was a self-criticism session. Without any ideological training, or indeed any foreign interference, the generals quite unconsciously adopted the technique that the Viet Minh had institutionalized to settle personal and political conflicts without violence. What the Americans failed to appreciate in both instances was that the whole drama looked both natural and necessary to the participants. Self-criticism is, in other words, as acceptable to the Vietnamese as majority rule is to Americans.

Ky himself declared in public afterwards, "All Vietnamese must make sacrifices in order to achieve unity and maintain the prestige of the armed forces. We can sacrifice our very life . . . or anything, including the renunciation of titles." (Critchfield, *Long Charade,* p. 339.)

11. Shaplen, "Letter from Saigon," p. 154, and Jean Taillefer, "Les Élections au Sud-Vietnam," pp. 453–456. According to the French journalist Taillefer, certain of these officers did not even bother to hide the fact that they reported a 90 percent turnout when only 20 percent of the people who registered actually voted. "In certain districts," he concluded, "it would be difficult to argue that the elections took place at all."

12. Shaplen, "Letter from Saigon," p. 154.
13. Ibid., and Taillefer, "Les Élections."
14. Shaplen, "Letter from Saigon," p. 157.
15. Ibid., p. 157.
16. Ward Just, in the *Washington Post,* 28 October 1968.
17. The election marked the beginning of the decline in the real, as opposed to the symbolic, power of Nguyen Cao Ky. Over the next few months Thieu slowly but systematically went about the business of removing all of Ky's supporters from the provincial commands until there was nothing left to support his establishment in Saigon. Towards the end of the process both the Americans and the NLF helped Thieu substantially in their own characteristic ways. During the Tet offensive an American helicopter pilot accidentally dropped a rocket into a suburban building where Ky's three or four closest political supporters happened to be standing. Not long afterwards, the NLF in full malice aforethought shot and badly wounded General Nguyen Ngoc Loan.

12: *The Downward Spiral*

1. Robert Komer. Press conference.
2. This rectification of figures and ambiguity of names undoutedly accounted for an experience Dr. Henry Kissinger had as a consultant to Governor Nelson Rockefeller. While visiting Vietnam one year, Kissinger went to see a certain Vietnamese province chief and asked, among other things, how the pacification program was going. "Very well indeed," said the province chief. "We've made great gains this year. Eighty percent of the province is pacified." The next year Kissinger returned to Vietnam and put the same question to the same province chief. "Excellent," was the answer. "We've been making great progress since you were last here. Seventy percent of the province is pacified."
3. Robert Komer, Press conference.
4. Richard Critchfield, *The Long Charade,* p. 173.
5. Robert Komer. Press conference.

6. William C. Westmoreland, *Report on the War in Vietnam*, p. 137.

7. Thomas Whiteside, "Defoliation," p. 32, 38.

8. *Newsweek*, 27 March 1967.

9. Frances FitzGerald, "The Tragedy of Saigon." This article is a description of the condition of Saigon in late 1966 and an argument concerning the uses of American aid in Vietnam. The city budget of Saigon for 1966 was equivalent to that of Lynchburg, Va., or Allentown, Pa.

10. William R. Corson, *The Betrayal*, p. 173.

11. David Halberstam, "Return to Vietnam," p. 53.

12. Ibid.

13. Pham Ngoc Nguyen, "House for Rent," in *Between Two Fires*, ed. Ly Qui Chung, p. 70.

14. *New York Times*, 26 November 1967.

15. R. W. Apple, "Vietnam: The Signs of a Stalemate." The irony was that though Apple used the story to illustrate the perfidy of the Vietnamese officer corps, certain analysts in Saigon might well have assumed that the adviser told it to illustrate his success at getting a unit of the Twenty-fifth Division out of its base at night.

16. Alec Woodside, "Some Southern Vietnamese Writers Look at the War," pp. 54–55.

17. Robert Jay Lifton, the Yale psychologist and social historian, also mentions this phenomenon, which he labels "counterfeit nurturance," in his paper, "The Circles of Deception — Notes on Vietnam."

18. Woodside, "Writers Look at the War," p. 54.

13: Prospero

1. In 1966 the mission, after a trial run, decided to increase the numbers of IVS workers severalfold.

2. Don Luce and John Sommer, *Viet Nam: The Unheard Voices*, p. 316.

3. William Pfaff, "A Vietnam Journal," p. 20.

4. The Advanced Research Projects Association (ARPA) was the cover-all name for Defense Department research projects based in Vietnam.

5. Simulmatics first achieved prominence by doing the polling and voter analysis for the John F. Kennedy campaign in 1960. The company was dissolved in 1968 as a result of overdependence on, and difficulties with, the Defense Department.

6. Richard M. Pfeffer, ed., *No More Vietnams?*, p. 146.

7. "The Michigan Winter Soldier Investigation," *Harvard Crimson*, 14 May 1971. Testimony from Scott Camile, 24, Sergeant (E-5), First Battalion, Eleventh Marine Regiment, First Marine Division. (In Vietnam, August 1966 to September 1967.)

   "The way that we distinguished between civilians and VC, VC had weapons and civilians didn't and anybody that was dead was considered a VC. If you killed someone they said, 'How do you know he's a VC?' and the general reply would be, 'He's dead,' and that was sufficient."

8. John T. McAlister, Jr., "America in Vietnam," p. 10.

9. In 1967–1968 the journalist, Harvey Meyerson, documented this process in detail during his several months' stay in Vinh Long province (Harvey Meyerson, *Vinh Long*). The syndrome was by then well established in history. In 1962 Colonel John Paul Vann, the Seventh Division adviser in My Tho, was known to American reporters to be the only adviser who reported on the deterioration of the GVN. Vann had to leave the Army as a result.

10. In a televised interview some of the prisoners said that many of them had become partially paralyzed by the confinement, that they had lung diseases from the lime the guards flung down at them, and that they were given so little water that occasionally they were forced to drink their own urine. Those prisoners

interviewed were Buddhist students. The American official who later briefed the press in Saigon said that the "bulk of the inmates are either hard-core Communist defenders or they are serious professional criminals" and that he "thought" the prisoners were "reasonably well-treated and that they looked in reasonably good health." (*New York Times,* 17 July 1970.)

11. *New York Times,* 18 July 1970.
12. Ambassador Bunker also played an important role in the affair of Tran Ngoc Chau in the spring of 1970. President Thieu arrested and imprisoned Deputy Chau on charges of cooperating with the Communists. Though these charges were false and Chau had important friends in the U.S. mission, Bunker washed his hands of the matter and allowed Thieu to imprison Chau.
13. *The Vietnam Hearings,* pp. 182–183.
14. The argument was often made by those people far from power, but the logic existed — and sometimes just below consciousness — for those people whose job it was to make the distinction. When asked in 1968 why he believed the United States could win the war in Vietnam, one high CIA official not directly concerned with the war gave a long speech about the virtues of democracy and the vices of Communism — a moral argument to a power-political question.
15. *Boston Globe,* July 1970.
16. "Michigan Winter Soldier Investigation," p. 7. Testimony of Steve Pitkin, 20, SP/4, "C" Company, 2/239, Ninth Infantry Division. (In Vietnam from May 1969 to July 1969.)
    The training that they gave us, the infantry, really amounted to nothing but familiarization with the small-arms weapons and the explosives you would use once you got over there. We attacked a mock Vietnamese village in the snow at Fort Dix. An interesting point: a lot of times when we were put on line to attack a point of something, you were told not to fire until your left foot hit the ground. I remember asking a drill sergeant, "Do they really do this in Nam?" "Yeah, you know."
    When I got to Nam, it was like black had turned to white because I was totally unprepared. I was put into a recon unit operating in the Mekong Delta. I hadn't been taught anything about the weather, the terrain. I had been taught a little bit about booby traps, but that's really up to the guy who lays them; they can just be anything. It was just a hit and miss thing. You go over there with that limited amount of training and knowledge of the culture you're up against and you're scared. You're so scared, that you'll shoot at anything.
17. "Michigan Winter Soldier Investigation," p. 3. Testimony of Scott Camile.
18. Ibid., p. 7. Testimony of Steve Pitkin.
19. Ibid., and Richard Falk et al., letter to the *New York Times,* 22 April 1970.
20. *New York Times,* 31 March 1971.
21. Calley's statement reminds one of the "legalism" of one Marine unit that, as one GI testified, "went through the villages and searched people [and] the women would have all their clothes taken off and the men would use their penises to probe them to make sure they didn't have anything hidden anywhere and this was raping but it was done as searching." ("Michigan Winter Soldier Investigation," p. 3. Testimony of Scott Camile.)
22. McAllister, "America in Vietnam," p. 12.
23. Jonathan and Orville Schell, letter to the *New York Times,* 26 November 1969.
24. *New York Times,* 7 January 1967.
25. Douglas Pike, "The Viet Cong Strategy of Terror," p. 9.
26. Ibid., pp. 19–20.
27. Ibid., p. 8.

14: Guerrillas

1. Frantz Fanon, *The Wretched of the Earth,* p. 43.
2. Alec Woodside, "Some Southern Vietnamese Writers Look at the War," p. 55.

3. *Le Monde* (*sélection hebdomadaire*), 14–20 May 1970, by Jean-Claude Pomonti.
4. Ibid.
5. Woodside, "Writers Look at the War," p. 55.
6. *New York Times,* 10 October 1967.
7. Ibid.

15: *The Tet Offensive*

1. *Newsweek,* 12 February 1968.
2. William C. Westmoreland, *Report on the War in Vietnam,* pp. 157–164.
3. *Newsweek,* 12 February 1968.
4. All the information on troop movements, on Giap's plan, and on Westmoreland's own estimates come from Westmoreland's *Report.*
5. Westmoreland, *Report,* p. 160.
6. *New York Times,* 21 February 1968.
7. Ibid., 9 February 1968.
8. *Newsweek,* 12 February 1968.
9. These discussions were so general in Saigon that Ambassador Bunker and General Thieu finally had to issue statements denouncing the rumors (*Washington Post,* 11 February 1968).
10. *Washington Post,* 1 March 1968.
11. *New York Times,* 15 March 1968.
12. Ibid., 8 March 1968.
13. *Washington Post,* 1 March 1968.
14. *Observer* (London), 3 March 1968. See also Westmoreland, *Report,* p. 160.
15. *New York Times,* 1 March 1968.
16. Robert Shaplen, *Time out of Hand,* p. 414.
17. *New York Times,* 28 February 1968.
18. Ibid.
19. Shaplen, *Time out of Hand,* p. 414
20. *Washington Post,* 19 February 1968.
21. Westmoreland, *Report,* p. 169.
22. John Bronaugh Henry, "March 1968: Continuity or Change?" This fascinating account of the events of March 1968 was written on the basis of personal interviews with General Wheeler, General Westmoreland, Clark Clifford, and others. Wheeler read the completed account and confirmed the facts above mentiond.
23. Jean Lacouture and Philippe Devillers, *La Fin d'une guerre,* p. 19. The Debré quotation is from the *Journal officiel,* débats parlementaires, Conseil de la Republique, 1953, p. 1741.
24. *Washington Post,* 25 October 1968.

16: *Nixon's War*

1. *Washington Post,* 29 October 1969.
2. The age span, perhaps, seemed reasonable enough to Americans because it would not have been excessive for the American population. But in a country where the average life-span cannot under normal conditions be much above forty-five to fifty, the drafting of men of forty-three meant the drafting of grand-fathers.
3. *Army* magazine estimated that the regular, uniformed soldiers amounted to 6 percent of the entire population of 17,400,000 people (this is not counting the self-defense forces, which amounted to another 6 percent). But over a half of

the total population must have been children under fifteen, over a half of the remainder, women, and a good percentage of the remaining 25 percent disabled or beyond the age limit.

According to *Army* the armed forces of the ARVN in October 1969 included ten regular infantry divisions, 46,000 "elite striking forces" (Marines, paratroopers, and rangers), 391,000 RF-PF, some 182,000 paramilitary troops (RF, PRU, CIDG, etc.), and an air force of eighteen squadrons with four hundred planes. (*Army,* October 1969, pp. 113–114.) This force was to be expanded a bit later.

4. *New York Times,* 4 October 1969.

5. *New York Times,* 4 October 1969.

6. Nixon's statement was doubly ironic as the period 1968–1969 was the period of some of the most brutal of the American massacres. In a single six-month operation, for example, the U.S. Ninth Infantry Division reported eleven thousand "enemy killed" and seven hundred weapons captured. When asked about discrepancy between these two figures, the commanding general, Julian Ewell, said: "The Ninth Division is so good we get them before they have a chance to pick their weapons up." The general did not, in other words, even attempt to cover up for the fact that a great proportion of "enemy killed" were civilians.

7. *New York Times,* 18 February 1970. Some long-term observers of the weekly "enemy killed" statistics from the ARVN have noticed that these numbers hardly ever end in a zero or a five. The Vietnamese, perhaps, realized that these would not seem quite "random" enough for MACV or the American press.

8. *New York Times,* 18 August 1969.

9. Ibid., 18 February 1970.

10. Dr. Samuel L. Popkin of Harvard University uncovered these incidents in the course of academic research in Vietnamese village politics.

11. Dr. Popkin and this writer presented this thesis in a memo to Dr. Henry Kissinger in the fall of 1969. U.S. field officers said the official figure of 13,668 enemy dead was inflated.

12. Secretary of Defense Melvin Laird called the North Vietnamese attack "vicious" — an indication, perhaps, of his surprise and alarm. Once again, the U.S. military command appears to have underestimated its enemy. The *New York Times* and various television newcasters reported that MACV did not anticipate the use of tanks or prepare the Vietnamese for the size and strength of the attacking forces.

13. This figure came from the ARVN spokesman at the operational headquarters.

14. Daniel Ellsberg, "Laos: What Nixon Is up to," pp. 13–17. Signaling, as opposed to militarily effective measures, was the primary intention of the Johnson administration in the first of the "Rolling Thunder" air operations against the north.

15. The United States dropped slightly more than two million tons of bombs during the Second World War. It dropped 2,539,743 tons in Indochina from the time of Nixon's inauguration until March 1971, according to Pentagon statistics. (Noam Chomsky, "Mayday: The Case for Civil Disobedience.")

16. Previously, air operations in Laos had been conducted principally against the Ho Chi Minh trail and the area held by the Pathet Lao in the north. Targets had to be approved by the American ambassador in Vientiane, William Sullivan. From the start of the Nixon administration all civilian restrictions were put aside, and the air force bombed populated areas in most parts of the country almost at random. (Fred Branfman, "Presidential War in Laos, 1964–1970," in *Laos: War and Revolution,* ed. N. Adams and A. McCoy.)

17. Neither the U.S. nor the Cambodian government would release data on American air strikes in Cambodia. Owing to poor communications it was simply impossible to tell how many civilian casualties and how many refugees there were. It was difficult enough to determine how many casualties Lon Nol's army took.

18. *Boston Globe,* 4 June 1971.

19. *New York Times,* 19 October 1970.

20. Ibid., 4 July 1970.

21. The *Le Monde* correspondent, Jacques Decornoy, had a number of these articles translated.
22. Robert Shaplen, "Letter from Saigon," *New Yorker*, 20 September 1969, p. 116, and *Time*, 29 June 1971.
23. In the spring of 1970 the black market rate rose from its normal level of 250–300 piastres to the dollar to 400 piastres to the dollar. The government rate was then still 118–1.
24. *New York Times*, 21 June 1970.
25. Ibid., 12 June 1970.
26. General Abrams himself was forced to warn against such practices after a North Vietnamese sapper entered one military compound and killed thirty Americans who, against regulations, were taking cover in the same bunker.
27. *Boston Globe*, 4 June 1971.

17: *Fire in the Lake*

1. Extract from Tru Vu's "The Statue of the Century," translated by Nguyen Ngoc Bich. In Nguyen Ngoc Bich, "The Poetry of Vietnam."
2. The name Bui Phat is a contraction of the names of the two Catholic bishoprics in the north, Phat Diem and Bui Chu, from which the first population of the district came.
3. *Le Monde* (*sélection hebdomadaire*), 14–20 May 1970. Jean-Claude Pomonti.
4. Ngoc Ky, "A Visit to My Village," in *Between Two Fires*, ed. Ly Qui Chung, p. 90.
5. Samuel Huntington, "The Bases of Accommodation," p. 655.
6. *New York Times*, 7 April 1968.
7. Cynthia Frederick, "The Vietnamization of Saigon Politics," pp. 9–13.
8. Henry Kissinger, "Viet Nam Negotiations."
9. *Le Monde* (*sélection hebdomadaire*), 14–20 May 1970.

Bibliography

Alsheimer, Georg W. *Vietnamesische Lehrjahre: Sechs Jahre als Deutscher Arzt in Vietnam*. Frankfurt am Main: Suhrkamp, 1968.

Apple, R. W. "Vietnam: The Signs of a Stalemate." *New York Times*, 7 August 1967.

Arlen, Michael. *The Living-Room War*. New York: Viking, 1969.

Bodard, Lucien. *The Quicksand War: Prelude to Vietnam*. Translated by Patrick O'Brian. Boston: Atlantic–Little, Brown & Co., 1967

Bouscaren, Anthony T. *The Last of the Mandarins: Diem of Vietnam*. Pittsburgh: Duquesne University Press, 1965.

Bowles, Chester. Excerpts from testimony to the Joint Economic Committee of Congress, January 1971. *Boston Sunday Globe*, 14 February 1971.

Branfman, Fred. "Presidential War in Laos, 1964–1970." In *Laos: War and Revolution*, edited by N. Adams and A. McCoy. New York: Harper and Row, 1970.

Browne, Malcolm W. *The New Face of War*. Indianapolis: Bobbs-Merrill Co., 1965.

Burchett, Wilfred G. *Vietnam: Inside Story of the Guerilla War*. New York: International Publishers, 1965.

———. *Vietnam Will Win!* New York: Monthly Review Press, 1968.

Buttinger, Joseph. *The Smaller Dragon: A Political History of Vietnam*. New York: Praeger, 1958.

———. *Vietnam: A Dragon Embattled*. 2 vols. New York: Praeger, 1967.

Cadière, Léopold. *Croyances et pratiques religieuses des viêtnamiens*. 3 vols. Saigon: École Française d'Extrême Orient, 1955–1958.

Carver, George. "The Faceless Viet Cong." In *Vietnam: Anatomy of a Conflict*, edited by Wesley R. Fishel. Itasca, Ill.: F. E. Peacock, 1968, pp. 292–311.

———. "The Real Revolution in South Vietnam." *Foreign Affairs* 43 (April 1965): 387–408.

Chomsky, Noam. *American Power and the New Mandarins*. New York: Random House, Vintage Books, 1967.

———. *At War with Asia*. New York: Random House, Pantheon Books, 1970.

———. "Mayday: The Case for Civil Disobedience." *New York Review of Books,* 17 June 1971.

Clark, Blair. "Westmoreland Appraised: Questions and Answers." *Harper's,* November 1970.

Confucius. *The Analects of Confucius.* Translated and annotated by Arthur Waley. New York: Random House, 1938.

Conley, Michael Charles. *The Communist Insurgent Infrastructure in South Vietnam: A Study of Organization and Strategy.* Department of the Army Pamphlet No. 550-106. Washington, D.C.: Center for Research in Social Systems, American University, 1967.

Corson, William R. *The Betrayal.* New York: Norton, 1968.

Critchfield, Richard. *The Long Charade: Political Subversion in the Vietnam War.* New York: Harcourt, Brace and World, 1968.

Davison, W. P. "Some Observations on Viet Cong Operations in the Villages." RAND Corporation Collection RM-5267/2-ISA/ARPA. Santa Monica, Calif.: RAND Corporation, July 1967.

Devillers, Philippe. *Histoire du Viêt-Nam de 1940 à 1952.* Paris: Éditions du Seuil, 1952.

———. "The Struggle for the Unification of Vietnam." *China Quarterly* 9 (January–March 1962): 15.

Dorsey, John T., Jr., "Bureaucracy and Political Development in Vietnam." In *Bureaucracy and Political Development,* edited by Joseph LaPalombara. Princeton, N.J.: Princeton University Press, 1963.

Duffett, John, ed. *Against the Crime of Silence: Proceedings of the Russell International War Crimes Tribunal, 1967.* New York: Simon and Schuster, Clarion Books, 1970.

Duncanson, Dennis J. *Government and Revolution in Vietnam.* New York: Oxford University Press, 1968.

———. "How and Why – The Viet Cong Holds Out." *Encounter,* December 1966, pp. 77–84.

Duong Son Quan. "Land Reform?" *Thoi Bao Ga,* 10 October 1970.

Duong Van Minh. "Vietnam: A Question of Confidence." *Foreign Affairs* 47 (October 1968): 84–91.

Ellsberg, Daniel. "The Day Loc Tien Was Pacified." RAND Corporation Collection P-3793. Santa Monica, Calif.: RAND Corporation, February 1968.

———. "Escalating in a Quagmire." Paper read at annual meeting of the American Political Science Association, 8–12 September 1970.

———. "Laos: What Nixon Is Up To." *New York Review of Books,* 11 March 1971.

Falk, Richard A.; Kolko, Gabriel; and Lifton, Robert Jay; eds. *Crimes of War: After Songmy.* New York: Random House, Vintage Books, 1971.

Fall, Bernard B. *Last Reflections on a War.* Garden City, N.Y.: Doubleday, 1967.

———. "The Political-Religious Sects of Viet-Nam." *Pacific Affairs* 28 (September 1955): 235–253.

———. *Street Without Joy: Insurgency in Indochina, 1946–1963.* 3rd ed. Harrisburg, Pa.: Stackpole Books, 1963.

———. *The Two Vietnams: A Political and Military Analysis.* New York: Praeger, 1963.

———. "Viet-Cong – The Unseen Enemy in Viet-Nam." In *The Viet-Nam Reader,* edited by Marcus G. Raskin and Bernard B. Fall. New York: Random House, Vintage Books, 1965.

———. *The Viet-Minh Regime: Government and Administration in the Democratic Republic of Vietnam.* Rev. ed. New York: Institute of Pacific Relations, 1956.

———. *Le Viêt-Minh: La République démocratique du Viêt-Nam, 1945–1960.* Paris: Colin, 1960.

———. *Viet-Nam Witness, 1953–1966.* New York: Praeger, 1966.

Fanon, Frantz. *Black Skin, White Masks.* Translated by Charles Lam Markmann. New York: Grove Press, 1967.

———. *The Wretched of the Earth*. Translated by Constance Farrington. New York: Grove Press, 1965.

Fishel, Wesley R., ed. *Problems of Freedom: South Vietnam Since Independence*. New York: Free Press of Glencoe, 1962.

———. *Vietnam: The Anatomy of a Conflict*. Itasca, Ill.: F. E. Peacock, 1968.

Fishel, Wesley R. "Vietnam's Democratic One-Man Rule." *New Leader*, 2 November 1959, pp. 10–13.

FitzGerald, Frances. "The Tragedy of Saigon." *Atlantic Monthly*, December 1966, pp. 59–67.

Frederick, Cynthia. "Cambodia: Operation Total Victory No. 43." *Bulletin of Concerned Asian Scholars* 2 (April–July 1970): 3–19.

———. "The Vietnamization of Saigon Politics." *Bulletin of Concerned Asian Scholars* 3 (Winter–Spring 1971): 5–14.

Friedman, Edward, and Selden, Mark, eds. *America's Asia: Dissenting Essays on Asian-American Relations*. New York: Random House, 1971.

Gobron, Gabriel. *History and Philosophy of Caodaism; Reformed Buddhism, Vietnamese Spiritism, New Religion in Eurasia*. Translated by Pham Xuan Thai. Saigon: Tu Hai, 1950.

Gosselin, Charles. *L'Empire d'Annam*. Paris: Perrin, 1904.

Gourou, Pierre. *L'Utilisation du sol en Indochine française*. Paris: P. Hartman, 1940.

Greene, Graham. *The Quiet American*. New York: Viking, 1956.

Halberstam, David, *Ho*. New York: Random House, 1971.

———. *The Making of a Quagmire*. New York: Random House, 1965.

———. "Return to Vietnam." *Harper's*, December 1967, pp. 47–58.

———. "Voices of the Vietcong." *Harper's*, January 1968, pp. 45–52.

Hammer, Ellen J. *The Struggle for Indochina*. Stanford, Calif.: Stanford University Press, 1954.

Hendry, James Bausch. *The Small World of Khanh Hau*. Chicago: Aldine, 1964.

Henry, John Bronaugh, II. "March 1968: Continuity or Change?" B.A. thesis, Department of Government, Harvard University, April 1971.

Herbert, Jean. *An Introduction to Asia*. New York: Oxford University Press, 1965.

Hickey, Gerald C. "Accommodation and Coalition in South Vietnam." RAND Corporation Collection P-4213. Santa Monica, Calif.: RAND Corporation, January 1970.

———. "Accommodation in South Vietnam: The Key to Sociopolitical Solidarity." RAND Corporation Collection P-3707. Santa Monica, Calif.: RAND Corporation October 1967.

———. *Village in Vietnam*. New Haven, Conn.: Yale University Press, 1964.

Ho Chi Minh. *Ho Chi Minh on Revolution: Selected Writings, 1920–1966*. Edited by Bernard B. Fall. New York: Praeger, 1967.

———. *Prison Diary*. Translated by Aileen Palmer. Hanoi: Foreign Languages Publishing House, 1962.

Hoang Van Chi. *From Colonialism to Communism: A Case History of North Vietnam*. New York: Praeger, 1964.

Hosmer, Stephen T. "Viet Cong Repression and Its Implications for the Future." Report prepared for Advanced Research Projects Association. RAND Corporation Collection R-475/1 ARPA. Santa Monica, Calif.: RAND Corporation, May 1970.

Huard, Pierre, and Durand, Maurice. *Connaissance du Viêt-nam*. Hanoi: École Française d'Extrême Orient, 1954.

Huntington, Samuel. "The Bases of Accommodation." *Foreign Affairs* 46 (July 1968): 642–656.

I Ching, or *Book of Changes*. Translated by Richard Wilhelm and Cary F. Baynes. 3rd ed. Princeton, N.J.: Princeton University Press, 1967.

"Interviews Concerning the National Liberation Front of South Vietnam." RAND Corporation Documents from Series FD and G. Santa Monica, Calif.: RAND Corporation.

Jumper, Roy. "Mandarin Bureaucracy and Politics in South Vietnam." *Pacific Affairs* 30 (March 1957): 47–58.

Just, Ward S. *To What End: Report from Vietnam.* Boston: Houghton Mifflin Co., 1968.

Kahin, George McTurnan, and Lewis, John W. *The United States in Vietnam.* New York: Dial Press, 1967.

Kissinger, Henry. "Viet Nam Negotiations." *Foreign Affairs* 47 (January 1969): 211–234.

Knoll, Erwin, and McFadden, Judith Nies, eds. *War Crimes and the American Conscience.* New York. Holt, Rinehart and Winston, 1970.

Komer, Robert W. "The Other War in Vietnam – A Progress Report." *Department of State Bulletin,* 10 October 1966, pp. 549–600.

Lacouture, Jean. *Ho Chi Minh: A Political Biography.* Translated by Peter Wiles. New York: Random House, 1968.

———. *Vietnam: Between Two Truces.* Translated by Konrad Kellen and Joel Carmichael. New York: Random House, Vintage Books, 1966.

Lacouture, Jean, and Devillers, Philippe. *La Fin d'une guerre: Indochine 1954.* Paris: Éditions du Seuil, 1960.

Ladejinsky, Wolf I. "Agrarian Reform in the Republic of Vietnam." In *Problems of Freedom: South Vietnam since Independence,* edited by Wesley R. Fishel, pp. 153–175. New York: Free Press of Glencoe, 1962.

Lancaster, Donald. *The Emancipation of French Indochina.* New York: Oxford University Press, 1961.

Lansdale, Major-General Edward G. "Two Steps to Get Us out of Vietnam." *Look,* 4 March 1969, pp. 64–67.

———. "Vietnam: Do We Understand Revolution?" *Foreign Affairs* 43 (October 1964): 75–86.

Lao Tzu. *The Way of Life: Tao Te Ching.* Translated by R. B. Blakney. New York: New American Library, Mentor Books, 1955.

Lartéguy, Jean. *Yellow Fever.* Translated by Xan Fielding. New York, Dutton, 1965.

Le Chau. *La Révolution paysanne du Sud Viêt-Nam.* Paris: Maspero, 1966.

Lederer, William J. *Our Own Worst Enemy.* New York: Norton, 1968.

Le Duan. "Under the Glorious Party Banner, for Independence, Freedom and Socialism, Let Us Advance and Achieve New Victories." Vietnam Documents and Research Notes, no. 77, U.S. Mission, Saigon, April 1970.

Leites, Nathan. "The Viet Cong Style of Politics." RAND Corporation Collection RM-5487. Santa Monica, Calif.: RAND Corporation, May 1969.

Le Thanh Khoi. *Le Viét-nam, histore et civilisation.* Paris: Éditions de Minuit, 1955.

Le Van Dinh. *Le Culte des ancêtres en droit annamite.* Paris: Éditions Domat-Montchrestien, 1934.

Lévi-Strauss, Claude. *Structural Anthropology.* Translated by Claire Jacobson and Brooke Grundfest Schoepf. Garden City, N.Y.: Doubleday, 1967.

Lifton, Robert Jay. "The Circles of Deception – Notes on Vietnam." *Trans-Action,* March 1968, pp. 10–19.

Luce, Don, and Sommer, John. *Viet Nam: The Unheard Voices.* Ithaca, N.Y.: Cornell University Press, 1969.

Ly Qui Chung, ed. *Between Two Fires: The Unheard Voices of Vietnam.* New York: Praeger, 1970.

McAlister, John T., Jr. "America in Vietnam." Portion of unpublished MSS, Princeton University, 1969.

———. *Vietnam: The Origins of Revolution.* New York: Alfred A. Knopf, 1969.

McAlister, John T., Jr., and Mus, Paul. *The Vietnamese and Their Revolution.* New York: Harper and Row, 1970.

McCarthy, Mary. *Hanoi.* New York: Harcourt, Brace and World, 1968.

Mandelstam, Osip. "An Interview with Ho Chi Minh, 1923." *Commentary,* August 1967, pp. 80–81.

Mannoni, Otare. *Prospero and Caliban: The Psychology of Colonization.* Translated by Pamela Powesland. New York: Praeger, 1964.

Mecklin, John. *Mission in Torment.* Garden City, N.Y.: Doubleday, 1965.

Meyerson, Harvey. *Vinh Long*. Boston: Houghton Mifflin Co., 1970.

"The Michigan Winter Soldier Investigation." Excerpts from the *Congressional Record*, 6–7 April 1971. *Harvard Crimson*, 14 May 1971.

Mitchell, Edward J. "Inequality and Insurgency: A Statistical Study of South Vietnam." *World Politics* 20 (April 1968): 421–438.

Moore, Barrington, Jr. *The Social Origins of Dictatorship and Democracy: Lord and Peasant in the Making of the Modern World*. Boston: Beacon Press, 1966.

Mus, Paul. "The Buddhist Background to the Crises in Vietnamese Politics." Mimeographed. New Haven, Conn.: Southeast Asia Studies Program, Yale University.

———. "Cultural Backgrounds of Present Problems." *Asia* 4 (Winter 1966): 10–21.

———. "Les Religions de l'Indochine." In *Indochine*, edited by Sylvain Lévi. 2 vols. Paris: Société d'Éditions Géographiques, Maritimes et Coloniales, 1931.

———. "The Role of the Village in Vietnamese Politics." *Pacific Affairs* 23 (September 1949): 265–272.

———. "The Unaccountable Mr. Ho." *New Journal*, 12 May 1968, p. 9.

———. *Le Viêt-Nam chez lui*. Paris: Paul Hartman, 1946.

———. "Viet Nam: A Nation Off Balance." *Yale Review* 41 (Summer 1952): 524–538.

———. *Viêt-Nam: Sociologie d'une guerre*. Paris: Éditions du Seuil, 1952.

Nghiem Dang. *Viet-Nam: Politics and Public Administration*. Honolulu: East-West Center Press, 1966.

Nguyen Du. *Kim Van Kieu*. Translated by Xuan Phuc and Xuan Viet. Paris: Gallimard, 1961.

Nguyen Ngoc Bich. "The Poetry of Vietnam." The Asian Literature Program of the Asia Society. Reprinted from *Asia*, Spring 1969.

Nguyen Thai. "The Government of Men in the Republic of Vietnam." Thesis. Michigan State University, East Lansing, Mich., 1962.

Nguyen Van Phong. "La Diffusion du confucianisme au Vietnam." *France-Asie* 21 (Winter 1966–1967): 179–196.

Oka, Takashi. "Buddhism as a Political Force. No. 5: Danang and Afterwards." Paper for Institute of Current World Affairs. 29 May 1967.

Osborne, Milton E. *Strategic Hamlets in South Vietnam*. Data paper No. 55. Ithaca, N.Y.: Southeast Asia Program, Department of Asian Studies, Cornell University, 1965.

Pfaff, William. "Rhetorical Escalation." *Commonweal*, 17 March 1967, pp. 673–674.

———. "Rivals for the Vietcong?" *Commonweal*, 3 March 1967, pp. 615–617.

———. "A Vietnam Journal." Discussion paper. Hudson Institute, N.Y., HI-807-DP. 23 February 1967.

———. "What Else Can We Do?" *Commonweal*, 10 March 1967, pp. 641–642.

Pfeffer, Richard M., ed. *No More Vietnams?: The War and the Future of American Foreign Policy*. New York: Harper and Row, 1968.

Phan Boi Chau. *Memoires*. Edited by Georges Boudarel. *France-Asie*, 22 (Autumn 1968): 263–471.

Phan Thi Dac. *Situation de la personne au Viêt-Nam*. Paris: Centre national de la recherche scientifique, 1966.

Pike, Douglas. *Viet Cong: The Organization and Techniques of the National Liberation Front of South Vietnam*. Cambridge, Mass.: MIT Press, 1966.

———. "The Viet Cong Strategy of Terror." Monograph. U.S. Mission, Saigon. February 1970.

Pond, Elizabeth. "The Chau Trial II: Denouement." April–July 1970. New York: Alicia Patterson Fund, 1970.

———. "The Chau Trial III: Aftermath." October 1970. New York: Alicia Patterson Fund, 1970.

Pool, Ithiel de Sola. "Political Alternatives to the Viet Cong." *Asian Survey* 7 (August 1967): 555–566.

Popkin, Samuel L. "The Myth of the Village: Revolution and Reaction in Vietnam." Ph.D. dissertation, Department of Political Science, Massachusetts Institute of Technology, February 1969.

Pye, Lucian W. *Guerrilla Communism in Malaya*. Princeton, N.J.: Princeton University Press, 1956.

Race, Jeffrey. "How They Won." *Asian Survey* 10 (August 1970): 628–650.

Raskin, Marcus G., and Fall, Bernard B., eds. *The Viet-Nam Reader: Articles and Documents on American Foreign Policy and the Viet-Nam Crisis*. Rev. ed. New York: Random House, Vintage Books, 1965.

Rostow, W. W. *The Stages of Economic Growth: A Non-Communist Manifesto*. New York: Cambridge University Press, 1960.

Sacks, I. Milton. "Marxism in Viet-Nam." In *Marxism in Southeast Asia*, edited by Frank N. Trager, pp. 102–170. Stanford, Calif.: Stanford University Press, 1960.

———. "Restructuring Government in South Vietnam." *Asian Survey* 7 (August 1967): 515–526.

Sansom, Robert L. *The Economics of Insurgency in the Mekong Delta of Vietnam*. Cambridge, Mass.: MIT Press, 1970.

Scheer, Robert. *How the United States Got Involved in Vietnam*. Santa Barbara, Calif.: Center for the Study of Democratic Institutions, 1965.

Schell, Jonathan. *The Military Half*. New York: Random House, Vintage Books, 1968.

———. *The Village of Ben Suc*. New York: Random House, Vintage Books, 1967.

Schell, Jonathan and Orville. Letter to the *New York Times*, 26 November 1969.

Schlesinger, Arthur M., Jr. *The Bitter Heritage: Vietnam and American Democracy, 1941–1966*. Boston: Houghton Mifflin Co., 1967.

Scigliano, Robert G. "Political Parties in South Vietnam Under the Republic." *Pacific Affairs* 33 (December 1960): 327–346.

———. *South Vietnam: Nation Under Stress*. Boston: Houghton Mifflin Co., 1964.

Shaplen, Robert. "Letter from Indochina." *New Yorker*, 9 May 1970, pp. 130–148.

———. "Letter from Saigon." *New Yorker*, 18 February 1967, pp. 150–166; 17 June 1967, pp. 37–92; 7 October 1967, pp. 149–175; 20 January 1968, pp. 35–82; 2 March 1968, pp. 44–81; 23 March 1968, pp. 114–125; 29 June 1968; pp. 37–61; 21 September 1969, pp. 100–150; 31 January 1970, pp. 40–55.

———. *The Lost Revolution: The U.S. in Vietnam, 1946–1966*. Rev. ed. New York: Harper and Row, Harper Colophon Books, 1966.

———. "A Reporter at Large." *New Yorker*, 16 November 1968, pp. 193–206; 12 July 1969, pp. 36–57.

———. *Time Out of Hand: Revolution and Reaction in Southeast Asia*. New York: Harper and Row, 1969.

Sheehan, Neil; Smith, Hedrick; Kenworthy, E. W.; and Butterfield, Fox. *The Pentagon Papers: The Secret History of the Vietnam War . . . as Published by the New York Times*. New York: Bantam Books, 1971.

Sheehan, Susan. *Ten Vietnamese*. New York: Alfred A. Knopf, 1967.

Solomon, Richard H. "The Chinese Revolution and the Politics of Dependency." Mimeographed. Center for Chinese Studies, University of Michigan, Ann Arbor, Mich., August 1966.

———. "Communications Patterns and the Chinese Revolution." Paper prepared for Annual Meeting of the American Political Science Association, 5–9 September 1967, in Chicago.

———. *Mao's Revolution and the Chinese Political Culture*. Berkeley, Calif.: University of California Press, 1971.

Sontag, Susan. *Trip to Hanoi*. New York: Farrar, Straus and Giroux, 1968.

Starobin, Joseph R. *Eyewitness in Indochina*. New York: Greenwood Press, 1968.

Stavins, Ralph. "Kennedy's Private War." *New York Review of Books*, 22 July 1971.

Steinberg, David Joel, ed. *In Search of Southeast Asia: A Modern History*. New York: Praeger, 1971.

Stone, I. F. "A Reply to the White Paper." In *The Viet-Nam Reader*, edited by Marcus G. Raskin and Bernard B. Fall. New York: Random House, Vintage Books, 1965.

Taillefer, Jean. "Les Élections au Sud-Viêtnam." *France-Asie* 21 (Spring–Summer 1967): 447–458.

Tanham, George K. *Communist Revolutionary Warfare: The Vietminh in Indochina.* New York: Praeger, 1961.

Taylor, Milton C. "South Viet-Nam: Lavish Aid, Limited Progress." *Pacific Affairs* 34 (Fall 1961): 242–256.

Taylor, Telford. *Nuremberg and Vietnam: An American Tragedy.* New York: Bantam Books, 1971.

Thich Nhat Hanh. *Vietnam: Lotus in a Sea of Fire.* New York: Hill and Wang, 1967.

Thompson, Sir Robert. *Defeating Communist Insurgency.* New York: Praeger, 1966.

———. *No Exit from Vietnam.* New York: McKay, 1969.

Thompson, Virginia. *French Indochina.* New York: Macmillan Co., 1937.

Thomson, James C., Jr. "How Could Vietnam Happen: An Autopsy." *Atlantic Monthly,* April 1968, pp. 47–53.

Thuong Vinh Thanh, ed. and trans. *La Constitution religieuse du Caodaisme.* Paris: Éditions Derby, 1953.

Trager, Frank N. *Why Vietnam?* New York: Praeger, 1966.

Trager, Frank N., et al. *Marxism in Southeast Asia: A Study of Four Countries.* Stanford, Calif.: Stanford University Press, 1960.

Tran Van Dinh. *No Passenger on the River.* New York: Vantage Press, 1965.

Truong Buu Lam. *Patterns of Vietnamese Response to Foreign Intervention, 1858–1900.* Monograph Series no. 11. New Haven, Conn.: Southeast Asia Studies, Yale University, 1967.

Truong Chinh, pseud. [Dang Xuan Khu]. *President Ho Chi Minh: Beloved Leader of the Vietnamese People.* Hanoi: Foreign Language Publishing House, 1966.

U.S. Department of State, Office of the Deputy Ambassador, Saigon. "Ky's Candidacy and U.S. Stakes in the Coming Elections." Memorandum for the Record, by Daniel Ellsberg. 4 May 1967.

Valéry, Paul. Extract from *History and Politics No. 10. New York Times,* 25 March 1971.

The Vietnam Hearings. Excerpts from the Senate Committee on Foreign Relations hearings on Vietnam, January–February 1966. New York: Random House, Vintage Books, 1966.

Vo Nguyen Giap. *People's War, People's Army: The Viet Cong Insurrection Manual for Underdeveloped Countries.* New York: Praeger, 1962.

Warner, Dennis. *The Last Confucian.* Harmondsworth, England: Penguin Books, 1963.

Weber, Max. *The Sociology of Religion.* Translated by Ephraim Fischoff. Boston: Beacon Press, 1964.

Weiss, Peter. *Notes on the Cultural Life of the Democratic Republic of Vietnam.* New York: Dell, 1970.

Westmoreland, William C. *Report on the War in Vietnam.* Washington, D.C.: Government Printing Office, 1969.

Whiteside, Thomas. "Defoliation." *New Yorker,* 7 February 1970, pp. 32–38.

Wolf, Eric R. *Peasant Wars in the Twentieth Century.* New York: Harper and Row, 1969.

Woodside, Alec. "Some Features of the Vietnamese Bureaucracy Under the Early Nguyen Dynasty." *Papers on China,* vol. 19. Cambridge, Mass.: East Asian Research Center, Harvard University, December 1965.

———. "Some Southern Vietnamese Writers Look at the War." *Bulletin of Concerned Asian Scholars* 2 (October 1969): 53–58.

———. *Vietnam and the Chinese Model.* Cambridge, Mass.: Harvard University Press, 1971.

Wurfel, David. "The Saigon Political Elite: Focus on Four Cabinets." *Asian Survey* 7 (August 1967): 527–539.

The Year of the Pig. Documentary film. Directed by Emile de Antonio. 1969.

Zasloff, J. J. "Origins of the Insurgency in South Vietnam, 1954–1960: The Role of the Southern Vietminh Cadres." RAND Corporation Collection RM-5163/2-ISA/ARPA. Santa Monica, Calif.: RAND Corporation, May 1968.

———. "Political Motivation of the Viet Cong and the Vietminh Regroupees." RAND Corporation Collection RM-4703/2-ISA/ARPA. Santa Monica, Calif.: RAND Corporation, May 1968.

Index